THE FIRST NEW ENGLAND CATALOGUE

When the Whole Earth Catalogue group decided to publish, regretfully, the LAST Whole Earth Catalogue, we at Pequot decided to carry on the idea and great spirit of their work in a more modest portion of our universe. We selected the area we love and know best, New England.

What started as a simple search for things, places, and activities particularly New England became a huge project of endless fascination. While we have not yet found anyone making oil well drilling-rigs in New England, we would not say that there is not one.

New Englanders seem to produce and do, unpredictably, just about anything and everything. We know that there are many items we have missed, but we plan to publish the New England Catalogue over the years and can use your help (See box headed NO PAID ADVERTISING).

We did feel that the concept of a catalogue with no paid advertising would be a welcome relief in the commercial information explosion we live in. This afforded us the chance to give a dispassionate review of products, books, activities and places of special interest.

To this end we set up the following publishing rules for the inclusion of an article or item in the Catalogue:

1. **It must have a New England address.**

2. **It must exemplify the idea that New England is not just a place ... It is a way of life.**

3. **It must give more than it takes.**

Most entries have been written logue staff or, upon request, by book reviews, articles and reports to visit are signed with the initials or member or the name of a contributo general, product reviews have not b signed except when the reviewer injected personal observation.

Whenever possible, excerpted passages from reviewed books, supplier's brochures and other source material are given to illuminate the product description.

So we hope you enjoy relaxing with our potpourri of products, places, activities and notes on this small but wonderful corner of our Country.

AND ... if you are an author with a special interest manuscript that is not fiction or poetry, we hope you will think kindly of Pequot. Our basic publishing philosophy is, in so far as is possible, to translate special interest books into viable commercial enterprises.

The door at Pequot (our "clement" New England weather permitting) is always open during reasonable working hours to authors, readers, friends and even an occasional disinterested observer.

ABOUT THIS FIRST EDITION

Ordering:
- Address orders to the supplier, not to The Pequot Press. Send check or money order. No C.O.D.
- Add state sales tax if applicable.
- Consult post office for parcel post delivery costs.

Products:
- To the best of our knowledge, all products in the Catalogue are currently available and upon order will be delivered within a reasonable period of time. Correspondence concerning products should be directed to the supplier.
- Prices of products and addresses of suppliers may have changed since the Catalogue went to press.

The First New England Catalogue

The Pequot Press

Publisher: J. Chandler Hill
Editor: Marie S. Hall
Editorial Assistants: Pidge Eastland
                    Sara Ingram
Editorial Design: Gina Rosencrantz

The Pequot Press, Inc.
Chester, Connecticut 06412

President and Treasurer: James F. Mottershead
Executive Vice President: Robert W. Wilkerson
Vice President, Marketing: Reese H. Harris III
Secretary: Muriel E. Mottershead

EARTH

Library of Congress Catalog Card Number: 72-12224

ISBN: 0-394-70662-5

Manufactured in the United States of America

First Edition

Earth Index

A

Amateur Sugar Maker 12
Animals 18, 25
  accessories 19, 20, 21
  bears 19
  birds 20
  cats 19, 20
  cows 18, 19
  dogs 19, 20, 21
  fowl 20
  frogs 19, 25
  goats 21
  horses 17, 18
  ointments 18
  repellents 24
  sheep 17, 18
  tonics 18
  wild 19, 23
  wildlife sanctuaries 29
Animals Nobody Loves 19
The Art and Practice of Hawking 20
Audubon Societies
  Massachusetts 5, 15, 25, 29
  Rhode Island 25
The Ayrshire Digest 19

B

A Beachcomber's Botany 26
Bees 22
Bird Banding 23
Birds 21.
  birdwatchers supplies 24
  feeders 23, 24
  field guides 21, 24
  hawks 20
  houses 23
  taming 20, 23, 24
Blacksmiths 18
Block Island Summer 31

C

Cape Cod Pilot 28
Clocks
  sundials 33
Companion Plants and How to Use Them 14
Conley's Gardening Handbook 6
The Connecticut Conservation Reporter 15
Conservation Associations
  Chatham, Massachusetts 29
  Connecticut 25
Cookbooks 9
Copper
  weather vanes 35

D

Down East 13
Dowsing 30
Dowsing
  instructions 30
  kits 30
  society 30
  supplies 30
Drinking Water Filter 27

E

East of America 31
Ecology 11, 14, 15, 25, 29
  nature centers 6, 14, 15, 29
Enjoying Maine Birds 21
Environ/Mental Essays on the Planet as a Home 14

F

Farming 6
  haying equipment 11
  tools 9
A Field Guide to the Birds 24
Fireplaces
  equipment 18, 35
Fish
  lobsters 27
  whales 21
Fishing
  eels 28
  lobster traps 26
The Flora of New England 4
Furnishings 26

G

Gardening 5, 6, 11, 14, 16
  blueberries 5
  bulb grower 10
  bulb planter 10
  bulbs 10
  center 6
  coldframes 10
  dwarf plants 11
  fertilizer 6
  flowers 4
  greenhouses 13
  herbs 8, 9, 12, 15
  indoor kits 12
  indoor plants 4, 7
  organic 15
  organic fertilizer 6
  plant food 5
  potting soil 4
  seeds 6
  soil conditioner 4, 5
  soil testing equipment 6
  strawberries 6
  tools 13
  wild flowers 8
Gardens
  botanical 8
  lighting 5
Glass
  blowing 35

H

Hand-Taming Wild Birds at the Feeder 23
Heavy Equipment Repair 12
Herbs 8
  gardening 8, 9, 12, 15
  insect repellent 15
  kits 9
  sprays 15
Hill Country Harvest 11
Horses 17, 18
  harnessmaker 19
  horseshoeing 18
  ointments 18
  riding equipment 19
Horticulture 5
The House on Nauset Marsh 26

I

Instruments
  weather 32

L

Leather
  preservative 20
Lighting 35
  gardens 5
The Lightning Book 36
Living the Good Life 15
Look What I Found! 23

M

Machinery Around Your Country Home 34
Man and Nature 25
Maple Sugar 12
  equipment 11
The Maple Sugar Book 16
Maps 13, 16
Mass. Soc. Prev. Cruelty to Animals 18
Minerals
  guide 32
M.I.T. Technology Review 29
Museums
  Americana 17
  maritime 26
  natural history 6
My Own Cape Cod 27

N

The New England Butt'ry Shelf Almanac 9
The New England Colonial Gardens 16
The No-Work Garden Book 11

O

The Old Farmer's Almanac 32

R

Recipes
  frog's legs 19
  lobster stew 27
Records
  Yankee humor 31
Rock Hound's Guide to Connecticut 32
The Rocky Shore 26

S

The Sandy Shore 26
Sea Born Island 30
Sea Fever — The Making of a Sailor 27
Seaweeds of the Connecticut Shore 14
The Shepherd 18
Starting Right With Bees 22
Starting Right With Milk Goats 21
Starting Right With Poultry 20
Summer Island: Penobscot Country 31
Sundials
  clocks 33
Supplies
  dowsing 30

T

That Quail, Robert 24
Tools
  farming 9
  gardening 13
Trees 6, 7, 8
  dogwood 6
  rare 6
  seeds 12

U

Using Wayside Plants 13

W

Weather
  forecasting 32
  instruments 32
  lightning 36
  snow removal 34
Weather Vanes 18
  copper 35
Weekly Market Bulletin 6
Whales 21
What Is It? . . . at the Beach 27
The White-Flower-Farm Garden Book 5
Wild Flowers of Martha's Vineyard 13
Windmills 16
Witch Hazel 7

Y

The Year of the Whale 21

From ABELIOPHYLLUM (a-bee-leo-fill'um) to ZANTEDESCHIA (zan-tea-desh'ee-uh)

The Garden Book of White Flower Farm is literally an A to Z on flowers, flower gardens and how to care for them. Even if your interest in such beautiful matters is as barren as the moon, you can't help being impressed with this exceptionally informative catalogue. If, on the other hand, you are a gardener and haven't seen *The Garden Book*, one can not tell to what extent your enthusiasm will abound. Exquisite line drawings and telling half-tone photographs enrich the informative pages. Phonetic spellings of all botanical names is only one of many assists the catalogue gives the gardener in his pursuit toward beautification of his world. *Summer Notes*, like its smaller siblings, *Spring* and *Winter Notes*, is published as a supplement to the catalogue. These Notes clarify cultural information that seems to be bothering some gardeners and, among other things, call attention to choice new varieties that are making headway in a genus. White Flower Farm is a nice place to visit, too — with or without *The Garden Book* in hand.

JCH

White Flower Farm
The Garden Book
Litchfield, Connecticut 06759
1972; 112 pp., paper
$2.50 — includes current Notes, plus $2.00 credit on first order of $15.00 or more

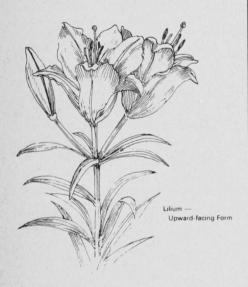

Lilium —
Upward-facing Form

L. Green Magic. 736. An outstanding trumpet, chartreuse and white in color. Grown well, the stems rise to 7 feet. A beaut. Flowers in July. 9- to 10-inch bulbs.   Each $1.00, Three $2.85, Doz. $10.75

L. Harlequin Hybrids. 738. Pretty gay, this one, with as much of the rainbow as can be captured in Lily chromosomes—each bulb is a different color. Vigorous, too. Flowers in June-July on 3- to 5-foot stems. 5- to 7-inch bulbs.
Each $1.00, Three $2.85, Doz. $10.75

L. Honeydew. 739. Mimosa-yellow and lettuce-green, the chart says—and that's Honeydew. Blooms hang down, a score or more of them, from the top of 5-foot stems. Bulbs 7 to 8 inches.
Each $2.30, Three $6.55, Doz. $24.80

L. Imperial Crimson Strain. 740. A strain. White with crimson centers. It flowers in August on 5- to 7-foot stems. A lovely thing. 6- to 7-inch bulbs.
Each $1.40, Three $4.00, Doz. $15.10

L. Imperial Gold Strain. 741. This de Graaff strain is truly imperial, each petal measures up to 3 inches in width, and we refuse to tell you the number of petals on each bloom. Color is purest white, heavily dotted with maroon spots. A heavy gold stripe shades down each petal. Height: 5 to 8 feet; it flowers in August. 6- to 7-inch bulbs.
Each $1.70, Three $4.85, Doz. $18.35

L. Imperial Silver Strain. 742. A huge all-white Lily in imperial size. Height 5 to 6 feet

Earth

The Flora of New England

I suspect that this book would be of more use to qualified botanists, rather than dilettante gardeners like myself. Not for the casual browser, it is extremely comprehensive, with each plant given a detailed description right down to the last "m." As there are approximately 3200 species of flora in New England, it is a rather large book; too much so, in fact, to be used comfortably in fieldwork. Since it is the only comprehensive manual on New England flora, it certainly deserves a spot on any serious gardener's bookshelf.

Anne Ward

The Flora of New England
by Frank Conkling Seymour
1969; 596 pp.
From: Charles E. Tuttle Co., Inc.
        Rutland, Vermont 05701
        $12.50

THE FLORA OF NEW ENGLAND

A Manual for the Identification of All Vascular Plants Growing Without Cultivation in New England

by FRANK CONKLING SEYMOUR

Autumn

The morns are meeker than they were,
The nuts are getting brown;
The berry's cheek is plumper,
The rose is out of town.

The maple wears a gayer scarf,
The field a scarlet gown.
Lest I should be old-fashioned,
I'll put a trinket on.

Emily Dickinson

Rare and Exotic House Plants

Continuing in the old tradition, Sam Richards is a one-man business which concentrates on useful items and avoids gimmicks. No catalog, but he'll send you product descriptions. He also offers an interesting assortment of *rare and exotic house plants* at reasonable prices. Live delivery is guaranteed. If plants are dead on arrival, he will replace them at no cost to you.

"It's only natural that I should be drawn to the business of selling gifts and necessities," Sam says. "My great grandfather, Samuel Stephen Newton of Connecticut, was a well-known country peddler in the 1850's. The S.S. Newton wagon was a welcome sight to lonely farm wives and residents of remote areas in those days. It brought knitting needles, magnifying eyeglasses, flour, cornmeal, seeds, salt, sugar, spices, boots and brooms, yardgoods and buttons, hats and toys. The outside of the wagon was hung with wash tubs, pots and pans — clanking against the axle along with axes, shovels, hammer and tongs to announce his long awaited arrival.

"The country peddler of the 19th century was much more than a traveling salesman. People on the farms depended on him to bring news of the outside world, to deliver mail and messages from friends wherever he went, and expected him to spend the night with the family he visited late in the day . . . for which S.S. Newton always insisted on paying 50¢ for himself and 25¢ for his horse!"

Sam Richards Trader
Box 456
Bantam, Connecticut 06750

```
NORFOLK ISLAND PINE (Araucaria
heterophylla) Culture A, E, H, J
        An evergreen house plant that
        looks like a perfect pine tree.
        Tropical and not hardy out doors.
Stock No. A186        $2.25


BLACK BEAUTY BEGONIA
Culture A, E, G, K
        The leaves are like black
        velvet. The plant is easy to
        grow. A truly different
        begonia.
Stock No. A177        $2.25
```

The White-Flower-Farm Garden Book

Definitive is the word for this book, yet its explicitness does not preclude a sense of humor by the author. Amos Pettingill (William B. Harris) knows whereof he writes. Founder of the unusual White Flower Farm in Litchfield, Connecticut, Mr. Pettingill and his wife Jane have gardened since the late 1930's. The book is an A to Z of invaluable gardening information. A delightful compendium, profusely illustrated, exacting in detail, warmly written.

The White-Flower-Farm Garden Book — JCH
by Amos Pettingill
Drawings by Nils Hogner
1971; 365 pp.
From: Alfred A. Knopf, Inc.
201 E. 50th Street
New York, New York 10022
$10.00

From the introduction:

... The reader will recall that the first time I produced perennials, the 6- to 7-foot Delphinium stalks were so sensational that I gave up golf for gardening. Then it took me 10 years to reproduce that first crop. Why? Because I had done everything right the first time — without knowing it. The garden books say, "Feed Delphinium heavily," and they obviously don't define "heavily" because their cautious authors have no idea how well fertilized borders already are or the strength of available fertilizers. My first border was loaded with plant food. I was a rank beginner. Enthusiastic. Not only had the border been double-dug, but I had laced it with twice as much manure and humus as the instructions required and then top dressed it with commercial organic fertilizer, reasoning that if a little fertilizer would be good, twice as much would be better. . . .

Horticulture

Horticulture. is America's oldest gardening magazine. For gardeners — green thumb or not — it's a must.

JCH

Horticulture
300 Massachusetts Avenue
Boston, Massachusetts 02115
$7.00 — 12 issues per year

————◆————

Plant Food/Soil Conditioner

All plants require certain trace elements for their metabolism in much the same manner as humans require vitamins. *Multi-Mer Science* develops two unique products, *Multi-El,* a plant food supplement, and *Multi-Con,* a soil conditioner, which fulfills plant needs.

The combination of *Multi-El* and a commercial fertilizer is indeed a complete plant food. It should guarantee optimum plant health and growth.

Most outdoor soils lack the correct balance of moisture retention and drainage, *Multi-Con* can produce this desired balance.

Multi-Mer Science provides helpful information and instructions on how to use their products for the commercial and home gardener.

Multi-Mer Science
Box 208, Arlington, Massachusetts 02174

Multi-El — 1 quart (makes over 100 gallons) $4.98
Multi-Con — 1 lb. (conditions 200 qts. soil) $7.98

It's interesting to note that "Tobacko" was not very welcome in early New England. In fact, it was forbidden to be planted, except in very small amounts, which were used only for preservation of health. An early Connecticut law permitted a man to smoke only once a day, and that only if he went on a journey of 10 miles or more — and *never* in another man's house — and absolutely *not* on the Sabbath!

————◆————

Cultivated Blueberries

This nursery offers hardy northern grown, finished stock at very reasonable prices. Send for their brochure which lists the many items they have available.

Giant Cultivated Blueberries

No other fruit has undergone greater improvement within the past few years. Improved new varieties now offered have created a demand for this fruit — fresh, frozen or canned.

Hybrid blueberries make a profitable crop and an attractive ornamental shrub for lawns, or hedges. In spring there are (bell-shaped blossoms), summer (blue fruit), fall (coppery red foliage). Blueberries require an acid humus soil. If your soil is not humus and acid, we recommend making a heavy application of peat moss, rotted sawdust, decayed leaves or some other such materials.

Three or four different varieties should be planted to pollinate. They can be planted in any good garden soil. Use no fertilizer the first two years. Complete planting and growing instructions will be sent with order — mailed in advance, if requested.

Common Fields Nursery will send a selection of best varieties suitable to your area.

Common Fields Nursery
Town Farm Road
Ipswich, Massachusetts 01938

3 yr. heavy berries	12 for $ 9.75
4 yr. heavy berries	12 for $10.75
5 yr. heavy berries	12 for $19.20

————◆————

Garden Lighting

Ludlow, the frog; Caladium Leaf; Tulip and Driftwood. Unique garden lighting from:

Browser's
Belden Station
Norwalk, Connecticut 06852
Bird House Light $17.00
Tulip Light $17.00

BIRD HOUSE LIGHT

Rustic Pine Bark
Color: Natural Wood
6'' Diameter with 8'' x 8'' Roof
8'-0'' Green Plug-In-Cord

DOWNLIGHTS PATIOS, TRAILS, STEPS, ROCK GARDENS AND GROUND COVER.

TULIP LIGHT

Cast Aluminum
Color: Garden Green
3'' x 4'' with 18'' Stem
6'-0'' Green Plug-In-Cord

BORDER LIGHT; ILLUMINATES WALLS, CASTS DRAMATIC SHADOWS.

Sanctuary

The *Ashumet Holly Reservation* is one of more than 30 Massachusetts Audubon Sanctuaries and open spaces. Its 45 acres, located in East Falmouth, Massachusetts were given to the Society to preserve the famed holly collection assembled by the late Wilfrid Wheeler. On these grounds, near the northern perimeter of the native range of American holly, grow many of the parent trees from which were developed famed commercial strains of northern winter-hardy holly trees. The Reservation also contains a broad selection of European and Oriental hollies, as well as other native plants of interest.

Earth

Seedsmen

Hard-to-find materials.

These seedsmen are innovative, modern with an ecological sensitivity. Among their specialty fertilizers is an unusual one called *Lyon Old New England.* 100% of its nitrogen content (6% nitrogen, 8% phosphoric acid, 3% potash) is naturally organic made from leather in a New England tannery. Being all organic, *Old New England* does not burn. Use it on all trees, shrubs, flowers, evergreens, roses, clematis, rhododendrons, perennials, ground covers — just once a year.

Lyon offers many other worthwhile seed mixtures and fertilizers as well as providing consulting service for your lawn and garden problems.

Catalog available.

John D. Lyon, Inc.
143 Alewife Brook Parkway
Cambridge, Massachusetts 02140

Brimfield Gardens Nursery

A large selection of rare trees, shrubs, and dwarf evergreens are offered by this firm. Send for their catalog.

Brimfield Gardens Nursery
245 Brimfield Road
Wethersfield, Connecticut 06109

DELUXE KIT
(Model A)

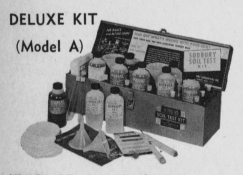

The Good Earth Can Do You Dirt

Sudbury Laboratory, Inc. is the leading manufacturer of soil testing equipment in the world today. Their kits are designed as simply as possible, so that the average consumer can readily determine soil deficiencies in his own back yard in a matter of minutes. *Sudbury* makes fertilizers, repellents and things to help keep your pets from scratching, as well as a variety of soil test kits.

Sudbury Laboratory, Inc.
Sudbury, Massachusetts 01776
Kits from: $6.95 – $42.95

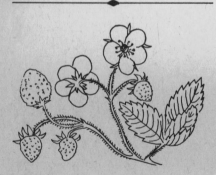

Strawberries

Over a million and a half substantially virus and disease free strawberry plants sold in New England. *Lewis Farms* keeps in touch with university and state agriculture experimental laboratories to keep its program up to date. Catalog available.

Lewis Farms, Inc.
New England Strawberry Nursery
RFD So. Deerfield, Massachusetts 01373

Earth

Dogwood Festival

Each year in May one of the Country's outstanding displays of pink and white flowering dogwood trees may be seen in Fairfield, Connecticut. During the two-week period, when blooms are at their height, the Greenfield Hill Church (located in the heart of dogwood country) sponsors the town's annual *Dogwood Festival.* Daily activities give the thousands of persons who flock to the area to enjoy the blossoms, a chance to participate in all the activities of a typical New England church fair.

The Cape Cod Museum of Natural History
Brewster, Massachusetts 02631

This Museum is a resource institution where questions about the natural environment are answered. Children can attend field natural history classes in such subjects as Geology, Pond Life, Botany, Insects and Marine Life. These classes are conducted by highly qualified instructors, most of them holding a degree in science. The Museum's Environmental Educational Program is designed to foster an ecological awareness in children, and to stimulate them to learn more about their external surroundings. Conservation practices, which will preserve our vanishing natural resources, are stressed. Lectures and field trips for adults are also a regular part of the program. The Museum is developing an extensive library of books and periodicals which will serve as a reference point for all groups interested and active in natural history and conservation on Cape Cod.

All those who believe in Cape Cod and have an interest in its preservation as a place where the natural environment can be seen and appreciated are urged to become members.

Weekly Market Bulletin
New Hampshire Department
of Agriculture
Bureau of Markets
ROOM 201
STATE HOUSE ANNEX
CONCORD, NEW HAMPSHIRE 03301
Tel. 271-2505

Second class postage paid at Concord, New Hampshire. Issued weekly at the State House, Concord, N. H., by the Bureau of Markets.
Subscription $3.00 per year

Gone back to earth — going to do some farming? This is the place to look for used farm equipment, cows, horses, pigs, poultry, sheep — even a farm. It also lists the weekly wholesale market prices for farm produce — very helpful in selling the fruits of your labors.

Conley's Gardening Handbook

A guide to hundreds of Maine-hardy plants acclimated to most New England conditions. Many short, informative articles are woven throughout. How to have a better lawn — foundation planting — spacing of plants and shrubs — fertilizers and their use — the why of mulching — the how-to of pruning and many more, are discussed. A list of shrubs and plants is available by mail order.

MSH

Conley's Gardening Handbook
by Ervin G. Conley
1971; 200 pp., paper
From: Conley's Garden Center
Boothbay Harbor, Maine 04538
$3.30 ppd.

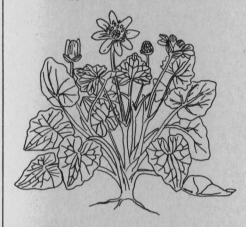

Autumn Color

When the first splash of color appears, though it may be a single branch on a roadside tree, we begin to think of the spectacular color pageant which will soon unfold throughout our wooded areas. If this preview is premature, we may think we are in for an early fall or that there might have been a tinge of frost during the night. Actually frost is not essential for leaf color and premature coloring often occurs in weak trees even in mid-summer.

Leaves turn color due to their own chemistry aided by certain climatic conditions. Through the action of photosynthesis, leaves manufacture sugars and other materials and the amount retained in the leaves as fall approaches has a great deal to do with the extent of color. For it is in cell sap that these sugars and certain pigments are suspended. The most prominent pigment is chlorophyll which gives leaves their green color. Chlorophyll also masks the carotinoid pigments (xanthophyll and carotene) which provide the yellow and orange shades that, though hidden, are present all summer. These are the same chemicals which produce similar colors in flowers, fruits and vegetables and the yellow of butter and egg yolks.

As photosynthesis slows down due to shorter days and reduced light, chlorophyll is no longer produced, allowing the cartinoid pigments to become visible, resulting in the beautiful yellow and orange colors. It is at this time the pigment anthyocyanin is released from the cell sap trapped in the leaves by the formation of corky cells at the base of the leaf stems. This pigment is responsible for the brilliant red and purple fall colors. It is also responsible for the reds and purples in the leaves of such trees as the copper beech and Japanese maple during the spring and summer months. The brown colors of beech and oak leaves which remain in them all winter are due to the astringent tannin.

For best autumn color, days should be warm and sunny, evenings cool, so that accumulated sugars remain in the leaves. Ample rainfall, location of plants, type of soil are all important to good color. It is probable that the yellow color will be good regardless of the weather, but if the days are not warm and sunny and the nights cool, the sugar accumulations in the leaves move into other parts of the tree for storage resulting in the loss of the red and purple colors.

Eat your pineapple and grow it, too.

by DORIS WILSON WEINSHEIMER

If you have enough space for a generous-sized container, why not raise a pineapple? Not only will the plant yield a full-sized pineapple, *Ananas comosus*, but the exotic foliage will add a dramatic touch to your house plant collection. Indoor pineapple farming is fun, too, and ridiculously easy.

The next time you prepare a fresh pineapple for table use slice off the leafy top with about 2 inches of fruit attached. Scoop out with a spoon the meaty part, being careful not to injure the tough little stem in the center.

Now, air-dry this clean-scraped lid until it is partially dry. In the meantime crock an old-fashioned clay pot by putting a curved shard over the drainage hole. Cover with a layer of smaller pieces before adding a thin spread of sphagnum moss. The latter not only prevents the fine soil particles from washing out but it forms a tiny reservoir for moisture. It also admits air freely.

Next, place your clay pot into a jardiniere or small wooden tub. Check your potting soil. If it tends to be heavy and clayish, remedy this by mixing with it an equal amount of peatmoss plus enough sharp sand to make it loose and friable. Then add about three parts of finely-broken charcoal to assure excellent drainage and to keep the soil sweet.

Of course, if your soil is light and sandy, add only one-half the amount of charcoal and no sand. Either way, mix it thoroughly.

Next, pot the pineapple top just deeply enough to cover the skin adequately but keep the leaves exposed. Place your new plant in a draft-free, sunny spot and groom it by nipping off any damaged leaves and water daily from the bottom.

Then, wait for the red bud. This is an arresting collection of many more than a hundred smidgen-sized flowers which, beginning at the bottom of the cluster, open into blue-violet blooms. Each lasts but a day but each remaining flower head develops into one small segment of the mature fruit as we know it. Then all you need to do is to water and feed it as you would any house plant.

Reprinted from *Horticulture*, May 1972 by permission of the Massachusetts Horticultural Society.

PINE APPLE

Witch Hazel From the Indians

Lest we need it, here's another reminder of the heritage left us by the Indians. This time it's the story of Witch Hazel.

The Hamamelis bush with its golden-flowered blossoms was discovered to have magic powers by Indian "medicine men." They found it soothed the aching muscles and bleeding wounds of their warriors. Squaws, too, got relief from their back-breaking toils when the powerful lotion was rubbed on the skin.

The story goes that late in the autumn, the sage Indian fathers noticed the mysterious blossoming of a bush, which occurred, to their astonishment, after the leaves had fallen and when the branches were bare. This striking peculiarity, so different from nature's general rule, led them to believe that the Great Spirit had revealed a shrub possessing magic properties. They collected the twigs, boiled them and suddenly the phantom-like form of a beautiful maiden could be seen through the steam above the caldron. The spirit was Witch Hazel.

It was understandable that the early settlers, who developed their own set of head-to-toe aches and pains, also found comfort in the healing properties of Witch Hazel. In fact, it served them as a general remedy, relieving not only wounds but softening weather-beaten skins and taking the sting out of insect bites.

DICKINSON'S

DOUBLE DISTILLED

WITCH HAZEL

THE E.E. DICKINSON CO. ESSEX CONN.

WITCH HAZEL

ALCOHOL 14% ABSOLUTE

A VALUABLE LOCAL REMEDY
INDICATED FOR THE RELIEF OF CUTS,
WOUNDS, SPRAINS, BRUISES, BURNS, ETC.
ALSO USED AS GARGLE AND LOTION.

Simples

Early New England housewives' cupboards were full of "simples." Many of these home remedies were learned from the Indians, others had been passed down from generation to generation. Written collections of remedies for use in the household were an important part of their lives and every household had its favorites, some of which have been incorporated into our Catalogue. Caution: You must make the judgment as to whether or not they can be applied today.

A New England Simple — To Cure Canker

Use the bark from the white poplar root steeped in water. Swab the mouth and drink a little.

Trees

It's refreshing to find an "industry" giving something back to "Mother Earth." Prices are reasonable, and the product is guaranteed. They do request that full payment accompany each order. Brochure available.

Western Maine Forest Nursery Co.
Fryeburg, Maine 04037

Two examples:

10 Blue Spruce — $3.00 ppd.
Ideal for Christmas trees or landscaping. These are four-year-old transplants, not seedlings. Five to ten inches tall, hardy, vigorous, heavy-rooted.

10 Evergreens — $6.00.
A good variety for home landscaping. Good transplants, five to ten inches tall. Two of each of these five varieties: American Arborvitae, Canadian Hemlock, Mugho Pine, Upright Yew, Colorado Blue Spruce.

Since 1866, the *E. E. Dickinson Company* in Essex, Connecticut has been helping modern man and woman to ease the bruises of their hectic life. From the beginning, the product was known as Dickinson's *Yellow Label* — double distilled — not double diluted. The company has not departed from the high standards set in the early years of production. It is used world-wide for many different ailments — soothing the skin of millions of modern-day aching muscles and bleeding wounds.

E. E. Dickinson's pride in its high quality Witch Hazel is based on its careful selection of the bush it uses (found in the vicinity of Essex), the water used in distilling, the pureness of the alcohol blended, the time of distillation and the sanitary handling of the lotion from still to barrel or bottle.

Today, the Dickinson plant — operated by the fourth generation of the family — is the world's largest and most efficient plant for the manufacture of Witch Hazel.

E. E. Dickinson Company
Essex, Connecticut 06426

Earth

The Herb Farm

Carol and Walter Pflumm run *The Herb Farm*. They welcome visitors (May 1 to Snowfall) to wander around, pick a posie to smell and visit the herb shop which was the old hired man's cabin.

Carol writes: "Our business is an at-home thing that grew out of a much loved hobby and is now an ever-enlarging proposition! I dry lavender, stitch moth bags, sterilize jars, blend potpourris. My husband pushes the rototiller and is my weekend weeder. It's a low key enterprise and fun place to come with the family. Ours is truly a rural town, where the main industry is still picking wild blueberries."

A catalog listing about 70 herb plants points out that the plants cannot be shipped. They are available only at the farm. Books on herbs are also for sale as well as Christmas cards with attached herbs, spices and recipes.

Fred Welsh

The Herb Farm
Barnard Road
Granville, Massachusetts 01034

Storing Fruits and Vegetables

To maximize your gardening efforts, try storing some of the surplus. To get the best information on the proper storage conditions, ask your county agent for a copy of the USDA Home and Garden Bulletin on storing vegetables and fruits in basements, cellars, outbuildings and pits. Or write to Publications, Morrill Hall, University of Vermont, Burlington, Vermont 05401.

Herbs

Herbing, an ancient and honorable avocation, is enjoying a resurgence in popularity today. Herbs are "in" things, and not just among the natural food cultists.

There are many good reasons why people are rediscovering herbs. To the cultists, it's a back to nature route; to the gardener, next to weeds, herbs are the easiest plants to grow; to the cook, a pinch of fresh herb does wonders for any dish; to the reader, there's a wealth of fascinating lore – sage grows well only where the woman rules the household, for example. To the aesthete, colors, textures and scents are particularly pleasing; and to the gift-maker, herbs present an abundance of possibilities from lavender sachets, dried arrangements to vinegars, jellies, teas, perfumes and liqueurs.

And these are but a few of the reasons that put herbs in the marketplace, herb books in the bookstores, herbs at country fairs, herbs in the kitchen and herbs under the Christmas tree.

Herbing is a practical, useful, sensible, historic, romantic, but most of all, fun thing to do.

Sally G. Devaney

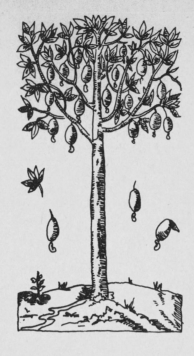

ar-bo-re-tum: A place for the scientific study and public exhibition of rare trees
Over 100 years old and still growing.

Arnold Arboretum: Centennial Year
By Bebe Miles

A century is a long time in man years; it is even a decent interval in the life span of a tree. For an American arboretum it is a real milestone, reason enough for hearty congratulations to the Arnold Arboretum on its 100th anniversary last year.

In fact this great collection of hardy woody plants near Boston has been a public arboretum longer than any other in this country. It contains some of the oldest specimens of certain trees and shrubs to be found in the entire United States.

For gardeners, however, its importance transcends mere age. First, because the grounds were laid out by the noted landscape architect, Frederick Law Olmsted, the collections are aesthetically arranged. The average visitor does not even realize the trees and bushes are grouped by genus until he studies labels. By applying ingenious attention to the differences in terrain, the arboretum's designers have achieved a magnificent blend of natural and artificial.

Second, Arnold Arboretum policy is to grow all possible species, varieties and cultivars of a genus for comparative purposes. In one short walk a gardener may see nearly three dozen different forsythias or magnolias, at least 75 willows or more than 60 species of pine.

Lilacs total just under 500, one of the most complete collections in the world. More than 250 crab apples are available, and there are notable numbers of maples, roses and honeysuckles, to single out only a few. In such surroundings it is easy to pick out varieties with superior flowers, fruits or foliage.

Age of course enters into the gardener's appreciation of what the Arnold Arboretum has to offer. A nursery can display only small specimens of a plant to facilitate carrying and transplanting. Too often the "darling little pine" soon outgrows its home and welcome. An alert gardener can learn much about the size of mature trees and shrubs by touring a collection like this.

In all, the living collections contain some 6,000 different kinds of woody plants from all over the North Temperate Zone. Nearly as many more are growing in the arboretum's nurseries as replacements or improvements. There are notable collections of plants for special purposes, too; dwarf varieties, a bonsai collection, woody vines, more than 100 kinds of hedge plants and ground-cover demonstration plots.

Actually the Arnold Arboretum has three facilities. The arboretum itself covers 265 acres at Jamaica Plain, just southwest of Boston. There are good access roads, or you can reach it from Boston by Arborway trolley. The aim there is to display all the woody plants hardy to the area.

In addition there is a library containing some 78,000 volumes plus photographs and slides and a herbarium of more than 900,000 sheets. Portions of these are located on the Harvard campus in Cambridge, across the Charles River from Boston.

The newest section, the Case Estates, dates from 1942 and is located in Weston, not far from the Massachusetts Turnpike. These trial gardens take up more than 100 acres but are not formally landscaped. Here are wonderful demonstration plots of ground-covers, street trees, mulching and pruning practices and low maintenance plants – all techniques relevant to today's gardening. Plants which will eventually go to the arboretum itself spend their first trial seasons at Weston where the climate is 10 degrees colder than at Jamaica Plain.

All this began with an old farm where the first head of the arboretum counted 123 species of woody plants *in situ* on an early tour. He was Charles Sprague Sargent, and for 54 years he guided the fortunes of the arboretum. In a very large sense it was his imagination, hard work and devotion that created this great institution.

On Sargent's death, Ernest Henry "Chinese" Wilson assumed overall responsibility. An intrepid explorer, Wilson had the talent to recognize worthy new species he encountered on his expeditions to the Orient. Equally clever at packing specimens, he introduced close to 1000 new kinds of plants into cultivation during his lifetime. These were skillfully propagated by the arboretum staff.

Other famous names associated with the arboretum over the years include Alfred Rehder and Donald Wyman. The latter has only recently retired as arboretum horticulturist and has authored several of the most useful books on woody plants for gardeners.

Publications of the arboretum include the *Journal of the Arnold Arboretum* for technical papers and *Arnoldia* for horticultural and general articles for the public.

Excerpted by permission from May 1972 issue
Flower and Garden Magazine
4251 Pennsylvania Avenue
Kansas City, Missouri 64111

Wildflowers

An old, well-established nursery specializing in native, hardy wildflowers, ferns, trees, shrubs, perennials and herbs. They emphasize that wildflowers can only be shipped in the Spring, before mid-April and in the Fall during September and October. Write for free catalog.

Putney Nursery, Inc.
Putney, Vermont 05346

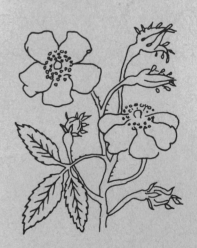

Garden-by-Number Herb Kit

If you've ever slaved over the planning and planting of an herb garden only to find by harvesting time that your orange mint has choked your thyme to death, and you've demolished your basil thinking it was a weed, there's a welcome solution for you.

The people at *Off The Beaten Path* have packaged a Garden-by-Number Kit for the herb enthusiast. It includes a pattern, adapted from a historic design, but reduced to practical proportions; seeds, garden stakes and a book covering everything from indoor seed propagation to herb gift ideas.

The kit retails, reasonably, for $7.00, is mail orderable, and is available wholesale to gift shops.

Claudia

Off The Beaten Path
P.O. Box 324
Southport, Connecticut 06490

full 5' diameter

Choose from 3 distinct designs

5' x 2.5' rectangle ▭

— 5' circle ◯   5' square ▢

✳ OFF THE BEATEN PATH, LTD.

✳ BOX 324 ✳

SOUTHPORT, CONN. 06490

What is a Garden?

A garden is an experience. It is not flowers, or plants of any kind. It is not flagstone, brick, grass or pebbles. It is an experience. If it were possible to distill the essence of a garden, I think it would be the sense of being within something while still out of doors.

James Rose

Reprinted from *Horticulture,* February 1972 by permission of the Massachusetts Horticultural Society.

The New England BUTT'RY SHELF ALMANAC

Being a Collation of Observations on New England People, Birds, Flowers, Herbs, Weather, Customs and Cookery of Yesterday and Today

MARY MASON CAMPBELL

Illustrated by Tasha Tudor

"Happiness is an herb garden."

A charming story about *Greene Herb Gardens,* Greene, Rhode Island, and the two lovely ladies who run it has been written in the New England Butt'ry Shelf Almanac, parts of which are reprinted below.

MSH

The New England Butt'ry Shelf Almanac
by Mary Mason Campbell
Illustrated by Tasha Tudor
1970; 302 pp.

From: World Publishing Co.
110 E. 59th St.
New York, New York 10022
$6.95

The Greene Herb Gardens are situated on the large, well-kept estate of one of Rhode Island's oldest families, and they are famous all over the country wherever people live who are interested in growing things, especially herbs. The Gardens consist of the large main house, with a small aromatic shop located across the carriage drive where the dried herbs which are the product of the Gardens are on display for sale; a greenhouse, drying shed, various other outbuildings, a number of acres of growing plants, and several delightful knot herb gardens which are a joy to wander in any day of the growing year, even in the rain, when the dampness seems to release the fragrance of the plants.

The Greene Herb Gardens were established in 1942 by Miss Mittie Arnold and Miss Margaret Thomas. They had found a mutual interest and challenge in growing and using herbs and decided to pursue it as a business. Miss Arnold's own home was a perfect site with its quiet location in the hills, surrounded by stone walls, great trees, farms, and fields . . .

. . . "Our real interest all these years," Miss Thomas said, "has been seeing this thing which we love — the growing and use of herbs — take hold of other people. We have done our best to encourage this interest by dispensing seeds, plants, plans for gardens and uses of herbs, and other information. It is so much better for a housewife to go out of her own kitchen door and pick off snippets of the fresh herbs she needs than it is to buy them packaged at the supermarket — who knows how long they have been on the shelf?"

They take pride in having helped Old Sturbridge Village lay out the early-nineteenth-century herb garden which is so well displayed at the restoration village in Massachusetts . . .

The interesting Dye Garden which has been established at the old Slater Mill restoration in Pawtucket, Rhode Island, was partially supplied from Greene Herb Gardens . . .

A New England Simple

If a broom is wet in boiling suds once a week, it will become very tough, last much longer, and always sweep like a new one.

Hoe, Hoe, Hoes

Probably man's first primitive farm tool was the bent stick hoe. In Higganum, Connecticut there is a company that has been making a science of the hoe for over 175 years.

To name but a few of the many types of hoes, there are the "Grub Pattern," "Italian Grape Pattern," "American Pattern," "Scovil Pattern," and, best of all, the "Southern Belle" which is a double-ended hoe described as the finest all purpose gardening cultivator and hoe ever developed. To me, it conjures up a picture of Scarlett O'Hara grubbing for the last few turnips in the ruins of Tara.

Romanticism aside, apparently the right hoe for the right job is a sound gardening dictum. A green thumb and a wrong hoe is bad news.

You can buy blades and handles separately if you wish. Scovil Hoes are available at fine hardware stores everywhere. Prices are right, with a Grub Hoe at $3.29 to the Italian Grape Hoe at $7.49. We assume the latter will work with good New England Concords as well.

RWW

Scovil Hoe Co.
Higganum, Connecticut 06441

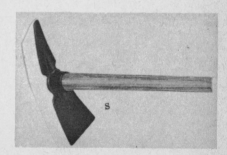

SCOVIL HOE CO.
Higganum, Conn. 06441, U.S.A.

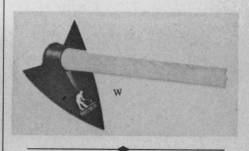

Mulching Strawberries

Spruce humus or needles, applied in the form of a mulch to strawberries, produces upright stems, thus helping to keep the berries clean, and yields berries that are both large and tasty.

Radishes grown near a border of chervil will be sharp in taste.

Earth

Flowering Bulbs

A fine, reputable firm with an extensive collection of Spring and Fall flowering bulbs.

Not only are their prices fair but the planting information given couldn't be clearer.

P. DeJager & Sons, Inc.
South Hamilton, Massachusetts 01982
Send $.25 for catalog.

HYACINTHS IN PLASTIC BULB GROWER

This old-fashioned way is in favour again now that the proper growers are on the market.

Fill the grower with water (rainwater preferred) almost to touch the base of the bulbs. The next procedure is the simple one of placing the growers in any dark cool room, cellar or cupboard until the sprouts are about 3 inches high, then they may be brought gradually to the full light.

De Jager Plastic Hyacinth Bulb Grower with specially designed holder for the bulb for easy indoor culture.

Specially prepared Hyacinths for Xmas flowering. 1 white, 1 blue and 1 pink
P-5000 set of 3 bulbs and growers **$3.00**
P-5100 3 bulbgrowers without bulbs **$1.50**

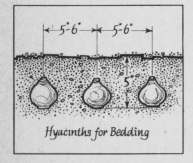

Hyacinths for Bedding

OUTDOOR CULTURE

For successful cultivation in the open air, Hyacinths may be planted any time from September to December. September and October are the best months; they like a light rich soil, the ground should be well-drained. Plant the bulbs at equal distances apart in circles or in straight lines and about 5 inches deep. Never plant the bulbs when the ground is wet. They require a little covering of straw or a thin layer of leaves during the winter to protect them from frost.
Those marked* are easy forcing varieties and especially suitable for indoor culture

CULTURE IN POTS AND BOWLS

Hyacinths should be potted either in soil or fibre early in September for Christmas flowering and every fortnight thereafter for succession. Plunge pots in the coolest place of the garden, or place in a dark, cool cellar, in which case it may be necessary to give water from time to time.
After not less than 8 weeks remove to the forcing house as required, but care should always be taken that the bulbs are well-rooted and the buds well out of the neck of the bulbs before beginning to force as successful cultivation depends on these points. To keep the foliage dwarf and to assist the perfect colouring of the flowers, they should have occasionally a supply of liquid manure during the growing period. Always use clean old pots.

A New England Simple

A pinch of snuff mixed into the top soil of a house plant will kill any worms present.

For planting any type of bulbs

The ideal bulb planter

This Ideal Bulb Planter has been specially designed for planting Daffodils and other bulbs in grass, orchards and borders. The use of the Ideal Bulb Planter enables a large number of bulbs to be planted in a very short time and without disturbance of the sward. Sturdily made, with steel cup, length overall 38 inches, weight 3½ lb. to cut circular hole 2¼ inches diameter.
P 4000—$ 12.50

DAFFODIL PLANTING

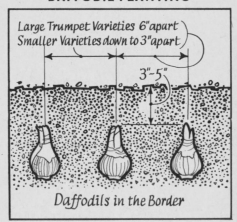

Daffodils in the Border

Soil and its Treatment. Daffodils and Narcissi will thrive in any well-cultivated and well-drained garden soil. In preparing the ground for planting, dig deeply and if well-rotted stable or cow manure is available this may advantageously be worked in 10 to 16 inches deep so as not to come into immediate contact with the bulbs. Never use fresh manure of any kind at planting time. On poor and dry sandy soils we recommend a dressing of bone meal at a rate of about 1 oz. per square yard to be sprinkled over the surface of the ground after planting. The bulbs should be covered with soil to a depth of once and a half to twice its own depth, measuring the bulb from base to shoulder.

Growing Daffodils in the greenhouse or indoors. Many Daffodils and Narcissi are suitable for this purpose some varieties responding better than others to forcing. Pot up the bulbs on arrival and if ordinary pots are used take a good loamy soil, adding sufficient sand and peat to keep the mixture open. A light dusting of bone meal is also useful. Pot firmly in well-crocked pots. For bowls without drainage holes use a good fibre. Plunge the pots and/or bowls in the coolest place of your garden and in the absence of garden space the pots may be placed in a cool cellar (35–40°F) where watering from time to time is necessary. When the shoots are about 4 inches long and the flower buds well out of the neck of the bulbs, the pots may be removed into a warm room. Heat should be gradually increased from 50° to max. 60°F. It is advisable to remove the foliage of the sideshoots, if these do not show a flower bud. Just before the buds are open, water should be sprayed lightly over the buds, when they are in bloom less water should be applied.

Daffodils and Narcissi are suitable for naturalizing but in very heavy soils, preference should be given to stronger growing kinds e.g. Trumpet varieties and many Large-Cupped. They are all admirably adaptable for grassy slopes and banks, where they should be freely planted. A splendid effect is obtained when Trumpet and other varieties are grouped separately, scattered on the ground and planted where they fall.

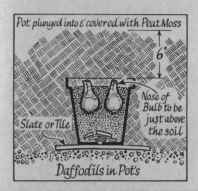

A Portable Coldframe hurries spring along. You can start your annuals ahead of the season. Portable Coldframe is durable aluminum and greenhouse polyethylene. It's 4'L x 2'W x 1½'H, with no wasted space inside; disassembles for storage. Portable Coldframe Kit #132 is $8.95 postpaid (plus 27¢ tax in Mass.). A. S. Margulies Co., 34 Porter Rd., Chelmsford, Mass. 01824.

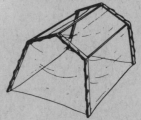

G. H. Grimm Company

"Sugaring is fun" but it takes a tree 40 years old to hold one bucket which is emptied daily for six weeks to produce enough sap to yield one quart of syrup.

Whether you have one 40-year-old sugar maple or one thousand, Robert Moore and sons of *G. H. Grimm* can supply you with every conceivable item for making maple sugar. *Grimm* not only manufactures these materials, but designs many of them as well. They include sap spouts, bits, drills, power tapping machines, buckets and covers, gathering pails, storage tanks and large evaporators.

Later in the year, long after the maple sugar season, you've got to get the hay in. *Grimm* can provide you with a "Super 16 Hay Tedder" — teds 16 feet wide at seven miles per hour. Two other standard models are also available. After the haying season, you can sit the winter out and look forward to the days when the sap will run again.

G.H. Grimm Company
Rutland, Vermont 05701

No-Work Garden Book

My husband — the vegetable gardener of the family, read this book through at one sitting and then proceeded to copy sections of it into his gardening notebook (he has no faith in Santa Claus).

As he wrote he muttered "Why didn't I think of this. . .it's so simple. . .mulch. . .mulch. . .mulch!"

And that is what this book is about — mulch. And those of us who are devoted to other aspects of organic gardening besides mulching — such as companion planting, composting or organic garbage — don't get much mention or support. But, this is a virtually no-work method — and it is easier to toss hay than spade compost!

Anne Ward

The No-Work Garden Book
by Ruth Stout and Richard Clemence
1971; 218 pp.
From: Rodale Press, Inc.
    Emmaus, Pennsylvania 18049
    $6.95

The ROCK GARDEN

STORAGE TANKS

Heavy Duty 20 ga. Galv. with steel angle around top:

175 gal.	60" x 30" x 24"		$54.00
210 "	72" x 36" x 24"		61.00
	1" Outlet extra		3.00

GATHERING PAIL

18 Qt. Galvanized Steel. Low Handle. Weight 4 lbs.		$7.80
20 " " " " " " with pouring rim		9.50

GATHERING TANKS OR HAULING TANKS

Made from smooth, galvanized steel sheets—20 gauge. Riveted and soldered. Rust resisting. Large dumping chamber with removable cone strainer. 2" Tip-down drain pipe, light weight, rubber gasket and wood top plug. 1 Barrel equals 31½ gallons.

Round Tanks -- 20 gauge.

Capacity	Height	Diameter	
3 Barrels	27 inches	35 inches	$ 84.00
4 "	" "	39 3/8 "	93.00
5 "	" "	43	104.00
6 "	" "	47 1/2 "	114.00

Oval Tanks - 20 gauge. Galvanized Sheets

	W x H x L	
5 Barrels	31" x 24" x 58"	$159.00
6 "	35" x 24 x 71"	165.00
7½ "	35" x 26" x 71"	184.00
10 "	44" x 26" 84"	278.00
15 "	44" x 26" x 120"	325.00

Oval tanks have heavy center cylinder and splash baffles, also lifting handles.

SAP STORAGE TANKS -- RECTANGULAR

24 gauge galvanized steel sheets. Steel reinforcing bars all around the top. Corners are double seamed and soldered. Sizes 5, 8, 10 and 15 bbl. have straight sides; 20 bbl. has folded-in center rib; self supporting. Outlet placed in bottom at one end unless otherwise specified. These tanks are ideal for water supply systems.

Capacity	W x H x L		
5 Barrels	34 x 23 x 48	160 gal. 1" Outlet	$ 52.00
8 "	27 x 24 x 96	250 gal. " "	67.00
10 "	34 x 24 x 96	315 gal. " "	80.00
15 "	47 x 24 x 96	475 gal. 1¼" "	98.00
20 "	52 x 32 x 96	630 gal. " "	121.00

STORAGE TANKS, ROUNDED BOTTOM

24 gauge galvanized steel; wood supporting frame, treated for weather resistance. 1¼" outlet flange at one end. (2" outlet available on special order).

Capacity	W x H x L	
15 Bbl.	54" x 30" x 7'6"	$115.00
20 "	54" x 30" x 10'0"	138.00
25 "	54" x 30" x 12'0"	149.00
30 "	54" x 30" x 14'9"	179.00
30 "	58" x 42" x 10'0"	185.00
35 "	58" x 42" x 12'0"	215.00
50 "	58" x 42" x 15'3"	330.00

CONDUCTOR PIPE

3" Conductor Pipe, 10' Lengths—Galv.	each $3.50
3" Conductor Funnel Head Sap Receiver	each 12.50

GERMICIDAL LAMP & FIXTURE

36" Long	$19.00

STORAGE TANK

GATHERING PAIL

ROUND GATHERING TANK

OVAL GATHERING TANK - 5, 6, 7½, 10 AND 15 BBL.

RECTANGULAR STORAGE TANKS

ROUND BOTTOM STORAGE TANK

Hill Country Harvest

This is one of the most exhilarating books I have ever had the good fortune to read! Beautiful, poignant, haunting, fascinating in its lore and detail, quiet sometimes, but never dull, the book is an environmental essay that made me stop, look and listen, and try to perceive the world around me anew. Doorbuilding barnswallows, Queen Anne's lace, woolybears, peepers — oh, a multitude of natural phenomena that urban dwellers miss altogether, and country folk take for granted. Mr. Borland sums up:

"It is easier to maintain perspective on life and mankind somewhat apart from the crowd. That perspective involves certain natural phenomena . . . man should know the earth of his own origins . . . and the benevolence of rain . . . Otherwise he becomes so ingrown, so overwhelmed by the crowd, that he forgets who he is, or where he is."

Anne Ward

Hill Country Harvest
by Hal Borland
1967; 377 pp.
From: J.B. Lippincott Co.
    E. Washington Square
    Philadelphia, Pennsylvania 19105
    $6.95

To The Builders of Old Stone Walls.

They call me, these places, I do not know why,
Unless it's the open, the sun and the sky.
The haze of September, with dreams woven
through of life long ago, and a faith that was true.
The old stone walls with woodbine so red,
And cranberries redder that hang overhead.
Small fruits scattered round, a rainbow in hue
No fairer a garden Persephone knew.
Green grapes and pomegranates, pink crab apples, too.
I rest awhile and close my eyes.
Heaven's best gifts surround me.
A leaf falls gently, and from a tree
A bird's song floats along to me.
It seems to come from the pine by the pool
Or was it the notes of a singing school?
And what was that elfin laugh of glee?
Echoes perchance from a husking bee.
A soft breeze touches the golden rod
And makes it nod approvingly.
Then passes by with a wistful sigh
As if it would say to you and I
"Tis better so exceedingly."
I rise and homeward wend my way
Shadowy fingers beckoning.
My heart cries out with joy to know
That once there lived such folks as you,
Honest workers, brave and true.

Grace Shaw Tolman (89)

Earth

All sorts of interesting plant material and arranging accessories for the Bonsai/Saikei/Terrarium "afficionada." His unusual catalog also offers how-to information, plus an interesting line of kits — three of which are shown below. Add 15% postage East of the Mississippi, 25% West.

Arthur Eames Allgrove
North Wilmington, Massachusetts 01887

KIT SB - MINIATURE INDOOR SAIKEI KIT
This kit makes up into the cutest little Oriental Dish Garden we've yet seen. A real, miniature gem - includes:

1 Serissa   or
1 Iva Lace (your choice)
1 Saikei Oval Container (200)

   Oriental figurine (our choice)
1 Piece of Featherock
1 Small Driftwood
1 British Soldier
Moss, Soil, Directions...Each Kit, $4.95, 3 for $12.95 Plus Postage.

KIT IB - INDOOR BONSAI KIT
Includes the following:
1 Serissa   or
1 Japanese Boxwood (your choice)

1 Bonsai Pot (1S1, 1H1, 1O1 - our choice)
Soil
Bottom Hole Screen
3 Small pieces Featherock
Moss
Oriental Figurine (our choice)
Complete Directions...Each Kit $4.95, 3 for $12.95 Plus Postage.

Herbs

Caprilands: everything for the herb gardener. These products may be purchased at the Farm or through the mail. The gardens contain over 200 varieties of herbs and scented geraniums. How-to paperback booklets are also available from $1.00 to $1.50.

Caprilands Herb Farm
Silver Street
North Coventry, Connecticut 06238

KIT TB - TERRARIUM BOWL KIT
Includes the following:
8 Partride Berries
1 Rattlesnake Plantain
3 Stems Shining Club Moss
1 Stem Striped Pipsissewas
Kelley and Green Sphagnum Moss
      Apothecary Bowl with cover
Directions...Each Kit $4.95, 3 for $12.95 Plus Postage.

Tree Seeds

Maple, holly, magnolia, rhododendron, and fruit tree seeds are just a few of the many interesting types they offer. Catalog available.

F. M. Schumacher Co.
Horticulturists
Sandwich, Massachusetts 02563

Heavy Equipment Repair

This is a book for mechanics and would be of little use to the casual reader or the home handyman. For someone going into the repair business, or the owner-user of heavy equipment, whether it be tractor or steam shovel, it gives the ins and outs of engine repair and upkeep. All the basic information needed to keep heavy equipment in good running order is in this book.

                                        Lance S. Hall

Heavy Equipment Repair
by Herbert L. Nichols, Jr.
Illustrated by Helen Schwagerman
1964; 621 pp.
From: North Castle Books
      212 Bedford Road
      Greenwich, Connecticut 06830
      $12.50

Courtesy of International Harvester Co.
Fig. 17-70. Hydrospring shock absorber in hoist line
469

Amateur Sugar Maker

The story is of a college professor who fashions himself a sugarhouse for $91.03, and takes up maple sugaring in a small Vermont town. In simple and personal terms, author Noel Perrin captures the spirit of self-reliance, and lovingly traces the triumphs and failures of his "prentice" year. Complete with illustrations and prices of equipment, Perrin bubbles sugar lore and optimism for the beginner. How-to-do tips include the art of tree tapping, purchase of a two-pan evaporator rig, a spot of cream to keep syrup from boiling over. "Might's well come look" at *Amateur Sugar Maker.* It's a Grade A source of sap from tree to table. An honest testament of what "one man can do alone with just his hands and a few tools."

                                               SJI

Amateur Sugar Maker
by Noel Perrin
1972; 104 pp.
From: University Press of New England
      Hanover, New Hampshire 03755
      $4.50

Amateur Sugar Maker

BY NOEL PERRIN

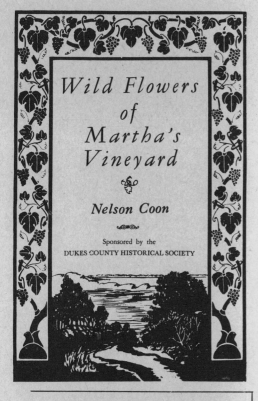

State of Maine County Maps

• **Detailed** • **Accurate** • **One Scale**

Androscoggin, Kennebec, Sagadahoc, Lincoln (One Plan); Hancock, Piscataquis, Penobscot Somerset, Washington, Aroostook (North Part), Moosehead Lake Region, $1.25 each; Cumberland-York (One Plan), Franklin, Oxford, $1.00 each; Waldo, Knox, Aroostook (South Part), 75c each. Complete set — flat for mounting — $10.00.

PRENTISS & CARLISLE CO., INC.

107 Court Street   Bangor, Maine

◆

Vermont Ware

A rugged, lightweight cart designed by truck body builders and made to last a lifetime.

Here are some of the details which make the Vermont Ware Cart reliable:

- large 20" wide-tread semi-pneumatic tires for easy rolling and stair climbing
- functionally placed wheels for balance and easy pushing or pulling
- holds more — 2 to 3 times as much as a wheelbarrow
- narrow enough to go through doorways
- stores easily — just stand on end or hang on a hook
- high handle makes pushing and pulling easier
- tight-welded, lightweight all steel body with wear-resistant finish

To top it off, after three months of use, if you are not satisfied with the cart, *Vermont Ware* will refund the full purchase price with no questions asked.

Vermont Ware
Hinesburg, Vermont 05461

Cart prices:
From $39.95 to $69.95 plus shipping

Using Wayside Plants – Wild Flowers of Martha's Vineyard

That Nelson Coon is a lover of gardens can be accepted through his credentials. That he is a man of love and reverence for all that exists in God's garden world — plants and animals — is evident in every page of these two books.

Using Wayside Plants is, as its name would suggest, a how-to-do-it book, a manual of 100 common, useful wayside plants found in the northeastern region of the country, with photographs and uses of each. It's a book with some delicious sounding recipes; chapters on medicinal usage, dyeing, crafts, amusements for children, and wild plants in and out of the house. There's a good working index, and a fascinating bibliography. It is a simple book, with no pretentions at being scholarly, but with every intention of being a useful one, which indeed it is.

Wild Flowers of Martha's Vineyard, by comparison, is more scholarly, giving Latin names, families, and quite detailed line drawings. This book is a compilation from various sources of plants to be found on Martha's Vineyard. It is not, the author states, complete, either in its listings or in the amount of information given on each plant. It is thoroughly adequate for the incidental wonderer-about-plants, and beautifully done, with short sections on birds seen when botanizing and interesting tidbits of history about the Vineyard.

Anne Ward

Using Wayside Plants
by Nelson Coon
1969; 288 pp.
$5.95
Wild Flowers of Martha's Vineyard
by Nelson Coon
1969; 175 pp., paper
$3.95
From: Nelson Coon
          Box 1
          Vineyard Haven, Massachusetts 02568

Down East: The Magazine of Maine

From the deep water coast to the cold reaches of Moosehead, northeast to Fort Kent in Aroostook and back down to Kittery is a long distance marked by topographical extremes. But many states in the U.S.A. are endowed with as varied and beautiful land as Maine, yet few possess such an individualistic way of living on it. *Down East* catches that rare flavor of this most northeasterly state in a provocative, readable manner. Maine goes very well on its own but being proud of its Yankee heritage, it is sensitive, indeed, to the ways its personality is depicted. Month in and month out, *Down East* speaks well for the Pine Tree State in its articles — giving a fare as varied and positive as its land and people. Doc Rockwell's sage "Newsletter" (he's the maker of fine cigar ashes since 1889), Gene Letourneau's "Outdoor Maine" for the sportsman and the poignant "Room with a View" are some of the monthly features which touch on the pulse of Maine's heartbeat. For the prospective property buyer, serious or otherwise, there's page after page of houses and land tempting the eye and pocketbook. If all of this doesn't motivate you to hop into the nearest car, bus, train, plane or boat and head down East with a copy of same under your arm, then you haven't read *Down East* thoroughly.

Down East   JCH
Camden, Maine 04843
$6.00 per year, 10 issues

USING WAYSIDE PLANTS

Nelson Coon

Stairhouse Greenhouse

Transform an unattractive cellar entrance into a year-round garden under glass.

The *Stairhouse Greenhouse* attaches directly to the house wall. It is intended as a replacement for an existing bulkhead with minimum alteration needed. It is equally adaptable to ground level exits where no stairs are involved.

The design of *Stairhouse* provides maximum sunlight with double strength greenhouse glass from ridge to sill, set in a frame of structural extruded aluminum. The entire unit is completely prefabricated and can be easily assembled by any handyman. Send for illustrated brochure.

Priced from $425.00.

Verandel Company
P.O. Box 1568
Worcester, Massachusetts 01611

◆

Toss coffee grounds, egg shells and vegetable scraps on the mulch pile to help make a fertilizer that is much better than any that you can buy.

◆

He "Built a Better Mousetrap"

Very shortly after purchasing an income-producing apple orchard, Mr. Wheeler found a need for a better pruning saw than those that were commercially available — so he designed one. It has grown in popularity over the years and is now widely used by fruit growers, tree farmers and nurseries everywhere.

Mrs. Wheeler writes that since her husband's death, she is carrying on the business tradition of offering a quality product at a fair price.

The Wheeler Saw Co.
Belchertown, Massachusetts 01007

HANDY SAW

H   **4.50** ppd.
                              Patent No. 2,817,899

Still the best saw you can buy for pruning and trimming. It has been called a "lady's saw", but don't let that fool you. Designed for use in the orchard and woodlot, it is made of finest materials and will bear hard use. 16" replaceable blades now 90¢ each. Just attach your name, address, and a check to this ad and mail to

WHEELER SAW COMPANY, Belchertown, Mass. 01007
(Mass. residents add 3% for Sales Tax)

Earth

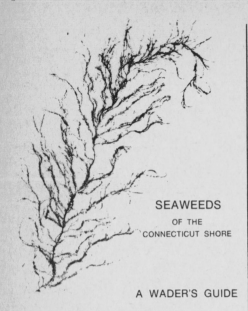

SEAWEEDS
OF THE
CONNECTICUT SHORE

A WADER'S GUIDE

In the foreword of this Bulletin, Dr. William A. Niering, Director of the Arboretum, says:

Anyone who has strolled along the shore of Southern New England has encountered the tremendous array of seaweeds cast up on the sandy beaches. After storms the quantity of this marine produce can be measured in tons. Even the casual observer will have noted the colors range from green to reddish brown. Green lettuce-like fragments—sea lettuce, brown belt-like straps, several feet long—the kelps, and highly branched delicate rods represent the three major groups of seaweeds. Have you ever wondered whether you could identify this great diversity of forms? Here is your opportunity to be guided by two students of phycology.

There is no environment in greater jeopardy today then the coastal zone. Sixty percent of the nation's population lives in a band 250 miles wide along our shoreline. It is worth recognizing that the beauty and diversity illustrated in the pages of this Bulletin represent millions of years of evolution. Yet in a few decades much of what we see here could be lost. There is no doubt that one of man's greatest future challenges will be the preservation of the tremendous floristic and faunistic diversity that has evolved in the coastal zone.

The Connecticut Arboretum
Connecticut College
New London, Connecticut 06320
$1.00

___

Companion Plants and How to Use Them

What causes certain species of plants to grow better in the presence of other plants? Learn that answer and more in this valuable little book which ought to be a reference for every gardener.

"Anise seed will germinate and grow better if it is sown with Coriander seed; apple trees infested with scab have been helped by chives growing near their roots; after carrots are harvested, do not store them in a cellar near apples, the latter will make the carrots bitter." These are just a few of the many interesting and helpful gardening hints in this book.

MSH

Companion Plants and How to Use Them
by Helen Philbrick and Richard B. Gregg
1966; 113 pp.
Published by The Devin-Adair Company
One Park Avenue
Old Greenwich, Connecticut 06870
From: John and Helen Philbrick
P.O. Box 96
Wilkinsonville, Massachusetts 01590
$4.95

Environ/Mental Essays on the Planet As A Home

If you believe that expansion and development mean progress — read this book! The social and psychological consequences of overpopulation are emphasized and esthetic issues are woven throughout this group of nineteen essays written by leading ecologists, sociologists and economists. Certainly important reading for those concerned with the state of the world around them.

MSH

In the headnotes introducing an essay by F. Fraser Darling, world-renowned conservationist, Editor Paul Shepard writes:

It is now possible to travel hundreds of miles in many parts of the United States without seeing domestic farm animals. Landscapes once animated by cows, horses, pigs, sheep, goats, chickens, and other fowl are fast disappearing. In part this is a result of the specialization, geographic localization, and individual farm economy of modern agriculture. It also marks the disappearance of such animals as the plow horse.

The absence of animals on the bulk of the land signifies more than a change in farm economics, however. As browsers, grazers, scavengers, and manure-makers, animals have been the principal agents in the creation of the rural environment for perhaps 5000 years. They have been the intermediaries, the tools, connecting men to the soil and the vegetation. As such they have carried in their genes certain behaviors and physical needs which left their mark on that environment and on the rhythm of farming and herding. In some ways these animal traits acted as a kind of restraint on the hand of man; in others, they simply limited the capacity of the human enterprise.

The pastoral countryside molded by animals was vastly different from that which is emerging now. It is common to hear the transition to "industrial agriculture" extolled in the news media as an unqualified achievement. But we know almost nothing about the long-term effects of these new procedures on rural people themselves, both on the farm and in town, or on the natural processes which are the source of agricultural wealth.

The history of husbandry is littered with geographic wreckage and its human consequences. Will we ignore its lessons on the assumption that they do not apply to us?

Environ/Mental Essays on the Planet as a Home
Edited by Paul Shepard and Daniel McKinley
1971; 308 pp., paper
From: Houghton Mifflin Company
2 Park Street
Boston, Massachusetts 02107
$4.50

___

The music that can deepest reach, And cure all ill, is cordial speech.

Ralph Waldo Emerson

___

Arcadia: rare, beautiful and mysterious.

Arcadia occupies an ancient oxbow of the Connecticut River. It is a valuable laboratory for the study of how the land was formed, and a center of concern for what man is doing to the land.

When the first English settlers arrived here in the mid-seventeenth century, Arcadia was the scene of Indian encampments and raids, river floods and agriculture. The varied habitat of the meadows attracted myriads of wild creatures, and it has remained a rich environment for both plants and animals.

The Land

Arcadia now stretches along the last mile of the Mill River, bordering the famous Ox Bow of the Connecticut River. The 450 acres of the sanctuary include the largest river marsh in the central Connecticut Valley, part of which may be viewed from a special observation tower. The marsh attracts major waterfowl concentrations during spring and fall migrations. Upland woods are occupied by nesting hawks and owls, songbirds, and many native mammals. Large agricultural fields are skimmed by swallows and are nested upon by bobolinks. Deep swamplands echo the calls of wood ducks and green herons. Millions of gallons of flood water are stored here during the spring freshet, replenishing the ground water supply and maintaining the flood plain forest. The spring flood is, itself, a natural wonder of impressive magnitude.

Arcadia is administered in three land-use categories: the managed area where food and cover plantings for wildlife have been created and maintained; the interpretive area with well-marked and labeled trails; and the wilderness area where the influence and intrusion of man is minimized.

Arcadia Nature Center and
Wildlife Sanctuary
Easthampton, Massachusetts 01027

Natural Resources

Preserve our natural resources is their message of concern. It's vital to join your local or state conservation association — wherever you live.

The Connecticut Conservation Reporter
Northrop Street
Bridgewater, Connecticut 06752
$1.00 yearly to members. Write for information.

The following is excerpted from The Connecticut Conservation Association March 1972 issue.

Wetlands today are faced with perhaps the greatest threat since settlement of this continent. Each wetland drained, filled or polluted comes from a greatly reduced natural resource base. Individual wetland types and the total natural wetland resource are rapidly approaching a stage where they can be placed in a remnant or rare category. Preservation of every acre is important. It is not too late to save this resource, but to do so, we must have action now. If we will act now, we can retain the many values, the variety and productivity of North American wetlands.

Conservation Terms

Wetland: Any area that is more or less regularly wet or flooded, where the water table stands at or above the land surface for at least part of the year. These are distinguished according to the condition of wetness and the resulting type of vegetation into marsh, swamp and bog.

Marsh: An area normally covered with shallow water the year round. Typical marsh vegetation is rooted in the underwater soil and may be totally submerged, float at the surface, or emerge above the water. Characteristic marsh plants are water lilies, pond weeds, cattails, sedges, arrowhead, and marsh marigold.

Swamp: An area that is flooded or water-logged in winter and early spring, but usually dry at the surface in summer. Ordinarily it is covered with wet-tolerant trees and shrubs. Typical are red maple, black gum or tupelo, willow, alder, sweet pepperbush, and highbush blueberry.

Bog: This develops in an essentially undrained depression with no outlet or where outflow is drastically impeded. Normal decay is extremely slow, and dead organic matter accumulates as peat. The water is cold, strongly acid, and practically devoid of oxygen and available nitrogen. Bogs harbor a distinctive group of plants that includes many members of the heath family such as cranberry, leatherleaf, and Labrador tea, as well as the insectivorous pitcher plant and sundew. Typical trees of northern bogs are tamarack and black spruce, while southern white cedar is most common in southern bogs. Also typical is sphagnum or bog moss that forms a thick, spongy, water-holding mass in which other plants may find a root-hold.

Flood plain: A flat, low lying area bordering a river or stream; not strictly a wetland, since it is flooded only at times of very high water. All rivers flood periodically, however. In fact, it is the silt deposited during flood stages through the centuries and millennia of which the flood plain is constructed. One can expect that flood plains will continue to be flooded at intervals, a fact that should be considered in deciding how they are to be used.

Insect Repellent Herbs and a Spray

Garden without DDT or other chemical insecticides, according to owners of *The Herbary and Potpourri Shops.*

Herbs offer protection through combination planting. Send for their extensive list of insect repellent herbs which offers information such as:

Chives — repels aphids when planted near lettuce and peas.

Lavender — repels ticks.

Horse Radish — used in combating fungi.

Pyrethrum — usage dates back 2000 years in China. It breaks down rapidly on exposure to sunlight, so can be used as a pre-harvest spray, and is considered safe for this purpose by the U.S. Department of Agriculture.

Medicinal, culinary, dye and native Cape Cod herb assortments are also offered. Descriptive price list available.

The Herbary and Potpourri Shop
P.O. Box 543
Childs Homestead Road
Orleans, Massachusetts 02653

Beachbuggy Wildlife Tours

The Massachusetts Audubon Society offers *Beachbuggy Wildlife Tours of Monomoy Island,* off Chatham, Cape Cod. A Federal wildlife refuge since 1944, this fragile area of beach, dune and sheltering thicket — giving protection to the rigorous domain of wildlife — is protected from alteration by man.

The wildlife tours conform to the wilderness concept. A vehicle is used only in accepted areas with most of the exploration traversed on foot. Be prepared for up to four miles of walking and wading, interspersed with some insects.

Detailed information available from:

Wellfleet Wildlife Sanctuary
Box 236
South Wellfleet, Massachusetts 02663

Organic Gardening

Whatsoever a man soweth, that shall he also reap. (Gal. VI-7)

The Natural Organic Farmers' Association is a non-profit cooperative dedicated to rebuilding the soil and rural lifestyle of New England. The association joins together to market its produce and share its experiences and knowledge. By working freely together, family farmers benefit from markets far afield. Speakers and printed material are available.

Natural Organic Farmers' Association
Box 321
Putney, Vermont 05346

Watershed Council

By joining, you will be helping each other.

Through the efforts of the *Connecticut River Watershed Council* and its Land Conservancy Program, many natural areas and scenic landscapes are being preserved for the use and enjoyment of present and future generations. As a private conservation organization supported entirely by membership contributions and foundation grants, the Council is quietly working to preserve the Connecticut Valley landscape in the states of Vermont, New Hampshire, Massachusetts and Connecticut.

The Land Conservancy Program is one of many projects undertaken by the Council since its founding in 1952 by a group of concerned, conservation-oriented citizens. The Council is actively engaged in water pollution abatement, fisheries restoration, controlling riverbank development along the main river and its numerous tributaries, and solid waste management, to list a few of its programs. These projects are undertaken by council members who are assisted by a full-time professional staff.

When you take a trip through the Connecticut River Valley and see a beautiful hillside or riverscape, it could be very possible that this conservation association is already hard at work to protect that area so that you may always enjoy it.

Membership in the *Connecticut River Watershed Council, Inc.* is open to anyone interested in subscribing to its conservation purposes. For further information, contact:

Christopher Percy, Executive Director. CRWC
125 Combs Road
Easthampton, Massachusetts 01027

Living the Good Life

More than thirty years before the advent of contemporary communal or independent living, Helen and Scott Nearing pioneered to a farm in the Green Mountains of Vermont to escape a society whose ways no longer appealed to them. They sought out a life of "economic self-containment" to be accomplished by good planning and "bread labor" with plenty of time for cultural and creative activity.

Their efforts proved to be an outstanding success in developing a productive farm with handsome, durable buildings, a year round supply of good food, and enough cash crops to supply any needed money. Friends or strangers were always welcome so there was a constant stream of visitors who stayed a night or for months, and who cooperated in varying degrees.

Breakfasts of apples, sunflower seeds and a black molasses drink — or lunch of raw cauliflower and boiled wheat would not appeal to everybody, but their vegetarian diet kept the Nearings in great good health all during the twenty years of this remarkable and satisfying Vermont sojourn.

Ellen Hill

Living the Good Life
by Helen and Scott Nearing
1970; 213 pp.
From: Schocken Books
67 Park Avenue
New York, New York 10016
$4.95

Earth

Maps

Clear — Correct — Complete maps.

The map described below is one of many offered. New England:

A beautifully lithographed, medium-scale map of the six New England states. Interstate and state highways are stressed on this map. It measures 3 feet by 4 feet. Scale: 1:570,000 or about 9 miles to the inch. Many unusual features, such as airports, ferry routes, etc., are shown. Available unmounted, on paper — $8.50.

The National Survey
Chester, Vermont 05143

The New England Colonial Gardens

The long, hard winter tended to restrict the size of Northern colonial gardens. Usually kept compact, nestled close to a building and surrounded by a tall hedge or wall, they were not so much for show as for utilitarian purposes — an important part of the household economy presided over by the house-wife.

MSH

The New England Colonial Gardens
by Rudy J. Favretti
1964; 32 pp., paper
From: The Pequot Press, Inc.
      Chester, Connecticut 06412
      $1.50

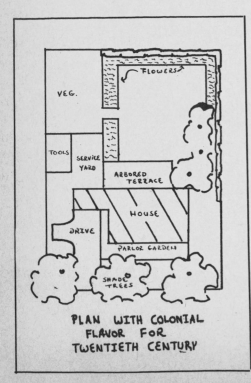

PLAN WITH COLONIAL
FLAVOR FOR
TWENTIETH CENTURY

There is a sumptuous variety about the New England weather that compels the stranger's admiration — and regret. The weather is always doing something there; always attending strictly to business; always getting up new designs and trying them on people to see how they will go. But it gets through more business in Spring than in any other season. In the Spring I have counted one hundred and thirty-six different kinds of weather inside of twenty-four hours.

Mark Twain

Earth

The Maple Sugar Book

An exhaustive search of rare books and forgotten documents plus much practical knowledge has been combined in these pages and anyone who enjoys a well-written book on an interesting topic will find satisfaction here.

Charles T. Letson

The Maple Sugar Book
by Helen and Scott Nearing
1970; 273 pp.
From: Schocken Books
      67 Park Ave.
      New York, New York 10016
      $5.95

Convenient groups of maple trees do not in themselves constitute a sugar bush. They must also meet climatic requirements. All maple trees run sweet sap in the spring. To make syrup production commercially feasible, however, the sap season must be of relatively long duration — at least three or four weeks.

Maple sap can be turned into edible syrup at any time from the first spring thaw until the leaf buds burst. The best or "first-run" syrup is made before the buds begin to swell. Syrup production is therefore possible in direct proportion to the length of time between the first thaw and the swelling of the leaf buds. The longer the time, the more sap and syrup.

Tools for Obtaining Sap

Tapping tools are simple. They consist of a brace and bit and a light hammer or hatchet. We use a breast drill instead of the ordinary brace. We prefer the breast drill because it is somewhat faster and the motion is less tiresome than that of the common brace. The size of the bit varies slightly according to the size of the spout used. The regular tapping bit is usually seven sixteenths of an inch in diameter, about five inches long, and rather fast cutting.

Sap is obtained from the tree by boring a hole, inserting a spout, and hanging a covered sap bucket on the spot. In the olden days, as told in chapter three, spouts were made of elder, sumac, birch, or balsam wood. Maple producers now use metal spouts. They are about three inches long, made with a tapered shank that is driven into the tree, a channel through which the sap runs from taphole to bucket, and a hook on which the sap bucket hangs. The ideal spout should not corrode, should allow free flow of sap, exclude all air from the hole, be strong enough to hold a full bucket, and yet be as light as possible so as not to damage the tree unduly. . . .

Sap Weather

The most important single factor in sugaring is the weather. Those who wrest a living from nature — farmers, herdsmen, woodsmen, fishermen, hunters — are keenly weather conscious, because the pursuit of all of these occupations is determined to a considerable degree by the weather. Among the weather-conscious farmers, sugar makers rank high in the list, because sap production is tied tight to weather.

Sap is available in quantity only after severe freezing. It cannot run when the thermometer reads below 30 or 32 degrees. It stops running when the mercury rises to around 50 degrees. It will not run when the trees are in leaf. With autumn and early winter out on account of the low sugar concentration in the trees (the sugar accumulations having been devoted to summer tree growth), the sugar maker is limited to the few warmish days or weeks that intervene between the breakup of winter and the burgeoning of spring. . . .

Maple Custard Pie

Line pie plate with fluted-edge pastry. Fill with the following custard: 1 packed cup maple sugar, 2 tablespoons butter, 1½ cups scalded milk. Stir over fire till sugar dissolves and mixture bubbles. Dissolve 1 tablespoonful cornstarch in ½ cup cold milk, 3 slightly beaten eggs, and ½ teaspoonful salt. Add to sugar mixture and pour into pie plate. Sprinkle nutmeg lightly over top of custard. Bake 10 minutes in a hot oven, then reduce heat and finish baking in moderate oven for about 25 minutes, or until knife inserted comes out clean.

Windmills Most Any Size

From complete windmills 8 1/2' high to four post, galvanized steel windmill towers 80' high that weigh some 2,691 lbs., and are called, implausibly, "Appeal" towers, *Edward A. Larter, Jr.*, of Dunstable, Mass., has them. Other odd tower code names are "The Amenia," "The Amery," "The Appraise," and "The Amity." The 8 1/2' high complete windmill (called a bit more plausibly the "Mini-Mill") sells for $95.50 f.o.b. Lowell, Mass., but we do not have prices on the bigger mills or towers.

Mr. Larter sells the BAKER RUN IN OIL WINDMILLS, and they need oiling but once a year. He also can supply any parts you might need plus windmill mechanisms, pumps, gears, and ancillary equipment.

It was not until we read Mr. Larter's engaging literature that we learned a windmill when in gear faces the wind and when out of gear faces fully out of the wind.

RWW

Edward A. Larter, Jr.
Main Street
Dunstable, Massachusetts 01827

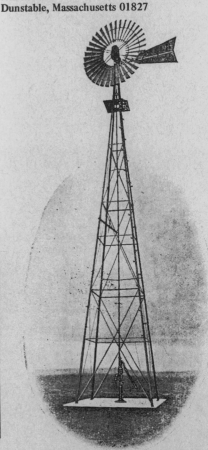

The living legend that is America is famous throughout the world. In song and story and poem, its growth can be charted from Plymouth to the Golden Gate. A bit of this legend is with us today whenever a Morgan horse carries a saddle-weary cowhand down off a Montana mountain; works his cow well and efficiently in a Wyoming cutting contest; doubles with a team-mate to pull the carriage for an Iowa mayor on the Fourth of July; carries the grandchild along Vermont's Green Mountain pathways while grandfather rides along on another — or flashes around the showrings from California to Illinois to Massachusetts. For the Morgan Horse, our country's oldest breed of light horse, is as much a part of America today as he was almost two centuries ago.

Justin Morgan himself was a living legend. As a small, rough-coated colt named Figure, he and his owner, the quiet-spoken schoolteacher Justin Morgan, left Springfield, Massachusetts late in 1789 to try for better fortune in Vermont. The little colt's predominantly Thoroughbred and Arabian ancestry showed even then, in his straight clean legs, the deep muscling over quarters and shoulders and his short, fine head with its large, expressive eyes and short, pricked ears. But even with all that, his lack of size was such that he found no buyers along the journey. It was Fortune's whim that no one should realize what a Little Giant he was. Over the years in Vermont, and for a variety of owners, the little bay stallion worked hard. Gradually his exploits gained him a kind of rough hard-earned fame. There was the time when he alone pulled that log a draft horse could not budge. There was the day he carried a President on a muster-day parade ground. And the time he out-ran the winningest quarter-mile racehorse central Vermont had, until that day, ever known.

As his saga grew, there came countless sons and daughters in his image. For little Figure, now known as Justin Morgan in honor of the man who brought him to Vermont, was also one of the greatest breeding horses of all time. Sons Sherman and Bulrush and Woodbury were of the same mold; strong, willing, able light horses, the kind that made it possible to log off rugged Vermont mountainsides and convert them into farms. But they weren't mere workhorses, for a Vermonter took just pride in the beauty of his trappy little horse. Coats curried, long, full manes and tails brushed out, harness or saddle brasses shined, Morgan

The Morgan Horse

horses filled city horsemen's eyes and still their fame grew and their colts sold. The good broodmares earned their oats on the farm, but sent sons and grandsons in ever-increasing numbers to be smart roadsters for Boston and New York financiers. Trotting racing reached a hey-day in the 1850's and the World's Fastest Trotting Stallion was Ethan Allen 50, old Justin's handsome, bay, great-grandson. New England men answered the call of gold and headed for California on Morgans, leaving hoofprints for lesser horses to follow. Came the Civil War and the famed Vermont Cavalry — all mounted on Morgan horses. Then Indian wars and the only survivor of the Little Big Horn, Keogh's Morgan-bred horse Comanche. For if all of the pathways of history are paved with the bones of the horse, then surely America's were laid there by Morgans.

The great stamina and vigor of the Morgan, together with his excellent conformation and way of going, have gone to make other American light horse breeds what they are today. There has never been a Standardbred to beat 2:00 for a mile, from Greyhound to Billy Direct, that has not had Morgan blood. In the 1860's the Morgan stallion Shepherd F. Knapp was exported to England where his trotting speed became a byword. Today, many English Hackneys carry his name on their pedigrees. In American Saddlebred history, such famous champions as Edna May, Bourbon King and Rex Peavine trace to Justin Morgan. Rated the best of all time, mighty Wing Commander himself is another descendant. The foundation sire of the Tennessee Walking horse, old Allen F-1, was a grandson of the Morgan stallion Bradford's Telegraph. Good Morgan mares went to Texas, only to lose their breed identity in Quarterhorse bands - and to make them greater for it. The American Albino and Palomino owe much to early infusions of Morgan blood. The oldest of all, only the Morgan was strong enough to contribute greatly to every other

one of America's light horse breeds — and yet to retain his own identity across two centuries.

The original Justin Morgan was a small horse. Barely over fourteen hands, he never weighed much over a thousand pounds, not an ounce of which was mere fat. The muscling over his quarters, along his back, down through thighs and gaskins and forearms was deep and strongly laid onto dense flat bones. Only such a horse could live almost thirty years and do the work of a good draft team for some twenty-eight of them. When you add the quality of clean, relatively hairless fetlocks, a thick but silky mane, a clean-cut throatlatch, a lovely head with huge, alert eyes and tiny, eager ears— then you have the physical conformation of the ideal lighthorse. Justin Morgan was up to any amount of work his many owners asked of him. Doing it all and doing it well, he remained sound of eye and wind and limb throughout a lifetime of two ordinary horses. That should have been enough but he added still more — trappy, alert, gaits with speed to spare at any one of them — a disposition that made him safe for a child to handle yet with spirit to spare for any horseman — beauty that men were to recall long decades after his death — and that rare, high courage that made men who lost wagers on him still lift their flagons of rum and say "To the little Morgan," and drink deeply.

Present-day Morgans differ remarkably little from their mighty progenitor. Some selection has had to be made over the past century in order to adapt the breed moderately to modern usage. Originally, his major use was as a harness horse. Today, it is under saddle. Therefore, his breeders have selected among his numbers for a little added size and somewhat sharper withers. Nothing of his courage, his disposition, his substance or his type has been sacrificed in the process. You may visit farms from New England to California and see bands of Morgan mares with the same deep bodies, lovely heads and straight clean-boned legs that roamed Vermont pastures over a century ago. In barns and show rings from one end of this country to the other are the stallions; heads high, eyes and nostrils wide, Morgan quality showing in every hair on gleaming, muscular bodies.

Reprinted with permission from
The American Morgan Horse Association.

The Morgan Horse
Box 265 West Lake Moraine Rd.
Hamilton, New York 13346

$6.00 yearly — members
$7.00 yearly — non members

Fleeceless Sheep?

Old Sturbridge Village has taken the unusual course of trying to "un-improve" modern farm animals and is importing three rare sheep from Australia as part of the program.

The sheep, two ewes and a ram, are Horned Wiltshires, believed to exist in very limited numbers only in Australia and England. Because of British quarantine regulations, the Village has been forced to bring the animals thousands of miles from Australia.

Horned Wiltshires are fleeceless, fat animals that gain weight rapidly. Research by the Village indicates that crossing the Horned Wiltshires with its own Dorsets will produce an animal resembling the "common sheep" of New England, circa 1790-1840. These "common sheep" were relatively small, with little or no fleece. It was their lack of wool which led to their abandonment as farm animals in the region.

The program to return the museum farm animals to their earlier forms is already under way, with plans to breed back cattle, chickens and pigs. Some chickens already have been returned to their earlier forms.

A group of gray seals are making their home along the northwestern shores of Nantucket Island. This herd is the only one known to exist in waters surrounding the U.S.

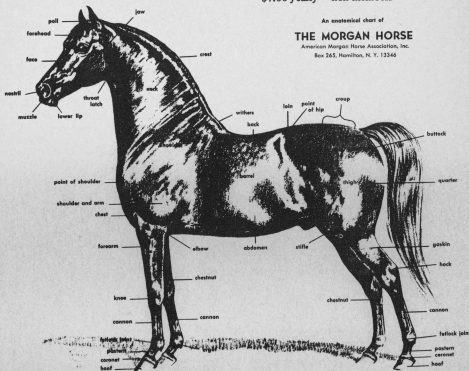

An anatomical chart of

THE MORGAN HORSE
American Morgan Horse Association, Inc.
Box 265, Hamilton, N. Y. 13346

Earth

18

For Cow and Horses

In 1890 Kow-Kare, a tonic for cows, was first manufactured by *Dairy Association Company*. In 1910, an ointment called "Bag-Balm" was made. They've been going strong every since. Other products added include Bag Balm Dilators, Kalf-Kare, Green Mt. Hoof Softener and Horse-Kare. Humans have discovered that bag balm is great for a lot of problems cows never heard of; for instance, squeaky bed springs, burns, cuts, bruises, and night cream. The Dairy Association recommends its products for use as prescribed — on cows and horses.

Dairy Association Co., Inc.
Lyndonville, Vermont 05851

Green Mt. Hoof Softener 1 lb. $2.50
Bag Balm Pail 4½ lbs. $9.50
Bag Balm 10 oz. $1.25

Convenient 4½ lb. Pail

Popular 10 oz. CAN

All Purpose Ointment for Horses and Cattle

GREEN MT. Hoof Softener

For softening hardened, dry pinches or contracted hoofs and quarter cracks

M.S.P.C.A.

To their knowledge, *The Massachusetts Society For The Prevention of Cruelty to Animals* publishes the only magazine in the world devoted entirely to animals. It is available at $3.00 per year by writing the Society at:

M.S.P.C.A.   MSH
180 Longwood Ave.
Boston, Massachusetts 02115

A New England Simple

Fleas and vermin on dogs may be destroyed by bathing them in a strong infusion of lobelia for two or three mornings, washing with soap and water after each application.

Earth

GUARD YOUR HORSE'S FEET

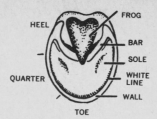

Your horse is an athlete. Proper hoof care is a must. "No Hoof — No Horse" is an old adage that all owners of horses should remember. GREEN MT. HOOF SOFTENER containing LANOLIN will help you.

A healthy frog is soft, moist and elastic to a remarkable degree. It is the function of the frog to destroy shock and to prevent slipping. Because of its soft structure, puncture wounds or any type of wound should be cared for immediately.

A. CANNON BONE
B. LONG PASTERN
C. SHORT PASTERN
D. COFFIN BONE
E. NAVICULAR BONE
F. FETLOCK JOINT
K. COFFIN JOINT
P. PASTERN JOINT

a. Extensor Tendon
b. Deep Flexor Tendon
c. Perioplic Ring
d. Coronary Band
e. Plantar Cushion
f. Sensitive Frog
g. Horny Frog
h. Periople
i. Sensitive Sole
j. Horny Sole
k. Sensitive Laminae
l. Horny Wall
wl. White Line
x. Ergot

To perform satisfactorily your horse's feet must be sound. To help keep them in good condition the following routine is suggested:

1. Check each hoof daily, paying particular attention to the area around the horn of the frog. Clean out between the frog and bar, to make sure no stones, nails, etc. are imbedded to cause lameness.
2. When the heel and frog are too dry and hard, clean out any pockets and pack daily with GREEN MT. HOOF SOFTENER.
3. For dry, contracted hoofs and quarter cracks apply GREEN MT. HOOF SOFTENER daily around the coronary band and wall of the hoof to help keep it soft.
4. Trim the frog sparingly.
5. Do not trim the bars excessively.
6. The sole should be trimmed if there is evidence of excessive growth.
7. Roll or round the edges of the wall to prevent chipping and breaking.
8. Shoe or trim the horse's feet every four to six weeks.
9. Keep the correct hoof angle. The angle of the hoof should be the same as that of the pastern and shoulder.

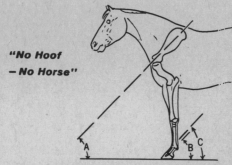

"No Hoof — No Horse"

Angle A = Angle B = Angle C (shoulder, pastern, hoof)

The Village Blacksmith

Under the spreading chestnut tree,
The Village Smithy stands.
The Smith, a mighty man is he,
With large and sinewy hands
And the muscles of his brawny arms,
Are strong as iron bands.

Henry Wadsworth Longfellow

In the summer, *Stephen Parker* shoes horses. The remainder of the year is spent making weather vanes, fashioning bed-warmers or creating a variety of functional fireplace tools. Sparks fly high and wide as metal begins to soften — muscles bulge and sweat runs freely as lifeless metal is twisted and turned into various shapes.

Local boys and girls know that if they hang around long enough, he'll eventually fashion a horseshoe nail ring for them.

Stephen Parker, Blacksmith
Box 40
Craftsbury, Vermont 05826

Bedwarmers	$100.00
Andirons	$ 60.00
Crane Jacks	$ 40.00

Weather Vanes — Priced to fit the job.

A Maine Blacksmith

David Court's work covers a wide area of general blacksmithing — shoeing horses, making shoes, redressing tools, repairing general equipment and antiques, designing and building ornamental and functional pieces.

Prices upon inquiry.

David Court
R.F.D. 2
Limerick, Maine 04048

SHEFFIELD, MASS. 01257

The sheep industry's production and management paper. Published monthly.

$3.50 yearly   MSH

Riding Equipment

Having served the horse community for nearly ten years, this English riding shop has become a kind of "headquarters" for families who enjoy horses.

Mr. and Mrs. Aquino, who preside at *The Saddler*, make regular junkets to England to keep up with the appurtenances of riding. Their shop features proper clothing and equipment, plus an array of gifts and accessories of the trade.

The Saddler's Sporting Gallery, for example, includes one of the most fascinating collections of hunting and riding prints. And there are original pins and jewelry, crystal, pewter, Spode, books, stable and grooming supplies, and even clothing for the horse. It is a museum for people who love horses. The horsey set is most welcome at *The Saddler*. A purchase is not necessary.

THE SADDLER
FOR ALL YOUR RIDING NEEDS
9 DANBURY RD. • WILTON • CT.
0 6 8 9 7

There's Still B'ar In Them Thar Hills . . .

or so say the folks in Jacksonville, Maine, and they ought to know! In the Spring of '72 a 370 pound bear tore a man-sized hole in the side of Alex Kennedy's barn and made off with his young veal calf. It took four days to trap the big animal – but Mr. Kennedy finally got his revenge.

In Maine, bear is protected by a closed season. However, when one becomes as bold as this animal did, there's a strong possibility that it will strike again – only the next time it could be someone's child. So all effort must be made to destroy it.

Suggested by Jay and Susan Lowe

A beaver must have a natural habitat with plenty of wood to chew on. In fact, his front teeth grow so fast that if he didn't chew on wood to keep them worn down – his back teeth wouldn't close and he'd starve to death.

Doggie Life Vest

Doggie Life Vest. Soft vinyl foam of vibrant orange. 3 sizes. Small 10" to 14" chest. Medium 14" to 18" chest. Large 18" to 22" chest. Adjustable buckles for best fit. $6.95 + 95¢ postage and handling.

Fore 'N Aft
P.O. Box 259
Marblehead, Massachusetts 01945

Frog Baitin' . . .

A sport my grandfather excelled at. By the time I came along, he'd given it up, but I never tired of the tales woven around his frog catchin' days. There was a time when he was considered "the best damned frogger in three counties" and he went to great lengths to uphold that reputation. Only a willow branch would do for the pole – one with the spring of a taut rubber band. The hook, fashioned out of a piece of wire and one end sharpened to a razor-like point, was tied at the end of a long piece of string attached to the pole. A piece of last winter's red flannels torn into a three inch strip and attached to the hook completed the outfit.

You dangled that line just right, in front of a big bullfrog – and if he took the bait you'd have one hell of a fight on your hands. Granpa used to say that he'd yet to see the trout that could give you the fight a solidly hooked bullfrog gave.

This wasn't as easy as it sounds – because first you'd sneak up on the "wary old frog" – positioning yourself behind him in such a way that he wouldn't know you were there. You slowly dangled the red flannel about six inches in front of him – then twitched the pole slightly, just enough to set the piece of flannel in motion. Weren't many frogs that could resist the lure and frog's legs were eaten at least once a week at his house. Granpa always said, "there was no one who could cook frog's legs like my mother with the meat so sweet and juicy that they tasted far better than any chicken I've ever eaten." He may have been right – though the thought of eating any part of a frog has never appealed to me. Here's one of her recipes for anyone who cares to indulge.

Frog's Legs

Wash the legs with salted water, dry them and dip into a bowl of flour. For twelve legs, put about 4 walnut sized pieces of butter in a heavy iron skillet and heat until it foams up. Add 2 minced cloves of garlic and cook for a few minutes; add the frog's legs and fry 'til they are golden brown on each side. Add salt, pepper, chives and parsley to taste. Cook a few minutes longer. Serve immediately.

MSH

Accessories for pets

Harnesses, nail clippers, leads, carriers and many other worthwhile items.

R. D. Symonds
58 John Street
Clinton, Connecticut 06413

Safeguard Harness
$1.50

New Haven, Connecticut was the first "cattle-town" in the country – minus the brawling and bars associated with the later western ones. There and in other frontier Connecticut towns, such as Farmington, techniques of breeding, feeding, and veterinary care were improved. Branding and recording of brands were also worked out. All of these things were the basis for the great cattle industry in the West, once it was discovered.

Animals Nobody Loves

The author, who has his M.S. in Wildlife Management, has written many natural history books for adults and children, and he obviously loves *all* wildlife, including many species that most of us either fear or dislike.

In chatty, informal style, he tells about twelve "creatures," how they act and look, and what fears and superstitions people have had about them through the years. Pigs are really good housekeepers if given half a chance. "Animal behavior experts say the hog has one of the highest I.Q.'s of domestic animals." Vultures are an essential part of nature. A carrion feeder "eliminates a potential source of disease and pollution. With splendid efficiency it quickly returns minerals and organic compounds to the world of the living." Bats are important in the war against insects. They "keep right after the bugs all night until the birds take over in the morning."

I needed no encouragement to see the finer side of wolves, coyotes, and even spiders, but no amount of persuasion could bring me to see any merit in fleas, mosquitos or rats, though it was fun to read about them.   Lephe Symmes

Animals Nobody Loves
by Ronald Rood, illustrated by Russ W. Buzzell
1971; 215 pp.
From: Stephen Greene Press
Brattleboro, Vermont 05301
$6.95

Harness makers for three generations.

The Sanborns make and repair harnesses and saddles of many kinds. Hard-to-find parts are also their specialty. If you have an elephant who needs a harness or a llama without a bridle, the Sanborns can fill that bill. They have recovered dashers for buggies, releathered shafts and surrey fenders. Fine workmanship and pride in it, best advertise *H. N. Sanborn & Son*.

H. N. Sanborn & Son
Chelsea, Vermont 05038

Earth

THE ART AND PRACTICE OF HAWKING

E.B. MICHELL

The Art & Practice of Hawking

Mr. Michell's book is undoubtedly one of the best of its kind available.

Even to the layman with just a slight interest in hawking (or an intellectual curiosity), the book proves both interesting and informative. How many of us, for instance, realize that the only true falcon is the female peregrine?

Mainly, however, the book is aimed toward the experienced falconer. Not only is a short history of falconry given, but Michell identifies all varieties of hawks and eagles known to be useful in the sport, the necessary appliances for keeping and training hawks and methods of training, maladies common to hawks (with suggested cures), and a listing of the virtues and vices of hawks is given. In short, this book may be called the falconer's Bible.

Also included are specific chapters dedicated to rook hawking, game-hawking, the goshawk and the sparrow hawk.

Originally published in 1900, the book has little practical value today, save for remote places on the globe where land is still free and unencumbered by civilization or forests. Woodlands are taboo for the falconer, as are undulating or steep hills, thereby rendering New England unsuitable for the sport.

However, the western United States could conceivably be a falconer's delight, if he would be satisfied with mostly game rather than winged targets.

Mr. Michell's book is enlighting in its explicit detail and is uplifting to the sport as it raises it far beyond a craft and nearly to the point of an art.

Martin Robbins-Pianka

The Art & Practice of Hawking
by E.B. Michell
1971; 291 pp.

From: Charles T. Branford Company
Newton Centre, Massachusetts 02159
$7.00

Tackmaster

Used for years by tanners, *Tackmaster* is a one-step, all purpose cleaner, preservative and conditioner which thoroughly penetrates the leather, helps to prevent mildew and restores natural oils.

Green Mountain Horse Products
Division of Dairy Association Co.
Lyndonville, Vermont 05851
1 Pint Plastic Bottle $1.50

STARTING RIGHT with TURKEYS

The "Have-More" Plan Reference Library

Starting Right with Turkeys

For the homesteader, 4-H'er or just anyone who's looking for an unusual business, these two books give all the how-to's of housing, breeding, feeding, cutting up, freezing and even cooking, turkeys and chickens.

MSH

Starting Right with Turkeys
by G.T. Klein; Edited by Ed Robinson
1972; 126 pp., paper
$3.00

Starting Right with Poultry
by G.T. Klein; Edited by Ed Robinson
1972; 177 pp., paper
$3.00

From: Garden Way Publishing
Charlotte, Vermont 05445

Can Turkeys and Chickens be Raised Together:

It is never safe to raise turkeys and chickens in the same pen because of the danger of Blackhead, the notorious turkey disease. The chicken acts as a carrying host for the Blackhead organism. This does not mean that it is impossible to raise chickens and turkeys on the same lot or in the same building, provided their housing units are separated.

In fact, it is entirely practical to use the poultry house for raising young turkeys as well as young chickens. The project would be worked out something like this:

Late May — Move laying hens out of the poultry house and build a shelter for them. This can be very crudely constructed. Use the poultry house and sunporch for brooding young turkeys, but be sure to disinfect thoroughly first.

August 1 — Confine the turkeys to the sunporch; build a roof over part of the sunporch for protection. Keep the turkeys on the sunporch until slaughtered. House new pullets in the poultry house.

Obviously, after chickens and turkeys are separated as explained above, you must be careful not to walk directly from the poultry house into the turkey pen. Infection can be easily carried on the shoes and this might set off an outbreak of Blackhead that would be disastrous. Have a pair of rubbers just outside the turkey pen and always wear them when you go into the turkey pen. Take them off as you step outside.

Doors For Pets

Creators of the well-known *Flexport* door units for pets — now offer a unique drinking fountain as well.
Turen, Inc.
Danvers, Massachusetts 01923

THE SAFE AND WONDERFUL
PET DOOR

automatic drinking fountain

Stops thirsty whining and improves health.

Refills as your dog drinks to provide a constant supply of fresh, clean drinking water. Price includes 2 ft. hose, couplings, bracket, pipe, valve and bowl.

Complete $11.75

Earth

Huskies

If your preference in dogs runs along the toy poodle line, forget a visit to *Norvik Kennels*. Their specialty is Alaskan and Siberian Huskies — strong, working dogs who also have a reputation, despite their wolf-like appearance, for kindness and intelligence.

In addition to the sale of dogs, the kennel stocks harnesses, collars, racing and driving sleds, fur parkas, skins and robes. You can also arrange to hire a single dog, or a dog team, for "special occasions." I can't precisely imagine the "special occasion" that would require the presence of sixteen speedy Alaskan huskies with sled — perhaps I lack imagination.

Claudia

Norvik Kennels
Center Harbor, New Hampshire 03226

Starting Right With Milk Goats

Get a goat and it'll soon be turning your brush, weeds, grass clippings, hay — and anything else it can reach — into good tasting, naturally homogenized milk, cream, butter, cheese and ice cream. A milk goat should average two to three quarts of milk daily — quite a saving when you consider that milk and milk products account for about 25 per cent of the average family's food budget. Many other reasons for raising goats, along with all the how-to, are included in this book.

This reviewer was raised on goat's milk and can attest to its goodness. However, having also watched a cantankerous buck tow mother across the back fields at the end of a ten foot rope (travelling at a mighty fast clip), I can attest to their unpredictability!

MSH

Starting Right With Milk Goats
by Helen Walsh; Edited by Ed Robinson
1947; 138 pp., paper
From: Garden Way Publishing
Charlotte, Vermont 05445
$3.00

A New England Simple — To Discourage Mosquitoes

Oil of sassafras left uncorked in a room at night will keep mosquitoes away. It also relieves the itching of bites.

Enjoying Maine Birds

The subtitle of this book, "An Aid to Finding, Studying, Identifying, Photographing and Attracting Birds in Maine," is a comprehensive and eminently fair description of this attractive offering of the Maine Audubon Society. The color photographs on front cover, (Common Puffin in Full Breeding Attire) and back cover, (Young Cedar Waxwing) raise expectations in the reader that are not wholly fulfilled in the section given over to identification and description. However, the black and white drawings are first-rate; the accounts, readable and authentic.

Only eighty Maine birds are presented; most are common, some uncommon. Inasmuch as 270 or so species are reported in Maine annually, it may be wise to keep Roger Tory Peterson in another pocket on your next bird walk down-east. Of special interest is the section on "Where to Find Birds in Maine," by Dr. Pettingill; the Check-List (with key to habitats) by Dr. Huntington; and the bibliography, "Sources of Information on Birds," also by Dr. Huntington.

Fessenden Wilder

Enjoying Maine Birds
Edward F. Dana
1972; 80 pp., paper
From: Maine Audubon Society
Portland, Maine 04101
$1.50

Herring Gull
Larus argentatus

This familiar white "sea gull" is less a bird of the sea than of the tidal flats, harbors, inland rivers and lakes, and garbage dumps. It can be found at any time of the year.

Larger than a Common Crow, the adults are pure white except for gray wings and back, black wing tips with white spots. Bill bright yellow with red spot; legs pinkish. Young birds are very dark, appearing black at a distance, and second-year birds are intermediate, showing much white on body, and gray on wings, but with dark tail and black-tipped bill. Sexes alike. Spring calls are high-pitched, repeated screams — *keeow, keeow, keeow*, etc. Alarm note is *ha-ha-ha, ha-ha-ha*, given at breeding colony.

Nest in colonies on coastal islands or islands in large lakes. The bulky nest, made of seaweed, grasses and debris, is placed on ground or sometimes in low evergreens. Eggs: 2 or 3, bluish or brownish, spotted and blotched with brown and gray. Incubation: 28 days, by both sexes. Both parents care for young. Chicks are fed on regurgitated food held in parent's beak or dropped on ground. They swim well and fly in about 6 weeks.

Herring Gulls feed on garbage and scraps from fishing boats; also live fish, molluscs, crustaceans, sea urchins, and starfish; sometimes frequent cultivated fields where they eat insects and their larvae. Very bold in taking scraps at picnic areas. Capture food while flying, plunging into water, swimming, walking, or wading. Occasionally take food from other birds.

SEPTEMBER

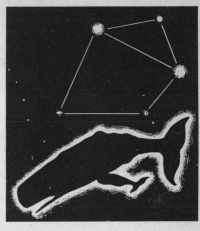

The Year of the Whale

"It is early September when for the first time the Little Calf sees light — a blue-green, dancing light. He slips easily from his mother's body beneath the surface of the Pacific Ocean two hundred miles west of Mexico, on the Tropic of Cancer. He trembles, for the water is cold and he has lain for sixteen months in a warm chamber at ninety-six degrees. He gasps for air as his mother nudges him anxiously to the surface with her broad snout. He breathes rapidly and desperately for a while, puffing with each breath a small cloud of vapor down the autumn breeze."

So begins one of the most interesting and beautifully written books I have ever read. The story, written as fiction based largely on fact, gives a rare insight into the mysterious and wild environment of the sperm whale. From birth in September, to gradual weaning from the mother sperm, one year later, in August, the reader shares in an experience which leaves him feeling slightly awed, and with a tender appreciation for what is considered "the grandest of the toothed cetaceans."

From the time of Moby Dick to present day, the sperm whale has held a special, mystical meaning. Moving through a dark, watery world, the whale is timeless — ancient. It prowls the ocean floor, half a mile down, under the guidance of powers and senses that scientists are only beginning to understand.

In writing about one particular whale, the author tries to show how men feel about whales, what they do to whales and what whales do to men.

Mr. Scheffer occasionally departs from the fictional part of a young sperm's life to give information about the study of whales, about whaling, past and present, about conservation and other matters related to the sperm whale.

It's easy to see why this book was the winner of the Burroughs Medal for the year's best book in the field of natural history.

Each chapter is named for a month of the year and the decoration by Leonard Everett Fisher that opens each chapter depicts the zodiacal constellation of that month and a different position or activity of the Little Calf or his companions, as described in the text.

MSH

The Year of the Whale
by Victor B. Scheffer
Decorations by Leonard Everett Fisher
1969; 213 pp., paper
From: Charles Scribner's Sons
597 Fifth Avenue
New York, New York 10017
$2.45

Have you heard of the wonderful one-hoss shay,
That was built in such a logical way
It ran a hundred years to a day?

Oliver Wendell Holmes

Earth

The Social Insects – Bees

Beekeeping is older than recorded history. One of the earliest known paintings of bees in existence was painted in a cave in Spain more than 15,000 years ago. The bee has survived some 19 million years with slight change from its original form and way of life, lasting proof that it has found the formula to meet and overcome those challenges of nature which proved too much even for the giant dinosaurs.

Though controlled by man, the honeybee has never actually been domesticated. Honey and beeswax are produced over a wider geographical range than any other agricultural crop. In fact, there is scarcely a country in which honeybees are not kept. The United States annually produces millions of pounds of honey and beeswax – New England being a major contributor to this natural wealth.

In a colony, the queen is capable of laying 2,000 eggs every day. She has the ability to control the sex of each of these eggs, and determines whether an egg shall hatch as a worker (female) or drone (male). There is no such thing as a "queen bee egg." It is impossible for a queen bee to reproduce one of her own kind. The creation or conception of a potential queen bee is solely the decision of worker bees.

When an old queen dies or abdicates, potential queens are selected by the workers. Any worker egg or larva, not more than three days old, may be chosen for the dubious honor. Incredible as it may seem, a worker egg left to develop without interference produces the complex organism that is a worker bee. She nurses the larvae, makes wax and comb, keeps the hive clean, guards against intruders, then spends the last days of her brief life, toiling without respite, foraging in the fields for pollen and nectar. At the height of the honey flow, the worker bee has a life expectancy of six weeks. Three weeks taking care of her hive duties and three weeks afield foraging for food. The worker bee performs all the chores that are necessary for the welfare of the colony with one exception, that of egg laying. But give that same worker larva a little more "Lebensraum", keep it on a strict diet of "royal jelly" and it becomes an equally complex organism – that of the queen bee – following an entirely different route of development and accomplishment. One notable change is the queen's life span, which may extend six to eight years in comparison to the worker's short six weeks.

A queen bee does not gain her high office by descending from a royal line or by divine right. She and several other worker eggs are nominated candidates by groups of their peers throughout the hive. Those selected are given special attention and fed royal jelly, which actually transforms and prepares them for their royal duties.

When the workers have chosen an egg or larva, harbinger of a queen that may eventually reign over them, they tear down the walls of the cell in which the candidate lies and start building a queen cell around her. When completed, a queen cell, made of wax and usually attached to the side of the comb, resembles a peanut shell in size, shape and color.

As the princess advances through the larval stage, she is fed by nurse bees. The candidates are fed so copiously, they actually float in a sea of royal jelly inside their cell. Royal jelly is a secretion produced by glands in the nurse bee's head; regurgitated, it is fed directly to the larva or added to the reservoir of this special food in the cell. To accomodate the fast growing larva, the queen cell is steadily enlarged or "drawn out." At the end of the princess' larval period the tip of the cell is capped off by the workers and the entombed princess passes through the pupal stage with no further assistance by her nurses. Sixteen days after the egg is laid, the fully matured princess gnaws her way out of her cell to declare her sovereignty.

Once free of confining quarters, she sounds a high pitched challenge to any other pretenders who may be ready to contest her right to be queen. Customarily, the workers nominate more than one candidate to strive for the high office of ruling monarch and build several queen cells at about the same time. The first princess to emerge rushes to those queen cells from which come answers to her challenge; tearing the cells to shreds, she stings her competitors to death. These assassinations continue until all her rivals have been vanquished, after which she takes a well earned rest, then swiftly walks about on an inspection tour of her domain. She is not yet accepted by her sisters, they do not crowd around her, she must first prove herself by returning from a successful nuptial flight.

Four to ten days after the victory over her rivals, the surviving princess prepares for' her wedding flight. On a bright, sunshiny day she takes wing, to mate, high in the air, with the fastest flying drone of those who pursue her. He couples with her in mid-air, dying in the act, actually exploding and depositing millions of spermatozoa in a pouch within the bride's body. The queen seldom mates more than once in her lifetime, thereafter becoming both mother and father to all the eggs she may lay. This is the most important day of her life, the culmination of all the preparation and manipulation to accomplish this feat. She is now truly a queen and returns triumphantly to her colony.

Arriving home, she is immediately surrounded by her royal attendants who take care of her every need from this moment on. They wash, clean, massage, comb, and feed her.

The new queen starts laying within 48 hours after mating. She inspects each cell carefully to see that it is properly cleaned and polished. Having satisfied herself that a cell is ready to receive an egg, she straddles the cell, inserts her long slender abdomen into it and leaves a single egg. Even during the few seconds required to lay the egg, the queen's royal ladies-in-waiting groom and feed her. The queen may lay eggs for five or six minutes, then rest for a few seconds, when her royal attendants again surround and care for her needs.

The endless round of egg laying is repeated over and over for the rest of the queen's life. She is now more a simple egg laying machine, rather than a royal personage. A queen may lay millions of eggs in her lifetime. She controls the sex of each egg by touching it with a speck of the father's sperm to produce a sterile female worker or withholding the sperm to produce a drone. But, she does not decide when or how many eggs to lay, this decision is made by the nurses. When there is sufficient pollen being harvested to feed the larvae, the nurses stuff the queen with royal jelly and she continues to lay at top speed.

When the pollen supply falls off, the nurses restrict the queen's intake of royal jelly and she immediately slows down or stops her egg laying activity.

This well-organized life in the beehive is considered to be the highest development of division of labor found in any animals lower than man. It occurs within some ant and wasp groups, but nowhere is it carried to a higher point of development than among the bees.

Eugene Keyarts

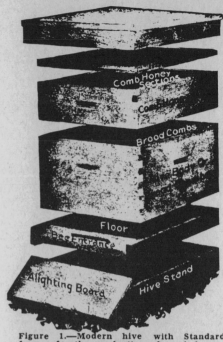

Figure 1.—Modern hive with Standard frames for the production of comb honey. (Any style of comb-honey super may be used.) The honey is stored in square boxes or sections. The sections are held in place by section holders.

Starting Right with Bees

If you have any inclinations toward raising these busy creatures, this beginner's handbook on beekeeping will get you off on the right foot. Twenty chapters provide step-by-step procedures, accompanied by numerous illustrations.

Beginning with a chapter on "Who Can Keep Bees" this guide goes into building hives, handling bees, wintering, producing comb honey and marketing it.

"Beekeeping is an occupation for old or young, rich or poor. It is for the professional man or woman, tired and worn with office work; and it is also for the vigorous man in his prime who seeks profit and pleasure alike from its pursuit."

Surely most everyone qualifies. How about you?

Charles T. Letson

Starting Right with Bees
1971; 96 pp., paper
Published by: The A. I. Root Company
Medina, Ohio
From: Garden Way Publishing
Charlotte, Vermont 05445
$1.00

Barrels make colorful displays. A large barrel with a keg on each side is an eye-catching arrangement or you can use a large barrel as a main display with smaller kegs set down the road as "come ons".

Audubon Approved Birdhouses

Birdhouses designed to last ten years or better are Mr. Thibault's claim. A one man operation, only the finest materials are used, and each design has been approved by the Audubon Society. If, for any reason, you are not satisfied, he will cheerfully refund your money.

Jeremiah J. Thibault
R.F.D. #2
Winchester, New Hampshire 03470

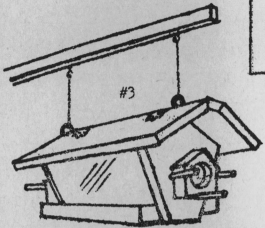

#3

$11.95

#3. JUMBO FEEDER DISPENSER 9 x 11 x 18"L. Half of roof swings on 2 strong hinges for easy loading, glass sided to contain 10 lbs. of seed. A suet block at ea. end will contain ½ lb. suet ea.

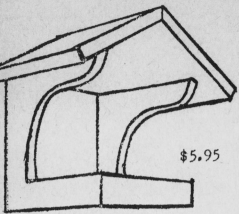

$5.95

#11 Robin House Robins like an open area with roof to build a nest, this house provides this. May be placed on Tree, Post or Building with screw provided.

Bird Banding
A Journal of Ornithological Investigation

A flock of facts for serious birdwatchers. Scientific articles of investigation range from "A Generalized Computer Program in Fortran IV for Listing All Possible Color Band Permutations" to "Red-Winged Blackbirds Wintering in a Decoy Trap." Probably the most useful aspect of *Bird-Banding* is two sections entitled "General Notes" and "Request for Information." In each, birdlovers can share, compare or request specifics on individual banding projects. Current ornithological publications are listed and reviewed. Nesting, reproduction, migration or psychology — every imaginable aspect of bird life is displayed. With scholastic dedication, *Bird-Banding* is a well-formed tribute to the many people who are actively working for the preservation and conservation of all birds.

SJI

Bird Banding
A Journal of Ornithological Investigation
From: Northeastern Bird-Banding Association
      Rutland, Vermont 05701
      $8.00 yearly subscription; quarterly

Look What I Found!

The time is right for this appealing book. Children have always wanted to bring home injured or orphaned wildlife, or to have small wild animals as pets, but their efforts have not usually met with success. Mr. Case tells which animals will survive — and even thrive — in the home atmosphere, how to care for them, and, most important of all, when and where to return them to their natural habitat. One can even learn to build an "ant observation house" or a "meal worm farm" which will provide food for turtles, snakes, frogs and fish.

With the growing interest in conservation education, this is a welcome book, attractively illustrated with photographs and drawings, and written for both the youthful and adult reader.

Lephe Symmes

Look What I Found! The Young Conservationist's Guide To The Care and Feeding of Small Wildlife by Marshal T. Case
Drawings by Mary Lee Herbster
1971; 95 pp.
From: The Chatham Press, Inc.
      Riverside, Connecticut 06878
      $4.95

PINE GROSBEAK
and his friend, Al Martin

Hand-Taming Wild Birds at the Feeder

What a beautiful little book this is! The author says he isn't much on writing words, but the simple ones he has used are more than adequate. They convey love, sensitivity, common sense and beauty. They instruct as well as entertain.

A very detailed and effective manual for the hand-taming of birds (and I have personally tried his methods and can attest to them). This little book also contains some of the most delightful stories of birds, small animals and people I have ever read.

Besides the basic rules for hand-taming wild birds, there are instructions on bird feeders, bird baths, seed mixtures, care of sick and injured birds, photography, identification and how to deal with predators, tame (your neighbor's cat) or wild (from chipmunks to hawks). The book is small enough to take into the field, enjoyable enough to read by the fire. It is short on photographs, and as the author is a competent bird artist, it seems a shame that more of his own work is not used to illustrate the book — but perhaps that would be superfluous, as his words are so graphic. The contents page is very workable, even in a hurry, and there is a list of North American birds in the back.

Anne Ward

Hand-Taming Wild Birds at the Feeder
by Alfred G. Martin
1971; 145 pp.
Publisher: The Bond Wheelwright Company
           Freeport, Maine 04032
From: Duncraft
      25 South Main Street
      Penacook, New Hampshire 03301
      $2.95

Mr. Martin writes:

You may have heard that hummingbirds will sometimes travel south in the feathers of a wild goose. You have never heard of a hummingbird being seen actually getting on a goose to take the trip. Many of you have accepted the story as nothing but a fairy tale. Unless you were a wild goose or could talk to a goose, it would be difficult to prove.

"One evening a friend called at my studio and laid a Canada goose on the table, then took a male ruby-throated hummingbird from this tobacco pouch and placed it on the head of the goose.

"Al," he said, "I shot this goose down on the Cape this morning, and when I picked him up, this little fellow rolled out of the feathers. He was still alive but died in my hand."

"I am just as sure that ruby-throated hummingbirds will ride a goose as I am that aviators ride planes."

There warn't anybody at the church, except maybe a hog or two, for there warn't any lock on the door, and hogs likes a puncheon floor in summertime because it's cool. If you notice, most folks don't go to church only when they've got to; but a hog is different.

Mark Twain

Earth

Birdwatchers

Attention — birdwatchers and friends of birds. Everything you need from:

Duncraft
25 South Main Street
Penacook, New Hampshire 03301
Catalog $.25

A New England Simple

To clear a room of tobacco fumes, place one pint of hot water and three tablespoons of ammonia in a glass bowl. Let it sit overnight.

A Field Guide to the Birds

Widely used by beginner and expert — this guide clearly emphasizes the field marks and characteristics of all birds found East of the Rockies, and is particularly helpful in identifying birds when seen at a distance.

MSH

A Field Guide to the Birds
by Roger Tory Peterson
1947; 230 pp.
Houghton Mifflin Company
2 Park Street
Boston, Massachusetts 02107
Order From: Duncraft
25 South Main Street
Penacook, New Hampshire 03301
$6.10

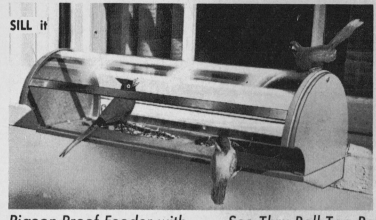

That Quail, Robert

Little did the Thomas Kienzles know when they rescued an egg from an abandoned nest, that it would hatch into a baby quail, soon to become a cherished member of their Cape Cod household. Robert's habits and adventures are lovingly recorded in this book.

Although the story may seem somewhat sentimental to the more sophisticated reader, it will appeal to the young adult interested in nature study.

Esmé Willis

That Quail, Robert
by Margaret A. Stanger
Drawings by Cathy Baldwin
1966; 127 pp.
From: J.B. Lippincott Company
E. Washington Square
Philadelphia, Pennsylvania 19105
$4.95

LEAST FLYCATCHER

— or —
chebek chebek

Grayest of the group

Habitat: — Farms, orchards, groves, open woods; northern U.S. and Canada

ACADIAN FLYCATCHER

spit-chee!

Greener than Least or Alder

Habitat: — Deciduous woods, wooded swamps; fond of beech trees; southern and central states

Eye-ring
Wing-bars

There are four Empidonax Flycatchers in the East. Only the Yellow-bellied can be told with fair certainty by appearance. Identify the others by voice and habitat.

ALDER FLYCATCHER

wee-be-o

Brownest of the group

Habitat: — Alder swamps and wet thickets, usually near water; northern states and Canada

YELLOW—BELLIED FLYCATCHER

chu-wee

Breast washed with yellow

Habitat: — Coniferous woods, cold bogs; Canada and northern edge of U.S.

THE SMALL FLYCATCHERS

Earth

Man and Nature

This magazine is dedicated to bringing an awareness of the plant and animal life around us.

The article reprinted from the June 1972 issue of *Man and Nature* is an example of the interesting things you'll read in this publication.

MSH

Fig 1

Man and Nature

JUNE, 1972

(Consolidating: Connecticut Conservation, Massachusetts Audubon and Narragansett Naturalist.)

"Man and Nature" is published co-operatively as the quarterly journal of:

The Audubon Society of Rhode Island
40 Bowen Street
Providence, Rhode Island 02903

The Connecticut Conservation Association
Northrop Road
Bridgewater, Connecticut 06752

The Massachusetts Audubon Society
South Great Road
Lincoln, Massachusetts 01773

Published on the first day of March, June, September, and December. Subscription available through membership only.

Fig 4

FISH and ESTUARIES

ROBERT D. ANDERSON

AN estuary can be defined as a semi-enclosed body of water with a free connection to the open sea, measurably diluted by land drainage. This productive ecosystem is habitat for a diverse assemblage of fauna and flora. The fishes, while less conspicuous than many of the shellfish inhabitants, account for a substantial portion of the estuarine fauna.

The importance of estuaries for fishes is six-fold. Each species falls into one of the following six categories depending on its mode of life:

1. Resident — spends entire life within the estuary.

2. Anadromous — inhabits the estuary on journeys between the ocean and freshwater spawning grounds.

3. Catadromous — inhabits the estuary on journeys between freshwater and ocean spawning grounds.

4. Feeding — enters the estuary to forage seasonally.

5. Reproductive — utilizes the estuarine environment to spawn in and/or for nursery grounds.

6. Marine — visits the estuary sporadically during coastal migrations from the open sea.

One of the more commonly encountered estuarine residents is the mummichog *(Fundulus heteroclitus)* (Fig. 1). This fish and the other forage species in the estuary find some use commercially as bait for the fisherman's hook. However, their most important function is as natural food for larger carnivorous fishes.

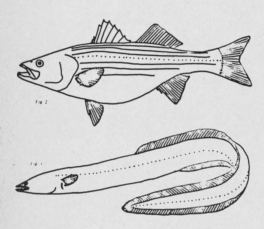

Fig 2

Fig 3

The striped bass *(Morone saxatilis)* (Fig. 2) needs no introduction. This anadromous species moves from the coast to spawn in fresh-water conditions, as do the salmons.

Catadromous species of fish are few compared to the number of representatives from each of the other categories. The American eel *(Anguilla rostrata)* (Fig. 3) falls into this reference. It descends from fresh water to spawn in a restricted area of the Atlantic Ocean, off the Florida coast, called the Sargasso Sea.

Seasonal feeders in the estuary are represented by the bluefish *(Pomatomus saltatrix)* (Fig. 4). Like the striped bass, this fish is extremely popular among sport fishermen and has some commercial value. The bluefish enters the estuaries during warmer months to feed voraciously on a va-

riety of smaller fishes.

The winter flounder *(Pseudopleuronectes americanus)* (Fig. 5) spawns in the estuary and the juveniles use it as a nursery ground. This is one of the most important, yet inconspicuous, uses of the environment by many fishes. The winter flounder is a valuable coastal resource to both sport and commercial fisheries' interests.

The species which are in the marine category have no apparent estuarine requirements. The Atlantic mackerel *(Scomber scombrus)* (Fig. 6), for example, could exist capably without estuaries.

The great majority of fishes, of monetary significance or not, fall into categories one through five. At some time in their life cycles they depend for their existence on the continuation of unaltered estuarine habitat.

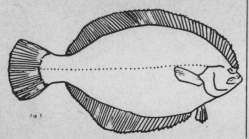

Fig 5

Frog Jumping Contest

"Keep those frogs wet!" So goes the cry at the annual frog jumping contest held each year in the spring on the grounds of the Mark Twain Memorial in Hartford, Connecticut.

The contest is open to kids from 6-16 and the frogs — not toads — must be Connecticut born and raised. The frogs are given their chance in three consecutive jumps. Each frog's official distance will be determined by measuring in a straight line, from the starting point to the end of the third hop. The three longest distances determine the winner. The top frog in last year's contest leapt 66 inches to victory!

Write for information.

Mark Twain Memorial
351 Farmington Avenue
Hartford, Connecticut 06105

Earth

HENRY
BUGBEE
KANE

The House on Nauset Marsh

Do you know why the cricket has such a long tail?

One of the qualities that makes this book immensely worthwhile is its easy, enjoyable readability. Filled with anecdotes and information presented in a lively, interesting manner, it is at once a journal reminiscent of Walden Pond and a personal letter inviting the reader to make a journey to Nauset Marsh on Cape Cod.

The combination is successful and the reader feels rewarded by the useful information about nature and pleased to be considered "one of the family" at the farmhouse on Nauset Marsh.

Like all salt marshes, Nauset contains a kaleidoscope of natural phenomenon. Added to this fact is its location at East Chatham, a place where the Cape is no more than four miles wide, the distinctive weather, and the migratory paths of fish and fowl as they pass the Cape going north and south, add to its charm.

Based on lifelong observation and experience, Mr. Richardson's comments are never dull or stilted. His theories are homespun and have the flavor of a home-style recipe — which is delightful for its sincerity and believability. Even when he states that the growth cycles of eelgrass coincide with economic depressions and inflations, I was inclined to "stick tongue in cheek" and go along with him.

If you've never visited a salt marsh or been to Cape Cod, this book will whet your appetite for the real thing.

By the way, if a cricket had no tail, he would starve because he lacks a neck. To forage for food, he presses his tail to the ground, which jacks up his rear end, which in turn, lowers his mouth to the waiting morsel.

Martin Robbins-Pianka

The House on Nauset Marsh
by Wyman Richardson
1972; 223 pp., paper
From: The Chatham Press, Inc.
    Riverside, Connecticut 06878
    $2.95

My life is like a stroll upon the beach,
As near the ocean's edge as I can go.

Henry David Thoreau

Earth

Build Your Own Lobster Trap

Albert Belanger of Oxford, Maine, will not build you a lobster trap but he will sell you all the wood stock you need and cut the bows for the ends. All stock is from No. 1 green oak bolts.

Prices are:
No 1 laths 7/16 x 1 1/8 x 50
    @$50.00 per thousand
Runners 1 x 2 x 50
    @   .16¢ each
Bows & Yokes 24 to 27
    @   .50¢ each
Door cleats
    @   .05¢ each
Sq frame with 13 1/2 dowel, 22 x 26
    @   .38¢ each

Belanger will also make bed slats and pallets.

Pinewood Products
Box 127
Oxford, Maine 04270

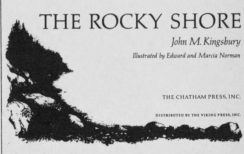

THE ROCKY SHORE
John M. Kingsbury
Illustrated by Edward and Marcia Norman

THE CHATHAM PRESS, INC.

DISTRIBUTED BY THE VIKING PRESS, INC.

The Sandy Shore — The Rocky Shore

The suburbanite who makes a yearly pilgrimage to the shore does not realize the intricacies and interdependence of plants and animals of the Northeastern seashore.

These two beautifully illustrated books ask that we take notice of the life that inhabits our shores.

The authors attempt to raise our consciousness and inspire a sense of wonder by providing information about the life that inhabits a very minute section of the earth.

The Sandy Shore is centered on Cape Cod and its environs, while *The Rocky Shore* explores the coast of Maine. Both books are of value as elementary field guides, owing to the precision of the accompanying illustrations.

B. Robbins-Pianka

The Sandy Shore
by John Hay
Illustrated by Edward and Marcia Norman
1968; 64 pp.
$3.95

The Rocky Shore
by John M. Kingsbury
Illustrated by Edward and Marcia Norman
1970; 77 pp.
$4.95
From: The Chatham Press, Inc.
    Riverside, Connecticut 06878

Also by John Hay:
THE ATLANTIC SHORE
(With Peter Farb)
THE GREAT BEACH
NATURE'S YEAR
THE RUN

1936   1972

Penobscot Marine Museum

The Penobscot Marine Museum

The Penobscot Marine Museum is the oldest maritime museum in the State of Maine. It was founded in 1936 by Clifford N. Carver and Lincoln Colcord, both direct descendants of Searsport sea captains.

Years ago, Penobscot Bay teemed with commercial maritime activity. Two, three, and four masted schooners ran up the Bay with a fair northeast wind to load cargoes for all parts of the world. Steamers and ferries carried passengers the length and breadth of the Bay when travel by water was far easier and faster than travel by land.

One of Searsport's finest traditions is that of shipbuilding. Ships such as the John Carver, William H. Connor, Lucy Nickels and many others were built at shipyards in the community. In all, eleven shipyards were located here. One tenth of all the captains in the American Merchant Marine during the 1870's were Searsport men. Throughout its history, the town has produced more sailing shipmasters than any other town of its size in the entire world.

These are the stories that the Penobscot Marine Museum reveals. Here you will get a view of the homes of former ship owners and captains, of original half models from which the lines were established for a ship's construction. You will also see original tools which were used to build the ships, and the instruments by which they were navigated on the high seas, as well as historic paintings and prints showing those ships at sea.

In addition, the Museum's five exhibit buildings house a fine collection of ship models, and small craft indigenous to the Penobscot Bay and River areas. Also displayed are 19th century American and Oriental furnishings brought to this country by shipmasters. The library houses shipping records, papers and 1300 volumes for those who wish to carry out research in the maritime field.

JCH

The Penobscot Marine Museum
Searsport, Maine 04974
Open: June — September 30
Adults: $1.00   Children: $.25

A Beachcomber's Botany

Delicate pencil drawings assist the reader in identifying the plant life which abounds along Cape Cod shores. Much of the flora illustrated will also be found in other sections of the northeastern seaboard.

A lovely book to own; by purchasing it you will be helping The Chatham Conservation Foundation to preserve valuable and irreplaceable marshes, beaches and uplands, as all sales proceeds go directly to them.

Esmé Willis

A Beachcomber's Botany
Essays and Comments by Loren C. Petry
Illustrated by Marcia G. Norman
1968; 158 pp., paper
From: The Chatham Conservation Foundation,
    Inc.
    Box 317
    Chatham, Massachusetts 02633
    $3.95

What is it? . . . at the Beach

Pennaria Tiarella, Callinectas Sapidus, Paguras Bernhardus, all commonly found along New England shores.

Take this book along on that next trip to the seashore and you'll be amazed at what you learn. The beach is made up of hundreds of interesting creatures and plant-life, now find out what they are — from seaweeds to chitons. Generic names and accurate descriptions are given along with clear, life-like drawings, enabling the reader to make positive identification.

A marvelous learning tool for children.

MSH

What is it? . . . at the Beach
by Paul Giambarba
1969; 63 pp., paper
From: Barre Publishers
 Barre, Massachusetts 01005
 $2.95

MOLLUSKS – BIVALVES (2 SHELLS)

ANOMIA SIMPLEX (COMMON JINGLE SHELL) IS SCALY, VARIOUS SHADES OF YELLOW, FROM 1" TO 3" IN DIAMETER. VERY COMMON, FOUND CAST ASHORE ON BEACHES ALONG THE ATLANTIC COAST.

ARCA PEXATA (BLOODY CLAM) IS WHITE WITH A THICK BROWN EPIDERMIS. 2" TO 2½" LONG. IT HAS RED BLOOD, HENCE ITS POPULAR NAME. VERY COMMON CAPE COD TO NEW JERSEY.

MYTILUS EDULIS (BLUE MUSSEL) HAS A PURPLE SHELL, COVERED WITH A DENSE BLUE-BLACK EPIDERMIS. 2½" LONG. VERY COMMON, NEW ENGLAND COAST.

THIS MUSSEL IS A SEAFOOD DELICACY IN FRANCE (MOULES) AND ITALY (COZZE). **MODIOLA MODIOLUS** (HORSE MUSSEL) NOT SHOWN, IS LARGER, 4" TO 5," HAS A DEEP BROWN EPIDERMIS, RED-ORANGE ANIMAL INSIDE. FOUND ALONG THE NORTHERN ATLANTIC AND PACIFIC COASTS. **MODIOLA PLICULATA** (RIBBED MUSSEL) HAS RIBS, A DINGY SHELL, 3" LENGTH, SILVERY WHITE INSIDE THE SHELL. MAINE TO THE CAROLINAS.

PINNA MURICATA
PINNA SEMINUDA
PEN SHELLS (LEFT) ARE COMMON IN FLORIDA. THEY ARE THIN AND FRAGILE, ABOUT 4" TO 10" LONG. DULL COLOR.

Sea Fever

Until man in his endless "progress" figures out a way to pave the seas, the seas will be there, and people, prepared and otherwise, will fill their dreams by venturing upon them.

The books, songs, and tales about the sea are endless and in "Sea Fever" we have another story of the young man and the sea. To the literary critic this may be just another tale. To the hopelessly sea-addicted, as I am, it is another view of a limitless attraction.

Put it aboard for a few days of fog in Cuttyhunk or Frenchman's Bay.

RWW

Sea Fever — The Making of a Sailor
by Emery N. Cleaves
1972; 283 pp.
From: Houghton Mifflin Company
 2 Park Street
 Boston, Massachusetts 02107
 $6.95

Of Lobsters . . . and Lobster Stew

The delicate, distinctive flavor of the North American lobster is a gourmet's delight, and enhancing this flavor has challenged many a chef. Some of the best ideas in lobster cookery have come from New England where the approach, while admittedly direct, is nonetheless effective.

Many a New England "lobster catcher" has made a quick feast of a few "sho'ts" boiled in seawater on the galley stove, or lacking the latter has baked a few tails on the hot manifold of the engine. No doubt a ravenous appetite from a day on the sea made up for the lack of subtlety in the dish.

There are certain basic rules to observe in lobster cookery, and the closer they are observed the better the results. These are:

— Hot dishes have more flavor than cold ones.
— "Wet"cooking (boiling, steaming) retains more flavor than "dry" cooking (baking, broiling).
— Salted water should be used (½ cup per gallon) for boiling or steaming; fresh, clear seawater is even better
— Don't overcook; 12 minutes for 1 to 1½ pounders, 20 minutes for 2 to 3 pounders, 30 minutes for 4 and up. Halve these times if the meat is to be extracted and reheated in a stew, newburg or casserole
— Don't overseason; the use of "boil spices" or court bouillon containing strong flavors — celery, onion, etc., will mask the lobster flavor

A word about buying lobsters: whenever possible, buy them alive and cook them yourself. Never accept an uncooked dead one, and if cooked, be sure the tail is curled securely under the body, an indication that it was alive when cooked. The harder the shell, the more meat you'll get; soft shell lobsters contain lots of water. However, at certain times of the year they're unavoidable.

Small lobsters, 1¼ pound and under, are the tenderest but the least economical since the larger the lobster the less waste there is. For individual servings in the shell, 1 to 3 pounds is a good size, depending on your appetite or your affluence. For recipes involving extracted meat buy the largest one you can use. It takes five one-pounders to make a pound of meat, whereas a five pounder will produce a pound and a half. Offshore fishermen bring in huge jumbos of up to 20 pounds, and since these bring the lowest price, they are the best buy if you're planning a party. However, you'll need a *big* pot!

And if you are planning a party, one of the finest lobster dishes you can prepare, and one of the simplest, is Lobster Stew. This ancient New England favorite capitalizes on the symbiotic relationship between lobster, milk and butter. Here's how:

Allow one pound of lobster (in the shell) for each person to be served. Boil or steam, and remove the meat. In a jumbo you'll find meat in all the little legs and flippers, and a great deal in the body. If there is red coral (roe), crumble it and add to the meat. Also add the tomally — this green material has lots of flavor in a stew. Cut the meat into bite-sized pieces.

Allow a quart of whole milk for each person and select a suitably sized pot. Allow 1/8 pound of butter for each gallon of milk.

Melt butter in pot over low heat; add lobster meat and sauté until thoroughly heated thru. Add milk. Heat over medium heat until steaming hot. Do *not* allow to boil! Season to taste with salt, pepper, and monosodium glutamate. A little paprika will improve the looks. Hold at low heat for a half hour.

Now — the most important ingredient: time. Cover the stew and place it in a cool place for from 6 to 24 hours. The longer it "sets" the better it will be. An hour before serving, re-heat it to steaming hot, but again, *do not allow to boil*. Serve with oyster crackers.

This is a rich, main-dish type of stew, and you can fully expect a demand for seconds.

Harry U. Snow

Drinking Water Filter Kit

Before you decide that booze is not being made the way it used to, better check the water you have been using to make the ice cubes. Almost all water lately has been tasting either like an old boot or the chlorine vat in a shirting factory.

Here is a pretty good solution for only $5.95 (plus the inevitable 65c for postage) — holds six cups. You can get two for $10.70.

P.B. Enterprises
Box 2251
Noroton Heights, Connecticut 06820

THE FABULOUS FILBROOK DRINKING WATER FILTER

My Own Cape Cod

A seasonal account of a year on Cape Cod by the well known writer of "Stillmeadow" journals. Mrs. Taber gives the reader a feeling of belonging. She says "Perhaps the greatest gift of the Cape is the intimacy we have with the sky and sea and shining sands, and as we enter the space age we shall be more grateful than ever for this narrow land where the tides are not regulated by computer and the skyway travelers are the wild geese going over and the red-wings announcing spring and the seagulls swooping against the fire of sunset."

My Own Cape Cod   Jean Allen Skiff
by Gladys Taber
1971; 251 pp.
From: J.B. Lippincott Co.
 E. Washington Square
 Philadelphia, Pennsylvania 19105
 $5.95

Earth

Cape Cod Pilot

While the paperback edition originally appeared in 1937 as part of the Federal Writers' Project, it has been reissued in 1969 mainly because it gives an unusually good picture of Cape Cod, its folklore and yarns. For anyone planning to visit this picturesque spit of land, *Cape Cod Pilot* would qualify as an ideal guide.

Many of the well-known Cape towns, from Sandwich to Provincetown, are the subjects of chapters and the author tells the reader some history of each town, something of its lore, and before you know it, you are itching to visit the towns and search out their spots of interest.

The author is equally at home in describing the glass industry of Sandwich or the first meeting house where Truro came to worship. "When the meeting house was completed, the first thing the town fathers did was to vote the purchase of a cushion for the pulpit, and an hourglass. The cushion was for the protection of the minister, and the hourglass, timing the sermon, for the protection of the flock."

Nor does the author neglect to pay homage to the beautiful and fearsome waters that pound the long stretches of beach. For it was to these that the local residents looked for food and industry. Shipwrecks abound and every town has its lore of how the local inhabitants lured unsuspecting mariners onto its rocks and sandbars. "Harwich was loudest of all the righteous towns that cried out against the 'dirty doings' on the beaches of Chatham; for Harwich, so close to the scene at Monomoy and the other ships' graveyards, was on the lee side, and her own beaches were therefore innocent of worthwhile wrecks. It was not only disgraceful, this mooncussing that went on in Chatham — it was heartbreaking."

Cape whaling ranked with that of Nantucket or New Bedford. Provincetown whalemen chased the ambergris monsters shortly beyond the turn of the century and had their share of lore concerning the long voyage involved, together with their rich rewards or their tragic endings.

Just the names of some of the villages are enough to evoke yearnings for a trip to the Cape: Barnstable, Yarmouth, Wellfleet, Truro, Hyannis, Mashpee. This is the Cape as the Capers see her "happily caught and recorded for future generations."

Charles T. Letson

Cape Cod Pilot
by Josef Berger
First MIT Press Edition 1969; 401 pp., paper
From: The MIT Press
      Cambridge, Massachusetts 02142
      $3.45

---◆---

Chappaquiddick

Recent world-wide publicity has changed things for the Island of Martha's Vineyard. Change is inevitable, so they say. Or is it?

In all New England there's no place
Which really'd rather hide its face
Than over-written Vineyard isle
We'd like to secede for awhile.
Unhappy, tragic, world publicity
Has joined most islanders in complicity
To help discourage tourist hordes
Who jam our by-ways, act like lords
With overbearing, noisy ways
And interrupt idyllic days
With "Where's the Bridge? Now, Babe, look limber
You stand on presidential timber."
So — friends of islands, join us well
And help reduce this horrid swell.
Don't write a word, or take a "snap"
Just let us have a few years nap!

Mary Murray Brown

Earth

Capt. Norman Benson Has Been Eeling for Four Score Years

He Pulls and Sets Pots to Supply Bait for Fishermen and a Delicacy for Gourmets

By Douglas Cabral

To a man who once caught a whale, eels are nothing. Back in October of 1928, Capt. Norman Benson discovered that his large trap near Quisset in Buzzards Bay contained a 20-foot sulphur bottom whale. The big mammal lay in a deathly repose among the schools of other fish captured in the trap, and Captain Benson only had to drag the carcass away.

Well, the era of the trap fishermen has passed and there are no whales in James' Pond near his house, but there are eels — and plenty of them, as Captain Benson will tell you. He traps them in small round wire pots which he sets and pulls from a skiff.

Captain Benson has been eeling every year since he was seven years old, and he's almost 87 now. Back in the beginning, when the itch for a boat of his own was too great to deny, his father told him that if he learned to swim a boat would be forthcoming.

Captain Benson says he did a good deal of "splashing around" that summer before his seventh birthday, and sure enough he got a skiff, the finest skiff he'd ever seen. And with it came a Josiah Cleveland eel pot, totally different in design from those he uses today.

"God," he says, "in those days, if I got three eels, I thought I hit 'em hard."

Each Morning

Now, each morning when the sun is well up, Captain Benson walks slowly down a long wide grassy path to James' Pond where it touches the back of his property. He carries a pink plastic bucket in the stiff fingers of one hand. The bucket will hold the eels he captures, and it has to be a deep one, because eels are slippery and they'll climb right up the sides if you give them half a chance.

He generally wears a warm checked shirt buttoned up to his throat and a fisherman's hip boots with the tops turned down a bit. Clamped firmly in his mouth is a pipe, not always lit, but stuck there where it belongs. He is a man who's worked very hard his whole life, but he knows how to work without wasted effort, without a single inefficient movement, in a milieu which preserves him.

He slips the skiff into the pond and steps to the rowing thwart, where he sits facing the stern and rowing in that direction. The pond is quiet. There is no breeze, and the air is still and hot. The shore is thickly bordered with trees and a very few buildings, and his boat is absolutely alone on the surface.

There are more eels to be found elsewhere, notably Tisbury Great Pond, Captain Benson says, and he will begin fishing there soon. Generally, he supplies the bass fishermen with eels for bait and during the height of the season the captain's son comes in with him in the eeling business. Last year, the two of them barely kept up with the demand.

Of course many people eat eels, and some people like to eat them very much, and Captain Benson's twisty captives are as flavorful as any. There are summer people, he says, who are just crazy for them.

"In fact, I'm quite apt to skin out a mess myself."

Four Pots Pulled

The morning I visited Captain Benson, he pulled only four pots. He was in a hurry to catch up with his son, Franklin, who's fishing lobsters in the Sound. The four pots brought him 17 eels, for which he had a buyer coming later that day. All the fishing was done in just two of the pots, and the captain was rather put out with the pair of shirkers.

"Never set there again," he muttered.

The two pots which failed were set near rocks, and the others in open water on the grass and mud bottom. He made careful note of this.

I don't mean to make it sound as though Captain Benson was all business. To set four light eel pots in James' Pond and pull them in the mid-morning of a fine, warm spring day is not apt to make a man a driver. The skiff slipped through the water and the captain slipped through his work, both as easy as could be.

While he worked, Captain Benson talked about bait, what was best and what he used. Menhaden or pogies, an inedible and generally abundant species, were the most attractive to the eels, but he found them too difficult to come by, he said. Instead, he uses horseshoe crabs, hacked into large, and, I imagine, fragrant chunks. The two pots which didn't fish contained the bait untouched. You'd think that economy would dictate the re-cycling of the uneaten morsels, but Captain Benson looked at it another way.

"Fresh stuff'll smell better," he said as he flipped the remains overboard.

Pulling the pots aboard didn't seem to tax the captain a bit. His pipe didn't so much as quiver in his mouth. As the mesh pot surfaced, the slimy flip flop of eel tails brought a grunt of satisfaction from the captain.

"They should all be like that," he said.

Heading Home

With the four pots in the boat, he stroked easily toward the shore, and finally, the stern bumped gently against the matted grass of the landing. He wasted no time opening the pots and dumping the eels into his bucket. Some tried to glue themselves to the bottom of the wire mesh where it joins the wooden end, but he shook and rolled the pot until every one had fallen through the small door.

As he walked up the rise to his house, the captain held the bucket in front of him in both hands. He talked a little as he went, and breathed more heavily. He explained that this eeling was a business, not a hobby, that he had a vendor's license which allowed him to sell what he caught. There are others who vend eels without benefit of such formalities, but "I don't squeal on 'em," the captain says.

When he reached the house, Captain Benson hid the catch in the cool shade of his cellar bulkhead. Later, in the early evening, when the time was right, he'd bait the pots and set them again.

(Captain Benson's adventures as a trap fisherman during 57 consecutive trap fishing seasons will appear in book form in late June, 1972. Salt Water In My Veins, a collection of Captain Benson's tales as told to Dr. William Peltz, is being published by Stanley Hart and the Vineyard Press of West Tisbury.)

M.I.T.

M.I.T.'s *Technology Review,* though geared toward the technically-oriented person, does have short, thought-provoking articles which appeal to any thinking person.

MSH

You may subscribe by writing:
M.I.T.
Room E-19-430
Cambridge, Massachusetts 02139
Enclose a check for $9.00 ($10.00 in Canada and elsewhere outside the U.S.)

Coastline: Private Or Public Good?

The free-enterprise market system (the idea that prices take their level on the basis of supply and demand) is leading the country to a crisis in seashore resources, says Dennis W. Ducsik, an M.I.T. graduate student.

The problem is that the private market system implies that those who cannot—or will not—pay for a product must be denied its use. But this principle is simply not applicable to coastline, which is now in such short supply that it is no longer possible or in the public interest to restrict access to buyers.

So we must now consider the shoreline as a "public good," writes Mr. Ducsik. "It has an intrinsic value to society as a recreational resource, in that everyone in a democracy has an inalienable right to derive equal benefit from the value of shoreline recreation . . ."

If not by private market, then how do we set priorities for shoreline land uses and values? The responsibility obviously lies with government, but there is no obviously correct answer. In one of a series of papers on land-use policy prepared for the Senate Committee on Interior and Insular Affairs late last year by M.I.T., Boston University, and Woods Hole Oceanographic Institution students in a seminar conducted by Carroll L. Wilson, Professor of Management at M.I.T., Mr. Ducsik offers this proposal:

☐ Let the states make master plans for their own coastline resources that take into account as best they can local, regional, and national interests and the competing needs of industry, conservation, and recreation (among others).

☐ Let the federal government set guidelines to ensure that each state's plan is compatible with those of its neighbors, and to show states how to make decisions when they encounter conflicts in costs and benefits.

Though most shoreline laws now under consideration are consistent with his proposal for states' responsibilities, Mr. Ducsik says all are "seriously deficient" in failing to provide for strong federal involvement.—*J.M.*

Happy is the house that shelters a friend.

Ralph Waldo Emerson

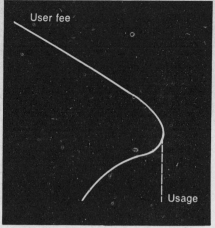

Are user fees a good way to apply supply-and-demand market characteristics to a recreational park? Not necessarily, says W. Robert Patterson, an M.I.T. graduate student, in a land-use report prepared for the Senate Committee on Interior and Insular Affairs last year. Fees can be set to support whatever policy is desired: very high, to discourage use; at some medium point to encourage highest possible use (dashed line); or at some point (not described on the chart) to maximize cash income. The issue would be far more complex, writes Mr. Patterson, if the toll related to a system of recreational resources instead of to a single park.

I've read somewhere that some early New Englanders made sugar with the sap of the birch tree. It is supposed to be a much richer, sweeter one. Have any *New England Catalogue* readers ever tried this, or have any knowledge of it?

MSH

Chatham Conservation Foundation

Many attractive features draw both visitors and permanent residents to the Town of Chatham, not the least of which is its varied and delightful physical characteristics — protected bays and beaches, salt and fresh water ponds, lovely marsh lands and tidal areas.

Fear of their loss prompted a group of Chatham citizens to look for the means of preserving, in their natural state, these precious areas that otherwise might vanish under the steady encroachment of what some have dubiously termed "progress."

Chatham Conservation Foundation, Inc.
Chatham, Massachusetts 02633

The New Alchemists
To Restore the Lands, Protect the Seas, And Inform the Earth's Stewards

A small, international organization devoted to research and education on behalf of man and the planet, they are seeking solutions that can be used by individuals or small groups who are trying to create a greener, kinder world. One of their major tasks is the creation of ecologically derived forms of energy, agriculture, aquaculture, housing and landscapes, that will permit a revitalization and repopulation of the countryside.

The Institute has an Associate Membership of $25.00 per year (tax deductible) which is available to anyone interested in their goals.

The New Alchemy Institute East
P.O. Box 432
Woods Hole, Massachusetts 02543

PETER RABBIT AS DRAWN BY HARRISON CADY

Laughing Brook Nature Center

Remember Peter Rabbit, Blacky the Crow and Reddy the Fox? — just three of Thornton Burgess' beautifully illustrated stories — still enjoyed by today's children.

They've come to life and can be seen at *Laughing Brook,* Mr. Burgess' former home and grounds, which has been made into an Education and Wildlife Sanctuary by the Massachusetts Audubon Society. *Laughing Brook*'s collection of animals reflects Mr. Burgess' interest in native wildlife. Lightfoot the Deer, Bobby Coon, Jimmy Skunk and Sammy Jay are but a few of the permanent animal exhibits. Both the animal center and the nature center display live animals, with outside exhibits constructed to simulate their natural habitats. There are several miles of trails and tours are conducted year round.

For information write:

Laughing Brook
789 Main Street
Hampden, Massachusetts 01036

Earth

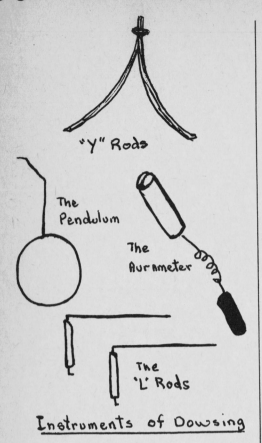

"Y" Rods

The Pendulum

The Auxometer

The 'L' Rods

Instruments of Dowsing

Dowsing – for locating water only?

Not so! Among its many uses are finding mineral deposits, lost persons, downed airplanes and hunting game. It's even been used to tell the genuine painting from the forgery.

MSH

Dowsing
by Gordon MacLean, Sr.
1971; 43 pp., paper
From: Gordon MacLean, Sr.
    30 Day Street
    South Portland, Maine 04106
    $1.25

Water location is a very small part of the potentialities of dowsing ... A typical example of these other uses is in the checking of soils as to their suitability for the particular plants you intend to propagate. As you gain skill, you will find many other uses.

It has been found that the younger you start dowsing, the greater is your chance of getting the dowsing reaction and the easier it will be to become an expert dowser. Children of five are almost 100% sensitive to the reaction and are extremely easy to train ...

... Always have your Y rods with you when you go out in a boat, for in the event of a heavy fog closing in, you can guide the boat to its dock with precision if you are a good enough dowser and have practiced this type of use for the rods.

Dowsing Society

This is a non-profit, non-commercial, non-stock, educational organization, open to all interested persons, and international in scope and membership. The Society says "dowsing can be quite consistently demonstrated and a dowsing *response*, after a bit of practice, can be experienced by almost anyone."

If you develop an interest in dowsing, apply for membership in *The American Society of Dowsers, Inc.*, Danville, Vermont 05828.

$6.00 per year

Earth

Dowsing Supplies

All articles sold by the *Dowsing Supply Company of America* are supplied with complete instructions, a reading list or bibliography, plus a list of societies and foundations involved with dowsing and parapsychology (ESP). The material is sufficient to provide both lay personnel and scientists complete background for further study of the phenomenon of dowsing.

Beginner's "Y" Rod Kit. These rods are similar to the classic "forked sticks" used by dowsers for centuries. They were originally made from wood, however, modern professional dowsers usually use synthetic materials, such as the rod included in the kit. The beginner's kit includes a professional but inexpensive plastic Y rod, complete with instructions. $1.50.

Beginner's Pendulum Kit. A handsome plastic ball pendulum used by most dowsers in Europe. Can be used for water, mineral or oil dowsing, as well as map, missing persons, treasure dowsing, etc.

Clear, sparkling ball	$1.25
Luminescent ball	$1.50

METAL DETECTORS
BY
· BOUNTY HUNTER
· COMPASS
· WHITE
· JETCO

FIND TREASURE

FROM 39⁹⁵

Now the Electronic Dowsing Rod

If you are one of those people who have tried dowsing and have never had even a twitch from the rod, perhaps you better bow to science over metaphysics and enter the electronic age with a metal detector from *The Foto Shop* in Barre, Vermont.

They claim the following test statistics for the detector called the Bounty Hunter:

Test Object	Distance from Search Coil
Mercury Dime	6½"
Copper Penny	7 "
Silver Quarter	7½"
Gold Wedding Band	8 "
Silver Half Dollar	9 "
Silver Dollar	11½"
3½" Jar Lid	17 "
Old Adz Head	18½"

You can start from as low as $39.95, admittedly a bit above a cut willow wand, and if you are really out after Captain Kidd's treasure (which has been hidden in so many places that Kidd must have been the master ditch digger of all time), you can go as high as $269.00.

Quite complete literature from:

The Foto Shop
129 North Main Street
Barre, Vermont 05641

About the New England Simples: These home remedies, most of unknown origin, may be of dubious effectiveness. They were used faithfully by housewives long before modern science surfeited us with "miracle" solutions to many of our problems. *Make your own judgment* as to whether or not the remedies are applicable today.

Sea Born Island

The birds, the sand dunes, the churches, the flowers, the land and the people of Martha's Vineyard are all here in this delightful collection of poems by a native Vineyarder, descendant of the earliest settlers of the island. What is the Vineyard but a compact piece of New England? You can almost taste the salty brine in some of the poems or hear the migrant bird. Enhancing the verses in this lovely little first volume by the author are blockprints by the author's husband.

Sally G. Devaney

Sea Born Island
by Dionis Coffin Riggs; illus. by Sidney Noyes Riggs
1969; 77 pp.
From: Noone House
    Peterborough, New Hampshire 03458
    $3.95

SEA BORN ISLAND

This sea born island
Is a salty thing
Where sea gulls mourn;

A thing of mist and fog
Where herons stand,
One-legged, in the bog;

A thing of sun and sea
Where catbirds nest
In the lilac tree.

East of America

In seeking poems for *East of America*, John Hinshaw has included poetry that has a "world view." As the poems are presented by order of the birthdates of the poets, we can see how poetic form has changed from the late 1800's to the present 1970's. However, man's desire to create a "view of the world," has changed little. Most of the poems in *East of America* are devoid of man-made complexities. The work-a-day world is obscured and gladly forgotten. Line drawings by Richard Fish complement the mood of the collection; for like the poems, they are not often about people. Instead, favorite objects associated with the outdoors, weather, the sea and shore are described and personified. With nature as subject matter, man seems to be more himself, and being more himself, capable of coping with the world.

East of America — the beauty of Cape Cod preserved in verse and art. If you have ever lived on the Cape, you will want to go back this way. If you have never visited, you will soon weigh anchor.

SJI

East of America
A Selection of Cape Cod Poems
Edited by John V. Hinshaw
Drawings by Richard Fish
1969; 80 pp.

From: The Chatham Press, Inc.
    Riverside, Connecticut 06878
    $4.95

Summer Island: Penobscot Country

At first glance, this slender Sierra Club abridgement is simply a superb photographic record of the flora and fauna of an obscure island in Penobscot Bay. The black and white and color detail of woods, beaches, rocks, flowers, birds and houses are not the chance snapshots of a compulsive amateur photographer; they are the careful delineations of a seasoned professional who has long lived with and studied the variety, mystery and beauty of Maine's sea-swept islands.

However, with its appropriate captions and quotations from such observers as Henry Beston, Rachel Carson and Sarah Orne Jewett, the little book is considerably more than a collection of photographs. It is a highly personal and loving account of life, enjoyed for the most part in summers, on Great Spruce Island, and of forays in the general vicinity. So fascinated did Eliot Porter become with his island world and the sea around him, and so encouraged in his photography by Ansel Adams and Walter Steiglitz, he gave up his career in bacteriology for a full-time vocation as a nature photographer.

Summer Island is basically a plea to save the unspoiled natural beauty of a "microcosm of life." The account, always absorbing, gives way to perceptions, oft thought but ne'er so well express'd, that match what is creative and innovative in the photography. For example:

"To be out in the bay in a small boat — a white wall of fog narrowing your world to a fifty-yard circle of visibility — is, paradoxically, a broadening experience. Although the world you can see has shrunk, it is all yours — the boat and the little pond you are moving on is all you have — you are on your own completely and irrevocably; there is no calling for help; whatever happens is yours alone to deal with."

Fessenden Wilder

Summer Island: Penobscot Country (abridged)
by Eliot Porter, edited by David Brower
1968; 160 pp., paper

From: Sierra Club-Ballantine Books
    101 Fifth Avenue
    New York, New York 10003
    $3.95

Which Way to Millinocket?

Capitalizing on the plain Yankee wit and wisdom — Bryan and Dodge have skillfully recreated the old folk art of "story-telling."

A city-slicker who has lost his way is just one of the down-east stories realistically narrated. All records are mailed first-class.

$5.98 each

Block Island Summer

Elizabeth and Klaus Gemming use the authenticity of black and white film, and well-chosen words to capture the character of the windswept island that lies off the Rhode Island shore. Originally known by the Manisses Indians who inhabited it, as the "Isle of the Little God;" it was named "Adriaen's Eylant" in 1614 by Adriaen Block, a Dutch fur trader who noted the beautiful island, and labeled it on his chart. In 1616, "Block Island" as it was later called, became the home of sixteen settlers who answered to threats of 300 Indian braves by confronting them face to face and unarmed. A truce was reached, and Indian and white man shared an island.

The settlers of Block Island have always been rugged, courageous, and peace-loving. During the War of Independence the islanders were left by the Colonies to fend for themselves against British ships. In 1738, a storm brought the German ship Palatine crashing upon an island reef. The islanders spent days and nights carrying survivors to their small cottages. In the War of 1812 they remained neutral and seceded altogether, often providing the British with water and provisions.

Today in 1972, Block Islanders still go out of their way to make you feel at home. Once a large summer resort at the turn of this century, there are less conveniences than one would find at other shores. There are no golf courses, few hotels, and fewer people. The 1970 census showed 489 permanent residents (900 fewer than in 1900). Zoning laws have been established to let things stay as they are. Since the residents make more than one half of

their annual income through summer trade, they cater to the yachtsmen and tourists with friendly, conveniencing small-time enterprises. Reviving a form of the New England "journey cake," yachtsmen nowadays are treated to a local muffin man, who in the early morn goes to each docked ship, selling hot, homemade muffins for hungry travelers heading out to sea.

As the Gemmings explore each area of the island — from the meadowed hill overlooking the Great Salt Pond, to the bustle of the Old Harbor where the ferry boat comes in; from the moorish West Side, to the Southeast, lure of many shipwrecks — their photos and comments are indicative of the various topography and atmosphere found in each area.

After having visited "Adriaen's Eylant" many times, I can testify that its spirit is contained in the pages of *Block Island Summer.* Having wondered about the history of the lonely island while sailing her waters, I now feel akin to the Indians and Colonial sailors who also experienced the Island's fog and hurricane winds. I guess they too, knew the peace of the Great Salt Pond at dusk, as something to come home to. The movement of progress has stopped on Block Island. Just that, makes me go back.

SJI

Block Island Summer
by Elizabeth Gemming
Photographs by Klaus Gemming
1972; 119 pp.

From: The Chatham Press, Inc.
    Riverside, Connecticut 06878
    $8.50

Weather Forecasting

Do your own forecasting with these *weather instruments* designed by a New Englander and manufactured in Maine, New Hampshire and Massachusetts.

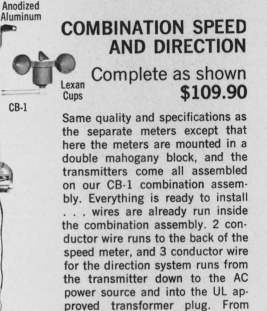

WIND SPEED
$69.95 complete

WIND DIRECTION
$69.95 complete

5" ALL BRASS CASES

Quality wind tunnel-tested wind measuring systems with polished brass cases, even the back plate. Large easy to read 4½" dial. Has very low starting speed for accurate readings. Wind vane also responds to slight changes in wind direction. 2 conductor wire from speed transmitter to speed meter. 3 conductor wire from direction transmitter to AC power source and into UL approved transformer plug, then 2 conductor wire to rear of meter.

Also comes with matching all brass case barometer for only (See opposite side)

Lexan Cups

10" mast

Universal Mounting Bracket

60' wire

Anodized Aluminum

10" mast

Universal Mounting Bracket

60' wire

Available with combination bar CB-1 when used together. See opposite page.

Anodized Aluminum

14" mast

CB-1

Universal Mounting Bracket

60' wire

Lexan Cups

COMBINATION SPEED AND DIRECTION

Complete as shown
$109.90

Same quality and specifications as the separate meters except that here the meters are mounted in a double mahogany block, and the transmitters come all assembled on our CB-1 combination assembly. Everything is ready to install . . . wires are already run inside the combination assembly. 2 conductor wire runs to the back of the speed meter, and 3 conductor wire for the direction system runs from the transmitter down to the AC power source and into the UL approved transformer plug. From there a 2 conductor wire runs to the back of the direction meter.

Can be installed, checked out and working in a matter of minutes. Fully guaranteed for one year.

WV-WD-1W with CB-1

Meter block measures
9" x 4" x 1½"

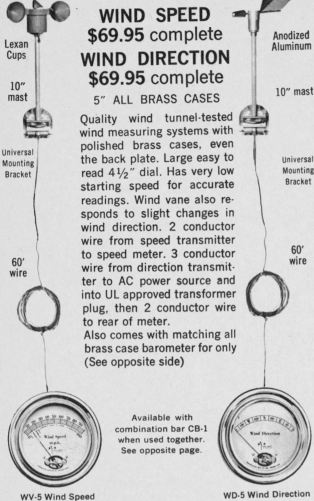

WV-5 Wind Speed

WD-5 Wind Direction

The Old Farmer's Almanac

For a publication which has been around for more than 180 years, it could be assumed that its longevity breeds complacency. "Why change," the editors might state. Not so, with *The Old Farmer's Almanac*. In fact, the reason it has survived close to two centuries is because it has "kept up with the times." The original editor of the Almanac, Robert B. Thomas, stressed the need to include "new, useful and entertaining matter."

Annually, *The Old Farmer's Almanac* is eagerly awaited by thousands of readers. Its weather predictions alone, are quoted over and over again. "The Old Farmer's Almanac says it's going to be a hum-dinger of a winter in these parts. . . ." and how often it is correct! But there's more to this popular annual — there must be for it to survive. New ideas, encompassing feature articles, subtle changes in format and an awareness of today's interests basically are what sustains the Almanac and insures its future — hopefully for another 180 years!

JCH

The Old Farmer's Almanac
Dublin, New Hampshire 03444
$.60 annually

A friend is a person with whom I may be sincere. Before him, I may think aloud.

Ralph Waldo Emerson

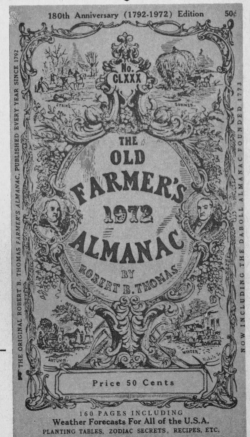

180th Anniversary (1792-1972) Edition   50¢

No. CLXXX

THE OLD FARMER'S 1972 ALMANAC

BY ROBERT B. THOMAS

Price 50 Cents

160 PAGES INCLUDING
Weather Forecasts For All of the U.S.A.
PLANTING TABLES, ZODIAC SECRETS, RECIPES, ETC.

Rock Hound's Guide to Connecticut

Grab your knapsack, sledge hammer and cold chisel — put a copy of *Rock Hound's Guide to Connecticut* in your back pocket — and you'll soon be involved in a fascinating hobby.

What to look for and where to find it? This handy little guide gives all that information — along with suggestions such as, get permission *first* before entering any area not public, and occasionally expect to pay a small fee to work sites located on private property.

A listing of basic equipment is helpful for the beginner.

MSH

Rock Hound's Guide to Connecticut
by Kathleen H. Ryerson
1972; 60 pp., paper
From: The Pequot Press, Inc.
    Old Chester Road
    Chester, Connecticut 06412
$2.50

A New England Simple

To prevent damp and rust from attacking the wires of a piano, tuck a small bag containing some unslaked lime inside the piano just underneath the cover. This will absorb all moisture.

 **Sundials**
New Ipswich, N.H.
03071 603—878-1000

 GNOMONICS, the art of telling time by the sun's shadow, dates back nearly 22 centuries. Before the birth of Christ in ancient Egypt, China and India there were accounts of men scientifically recording time by the sun's shadow. Later in ancient Greece and Rome the art of dialing or gnomonics was still further developed.

The first Spanish explorers to the New World in the 15th Century found that the Aztecs of Central and South America were using sundials very extensively. It wasn't until the 18th Century, when clocks began to be mass produced, that the sundial became primarily a decorative item. As late as 1900 sundials were used by the French railroads for checking the accuracy of and setting watches. Today throughout the world sundials are used extensively as a focal point in gardens.

There are two major parts to a sundial. First, the **dial** which comes from the Latin word meaning day and, second, the **pointer or gnomon** from the Greek word meaning **one who knows or explains.** In actuality, the gnomon casts a shadow onto the calibrated surface of the dial, thus recording time in a fashion which we can interpret.

Probably the earliest sundial was the shadow cast by a tree onto the ground at its base. Later, cavemen most likely found that the shadow cast by sticks of equal length were the same and could be used by two people in different locations to perform tasks at similar times. For example, Mrs. Caveman might well have said to Mr. Caveman, "Start home when the shadow is the same length as the stick." The earliest known sundial looked like a T fastened to one end of a graduated bar. As the sun rose and set, the shadow cast by the T moved along the graduated bar recording the time of day. The major problem with this dial was that at noon someone had to remember to turn it around so that the T was constantly facing into the sun.

About 250 B. C. the Babylonians developed a bowl-shaped sundial. The inside of the dial was calibrated with sweeping lines and as the sun moved across the sky, the edge of the bowl acted as a gnomon casting a constantly changing shadow into the bowl, thus recording the time.

For many centuries we relied on the sundial to give us one major time reference each day. For example, to navigators and others interested in fixing a point in the day, the **noon mark** became very popular. This dial was constructed to record only high noon each day. As a result, it took on some most fascinating configurations. One of these contained a magnifying glass that at noon concentrated the sun's rays onto a wick in a small cannon. When the wick had burned down, the cannon exploded telling all within ear-shot that it was noon. This more than likely was the first alarm clock. During the 18th and 19th Centuries clock-makers frequently included a sundial with their clock, the reason being that in many instances there was no other means by which to get a correct time reference for setting the clock. In the late 19th Century an international agreement was reached to fix time zones around the world, with Greenwich, England, being the starting point and then moving west with the sun. Before that time, noon in Boston was not the same as noon in New York, even though both are within the same time zone. Certainly in solar time, when the sun is directly over Boston, it cannot be directly over New York. In reality, there is a few minutes between the two solar noons. Until our communications network became as sophisticated as it is today, the few minutes' difference between cities was relatively unimportant. This is an important point to remember when you are using a sundial to tell time. The dial records solar time very accurately, but because of the time zones by which we set our watches (mean time), it is nearly impossible to get the two to agree.

SUNDIALS tell sun time (apparent time), while clocks record mean time. There are only four days during the year when a sundial and a clock will agree. The difference is referred to as "equation time". Today, since sundials are more decorative than functional, they are generally set for an average latitude to tell approximate time. However, our equatorial and armillary dials can be adjusted by you to tell accurate "apparent time." Each of our dials are cast and finished by hand to bring out the natural beauty and warmth of the metal. Most are cast in solid bronze to capture their everlasting beauty and patina which improves with age.

THE DOVER ▲

An unusual vertical dial because of its compact size (4½" x 7½"). Can be mounted on almost any wall or fence post that faces south. A thoughtful small gift of solid bronze, natural finish .... **$7.00 ppd**

THE LEXINGTON ▲

A beautiful solid bronze, extra heavy sundial for those who prefer no motto. Instead, it carries an emblem showing the points of the compass and has Roman numerals. It is 7½" in diameter, natural finish and has a figurine gnomon .... **$20.00 ppd**

THE SHIP'S BELL

Basic nautical motif of the Ship's Bell has been the basis for the reputation "Timekeepers of the Sea." Shipbuilders and designers consider this a mandatory part of on-board instrumentation. Stop-strike switch is incorporated. Case is solid polished brass with hinge bezel, 8-day springwound, 11 jewels, ship's bell strike, 5½" diameter.

	$200.00
Mahogany display base	**$26.00**

Earth

Machinery Around Your Country Home

With labor charges skyrocketing today, needed repairs to house and grounds are often put off. Then again, many do-it-yourselfers hesitate to get involved in projects because they simply don't know where or how to begin.

Herb Nichols has given the basic information for just about any home project you might tackle — and some that you wouldn't! A gamut of machinery, from lawnmower to bulldozer, is explained in detail, along with graphic examples of their use. Enough, in fact, to encourage the most ambitious undertaking.

If you're at all handy, this book will help you to do a professional job at a very substantial savings, and perhaps a considerable amount of self-satisfaction.

Lance S. Hall

Machinery Around Your Country Home
by Herb Nichols
Illus. by Helen Schwagerman
1957; 407 pp.

From: North Castle Books
212 Bedford Road
Greenwich, Connecticut 06830
$7.50

SNOW PLOWS

✧✧✧✧✧✧✧✧✧✧✧✧✧

A snow plow may be a most important piece of equipment, that in itself can justify or make necessary the purchase of a tractor. However, it can be a most disappointing investment, as there may be no snow for years, it may come at a time when the owner-operator is away, so that a plow must be hired, or worst of all, the plow may prove incapable of handling an unexpectedly heavy fall...

DEPTH OF SNOW

It is impossible to set up any rules for the depth of snow that can be plowed by any particular unit, because of variation in the weight and cohesiveness of snow, in traction, and in condition of the tractor and the blade.

In light dry snow a push plow might handle a depth almost equal to the height of its blade, and roll it up well over the top of the blade. The following depths can usually be plowed:

Garden tractor	6 to 12 inches
Farm tractor	9 " 20 "
Jeep	12 " 24 "
Truck, rear drive	12 " 24 "
" four wheel drive	18 " 36 "

Occasional deeper drifts can be handled, but drifted snow is sometimes so tightly packed that it has as much resistance as soft wet snow...

CHAINS

Any wheeled vehicle used for snow plowing should have chains on all driving wheels. While much light plowing can be done without them, there is a probability that the tires will spin if a hard push is encountered, and that the machine will get stuck easily. Chains on non-driving front wheels are useful for steering but are not essential...

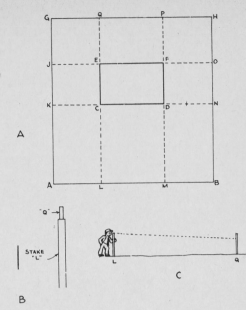

Fig. 1-19. Staking without instruments

WITHOUT INSTRUMENTS

Simple location work can also be done without instruments. Figure 1-19 shows the same square building plot. Lines are drawn on the print or tracing prolonging each side of the house to the plot boundaries, from where the distance to the corners is measured. These distances are then measured off on the ground and stakes set.

The distances of the house corners from the boundary lines may be scaled from the map and measured on the ground in directions found by sighting between pairs of boundary stakes.

Sighting may be done by placing a thin straight stake, as at L and another at Q. A man may stand behind the stake at L in such a position that, when he looks with one eye, the stake at Q is centered on L and just above it, as in Figure (B). Another man, carrying a third stake, measures the distance QE, keeping on the line LQ in response to directions from the observer. The measuring is best done by pinning the tape to Q. The stake is set at E so as to be directly in line between stakes L and Q. The distance EC is then measured and stake C set in the same way. CL is measured for a check...

Fig. 13-27. Trimming a hedge

CUTTING TO SHAPE

If the hedge is to be an even height above the ground, three light sticks can be fastened into a guide frame such as is shown in Figure 13-27.

Cutting should be stopped frequently to check with this. A string stretched along the ground between stakes will provide a guide for keeping it in line. This string should be checked after placement by measuring out from enough plant bases to make sure that it is parallel with the planting. A carpenters' rule or a steel pocket tape will do this without the need of crawling into the thicket.

If the hedge top is not to follow the ground contour, an offset string can be stretched between posts at the desired height and measurements made from it as cutting progresses. It may be necessary to slacken the cord while working, and draw it tight only for checking.

The accuracy of vertical cutting on the sides can be checked by a carpenters' level on the guide sticks, or by a plumb bob or stone suspended from a string at the top edge.

If the trimming is so drastic as to get back among thick branches, it should be done with a parrot bill or other heavy pruner, and the cut should be several inches deeper than the desired surface. When the sprouts are trimmed accurately at the next cutting, there will then be no coarse stubs at the surface to catch and damage the trimming tool if a slight error is made...

SOIL MOISTURE

✧✧✧✧✧✧✧✧✧✧✧✧✧

WATER TABLE

Subsurface water exists in three states or zones. The lowest of the series is hydrostatic or free ground water. Its upper surface is known as the water table, or ground water level. It follows the contour of the land in a general way, but tends to be farther under the surface in hills and pervious soils than in hollows and heavy soils. If it rises to or above the surface, it makes swamps, ponds, or springs.

The actions of this water are controlled by gravity, causing it to seek lower levels by the resistance of the soil to its movement, and by fresh supplies of water reaching it from the surface.

The water table may be static, or fluctuate only slightly, or it may shift up and down widely in response to season or rainfall.

Soil which is saturated with ground water is usually unstable under load, will turn to mud if disturbed, and does not permit the growth of roots of most plants because of their need for air.

If a hole is dug below the water table, it should fill with water....

Ornamental Iron & Copper Work

All sorts of good-looking iron and copper pieces ... we were especially attracted to some of their weather vanes, but then we are a little ape about horses, whales and sailboats. All this from a two man shop!

RWW

PALUMBO

ORNAMENTAL IRON & COPPER WORK

HANOVER STREET
NEWBURY, MASS. 01950

WEATHERVANES · LANTERNS
HANDCRAFTED ITEMS · WELDING
GOLD LEAFING · IRON RAILINGS
FREE ESTIMATES

No. C-75 Beautiful Iron Cat Andirons
17½'' High, 17½'' Deep
No. 76 Woman Figurine Andiron
No. 77 Key Andiron

$20.80

Sailing Sloop
28'' Long - 20'' High
$148.00

Whale Weathervane
30'' Long - 12'' Overall Height
$174.50

Authentic Whaling Harpoon $58.50
4½ foot Wood
Harpoon & Cone 36'' overall
8 foot Overall

CAPE COD CUPOLA CO., INC.
P. O. Box A-2096
New Bedford, Mass. 02741

Unusual weather vanes, cupolas, wall eagles.

CELEBRATED FULL-BODIED WEATHERVANES

These celebrated, old-fashioned, copper weathervanes are handmade on rare, old molds over 100 years old.   The motifs are hand-hammered of pure copper, beaten down into the old molds by hand, made in two halves, soldered together.   Some are gold leafed, some are antique verde green. The compass cross arms are cast aluminum, 22" wide with 5" letters.   The spire is 4' long and ¾" in diameter.   The shaft is long enough to allow mounting down through your cupola or barn roof.   Each weathervane comes complete with motif, shaft, compass letters and two balls; on gold vanes the balls are gold leafed, also the four letters.   On antique verde green vanes, all other parts are verde green also.

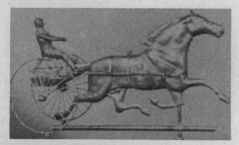

ST. JULIAN WITH HIGH-WHEEL SULKY
No. NE 3, 33" long, Antique Verde Green
$306.00 plus parcel post charge

Cosmo Glassworks

After graduating from Rhode Island School of Design, Alexander Moore discovered glassblowing, and set up a studio to practice the art. He makes a variety of utilitarian pieces — vases, bowls, glasses, plates — as well as decorative pieces. Not only is each piece designed and made by hand, but he also makes the glass from scratch, in a wonderful variety of colors: amethyst, cobalt blue, bottle green, teal. Prices range from $5.00 to $100.00. Alexander Moore encourages those interested to visit his studio. Call or write first for appointment.

Cosmo Glassworks
16 Pratt Street
Providence, Rhode Island 02906

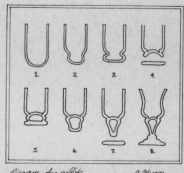

Diagram of a goblet   A. Moore

Earth

The Lightning Book

Lightning never strikes the same place twice. Fact or fallacy? Learn the answer to that and many other things. Well-researched and written for the layman, the author also includes an extensive bibliography for those who wish to delve further into this natural phenomenon. The book explains why it happens, what it does and what you can do about it.

For those who scoff at warnings to be cautious during electrical storms — it will give serious food for thought, and for others who react much too strongly and timidly when storms approach — it will enable them to understand and be aware of what's happening — helping to overcome unreasonable fears.

MSH

The Lightning Book
by Peter E. Viemeister
Diagrams by Read Viemeister
1972; 316 pp., paper
From: MIT Press
        Cambridge, Massachusetts 02139
        $1.95

Fulgurites

If lightning strikes sand of the proper composition, the high temperature of the stroke may fuse the sand and convert it to silica glass. "Petrified lightning" is a permanent record of the path of lightning in earth, and is called a fulgurite, after fulgur, the Latin word for lightning. Fulgurites are hollow, glass-lined tubes with sand adhering to the outside. Although easily produced in the laboratory in an electric furnace, silica glass is very rare in nature. The glass lining of a fulgurite is naturally produced silica glass, formed from the fusion of quartzrose sand at a temperature of about 1800° centigrade.

Most people have never seen a fulgurite and if they have they might not have recognized it for what it was. A fulgurite is a curious glassy tube that usually takes the shape of the roots of a tree. In effect it gives a picture of the forklike routes taken by lightning after striking sand. One of the largest ever found was discovered in South Amboy, New Jersey. When scientists dug the sand away from around the fulgurite, it broke so that the largest single piece was only six inches long; however, when put together, this Jersey fulgurite was almost nine feet long. It was virtually a straight tapering tube with only a few branches coming off the main stem. It was three inches in diameter near the surface of the ground and tapered down to about three-sixteenths-of-an-inch diameter at the lowest recovered piece. The thickness of the tube wall was on the order of a thirty-second of an inch.

Fulgurites have been found in all parts of the United States as far south as Florida and Mississippi and as far north as Waterville, Maine. Next time you are at a beach after a thunderstorm, look around, perhaps you will be lucky enough to find a fulgurite. You can recognize it as an approximately circular section of tube that would go down into the ground. A fulgurite is quite brittle. Dig around it carefully so that it can be removed with a minimum of breakage. Fulgurites vary in color, depending upon the type of sand from which they were formed. They are usually tan or black, but an, almost translucent, white fulgurite was found in Pensacola, Florida. The inside tends to be lustrous and somewhat irregular and the outside is rough sand which adheres to the fused areas. The glassy portion usually includes tiny bubbles which are formed by moisture trapped when the fulgurite cools suddenly after the lightning has passed.

Thunder is good, thunder is impressive; but it is lightning that does the work.

Mark Twain

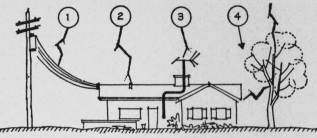

Fig. 56 How lightning could enter your home. (1) Strike or induced surge may follow utility lines into building. Arresters can divert these. (2) Direct stroke to building. Lightning rods can intercept these and lead them to ground. (3) Strike to TV or radio antenna. Good ground connection on mast and arrester on lead-in will keep these strokes out. (4) Side flash from nearby tree struck by lightning. Keep trees away from house or install conductors on house and trees.

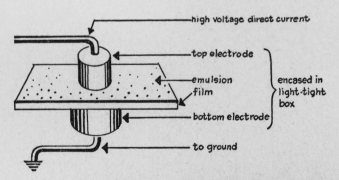

PLATE XLII, above. "Petrified lightning," or fulgurite, is made of sand fused by lightning. (See Chapter 10)

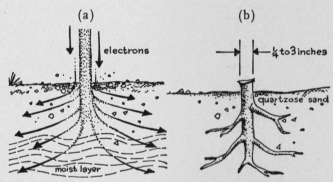

Fig. 44 (a) When lightning strikes the earth, electrons flow outward in all directions. (b) Petrified lightning or fulgurite is sometimes made when lightning strikes and fuses certain types of sand. Formed on beaches or shores, a fulgurite is usually covered with shifting sand and goes undiscovered. Eroding sand may expose a fulgurite. See Plate XLII.

Fig. 8 Klydonograph is inexpensive instrument for measuring lightning current that leads current through a sensitized photo film. Developed image is a "klydonogram" whose size indicates magnitude of current and whose shape reveals polarity.

EDUCATION

38

Education Index

A

The American Neptune 45
Archaeology in Vermont 39
Architecture 48

B

A Book of New England Legends and Folklore 43

C

Chemicals 42
The Community Press of New England 56
Connecticut 47
Connecticut Town Origins 44

D

Dynamics of Growth in New England's Economy, 1870–1964 46

E

Ecology
  kits 54
  schools 52, 55

F

Fishing
  schools 52

G

Good Old Days 49

H

Hands to Work and Hearts to God 57
Haunted New England 43

I

The Independent School Bulletin 44
Indian
  museums 50
The Indian in Connecticut 45

J

Jewelry
  minerals 48
The Junior Scientist Newsletter 42

K

Kalliroscope 42

L

Learning
  games 54
  kits 54
  tools 53, 54
Libraries 42
Life in an Old New England Country Village 47

M

The Maine Catalog 51
Maine's Treasure Chest – Gems and Minerals of Oxford County 39
Marblehead – The Spirit of '76 Lives Here 46
Medicine in New England 45
The Metaphorical Way of Learning & Knowing 53
Minerals 39
  granite 39
  jewelry 48
  stores 39
Museums
  Americana 47, 51, 57
  Indian 50
  science 40
Mysterious New England 43

N

New England Men of Letters 43
New Hampshire Echoes 46
New Hampshire Folk Tales 49

O

Old Landmarks and Historic Personages of Boston 44
Optics
  microscopes 40, 41
  telescopes 41

P

People From The Other World 43
Plantation in Yankeeland 46
Pottery 53
Printing
  Americana 51, 54
  limited editions 44, 47
Prints 54

R

Rhode Island Yearbook 49

S

Schools
  alternative 53
  bartending 52
  ecology 52, 55
  film 54
  fishing 52
  maritime 52
  private 44, 55
  travel 52
Shakers 57
Sky & Telescope Magazine 42
Stores
  minerals 39
The Story of Dorset 47

T

Tales of Old Wallingford 48
Tools
  learning 53, 54

V

Vermont Afternoons with Robert Frost 49
Vermont Life 49

W

The Wild River Wilderness 50
Window of Vermont 45

Granite

A look at the map of the State of Vermont shows a mountain ridge running down its spine. The range is the Green Mountains — famous for its beautiful valleys, scenic views and mantle of snow which buries quaint villages and delights frenetic skiers. Deep beneath these mountains is another kind of beauty which for over 100 years has been as important to Vermont as its scenery, cows, cheese and skiers.

These mountains contain huge deposits of hard, close-grained granite rock, most of which is nearly as hard as the sapphire. What is granite? How did it come into being?

Granite's principal ingredient is gray feldspar, next there is mica which gives it sparkle, and then there is the most resistant of all common materials — quartz. Fundamentally, all rocks sprang from the original molten process. This was not a placid happening. It took place with a violence that marks the birth and death of the volcano and the earthquake — multiplied a million fold. As the earth's crust cooled and contracted, pent-up gases and molten masses were confined at enormous pressures. Some broke free and overran the solid surface, mixing, melting, molding and making the varied strata of the earth. Rain fell, and running water wore away the high places, filling in the low ones with sediments.

Even then the earth was not yet finished. Changes are going on today, as the world is jarred by earthquakes and scorched by volcanic eruptions, deeply buried rocks become so heated that they are melted, time and again, and are squeezed upwards into the covering strata of younger rocks. New granites form and are brought to the light of day by the slow, steady processes of erosion.

The structure of granite is such that it is seldom quarried by blasting because this could shatter it. In the old days of quarrying, much granite was removed by blasting. A visit to a quarry will reveal rocks that were badly shattered by the use of high explosives.

Today, two methods — drilling and jet piercing — are used to cut the granite out of the quarry. In drilling, vertical holes are drilled about one inch apart to the desired depth (up to 20 feet) and the granite remaining between the holes is later removed by secondary drilling. In jet piercing, a high velocity flame like a blow torch is directed at the granite to be removed, causing a continuous flaking action. As the flame nozzle is moved back and forth, a deep channel is created in the granite. Granite has a grain like wood. In one direction it can be split; in the other direction it must be cut. The derricks used in hauling the granite out of the quarry are usually made of 115-foot lengths of Oregon fir. The importance of the derricks is obvious — without them, there'd be no deep quarry or granite. Most of the derricks have a lifting capacity of between 40 and 50 tons. The average block taken from the quarry is 20 tons. For easy figuring, the quarrymen use 200 pounds per cubic foot as a basis for estimating weights of blocks. Actually, a cubic foot of granite weighs about 170 pounds.

Once the granite is out of the hole, the finishing process begins — sawing, polishing, sandblasting and carving. Most granite is cut by wire saws made of hard steel wires about ½" in diameter. The wire passes over the surface of the granite carrying a silicon carbide abrasive mixed with water. When the cutting is complete, the block is separated into flat slabs ready for polishing.

Granite is polished by large metal discs that spin on top of the slab. An abrasive mixed with water is used in the process. The final polishing process, utilizing a powder similar to a jeweler's paste and a felt disc, provides a sparkling gloss and a finish as smooth as glass.

Beautiful designs and names can be etched on the polished slab by sandblasting. A flat sheet of rubber is first placed on top of the granite and the design is cut out of the rubber. Fine particles of

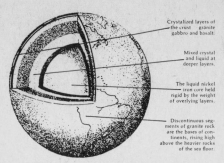

Theoretical section through the earth
which shows how granite forms a thin discontinuous crystal layer, just beneath the mantling surface rocks.

abrasive are then blown by air pressure against the slab. The abrasive cuts away the unprotected granite so that when the rubber is removed, a design etched in the granite is left.

The hand cutting of granite is done by skilled carvers with sharp chisels powered by compressed air. The master carver can create full figures or small, delicate flowers and intricate designs out of the granite. He is truly an artisan whose craft is perfected through years of dedication.

When you pass a monument or the gleaming white pillars of a stately building, pause for a moment and think about the chaotic turbulence that gave birth to the rock itself and then about the work of man before that granite was placed on its site.

Based on a booklet prepared by:

The Barre Granite Association
Barre, Vermont 05641

The Rock of Ages Granite Quarry and Craftsman Center have free guided tours daily from May 1 through October 31.

Wilk says —

Back a few years at Caspian Lake, in northern Vermont, lived the last of a passing breed named Sam Ladd, then 94 years old and still delivering all the Railway Express packages including outsize trunks sent up by summer visitors. One of these visitors, just past his fiftieth birthday, asked Sam one day what he did about the growing number of errant aches and pains that start after fifty and grow more numerous with age. Sam's reply was normal Vermont size. He said, "I just grunt and go on."

Archaeology in Vermont

This book offers a glimpse into New England's pre-Columbian past. There's detailed information on fourteen important archaeological sites discovered in Vermont and some background on two areas of pre-Columbian habitation: the Champlain Valley and Connecticut River Valley.

Many clear plates and pictures enable the reader to visualize better some of these important archaeological discoveries.

MSH

Archaeology in Vermont
Compiled by John C. Huden
1971; 107 pp., paper
From: Charles E. Tuttle Company
        Rutland, Vermont 05701
        $3.50

Minerals

For the rock-hound, Perham's is a mecca.

Perham's had its beginning when Stanley Perham was twelve years old. He made a collection of all things of nature and began to sell some of his duplicate pieces in order to enlarge his collection. As time passed, he settled on his real love of minerals. By the time he reached his twenties, his knowledge was such that people traveled far and wide to consult him. From this evolved the interesting shop he now runs.

Thousands come to Maine each year to collect minerals and Stanley Perham happily offers appropriate equipment for sale for grinding, cutting and polishing stones. He owns five quarries — all of which are open to interested collectors. No fee is charged, even maps are provided.

A book written by Mr. Perham's daughter takes you on an "armchair" treasure hunt, spanning 153 years of search for the magnificent gems and minerals of the Oxford Hills in Maine.

JCH

Catalogue available.
Perham's Maine Mineral Store
Trap Corner
West Paris, Maine 04289
Maine's Treasure Chest — Gems and Minerals of Oxford County
by Jane Perham Stevens
1972; 216 pp.
From: Perham's Maine Mineral Store
West Paris, Maine 04289
$5.95 — paper
$8.95 — cloth

Microscopes

If you want to look up or if you want to look down, *Unitron* has the instrument — microscope or refractor — to do the job. The wide range of microscopes includes those for the metallurgist, the toolmaker, for the laboratory, the clinic and the student. For example, metallurgical microscopes, series MMU, offers professional performance at prices associated with student models. For the astronomer, carefully designed, precision mounted refractors are equally reasonable in price, starting with Model 114 at $145.00 to a 4″ Photo-equatorial refractor, Model 166, at $1470.00.

Unitron Instrument Company
66 Needham Street
Newton Highlands, Massachusetts 02161

Series MMU Monocular Metallurgical Microscopes
Model MMU-055 — $345.00
Model MMU-155 — $434.00
Model MMU-MPL — $606.00

SPECIFICATIONS: UNITRON SERIES MMU METALLURGICAL MICROSCOPES

STAND	Large monocular stand inclinable 90°. Drawtube graduated in mm. Built-in adjustable plane glass reflector. Rack and pinion coarse focus. Full range micrometer screw fine focus. Plain stage, with removable glass insert plate, drilled to accept accessory mechanical stage. Stage adjustable in height over 40mm range by rack and pinion. Quadruple revolving nosepiece. Stage clips. Plastic dustcover.
ILLUMINATING SYSTEM	High-intensity illuminator with condenser, iris aperture diaphragm, filter holder and green filter. Illuminator may be used to provide vertical incident, oblique or transmitted illumination. Built-in base transformer for 115 volts, A.C., two-intensity switch mounted in base. Accessory substage mirror and fork. Line cord and spare bulbs.
CHOICE OF THREE MODELS	**Model MMU-055:** Stand and Illuminating System as described above, plus: Three coated, achromatic, parfocal objectives: M5X(0.10 N.A.), M10X(0.30 N.A.) and M40X(0.65 N.A.). Two coated eyepieces: W10XP Widefield with built-in (but removable) pointer for reference, and Ke15X Kellner. (Total power 50X-600X).
	Model MMU-155: Stand and Illuminating System as described above, plus: Four coated, achromatic, parfocal objectives: M5X(0.10 N.A.), M10X(0.30 N.A.), M40X(0.65 N.A.) and M100X(1.25 N.A.) oil immersion. Two coated eyepieces: WFH10XR High-eyepoint Widefield Measuring with focusable reticle (0.1mm), and Ke15X Kellner. Polarizing filter and eyepiece cap analyzer. Additional daylight blue and yellow filters. Bottle of immersion oil. (Total power 50X-1500X).
	Model MMU-MPL: Stand and Illuminating System as described above, plus: Four coated, flatfield Planachromatic, parfocal objectives: MPL10X(0.30 N.A.), MPL20X(0.40 N.A.), MPL40X(0.65 N.A.), and MPL80X(0.90 N.A.). Two coated eyepieces: WFH10XR High-eyepoint Widefield Measuring with focusable reticle (0.1mm), and Ke15X Kellner. Polarizing filter and eyepiece cap analyzer. Additional daylight-blue and yellow filters. (Total power 100X-1200X, without need for oil immersion).

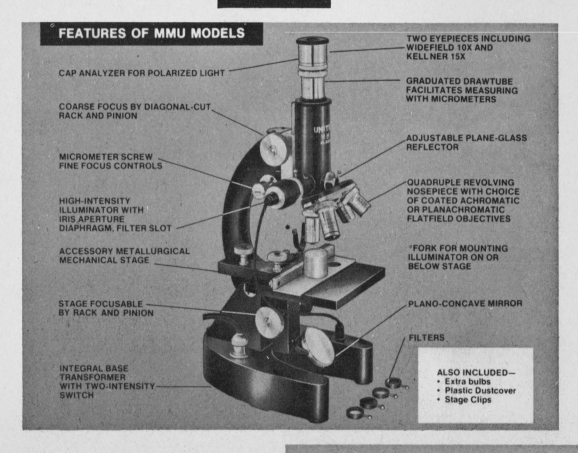

FEATURES OF MMU MODELS

- CAP ANALYZER FOR POLARIZED LIGHT
- COARSE FOCUS BY DIAGONAL-CUT RACK AND PINION
- MICROMETER SCREW FINE FOCUS CONTROLS
- HIGH-INTENSITY ILLUMINATOR WITH IRIS APERTURE DIAPHRAGM, FILTER SLOT
- ACCESSORY METALLURGICAL MECHANICAL STAGE
- STAGE FOCUSABLE BY RACK AND PINION
- INTEGRAL BASE TRANSFORMER WITH TWO-INTENSITY SWITCH
- TWO EYEPIECES INCLUDING WIDEFIELD 10X AND KELLNER 15X
- GRADUATED DRAWTUBE FACILITATES MEASURING WITH MICROMETERS
- ADJUSTABLE PLANE-GLASS REFLECTOR
- QUADRUPLE REVOLVING NOSEPIECE WITH CHOICE OF COATED ACHROMATIC OR PLANACHROMATIC FLATFIELD OBJECTIVES
- *FORK FOR MOUNTING ILLUMINATOR ON OR BELOW STAGE
- PLANO-CONCAVE MIRROR
- FILTERS

ALSO INCLUDED—
- Extra bulbs
- Plastic Dustcover
- Stage Clips

Museum of Science

Noted for its lively atmosphere, Boston's *Museum of Science* attracts more than half a million visitors a year who enjoy colorful, do-it-yourself exhibits and dramatic demonstrations. The musuem offers a smorgasbord of science, from astronomy in the Planetarium to zoology, from man's health to technology of the space age.

Museum of Science
Science Park
Boston, Massachusetts 02114

Adults: $2.00   Children: $1.00

SERIES MMU METALLURGICAL MICROSCOPES

The illuminator is powered by a transformer housed conveniently in the microscope base. This integral design eliminates the clutter of a separate transformer with long dangling wires. When the illuminator-condenser unit is installed on the body tube, it provides the usual vertical illumination needed for polished metal samples. Additionally the same illuminating unit also may be mounted on the microscope stage to give oblique darkfield-type illumination useful for studying opaque specimens at lower magnifications. Alternately the illuminator may be attached to the substage when transmitted light is needed for transparent specimens. An accessory mirror also is included to allow simultaneous transmitted and reflected light for counting of opaque particles dispersed in a transparent medium and similar applications.

Because of this versatility in types of illumination the MMU Models are not only microscopes for examining metallurgical specimens but also ideal general-purpose instruments where there is occasional need to examine samples by transmitted and oblique illumination as well.

Education

Telescopes

Kits, parts and accessories for the telescope maker, designed by experts, scientifically tested, and accurately manufactured.

Criterion Manufacturing Company
331 Church Street
Hartford, Connecticut 06101

KIT No. T-3

A complete kit for building a refractor telescope. No technical knowledge required as all parts are pre-fitted. You can assembly it complete in very little time by following easy simple directions included.

Focal length of objective lens is approximately 39". Air spaced achromatic objective lens is already mounted in cell, is 42MM diameter and corrected so that exquisite definition is obtained. Eyepiece holder is spiral focusing with click stops. Cells and holders are designed to slip over a tube and screws are provided. Combination eyepiece is adjustable to 40 and 80 power. Also included is a swivel-type mount with thumb screw for adjusting to any position.

The only additional material required is the main tube, which, if necessary can be purchased from us.

The finished instrument is comparable to ones selling for many times this price. You'll be able to see rings of Saturn, Moons of Jupiter, Moon's craters, — all with amazing clarity and in great detail. Even our technicians were surprised with the results!

COMPLETE KIT (less main tube)   No. T3   . .   **$21.50** Postpaid
Aluminum Tube of correct size   No. AT4   . .   **$3.00** Postpaid

A new optical method of positioning the outlined figures of the constellations on the night sky and directly naming the stars.

A precision instrument, not a gadget. Charts register accurately over the actual stars in the night sky. Complete sky coverage with 30 illuminated charts for your study and enjoyment.

With one eye to the instrument and one eye to the sky, optical illusion "projects" the battery-illuminated chart on the heavens to name the stars, locate the planets, and identify the constellations. Easily used. Battery included.

No. TG175 . . . .   **$3.50 postpaid**

A Contribution to Better Education

Independent study is an important part of the open education movement. *Selective Educational Equipment, Inc.* are suppliers of finely conceived and designed educational equipment at reasonable costs. They look for and develop materials which can be used to create a warm and effective learning climate for children and which will encourage teachers to be innovative and free in their approach to curriculum. *SEE* is constantly in touch with educators. Their comments and suggestions are evaluated and applied toward making better and more functional equipment. Materials for math, language art, science and social studies labs are available from:

Selective Educational Equipment, Inc.
Three Bridge Street
Newton, Massachusetts 02195

see-scope$_{tm}$

SEES01   basic see-scope$_{tm}$ $ 4.75
The see-scope (patent pending) not only satisfies the "teachers' requisites"(cover), but it also can be used as a water drop microscope and a microprojector. It can't be a "black box" to the student because he assembles it piece by piece in 1 or 2 class periods (no tools, glue, or other special materials are needed — the see-scope "snaps together"). There is no rack and pinion to wear out; the lens carrier (tube) focuses up and down via the movement of a non-wearing cam. The scope operates as a 60X simple microscope or, when the compound attachment is used, as a 120X compound microscope; the compound attachment has a telescoping tube which "zooms" the power even higher than 120X. The lens system does not use a bead lens, but, rather, uses a new type "disc lens". The see-scope is made of polypropylene, which makes it not only unbreakable, but also stain-proof (and dishwasher safe). The design of the concave mirror allows for adjustments of light intensity. Slight downward pressure on the see-scope lights the illuminator; when the pressure is released, the illuminator ceases operating. The lamp, then, is lit only when the student is viewing through the scope. Each see-scope, complete with compound attachment and lamp (but without D-cell), comes packed in an unbreakable polyethylene bucket with cover and handle; the bucket acts not only as a storage container for the scope, but also as a handy carrier for pond water.

Education

Chemicals for Research and Development

The *Ames Laboratories* list some 350 reagent and electronic grade intermediates with such tongue-twisting names as "2 Amino-1-propanol hydrochloride" (which, incidentally, sells for $200.00 per kilo). They also offer custom synthesis.

Then there is the story of a man who called up a chemical company at 5:30 pm one Friday and was answered by the janitor who, quite naturally, said, "Hello."

The caller asked, "Do you make Cyclohexydiethanolamine?"

The janitor said, "What did you say?"

The caller asked again, "Do you make Cyclohexydiethanolamine?"

To which the janitor answered testily, "Mister, when I said hello I told you everything I know."

Back to Ames; their products are deeply technical and are strictly for the research and development specialist. If this is your field, you should know about them.

RWW

The Ames Laboratories, Inc.
200 Rock Lane
Milford, Connecticut 06460

Junior Scientist Newsletter

Scientific material geared to young people and designed to keep them abreast of the latest scientific developments and events. An eleven year old boy writes, "There are many interesting things in *The Junior Scientist Newsletter* – such as articles about laser beams, colonies on the moon and even some bits of ancient history."

The Junior Scientist Newsletter   MSH
P.O. Box 581
Waltham, Massachusetts 02154
$4.00 yearly

KALLIROSCOPE
C O R P O R A T I O N

Kalliroscope – a new art form

Named from two Greek words: "kalliroos" (a beautiful current) and "skopein" (to see), *Kalliroscope* resembles a glass-fronted picture frame and is filled with a nonflammable cleaning fluid called perchloroethylene – a multitude of tiny flat crystals suspended in the liquid reflect light. Thus when *Kalliroscope* is held in the palm of a hand, or under a bulb, or near any source of heat or cold, or even spinning it on its back, it produces galactic spirals of enticing designs. "Squeeze to unwind," says Paul Matisse, the creator of *Kalliroscope.* "Its slow, soothing currents lull you to daydream."

Kalliroscope Corp.
145 Main Street
Cambridge, Massachusetts 02142

Viewer Model 2S	$10.00
Standing Viewer, Model 2S, 115v	$15.00
Picture Model 20S	$29.95

Education

Medicinal Purposes
Or, Great-Grandpa was a Resourceful Man

Back before the Civil War, there apparently must have been a form of limited Prohibition. A volume called "Colebrook Liquor Agency Book" has been given the News and Sentinel by Mrs. Floyd Dennison of Lancaster, hopefully for deposit with a local historical society. At a rough estimate, it contains 35 pages of entries running from May 24, 1858 through June 18, 1860, for quantities of rum, "alcohol", brandy, and gin, ranging from a half-pint to a couple of kegs. It takes only about a page and a half to list purchases, incidentally, most of them from the "State Agency." G.E. Hutchinson seems to have been in charge of the book, and presumably the sales. The only individual listed as a source is on March 3, 1859, Benj. Wittemore, "for liquor", $14.53.

The 800 or so entries for purchase are something else. Most are men's names, of course, but the pages are sprinkled with a lady's name here and there. New England rum cost 10¢ a pint, or 20¢ a quart. Gin was 25¢ a pint, "alcohol" 30¢ a half-pint.

The overwhelming majority of the purchasers weren't very original. They simply listed "medical", and a goodly number of them put down "mechanical". "Pickles" – perhaps the source of the phrase "getting pickled"? – and "camphor" were other popular reasons. The more imaginative citizens seem to have had quite a time keeping their horses in good health. For instance, on May 29, 1858, Simeon Carlton had to have a pint of rum "to doctor Horse"; on June 11, Burnham Rolfe got a half-pint of brandy "for linament to put on horse." Hiram Cummings got a pint of rum on June 4 "to wash horse breast", and had to come back the next day for another pint for the same purpose. On October 16 Henry Gathercole got a pint of rum "to wash horse," and J.B. Titus of Columbia needed a half-pint of "alcohol" to "doctor horse." The only other zoological note was the purchase by Richard Jackson of Colebrook on June 11, 1858 of a pint of rum "to wash calf."

On June 29 of the same year Zebulon Horn of Stewartstown got two quarts of rum "to make Bitters", and the same day Hiram Cummings of Stewartstown got 3 pints of the stuff "for Ed to make Bitters". The same day, Ezra Crawford of Clarksville picked up a pint of rum because "wife sick", on June 3 Gilman Coarser got a pint of rum "for bitters for Mother"; on June 9, 1858 Caleb Little needed a quart of rum because "Wife sick." On June 11, Hiram Cummings of Stewartstown bought a quart of rum for "bitters for boy", and Timothy Covell had to have a quart because "boy cut his foot." There was an epidemic of wives' ailments on June 15, when Daniel Young needed a pint of gin for "Wife sick", while the following day John Titus and Aaron C. Whipple of Columbia needed two pints of rum apiece for the same reason.

The essential kindliness of Colebrook citizenry was alive more than a hundred years ago, as witness entry of purchase by Archelaus Cummings of Colebrook June 17, 1858 of a pint of gin (25¢) for "Old Fred Atherton." The next day Timothy Covell got a pint of rum "to wash boy's foot." That leads, naturally, to the most picturesque and perhaps ultimate entry. On July 1, 1858, Merrit Gilkey of Colebrook bought a pint of rum for 10¢ "to use on corpse."

Reprinted with permission from the News and Sentinel, August 2, 1972.
Colebrook, New Hampshire.

A New England Simple

Face and hand lotion – Take 1/4 lb. of honey and warm through; add 1/2 lb. lanolin, then beat in 1/4 lb. of almond oil. Cool and bottle.

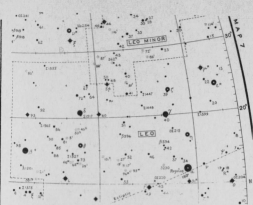

The constellation of Leo the Lion in *Norton's Star Atlas.*

NORTON'S STAR ATLAS AND REFERENCE HANDBOOK

An indispensable companion to all astronomers who take their stars seriously. The large, easy-to-read charts of this recent (15th) edition show the 9,000 stars of magnitude 6¼ and brighter, clusters, nebulae, and galaxies, plus many variable stars. Comet and asteroid paths may be readily plotted. The galactic equator and poles are drawn at the new official IAU positions, and the two supplemental Milky Way maps have been completely redone in this new system.

Preceding the atlas section is a veritable mine of essential information for observers using the naked eye, binoculars, or a telescope; of telescope design principles; of data on the moon (with a two-color lunar map keyed for hundreds of features); sun and planets, as well as an updated review of spectroscopy. There are astronomical tables of all kinds, and an elaborate index. Long lists of double stars with descriptions are given for each chart, and variables are similarly treated. The most impressive nebulae and clusters are described. The charts cover the sky from pole to pole, thus are usable anywhere.

The first edition of Norton's was published in the year 1910, so that for more than half a century this has been a standard reference work for every astronomer. Each map occupies a double page in the book, thus measures 16 inches high by 10 inches wide and presents almost one-sixth of the entire celestial sphere. There is a sizable overlap from one map to the next and no constellation is inconveniently broken up. The circumpolar charts overlap the others. This 114-page book is clothbound, 8½ by 11 inches.

Order A-3 NORTON'S STAR ATLAS . . . $7.25

Sky Publishing Corporation

Whether your interest in astronomy is amateur or professional, *Sky Publishing Corporation* may have something of interest for you. In addition to publishing a monthly magazine called *Sky and Telescope*, they offer a wide variety of books, pamphlets, atlases and catalogues. Send for their publication list.

From: Sky Publishing Corporation   MSH
4950-S1 Bay Street Road
Cambridge, Massachusetts 02138

Sky and Telescope Magazine
$8.00 U.S.; $9.00 Canada – yearly

The Francis A. Countway Library of Medicine

The Countway Library of Medicine, opened in 1965, houses two of the most extensive collections of medical literature in the United States: the Harvard Medical Library and the Boston Medical Library.

Seven years were spent in planning the Countway Library, but more than one hundred eighty years had gone into the development of the Harvard Medical Library and ninety years were behind the Boston Medical Library. The Countway Library contains excellent collections, both of old and rare books which relate to the history of medicine and the modern books which support current teaching, research and patient care. Of the older material, the Library contains virtually all of the great works of medical history from the fifteenth to the nineteenth centuries. In addition to its collections of books printed before 1501 and rare European books, New England imprints and Bostoniana are particularly well represented.

The Countway Library is intended primarily for use of students, faculty members and research investigators associated with schools of medicine in the Boston area. Others who have a serious purpose in using the technical literature may consult the books and periodicals upon request.

The Francis A. Countway Library of Medicine
10 Shattuck Street
Boston, Massachusetts 02115

Haunted New England

Short tales of horror and hauntings in New England, with companion photographs, make this book a highly entertaining one. To quote the author:

"... no section of America can claim a greater sense of mystery than old New England. The inexplicable nature of its sea, the special chill of Yankee weather, the heritage of Salem witches, and the bony, unyielding nature of the land and of New Englanders themselves cannot fail to lend a haunting tone to much of its folklore ... A hard land and a hard life have inevitably produced something other than a tradition of brightness and joy ... Yet horror and humor do have a strange proximity ... In any case, the Yankee character surely had a strong taste for the macabre."

The publisher has complemented these two talented women's efforts with good editing, splendid photographic reproductions, and beautiful binding.

Anne Ward

Haunted New England
by Mary Bolté; photographs by Mary Eastman
1972; 128 pp.
From: The Chatham Press
Riverside, Connecticut 06878
$8.50

FROZEN CITIZENS
Vermont

One of the more bizarre New England legends concerns the freezing of elderly or ailing citizens during the winter months in order to assure the young and the healthy of the area a sufficient share of the scanty food supply. In 1939, *The Rutland Herald* published an account of this practice. The unknown author claims that in one January during the last century, his grandfather had been present when six people, drugged and unclad, were taken from a cabin out into the bitter cold to be left overnight in the snow. The ceremony was conducted with equanimity and even lightheartedness by the practitioners, who afterwards returned to the cabin for a night of easy sleep. In the morning after a hearty breakfast, the group invited their visitor out to witness the rest of the proceedings. The lifeless bodies, partially covered by a fresh snowfall, were put into a ten-foot box and bedded down with cloth and straw. Boards were nailed over the top for protection against wolves, and the whole was covered with masses of hemlock boughs. All this was done with a matter-of-fact air, and the visitor was cordially invited to come again next spring to witness the process of resuscitation that would enable the frozen persons to help with the planting of corn. Upon his return in May, a small amount of snow was still on the ground and the bodies, when removed from their coffin, seemed as stiff as before. The visitor watched as large troughs were filled with warm water. The bodies were placed in these tubs, heads slightly raised, and boiling water was gradually added to the baths until color began to return to the flesh. When breathing began, small amounts of spirits were administered. This was followed by a hot meal in the cabin, after which all six seemed lively, talkative, quite rejuvenated after their four-month sleep, and ready for the spring planting.

As far as is known, this strange practice has not survived to the present day, though it is possible that many old Vermonters might still welcome such an escape from their long hard winters.

People From The Other World

Ghost stories should be short and simple. This one isn't. There are 423 pages of Col. Olcott's investigations in 1874 of the spirit materializations at the Eddy brothers' farm in Chittenden, Vermont, and 50 or so pages on several separate investigations. Scientifically, it is sadly lacking by modern standards; from a spiritualistic point of view it is intriguing. Pretty heavy going for one who does not have an avid interest in such things. What it is, quite basically, is a curio of its time, written in the 19th century, by a spiritualist and associate of Madame Blavatsky.

Anne Ward

People From The Other World
by Henry S. Olcott
Illus. Alfred Kappes and T.W. Williams
1972; 492 pp.

From: Charles E. Tuttle Company
Rutland, Vermont 05701
$8.25

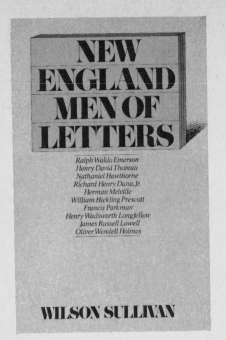

New England Men of Letters

"Build therefore your own world" Emerson's voice is heard today in youth's struggle to do his own thing. This is the theme that author Wilson Sullivan artfully pursues in *New England Men of Letters*. Many biographies have been written about the authors of the 19th century, but Mr. Sullivan has revealed, by a mere chapter, the literary prowess of each. As the reader recalls the lives of essayists Emerson and Thoreau; novelists Hawthorne, Dana and Melville; and poets Longfellow, Lowell and Holmes, he realizes how often their lives were interwoven. Historians Prescott and Parkman are of added interest, recording perspectives of world thought.

The idea that today's writers are thinking in likethought to those of the 19th century is brought out in the introduction by Dr. Hyatt Waggoner. Wilson Sullivan goes on to show that men do seek the same things. The ideas and ideals of transcendentalism, industrialism, anti-slavery and expansion of geographical horizons all find their counterparts in today's world. Even the desire to follow the "beat of a different drummer" is still part of our American spirit.

New England Men of Letters is a helpful volume for a student working on a thesis. Little known facts add dimension to already familiar writings. The book is also a useful tool for teachers who must compete with the multi-media of today, to paint a colorful picture of traditional American literature. If you have time to read leisurely, and think about it, Wilson Sullivan has shown in a quiet but convincing way, that there is no generation gap in the dreams and thoughts of good writers.

Lois Ingram

New England Men of Letters
by Wilson Sullivan
drawings by Thomas Evans Hinton
1972; 242 pp.
From: The Macmillan Company
886 Third Avenue
New York, New York 10022
$6.95

The Morning and Evening of Life

The following is an inscription on a tombstone in Massachusetts. It is beautiful:

"I came in the morning – it was spring,
And I smiled;
I walked out at noon – it was summer,
And I was glad;
I sat me down at even – it was autumn,
And I was sad;
I laid me down at night – it was winter,
And I slept."

A Book of New England Legends and Folklore

A long, delicious compilation of legends and stories of New England put together by an expert in the field. Every corner of New England has its own tales, many put into the public domain by such eminents as Whittier, Longfellow and Hawthorne. There are also the many lesser known accounts ranging from witch hunts to out right ghost stories which make intriguing reading and are a fascinating revelation of the history of New England as seen through the beliefs of its people.

Witch stories predominate, such as one about "Old Meg the Witch". History devolves into legend with the retelling of the Quaker persecutions. Small homilies of everyday life make intriguing reading. "Telling the Bees", reprinted below, is a good example. Among the ghost stories, the tale of "Peter Rugg, the Missing Man" is one of the most unusual.

This book is well put together, the stories grouped by geographical area and interestingly illustrated by photographs and drawings.

Anne Ward

Telling the Bees

Respecting bees, one very old superstition among others is, as I can strictly affirm, still cherished, surviving, apparently, through that peculiarity of the mind, which, the event being uncertain, elects to give it the benefit of the doubt rather than to discard it as a childish and meaningless custom. This is the common belief that bees must be made acquainted with the death of any member of the family, otherwise these intelligent little creatures will either desert the hive in a pet, or leave off working and die inside of it. The old way of doing this was for the goodwife of the house to go and hang the stand of hives with black, the usual symbol of mourning, she at the same time softly humming some doleful tune to herself. Another way was for the master to approach the hives and rap gently upon them. When the bees' attention was thus secured, he would say in a low voice that such or such a person – mentioning the name – was dead. This pretty and touching superstition is the subject of one of Whittier's "Home Ballads."

A Book of New England Legends
by Samuel Adams Drake
1972; 477 pp., paper
From: Charles E. Tuttle Co., Inc.
Rutland, Vermont 05701
$3.25

Mysterious New England

Yankee says that this is "a collection of stories from the dark side of New England," – a fascinating collection it is!

Here is an assortment of New England characters, strong, fey and interesting. The ghosts are a fine lot – often authenticated as recently as today. They are as skilled and versatile as those of Ireland – no apologies needed.

There are animal stories, such as the last cougar, the mixed breed coyote-wolf-dog, a flight of hawks to be remembered and the rare and bloodied fruit.

Some of the stories dwell on disappearances, vampires and witches, horrors in the cold, forecasts of a hundred years ago, and towns best forgotten.

For the archeological minded – there are some fine accounts of stone carvings and caves; foundations of ancient ruins with all kinds of theories.

It's a fine selection of fifty tales unique to the area, and illustrated very handsomely.

Alice Rosencrantz

Mysterious New England
Compiled by the Editors of Yankee Magazine
1971; 320 pp.
From: Yankee, Inc.
Dublin, New Hampshire 03444
$7.50

Education

P. REVERE
REVERE'S PICTURE OF BOSTON IN 1768.

Connecticut Town Origins

Helen Earle Seller's book *Connecticut Town Origins* should be in every school and public library in Connecticut. The capsule early town histories make fascinating reading for all ages. Indian tribes are described so that their history is as vivid as that of the men and women who settled the various areas before their settlements were named. Genealogists and historians will delight in the names and short accounts of various founding families.

From the sketch of North Branford. "When Totoket was purchased from the Indians in 1638, two white families were already in residence here. One was Thomas Whitway, an Indian interpreter who lived in the vicinity of Foxon. A more extensive settlement was begun about 1720. Tradition says that for a long time these settlers were accustomed to leave their houses in the spring ... occupying the clearings at the base of Totoket Mountain ... returning to their houses with the approach of winter ... 'The Indian name of the place ... appears to have been Paug,' and so it was known for a great many years ... In May 1831 the Northford and North Branford Village Societies were united to form the town which was named for the latter."

Many of these town histories give the origin of the names. Preston is derived from the old English, meaning the priest's town or fen. Guilford is derived from the old English, probably meaning ford where the golden flowers grow.

The photographs are excellent. Tantaquidgeon, a Mohegan who maintains an Indian museum, and the covered bridge at West Cornwall over the Housatonic and Bride Brook in winter are especially appealing.

Helen L. Bush

Connecticut Town Origins
by Helen Earle Sellers
1942; 96 pp., paper
From: The Pequot Press
    Chester, Connecticut 06412
    $2.50

Old Landmarks and Historic Personages of Boston

Journalist and historian, Samuel Drake, realized that many of the old houses and public buildings built by the early residents of Boston and vicinity had been torn down as the city grew. He studied old books, maps, pictures and culled the memories of older citizens until he wrote this amazing book in 1872. From the words and pictures we are able to visualize the early landmarks and the people who settled Boston. In the Introduction, Drake gives the beginning history of Boston. In 1628, the first white settler, William Blackstone had a dwelling on Beacon Hill, called Shawmut, or Trimountain, by the settlers of Charlestown at that time. In 1630 it was ordered by the court that Trimountain be called Boston for old Boston in Lincolnshire, England. The first crude houses were of wood with thatched roofs and wood chimneys covered with clay. By the end of 1752, the first census was taken, and the people numbered about 18,000, with 2,776 houses.

Drake takes us on a tour of Boston Common, site in the early days of the Almshouse, the Workhouse ("for the confinement of minor offenders such as rogues and vagabonds"), the Massachusetts Medical College and the Common Burying-Ground.

The book is illustrated with early lithographs, engravings and woodcuts; especially interesting is Paul Revere's picture of Boston in 1768.

Helen L. Bush

Old Landmarks and Historic Personages of Boston
by Samuel Adams Drake
First Tuttle edition published 1971; 484 pp. paper
From: Charles E. Tuttle Company
    Rutland, Vermont 05701
    $3.25

GREAT IDEAS

"Great ideas, it has been said, come into the world as gently as doves. Perhaps then, if we listen attentively, we shall hear, amid the uproar of empires and nations, a faint flutter of wings, the gentle stirring of life and hope. Some will say that this hope lies in a nation; others, in a man. I believe rather that it is awakened, revived, nourished by millions of solitary individuals whose deeds and works every day negate frontiers and the crudest implications of history. As a result, there shines forth fleetingly the ever threatened truth that each and every man, on the foundation of his own sufferings and joys, builds for all." (Taken from the writings of Albert Camus for the Christmas card of Dr. and Mrs. Richard Day of Phillips Exeter Academy, 1971.)

From May, 1972 issue of
The Independent School Bulletin
4 Liberty Square
Boston, Massachusetts 02109

Imprint Society

For well-heeled bibliophiles — limited editions of unusual, enduring works in the fields of history, exploration, early travel, Americana, and literature. Each edition is limited to 1950 numbered copies, signed by an eminent author, scholar or artist who has contributed to it. Printed on the finest watermarked paper, all are beautifully illustrated and richly bound. The Society intends each book to embody the best of the tradition of bookmaking and to offer both pleasure and value to the connoisseur of fine books. Prospectus available.

Imprint Society
South Street
Barre, Massachusetts 01005

Poor Richard's Almanacks

Published by BENJAMIN FRANKLIN. *Poor Richard's Almanacks* are here presented for the first time in their entirety. First published in 1733, they eventually sold 10,000 copies a year, and had a score of imitators. What made Franklin's almanacs unusual—and memorable—were the line fillers: the wise sayings, proverbs and aphorisms that Franklin printed in the empty spaces in the monthly columns of data on the hours of sun, moon and tides.

The introduction is by Whitfield J. Bell, Jr., Librarian of the American Philosophical Society. The almanacs have been reproduced in their true size from originals selected by Harold Hugo. Printing is by The Meriden Gravure Company, design by Klaus Gemming. There are two portrait frontispieces, one cut on wood by Sidney Chafetz for this edition and the other an 18th century likeness. Two volumes. $50.00

Poor Richard, 1737.
AN
Almanack
For the Year of Christ
1737,
Being the First after LEAP YEAR.

And makes since the Creation   Years
By the Account of the Eastern Greeks   7245
By the Latin Church, when ☉ ent. ♈   6936
By the Computation of *W. W.*   5746
By the *Roman* Chronology   5686
By the *Jewish* Rabbies   5498

Wherein is contained,
The Lunations, Eclipses, Judgment of the Weather, Spring Tides, Planets Motions & mutual Aspects, Sun and Moon's Rising and Setting, Length of Days, Time of High Water, Fairs, Courts, and observable Days.
Fitted to the Latitude of Forty Degrees, and a Meridian of Five Hours West from *London,* but may without sensible Error, serve all the adjacent Places, even from *Newfoundland* to *South-Carolina.*

By RICHARD SAUNDERS, Philom.

PHILADELPHIA:
Printed and sold by *B. FRANKLIN,* at the New Printing-Office near the Market.

Education

The Indian in Connecticut

More and more people are becoming interested in America's downtrodden and vanishing breed, the pure-blooded Indian. This book, first of a series of Indians in New England books, gives not only an interesting account of the Indian before the white man's arrival, but also several reasons and explanations for the Indian's oftentimes tragic, and sometimes warranted demise. And along with word and picture descriptions of Indian tools and artifacts, this book also explains the derivation of many words and phrases that the Indian added to Webster's Dictionary — like *Indian-giving* and *powwow.*

The book seeks neither to glorify nor expunge the Connecticut Indian. It tells about the Indian and his complicated system of tribes and allegiances and lets the reader form his own conclusions. The book should be part of every Connecticut youngster's American history course. Subsequent books will deal with the Indians of Massachusetts, Rhode Island, Vermont, Maine and New Hampshire.

Sally G. Devaney

The Indian in Connecticut
by Chandler Whipple; illus. by Janice Lindstrom
1972; 95 pp., paper
From: The Berkshire Traveller Press
    Stockbridge, Massachusetts 01262
    $2.95

THE INDIAN IN CONNECTICUT

"WHITE PEOPLE . . . WHO ARE THEY?"   33
THE DISSOLUTE CAPTAIN STONE   39
"ARE YOU ANGRY, ENGLISHMEN?"   46
SASSACUS MOVES   52
THE PEQUOT WAR   57
DEATH OF A NATION   63
"MY MEN CAME TO FIGHT"   68
"I SHALL DIE BEFORE MY HEART IS SOFT"   73
WHERE ARE THEY NOW?   79

Window of Vermont

Here's a monthly newspaper, four-color in spots, representing the flavor, character and pastoral beauty of one of America's favorite states. Editorial features include skiing, home building, antiquing, places to visit, and country inns — all the things you expect to find in a publication devoted to the Green Mountain State.

JCH

Window of Vermont
The Burlington Free Press
Burlington, Vermont 05401
$3.00 yearly; 12 issues

A New England Simple — To Cure Inflammation of the Stomach
Drink the water in which onions have been boiled.

———————◆———————

The American Neptune is a quarterly journal devoted to the many aspects of American maritime history and is published as a noncommercial undertaking by The Peabody Museum of Salem, Massachusetts.

In each issue, documents of maritime interest, notes and book reviews are included. Although they do not publish articles dealing with the technique of model building, plans and information of value to builders of ship models are included whenever possible.

Published quarterly at a rate of $12.50 per year.

MSH

THE AMERICAN NEPTUNE

A Quarterly Journal of
Maritime History
published by
The Peabody Museum
Salem, Massachusetts

There's still much to discover in the field of medicine, but when you measure what has been accomplished since 1840, against what was done before, the advances are miraculous.

MSH

Medicine in New England — 1790-1840
by Barnes Riznik
1969; 26 pp., paper
From: Old Sturbridge Village
    Sturbridge, Massachusetts 01566
    $1.20

In colonial New England, contagious diseases like scarlet fever and diphtheria were carried along traveled roads by new settlers and traders. People often contracted disease at public meetings, in town schools, and from their doctors and ministers. But the "art of physic" was beginning to show signs of taking its place in a wider scientific revolution whose methods altered older traditions of learning. Early in the eighteenth century Massachusetts became the scene of the first organized efforts in both Britain and America to combat smallpox by immunization. Few of the grim, infectious diseases plaguing both Europe and the North American colonies were so widespread and fatal as smallpox, outbreaks of which were regarded with terror. Cotton Mather, who read in the Transactions of the Royal Society that inoculation for smallpox had long been successfully practised by the Turks, urged experimental inoculation to halt a smallpox epidemic in Boston in 1721. While Boston physicians at first refused to experiment with the new method, Mather and other leading clergymen continued to advocate inoculation. Only one medical practitioner, Dr. Zabdiel Boylston, was willing to give immunization a trial, but he proved that the risk of deliberate infection was worth taking. Of several hundred healthy persons who were inoculated in Boston at this time only a few died, and tradition-bound practitioners soon joined Mather and Boylston in the attack on smallpox.

... the majority of New England practitioners probably had less understanding of medical science than has the average high school senior today. Few doctors had even seen an institution for bed care of the sick. Although Philadelphia and New York possessed hospitals, only a few New England physicians knew those institutions. The slow development of general hospitals in New England meant a long, unfortunate delay in providing better care for the seriously ill and in studying diseases.

———————◆———————

A New England Simple — Cure for Dysentery
Adults — A tablespoon of castor oil and 25 drops of laudanum.

Education

New Hampshire Echoes

You don't have to live there to enjoy this interesting magazine with articles about New Hampshire people and places — known and not-so-well known, such as the one about the Bean Matchmaking Plant in their May-June 1972 issue.

MSH

New Hampshire Echoes
6 Odd Fellows Avenue
Concord, New Hampshire 03301
$3.75 per year

Every year people burn up and throw away five trillion matches, all over the world. That figure has three more zeroes at the end of it than anything the politicians and economists talk about. In the United States, one-tenth of the world's production — some 500 billion matches a year — are made and used. And to bring it closer to home, *D.D. Bean & Sons Co.* of Jaffrey, New Hampshire, produces 50 billion of them.

Matches are the world's No. 1 man-made object in terms of quantity. The rise from cave man to civilization was advanced by the discovery of methods of making the fire stick, long before the Boy Scouts invented this art.

You'll find way back in the Old Testament, in the prophet Elijah's time, that the Israelites were rubbing sticks together to start fire. And over the centuries inventors came step by step to the conveniences of modern life in America where something like 57 million matches are now lit every hour with a flick of the wrist.

There are many historical notes on the discovery of matches and the match business, but the match book was unquestionably invented by Joshua Pusey, the Philadelphia lawyer who also invented the roller coaster, the mail box, and those coin-operated opera glasses attached to theater seats.

Today, the match book is the "best read book" in America. A total of 12 billion of them are circulated during the course of the year in this country and each one is good for 20 readings.

More than nine out of ten of these match books are given away. Buy a pack of cigarettes, and you get a match book. Dine at a good restaurant, the cashier will offer a match book. In your travels, aboard a train, airplane or steamship, or in a hotel, there are match books for the taking. The reason, of course, is the advertising message on the cover, and it took a particular American type of genius to think of it.

Delcie David Bean, founder of *D.D. Bean & Sons Co.*, was born in Montpelier, Vermont, in 1883, and spent his childhood in Rindge, New Hampshire, where he went to public school and later into business, first with his father and then for himself.

In 1907, when he was 24, he moved to Jaffrey and five years later he brought his original business of manufacturing box shooks to the community. He founded the present company in 1938 with his two sons, and since that time, D.D. Bean & Sons Co. has grown and developed into a major international concern.

D.D. Bean died in 1964 and now his sons, son-in-law and several grandsons carry on the business, unique in that it still remains a family affair.

In the formation of the company, D.D. Bean had the vision of the tremendous growth potential of the give-away paper book match. And long before the word "automation" was coined, he was using automatic machinery and conveyors for the efficient production of paper book matches.

Since the Bean company was founded 34 years ago, the growth of the book match business has roughly paralleled the cigarette industry, and consequently production has increased to meet increasing demand.

Today, *D.D. Bean & Sons Co.*, besides its factory in Jaffrey, has plants in St. Louis, St. Cesaire (near Montreal) and Toronto, Canada. This expansion has taken place largely in the last few years and, as new markets are opened up throughout the world, it is planned to start branch factories patterned after its present New Hampshire operations.

The growth and success of one of the Granite State's best-known companies is due to the wisdom and vision of Delcie David Bean. Wherever book matches are used — and that's practically everywhere in the world — you're likely to see the name:

"D.D. Bean, Jaffrey, N.H."

◆

The Dynamics of Growth in New England's Economy, 1870-1964

by Robert W. Eisenmenger

THE NEW ENGLAND RESEARCH SERIES: 2
SPONSORED BY THE NEW ENGLAND COUNCIL, AND PUBLISHED BY WESLEYAN UNIVERSITY PRESS

The Dynamics of Growth in New England's Economy, 1870-1964

This is a scholarly presentation of the economics of New England, "a poorly endowed region" with "few natural resources or locational features to attract and support industry and agriculture."

As the United States has grown, New England ports have diminished in importance. It is "out of the way" for rail connections, living costs and taxes are higher than in other areas, and the "rugged climate is generally not attractive to a growing number of retired people." Yet New England continues to grow and to maintain a higher per capita income and a lower unemployment rate than the rest of the nation.

Dr. Robert Eisenmenger examines this phenomenon through a factual study, many statistics, mathematical formulas, maps, graphs, etc., well beyond the average reader's desire for information. But economists and businessmen will find it a valuable source.

The final summations are pleasing to a born and bred New Englander. The area has prospered because descendants of those who were financially successful in the 19th century have chosen to remain in New England to cope with, and rise above, locational disadvantages and to continue to exert Yankee ingenuity.

A. C. Ambrose

The Dynamics of Growth in New England's Economy, 1870-1964
by Robert W. Eisenmenger
1967; 201 pp.
From: Wesleyan University Press
       Middletown, Connecticut 06457
       $9.00

Plantation in Yankeeland

For all who are interested in Rhode Island or New England history, or those looking for a socioeconomic study of the rise and fall of the plantation system of the region, this book is a treasure trove of information. It spans the history of one plantation, Smith's Castle at Cocumscussoc, Rhode Island, from the negotiations with the Indians in 1637 to its restoration and preservation by the Cocumscussoc Association in 1949. All the factors influencing the life of the plantation are explored, and we are given a summary of Indian and military affairs, education, social customs, politics and folklore. Also provided is a good outline of the establishment of the different religious sects in Narragansett. The economic structure of the plantation system itself, with its corollaries of slavery, agriculture and commerce are gone into in great detail. The genealogical procession is quite clear and uncomplicated with each individual and their contributions to the plantation and to history carefully delineated. The parade of passersby — Gilbert Stuart, Bishop Berkeley, and others, gives the history of the plantation a far wider scope than just Narragansett country.

This is not a book for the casual reader. But for those who are interested, it will provide a rich source of information. It is adequately illustrated, and contains a very complete index and a good bibliography.

Anne Ward

Plantation In Yankeeland
by Carl R. Woodward
1971; 198 pp.
From: The Pequot Press
       Chester, Connecticut 06412
       $8.95

◆

Marblehead — The Spirit of '76 Lives Here

As the two authors note, Marblehead has often been neglected in historical accounts of the development of New England. Priscilla Sawyer Lord and Virginia Clegg Gamage set out to record the heritage and history of this vital and fascinating town. Endless work and research went into the assembling and sorting of facts and legends, and this highly readable account presents the story of the nearly 350 years of this spirited town.

The book is divided into two parts. Marblehead: Its History, and Marblehead: Its Other Aspects. There are thirty-two pages of photographs, and the many line drawings that appear as chapter heads and interspersed throughout the pages are charming.

Louise Russell

Marblehead — The Spirit of '76 Lives Here
by Priscilla Sawyer Lord
and Virginia Clegg Gamage
Drawings by Marion Martin Brown
1972; 395 pp.
From: Chilton Book Company
       401 Walnut Street
       Philadelphia, Pennsylvania 19106
       $13.95

Education

The Story of Dorset

This history or autobiography, of an old Vermont town was first printed in 1924, then reprinted again in 1971. When the original idea for a history of the town was conceived, the people of Dorset were invited to contribute material, and the response was most gratifying. Letters came pouring in, old books and papers were loaned, anecdotes were related, every possible aid and encouragement was given. The result is a sort of town autobiography.

A charming story of the town from its earliest beginnings — geological formations, Indian habitation, colonial days, the Revolutionary War, into 19th century life and on up through World War I.

The author has tried to avoid as much as possible facts and statistics, except as they related to persons and events involved in a particular chapter. By using the material loaned by local residents, the author has recreated the life and times of this town.

For those who have visited Dorset, set in a lovely valley surrounded by mountains, this story should enhance their knowledge and understanding of the town. And who could resist a visit during the fall when the leaves are turning and the entire surrounding hills are an endless panorama of color? In all, this is a work to delight the hearts of historians, Vermonters, and connoisseurs of the American scene.

Charles T. Letson

The Story of Dorset
by Zephine Humphrey
1971; 298 pp.
From: Charles E. Tuttle Company
Rutland, Vermont 05701
$10.00

Laural Armstrong was born in 1806. Apparently he was an observant youngster with a retentive memory. In his maturity he became one of our most popular and influential citizens, a man whom everyone honored. It is with implicit belief that we may listen to him as he again speaks to us in the following paragraphs:

"I will begin by saying that the first rude log houses of our grand and great grandparents — had mostly given place to the second class of houses built — with an eye to something more than a bare shelter from the weather. The first and principal room was the kitchen in which was done the work of the household, where the family table was always set, where was done the washing and the little ironing that was done. The men's shirts of those days, commonly of red and yellow checked home-made flannel, collars and all, were guiltless of starch and ironing. Sometimes a home-made shirt of linen was put on over the woolen and coming down as low as our vests do now, was guilty of a little potato starch in the collar for Sunday wear or nice occasions. Also during the heat of summer many of the men wore shirts and pants made with linen warp and filled with the tow which was separated from the flax by the process of hetcheling. — It may not be uninteresting to some of these young misses to describe the process by which their great-grandmothers used to wash these tow trousers, to cleanse them from the smut and crock of rolling the blackened logs into great heaps to be burned. None of your chemical soaps and patent washing fluids would do the thing. No, no, a kettle of good strong hot lye, a wash tub, a battle board and battler were the needed tools. The wash woman was clad in a petticoat and short gown with short or no sleeves at all. — Thus equipped in pleasant summer weather, you could see them on the shady side of the house or down by the spring or at the well side, with the battler in the right hand, shaped like an over-grown pudding stick, the battle board some four feet long by one foot wide, smooth and rounded at the lower end, standing in the tub and the upper end resting against the person. The garment is now taken by a corner with the left hand, dipped ever and anon into the lye, and then laid on the board. Then down comes the battler with quick and oft repeated blows and with a spanking sound which echoes from many a hill around. But woe to the urchin toddling about whose eyes are just on a level with the spurting fluid, and woe to the boys of larger growth whom a handsomely rounded arm and a rosy cheek glowing with inspiring exercise may have drawn admiringly too near! Cleansed from the fallow smut and dipped into the running brook, then spread to whiten on the grass, and next Monday morning the admiring lover or the doting husband walks about in snowy linen, clean and white, that a prince might envy. . . ."

The Stinehour Press

Stinehour has achieved a wide reputation for excellence in printing. This Press prints on order principally for scholarly and academic publishers and institutions. *Stinehour* specializes in the production of difficult and demanding books and journals in limited or small editions. Typographic resources are considerable, as well as are talents for editorial and design services. The Press takes pride in a craftsmanlike approach to type composition, presswork and binding. Each project is priced individually.

The Stinehour Press
Lunenburg, Vermont 05906

◆

A New England Simple — To Clean or Sweeten Cider Barrels

Wash the barrels with a mixture of ashes and water, rinse thoroughly and put in a pint of clear water, and one large spoonful of oil of vitriol, well shaken. Then rinse with cold water. Beef and pork barrels can be cleaned in the same way.

◆

Brookline, Vermont has the only round school-house in the country. It was built in 1822 of brick by Doctor Wilson, an eccentric schoolmaster wanted in Europe for highway robberies committed under the name of "Thunderbolt."

CONNECTICUT

Connecticut

Connecticut, along with its fine magazine counterparts in New England, focuses on interesting, important issues in the Nutmeg State. The magazine *Connecticut,* of and about the state, brings into perspective crucial points which need thoughtful observation after the first blush of the daily newspaper has faded. Who's doing something about the oil slicks on Long Island Sound? Cable TV is moving in. What about it? What's happening to your purchasing dollar? Is there anything funny about the lottery? These are examples of the concern *Connecticut* has for keeping its readers informed. There's a good mix here — issues, things to do, book reviews, humor — for native nutmeggers and others interested in Connecticut.

JCH

Connecticut
2505 Main Street
Stratford, Connecticut 06497
$7.50 a year/10 issues

◆

Life in an Old New England Country Village

Reading this book is like taking a walk into the past. Here is rural New England in the early nineteenth century. It's a specific place, Old Sturbridge Village, but it's more than about a museum; the book, like the village *is* old New England, the place, the buildings, the feelings of a time gone by, but one whose influence still exists.

The text is interesting, informative and very readable, and the illustrations are apt and descriptive.

Life 150 years ago had its drudgery and seemingly ceaseless chores, but it was also here that humanitarianism burgeoned with free education, prison reform and care of the poor, sick and handicapped.

Along with the kind of life then, the book also deals with the structures, the meeting house, school, barns, mills, residences, gardens and land.

Reading the book is the next best thing to going backward in time to the recreation of a way of life that is Old Sturbridge Village and old New England.

Sally G. Devaney

Life in an Old New England Country Village
by Catherine Fennelly
1969; 211 pp.
From: Thomas Y. Crowell Company
201 Park Avenue South
New York, New York 10003
An Old Sturbridge Village Book
$10.00

Education

Tales of Old Wallingford 1670 – 1970

"The Yankee peddler was more than just a picturesque medicine man who hawked his wares to captive audiences. A purveyor of Yankee ingenuity and good news; vendor, mailman, doctor, minister, musician, standup comic, politician, stoic, teacher, mechanic, lover, scout and explorer, his was a reign of 'great historical significance'," says Clarence E. Hale in this book.

Created by the economic conditions of a new country, with its products developed under the harsh necessities of New England life and family activities, the Yankee peddler flourished until the middle of the nineteenth century with its growth of cities and towns, and their ample merchandising facilities — the time of railroads, steamboats, waves of immigrants — when there was a gradual transition from peddler to traveling salesman.

"At first," says Hale, "the tendency was for the peddler to carry only one item, made by his family or by a small group. Thus Amos Stanley of New Britain made hats, took them west and bartered them for beaver skins and other pelts, and returned to make more hats. Another planted broom corn, made and sold a few brooms, and each year increased his acreage and the area of his market."

"The early peddlers of silverware, from Wallingford and Meriden, apparently sold nothing else."

"As roads improved and it was possible to push a hand cart or to use horse and cart, peddlers became independent of the individual manufacturer and took on as varied a line of goods as can be found in a small department store."

Brass buttons from Waterbury, jewelry from Attleboro, silks from Manchester, clocks from Bristol, locks from New Britain, bells from East Hampton, indigo from the Carolinas, Bennington crockery, dress goods, baskets, laces, hardware, tin ware, Paisley shawls, and later, drugs and patent medicines. "The list is almost endless," says Hale.

"The spirit of adventure was everywhere. One young peddler encountered John Jacob Astor out searching for furs and went along with him to Canada.

"Some joined in the gold rush to California in 1849. Marshall Field grew tired of peddling and settled down in Chicago. Later, Benjamin Altman and Adam Gimbel, both peddlers, did the same in New York. A Connecticut Yankee, Benedict Arnold, peddled woolen goods up the Hudson and into Canada for his father-in-law, thus doubtless familiarizing himself with West Point and Quebec, destined to become his shame and his glory respectively."

Most peddlers evolved regular routes and stopping places, established social relations with customers and in the villages often joined in the dances and parties, sometimes providing the music and were generally welcomed as honest men.

"The dishonest salesman rarely returns to the scene of the crime. Let it be said," emphasizes Hale, "the Yankee peddler traded hard but, with exceptions doubtless magnified, was generally as fair as the times and circumstances permitted."

Hale's explanation of the wooden nutmeg is as a simple goodwill gesture rather than an outright sham. He says the peddlers made it a practice of giving a housewife a gift to encourage business and a nutmeg was a sensible and useful item. When real nutmegs ran out, the peddlers substituted wooden ones so as not to disappoint the ladies.

"Even the wooden nutmeg was just another manifestation of the Yankee's ingenuity and resourcefulness, when he had to 'make do'," says Hale. And it also shows his dry sense of humor. "What could be dryer than grated wooden nutmeg?"

"The peddler was his own doctor and often was called in to help others. He usually did his own cooking; and had to have mechanical skill when a wheel broke or in repairing for resale, articles taken in trade. The peddler had to be resourceful in emergencies, pleasant in manner, loquacious with gossip-starved women, knowledgeable in politics and farm matters with the men, merry with the children and attractive to the girls.

"To the young men of New England with the large families of the period crowding the house, the opportunity to escape and see the world by peddling some neighbor's wares was too good to be overlooked," Hale says. "Apparently youth found the parental yoke just as galling in 1790 as in 1970 and seized upon a chance for freedom and the open road." It was a chance to earn their living and, incidentally, to travel to the far places of their small world.

The Yankee peddler continues to fascinate and enthrall. To the economist, he supplied demands — his was a hungry market. To the merchant, he employed methods that continue to the present — attractive displays, sales spiels. To the adventurer, he was one of the main influences in opening up the west to settlement — sometimes, preceding the trappers and explorers.

Sally G. Devaney

Tales of Old Wallingford
by Clarence E. Hale
1971; 154 pp.
From: The Pequot Press
Old Chester Road
Chester, Connecticut 06412
$6.00

The Jewel Mill

This mill has been in almost constant operation for over three hundred years. The big waterwheel is still used everyday to grind and polish gems. Necklaces, bracelets and earrings are available in all the range of gemstones from New England — and the world.

Suggested by Muriel Peterson

The Jewel Mill
Newburyport Turnpike
Rowley, Massachusetts 01969
Prices from $2.00 to $6.50

Who'd ever think that a town in northeastern Vermont would be the scale manufacturing center of the world? It is — and descendants of Thaddeus Fairbanks, inventor of the platform scale, still live in St. Johnsbury, Vermont.

Where in New England Is This Strange Device?

Originally constructed in 1857, destroyed by fire in 1864, and reconstructed in 1874, this is the famous Moorish Dome on top of the *Colt Industries* factory in Hartford, Connecticut.

Since its creation and up until the advent of our vertical-minded architects it has dominated the sky-line of Hartford.

One story claims that Col. Samuel Colt, founder of the world-famous company which still bears his name, was so delighted with the architecture of Egyptian mosques that he had a similar model constructed on the Hartford plant.

Another story which has been told claims that a maharajah, knowing of Colonel Colt's interest in this type of architecture and wanting to show his gratitude for an exceptionally fast delivery of Colt Firearms to his country (India), had the materials shipped to Hartford and the dome consequently assembled.

Still another story, and possibly the most plausible, is that Colonel Colt, who was well-known for his promotional efforts, had this unusual architectural shape constructed on his factory so that every visitor to Hartford would gaze at it in wonderment and remember it long after the visit had been completed.

The gold, rampant colt horse mounted on top of the gold replica of the world is over six feet in length on a perpendicular plane. The significance of a single broken spear (two pieces) is that the horse has lost its rider in battle and has picked up a spear to return to the battleground.

It can be seen today, hard by Interstate Route 91, but a caution. Do not take your eyes off the road too long to look at the dome; for that particular section of Route 91 must have been created when the highway designers were out to lunch. Its proper name would be Spaghetti Junction.

RWW

Colt Industries
150 Huyshope Ave.
Hartford, Connecticut 06102

Education

Rhode Island Yearbook — 1972

The idea of a state yearbook makes sense. It's an opportunity for the state to highlight annually important events, articles of historical significance and other appropriate matters. Although the *Rhode Island Yearbook* does not conform strictly to the definition of a yearbook — the 1972 edition might apply to any year — perhaps the way the editors treat the contents allows for more freedom and interest. The range of the contents includes such diversified subjects as folklore, human interest articles, landmarks, history, anniversaries and special features about people, places and things. The result is a varied selection of reading material, generously enhanced with many halftones, line drawings and photographs in black and white and full color. The 1972 Yearbook might serve as a basic model for other states to follow.

Rhode Island Yearbook   JCH
Rhode Island Yearbook Foundation
1 Peck Avenue
Riverside, Rhode Island 02915
$2.00 annually.

Vermont Afternoons with Robert Frost

Written as a tribute to Robert Frost, a close personal friend of the author, this book combines letters from Frost, poems by Vrest Orton and quiet wood engravings by Thomas Bewick.

Flo Laffal

Vermont Afternoons with Robert Frost
by Vrest Orton
1971; 63 pp.
From: Charles E. Tuttle Co., Inc.
      Rutland, Vermont 05701
      $4.00

Vrest Orton writes:

There are few perfect moments in a man's life. One is when he sees genius plain. Millions now living will die and never know this ecstatic pause in eternity because there is, of course, not always a genius in every lifetime; more often there are none in several . . . In the presence of genius the world falls away and a human being is one with the cosmos. The privilege of being moved by Rubinstein and by Frost into perfect grace is too rare and unique an experience to bear examination, or to explain . . . I began to assimilate Robert Frost's conversation and verse forty years ago; I have never been the same since. . . .

A letter from Robert Frost begins:

"Sometime in the fall when the flood of summer people has subsided, you and I will be left, still clinging to the rocks of Vermont. . . ."

1976 will be the year of the U.S. Bicentennial celebration. All over the country — people will have special activities, but in the town of Concord, Massachusetts, they've started early preparations. Minuteman National Historical Park, consisting of 750 acres is being put together for the celebration. It contains the "rude bridge that arched the flood," the battle field site, and stretches of the "battleroad" along which the British retreated.

Some Characters I Have Known

The other day I received a letter from a summer resident, a lady who lives down in the City, and who says, "You are always talking or writing about the old timers up there in the North Country. Yankees, you call them, crusty lot, it seems to me and I'm wondering just who they thought they were."

Well, most of the old time Yankees that I knew were a bunch of characters and some were mighty stubborn, small-spoken, scowling over their spectacles like old Will Wishman who used to run the village store up in Campton. All that Will wanted was to be left alone. He would sit in his rocking chair by the stove and growl at any customer who came, "Now, what in the devil do you want?" His attitude toward the world was best expressed one morning when I found him washing the big show window in front of the store, removing a year's accumulation of cobwebs and grime. "Cleaning the window so people can see in?" I asked. "Naw," he grunted "so I can see out."

Old Timers up this way are by nature independent. They can be as sociable as anyone else, but they don't choose to be rushed. Old Joe Fisher Hobbs up in Ossipee Valley hired out as a fishing and hunting guide and one day a summer resident here at the lake said to him, "Be at the pier at two o'clock sharp." "Be there as near as I can make it," Joe replied with true Yankee independence, ' Ain't no time sharp in these parts."

Our old timers were instinctively suspicious of strangers. Take old Jeb Blodgett who lived up in Conway — the first trip he made down to Boston folks were waiting at the station when he got back and when asked if anything happened Jeb replied, "Waal, I was walking down Washington Street and a feller came up to me and he said, 'Have you got the time?' and I said, I have, and I shall keep it, and I kept right on walking down Washington Street." Old Jeb mistrusted everybody. He presented a twenty-five dollar check to be cashed at the bank one day, and watched sharply as the teller counted out four fives and five ones. Then he picked up the bills and counted them over again, very carefully. "Did I give you enough money?" the teller inquired sarcastically. Jeb glared at him "Just barely," he said.

Old time Yankees, up here in the North Country had a pretty good idea of themselves and they didn't care a tinker's hoorah what anybody thought about it.

John Noyes

Reprinted with permission from the author and the Carroll County Independent, July 20, 1972.
Center Ossipee, New Hampshire.

New Connecticut

Between 1667 and 1713, Connecticut colony sent out more emigrants than any other New England colony. One of the many "New Connecticuts" that popped up when the Yankee needed more elbow room was Westmoreland Township, extending 170 miles westward from the Delaware River. This Township eventually became known as the Western Reserve of Connecticut, and later still as "Ohio".

Photos, songs, cartoons and stories of "the good old days."

Published monthly by:

Tower Press, Inc.
Folly Mill Rd.
Seabrook, New Hampshire 03874
$4.00 yrly., U.S.; $4.50 Canada

Vermont Life

Published four times a year, to coincide with the seasons, *Vermont Life* contains no advertising — just 64 pages of good reading and outstanding color photography, bringing to the reader the flavor of life in Vermont, past and present.

Vermont Life   MSH
61 Elm Street
Montpelier, Vermont 05602
Subscription rate $3.50 yearly

New Hampshire Folk Tales

Beginning with stories from before the advent of the white man, this volume compiled by the New Hampshire Federation of Women's Clubs, aims at keeping the folk history of New Hampshire intact.

Written in a homey style, these folk tales impart the bravery, superstitions and curious adventures of the early homesteaders as they have been passed down from generation to generation. As such, they should not be judged on their literary merit or demerit, but on the fulfilling of their intention — the preservation of tradition.

In the earlier tales, one can find the origin of the names for such places as Great Stone Face, Lake Winnipesaukee and the Salmon Falls, therefore, they will be valuable to anyone interested in the New Hampshire segment of New England history.

Of the later stories, those on witchcraft, superstition and haunted houses are the most interesting and prove enjoyable reading.

For storytellers, they will prove to be a find, since, with the proper dramatic embellishments, some would make excellent campfire tales.

Martin Robbins-Pianka

New Hampshire Folk Tales
by Eva A. Speare, Editor
1964; 279 pp.
From: Courier Printing Co., Inc.
      Littleton, New Hampshire 03561
      $5.00

Legend of Salmon Falls

Another famous rocky ravine is found in southern New Hampshire where the Salmon Falls River descends to sea-level by a series of cascades. This name is said to have been given to the stream by the Indians because at the time when salmon ran from the sea to spawn in the fresh waters of the river, they pressed themselves into so crowded a mass against the rocky barrier of the cliffs that the Indians were accustomed to walk across the wide stream on the backs of the salmon as on a natural bridge. Strange to tell, not one fish enters the river at the present day.

Elizabeth P. Pope

A New England Simple — For Bladder Infections
1 oz. crushed spearmint dissolved in a pint of warm water. Drink a wineglass-full every half hour until pain stops.

Education

The WILD RIVER WILDERNESS

A Saga of
Northern New England
by D. B. Wight

The Wild River Wilderness

The Wild River Country flourished for about a century but, like so many other areas of New England, died when big logging moved westward in the early 1900's.

The author tells of the history of this region, a border area partly in the White Mountains of New Hampshire and extending over into Maine. A railroad eventually served the villages and logging camps along the way. The author presents pictures, maps, town records, wills, deeds, newspaper reports, anecdotes and other information on the history of the period. He describes early life of the settlers and the Indians. He takes us on a bear hunt. He tells of the wrecks on the railroad. We learn how L.L. Bean came to make his famous hunting boots. He shows how early logging gave way to wholesale methods that laid waste to many of the virgin tracts of forests.

It is, as the author states, a summary of events that took place in this area. It would provide excellent background data for the prospective author contemplating an historical novel dealing with life and times of the period and region.

Charles T. Letson

The Wild River Wilderness
by D.B. Wight
1971; 158 pp.
From: Courier Printing Co., Inc.
Littleton, New Hampshire 03561
$6.95

Bears have always been a good subject for stories. The Heath family were among the early settlers of Gilead, and Alonzo Heath, better known as Grandfather Heath, for over 40 years told a better bear story than anyone in that area. Everyone around there knows the story which took place in the 1800's. Grandfather would start by asking if you had ever heard his "B'ar" story. If the answer was "no", he would say "that's too bad" and go on with the tale.

Remember him? Why tarnation if I didn't. I've got these scars on my arm to liven up my memory of that scrimmage. We was living on the further side of Wild River and, I'm telling you, this upper section of Maine was a pretty big wilderness in those days.

Reckon I was a little feller – not much more than knee-high – kind of sprightly for my age. It was one of them spring-summer days. Day when birds were singing; when you could see the grass a-growing; smell the flowers and hear the bees a-buzzin'; one of the days that makes the school seats seem harder and makes a fellow want to get right out into the sunshine. Prob'ly I'd skipped school that

day. Anyhow, curious what a boy will do, for I don't see no other way for me to be sitting under the hemlocks by the river a-watching the kingbird chasing the robin and a-listening to the rippling of the river a-bobbing my stopper-float under the shady bank before the wary speckled beauties a-sunning themselves there.

I remember I'd twisted my leg around the alder pole to keep it over the water and with my hands free was a-whittling a hemlock limb into some dumb deviltry, when I see the brakes and ferns a-waving further up the bank. Reckoned 'twas a squirrel, or a rabbit maybe, that was a-frisking around the trees there, and I hove my club into the bushes. Zip! Crash! Bang! Lord sakes, I was a mile behind for slowness. Quicker than you can say scat that b'ar was on me. Yes, it was a b'ar! and a tarnal big one too.

Swish! she pounced on me. snarling and growlin'. I could feel her hot breath and just one swoop of her powerful paw tore half my vest away, and clean through to my shirt. I was rags and tatters. You never saw the like; my arm was a-bleeding and the b'ar was just a-gitting her paws around me for another hug. then I happened to realize I had my knife in my hand and I just stabbed her good and hard. Tore a gash long's the blade in her shoulder, and now I tell you there was scratching and a-scrambling and in a twinkling the b'ar was on the ground all ready for another leap.

I didn't wait for her, and mind you all this was happening in a pretty short space of time, and when the b'ar stuck the ground, I was on my feet and a-streaking it for home. Barefoot, of course. The old b'ar give me a tarnal scratch across my legs that sent me sprawling into the bushes, but I was up again and running for dear life. The road followed Wild River pretty near to the settlement and that b'ar followed right along in the bushes side of the path all the way home.

A-panting and covered with blood from head to foot I dropped into the kitchen door frightening the wits nigh out of the women folks. All the men were working in the woods, and by the time they was home at night the b'ar had disappeared.

Some of the neighbors went out to the main road and got a trap and set it by the river, and in three days the b'ar skin was stretched on our barn door. The two cubs followed the mother to the trap and father took the little fellers by the napes of their necks and fetched them home to me.

Skipping school? No, there war'nt a word said about it. Father give the cubs to me and I kept them all summer. Used to feed them milk and let them sleep in the barn. About Christmas there come a blinding gale, and we missed the cubs from the barn, and when we followed their winding tracks down across the garden to the maple orchard, there was a round hole where they'd burrowed into the snow according to their nature, to den up and fall asleep....

. . . . . .

In 1943 C.B. Cummings of Norway, Maine purchased some white birch stumpage from the National Forest about seven miles up Wild River from Gilead. He employed one man, Wildred Caron, to cut and yard it out to the road.

On the night of November 28, one of the worst blizzards of the winter occurred. Around 9:00 P.M. Mr. Caron went to bed in his little cabin, taking with him Tip, his pet cat. At 11:00 o'clock the cat jumped from the bed just as a yellow birch, 20 feet high and two feet through at the butt, crashed through the roof. The heavy tree and the top bunk pinned Caron down in the lower bunk. The fall of the tree forced open the door of the camp and the snow came blowing in. He tried to free himself in the dark but was unable to do so.

At daybreak he was covered with two feet of snow and was so cold that it wasn't until about nine hours later that he became aware of how badly he was injured. He was able to reach a bucksaw and sawed the tree away. Releasing himself from the

bed he attempted to stand but fell on the floor. Finally he was able to drag himself to the stove and start a fire. He closed the open door through which snow was still blowing in. He then made himself a pair of crutches out of spruce boards two inches through and four feet long.

He started to shovel through the four foot snow to the hovel where his horse Jerry was stabled. He fell down several times while shoveling the 150 foot stretch from the camp to the hovel. This took him three hours. Finally he reached and fed Jerry. Later the horse repaid his master by hauling him down the steep incline in a sled which the injured man spent an entire day building from boards taken from the hovel. He took his meat box for a seat and an egg box in which to carry Tip to safety. It took him an hour and a half to harness his horse to the hand-made scoot before he left to start for Gilead.

When one and one-half miles from camp he struck a fallen tree and was tipped into a snow bank. It took another one and one-half hours to extricate himself and get started down the unbroken road. Three miles from the camp he arrived at a ranger camp. It was located 500 feet from the road and there were no tracks into the camp. Caron attracted Ranger Steve MacLain's attention by shouting. The ranger went out on snowshoes in the dark, and upon learning Caron's condition, provided blankets to bundle him up in, and on his snowshoes he led Caron's team four miles over an unbroken road. He had to use his axe to clear away 40 trees blown across the road before arriving at Gilead post office.

Tantaquidgeon Indian Museum

This unique museum, built in 1931, houses a collection of objects made and used by Mohegan and other New England Indian artists and craftsmen — past and present. Some of the stone treasures date back to the early 1600's and others have been made more recently. John Tantaquidgeon, a skilled woodworker, passed on the art to his son, Harold, who continues to practice and teach the skills learned from his father. There are stone artifacts on display, many of which have been found in the Mohegan area.

In 1958, a second room was added in which are displayed examples of the expert craftsmanship of the Indian tribes of the Southwest and Northern Plains areas.

To the rear of the Museum, surrounded by a stockade, are reproductions of a wigwam and a longhouse, typical of the early type dwellings used by Indian tribes of southern New England. A Council Circle and fire pit provide a perfect setting for cooking and storytelling around a camp fire. There is also a small grove which is frequently used for picnics and by overnight campers.

The purpose of the Museum is to preserve and perpetuate the history and traditions of the Mohegan and other Indian tribes.

Tantaquidgeon Indian Museum
Route 32, Norwich-New London Road
Uncasville, Connecticut 06382
Open: May through October

The Shelburne Museum

What makes a place great — better than any other place? Imagination? Creativity? Money? Ah, yes, money! But there's more. There must be a dream, a desire, a determination to make a worthwhile contribution and knowing how to achieve it with taste. That's what makes the difference!

Generations to come will enjoy the tales that are told about the time a museum came inching its way along to Shelburne. Today, visitors remark, "Incredible!" "What an undertaking!" The hauling of the S. S. Ticonderoga from Lake Champlain to Shelburne may stand out as the most remarkable physical feat in the Museum's history. It was an accomplishment of enormous complexity, yet the "Ti" is only one chapter in the unusual Shelburne story.

It was just after World War II when Electra Havemeyer Webb first thought about starting a museum. She wanted a place to exhibit many of the treasures she had collected since her marriage to James Watson Webb. From that time until her death in 1960, Mrs. Webb never stopped "forging ahead" with her dream to contribute something worthwhile to America's heritage. That "something" is the Shelburne Museum, now administrated by members of the Webb family.

The Shelburne Museum depicts life in the 1800's, yet, it is not the life of any one village. It is representative of the life in many towns and villages of early New England. Locating buildings for the Museum was hardly a problem for Electra Webb, as scouting the countryside for likely additions was one of her favorite pastimes. Getting the treasures to Shelburne offered real challenges. Many of the obstacles would have defeated a less dedicated, determined person.

Hundreds of old barns, shops and homes lay hidden along back roads and country lanes of northern New England, vacant and declining in a state of picturesque decrepitude. For an elect few of these buildings, on the brink of oblivion, the future would bring rebirth in new, idyllic surroundings. From East Dorset came the Dorset House, the Dutton House from Cavendish, the Stone Cottage from South Burlington, the Diamond Barn from Shaftsbury and the Covered Bridge which crossed the Lamoille River from Cambridge. Twenty-one buildings and other structures were moved either intact, inching their way overland from their original site by the nudging of patient, skilled men, or they came in bits and pieces of interior panelling, floorboards, roofs, clapboards and bricks, carefully wrapped and coded so that they could be reconstructed in their new home at Shelburne.

The most difficult — and most publicized — undertaking was moving the Ticonderoga from Shelburne Harbor on Lake Champlain, 9,250 feet to her new berth at the Museum. This story is one of Yankee ingenuity, perseverance and courage. It took 65 harrowing days to budge the 220-foot, 900-ton steel-hulled side-wheeler. Freezing weather and unseasonable warm spells nearly brought disaster. But the valiant moving crew prevailed and "Ti" came to rest at her newly constructed berth on April 6, 1955. Her water history far behind her, she rests like an old veteran retired from active service, who, having outlived all her comrades, is content to live on in quiet leisure.

Shelburne is not to be visited in a day. There's too much to see, too much that is exquisite, compelling and lovely to be brushed through on the run. Like the Museum itself, preparation and thought should be given before traversing its 45 acres. There are paintings to study in the Webb Gallery; clocks, dolls, weathervanes, molded glass, toys, furniture, stage coaches and sleighs — each to be seen in a lovely, appropriate setting.

Then there is the beautiful Electra Havemeyer Webb Memorial Building which, like it neighbors at the Museum, was moved to Shelburne from another place. It is fitting that the children of Watson and Electra Webb decided to bring their mother's idea to a reality and construct a building which would house the Havemeyer art. For this there was nothing more suitable than their apartment at 740 Park Avenue in New York. In 1960, a seven-year venture began!

Six rooms were removed from the apartment and brought in their entirety to Shelburne. They were reconstructed and refurbished. So exact was the result that the rooms appear to the visitor as if Mr. and Mrs. Webb had just stepped out for a minute. This beautiful Greek revival-type building, overlooking the Museum, was opened to the public in 1967. It is an impressive memorial to the founders and guiding spirit of the Shelburne Museum.

The Shelburne Museum — JCH
Shelburne, Vermont 05482
Open: May 15 – October 15
Adults: $3.50   Children: $1.50

Americana Archives Publishing

If nostalgia and yesteryear appeal to you, you'll love the choice of reprints available from *Americana Archives Publishing*.

There are bandit reward posters, recruiting posters, old-time cookbooks, children's books and historic aviation patents. Send for their catalog.

Americana Archives Publishing
Box 314
Topsfield, Massachusetts 01983

The Maine Catalog

We have a special understanding of, and appreciation for, the work which has gone into the publishing of the *Maine Catalog*. Gathering together a wide variety of unrelated material, sorting it out, editing it, pasting it up and attending to the myriads of miscellaneous details has been the task of The First New England Catalogue staff.

We examined the *Maine Catalog* carefully and with curious interest. The product reviews have a nice, honest touch in their approach to the background of the people behind the craft and the number of subjects covered is broad. Doing an in-depth research for catalog entries becomes encyclopedic in proportions and the State of Maine must have loomed more and more formidable as their group dug deeper into its wonderful resources. A second annual edition should be in the works.

JCH

Suggested by Ruth Pullen

The Maine Catalog
Eosphonic Institute
Box 1770
Portland, Maine 14104
$1.95 annually

Webster's Copyrights

Noah Webster probably got more for his Spelling Book than was ever paid for any other book in the United States at that time. His large Dictionary, a work on which he spent the greatest part of his life, never yielded him a tenth part of the profits of his Spelling Book.

GOOD CHILD'S PRIMER

The charming woodcuts in this 1840 children's reader show the picture-word association by which great grandma learned to read. Coming straight from the narrow shelf under the scarred wooden desk of the one-room schoolhouse, this booklet is a combination of phonetics and Sesame Street that will amuse the new generation and bring back memories to the old. Over 50 woodcut illustrations, plus spelling, grammar and little tales to learn by.

#606, $1.50

E e

COMICALITIES: OLD NEW ENGLAND CARTOON HUMOR

Selected from diverse sources by our Staff Wit, these cartoons from yesterday are the unique New England Kind, offering a brand of humor that permeates our cultural heritage. And they show, too, there is little new in our world, for here are social commentaries on such current subjects as the Generation Gap, Woman's Lib, Smoking . . . and an amazing amount of spoof about things the young generation thinks it made up, like UNIsex, children in adult roles, long hair, etc. A delightful book of a kind of humor that is part of our daily life. Also included: some historical notes about New England humor.

#604, $2.00

Education

Trailside Country School

Each year, 15-20 boys and girls participate in a fully accredited one year high school ecology and environmental studies travel program sponsored by *Outdoor Travel Camps, Inc.*

More information from:

Outdoor Travel Camps, Inc.
Killington, Vermont 05751

ABOUT CURRICULUM:

The school being a group living experience needs no artificially pre-conceived curriculum. Direct, raw exposure of the group to the values and realities indigenous to varying environments, the web of life, and itself, provides the most natural and meaningful kind of educational direction. In reality our itinerary is our curriculum determinate.

All facets of life on earth, including human life, have developed relationships which promote and keep alive life in its present forms. An adequate food supply and habitat for all forms of life is kept alive as well. The culture of humanity is one of mankinds adaptations to the environment in which he finds himself on this planet. Human culture in varying environments becomes part of the total picture unfolded during the school year. It is curriculum.

Through travel, the group visits areas which are historically significant and representative in terms of both their natural and human history. All aspects of modern and past life are viewed and considered equally in relation to the earth and its life forms as discerned geologically, phylogenetically, ecologically, anthropologically as well as socioeconomically, culturally and politically. Therefore, the base rocks in which lie the roots of Manhattan Island and its important harbor become no less significant than Mayor Lindsay's relationship today with the transit union, or, for that matter, the philosophic impossibility of any life existing in NYC were it enclosed by a large glass dome. This is also curriculum.

Bartending School of Mixology, Inc.

Did you ever watch a bartender adeptly juggling three or four glasses — mixing one exotic drink after another without batting an eyelash, and wish you could do the same?

This school will make you a creditable bartender with only a small investment of your time and money.

Bartending School of Mixology, Inc.
635 Farmington Avenue
Hartford, Connecticut 06105

Education

ORVIS Operates Fly Fishing Schools

for Beginners, for Intermediates, for Experts . . . 3 days of casting coaching and illustrated lectures, with good meals and comfortable room, all for $125 (which includes a 3-day Vermont Fishing License)

Summer 1972 is the sixth year of the Orvis Fly Fishing Schools. "Students" of all ages and both sexes assemble each Friday through luncheon Sunday . . . to learn or to perfect fly casting techniques, to hear lectures on flies, fly lines, leaders and fly rods, probably to fish the evening rise on the Battenkill, and certainly to enjoy congenial companionship in the lounge of their luxurious motel.

The Orvis School boards it's "students" beside a pleasant swimming pool and provides delicious meals from luncheon Friday through luncheon Sunday. All very relaxing and delightful.

But the **excitement** of the 3-day session is the **learning** . . . and the "students" do learn and do get very excited about it. A corps of dedicated Orvis instructors take great pride in creating an effective fly caster from a neophyte or youngster. Lectures with color slides make clear the relation between stream entomology and what artificial flies to use when and how and why . . . and with diagrams that simplify the right balances of rod and line and leader.

Fathers-and-sons, husbands-and-wives, and plenty of "loners" gather for these 3-day sessions. It's fun to learn to fish with the fly. Or to polish your techniques. Incidentally it is a fine opportunity to try out the various famous Orvis Fly Rods. Tackle for the School sessions is supplied (and/or, of course, bring your own if you choose).

Schools start the weekend of May 5th with a 3-day session every week-end all summer except July 4th. You are cordially invited to attend. Just drop a card or note, indicating the weekend of your probable choice, to

Orvis Vermont Fly Fishing School
The Orvis Company, Inc.
Manchester, Vermont 05254

We will promptly send you a brochure about the Schools and a Registration Form.

Hurricane Island OUTWARD BOUND School
P. O. Box 729
Concord, Massachusetts 01742

Hurricane Island

The Hurricane Island School is located on an island of the same name in the lower Penobscot Bay along the coast of Maine. Temporary bases are established on other islands from time to time. Extensive seamanship and navigation training, ocean sailing expeditions, rock climbing, community service and an isolated island solo highlight the course.

The first days of the course are spent in physical conditioning and skills training out of a base facility. After that, students operating 12-man, open 30-foot pulling boats travel the coast from Hurricane Island to some of the most remote offshore islands on the eastern seaboard. Participants share in the beauty of this unique environment while they learn to cope with rough seas, night navigation, extended calms and long sea passages.

Outward Bound Schools

Outward Bound began in 1941 at Aberdovey, Wales as a means for training young merchant seamen facing the demands of hazardous maritime service. Its success led to the establishment of several additional schools administered by the Outward Bound Trust. From this beginning, *Outward Bound* spread throughout the world.

Today there are 28 Outward Bound Schools operating on five continents, with seven in the United States alone.

Its reason for being is well expressed in the words of a student:

Only under the pressure of stress does a person get the chance to know himself. *Outward Bound* is not easy — it's not meant to be. It is something very good.

Catalog available.

A Degree In Human Ecology

The College of the Atlantic awards the Bachelor of Arts Degree in Human Ecology after four years. Its goals in part are:

To translate our goals and ideals into a curriculum that is both flexible and rigorous requires an unusual format. . .

Like the balance achieved in a salt marsh, the parts of our curriculum will each have their individual purposes as well as their relationship to the whole. The features of the curriculum will be group workshops, courses in human ecology, seminars, skill courses, independent study, tutorials and internships away from the college. While we will encourage students to develop an all-encompassing point of view, we realize that many students will want to achieve depth in at least one area. The acquisition of necessary skills will be provided for. We believe the program will allow students to prepare themselves to do something about the world in a rigorous, understanding and compassionate manner.

College of the Atlantic
Box 3
Bar Harbor, Maine 04609

Woodstock Pottery

In 1793 Thomas Bugbee began making brown-glazed ware, known as redware pottery.

The *Woodstock Pottery* has revived this production, 125 years later, making traditional redware bowls, mugs, pitchers and porringers based upon 18th and 19th century New England examples.

The *Woodstock Pottery* presents demonstrations and programs for schools, organizations and fairs throughout the area, and serves as a training base for local apprentices.

Suggested by Kathy Carrigan

Woodstock Pottery
Route 169
South Woodstock, Connecticut 06276

Synectics Education Systems

"Synectics" is a hell of a complicated word for what appears to be a really creative approach to education. "Synectics", as they define it, is the name for the metaphorical approach to creative process and learning, and in their literature they have the following quote:

"The greatest thing by far is
to be master of metaphor."

Aristotle

If education is your bag, either professionally or otherwise, send for their catalogue and be sure to ask for their flyer on a game they have called "Hang Up", which has to be a great name.

And, if you want to plunge all the way in right at the start, they have a complete book on the subject.

RWW

The Metaphorical Way of Learning and Knowing
by W.J.J. Gordon
1971; 263 pp., paper $8.00

Direct all inquiries to:
Synectics Education Systems
121 Brattle Street
Cambridge, Massachusetts 02138

Cardboard Carpentry and Other Things

The *Workshop for Learning Things* sells things like cameras, film and supplies; cardboard and the tools for working with it; things to build with, carve with, print with; furniture things . . . easels, workbenches, playground equipment, sand tables; storage things like cubbies and cubbyboxes; and books to help you get started and to learn what others have done, several by children.

The Workshop also offers a line of services to schools and others from advice on purchasing, illustrative photography, an olio of other things, and even to publishing books by children.

They have a great catalogue, and you can get it by writing:

Workshop For Learning Things, Inc.
5 Bridge Street
Watertown, Massachusetts 02172

Teacher Drop Out Center

Rigid, dull, bureaucratic institutions are on the way out — if Stan Barondes and Len Solo have their way. Ten years ago, the alternative school was just another idea, experimented with slightly and tossed about by many who were dissatisfied with the monotonous, inhuman type of education children in public school were getting.

Today, alternative schools are a very tangible thing, encouraged and supported by a large number of people who want their children exposed to a freer — more humane type of educational system.

To help this trend along, these two men created *Teacher Drop Out Center*, a nation-wide clearing house for information that would help teachers to find jobs in free innovative public and alternative schools. Now in their fourth year of existence, they have helped hundreds of teachers to find more satisfying and rewarding jobs. Information available upon request.

Teacher Drop Out Center
Box 521
Amherst, Massachusetts 01002

Visual-conceptual comparisons are so clear and distinct that analogy parallels as well as discrepancies reveal themselves in ways that might otherwise be hidden. For instance, a particular science section of the course deals with the eruption of a volcano. Cross sections show the earth in a pre-eruptive state and then in an eruptive state. A typical student made these connections when comparing the revolutionary American colonists with the activity of a volcano:

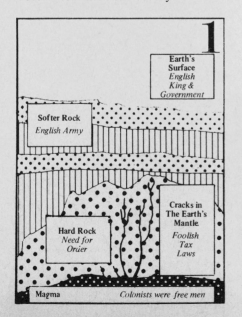

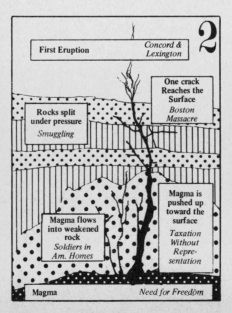

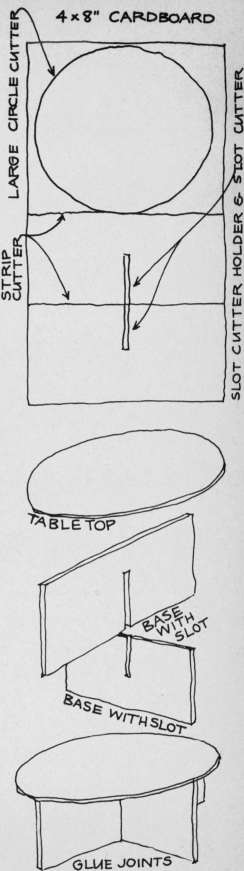

About the New England Simples: These home remedies, most of unknown origin, may be of dubious effectiveness. They were used faithfully by housewives long before modern science surfeited us with "miracle" solutions to many of our problems. *Make your own judgment* as to whether or not the remedies are applicable today.

Education

Exciting new learning tool.

$8.00

The REAL Numbers Game

The REAL Numbers Game is a handy and fruitful lead into EQUATIONS. The equipment for playing the five games in this series comes clipped to a ball-point pen ready for play anywhere that two or three minutes of time is available. Players find fun and frolic in dealing with real, rational, irrational, integer, and natural numbers. The deeper one's understanding is of these five concepts, the better player he (or she) is of the REAL Numbers Game.

WFF 'N PROOF P.O. BOX 71, NEW HAVEN, CONNECTICUT 06501

BATTLEDORES

Battledores represent the stage after the hornbook in the development of books for children. From worn old originals in the Boston Public Library collection, we have reproduced two battledores, one named The Horse and the other, Friendship.

50¢ each, postage 6¢

THE HORN BOOK, INC.
DEPT. HB, 585 BOYLSTON ST.
BOSTON, MASS. 02116

The Film School

An unusual alternative educational opportunity is offered to students interested in filmmaking, whether that interest be hobby or professional. The curriculum at this school is designed to provide a rich variety of filmmaking and viewing experiences.

Free of traditional academic structures, *The Film School*'s curriculum keeps pace with the constantly changing world of filmmaking. Continuous updating of equipment and facilities has included the incorporation of Super 8 mm sync-sound systems, a recording studio, 16 mm and 35 mm screening rooms and a fully equipped 16 mm sound, editing and mixing studio.

Film Syntax, Film History, Media Workshops for teachers and Videotape Lab are just a few of the courses offered to students between the ages of 16-65 in this unique school. Catalog available.

The Film School
Box C
1001 Massachusetts Avenue
Cambridge, Massachusetts 02138

Educational Development Center

"Open education," an idea that is becoming a reality. It is a process and a style of schooling that has arisen in many places in response to the changing needs of our society. Basically, its philosophy is that 1) children can best learn at their own rate and following their own curiosity and desire to learn; 2) the young learn responsibility by making real choices; 3) a teacher serves himself and his students best by helping them follow through on their questions and choices and; 4) schools should be flexible learning centers, full of imaginative materials and serving as a base for a variety of life experiences.

For the last ten years, *Education Development Center, Inc.,* a private, non-profit corporation, has steadily researched and produced materials to define and bolster the open education movement. These materials range from pre-school through university levels.

A wide variety of films and educational material is available from them.

Write for descriptive material.

From: Education Development Center, Inc.
55 Chapel Street
Newton, Massachusetts 02160

Simulation Gaming

Simulation Gaming is one of the fastest growing education technologies. This Guide is the basic reference in the field of simulation and gaming.

It contains complete information on over 400 games, organized and evaluated for the training director and teacher.

Their aim is not to compare one game with another, but rather to give the readers complete information on all simulation games available to them.

MSH

The Guide to Simulation Games for Education and Training
by David W. Zuckerman and Robert E. Horn
From: Information Resources
P.O. Box 493
Lexington, Massachusetts 02173
$15.00

Education

ABOUT URBAN SYSTEMS, INC.

Urban Systems is a young company located in Cambridge, Massachusetts. The main scope of our work is to acquaint children and adults with the problems of a rapidly changing environment. Through our concern we have developed a series of ecology kits and environmentally related games which have found their way into homes, schools and industrial training programs throughout the world. We feel that learning should be an enjoyable experience for children. Our products, while wholly educational in concept, are fun and easy to understand. Several of our games are completely color-coded---no reading ability is necessary.

Urban Systems was founded three years ago by a group of professors and graduate students from Harvard University and M.I.T. At that time, much of our work concentrated on air and water pollution reform via surveys for federal and private agencies. The President of the company, Dr. Richard Rosen, is responsible for a major portion of the research behind the current legislation on air and water pollution.

GAMES AND KITS BY URBAN SYSTEMS, INC.

DIRTY WATER-the water pollution game
SMOG-the air pollution game
ECOLOGY-the game of man and nature
POPULATION-the game of man and society
LITTERBUG-a color coded anti-litter campaign for kids
CLEAN-UP-beautify your very own town
WOMEN'S LIB?-a game of female rights
ECOKITS
POLLUTION DETECTION KITS
WATER TEST KIT
LITTLE GREENHOUSE GROWKITS
BIRD NESTING HOUSES
ENVIRONMENTAL TEST KITS

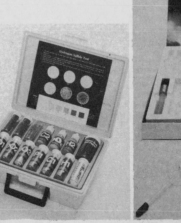

$15.00

Urban Systems Products, Inc.
1033 Massachusetts Avenue
Cambridge, Massachusetts 02138

$ 7.00

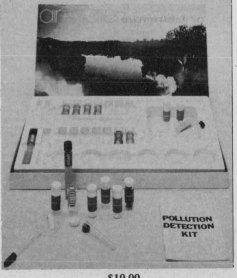

$10.00

Whatever Happened to the New Engand Prep School?

Not long ago a mother brought her carefully groomed son to visit a New England boarding school campus. She spent the morning visiting classes, dormitories and dining rooms with her son and student guide. She noted the long hair and casual dress in an increasing dismay that was amply evident when she returned to the director of admissions' office. "No," she said. "No, thank you. I think what we're really looking for is a traditional New England prep school."

The director scratched his head a moment searching for a helpful and reassuring answer. Finally he said, "I don't really know where you can find one of *those*."

With the end of the Civil War, New Englanders went considerably beyond beating their swords into ploughshares; they attempted to create new and broader educational opportunity. In the process a unique institution came into being – the New England Prep School. The initiative and a great deal of the financing came from the churches and from the early days until only recently, not only was church attendance mandatory in many schools, but so was allegiance to a religious code.

The founding idea behind most of these schools was to teach young men the gentlemanly arts away from the hurly burly of the sinful and noxious cities. Building on Benjamin Franklin's idea to teach "All things useful and all things ornamental," they went a step beyond the old academy, which taught the local gentry, and proposed to do their business in a cloistered environment.

The schools were, for the most part, straightforwardly WASP, and though they made no promises, the intention was to grease the ways into the prestigious Ivy League colleges, preferably the New England Ivy League colleges. And for the most part, they did their job admirably well. Even in the last decade, 65% or so of the freshman class at those colleges would be prep school graduates.

However, within this group and from the very beginning there were schools with different goals and ideas. For example, when Dwight L. Moody founded Mount Hermon School, he stated his intention to train "young men of sound bodies, good minds and high aims." His earlier experiment in education, Northfield School, had demonstrated the desire for education for its own sake and college entrance hardly mattered at all. In the early days of his schools, many students had trades and were expected to exercise them for the advantage of the schools. A work program was an ideal and an economic necessity.

The point of this is that, though there were many variants, the schools had one thing in common. They were independent. Indeed, many people prefer the term independent boarding school to "prep school." It was independence that enabled them to respond quickly and effectively to the needs of the times. A school set its own goals and parents either approved of these goals or chose another school. It was independence that fostered the development of curriculum that prepared students uncommonly well. They could select their students according to any criteria they desired and assemble as diversified a student body as they wished. If they found a German with no teaching certificate but an uncommon ability to teach youngsters to speak and enjoy German, they could hire that teacher, teaching certificate be damned.

Then, in the mid-nineteen sixties, young people everywhere expressed new concerns. In some schools, notably in the colleges, they shouted them. And made demands. They didn't want the world the adults wanted to hand them. They were skeptical and sophisticated. They attacked platitudes. They didn't like racial inequality and they wanted something done about it. They didn't like the war in Vietnam and they were going to do something about it. They recognized that women were not given equal treatment under the law and

they were going to do something about that too. To make matters more difficult, they had a bagful of disorderly knowledge that could confound the most circumspect teacher.

Neither teacher nor administrator was able to take such self-assertion in stride. It was a rocking prelude to ... what? A future that promises to be as raucous as the last few years? No one knows, but the dust hasn't begun to settle.

Yet prep schools were in a unique position to respond. They were free to interpret social trends and needs and to act accordingly without consulting ponderous and frequently self-serving bureaucracies. They could listen to their students, faculty, parents, alumni and decide for themselves how to respond.

In 1963, for example, a group of schools formed the Independent School Talent Search Program and actively began to look for students with high academic potential, but with little or no opportunity to develop it. This group, now known as ABC (A Better Chance), has nearly a hundred private school members, and places, an average of 400 students in boarding schools every year. At first, most of these students were black and came from the core cities. Now recruitment of students is much broader. Special efforts have been made to locate promising students among the Mohawk, Sioux, Navajo, Cayuga and other tribes.

What about integration of the sexes? Because coeducation is the rule in most public education, the widespread shift from strictly girls' and boys' schools to coeducation, has gone relatively unnoticed outside of the prep school sector. Nevertheless, for many of the schools, particularly the boarding schools, integration of the sexes has reflected a major change in basic policy. Even in the academies still committed to segregation of the sexes in the classroom, there is a concerted effort to bring them together more often in their other activities.

The changing needs of both boys and girls have been reflected most dramatically, perhaps, in the curriculum. Several schools have instituted courses in African studies; at least one offers a course on the history of women. Nearly all teach the use of the computer, and many have their own computer installations. One student taught the "thing" to write poetry. Others are studying the rivers and oceans at first hand to find some answers to environmental problems. And what about religion, the rock on which so many of the academies were founded? Traditional religious studies are still taught, but not traditionally. Chapel services often depart from older liturgical practice, and writers such as Tillich, Hamilton, Cox, and Bonhoeffer are studied along with Jesus Christ and Mohammed.

Clearly, it isn't only the courses that are taught, its the way they are taught, that makes the big difference. Teachers still address the head and recognizing the student's need for factual knowledge, they spend much more time talking to the heart. The very nature of boarding school life makes this possible. Students know their teachers, not just as teachers but as husbands and wives, as parents with youngsters of their own, as coaches, counselors, and even good friends. It is not that prep school teachers are better than others; they simply have a rare, if not unique, opportunity to help young people grow. Testimony of growth amidst innovation has been given enthusiastically at both ends of the spectrum. A young prep school teacher, addressing a trustees' meeting recently, expressed the common feeling among teachers that he was overburdened. He was teaching Latin, coaching three sports, was advisor to a dozen students, and was resident in a dorm. "Which of these activities would you like to give up?" asked a trustee. The teacher thought a minute and said he wouldn't give up any of it. He preferred to be overburdened!

When a group of boys and girls from one New England prep school spent their spring vacation in the Virgin Islands to study the ecology of the reef and beach, one of them said, "This is the way to

learn." They had covered a two or three term course in two weeks. But they also developed a reverence for life that wouldn't have happened if they had spent the term in the lab and classroom on campus.

One of the problems that doesn't want to go away is the resistance to the high cost of this kind of education. If a still small but growing number of students decide to postpone college, where does such a decision leave a "preparatory" school? This problem is not alleviated by the fact that many public high schools can point to a proud record of gaining admission to prestigious colleges for their students. Why spend around $4,000 a year if the young man or woman decides not to go to college, or can be readily accepted from the local high school?

Those who believe genuinely and deeply in the independent boarding school know that it is, or can be, a transforming experience in the life of a young person. The total learning environment functions twenty-four hours a day. Teachers make themselves available for counseling in all kinds of matters – academic, vocational and personal. They can help students cope with the changing mores of the society in the world around them.

Young people today are bent on transforming the world. They are asking for a reordering of priorities, so that a fuller measure of mankind's hopes may be realized. The New England Prep School provides an atmosphere where this transforming effort can thrive. How much is that worth?

Howard L. Jones
President, Northfield Mount Hermon School
East Northfield, Massachusetts 01360

The problem is I lived half my life before I realized it was a do-it-yourself job.

At Habitat everyone is encouraged to realize that living your life is a do-it-yourself job. Others will care for you and can help you, but you are the person who is ultimately in charge.

A Place To Work – A Place To Learn

Many young people have a deep concern for their environment. *Habitat* offers a means of acting on that concern in productive ways.

Some students at *Habitat* are taking a year off from college, others are fresh out of high school. All of them participate in practical as well as theoretical training in environmental problem solving.

Habitat strives to create an open, humanistic atmosphere in which work and play, learning and doing, self and others, are integrated into a meaningful life.

Students are expected to devote roughly half of their time working on environmental community service projects. These focus on actual problems. Students and staff collaborate in defining the problems, gathering data, exploring alternatives and implementing solutions.

Habitat actively solicits projects from outside organizations, such as town conservation commissions, the Massachusetts Department of Natural Resources, and the Environmental Protection Agency. The funding from these projects helps to finance the cost of education.

The program is based on the conviction that the individual student is an intelligent, resourceful person capable of making decisions about his own education and life.

Applications are open to both men and women. Minimum age is sixteen.

Habitat
Box 136 B
Belmont, Massachusetts 02178

Education

The Community Press of New England

Except in a few of the larger cities, the journalism of New England is a very personal thing. This is especially true of the weekly and semi-weekly newspapers, of which there are 250 by the latest tabulation, published in the six-state area. Even the smaller dailies, scattered throughout New England have "over-the-back-fence" flavor.

But don't for one instant think that the community press in New England is of little consequence or purely parochial. It can be argued successfully that the two hundred and fifty smaller newspapers exert a greater influence on the thought and lives of the area's residents than do all the large urban dailies combined.

The community newspaper has a place completely unfilled by the big daily. It chronicles the laughter and tears, the births and deaths, the marriages and divorces, and yes, the deeds and misdeeds of the residents of the towns as no other medium can do. Even more important, perhaps, it points the way through its editorials and feature columns in a manner quite impossible for newspapers or radio stations covering large urban territories.

A publisher of a community paper in New England plays an immensely important role in his town and has, at the same time, a job, the difficulties of which are usually underestimated.

Take, for example, an editor and publisher like Bill Slator of the *Addison County Independent* in Middlebury, Vermont. Slator, a former army colonel, has owned the Independent for nearly thirty years. At one time or another it's our guess, the name of every resident of Middlebury and surrounding villages has appeared in the Independent — some, of course, many times. Bill has come to know every resident (a large number intimately). So what he has had to say about a person, whether good, bad or indifferent, is said as directly as though Bill had met the man or woman mentioned waiting for the mail at the post office each morning, and told that person to his face what he was going to publish about him. There's no hiding behind anonymity, and Bill, or no other editor worth his salt, can always be nice.

No one can be in the news end of the community newspaper business without becoming wholly involved. What appears in the paper will not please everyone. It is the displeased reader, giving vent to his wounded feelings, with whom the newspaper editor must contend.

The community newspaper must perform a genuine service to the towns in which it circulates if it is to prosper — a service that can be performed by no other agency.

The community newspaper can be, and should be, the community conscience. It is this service function that sets it apart from the daily papers. The dailies cannot perform as well when it comes to supplying this service to a specific area.

There are many examples in New England of this remarkable community service. *The Newtown Bee,* for instance, of Newtown, Connecticut, runs a weekly tabloid section titled "Antiques," and not only regularly carries articles about antiques, art, books, etc., but has established a wide reputation for listing all the auctions in the lower section of New England. No one interested in antiques, or antique auctions can be without the paper because the feature is not found elsewhere in southern New England.

The Falmouth Enterprise on Cape Cod, and the *Vineyard Gazette* of Martha's Vineyard, Massachusetts (at one time both run by two remarkable and understandably famous Hough brothers) have established reputations for bringing the salty spirit of "down east" to their interesting pages.

The Milford Cabinet and *The Littletown Courier* in New Hampshire truly reflect the character of the Monadnock region and the White Mountains more completely than any other media.

Little Rhody is mirrored in the *Bristol Phoenix* through its interest in yachting, published as it is in this capitol of the nation's sailboat industry.

No person who has ever known and loved Maine can be oblivious to the way in which the *Aroostook County Republican* in Caribou, Maine has gathered to itself the feel of the pine woods, the expansive potato fields, and the best fishing and hunting in the east.

And the mention of these few newspapers by no means limits those which might have been cited.

The community press of New England is, by and large, prosperous and growing. It will survive as long as it continues to give to its readers what they cannot obtain elsewhere.

Curtiss S. Johnson

Police News

TUESDAY, JULY 11

12:20 a Phillips back man arrested on warrants.

1 a Determined that man gave false name when arrested. True name obtained.

8:15 a Her daughters' speed bike stolen from garage.

10:21 a Bike stolen from garage yesterday.

10:47 a Water D losing electrical power.

1:04 p Lost pair of glasses on 14.

1:07 p Capt Johnson back. Man arrested last p. Gave false name. Complaints changed to read his true name. Additional complaint of giving a false name to officer. He pled to that charge but NG to other 2 charges. Case con't to 7/20. Bail set at $1,000 on charge of using car w/o Auth.

2:10 p Wants to see officer re stolen outboard motor.

2:51 p 7 driveway lights taken & underground phone wire damaged since Sunday p.

4:10 p Boy driving family car on his own property & hitting trees.

4:20 p Car 12 finds car was stuck in mud. Mother home at time.

6:29 p Chelsea res in re car stolen last evening.

6:43 p Car passed his family walking on beach at high rate of speed & very close.

7:35 p His son just came home & said silver car was speeding on st. Was all over, Upland Rd. Listed to Dux. res.

7:55 p Elderly women fell. May have broken hip.

9:37 p Something just hit her picture window. Car 11 says it looks like 2 B-B holes.

10:03 p 251 wants cruiser to pick up commitment papers from M D & meet cruiser at Cox's Corner.

10:33 p Saw cars depositing & picking up beer & wine.

11:18 p Reported B&E.

11:23 p Pickup parked outside his house. Car 11 says car contained local people looking at moon.

11:42 p Complaint of noise from a car radio coming from Town Pier.

11:42 p Car 12 reports B&E . Bed is missing.

WEDNESDAY, JULY 12

8:37 a Pembroke res hit dog on 53.

9:11 a Dog missing.

10:23 a Owner of house being built wants patrol check.

11:44 a Food & Drug, Boston, says sample left there to be analized is ready.

12:25 p Big black horse on her lawn. Car 12 ties horse. Will find owner.

12:37 p Wedding & engagement rings missing.

1:35 p Woman found 4-year-old girl. Gave to car 14 & Dux. Beach Park.

3:31 p Girl says man in white car on Park St. w/o pants on. Cars 11 & 12 can't find him.

4:58 p Car just hit a phone pole on P.P. Ave. Gave to Car 11 & FD.

%09 p FD on way to hospital. Car 11 wants wrecker.

7:30 p Pembroke res in with res who got her foot caught under a lawn mower. Car 12 takes to hospital.

8:00 p Dog ran into his car at corner of Chandler & Summer sts. Dog ran into the woods.

9:03 p Customer came into store today & asked questions. Ask patrol check.

Reprinted with permission from the Duxbury Clipper, July 27, 1972. Duxbury, Massachusetts.

Education

Old Sturbridge Village

Rain cancelled a golf game one weekend back in 1926 and it was from this small caprice of nature that Old Sturbridge Village, the largest museum in northeastern United States, got its start.

A Massachusetts industrialist, Albert B. Wells of Southbridge, was in Vermont to play golf that now auspicious weekend but when it rained a friend suggested antiquing to fill in the time. "What's that?" Wells asked, or so the story goes.

Not only did he find out what it was, but he became such an avid antiquer that his collections of the furniture, tools and utensils of early-day rural New England soon outgrew his home, various additions, barns and even a bowling alley.

The Wells family incorporated the Wells Historical Museum in 1935 to share the collected Americana and in 1936 the idea for a living museum was conceived. "Why not create an outdoor museum so the collections could be displayed in buildings and a setting which could evoke the atmosphere of an early New England village?" suggested Wells' son. Wells' brother, also a collector, mostly of New England clocks, paperweights and glass, supported the plan. So on July 23, 1936, the original 167 acres in Sturbridge, Massachusetts, were purchased and work begun.

The next ten years were active ones with the excitement and enthusiasm of the Wells families and their friends outweighing the setbacks and tribulations of floods, hurricanes and World War II. Houses, mills, barns and shops were both reproduced and purchased with the acquired structures dismantled and moved for reconstruction on the site. More land was bought and more collections were added, both by gift and purchase. For these ten years the museum was called Quinebaug after the nearby river.

Renamed as Old Sturbridge Village, the living museum first opened its doors to 81 visitors June 8, 1946. In just twenty-five years, the attendance went up to 646,373, in 1971.

But it hasn't been just the steady growth of attendance that makes Old Sturbridge the largest in the northeast and one of the first 28 museums in the country to be fully accredited by the American Association for Museums.

There's also been a steady growth in ideas, educational programs, concepts, buildings, crafts, plans and scope — all with an emphasis on education and authenticity.

Old Sturbridge Village is now truly a living recreation of life in New England 150 years ago, 1790-1840. It's a three-dimensional living museum with everything in its place — activities, chores, skills and clothing as well as the buildings and their furnishings. The vast assortment of collections, including farm tools and equipment, woodenware, glass, firearms, clocks, carpentry and lighting are now on view in village peripheral buildings.

The visitor who steps onto the path to the village green is taken back to the 19th century, with houses, churches, barns and mills authentically furnished and equipped. The people — village hosts, hostesses and craftsmen — are dressed as they would have been dressed and are doing what they would have been doing — pickling cabbage, knitting, hoeing, washing, making soap, dipping candles, mending harness, harvesting, weaving, making pottery and cabinets. The animals — sheep, cattle, horses, chickens and even chipmunks — graze on the common, and in the pasture or perhaps even in the animal pound waiting to be collected — and doing what they would have been doing, whether it be pulling a plow, giving milk, getting fat to grace the table or just scampering along the stone walls.

Making it all possible is a highly efficient and talented 20th century staff. Nearly half the employees (there are more than 700 in all, including many part-timers, usually about 300 employees per day, about 100 in period clothing) work behind the scenes on administrative details that make the

whole thing financially feasible, and research, curatorial and educational projects that not only assure authenticity in the village, but also promote and maintain programs for learning. Some 82,000 school children went through the village in 1971 and the museum is now involved in a Learning Resource Center that teaches 19th century skills to 20th century children, in addition to many other specific educational training programs and projects.

Old Sturbridge Village is an independent, nonprofit educational institution that is maintained and run entirely on toll gate receipts ($3 for an adult with lower prices for children and groups), memberships (9,200 in 1971 that benefit with various discounts and publications), and merchandising (everything from penny candy to an $885 Hepplewhite sofa reproduced by Kittinger of Richmond, Virginia).

Although the artisans at the village make only about 10 per cent of the items sold at the museum shops, the merchandising staff operates on the premise of furthering the visitors' education with authentically reproduced articles for sale, all made to conform to high village standards.

No detail is too small for consideration and attention by the staff. They know, for example, exactly how many flat-headed nails were hammered out at the village forge and sold in 1971 — 6,556 — more than enough to build a house. The straw hats formerly worn at the village were not quite accurate, so a more suitable tall hat was copied from one in the museum collection and made on a newly-reproduced metal block.

Not content merely to show today's version of sheep, cattle and fowl, the museum is now in the process of a regressive breeding program that is actually downgrading the animals to show them as they were in the 19th century. By identifying genetic characteristics through several generations, the historical agriculture department is bringing back early strains of a poorer grade of animal. Durham and Devon Cattle were crossed to produce a "common cattle" and a combination of fourteen Florida Merinos and three Horned Wiltshires from Australia will eventually produce a hardy sheep with poorer quality wool. A similar process is at work for a truer representation of 19th century horticulture.

Everywhere there are people learning, studying, researching and demonstrating — in village basements and peripheral buildings. Whole temperature controlled buildings are filled with all kinds of clothing — outer and under, textures, fabrics, cuts, designs; artifacts — wrought iron, pewter, wood, tin; furnishings — clocks, tables, chairs, beds, cradles; and decorative arts — paintings, crewel, embroidery, decoys.

Curators work continually to stop the ravages of time. Registrars record and catalog every item from common pins to priceless portraits. Craftsmen pass on their skills in training courses. Maintenance men work on roads, paint buildings, beautify the grounds, but disappear to other parts of the village before the 9:30 a.m. bell sounds and the Green opens to visitors. Simple, appropriate chores are added to housekeeping activities. Herbal remedies are retried. And the researchers find excitement and information in an old invoice, antiquarian vaults and their own 18,000 volume museum library.

A current big project in the research and curatorial departments is work on the Asa Knight Store, found in Dummerston, Vermont, to replace the non-authentic Mashapaug House on the corner of the Village Green this year. A pickle barrel won't be in view. They don't date to pre-1840, but cracker barrels do. Old newspaper ads are helping prepare the stock for the shelves.

So the work goes on, not only for Old Sturbridge Village, the present rural re-creation of the past, but also for the planned re-creation of a manufacturing village to rise on 1,000 adjacent acres. Old Sturbridge began with collections, the shoe, not the foot, first, so to speak. The new, old milling town is beginning with research, or foot first. It's an exciting idea and one fraught with myriad challenges — there was child labor then, for instance, and no safety features on the machinery. How can you reproduce that authentically?

And visitors will expect the same excellence in the new re-creation as they are getting at Old Sturbridge Village, a step backward in time.

Sally G. Devaney

Old Sturbridge Village
Sturbridge, Massachusetts 01566

Hands to Work and Hearts to God

There has been a recent and quiet awakening in this part of the country to a creative force which had its origin in the late 18th century, reached its peak in the middle of the 19th, and became dormant until its "discovery" in the 20th century. This force came from several communities of "deluded fanatics" — Shaker Communities.

One of the basic teachings of the founder and unquestioned early leader of the Shaker movement, Mother Ann Lee, is found in the title of this fine booklet, *Hands To Work and Hearts to God*. This thought is the essence of the Shaker way of life and explains how, as a group apart from the main stream of the industrial revolution, so many original ideas and functional products were created.

In addition to a foreword devoted to the Shaker tradition in the State of Maine and a short essay about the Faith and its development, *Hands to Work and Hearts to God* captures their artistic achievement in a very fine series of 46 black and white photographs of furniture, houses, utensils and inspirational drawings.

The Shaker achievement is beautifully recorded in this booklet and it is worth owning.

RHH

Hands to Work and Hearts to God
Essay and notes by Theodore E. Johnson
Photographs by John McKee
1969; 46 pp., paper
From: Bowdoin College Museum of Art
Bowdoin College
Brunswick, Maine 04011
$2.75 plus $.50 postage

A New England Simple — To preserve clothes pins. Boil them for a few moments and dry quickly. This done twice a month will make them more flexible and durable. Clothes lines will last longer and keep in better order for washday service if occasionally treated in same way.

Education

LEISURE

Leisure Index

A

The American Boys Handy Book 63
Animals
  deer 74
  zoo 66
Antiques 64, 70
  automobiles 94
  toys 63, 64, 65
Appalachian Mountain Club 86, 90
Architecture 62
Automobiles 94
  antiques 94

B

Bicycles 95
  custom-made 95
  equipment 95
  tours 95
Bikes 95
Boats
  building 83
  canoes 84, 85, 86
  ferry 84
  footwear 76
  gear 76, 78, 80, 81, 82
  hardware 81
  kayaks 77, 84, 85, 86
  kits 77, 80
  models 80, 81
  motor 78
  museums 83
  plans 79, 81
  racing shells 78
  reproductions 82
  row 77, 78, 79, 80, 82
  sail 77, 78, 79, 81
Boston Architecture 62
Boston Magazine 61
The Boston Marathon 61
The Building of a Wooden Ship 83

C

Camping 86, 87, 88, 90
  canoe trips 86
  equipment 87, 88, 89, 93
  food 88
Canoeing on the Connecticut River 86
The Cape Cod Compass 93
Cape Cod Journey 60
Child Life In New England: 1790-1840 69
Clocks 74
The Cod 75
The Connecticut River 73
Country Inns and Back Roads 94
A Cruising Guide to the New England Coast 79
Cruising the Maine Coast 83

D

Dolls and Miniatures 64
Duck Decoys 74

E

Ecology 90
Enduring Friendships 81
Exploring Cape Cod 60
Exploring Connecticut 96

F

Fish
  anglerfish 73
  cod 75
  exhibition 66
Fishing 73, 75
  gear 72, 88
  regulations 75
Food
  camping 88
  hiking 88
Footwear
  boats 76
  canvas 76
Furniture
  miniature 64, 65, 67

G

Give Me The Hills 90
Growing Up In Old New England 64

H

Hardware
  boats 81
Hemmings Motor News 94
Hiking 86, 87, 88, 90
  equipment 87, 88, 89, 93
  food 88
Historic Mansions and Highways Around Boston 60
Home and Child Life in Colonial Days 63
The Horn Book Magazine 63
How to Make Dolls' Houses 67
Hunting
  decoys 74
  gear 88
  regulations 75

I

Instruments
  music 63, 70, 71

L

Learning
  games 68
  tools 61
Let's Go! Trips for Children in Connecticut and Rhode Island 66
Lighting
  portable 86

M

Maine Fish and Game 74
Maine Mountain Guide 86
Massachusetts and Rhode Island 86
42 More Short Walks in Connecticut 87
Mountain Flowers of New England 86
Museums
  Americana 64, 94, 96
  art 61
  boats 83
  children's 61, 67
  maritime 62
  railroads 60
  toys 65
  transportation 94
  whaling 62, 85
Music
  books 71
  dictionary 71
  instruments 63, 70, 71
  records 71

N

The National Fisherman 75
Natural History of Vermont 90
The New England Caller 70
New England Canoeing Guide 86
The New England Guide 62
Northwoods Tales and Unusual Recipes 87

O

Old-Time New England 70
On The Sound 82
Outdoor Fun 90
Overseas Travel Kit 61

P

Parachuting
  equipment 92
Playground Equipment 66, 67
Printing
  Americana 64

R

Railroads 60
  museums 60
Records
  music 71

S

Sail 79
The Salt Water Sportsman 73
Short Walks in Connecticut 87
Skinny-Dipping 91
Snowmobiles 92
The Snowshoe Book 93

Snowshoes 92
Soundings 77
Square Dancing 70
Striped Bass & Other Cape Cod Fish 75
Successful Ocean Game Fishing 75

T

Teachers Services 61
Tools
  learning 61
Toy Review 68
Toys
  antiques 63, 64, 65
  doll houses 66, 67
  dolls 63, 65, 66, 68
  games 66, 68
  kites 63
  stuffed 67, 69
  wooden 66, 68, 69
Toys and Banks 64

U

Understanding Boat Design 81

V

Vermont General Fish and Game Laws and Regulations 75

W

Whaling Wives of Martha's Vineyard 76
White Mountain Guide 86
White Water Handbook for Canoe and Kayak 86
Woodcarving
  decoys 74
  shipcarvers 84

Y

The Yachtsman's Guide to Dining Out in Maine 79
The Yankee Guide to the New England Countryside 61
Your Happy Valley Guide 86

Z

Zeb, A Celebrated Schooner Life 83

VIEW OF THE ANCIENT BUILDINGS BELONGING TO HARVARD COLLEGE, CAMBRIDGE, NEW ENGLAND.

Historic Mansions and Highways Around Boston

This book was written by Samuel Adams Drake, a journalist and historian in 1873. Mr. Drake takes us to almost every town, field, inn, shipyard, street, lane, church, house, cemetery and ale house in and around Boston. The author collected this information from old books, letters, manuscripts and interviews with older citizens. The battles of the American Revolution, heroes and ordinary soldiers, the founders and first years of Harvard College, the famous monuments, the homes of prominent citizens and plain townsmen — all combine to make this book a delight for the historian as well as the casual reader.

He describes old customs and gives many unusual bits of information. In describing a funeral the author says that "members of the family always walked in back of the hearse, a train of empty carriages brought up the rear, and bells were tolled to keep the devil at a respectable distance." Many photographs illustrate the book, as well as a wonderful selection of early drawings, prints and paintings. Particularly interesting is a 1775 map of Boston.

Helen L. Bush

Historic Mansions and Highways Around Boston
by Samuel Adams Drake
First Tuttle edition published 1971; 440 pp., paper
From: Charles E. Tuttle Company
Rutland, Vermont 05701
$3.25

Cape Cod Journey

The next best thing to going there is browsing through this lovely photographic essay of one of the loveliest places in the world, Cape Cod, Massachusetts. Here are the sand dunes, the beaches, the churches, houses, mills of antiquity and the fishing villages. One can almost smell the brackish waters and hear the screech of the sea gull overhead. Done with taste and simplicity, the book does credit to the art of the photographer and the beauty of the incomparable land.

Sally G. Devaney

Cape Cod Journey
by Katharine Knowles
1966; 95 pp.
From: Barre Publishers
Barre, Massachusetts 01005
$5.95

◆

About the New England Simples: These home remedies, most of unknown origin, may be of dubious effectiveness. They were used faithfully by housewives long before modern science surfeited us with "miracle" solutions to many of our problems. *Make your own judgment* as to whether or not the remedies are applicable today.

◆

Exploring Old Cape Cod

For those touring the Cape, this is a great guide to have along. Scenic drives, museums, old cemeteries, historical homes, fishing areas, art exhibits, beaches and churches are described in a succinct as well as pictorial manner. The graphic work of Richard Fish adds to the illumination of this little volume. *Exploring Old Cape Cod* fits nicely in tote bag or glove compartment.

Nancy Deveno

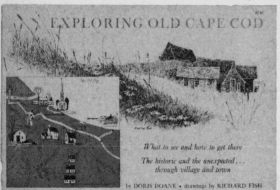

Exploring Old Cape Cod
by Doris Doane
Drawings by Richard Fish
1969; 40 pp., paper
From: The Chatham Press, Inc.
15 Wilmot Lane
Riverside, Connecticut 06878
$1.95

Steam — Short and Scenic

NEW HAMPSHIRE

Mt. Washington Cog Railroad. Sturdy, little steam engines have been huffin' and puffin' to the top of northeastern North America for over 100 years. The trains ascend from the base station at Marshfield (near Bretton Woods) and claw their way 6,288 feet up the side of Mt. Washington, affording the rider some of the most thrilling scenery in the United States.
$7.50; children under 12, $5.00

The White Mountain Central Railroad. Located at North Woodstock, this line operates on private property.

The Wolfeboro Railroad Company. This new corporation owns 12 miles of rail between Sanbornville and Wolfeboro. There's passenger service during the summer, freight year 'round.

VERMONT

Steamtown, U.S.A. The train operates on a 22-mile run from Bellows Falls to Chester. This is a high-speed trip along the scenic Connecticut and Williams Rivers, through rustic countryside of forests, farms and covered bridges.
$2.50; children under 12, $1.25

MASSACHUSETTS

Edaville, South Carver. Through the heart of cranberryland, the doughty Edaville steams along with vintage cars and happy passengers.
$1.75; children under 12, $.85

CONNECTICUT

Valley Railroad Company — Essex. Old Number 103 chugs its way 3.6 miles from Essex to Deep River and back again, in grand style for a pleasant country trip in the lower Connecticut River Valley.
$2.00; children under 12, $1.25

RHODE ISLAND

Narragansett Pier Railroad. From Peace Dale to Kingston, a distance of six miles, this railroad offers both passenger and freight service. It has been in business since 1876.

MAINE

"Boothbay Central." At the Boothbay Railway Museum, the inimitable "chuff" of steam signals the start of a ride on the narrow gauge railroad. Though not an old railroad line, the "Boothbay Central" does offer a fun-ride for kids of all ages.

Most New England scenic railroads operate during summer months. Best to check with the lines when making plans to visit them.

Railroad Enthusiasts

The New England Division of this active organization is the place to contact for those who are interested in a variety of day-long rail excursions in New England. Write:

The Railroad Enthusiasts, Inc.
Box 136
Ward Hill, Massachusetts 01830

A curious tomb of marble and granite with statues of an entire bereaved family, including the deceased himself, shown about to enter the mausoleum, is located in the small town of Cuttingsville, Vermont.

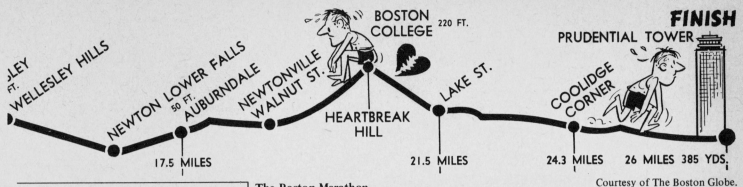

WELLESLEY HILLS · NEWTON LOWER FALLS 50 FT. · AUBURNDALE · NEWTONVILLE WALNUT ST. · BOSTON COLLEGE 220 FT. · HEARTBREAK HILL · LAKE ST. · COOLIDGE CORNER · PRUDENTIAL TOWER FINISH

17.5 MILES   21.5 MILES   24.3 MILES   26 MILES 385 YDS.

Courtesy of The Boston Globe.

Boston Magazine

If you're planning a trip in or around the Boston area, this magazine has information on where to eat, places to stay and things to do, and will entertain you with interesting and savory articles between trips.

JCH

Boston Magazine
38 Newbury Street
Boston, Massachusetts 02116
Monthly; $7.00 per year/U.S.A.; $9.00 other

". . . No other part of the country has retained so much of its character through the centuries as New England," writes L.E. Sissman in the Spring/Summer, 1972 issue of *The Yankee Guide to the New England Countryside.* Whether true or not, this part of the U.S.A. has an irresistable quality. A delightful assist for the visitor — and native, as well — is this new publication from the people of *Yankee Magazine* in Dublin, New Hampshire. As a guide, it does its job well. Although quite selective in coverage, the guide presents "a selection of those diverse and unusual parts that could reasonably be explored in a given season." Subsequent issues will choose more and different points of interest. Sprinkled generously through its 128 pages are articles expressing the Yankee flavor, full-color photographs, a sampler of New England Inns, a state-by-state schedule of activities, and, of course, an abundance of interesting advertisements.
JCH

Yankee, Inc.
Dublin, New Hampshire 03444
$2.00; bi-annually

The Boston Marathon

April 19th, Patriots' Day, marks the anniversary of the Battle of Lexington and Concord in 1775. It's celebrated in Maine and Massachusetts as a legal holiday. Not overshadowing this important holiday but crowding it closely for interest is the venerable Boston Marathon — 26 miles and 385 tortuous yards through the hills and dales of suburban Boston. The first race, in 1897, had 15 starters pitted against the winner, John J. McDermott of New York. Two early favorite speedsters, Hamilton Gray, a famous cross-country runner, and Dick Grant, a Harvard athlete, battled the New Yorker valiantly most of the race. Through the dust-raising convoy of bicycles and horse-drawn carriages, the three men fought stride for stride. Finally, the powerful McDermott overtook the others on the steep downhill in Newton Lower Falls. Gray, exhausted, walked — Grant battled for another mile before yielding, then finally in defeat, the Harvard athlete threw himself prone under a street-watering wagon to revive himself.

Today, the same heroics can describe this classic race rated second only to the Olympic race in international prestige.

The winning times are now faster, the number of entries has increased many, many fold, the runners come from the world over and the race goes on with unabated enthusiasm from the hundreds of thousands of spectators who line the streets. Some day, perhaps not too distant, a new entry will go into the record book of this famed New England tradition — it might read, "Winner of the Boston Marathon: Ms. Suzy Grant."

American Science and Engineering Co.

In partnership with The Children's Museum, this company is developing and marketing commercial versions of the *Match** Units for sale to school systems, curriculum centers and teachers' colleges. Write for detailed information.

*Materials and Activities for Teachers and Children.

American Science and Engineering Co.
20 Overland Street
Boston, Massachusetts 02215

Isabella Stewart Gardner Museum

Fenway Court, incorporated as a museum in 1900, houses the collection of paintings, tapestries, stained glass, furniture and other objects of art assembled by Isabella Stewart Gardner. The building is of Italian style and the central court has a display of flowers. Music programs are offered three times a week from September through June. Admission to the museum and to the concerts is free.

Isabella Stewart Gardner Museum
280 The Fenway
Boston, Massachusetts 02115

The YANKEE Guide to the New England Countryside
FALL & WINTER PRICE $2.00

SPECIAL FOLIAGE TOURS • AUCTIONS, ANTIQUES & INNS
NEW CALENDAR OF EVENTS: SEPT. '72-MARCH '73
SKI AREA LISTING • SNOW FORECAST • LAND FOR SALE

Christopher's Travel Discoveries

This is a travel service with a different twist. *Christopher's Travel Discoveries* has devised a solution for helping the traveler break the communications gap. They have published twenty-seven of the world's major languages used by travelers and linked them all to a unique numbering system. Using a wallet-size brochure, with language phrases keyed by numbers and picture symbols, an American traveling to Germany, for example, can use the same translator as a German uses visiting Spain, England, France or Italy. In one of the brochures, an International Menu Translator, over 1200 words are translated.

Christopher's also offers an "Overseas Travel Kit," including language menus, phrase translators, currency and tipping guide for twenty-seven countries and an up-to-date newsletter listing the most current bargains in the field of travel. There are other surprising bonuses in the kit and it is sold on a money-back guarantee.

Christopher's Travel Discoveries
Box 47
Milford, Connecticut 06460
Overseas Travel Kit $5.95 postage/handling extra

Leisure

The New England Guide

The New England Guide

Each New England state is given its own section, with a map, and is divided into geographical regions. There is an introduction which describes the scenic attractions of the state, historical data of interest, plus population figures, area size, wildlife, industry, state flower, etc.

The towns are listed individually and one learns what resort facilities are available, what historical buildings are open to the public and dates and hours of festivals, fairs and shows. Also, there are advertisements of restaurants and places to stay and stores for shopping. It's all here! A valuable tool for the traveler.

A.C. Ambrose

The New England Guide
From: Stephen W. Winship & Co.
      Box 108
      Concord, New Hampshire 03301
      Annual $.75

A View of Beacon Hill

Boston Architecture

Something old, something new, something borrowed . . . something blue . . .

The many faces of the city of Boston — a marriage of the old and new. A companion guide for those interested in a short course in the architecture of Boston and how it evolved, from the Commons to the new Aquarium, the Back Bay to the restored waterfront. Lots of photos, and clear consise comments. Includes a fascinating section on Boston's park complex (the granddad of the open space idea). This is a good book to carry on a walking tour as it is divided into districts and sections; including maps on which outstanding buildings are keyed for easy identification. Happy walking!

Donald Male

Boston Architecture
Edited by Donald Freeman
1971; 122 pp., paper
From: The MIT Press
      Cambridge, Massachusetts 02142
      $2.95

Leisure

The Mystic Seaport

The sea, which at the same time destroys and creates, has been a vital artery to New England's fast-beating heart for well over two centuries. It is fitting that a truly fine monument to the pulse of New England's seafaring past be established.

At the Mystic Seaport in Connecticut, with its 19th century village atmosphere and great ships from the age of sail, a step into yesterday is easily made. The Seaport, created by the Marine Historical Association, is on the site of the former George Greenman & Bros. shipyard — one of several shipyards that sent forth to the seas over 100 vessels. A visit to the Seaport is a delightful, inspiring experience in American history.

Walking through the cobblestone streets of this whaling port, an air of authenticity is felt. The old whaleship looms tall and proud at its berth. The smell of hemp, tar and possibly a whiff of whale oil accents an other-world existence. The formal museum buildings contain hundreds of priceless ship models, figureheads, scrimshaw and other nautical exhibits. In the Diorama Building, the replica of mid-19th century Mystic helps make this whaling port more vivid to the visitor's imagination.

All this just didn't happen by chance. In any fine artistic work, research, attention to detail, technical know-how, experience and tender loving care are the ingredients for its greatness. It is the dedicated work of many which goes on behind the scenes that makes the Seaport a worthy memorial to the rigorous days of hardy men and women.

Typical of the expertise that has put together the Seaport and is maintaining it with unabated enthusiasm is Henry Jarvis, head shipwright. He is responsible for the restoration on the whaleship Charles W. Morgan. So that his work and that of others at the port will continue in years to come, Jarvis runs an informal apprentice program in the techniques used in accurate, detailed restoration.

The Charles W. Morgan, pride of the Seaport, is worth every minute of attention given it. Built in New Bedford, Massachusetts in 1841, she made 37 whaling voyages and logged more miles and landed more whales than any ship of her time.

The Charles W. Morgan does not consume all of Jarvis' time. Boats which have long lost their identity under the unrelenting, shifting beach sands are dug up, and for Jarvis and his apprentices the challenge begins. Restoring a derelict, piece by piece, entails running tests to determine the type of wood, paint or varnish formulas which can be used to bring back "life" to the boat in as authentic restoration as possible.

Revel Carr, Curator of the Seaport observes, "We are the only ones involved in ship restoration today who are applying the disciplines and methods that have been used for years in fine art restoration. For example, recreating old paneling, with just a few pieces of the original and a faded photograph to go by, is one of the many jobs which calls for careful research and craftsmanship." It takes many craftsmen and artists to bring back a "lost" ship. One assisting in the Seaport's penchant for accuracy is Willard Shepard, the resident shipcarver. When a figurehead which once graced the bow of a ship has disappeared, Shepard creates the piece by carving from wood which matches the original almost identically. The wood most likely comes from the Seaport's lumber yard where rare pieces are stored.

Included in the restoration program is the repair of such diverse items as ship models, etchings, ship building machinery and the reupholstering of ship furniture. A difficult and challenging job which occurred recently was the renovation of a velvet settee that once graced the captain's cabin of an old whaleship. Extensive research turned up fabric that closely matched the original, with tracings of gold leaf along the bottom edge of the frame included.

New ideas also abound at the Seaport. Ray Pendleton, a ship model builder, with a draftsman and engineer drew up detailed plans for a scale model of an old steamship. They worked from a faded

etching and sail plan. The Seaport's know-how and experience provided these craftsmen with the patience to enable them to add one more exquisite reproduction to the museum's exhibits.

Complete records are kept of all restoration done at the Seaport. The minutest detail is recorded; from replacing a brass button on a sailor's middy to a new mast for the square-rigger Joseph Conrad. Artisans and craftsmen will explain and demonstrate early nautical techniques, a youth training center and program includes instruction in boat-handling, navigation and ship routing. A six-month summer graduate course in maritime history is offered and accredited by the University of Connecticut.

The Seaport is about an age gone by, yet, it couldn't be a true picture without the foresightedness of the people who maintain its existence today. Their dedication perpetuates the life and times of one of New England's proudest eras.

The Mystic Seaport   JCH
Mystic, Connecticut 06355
Adult: $3.00   Children: $1.25

As If To Beckon Us Aboard

This great ship of the past fills
books of history of seafaring days.

Her masts straight and tall, stood
strains unmatched by ships much younger.

The mighty Charles W. Morgan, permanently
moored in sand, still stained in whale oil,
is the last of its kind.

Onlookers, not picnickers of a century ago,
nor kibitzers, nor a salvage party,
nor shoremen waiting to unload
the precious heavy cargo from the hold,

But members of a treasured group of
ship lovers stand in misty rain,
waiting to hear the long-dormant sounds
of creaking rigging and see
the Sea Scouts quickly clamber atop
the lofty ship
and lower the full suit of massive square sails.

The gentle West Wind fills and billows each
sail, and when quieted, causes a restless flapping
as if to beckon us aboard for one last run
up the Connecticut Sound toward Martha's Vineyard
in quest of the great blue whale.

This recreated drama is a final tribute
to the brave men of the sea and their lady ship,
now commemorated as a National Historic Landmark
for all the world to see.

Katherine Carrigan

Home and Child Life in Colonial Days

This 357-page volume is not only encyclopedic in its information, but also chock full of interesting illustrations and delightful miscellany.

Edited by Shirley Glubok, it is an abridged and consolidated edition of two books published in the late 1890's by Alice Morse Earle, *Home Life in Colonial Days* and *Child Life in Colonial Days*. It's virtually a home study course on all aspects of colonial life — homes, light, fireplaces, meals, food and drink, babyhood, childhood, education, discipline, school books, writing, games, pastimes, toys, occupations, needlecraft, decorative arts, flax, wool and cotton cultures, dress, religion, neighborliness, flowers, travel, transportation and taverns.

The book is written so simply that a child can grasp the feeling of life in this by-gone era, and at the same time, the adult reader has his appetite whetted for more and more information. The 10-page index makes for easy access to little-known facts as well as additional information on assorted broad areas.

Sally G. Devaney

Home and Child Life in Colonial Days
Edited by Shirley Glubok
1969; 357 pp.
From: The Macmillan Company
866 Third Avenue
New York, New York 10022
$6.95

Attention Musicians!

There's something good in Bridgeport. Carl Barney, owner of *The Guitar Shop*, makes guitars — both classical and acoustic-electric. Mr. Barney will also repair any type of stringed instrument. In fact, his motto is "If it's repairable, I can fix it."

He writes: "Construction and price vary with each type of guitar. A classical one has a spruce top, with either rosewood or mahogany back and sides. Fine detailing, such as banding around all edges and a handmade inlay around the soundhole, are standard on all instruments. The type of wood used and extra custom detailing will determine the price, which ranges from $250.00 on up.

"An electric guitar is made of different materials and has a slightly different shape. The top and back are hand carved from solid blocks of spruce. The higher list price of the electronics, which start at $750.00, reflects the greater amount of time, work and material that go into their construction. Call or write for more information."

The Guitar Shop
780 Hancock Avenue
Bridgeport, Connecticut 06605

Attention — Doll Collectors

Elizabeth Andrews Fisher — writer, editor, publisher, teacher, collector — is probably one of the best-known doll people in the world.

Her newest contribution to the world of doll collectors, second only to stamps and coins as the largest hobby in this country, is a book called "Another Doll Stuff Again." It follows her earlier sell-outs "Doll Stuff," "Doll Stuff Again" and "Miniature Stuff."

For more than twenty-five years she wrote, edited and published a magazine called "The Toy Trader" that included articles and miscellany on dolls and toys, swap columns and collectors' advertisements. Published ten times a year, the magazine had thousands and thousands of subscribers in every country in the world except those under USSR domination. The magazine ended in July of 1972 when bound volumes were sent to the Library of Congress for cataloging and general reference.

In addition to all her writing, editing and publishing, this amazing woman somehow has found the time to teach courses in doll making and repairing, also porcelain and dress design; and to build and furnish a five-foot tall, eight-room doll house that attracts visitors from as far away as Alaska, California and Florida. She also makes miniature wooden kitchen utensils for the Jefferson City Museum in Missouri and carries a full schedule of piano classes.

Except for the piano, almost her entire life has been oriented to dolls. "I've worked *for* dolls ever since I can remember," she says, as she enthusiastically recalls dolls she's owned and dolls she's seen. (Her collection has been sold.) Some back issues of "The Toy Trader" are still available at $1.00 or $1.50 and the "Another Doll Stuff Again" may be obtained by writing to Mrs. Fisher. Because of her busy schedule she can be visited by appointment only.

Sally G. Devaney

Elizabeth Andrews Fisher
2112 Middlefield Street
Middletown, Connecticut 06457
Another Doll Stuff Again — about $8.00

Go Fly A Kite

Space-Bird kites are made in a "little old kite making plant" in New Haven. There are two fully guaranteed models with wing spans of 48" and 66" respectively. They are controllable, three-dimensional aeronautical kites. There's no need to run your legs off launching these birds. The wings flutter continuously and they will fly in all weather. Space-Birds are made of acetate taffeta cloth and come in seven sparkling colors. Go fly these kites.

Alan — Whitney Co., Inc.
780 State Street
New Haven, Connecticut 06502

Space — Bird: 48" wing span, 250' cord — $5.98
66" wing span, 500' cord — $8.95

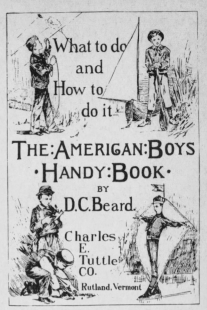

The American Boys Handy Book

Dan Beard wrote this book in 1882 and his advice to boys then, is screaming to be heard today. "Money spent on fancy sporting apparatus, toys, etc., would be better spent upon tools and appliances. Let boys make their own kites and bows and arrows, they will find a double pleasure in them, and value them accordingly — to say nothing of the education involved in the successful construction of their homemade plaything."

This book is an exact reprint of Beard's original work sometimes erroneously referred to as the first "Boy Scout Handbook;" for this book was done before Beard founded "The Sons of Daniel Boone" and "The Boy Pioneers," both of which were later absorbed into the Boy Scouts of America.

For a son of any age, or a husband, who still gets wistful at the sight of a kite, this book is a perfect gift. It has so many wonderful things to make and do, I know from first-hand experience. A friend has an original of this book and last Fourth of July I participated in the ascension of a paper balloon he had made to Beard's instruction on page 136. It was better than fireworks.

RWW

The American Boys Handy Book
by Daniel Beard
1972 edition; 391 pp.

From: Charles E. Tuttle Co.
Rutland, Vermont 05701
$4.50

The Horn Book Magazine

For 47 years *The Horn Book Magazine* has presented the best of children's books to adult buyers, and might be considered the ultimate guide for parents, teachers, and librarians in "getting their money's worth" out of the multitude of books published yearly. For easy reference, *The Horn Book* is indexed according to children's age and interest levels, while different publishers are represented by sketches of new books. Each issue contains articles by authorities discussing the varied aspects of juvenile literature, as well as special articles on prize winning books.

Back issues remain valuable for research. *The Horn Book Magazine* is published six times a year, "so you can keep up with it" — an enjoyable way to better our children's choice in the eyecatching world of books.

Lois Ingram

The Horn Book, Inc.
585 Boylston Street
Boston, Massachusetts 02116
$7.50 yearly; 6 issues

Leisure

64

Mehitabel and Arixene sang as they spun in the yard—I can still hear them. They made a duet and sent forth snatches of church hymns, transforming them into gay, lilting tunes, quite unconscious of eavesdroppers. These joyful airs echoed from hill to hill—I was sore afraid our minister might walk by and chastise them on the spot!

Growing Up in Old New England

Twelve youngsters, spending part of their summer at Old Sturbridge Village in Massachusetts, re-created life of colonial times in this charmingly put together book. Taking their cue from a journal written in 1836 as recollections of a New England Country Boy, the young boys and girls explore the world of 150 years ago with its hours and hours of hard work — churning butter, dipping candles, spinning and weaving cloth, hoeing corn, making fences, harvesting and haying, and going to school. There are fun, too, with spinning bees, picnics, parades and dancing. The text is lively and interesting, and the photographs capture not only the essence of the youngsters enjoying their learning experience, but also the flavor of life in old New England.

Sally G. Devaney

Growing Up in Old New England
by Marc and Evelyne Bernheim
1971; 100 pp.
From: The Macmillan Company
866 Third Avenue
New York, New York 10022
$6.95

Sand Pond Publishers

Mr. Tillinghast's business evolved from a hobby started years ago. An extensive collection of old trade catalogs has been reprinted so that others may enjoy them.
List available.

Sand Pond Publishers
Box 504 A
Marlow, New Hampshire 03456

Barbers Supplies $3.00 ppd.

Webster's Diffidence

Daniel Webster, when a schoolboy, succeeded very poorly in declamation. "Many a piece," he says, "did I commit to memory, and rehearse it in my own room, over and over again; but when the day came, when the school collected, when my name was called, and I saw all eyes turned upon my seat, I could not raise myself from it."

Victorian Miniatures

A Victorian fainting couch upholstered in tufted silk velvet, a chest on chest with eleven working drawers, the center one intricately carved are some pieces in this outstanding collection of beautiful furniture measuring one inch to the foot! Each piece is handmade by Mrs. Prescott, every one a masterpiece of detail and workmanship. Price list available.

Mrs. Blake Prescott
Box 177
Warrenville, Connecticut 06278

Silent Auction

Arrowheads, tomahawks, old watches, petrified wood, military medals, old magazines, jewelry, stamps and coins from all over the world, even an ancient pickle-fork piano tuner. Just a few of the items that you might find at *Willy Storz' Midas Coin Auction Shop.*

Most of the stuff he offers would be relegated to the junk box at a regular auction. Willy hangs each item on the bid-board, usually accompanied by a small description of what it is. You must be there in person to bid and it may involve going back two or three times before bidding is closed on the item you want.

Collectors of odd and unusual items seem to congregate there, hoping that the one thing they've spent years searching for may show up on the bid-board.

Midas Coin Auction Shop
Boston Post Road
Orange, Connecticut 06477

Toys and Banks . . . Dolls and Miniatures

Collecting antique dolls, toys, miniature furniture and banks has become a popular hobby and people are paying some pretty steep prices for some of these.

Maybe the doll collection Aunt Tizzy left you is quite valuable — or great grandpa's old mechanical bank is sought after by collectors.

These two books give prices, descriptions, and are well illustrated with color photographs. If your old doll, etc. isn't listed in one of the books, bring it to the Hopkinson's shop, and they'll be happy to tell you whatever they know about your particular piece.

MSH

Dolls and Miniatures with their prices at Auction
by Isabella and William Hopkinson
1970; 51 pp., paper
$4.95

Toys and Banks with their prices at Auction
by William P. Hopkinson
1970; 51 pp., paper
$4.95

From: Hopkinson's Antiques
R.F.D. #1
Tilton, New Hampshire 03276

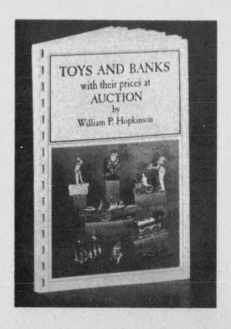

Leisure

Custom Miniature Reproductions

A six room saltbox doll house completely furnished with miniature furniture — that's the project Ed Norton took on as a graduation gift for a daughter who collects such things. His miniatures were admired by those who saw them and soon orders started coming in from other collectors.

All of his pieces have working parts and are carved from solid blocks of wood. He makes the brasses and hinges, as well as the tools used in this work.

The reproductions are definitely not children's playthings, but exquisite works of art to be cherished by collectors.

Custom Miniature Reproductions
Edward G. Norton
Wesley Avenue
Westbrook, Connecticut 06498

Braced-Back Windsor Chair $35.00

Queen Anne Desk (mahogany) $85.00

Block Front Bureau (cherry) $45.00

Doll Museum

Ellsworth's Doll Museum
12 W. Maple Street
Ellsworth, Maine 04605

1890 German-made Gibson Girl.

DOWN through the ages, man has created likenesses in his own image. From the first stone carvings to today's sophisticated mechanical dolls, toy images of the human form have enchanted children and intrigued adults for centuries. Today, collections of dolls represent an accurate and continuous historical portrait of man himself — his dress and bearing, his artistry and skill.

When Mrs. Helen Dickinson opened her Doll Museum in Ellsworth last year, she brought together under one roof, perhaps for the first time in Maine, a nearly priceless collection of dolls dating from the 15th Century. They range from life-size to three-quarters of an inch and include all races and several nationalities.

Like human beings, the dolls in Mrs. Dickinson's collection have had their ups and downs. One of the most elegant was rescued from a rubbish heap. And a tattered but still jaunty rag doll has traveled the world and even into battle in both World Wars.

An accomplished singer and pianist, Mrs. Dickinson zestfully tackles anything that interests her — whether it is writing, rebuilding dolls and toys or digging clams for her own homemade chowder. She jests about her varied talents: "If you believe in reincarnation and you're a merry old soul, you can do anything." ∎

Handmade Dolls

Loving hands create cloth dolls in the old-fashioned Yankee tradition. Each one is a faithful copy of its counterpart in history, dearly loved by children of bygone days. Only the finest quality materials are used and all clothes are removable. Dolls are 12" tall with a choice of blonde, brunette or redhead. They are custom made, so allow two weeks for delivery.

The Little Doll House
Stockbridge, Massachusetts 01262

EUNATEE
(pronounced "unity")

Our newest creation which is a faithful copy of a doll made about the turn of the century. She is really two dolls in one. On one side she is black with black hair and in bright calico dress and bonnet, and when you turn her upside down her dress falls and reveals her counterpart fair and blonde dressed in bright gingham with matching bonnet. (See small sketch.) The most colorful and fun doll we have, you'll love her when you see her. In yellow, blue, orange, pink, green, or purple calico.

$12.50

LITTLE ABIGAIL

The charm of Early Colonial America is evident in her bright calico dress and homespun pantalettes and petticoat. Her pointed basque, and sunbonnet is copied from that early Colonial period, and her purse matches her dress. Calico prints are in yellow, red, blue, pink, green, aqua, or brown.

$12.50

Leisure

Doll Houses

Practical dolls, whimsical ones and some for collectors, too.
Games, books and miniature toys — even a house for "Pooh."

Catalog — $.25

The Enchanted Doll House
Manchester Center, Vermont 05255

"THE POOH HOUSE" — 18" high x 9" wide x 9" deep. Two storied, two rooms. Decorated outside like a very Imaginative Tree. Wallpapered in Chintz.
16 – EP – $23.50 Postpaid
Appropriately furnished, add $15.00

POOH HOUSE
For your animal lover

Five years ago, we had a NOTION which is not considered UNUSUAL around here. Our feeling is that some times little girls get Doll Houses too early so we invented our little carrying Wooden Handmade, Handpainted, one and two-story houses. Each is wallpapered and each has its own padlock with two keys (one for Mother in case). They can be furnished any number of ways according to your child's taste. Some prefer people families, others animal families. We're ready to fill any requirement. We think we have all types of furniture and all prices.

"THE CHALET" – 18" high x 9" wide x 9" deep.

Natural wood, two storied, Swiss-flavored decoration.
16 – ECH – $23.50 Postpaid
16 – FR – $18.00

"THE CASTLE" – 18" High x 9" wide x 9" deep. Imaginatively handpainted, two storied house with red brocade wallpaper. White with Red Door and Pink Flowers. (Prince and Princess only by Special Order, $10.00 Each)
16 – EC – $23.95 Postpaid
Appropriately furnished, add $15.00

Leisure

Let's Go! Trips for Children in Connecticut and Rhode Island

Exploring the world around them is high adventure for youngsters and this booklet gives parents and their children a wide variety of interesting, educational and fun things to do — museums, green houses, zoos, amusement parks, science centers, theaters, art galleries, farms, sports, fairs and forays into the working world of manufacturing and craft demonstrations.

As well as listing places to go, this delightful and informative booklet also gives accurate directions, admission prices, eating facilities, when to go and a description of what you'll find when you get there.

Some longer trips are described such as the Plimouth Plantation in Plymouth, Massachusetts, the Old Sturbridge Village in Sturbridge, Massachusetts, but for the most part, *Let's Go* concentrates on Southern New England's own backyard.

Ever been to a piggery? What about a turkey farm or a silver manufacturer? And there are trip tips and travel games suggested, too.

Sally G. Devaney

Let's Go! Trips for Children in Connecticut and Rhode Island
Compiled by The Creative Playschool
Niantic, Connecticut
1969; 84 pp., paper
From: The Creative Playschool
Mrs. Fred Grimsey
35 Oswegatchie Rd.
Waterford, Connecticut 06385
$1.25

Children's Zoo

Baby animals from around the world. A complete New England barn. Young monkeys, alligators, sheep, goats, apes, otters, wolves, turtles, tapirs, parrots, swans, flamingos, ducks, and dozens of colorful birds in a walk-through outdoor aviary.

Children's Zoo
Franklin Park
Boston, Massachusetts 02121

Adults: $.75   Children: $.25

New England Aquarium

The New England Aquarium on Boston's waterfront has as its goal the advancement of man's knowledge of the fascinating world of water in education, research and recreation. The center of this intriguing structure is a 200,000 gallon Giant Ocean Tank, the largest glass enclosed salt water tank in the world. Aquatic animals, including some 2,000 exotic fishes, are exhibited in life-like environments.

New England Aquarium
Central Wharf
Boston, Massachusetts 02110

Adults: $2.00   Children: $1.00

Playground Equipment

A small company making a high quality product.

Child Life Play Specialties, Inc.
1640 Washington St.
Holliston, Massachusetts 01746
$23.50 + 23 lbs. parcel post charge

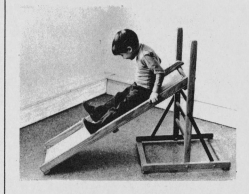

THE JUNIOR SLIDE

Here is a safe beginners slide designed so you can use it in many additional ways. The separate 4 ft. chute attaches to the ladder at any of 4 heights for adjustable steepness. Use it alone on the stairs indoors. The free standing ladder is ideal with our all-purpose board to make bridge, ramp or seesaw.

Age 2 to 4.   (p.p. 23 lb.) $23.50
Chute only   (p.p. 14 lb.) $13.50

A hobby horse — built to last for generations.

HOBBY HORSE

Cornwall Crafts
RD #2
Middlebury, Vermont 05753
$25.50 ppd.

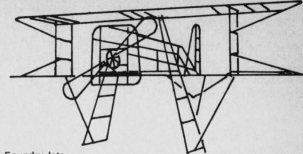

Grandmother's Soft Toy Shop

A young great-grandmother with a bustling career that began three years ago, when retirement age was only a jump away, Betty Winslow found herself with a full-time occupation, both gratifying and fun-filled. The toys are handcrafted with a combination of fine materials and excellent workmanship. Designs are obtained from a variety of sources, but many are the result of Betty Winslow's creative mind and artistic fingers. Orders for very special storybook creatures are accepted on a limited basis.

Mrs. Winslow does not retain an advertising manager, shipping clerk, or sales representative. Grandmother is all of those people. Ask her how she does it? Well, she takes vitamins regularly and works eight to ten hours a day.

Grandmother's Soft Toy Shop
P. O. Box 39
Fabyan, Connecticut 06245
Catalog $.20

Whale
14" long, navy corduroy with red
felt mouth $5.25 ppd.

Clown
16" tall, bright cotton print $7.95 ppd.

Furniture in Miniature

Miniature early American pine furniture, scaled 1" to the foot with working drawers and doors.
Send for price list.

Toncoss Miniatures
North Grosvenordale, Connecticut 06255

Blanket Chest, Bedside Stand

Drop Leaf Table, Four Drawer Chest

Bi-Plane Jungle Gym

Elliot Joslin of the Old Stonington Foundry lets his work speak for itself and it speaks very well. The Bi-plane Jungle Gym (makes one wish he were a kid again) sells for $500 and a companion gym in the form of a locomotive sells for $400. He also specializes in brass castings and hand-forged reproductions.

Suggested by James Scully

Old Stonington Foundry
230 North Water Street
Stonington, Connecticut 06378

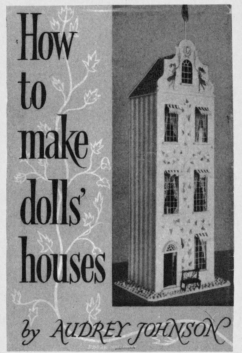

How To Make Dolls' Houses

The author of this book presents four dollhouse projects, ranging in difficulty from one that could be made easily by school children, to an elaborate nineteenth century draper's shop. Even in the more ambitious plans, it is obviously imagination and ingenuity, rather than laborious effort, that are most important in achieving the desired effect. For those with a minimum of pioneering spirit, Audrey Johnson has given her own ideas on the subject of furnishings. A four-poster bed, a Victorian bookcase, armchairs and footstools are all made from the strangest conglomeration of bits and pieces. There are plenty of drawings and diagrams to refer to during construction and suggestions are made for sources of needed materials.

With some assistance, a child can not only have a "fun" toy, but also experience the joy of making it himself.

Barrett Robbins-Pianka

How To Make Dolls' Houses
by Audrey Johnson
1968; 112 pp.
From: Charles T. Branford Company
      Newton Center, Massachusetts 02159
$3.95

The Children's Museum

Your children — and you — are invited to explore this fascinating museum. Free from the restrictions of formal education, *The Children's Museum* offers seven special workshops encouraging in-depth learning — all designed to supplement a child's formal education. The Museum staff finds that parents often enjoy them as much as the children.

Enter the world of the Massachusetts Algonquin Indian in the sixteenth century. Children will participate in the preparation of food and clothing, make corn husk dolls and soapstone beads.

A course in Animal Ecology deals with living things — how they affect each other and the world they live in. Children explore a turtle pond and a beehive tree. In an activity corner they can observe and learn to handle live animals. The computer revolution is barely older than many of the Museum's visitors. It has come upon us more swiftly and completely and will profoundly affect the lives of today's children. The Computer Center is dedicated to discovering new ways in which children can learn to use and be comfortable with this technological medium.

In a house donated by the city of Kyoto, Japan, children can take part in various aspects of Japanese life — a tea ceremony, brush painting, storytelling.

The Video Studio is designed for operation by the children themselves, to introduce them to the creative and personal capabilities of television. They learn to operate cameras, lights and programming monitors. Designing costumes and sets, acting and directing, all are part of the experience offered here.

What's New is a rotating exhibit of innovative concepts developed in collaboration with outside individuals and groups. Its focus is on familiarizing children with recent technological advances and inventions, and novel forms of old ideas.

MATCH (Materials and Activities for Teachers and Children): These kits are non-verbal systems of materials and activities that communicate. Designed for a relatively intensive treatment of a specific topic over a two or three-week period, they contain objects of all sorts — films, pictures, games, recordings, projectors, supplies and a detailed Teacher's Guide which structures the use of the unit.

MATCH Unit activities are designed to make learning the product of the child's own actions. Children study film strips to find out what various birds eat; they grind corn to make an Algonquin Indian food, nokake; they reconstruct life in ancient Greece by "reading" objects found in an excavated villa; they write, edit, illustrate and print their own book — and much more.

Sixteen rental MATCH Units are available — for a fee — from the Museum's Circulation Department. These units are not shipped outside the New England area. Write for more information.

The Children's Museum   MSH
Circulation Department
Boston, Massachusetts 02130

Leisure

The Young Man Who Worked at Playing

One June day in 1856, young Milton Bradley, just nineteen years old and burning with ambition, swung off the little train from Hartford, Connecticut and looked about at a place called Springfield, Massachusetts. Eager to work, he applied for a job at the Wason Car Manufacturing Company, leading manufacturers of railroad cars in the burgeoning railroad industry.

Though he seemed rather young to the superintendent who interviewed him, his training as a draftsman at the Lawrence Scientific School, later to be known as Harvard Engineering School, was enough to get him the job, at $1.25 a day. Unfortunately, a depression in 1858 forced the Wason Company to lay off many employees — Milton was one of them.

Young and eager, Milton Bradley decided to go into business for himself. Soon there was a neatly lettered sign on the door of a small, second floor office at 247 Main Street — "Mechanical Draftsman and Patent Soliciter".

Money was tight, the times were hard, and Milton found very little business coming his way. When he was about to abandon hope and close his office, early in 1859, help came from a strange source. The Pasha of Egypt had sent an order to the Wason Company for railroad cars which would cost $300,000! The Wason Company reopened its big doors and summoned Bradley and many other unemployed craftsmen to work again.

In 1860, yearning to be on his own again, he left the company and formed "Milton Bradley Co., Publishers — Lithographers." Business was slow, but a friend of Milton's, Samuel Bowles, the astute and eloquent publisher of the Springfield Republican, came up with an idea.

Bringing Milton a photograph of Abe Lincoln who, at that time, was considered the Presidential candidate likely to win the office, he said, "Lithograph and sell these — you'll make a fortune."

Throwing himself enthusiastically into the job, he turned out thousands of lithographed likenesses of Lincoln. For a time there was a steady sale of lithographs of the newly nominated President, then one day, a man strode into the office carrying one of the lithographs. He'd been deceived in buying this lithograph, he growled. Deceived? Bradley stared at him in astonishment. Yes, deceived, said the man. Abraham Lincoln had grown a beard! Bradley destroyed thousands of Lincoln lithographs which one day would become valued collector's items.

Discouraged after the Lincoln incident, Bradley might have given up, if it hadn't been for an old friend and business colleague, George W. Tapley. One evening, his friend took out an old game board, apparently made in England. That one incident changed the course of Milton Bradley's life. When he left the Tapley home that evening, he'd definitely made up his mind to invent a game, print, package it and sell it himself. Bradley, a devout Methodist, remembering that the times looked upon game playing as sinful, called it the "Checkered Game of Life." The games sold like ice in August; Milton Bradley was in the game business.

The company has continued to grow and currently enjoys a dominant position in the manufacturing of games, toys, puzzles, crafts, gifts, art and educational materials.

Milton Bradley Company
Springfield, Massachusetts 01101

A New England Simple

Uses of paraffine: Wine and beer casks are rendered tight by paraffine. Its introduction into the vacuum pans of the sugar industry is said to prevent frothing of the syrup. Plaster casts are coated with it; drawing paper is rendered transparent; parlor matches are tipped with it; sponges are kept elastic; cloth is rendered water tight and it is employed to keep shoemaker's wax soft and pliable.

Leisure

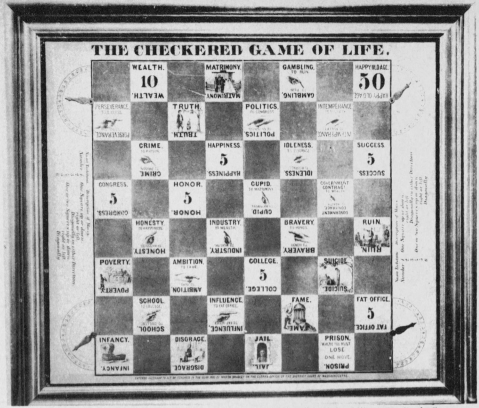

THE CHECKERED GAME OF LIFE.

The playing board for Milton Bradley's first game, published in 1860.

Contemporary version of The Game of Life.

This version offers dramatic evidence of how much life has changed in the last 112 years.

Mrs. Charlotte Hatch

Jointed wooden dolls with life-like faces are this talented woodcarver's specialty. Animals, sea captains and lobstermen are also brought to life with a few simple carving tools.

A talented artist as well, she specializes in seascapes. An interest, she tells us, fostered by her grandfather, a retired sea captain and artist whose many tales of the sea piqued a young girl's imagination.

There were lean times for Charlotte Hatch who, with a growing family to support and no husband to help, turned to house painting as a means of livelihood.

A job in a shipyard required her to work high up on a scaffolding, painting the smokestacks of the battleship "Oregon."

Now disabled, her painting and woodcarving help to bolster her income.

Mrs. Charlotte Hatch
RFD #1
Lincolnville, Maine 04849

A New England Simple

Spring Tonic — Mix 1½ oz. of sulphur and 1/2 oz. cream of tartar with 8 oz. of molasses. For children, give 1 teaspoon daily for four weeks.

Toy Review

Parents: Instead of rushing out to the store and buying the first toy you see for little Johnny or Janie, you would do well to examine an issue of *Toy Review*. The staff of this new magazine believes "that the time has come for a new and responsible approach to providing toys for children." This approach is based on the idea that most families would rather have honest information and opinion, rather than high pressure advertising about the toys they may buy for their children. To this end, *Toy Review* provides the following information on toys, games and books: 1) a description of each toy assembled from responses received; 2) recommended age range; 3) price; 4) manufacturer; 5) TR's stamp of approval, if appropriate.

The purpose of the reviews is to help acquaint the reader with various opinions about a wide variety of toy items. You may order any item which bears the TR stamp from the Readers Service Department.

Toy Review   JCH
383 Elliot Street
Newton, Massachusetts 02164
$2.00 — Four issues

By Michel

Child Life In New England: 1790-1840

This little book ought to be required reading for today's children. Quite an eye-opener.

MSH

CHILD LIFE IN NEW ENGLAND

1790–1840

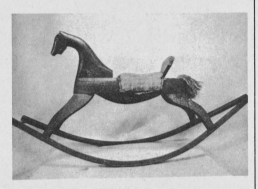

by Elizabeth George Speare

Child Life In New England: 1790-1840
by Elizabeth George Speare
1969; 28 pp., paper
From: Old Sturbridge Village
Sturbridge, Massachusetts 01566
$.75

The work of the household fell even more heavily on the shoulders of little boys. There was the never-finished sawing and chopping to keep the fireplace supplied; there were animals to be fed and watered and the full circle of sowing, weeding and harvesting. In addition, boys shared with their sisters feminine tasks at which a modern boy would rebel. Henry Ward Beecher, later to become the famous preacher, in the years he attended district school in Litchfield, hemmed towels and aprons and knit suspenders and mittens, with no thought that these arts were unmanly. In addition, he rose before dawn to start the kitchen fire. When the well was frozen in winter he drove oxen two miles to the river, broke the ice and hauled back the barrels of water for washday, and tunneled through the snow to reach the woodpile he had stocked in the summer months. "It is indispensable that children be early accustomed to profitable industry," wrote his father, Lyman Beecher.

... "I go to work before daylight," a little girl of eight or nine years was quoted as saying in Fitchburg, Massachusetts, in 1845, "and never leave it until it is dark, and don't make enough to support mother and baby."

The faces of these children haunt us, disturbing the nostalgic picture we should like to cherish of a sunny and untroubled age. Yet they cannot be ignored. These too were the children for whom the embattled farmers had stood. The little mill-workers were as truly sons and daughters of New England as the boys who bent over their Vergil in preparation for Harvard or Yale, or the Boston girls who wrinkled their delicate brows over "Feather work, Filagree, and Painting on Glass."

... It is often claimed that we can gain an understanding of the children of a particular age by a study of the books they read and loved. This is only partially true. There have always been om- nivorous readers, but only recently have children had any choice as to what they would read. When there was nothing else available, Puritan children read and reread Foxe's Book of Martyrs and Bunyan's Pilgrim's Progress, almost the only books

VERMONT WOODEN TOY COMPANY
The Old High School
Waitsfield, Vermont 05673

Vermont Wooden Toy Company

In today's world of plastic toys and painted dolls it's comforting to find someone who understands what children, toys and imagination are all about.

The prices may seem a little high to some, but consider the fact that long after the plastics have been thrown out in pieces, these will still be around.

We're not a very big company, and our job is a simple but sometimes difficult one. We are engaged in designing and building safe and beautiful toys for children that will last.

All toys are made of select woods, mainly pine, maple, and birch. They are hand assembled by skilled craftsmen using strong, well made parts held together by pegs and dowels. We use no nails, screws, staples, or plastics that could possibly hurt a child. We omit paint and artificial finishes because we want our toys to taste as good as they look, and we know paint is not good for children.

Our toys operate on child-power – there are no lights, batteries, or extra gimmicks to buy or replace. Naturally these toys are only as strong as the wood they are made from, and if tragedy does befall one of our toys, usually dad and a tube of glue can save the day.

We realize our toys are not perfect, but they are the very best that we can make them. They are safe, they are sturdy, we think they're beautiful and we hope you will. Above all, our most important purpose is to make children happy.

Vermont Wooden Toy Company
Old High School Building
Waitsfield, Vermont 05673

Block Wagon

A good sturdy wagon with 15 interesting blocks. They fit easily back into the wagon. 17" long, 12" wide, 5" high. Weight: 12 lbs. Price: $16.00
Postage and Handling: $2.00

VW Bus, VW Log Truck, VW Car

All three rugged and sturdy. We know that VW stands for Vermont Wooden.

Bus: 7" long
  Price: $3.00 post. & hand.: $.50
Log Truck: 7" long
  Price: $3.25 post. & hand.: $.50
Car: 6" long
  Price: $3.00 post. & hand.: $.50
Set of the Three: $8.50 post. & hand.: $1.00

Work consists of whatever a body is obliged to do ... Play consists of whatever a body is not obliged to do.

Mark Twain

other than the Bible which their parents had been able to bring to the new world. For more than a hundred years the New England Primer was the sole reading book for children in schools and homes. The rare books written for young readers were intended purely for religious instruction. A Token for Children, for example, published in 1700, chronicled the lives of "Children in whom the Fear of God was remarkably budding before they died in several parts of New England" and was "published for the Encouragement of Piety in other Children."

That young readers were sobered and sometimes terrified by these constant reminders of the near- ness of death and the certainty of judgment we know from the pathetic records that have come down to us. ...

VW Bus, VW Log Truck, VW Car

Block Wagon

Teddy Bears, Stuffed Tigers and Other Soft Things

Mary Meyer makes stuffed animals, including Teddy Bears (and for you under the age of 70 the name derives from Theodore Roosevelt of San Juan Hill fame). The small Teddy, 8" high is $3.00 and the 12" Teddy is $4.75.

Apparently some of Santa's elves have moved "south" to Townshend, Vermont; so if you have any small ones or grand small ones, here is a wonderful trove of gifts.

Full color catalogue, write: RWW

Mary Meyer Mfg. Co., Inc.
Mary Meyer Station
Townshend, Vermont 05353

Small Teddy – 8" high – $3.00
Medium Teddy – 12" high – $4.75

Leisure

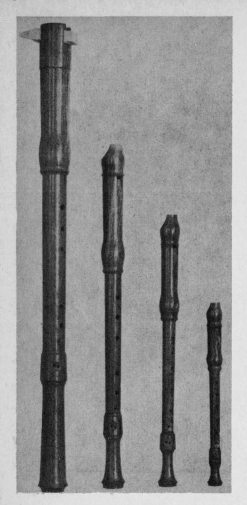

Recorders

Made in only one grade — the best.

William F. Koch spends many hours a month making recorders from a design originated by his father nearly 40 years ago.

Recorders bearing the *Koch* stamp are made of native black cherry or cocobolo wood from South America. The cherry is vacuum impregnated with waxes in a pressure tank designed and built by the late Mr. Koch, while cocobolo is an extremely heavy and dense wood packed with natural waxes.

The planks of wood are allowed to season for two years. Each instrument is then constructed in three parts from one block of wood so that the finished product is matched in color and grain.

Between the first rough borings and turnings, the pieces are stored for two months to release strains in the wood fibers, then finished to the correct shape, hand rubbed and varnished.

Before drilling the tone holes, cork joints are hand fitted and cemented in place, and a plug of soft wood, called a fipple, is fitted inside the mouthpiece.

Finally each instrument is checked on a stroboscope, an electronic machine which measures the accuracy of pitch.

Koch Recorders
Haverhill, New Hampshire 03765
From $10.00 to $100.00

Square-Dancing

A monthly magazine devoted to square-dancing!
MSH

The New England Caller
Norwell, Massachusetts 02061
$3.50 per year

Leisure

OLD-TIME NEW ENGLAND

A Quarterly Magazine Devoted to the Ancient Buildings, Household Furnishings, Domestic Arts, Manners and Customs, and Minor Antiquities of the New England People

BULLETIN OF THE SOCIETY FOR THE PRESERVATION OF NEW ENGLAND ANTIQUITIES

Articles are thoroughly researched and interestingly written. The paragraphs below are from an article in the Winter issue by *Barbara Lambert* entitled *"The Musical Puritans."*
MSH

141 Cambridge St.
Boston, Massachusetts 02109
$5.00 yearly

No known musical compositions by the Puritans in the Colonies were published until about 1770, and there are very few reports of musical instruments having been among their possessions. When these two long-accepted facts are coupled with ambiguous comments about music made by the Puritans themselves, it would seem that they disapproved of music outside psalmody. This is the conclusion drawn by most writers until about 1960.

Since 1960 the gulf of disagreement between the two factions has narrowed. Musicologists, such as Robert Stevenson, either evade the issue entirely, discussing only psalm singing, while others suggest the possibility that the Puritans may well have enjoyed various kinds of social music, but that under the stress of a survival-existence it most likely was simple and functional.

Oscar G. Sonneck, author of "Early Concert Life in America", turned up the fact that a public concert was performed in Boston as early as 1731. This was the first documented concert in the English colonies of North America. . . .

With such a rich musical heritage it is hard to imagine that the English settlers would have been content with psalm singing alone as their only form of musical expression. If the practice of musical art and the leisure it implies seems unlikely in a raw society among men who were commoners, we have only to look at the "musical parties" in the genre paintings by numerous seventeenth-century Dutch artists.

The musical life of the Puritans who did own instruments was a private affair. One played chamber music in the family, or invited in a neighbor to join in singing to the accompaniment of a virginal or a guitar. From the evidence presented in this study it would begin to appear that secular music was thought of as an innocent diversion and a pleasant escape from the rigors of daily life.

Musical Instrument

The Virginal — a rectangular harpsichord in which the strings run parallel to the front edge of the keyboard.

From the sixteenth through the eighteenth centuries, this instrument was commonly used for accompaniment and had widespread use as a home instrument. Because both bridges are on a free soundboard, the sound is quite different from the spinet. It blends nicely with other instruments.

In producing kits for the *Virginal*, Mr. Ross has strived to provide one of the best possible instruments that is satisfying musically, has good action and is easy to build. There is no compromise on design and the kit instruments he offers are the same as his personal ones which he has patterned after antique *Virginals* he has examined or restored.

Kit prices range from $345 to $1000. Write for more detailed information.

WILLIAM·POST·ROSS

HARPSICHORD MAKER

791 TREMONT STREET Room 515
BOSTON, MASSACHUSETTS 02118

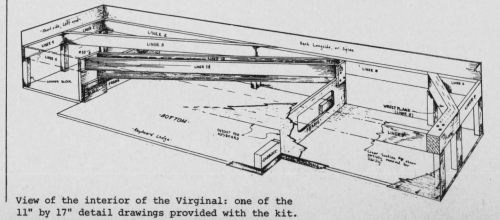

A virginal built from the kit and painted by Sheridan Germann of Boston.

View of the interior of the Virginal: one of the 11" by 17" detail drawings provided with the kit.

Harpsichord Kit

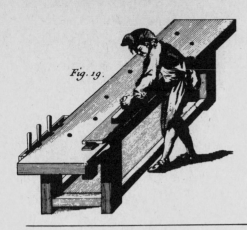

Fig. 19.

___ Three Centuries of Harpsichord Making.
Hubbard. (SBN 674-88845-6) $12.95

___ Instrumental Music Printed before 1600.
Brown. (SBN 674-45610-6) $19.50

___ The Lute Music of Francesco Canova da
Milano. *Ness.* (SBN 674-53955-9) 2 vols. in
one, paper $25.00

___ Harvard Dictionary of Music. *Apel.*
(SBN 674-37501-7) $20.00

☐ Check enclosed
(we pay postage)

All orders placed by individuals must be prepaid; Harvard University Press will pay shipping and postage. Libraries and other institutions will be billed on receipt of regular purchase authorization.

Harvard University Press
79 Garden Street
Cambridge, Massachusetts 02138

Music Synthesizers

Instrument for the "now generation."

Synthesizers are the new way of generating sounds by electrical means and may have enormous impact on musical instruments of the future.

ARP 2600P Portable Synthesizer is used by rock groups like "The Who", Stevie Wonder, Santana, etc., as well as by colleges and high schools.

6. ARP 2600: Popular portable professional performance and studio instrument built into two "suitcases" for easy carrying. Designed for colleges and demanding professional performers and rock bands. Electronics nuts' delight. Roughly $2490 retail.

ARP Instruments, Inc., 45 Kenneth St., Newton Highlands, Massachusetts 02161

Harpsichord Kits

If you have several hundred hours to spare and a well-equipped workshop at your disposal, you might like to consider building one of these authentic replicas of an 18th century French harpsichord.

In their basic form, the kits supply all parts needed, an accurate full-scale drawing, thirty detail drawings, elaborate instructions and a booklet on maintenance, voicing and tuning. The finished instrument is intended to be painted, as they were in the 18th century, but can be veneered if the maker wishes. Full instructions for either are provided.

Two versions are available — single or double keyboard. Either one may be purchased in any of several stages of completion. Details sent on request.

The Boston Symphony's harpsichord was assembled from one of these kits, as well as many of those used in well-known music conservatories throughout the world.

Frank Hubbard
Harpsichord Maker
185A Lyman Street
Waltham, Massachusetts 02154

Basic Kits: Single Manual Keyboard $600.00
Double Manual Keyboard $860.00

◆

the Vermont
UNI-BASS

- **instant music**

- **no practicing or expensive lessons**

- **fun for everybody**

- **make any musical group sound better or**

- **accompany your favorite records**

- **handcrafted in VERMONT**

- **inexpensive**

Send your check today for
$22.00 to:

UNI-BASS

P.O. Box 161
Jeffersonville, Vermont 05464

A five-gallon paint can, fingering board and a bass viol G string.

#600 — Drum Table — 20″ diameter, 25″ high.
Color: Red, white and blue — $100.00

The Old Drum Shop

In January of 1854, Silas Noble and James P. Cooley started making drums in the Noble's farmhouse kitchen. Their drum was an immediate success. A few weeks later they moved into a small building and after two years built their first factory. During the Civil War, the Company made drums for the Northern Regiment and business boomed. At this time, many changes occurred, with expansion to a larger factory and change from water power to steam engine, all influencing the continued growth of the Company.

Noble & Cooley Co. not only made military drums of all sizes, but also toy drums. In 1854 the Company produced 631 drums, by 1873 they were manufacturing 100,000 a year. Special machinery was designed and built to aid in the difficult process of steam bending, decorating and fabricating the drum parts. Many of these machines have been restored for use on their present line of reproductions.

Granville is a typical, small New England village in the foothills of the Berkshires. The business is still owned and operated by the descendants of James P. Cooley and retains the original firm name. Through the years, improvements in buildings and manufacturing processes have been made, but the company has retained much of its antiquity and charm.

Noble and Cooley are particularly proud of the historical background of two of their drums. In 1860, they made a drum from a rail split by Abraham Lincoln. This was used in political rallies in Massachusetts and Connecticut — eventually presented to the 10th Massachusetts Regiment and finally found a resting place in the United States Patent Office. A few years later they made the largest drum on record — eight feet in diameter. Made especially for use in Boston in 1868 at the First Grant Presidential Campaign, it was later used in the 1876 Centennial.

Noble & Cooley Company
Water Street
Granville, Massachusetts 01034

Benedictine Monks

At Weston Priory, thirteen Benedictine Monks farm the land, make bread, cider, pottery and jewelry.

The Brothers have recently published two record albums of songs composed by Brother Gregory of Weston and sung by members of the Priory. These sensitive recordings reflect the peace and simplicity at Chapel celebrations. Visitors are welcome.

Locusts and Wild Honey $5.50 ea.
Accompanying Song Book $1.70 ea.
Wherever You Go $5.00 ea.
Accompanying Song Book $2.20 ea.
From: The Gallery Shop
Weston Priory
Weston, Vermont 05161

Leisure

To Make An Orvis Bamboo Rod...

By nature a "tinkerer," *Charles Orvis* had the ability and inclination to design new products and improve on existing ones.

At an early age, he started building fly rods for his own use. Word spread rapidly that the Orvis rod was superior in both performance and workmanship and soon young Orvis was swamped with requests for them.

That was the beginning of a business which has been dedicated to quality and now offers a most complete line of equipment and accessories for the fisherman anywhere.

Orvis Bamboo Rods are **impregnated** . . waterproofed to the core with Bakelite resin. The finish is IN the rod, not on it. Not a surface varnish but permanent impregnation which makes the bamboo absolutely impervious to rain, snow, ice, saltwater, broiling sun, humidity. The rod is simply buffed to a high polish and, after 20 years, you can rub it up to this same high polish anytime. Impregnation not only waterproofs the "sticks" but also binds the fibres to prevent the rod from taking a set.

After impregnation, the "sticks" go for final inspection, calibration and grading before being mounted with ferrules, reel sear and guides. Again we have to repeat that at this stage too, **individual** judgment, skill and experience of fine rodmakers is what distinguishes a merely "good" standard production rod from a truly GREAT rod.

Each Orvis Impregnated Bamboo Rod is built, truly, for the fisherman who takes a deep pleasure in the "feel" of his fly rod.

THE ORVIS COMPANY, INC.
Manchester, Vermont 05254

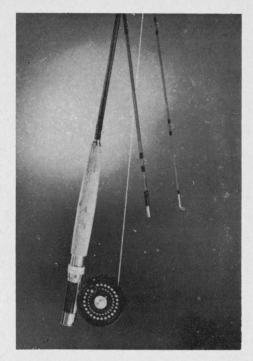

In mid-1971 the United States Government decided to permit, again, the importation of Tonkin Cane from China. Fortunately the Orvis supply of this cane had been adequate for the period of prohibition, but it is certainly fine again to be receiving our shipments of these beautiful staight canes, so incredibly strong in their recovery from perfect uniform flex.

Arundernaria Amabilis, known as Tonkin Cane, is a **cultivated** (not wild) product. It is grown in a small area about 25 miles long in the district of Wai Tsap in Kwangsi Province just south of Canton. This cane is definitely the finest material so far known for the fabrication of a superlative fly rod. It is straight, tough, with very finely compacted elastic lignified fibres. All attempts to grow bamboo of this quality in other areas (including our own South) have been unsuccessful. And the recovery rate, freedom from "fatigue" and sensitivity of selected Tonkin Cane can produce a fishing rod unequalled by rods of any other material.

The cane is sorted on arrival at Orvis, and all but the flawless rejected. The skill, judgment and experience brought to this sorting by Orvis is a **major** justification for your confidence in our rods. The selected cane is then heat tempered. At Orvis this process is a modernized version of **surface flame treating** NOT oven baking. What this does for the vitality, flexibility and freedom from all brittleness is, we believe, important.

Wesley Jordan designed **and personally built** our first rod segment milling machine many many years ago. Wes built it NOT to increase speed of production but **accuracy** of rod segment dimensions . . . which determine the taper and so the action of a rod. The accuracy of our present new modern miller is to tolerance of ¼ of 1/1000, very much more accurate than could be achieved by hand . . . any hand. However, when these milled segments are glued, Howard Steere personally inspects, mikes, constantly checks against his spec book for the tapers which will produce the action and "feel" expected of the particular rod design. Incidentally, the mismatching and glueing of the six segments is, again, a matter of great individual skill, judgement and experience. "Mis-matching" means the staggering of natural nodes in the six rod segments, to achieve uniform strength and perfect smoothness of flex.

Saltwater Tackle Box

For the guy who wants to order his fishing equipment from the catalog, *Salt Water Tackle Box* offers everything from rods and reels to lures of every description, plus every other imaginable item to make him a "complete angler."

Charles T. Letson

The Salt Water Tackle Box
P.O. Box 263
East Falmouth, Massachusetts 02536

TONY ACCETA PET SPOONS

The most effective salt water trolling spoon on the market. All sizes have a jewelry chrome finish and feature replaceable hooks. The spoon simulates a wounded minnow and drives the blues, stripers, tuna, and channel bass crazy!

C7B1	140	1/4 oz.	$ .79
C7B2	150	1/2 oz.	$ .89
C7B3	170	3/4 oz.	$ .99
C7B4	180	1 1/8 oz.	$1.19

Leisure

NEW

#747 PLANO Tackle Box

This king of the tackle boxes has a front panel that drops allowing three giant trays to be pulled out individually. Drawers are interchangeable, and the box has a patented locking arrangement to prevent gear spillage. It is beige and brown and measures 203/8" x 11½" x 12¾".

747	$28.89

One tray portable tackle box: This compact box has 6 good sized compartments in a single tray. It has a secure latch and a strong handle. Constructed of polypropylene and measures 12 7/8" X 6 1/4 X 5. Priced to sell and made to use.

2000	$1.69

2000

Fishing Preparation and Safety

If you plan to fish in the remote areas, please remember that they are remote — from stores, hospitals, gas and other supplies. Go prepared, and exercise sensible safety precautions. A good compass and map may be more important than your fishing or camping gear, but won't. do you any good unless you know know to use them.

From Maine Department of Economic Development
Augusta, Maine 04330

"The Voice of the Coastal Sport Fisherman"

The Saltwater Sportsman
10 High Street
Boston, Massachusetts 02110
$5.00 per year
The following was reprinted from the June 1972 issue.

Trick Or Treat?
The Delectable Goosefish!

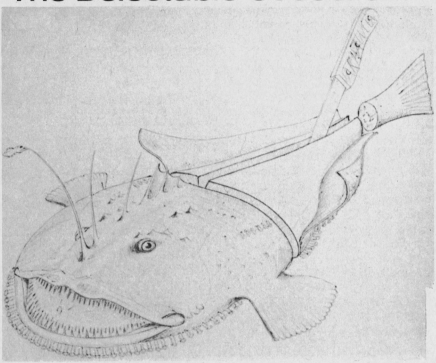

The business end of a goosefish is all ferocity and jellylike flesh, but there are two firm fillets aft of the dorsal which provide gourmet table fare and are said to taste like lobster. The species is regularly caught by commercial trawl fishermen and there is a ready market for its flesh.

When one fishes on bottom with such natural baits as skimmer clams, chunks of herring, mackerel, mullet, or the various seaworms between the Canadian Maritimes and North Carolina's Cape Hatteras, he is apt to hook many a strange and fearsome-looking creature of the deep.

Probably as fearsome-looking as any of these is the anglerfish, *Lophius piscatorius,* the mini-monster who is also known as the goosefish, the molligut, the allmouth, or the lawyerfish. Codfishermen in particular are apt to catch *Lophius,* a critter that may grow to four feet in length and weigh as much as 70 or 75 pounds.

Anglerfish is probably the most appropriate name for *Lophius,* for an angler is what this rather ugly, brownish-mottled fellow is. Shaped somewhat like a comet, his awesome lower jaw juts out like a rocky ledge. From that tooth-studded, prison-barred mouth, as well as other parts of his body, seaweed-like appendages resembling sponges and other marine organisms that decorate underwater rocks protrude. From *Lophius'* head extends a dorsal fin, which, like a fishing rod, can be waved tantalizingly.

Passing baitfish pause to nibble at it — and are gulped by the angler.

As many as a dozen herring or four or five haddock have been found in the gullet of an anglerfish. Seabirds such as ducks, geese, loons, gulls and terns been found there. One captured angler, in fact, was found to have seven ducks in its cavernous maw.

Many of the anglerfish, especially the larger ones I have accidentally hooked when bottomfishing, I've disposed of with haste. In some cases I've even sacrificed a heavy sinker and hook by cutting the line. But I seldom do that any more. Two years ago I learned from George Haas, a New York friend of mine, that the tail of an anglerfish contains meat that, when skinned, filleted and broiled, becomes "poor man's lobster."

Preparing anglerfish fillets for the broiler is far easier than it may sound. Simply chop away the tail fin with a cleaver or a hatchet, then fillet. The fillets are delicious when broiled and served with lemon or lime butter. Some of our guests have told us that they're even better than lobster because they are more tender. — *George Heinold*

The Connecticut River

About twenty-five years ago, when I was a senior at Dartmouth College, I canoed down the Connecticut River. Last spring, when my older son was a senior at Dartmouth, *he* canoed down the Connecticut River. So, we both know the river and we both love it and the land it touches in the 410 miles it flows from the boggy little lake in northern New Hampshire to the sand and marsh flats at Old Saybrook on Long Island Sound.

The love my son and I share for the river is also shared by author Evan Hill and photographer William F. Stekl, who have given us *The Connecticut River.* It is surely one of the finest books of its kind ever published in America. To anyone who knows the river, lives (or has ever lived) in New England and has some feeling for the desperate need in keeping our natural resources from turning into a vast cesspool, *The Connecticut River* is both a guidebook and a warning. Its guidebook aspects are clear: 143 pages of splendid black and white photographs and maps, combined with the author's informative, witty and profound prose. Evan Hill writes poetically about the river. Focusing on a quiet eddy near Deep River he writes:

"A scintilla of sunbeam. A pollen mote. A bird's clear cry. And always the steady, softly hissing presence of the river."

And of that gorgeous sweep of water at Lancaster, New Hampshire,

"Here the river's in no hurry; nor are the people on its banks. They're as peaceful as the land around them, as passive, and as permanent."

I said the book's a warning. It is. A warning to all of us that we have precious little time to save this river. Every one of Bill Stekl's photos and Evan Hill's words tells us the same thing. The river has been violated too long — too many dumps along the banksides, too much industrial sludge splashed into it, too little concern for one of this country's great rivers. It's late to save this natural wonder. It may be too late, especially the way Hill tells us about the land-grabbers, the industrial barons, the thoughtless little guys who figure that "just one more" beer can won't hurt the river.

But the Connecticut can stand just so much — and no more. Hill and Stekl have given us a magnificently beautiful book about a magnificently beautiful river. Let's hope their efforts aren't the final tribute to the Connecticut. It's been flowing through three centuries of man's abuse. Like all fragile and beautiful things, it can perish in time.

The Connecticut River is no coffee table volume, not one of those books that lies around as decoration. Look at it and read it. Over and over again! Think about what it tells us and shows us and act in a way to help save the Connecticut!

Alexander Medlicott

The Connecticut River
by Evan Hill
Photographs by William F. Stekl
1972; 143 pp.
From: Wesleyan University Press
Middletown, Connecticut 06457
$9.95

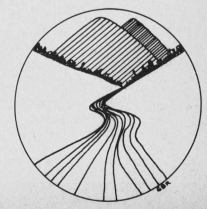

Leisure

DUCK DECOYS

HOW TO MAKE THEM
HOW TO PAINT THEM
HOW TO RIG THEM

EUGENE V. CONNETT, 3rd

ILLUSTRATED IN BLACK AND WHITE
AND COLOR
BY DR. EDGAR BURKE AND THE AUTHOR

Duck Decoys

Making duck decoys is to the waterfowler as tying flies is to the angler. This handsome book with its numerous illustrations takes the would-be maker of decoys step-by-step through the process, so that he should emerge an expert.

In addition to telling how to make them, how to paint them, and how to rig them, the book contains an invaluable store of information about ducks and successful ways to hunt them by using the proper decoys set out in the most advantageous ways.

Every duck hunter will find this unusual book of great interest, and value — whether he makes his own decoys or uses decoys made by others.

Charles T. Letson

Duck Decoys
by Eugene V. Connett, 3rd
Illustrated by Dr. Edgar Burke
1953: 116 pp.
From: The Stephen Greene Press
Brattleboro, Vermont 05301
$9.50

A North American Indian made the first duck decoy, maybe a thousand years ago. One of them was found in a desert cave; it was a canvasback made of reeds, and had some white feathers along its sides. There was no mistaking the species.

Since that time other Indians and many white men have fashioned decoys of all species with which to lure wildfowl within the range of their weapons. These men knew ducks and geese — their habits, their kinds, their worth. What some of them didn't know was that their seemingly untold millions could be reduced by drought and over-gunning to a dangerously low level. But we know that today, and we kill fewer of them, and we no longer toll them in with live birds. We rely on counterfeit birds, and we have learned that the more true-to-life we make these, the more effective they are, and the more pleasure we derive from their use.

. . . No matter how beautiful your decoys may be, and no matter how skillfully you may have rigged them out, all will be wasted if you don't remain ABSOLUTELY STILL when birds are coming in or flying around near you. I can count on the fingers of one hand the men I have shot with who don't grab for their guns or turn their heads for a better view of the birds when you whisper "Don't Move! Coming from the right!" It is, of course, important that you be well hidden in your boat or blind; but it is infinitely more important that you keep perfectly still in the presence of birds. I'd rather lie right out in the open and keep absolutely motionless than to have a good hide and move.

Several years ago I was shooting with a young friend and a guide on the Chesapeake. We were in a stake blind — the kind that is built several hundred yards from the shore and big enough to hold three or four men, with a space under it for the boat. The sun was shining in such a way that if we moved in the blind, a shadow was cast on the back wall of it. But I didn't discover this until three or four birds had swerved out of gunshot as they approached the rig. Then I noticed that on the approach of birds my friend and I would shift along the inside of the blind, well below the front of it, in order to take the best position from which to shoot. Although we couldn't be seen by birds out in front, our shadows certainly could, and we lost quite a few shots before we learned to hold perfectly still.

There just isn't any situation in which you can afford to move when birds are coming toward your rig, and unless you are willing to stay motionless, don't waste your time making a set of beautiful decoys.

Kamper Kraft

Attention campers, fishers, hunters — all you outdoor types: *Kamper Kraft* offers a transistor clock that will help to keep you on time for your appointed rounds.

Kamper Kraft
Box 127 Parcel Post Station
Mainline Industrial Park
Westfield, Massachusetts 01085
Transistor Clock: $19.95, includes battery and postage

Who Cares About Deer?

We don't know why people continue to let their dogs run loose in areas frequented by deer, but they do. It's unlawful. All the news media carry material about this problem. Department people mention it constantly in addressing clubs and other groups, and we know that people are aware that dogs will kill deer and that deer are especially vulnerable during snow time when the dogs have the advantage.

Still, dogs are turned loose without a thought. And deer die — often a pregnant doe, whose death brings about the premature death of one, two, maybe three fawns.

Wardens work on this problem, on the ground and from the air. They have success, but there are only so many of them, and there are too many dogs running free.

Still, people let dogs run loose. Don't they care about deer?

We don't know. But people caring about deer is all that will prevent dogs from killing deer. Period.

Courtesy of:

Maine Fish and Game, 1972
Maine Dept. of Inland Fisheries and Game
State Office Building
Augusta, Maine 04330
Published quarterly
$2.50 for two years

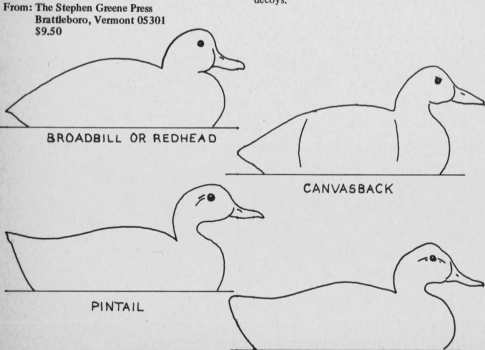

BROADBILL OR REDHEAD

CANVASBACK

PINTAIL

BLACK DUCK OR MALLARD

An informative booklet for the hunter and fisherman, General Fish and Game Laws and Regulations, may be obtained from:

Vermont Fish & Game Department
Montpelier, Vermont 05602

OUR INSIGNIA HAS MEANING

The top band of fourteen black and green alternate slashes represents the counties of the state.

The stylized green foliage framing the wildlife species represents our concern for the forest; this splash around the fish on the left, our concern for the waters of the state; and the band of grass on the right, our concern for the field and edgeland. Combined, these stand for our deep concern for good habitat needed to support our wildlife and the key to game management.

The species shown stand for the whole wildlife community. The deer, our most important single game species, stands for all mammals. The trout is symbolic of all fish. The ruffed grouse, Vermont's king of game birds, represents all birds.

The yellow gold background carries out the official state colors of green and gold.

The five converging wedges at the bottom of the shield depict the five Fish and Game districts focusing attention on the species and the habitat, neither of which can be considered separately.

The state superimposed over the districts depicts central direction from Montpelier to benefit the state as a whole.

Trout Fishing on the Cape?

Barnstable County has 77 fresh-water ponds (27 trout ponds) of 20 acres or more, a large number of smaller ponds, plus several coastal streams where native or stocked brook trout (salters) are available. Game fish include several species of trout (brown, brook, rainbow), black bass, pickerel, perch, pout and salmon.

Trout fishing on Cape Cod is comparable to any in New England. The State Fisheries and Game Division is constantly improving fishing facilities. Nonresident 7-day fishing licenses are $5.25, obtainable from Town Clerks.

Striped Bass & Other Cape Cod Fish

This fisherman's guide, primarily to the waters of Lower Cape Cod Bay, is by a commercial fisherman, charter-boat skipper, and writer, aimed for those who would become specialists in this absorbing pastime. The growing enthusiasm among sportsmen, for catching stripers, is ample justification for this highly personal, but thoroughly instructive, manual.

Everything on the subject is surely here. When and where you'll catch what kinds of fish; the art of spinning and free-spool surf casting; the best rods, reels, lines, lures; bottom rigs and bait; the ideal boat to own or charter; trolling for stripers and blues . . . plus interviews with other specialists on live-lining for stripers and going for mackerel.

Toward the end of April, no later than early May: let's go! This book will increase the ranks of the "fish-widow," unless she chooses to go along too. As the author puts it: "It's a Phil Schwind who blows no good."

Fessenden Wilder

Striped Bass & Other Cape Cod Fish
by Phil Schwind, Photographs by Bill Quinn
Drawings by John Quinn
1972; 128 pp., paper
From: The Chatham Press, Inc.
Riverside, Connecticut 06878
$3.95

Successful Ocean Game Fishing

This handsome volume is profusely illustrated with photographs of sport fishing from boats on salt water.

The author, Editor of Sportfishing Magazine, brings his professional know-how "to focus on topics that cover the fishing waterfront from flounders to swordfish, from selecting boats and tackle to using the proper fishing techniques." Frank Moss has augmented his own knowledge and writing skill with chapters by nine other famous fishing writers, specialists in their respective fields.

Among some of the exciting forms of the sport described are: fly fishing for tarpon, live mackerel fishing for striped bass, baiting and landing record billfish, battling giant sharks and many more.

Charles T. Letson

Successful Ocean Game Fishing
by Frank T. Moss
1971; 245 pp.
From: International Marine Publishing Co.
Camden, Maine 04843
$12.50

The Nantucketer, out of sight of land, furls his sails and lays him to his rest, while under his very pillow rush herds of walruses and whales.

Herman Melville

The Cod

Want to read a good fish story? A story about a fish that spawns ninety-eight million eggs per year, had a role in the "golden triangle" of rum, cod and slaves, can be caught in peach baskets and whose oil is labled the sunshine of the sea?

Albert C. Jensen has done a whale — or shall I say "cod" — of a job compiling the history, legend, habit, facts and likely future of this common but relatively unknown fish. Everything that touches on cod is faithfully and entertainingly reported. Some things, like the slave trade, are reported with gruesome accuracy. Other things, like the development of the cod industry, are reported with anecdotes and explanations. For instance, cod fishing has become extremely efficient. Once, the line and hook were used, then the line trawl (a line suspended between two anchors with numerous fish hooks attached to it) improved fishing; the gill trawl (a net with holes big enough for only the cod's head to go through, as he tried to back up the gills would catch on the netting and fasten him there) brought in still greater catches. Finally the otter trawl (which dragged along the bottom and gathered the fish in a sack net) revolutionized the industry until today, Jennings fears that the cod may be overfished and in danger of extinction.

Of course, there are many other contributors to this tragedy — pollution of the seas, for one — and Jennings takes it all into account.

This is truly a surprising and comprehensive book; undoubtedly the definitive work on the subject. Indexed and with an excellent bibliography, it reserves a prominent place in New England history for the cod.

Martin Robbins-Pianka

The Cod
by Albert C. Jensen
1972; 182 pp.
From: Thomas Y. Crowell Company
666 Fifth Avenue
New York, New York 10019
$7.95

The National Fisherman

A periodical every fisherman, sailor and lover of the sea should enjoy.

MSH

The National Fisherman
Camden, Maine 04843
$6.00 per year

Leisure

Nautical Items

Many interesting and useful items for the seaman.

Fore 'N Aft
P.O. Box 259
Marblehead, Massachusetts 01945

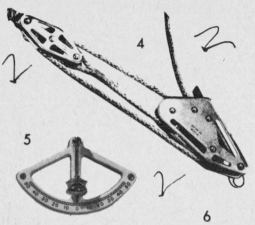

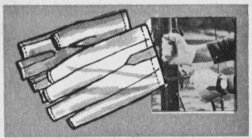

1. NC/01 SLIDE CHART SAIL TRIM GUIDE for racing and novice sailors. Made of durable waterproof plastic with pouch. **$8.95**

2. NC/02 CLEAT AND WINCH LABELS, waterproof, self adhesive ready to apply. **$1.95**

3. NC/03 DINGHY LABELS, waterproof, self adhesive ready to apply. **$1.95**

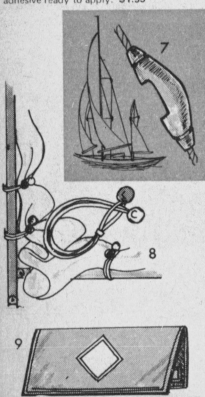

4. WC/01 KICKING STRAP JAMMING BLOCK ensures rapid adjustment either in or out with one hand only, stainless steel, 3/4" line recommended. Consists of a jamming block, single and becket block with clevis pin and ring and boom key with clevis pin and ring. **$11.95**

5. EG/02 CLINOMETER imported from England tells you angle of heel quickly and easily. **$3.25**

6. WO/02 SAILING GLOVES of chromed leather from England. Rot proof thread with red and green Port and Starboard tabs on wrists. Men's sizes: S,M,L. **$5.50 pr.** S,M. will fit women.

7. FM/01 STOP CHAFE protects sail chafe at cross-tree ends; can be fitted before or after mast is stepped. White rubber will not mar sails. Dinghy size for 3/16" dia. wire **$1.85 pr.** Size A for up to 1/4" dia. wire and crosstree end 1 1/4" X 1 1/4" or 1 1/4" dia. **$2.60 pr.** Size B for up to 3/8" dia. wire and crosstree ends 1 3/8" X 1 3/8" or 1 3/8" dia. **$3.50 pr.** Size C for up to 1/2" dia. wire and crosstree ends 1 1/2" X 1 1/2" or 1 1/2" dia. **$3.80 pr.**

8. IS/01 CARGUETTE TIES. Nonmarking super sail ties, twin nylon covered elastic lines with high density polyethelene ball ends. No rust. 11" long **.80 ea.** 16" long **.95 ea.** 20" long **$1.05 ea.** 30" long **$1.20 ea.**

9. AB/02 FLOATING WALLET for keys, credit cards, bills, made of nylon with velcro fastening and a luminous patch. Color orange. **$4.50 ea.**

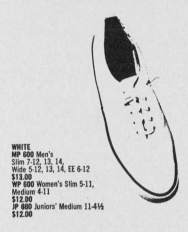
Whaling Wives of Martha's Vineyard

These tales of whaling voyages made in the middle of the 19th century are fascinating. Told from the woman's point of view, there is a poignancy to the efforts of sea-going wives to make a home aboard ship, and admiration for their courage in the face of hardship — terrifying storms, sickness and death at sea, insufferable heat near the equator and frigid cold in the northern waters, loneliness and the dangers of childbirth, far from home.

There were happy and exciting times too, as when several ships would meet — perhaps in Honolulu — and the wives of the captains would stay there together while the ships sailed north on an Arctic run.

Many of the voyages were three or four years in length. Wives who stayed at home had their own hardships. "The real and implacable enemy was separation."

Ellen Hill

Whaling Wives of Martha's Vineyard
by Emma Mayhew Whiting and Henry Beetle Hough
1965; 294 pp.
From: Dukes County Historical Society, Inc.
Edgartown, Massachusetts 02539
$4.50

Leisure

Kayaks

Build your own kayak — in one day! So *Dedham* claims. Any of our readers done it?

DEDHAM KAYAKS

BOX 207, W. LYNN, MASS. 01905

12' "WANDERER"
COMPLETE CONSTRUCTION KIT TO MAKE A KAYAK ... $ 49.95
NITRATE DOPE ... $ 6.50
CANVAS AND ADHESIVE FOR DOUBLE BOTTOM ... $ 12.75
PAINT AND VARNISH KIT ... $ 9.95

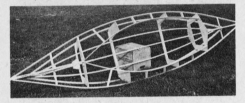

Some Yankee Weather Superstitions:

1. If pine needles hang together and are dark in color, a storm is coming.

2. A white-circled moon foretells a storm. The number of stars within the circle tells how many days away the storm is.

3. In the winter, the farmer's wife cuts a flock of geese across the crust of her pie, hoping to bring on an early spring.

SOUNDINGS

Soundings Magazine of Boats and Boating is much like the bumble bee that flies extremely well in spite of aerodynamists who say the bee does not have wingspan enough to get off the ground.

Some ten years ago SOUNDINGS was launched in Rocky Hill, Connecticut, a rather safe distance from any substantial amount of navigable water. The people who put it together, headed by Jack Turner, loved boats, especially sail boats, and were delightfully unaware that publishing experts had proved beyond doubt that the pleasure marine field could not possibly support another magazine.

With an accumulation of capital that would have been laughable for opening a shoeshine stand they scrabbled together a first issue and got it out.

The rest is heartwarming history. The latest issue resembles a Sunday New York Times just before Christmas. They have three editions covering central and northern New England, lower New England and New Jersey, and a Chespeake edition.

It is edited by Keith Taylor, an ex-New Zealander who makes a beef and kidney pie à la New Zealand you cannot believe until you eat it, and contains some of the finest boat photography being done today. Peter Barlow is the man with the camera.

Soundings is a tabloid format and is excellent reading for anyone who loves boats. Fifty cents per copy.

From: Soundings Publications, Inc. RWW
Box 210
Wethersfield, Connecticut 06109
$5.00 yearly.

Thus the Birch Canoe was builded
In the valley, by the river,
In the bosom of the forest;
And the forest's life was in it,
All its mystery and its magic,
All the lightness of the birch-tree,
All the toughness of the cedar,
All the larch's supple sinews;
And it floated on the river
Like a yellow leaf in Autumn,
Like a yellow water-lily.

from The Song of Hiawatha
Henry Wadsworth Longfellow

Boats

Fine design, fine performance comes from the *Cape Cod Shipbuilding Company*. Perhaps one of their most popular — and successful — sailboats is the Rhodes 18, designed by Philip Rhodes. Originally built in wood, it's now available in fiberglass. "Cape Cod" has a good selection for all the salts who want quality in their boats.

Cape Cod Shipbuilding Company
Wareham, Massachusetts 02571

RHODES 18 (Less Sails)
Centerboard Model ... 800 lbs. . **2190.00**
Keel Model ... 920 lbs. . **2095.00**
Mainsail and Jib, 165 sq. ft. ... **200.00**

Dories

Quality sailboats continue to be built in New England. *Cape Dory* is helping to maintain that tradition. This builder offers a wide variety of well-built craft from rowboats to a handsome Ted Hood-designed 30-foot cruising yacht.

Cape Dory Company, Inc.
373 Crescent Street
West Bridgewater, Massachusetts 02379

The Handy Cat 14

Price: $2,595.⁰⁰ *including Dacron sails*

Leisure

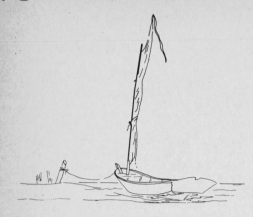

Mile Creek Boat Shop
John D. Little, Prop.

John Little is a man bucking a trend. He builds wooden boats as they were once built. He has his own design for a 17' lapstrake catboat — as far as I know the only lapstrake "cat" in existence. It can be powered with an inboard or fitted with an outboard. Extremely seaworthy, there's plenty of living space below, though, of course, not full headroom.

John also builds The Able Skiffs, so named because each one built to date has had a name ending in *able* — "Amiable," "Oarable" and "Unmentionable," to name a few. The Able Skiffs (based on Pete Culler's design) are excellent pulling boats, can be sculled, and are fitted with centerboard and sprit-rigged single sail. While not quite as sure to windward as an America's Cup racer, they are good sailors and will get you home.

The Able Skiffs, complete with sail and ready to go, are about $700, according to what fittings and grade of sail you choose. They can also be purchased rough-finished at substantially less. Of course, what John Little means by "rough-finished" is grade "A" joiner work to most of us.

Best of all, John builds these boats in the loft of a "70 ton barn" (so named because the barn held 70 tons of salt hay) on the backwaters of Mile Creek.

John will build almost any size or type of boat, though the biggest he has done in his loft is a 23' schooner.

There's nothing for immediate delivery, he builds only to order, but it's well worth the wait and the fun of working with a real boat builder.

RWW

Mile Creek Boat Shop
Old Lyme, Connecticut 06371
John D. Little, Prop.

Atlantic Sails

Sailing is a fun sport — sailmaking is a fun business, according to Graham Stone, head man at *Atlantic Sails*. Sailmaking is also a serious business, and Stone strives to bring modern manufacturing techniques into his expanding business. Although his number of employees is growing, he personally supervises the cutting and making of all sails. The pride of the ancient art is evident in all finished sails . . . from the head board to the clew grommet. *Atlantic Sails* specialize in making sails for 20'—30' class boats, but sails for larger classes can be made on request. For full details on all sails, write:

Atlantic Sails
22 Birch Knolls
Cape Elizabeth, Maine 04107

The Northern word "guess" — imported from England, where it used to be common, and now regarded by satirical Englishmen as a Yankee original — is but little used among Southerners. They say "reckon."

Mark Twain

Leisure

Fiberglass Boats

A New England firm designed these fiberglass boats around the concept of safety, reliability, seaworthiness and trailerability.

Gull of Bristol, Inc.
P.O. Box 204
North Dartmouth, Massachusetts 02747

15' Bristol Pilot — from $3,450.00 to $3,950.00 plus options
20' Bristol Helmsman — from $5,400.00 to $7,200.00 plus options

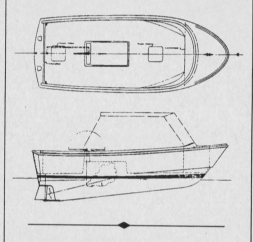

Identification of Buoys and Markers in New England Waters

Black Can — a black, cylindrical buoy marks the left side of channels entering from seaward.

Red Nun — a red, tapered buoy marking the right side of channels entering from seaward.

Horizontal Striped Buoys — Can or nun buoys, alternating black and red stripes, mark obstructions or junction of channels; principal channel, from seaward, lies to right of a "can" with black top stripe, to left of a "nun" with red top stripe.

Vertical Striped Buoys — Conical or nun buoys with black and white vertical stripes mark middle of channel; may be passed close on either side.

No special significance to shapes of spar buoys, bell buoys, lighted buoys, whistle buoys, gong buoys, or combinations. Color, number or light denotes purpose.

Lighted Buoy — warns of underwater obstruction. Color of light denotes type of buoy, at night.

Bell Buoy — long tapered pole, colored and/or numbered to denote purpose.

Day Beacons — of varying designs and colorings, marked or numbered according to their purpose. Placed on land or reefs.

Courtesy of the State of Maine Economic Development Commission.

ALDEN OCEAN SHELL

Alden Ocean Shells

"Add to your life with exercise" says Alden Ocean Shell designer, Arthur E. Martin.

The sudden interest in exercise and ecology has sparked a mushrooming enthusiasm for rowing. Unfortunately, it seems to be divided into two separate and distinct worlds. One is dominated by the competitive oarsman, who has been brought up in school and college with the ultimate in self-propelled speed on water: the racing shells. These beautiful boats call for great skill, are easy to damage and expensive to repair.

The other world of rowing encompasses sturdier, more seaworthy, and much slower boats without sliding seats. Fortunately, there are several good companies making these boats out of wood and fiberglass. Their use is not limited to sheltered waters and they offer good exercise and relaxation. The medical profession, however, seems to feel that leg exercise is most important for health, and this is unobtainable by rowing, unless the boat has a sliding seat.

Already there are lakes where no internal combustion engines are allowed. This kind of restriction must be extended if we are to preserve what is left of our heritage of natural waterways. The peace and quiet, clear water and wildlife of many a lake, river, or salt water inlet are being damaged each day by the noise, smoke and pollution of power boats. Younger and younger children, who might otherwise be learning to row or sail, are running around aimlessly in outboards which require no more effort to run than a TV set. They endanger the lives of themselves and others, and make life miserable for the many people who have come great distances to get away from the very environment that these boats create.

While no group could eliminate, or should even try to eliminate, outboard motors, a great deal can and should be done to restrict their use, and to encourage people, particularly the younger ones, to find something more constructive to do with their spare time. Perhaps the world of rowing will be able to make a more unified effort in this direction in the future. And certainly many more people can enjoy the good health and feeling of well being that rowing always brings.

This is the best boat for all-around use. It has a very low sliding seat, to keep the weight in the bottom, and increase the stability. Its short oars are easy to handle under any conditions. It is easiest for beginners, and best for children. It is also great for rough water, fishing and rowing in narrow or crowded waters.

Standard Model $425.00

Box 251 — Pepperrell Road
Kittery Point, Maine 03905

Dory Headquarters/Down East

Harold H. Payson has built well over 70 boats in his one-man shop. Among his most successful is the *Gloucester Gull Rowing Dory,* designed by naval architect, Philip Bolger of Gloucester, Massachusetts. Now, another Bolger-designed craft has been added to the line called the *Thomaston Galley.* It will row with the best of them, but also can be used with sail or power. Dory boat plans may be ordered in a wide selection of designs.

Harold H. Payson
Pleasant Beach Road
South Thomaston, Maine 04858

Gloucester Gull Rowing Dory 15' 6"

The Thomaston Galley 15'6" x 4'1"
$475.00 – rowing version

Gloucester Gull Rowing Dory 15'6" x 4'
$425.00 – includes oars and tie line

A Cruising Guide to the New England Coast

"The fog sifts through the spruce trees, the dark weed, swings in the tide, the distant surf on the ledges underlies every sound. The gentle motion in the harbor is never quite lost. Especially at night you feel you are far offshore, just on the edge of life beyond your own."

This Guide gives the sailor more than a description of harbors and facilities, information on piloting, sailing directions, weather conditions and longshore navigation from the Hudson River to the Bay of Fundy. What more is there?

The quote is from information on Matinicus, that interesting, fog-shrouded island some twelve miles off Vinalhaven, Maine. Sailors and lovers of the sea need to be informed of the constant changes wrought by the ever eroding sea. They also enjoy the stories of folklore and history of the coast they are visiting. The keen interest of the authors in these things adds much to this cruising man's "Bible."

A Cruising Guide to the New England Coast   JCH
by Roger F. Duncan and John P. Ware
1972; 603 pp.
From: Dodd, Mead & Company, Inc.
    79 Madison Avenue
    New York, New York 10016
    $15.00

The Yachtsman's Guide to Dining Out in Maine

"May you have good sailing and good dining." So wishes Paul Dale in his attempt at making dining out on the coast of Maine more convenient; and with this little book, a lot of fun! Dale has some solid criteria behind his guide. In addition to descriptions of what one might find in terms of restaurant food, prices, personnel, and atmosphere; he has included reproductions of the National Ocean Survey Charts for each harbor reviewed, to show what you might expect in terms of sea room. Although not for navigational purposes, the charts are keyed to show where you can expect a snug harbor, satisfactory anchorage, float or dock. With such help, you are bound to moor your yacht in a slip deep enough for your keel, and tie your dingy to the float closest to town.

For the person touring Maine by car, who desires a shore dinner, there is a road map coded to the restaurant listings. An index lists each town or harbor and restaurants, in alphabetical order. In keeping up with change, Mr. Dale has included a postage-paid card so that fellow diners might report back their findings of good food.

The Yachtsman's Guide — alive with information esoteric to each harbor. Take it along by land or sea. You'll surely find a top spot in the old town tonight!

SJI

The Yachtsman's Guide to Dining Out in Maine
by Paul W. Dale, Editor
1971; 45 pp., paper
From: The Guidebook Press
    P.O. Box 82
    Old Greenwich, Connecticut 06870
    $2.50

Sail Magazine

I liked what I read in *Sail* and *Sailboat & Sailboat Equipment Directory.* For the yachtsman, *Sail,* the monthly magazine, contains a wealth of worthwhile articles. In the "Techniques" section, for example, racing, the raison d'etre for every true sailor, is ably handled with a discussion on a variety of racing skills.

As with any successful magazine, *Sail* arms the reader with ideas and suggestions on how to do his thing better, more efficiently. Feature articles and technical information are interesting as well as helpful to the sailor. News of new boats, equipment and boating events rounds out each issue in the manner of a spanking breeze.

The annual *Sailboat & Sailboat Equipment Directory* would seem to me to be a must for every sincere sailor. The 1972 edition provided specifications for over 230 daysailors and cruisers. At the end of the directory, the "Sailor's Library" recommends books which can be a valuable addition to your own collection and appreciated gifts for sailing friends. The variety of books to choose from afford plenty of sack-time reading for the beginning or expert boat enthusiast.

JCH

Institute for Advancement of Sailing
38 Commercial Wharf
Boston, Massachusetts 02110
Sail
$9.50 yearly
Sailboat & Sailboat Equipment Directory
$2.00 annually

Leisure

Marine Supplies — Ship Model Kits

On a fresh spring morning in 1832 the Boston waterfront found itself with a new Ship Chandlery. Owner — young James Bliss. Supplies — spun oakum, candles, treenails, rum, pitch. Means of transporting goods to the docks — wheelbarrow.

Now, 140 years later, *James Bliss & Co.* with five stores serves local and distant boating customers with about the finest supplies available.

Send $1.00 for their two catalogues: *Ship Model Kits* and *Marine Supplies.*

James Bliss & Co., Inc.
Route 128
Dedham, Massachusetts 02026

288 PAGES

MARINE CATALOG $1

Charts & Books
Nautical Gifts
Galley Supplies
Wearing Apparel

Marine Hardware
Safety Equipment
Navigation Instruments

ACE RACING SLOOP

Operating model completely prefabricated. Balsa and mahogany hull with die cut parts, streamlined keel, 21″ birch mast, hemmed sails of fine grade muslin, rudder, all necessary top quality rigging and fittings.

$ 6.95

THE BLISS PRAM KIT
Fig. 2667

SPECIFICATIONS: Length 8′   Beam 48″   Weight 54 lbs.   Maximum Overall Depth 16½″

"STITCH AND GLUE" Method

Pram type hull with vee bottom designed for sheet plywood construction.

Children can build this pram. You stitch with copper wire and fiberglass the seams. Every wooden part is pre-cut and identified. No carpentry work is necessary — just assemble. Complete instructions for assembly are enclosed with each kit and everything but paint is included in the kit.

Use it as a ship-to-shore dinghy (it tows nicely), a rowboat or with an outboard motor (up to 3½ H.P.). Its 54 lb. weight is light enough to put aboard easily or to carry up on the beach. Perfect as a car top boat for fishing, etc. Its 48″ beam will fit into the back of most station wagons. Fun for the whole family both in construction and its final use.

VELACHERO

A very interesting model of a 19th century coastal merchant ship. Its trapezoidal sails evoke the trading vessels of much earlier days, and their variety makes this an unusual type. It is of fine design and has a marked decorative effect.

Length: 24½″
Height: 19¾″

No. U-606K Kit to build this model $42.50

STITCH YOURSELF A PRAM

The remarkable method of construction is simplicity itself. The oldest boat building method known, sewing, is used in building this pram. The Vikings used it; the Polynesians still do. They "stitch" the hull together — then waterproof the seams. This idea has been applied to the Bliss pram — with improvements. You stitch (or tie) with copper wire and fiberglass the seams. This makes an absolutely water-tight hull.

The six basic sheets of ¼″ thick marine quality plywood are shaped ready for stitching.

The two sheets forming the vee bottom are put together and "stitched" with twists of copper wire at eight inch centers — through pre-drilled holes — a process which makes the vee bottom take up its shape naturally. Next the fore and aft transoms are secured in the same way, then the two sheets forming the sides of the boat are slipped into place and secured with twists of wire. You then have a complete shell which is strengthened at the joints by 2 inch wide fiberglass tape and resin over the mating surfaces inside the hull. The copper stitching is then cut off outside and fiberglass tape and resin is applied over the outside joints making complete rigidity and watertightness to the entire hull. Seats, gunwales and keels are installed, some with screws and a pair of rowlocks is included.

Contents of Kit:
Pre-cut wooden parts
Copper stitching wire
Bronze screws
Fiberglass tape
Fiberglass resin
One 3″ brush
One pint acetone
One pair of rowlocks
Complete building instructions

Fig. 2667 BLISS PRAM KIT $64.50 F.O.B. Dedham

Optional Accessories:
Fig. 321 White rubber gunwale guard 19 feet @ **$0.75** per foot
Fig. 63P extra set of rowlocks and sockets **$4.50**
Fig. 475 Six-foot spruce oars **$16.50** per pair
Fig. 1900-1 Bronze towing ring **$1.90** each

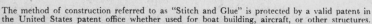

The method of construction referred to as "Stitch and Glue" is protected by a valid patent in the United States patent office whether used for boat building, aircraft, or other structures.

Leisure

Understanding Boat Design

A look around a boatyard shows an assortment of underbody shapes, rudders, keels, centerboards, gas engines, Diesels, sailboats and on and on. A reading of boating magazines reveals a host of fascinating designs and plans, adding confusion for the enthusiast who wants to know more. Why does a new, computer-planned boat win the Bermuda race one year and a 30-year-old design win another?

Understanding Boat Design introduces the fundamentals for the boat buyer, amateur builder and beginning yacht designer. The book adequately clears away many questions he has in a pleasantly readable style, amply supplemented with clearly executed black and white drawings from basic boat layouts to a portfolio of boat plans. Edward Brewer, co-author of the book, is director of the Yacht Design Institute in Brooklin, Maine, a correspondence school for the boating devotee who wants to move to the top of the field. Inquiries are welcome.

JCH

Understanding Boat Design
by Edward S. Brewer and Jim Betts
1971; 66 pp., paper
From: International Marine Publishing Co.
Camden, Maine 04843
$3.95

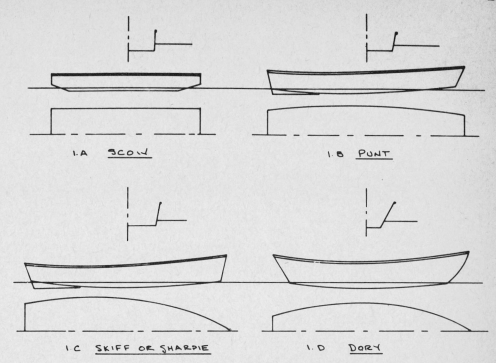

1.A SCOW

1.B PUNT

1.C SKIFF OR SHARPIE

1.D DORY

One Design Class Half Models

Norm Ross carves accurate wooden reproductions of the Blue Jay, Lightning, Sun Fish, Thistle and Star classes.

Reasonably priced at $15.00 each for a complete half model mounted on a walnut tone antiqued panel, edged with gold line yacht rope. Hull colors are appropriate and a chain is attached to the top for hanging. Custom models are also available at $25.00 each. Write to Norm for details.

Norman A. Ross
Bates Road
Chester, Connecticut 06412

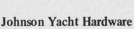

Johnson Yacht Hardware

The idea struck Curtiss S. Johnson, Jr., an ardent sailor from his childhood days, that there should be an improvement in the common turnbuckle — that important component on every sailboat. He put his industrial engineering background to work and designed a trouble-free, easy to use turnbuckle which once properly adjusted would hold its tension. The "Handy-Lock" turnbuckle is the result. Out of this idea evolved a whole line of well-made sailboat hardware. Catalog is available.

C. Sherman Johnson Co., Inc.
Main Street
Middle Haddam, Connecticut 06456

HANDY-LOCK/TURNBUCKLES, neat, compact stainless steel.
Positive locking without cotter pins or check nuts. No sharp corners to tear sails, threads fully protected. Adjustment is quick and requires no tools, just turn handles from lock position to adjust, even during a race. Toggle jaws are incorporated to avoid bending stresses at rod end.
HL04 series features stainless construction with forged body for maximum strength. Used wherever quality turnbuckles are required, especially backstays.
HL06 series is a long body backstay turnbuckle for larger boats. Two handles allow quick mast bending, even under strain. The body is machined high grade silicon bronze, chrome plated, while the rod ends and handles are stainless steel. This combination prevents galling under the most severe conditions.

SPECIFICATIONS & DATA

CATALOG NUMBER	TYPE	WIRE SIZE	†APPROX. BREAKING STRENGTH (LBS.)	THREAD SIZE	LENGTH CLOSED	LENGTH OPEN	PIN DIA.	WEIGHT	PRICE
HL04	Jaw & Jaw	⁵⁄₃₂, ³⁄₁₆, ⁷⁄₃₂	3,300	¼-28	7½"	10¼"	¼"	7 oz.	$16.50
HL04—5³⁄₃₂	Jaw & Swaged	⁵⁄₃₂	3,300	¼-28	8½"	11"	¼"	6 oz.	15.50
HL04—5½₂	Jaw & Swaged	⅛	3,300	¼-28	8½"	11¼"	¼"	6 oz.	15.50
HL04—5³⁄₃₂	Jaw & Swaged	⁷⁄₃₂	3,300	¼-28	8½"	11¼"	¼"	6 oz.	15.90
HL06	Jaw & Jaw	³⁄₁₆, ⁷⁄₃₂, ¼	8,200	⅜-24	13¼"	19¾"	⅜"	1 lb. 13 oz.	50.00
HL06—5³⁄₁₆	Jaw & Swaged	³⁄₁₆	8,200	⅜-24	13¾"	19¾"	⅜"	1 lb. 10 oz.	46.00
HL06—5⁷⁄₃₂	Jaw & Swaged	⁷⁄₃₂	8,200	⅜-24	13¾"	19¾"	⅜"	1 lb. 10 oz.	49.00
HL06—5¼	Jaw & Swaged	¼	8,200	⅜-24	13¾"	19¾"	⅜"	1 lb. 10 oz.	52.00

†We recommend a working load of not over 40% of these amounts.   Pat. No. 2913267

Enduring Friendships

And for good reason. Doughty, durable and designed for the complete sailing experience, Friendship Sloops have graced the waters of the Northeast for over 70 years. *Enduring Friendships* is an exceptional book worthy of its subject and a must for the library of each member of the Friendship Sloop Society. It's a well-written story of the Sloops with detailed plans of a famous Friendship, Pemaquid, fine half-tones (over 100) and data covering every boat registered in the Society which all sailors and those interested in excellent craftsmanship and sound tradition will enjoy.

JCH

Enduring Friendships
Edited by Al Roberts
1970; 74 pp. plus Catalog of Friendships
From: International Marine Publishing Co.
Camden, Maine 04843
$11.95

A New England Simple – To Remove Mildew
To remove mildew, wet the article and rub with a mixture of 1/2 chalk and 1/2 soap. Place in sun until gone.

MAN OVERBOARD DRILL:
At least two aboard at all times should know how to handle the boat, toss over aids, and get straggler back aboard. Why not let each member of crew take a turn at each role?

Leisure

Manchester Yacht Sails

As the name indicates, sail making is Manchester's bag — fine custom-made sails. All sails are manufactured to design specifications and are guaranteed in every respect. Manchester specializes in resolving sail problems and by working closely with the boat owner, there are few difficulties that can't be mutually smoothed out.

Also, Manchester manufactures a line of canvas bags, special awning poles and a variety of zipper products for fast spinnaker setting, reefing and sail setting. Inquiries relative to sails are welcome and price quotations will be given at no obligation.

Manchester Yacht Sails, Inc.
South Dartmouth, Massachusetts 02748

On The Sound

Sophisticated, slick and salty, *On the Sound* is good reading for those whose haunts string along New York and Connecticut's busy 90-mile waterway. Each month *On the Sound* offers a variety of interesting features for the golfer, fisherman, sailor, cook-outer and high-liver. If you are none of these, the magazine should hold your interest with its general departments which include letters to the editor, real estate and notes on happenings "Around the Sound."

On The Sound   JCH
235 E. 45th Street
New York, New York 10017
Yearly; 12 issues — $12.00

Frigate H. M. S. Rose

The Parimar Dory Skiff

A true fiberglass replica of its eighteenth century wood counterpart, retaining all the qualities of safety, ease of handling and use in rough waters.

Primarily a rowing boat, it will handle up to a 3 h.p. motor.

Parker River Marine, Inc.
Route 1A at Parker River
Newbury, Massachusetts 01950

H. M. S. Frigate Rose 1756-1779

Only full-sized ship of the Revolutionary War in existence.

The original Rose was built in Hull, Yorkshire, England in 1756. Its replica was built in 1970 and may be seen at the docks in Newport, Rhode Island. The Rose blockaded New England 1774-1776, making a great impression on the New England delegates to the Continental Congress who, as a result established the American Navy. In 1776 she was used by Admiral Lord Howe as part of his unsuccessful plan to persuade Washington to discuss peace at New York. In 1779 she was scuttled by her captain to prevent the French fleet from entering the narrow channel to Savannah, Georgia. A number of pieces of her have been recovered over the years, including one cannon. Usable parts were incorporated in the replica.

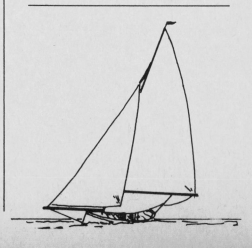

Specifications:

Hand laid up fiberglass of mat and roving construction.

Mahogany trim and mahogany seats.

Special non-skid floorboards.

Bronze Davis oarlocks.
LOA — 13'6"
Beam — 50"
Weight — 160 lbs.

Price — $490.00 FOB Newbury, Mass.

Leisure

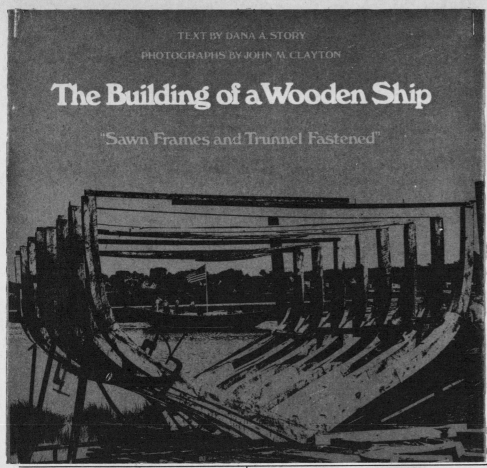

The Building of a Wooden Ship

This little volume is fascinating and nostalgic to those who, like this reviewer, witnessed the last throes of wooden shipbuilding at the end of World War II.

The superb photographs follow the building of a wooden ship in the yards in Essex, Massachusetts — the men who labored, and the tools they used.

Harry U. Snow

The Building of a Wooden Ship
by Dana A. Story
Photographs by John M. Clayton
1971; 102 pp.
From: Barre Publishers
      Barre, Massachusetts 01005
      $12.50

The great majority of the men who labored with heart and soul and aching backs to build the Essex vessels were never able to see their ships in the true environment for which they were intended, much less be aboard them in such a circumstance. There must have been many, however, who, through the long hours of hewing, adzing, planing, fitting, boring, caulking, painting, or whatever, dreamed of the day when the vessel would be out there in the midst of great seas and the worst of the elements. Perhaps as they did so they put just a little more care and pains into the job, remembering the lives dependent upon the skill of their hands.

ZEB

Zeb . . . a book about a man as hardy as the ship he sailed and loved.

Zebulon Northrop Tilton was a huge, cross-eyed schooner captain born in 1867. Before he died in 1952 he sailed his beloved "Alice S. Wentworth" to Chicago on a heavy dew, performed in a movie with Clara Bow, was struck by lightning (a mere incident to Zeb), and had his portrait painted by Thomas Hart Benton. All this and much, much more is true.

Well written, wonderful photographs, the book is a bit on the expensive side, but well worth it.

RWW

Zeb, A Celebrated Schooner Life
by Polly Burroughs
1972; 160 pp.
From: The Chatham Press, Inc.
      15 Wilmot Lane
      Riverside, Connecticut 06878
      $14.95

The Schooner Museum

There are so many things to see and do in Boothbay Harbor, Maine, you are bound to miss some, but do not miss the *Schooner Museum*.

"The Schooner Zwicker," about the last of the Grand Banks dory fishing schooners (and who can forget *Captains Courageous*), the "Seguin," the nation's oldest wooden, steam-powered tugboat (their literature says "tugboat" which is a landsman's term . . . a merchant seaman would only call it a "towboat") are two ships well worth seeing.

The Schooner Museum   RWW
Commercial Street
Boothbay Harbor, Maine 04538

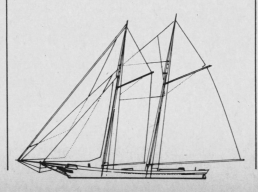

Cruising the Maine Coast

Real cruising begins in Maine. Would you say at Portland?

Morten Lund implies this in his generously illustrated narrative of a "model cruise" from Kittery to Roque Island for the skipper with limited time at his disposal, who wishes to recapture the magic of earlier discoveries and impressions. His *Slide* course (Straight Line Interesting Down East), gets you as far as the Machias River and back in just over two weeks.

Although our skipper is never restive, nor *Slide* wholly prescriptive, this is cruising under some pressure. Or so it often seems. Furthermore, although he does not say so, the incessant bleat of the twin Evinrudes, valiantly keeping *Puff* on schedule, might conceivably discourage him who is irretrievably indentured to cruising under sail.

But you can't have it both ways. What gives this informal account special appeal, aside from the maps and photographs, are the personal encounters, and touches of historical background, and the innumerable side-trips, many of which can *only* be negotiated by a relatively small power boat.

None of the classic havens (and few of the gunkholes) has evaded *Puff's* glancing, or inquiring, scrutiny: Quahog Bay, the Basin (both Basins, in fact), Robinhood Cove, Pleasant Point Gut, Winter Harbor (Vinal Haven's!), Horseshoe Cove, Sorrento, Lakeman's . . :; and although times have changed a bit even in Maine since 1967, most of the advice given on navigational aids, coaling stations, et al, is accurate. For more detailed information, get out "The Bible" *(Cruising Guide to the New England Coast,)* standard equipment aboard all coast-wide cruisers, to which the author pays handsome tribute.

Nevertheless, Morten Lund is both knowledgeable and persuasive. Go Down East, young man, go Down East!

Fessenden Wilder

Cruising the Maine Coast
by Morten Lund
1967; 224 pp.
From: Walker and Company
      720 Fifth Avenue
      New York, New York 10019
      $12.50

Leisure

Baldwin Boat Company

Established in 1966, this company set out to design and build a complete line of kayaks "at a time when, in this part of the world, only a few fanatics would even sit in one," says owner Earl Baldwin. A two-place family kayak was introduced first. It is a general-purpose, car-top model that a woman can easily launch.

From this start, came down-river kayaks and racing machines to compete with better European boats. A white water, open canoe — Natanic by name — is one of Baldwin's prizes. One expert and his wife report, "In this canoe, they no longer have to pick their way through rocky shallows; they look for the big 'haystacks' and drive on through."

Baldwin Boat Company
Hoxie Hill Road
Orrington, Maine 04474

FAMILY KAYAK — 2 PLACE

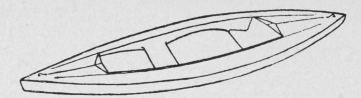

The Family Kayak is a general purpose boat popular with campers, for cruising, fishing, hunting, and moderately fast water. It is very stable; a person weighing 170 pounds can sit on the cockpit edge without capsizing. Molded seats are raised about five inches from the floor and placed so the boat is properly trimmed with either one or two occupants. An excellent boat in wind; any chosen course can be held, even with only one paddler. Easily cartopped and launched. Length 14'—Beam 38"—Depth 12"—Weight 60 lbs. Colors: Red, yellow, or light green deck on white hull. All bullrush tan. Price: $250   Packing Charge $15

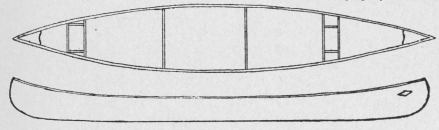

NATANIS WHITEWATER CANOE

NATANIS was born from a union of open canoe whitewater lore and a mathematical formula for underwater lines. She is designed for the ultimate in whitewater capabilities coupled with flatwater speed, light weight, and suitability as a traditional general purpose family canoe. She complies with the new racing rules of the Open Canoe Whitewater Committee of the American Canoe Association. Length 20' 6"—Beam 38"—Depth 15"—Weight under 100 lbs. Colors: White, light green, dark green.
Prices: Complete $389, Fiberglass Shell Only $255.
Packing Charge $15

Blount Marine Corporation

Blount says, "Do you have to transport 350 passengers across a rough water sound at speeds high enough to make the run profitable? What about 12 cars and 100 passengers across a river through severe ice conditions part of the year? Need an inland waterway cruise vessel that will allow clubs or organizations to sponsor their own charters at an average cost of as little as 72¢ per person?

"These are some of the problems that our customers have brought to us. We are proud to say that we have solved these — and a host of other equally difficult ones. Our experienced, versatile marine architects are equipped to design any type of passenger boat, vehicle carrier or combination of the two — from 65 to 250 feet, tailored specifically to meet your particular needs."

What more is there to say.

Blount Marine Corporation
461 Water Street
Warren, Rhode Island 02885

The Bean Hill Whittler

Want a name board or figurehead for your boat? How about a personalized sign for your home? *Ed LeRich* is the man to see. He is the man who was chosen to gold leaf and refinish the two original name quarter boards on the USCG training ship Eagle. His signs are hand carved and gold leafed or painted. Many different styles of lettering are offered in his illustrated brochure. Send for it.

Ed LeRich
The Bean Hill Whittler
49 Sholes Avenue
Norwichtown, Connecticut 06360

The 65-foot "Essex"

The 'Bean Hill Whittler' at Work

The 108-foot "H" class "M.S. Shahan"

Old Town

Old Town — Canoes. Canoes — Old Town. Which comes first? It doesn't matter, they are synonymous. Kayaks for surfing, white water-racing, downriver touring; power boats and accessories for the boating enthusiast are some of the other products from this quality manufacturer. Excellent dealer representation throughout the United States, Mexico, Puerto Rico and Virgin Islands.

Old Town Canoe Company
Old Town, Maine 04468

Rushton 10½' x 27" Weight 18½ lb.	$215.00
F.G. 14' x 36" Weight 69 lb.	$355.00
Surfer 10½' x 24" Weight 34 lb.	$295.00
Snapper 13' x 1½" x 24" Weight 31 lb.	$345.00

OLD TOWN Snapper

OLD TOWN Rushton

OLD TOWN F.G.

OLD TOWN SURFER

Whaling Museum

The largest ship model in the world greets one at the *Whaling Museum* in New Bedford. It's a complete and accurate model of the Bark Lagoda, typical of the whaleships which sailed out of New Bedford around 1850. The model is 60 feet long, large enough for visitors to go aboard.

There's more at this fascinating museum. Thirty-foot cedar whaleboats — the life blood of every whaleship — are on exhibit. With a little imagination you can hear "There she blo-o-ws" from the lookout and the scrambling of the crew into these lightly built boats.

Off they rowed, or sailed if the wind and sea was right, to the vicinity of the whale and there the encounter began. As the boat neared the whale, the harpooner reared back his arm and with an accurate aim threw the harpoon to which was attached 1300 feet of rope! With the weapon imbedded, the whale took off and the men were usually in for the ride of their lives. The "sleigh ride" was on. With great speed, the whaler was towed sometimes miles from the ship, but eventually the mammal's great strength ebbed, allowing the boat to come again alongside where a lance was thrust into the victim, killing it by hitting a vital spot.

After being towed back to the ship, the cutting of the whale began. While it was lashed to the side of the ship, men peeled the blubber off. These large slabs (blanket pieces) were hauled aboard and the blubber was then cut into two foot hunks (horse-pieces) which in turn were sliced into smaller pieces (bible leaves). These were boiled until reduced to oil in fires under the pots first started with wood, later fed by scraps of boiled blubber. From the pots, the oil was ladled into large barrels in the hold. On a good voyage, the ship would bring home about 2,000 barrels; the equivalent to 64,000 gallons.

The great days of New Bedford whaling extended from 1800 to 1900. At the height of the era, approximately 400 ships were registered out of that port. With the discovery of petroleum in 1859 and the introduction of kerosene for lighting, the industry started to decline. It survived the Civil War, but the fleet was decimated, so the great days of American whaling drew slowly to a close. A last whaling voyage was made from New Bedford in 1925.

A trip to this southeastern Massachusetts city can be memorable if a visit is made to the *Whaling Museum*.

Whaling Museum
Johnny Cake Hill
New Bedford, Massachusetts 02740

New Bedford Whaleboat

Honest Birchbark Canoes

Henri Vaillancourt sounds like our kind of purist, and here is what he said about his work:

I build birchbark canoes in traditional Indian manner. The wood for planking and ribs is all split out of white cedar and shaved by hand. The seams are sewn with split pine roots, and the lashings of the gunwales are also split roots. All fastenings are done with whittled pegs in the old manner. No power tools are used in the construction. The hand tools involved are the crooked knife, drawknife, plane, spokeshave, awl, froe, wooden mallets and wedges.

I build Malecite canoes, and the different types formerly made by this tribe can be seen in the chapter on Malecite Indian Canoes in the book "Bark Canoes & Skin Boats of North America" by Adney from U.S. Govt. Printing Office, Wsh., D.C. price $3.75.

I specialize in the St. Lawrence River type, but build the other tumblehome types as well. I also build the Tetes de Boule Fur Trade Canoe seen on page 136 of the same book.

As far as the canoes themselves, if a person wants a canoe he can abuse, let him get an aluminum or fiberglass. But if he's interested in taking care of his canoe and having something out of the pages of history, then he can consider buying a birchbark.

Because of the scarcity of good bark for canoes, I build only 6 canoes per year, and take orders in advance.

Henri Vaillancourt
Mill St. Box 179
Greenville, New Hampshire 03048

———— ◆ ————

Porta Lamp

The *Cordless Porta Lamp* operates on a long life, 6-volt battery — up to 100 hours of continuous light and satisfaction.

Sam Richards Trader
P.O. Box 456
Bantam, Connecticut 06750
$8.95 ppd.

———— ◆ ————

Habit is habit, and not to be flung out of the window by any man, but coaxed downstairs a step at a time.

Mark Twain

Leisure

Appalachian Mountain Club

A.M.C. New England Canoeing Guide

A handy guide for the recreational canoer. Book mentions many not so popular rivers and streams which equal or even surpass major canoeing streams with their beauty and historical interest.

Mountain Flowers of New England

Pocket size book of flowers with detailed illustrations and excellent photography. Drawings and photos are so important for such books. A helpful book for those who know little about flowers. This has to be one of the best!

A.M.C. White Water Handbook for Canoe and Kayak

Covers every situation a canoer might run into. Helpful in learning the difficult skills of kayaking. Anyone who questions learning how to kayak, will surely not question it anymore.

Thomas D. Archambault

———— ◆ ————

North Country Canoe Trips

The thrill of running the rapids or the tranquility of a mirror smooth lake are experiences to be remembered by participants in the *St. Croix Voyageurs* camp program.

Although there is a definite period of training, such as "setting pole," loading the canoe and other woodcraft, there is also time for swimming, fishing, wildlife photography, along with such special programs as geology and forestry.

The Voyageurs cruise for seven weeks on the watersheds of the St. John, Allagash and Penobscot rivers.

Because of a flexible itinerary, mail delivery is irregular and is usually forwarded to the camp via bush plane — so patience, please, in waiting for answers to inquiries. Write to:

The St. Croix Voyageurs
George L. Dwelley, Director
Box 47
Belgrade, Maine 04917

canoeing on the connecticut river

Upper Connecticut River: Canoeing — Fun in Happy Valley

A Vermont state law says every canoeist must have a life preserver . . . in case you plan any canoeing on the upper reaches of the beautiful Connecticut River. And don't go until you read the booklet *Canoeing on the Connecticut River*, prepared by Vermont State Board of Recreation and Water Resources Department. It contains a Canoeing Map of the river starting near the Canadian border showing dams, portages, bridges, camping areas, danger spots and points of interest. Unfortunately the map stops at the Massachusetts-Vermont-New Hampshire State Line . . . but it does tell you what every canoeist should know about that 237 miles of the upper river. There's still another 137 miles down to Long Island Sound.

Did you know the Connecticut River falls 2,600 feet from the Canadian border to the Sound . . . through what the New England Electric System calls "Happy Valley?" Friends of New England Electric System have put out another booklet, *Your Happy Valley Guide,* that tells you the best places to fish, camp, hunt, hike, picnic and boat in the valley . . . but only north of the Massachusetts-Connecticut State Line. This booklet, too, includes a map of Happy Valley showing landmarks of interest, plus places to watch birds or see dinosaur tracks.

Fred Welsh

Prepared by:
Vermont State Board of Recreation
Montpelier, Vermont 05602
And . . .
Friends of New England Electric System

PORTAGING

POLING

Lightweight Camping and Hiking Equipment

With the right equipment any healthy person can enjoy the beauty of the countryside, lake, sea or mountains. *Moor & Mountain* has that equipment; it's lightweight, durable and designed to a specific need.

Moor & Mountain
67 Main Street
Concord, Massachusetts 01742

NORFELL 4 MAN EXPEDITION TENT — This 4 man tent is designed to be both an excellent warm and cold weather tent which will shelter 4 men and most of their gear. The inner tent is 8½ ft. square and 5 ft. tall at the peak; built in a pyramid shape. The floor material is the heavy duty 2.5 oz. coated ripstop nylon and extends up the walls 4 inches to give sidewall protection. This fabric will take great abuse from rough ground without wear or puncture. The upper body of the inner tent is made of the .75 oz. polypropelene-nylon ripstop fabric which gives unusual breathability for both air and water vapor. There is a triangular door opening which is 4¼ ft. wide and 3 ft. tall which can be closed with two side nylon No. 5 zippers. Behind the door is a nylon insect netting panel with side nylon zips as well. When not in place the netting panel can be stored in a pocket behind the front sill of the tent. There are tape peg loops at each corner of the inner tent, and a hole in the peak to allow the single center pole to be placed through the tent and the inner tent suspended from the top of the pole with an adjustable cord.

The outer tent is made of the coated and waterproof 1 oz. ripstop nylon and designed to be suspended over the inner tent in two ways. The fly can be pitched down to the ground to form a double wall construction which has excellent insulation properties in cold weather. The fly can also be pitched about 6 inches off the ground using extra length peg so that air will circulate past the inner tent and out the ventilator in the top front of the fly. Thus the inner tent can be kept cool in hot weather while still completely protecting the inner tent from rain regard less of wind direction. The entrance to the outer tent is a single vertical nylon zipper. When the zipper is open the front flaps can be tied back for better visability. Peg loops are provided at the corners and the center of each side of the fly as well as tensioning points 1 ft. up each side to stop the fly from collapsing onto the inner tent.

In the space between the inner and outer tents, equipment can be stored in bad weather and cooking can be done without possibility of spillage inside the tent.

The tent color is medium blue. Tent is shipped complete with single adjustable pole, 18 aluminum pegs, 6 nylon cord tighteners, and 50 ft. of No. 3½ braided nylon line.

The weight of the tent without pegs, pole and cord is 5.5 lbs. and 7.0 lbs. complete. This low weight makes the NORFELL 4 man Expedition tent the lightest for its size while still providing maximum comfort in both cold and warm weather.

Cat. No. 108   Wt.: 7.0 lbs.   **$170.00**

GAITORS — For use with boots to keep out snow, ice, and brush; waterproof urethane coated 8 oz. nylon; velcro tape closure which will work in ice when zippers jam; cord under instep; hook on front edge to hold gaitor down to laces; elastic top and bottom with snaps. Two sizes: 7" and 16" high. Green.
Cat. No. 669 Wt.: .12 lbs. **$4.50**
Cat. No. 668 Wt.: .30 lbs. **$8.00**

Northmark Alpine Mummy Bag 4.75 lbs. $85.00

COMPLETE PACK MODEL 1

Sizes Med., lge., x-lge. Color — International Orange.
14.08 lbs. $44.00

Short Walks in Connecticut — 42 More Short Walks in Connecticut

These pocket sized books are written for those who enjoy a definite pattern for their walks. A general map of Connecticut is included with the individual walks marked on it. Each separate walk is well described with a map, excellent directions for how to reach the trail, the degree of difficulty, and the sights of interest.

A good sample is the chapter on Mushantuxet — page 72 of the first volume. The Mushantuxet segment of the Pequot trail is a small part of the network of trails used by the Indians. "The poles are clearly blue-blazed to point where the trail enters dense evergreen woods to the south. Trail descends gradually through a heavy growth of laurel to a brook, then continues on the south edge of a wide-spread cedar swamp. From the southwest end of the swamp the trail skirts the north end of the Western Pequot Indian Reservation, then passes over Slabs Hill with good views to the south and west."

Jean Allen Skiff

Short Walks in Connecticut
by Eugene Keyarts
1972; 85 pp., paper
$2.50
42 More Short Walks in Connecticut
by Eugene Keyarts
1972; 87 pp., paper
$2.50
From: The Pequot Press
Chester, Connecticut 06412

Hosteling

Feel rugged? SHP may not be for everyone, but if you're willing to expend physical effort on an extended bicycling/hiking tour or you're up to living for a month or more with nine other people — nine different personalities — then you'll "dig" this program. The tours range from a short trip (29 days) in Maine and Nova Scotia, to a longer one (40 days) in New England, to a distant one (44 days) in England, Scotland and Ireland. The groups travel and live simply — using campsites, hostels and mountain huts. They cook their own meals, of course! The goal is to provide the opportunity for motivated teenagers to learn about the world, the beauty of life and about themselves.

Full information from:

Student Hosteling Program of New England, Inc.
East Park Street
Rochester, Vermont 05767
Prices
Seacoast (Maine and Nova Scotia) — $485.00
New England (Vermont, New Hampshire and Maine) — $625.00
Great Britain (England, Scotland) $830.00

Northwoods Tales and Unusual Recipes

An ardent conservationist, Mr. Soule was Northeast Area Director for the Agricultural Stabilization and Conservation Service. His book relates dozens of amusing anecdotes, and includes many recipes for cooking whatever was caught on the expeditions. A few of these, such as roast racoon, roast beaver and roast porcupine are unlikely to find their way into many kitchens, but the fish chowders, beanhole beans, hunter's stew, graham muffins and many others sound delicious. Most can be cooked outside over a fire — others are better tried in the comfort of one's own kitchen.

S. S. Stowell

Northwoods Tales and Unusual Recipes
by Harris W. Soule
Sketches by Margo Holden
1971; 147 pp.
From: Essex Publishing Co., Inc.
Essex Jct., Vermont 05452
$5.95

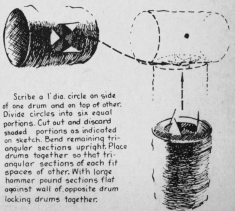

FOOD SMOKER

Scribe a 1' dia. circle on side of one drum and on top of other. Divide circles into six equal portions. Cut out and discard shaded portions as indicated on sketch. Bend remaining triangular sections upright. Place drums together so that triangular sections of each fit spaces of other. With large hammer pound sections flat against wall of opposite drum locking drums together.

Leisure

L. L. Bean, Inc.
With a world-wide reputation — *L. L. Bean* needs little introduction. They carry a complete line of equipment for the hiker/camper/fisherman/hunter. Catalog available — one of the best.

L. L. Bean, Inc.
Freeport, Maine 04032

L. L. Bean, Inc.
635 Main Street, Freeport, Maine 04032
Camping, Fishing and Hunting Specialties

Open 24 Hours A Day 365 Days A Year

Sven Saw

The ideal folding saw for campers, picnickers and home fireplace owners. Tempered Swedish steel blade quickly rips through firewood.

Strong, easily assembled, rigid triangular frame. Folds into compact 24" x 1¾" corrosion resistant aluminum handle. Protects blade and prevents tearing of other duffle. Weighs about one pound.
Price, $6.50 postpaid.
(Additional Blades: "Woodsaw" or "Meatsaw", price $1.75 each postpaid.)

Bean's Camp Saw
Coated with Teflon-S®

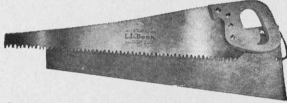

Manufactured for us in the Tuttle tooth design that frees blade of sawdust same as a one-man crosscut saw. Can cut firewood up to 8" in diameter. Unequalled as a pruning saw.

Blade coated with DuPont Teflon-S®. Resists sticking and prevents rust. Overall length 26¾". Weight 25 oz.
Price, $9.25 postpaid. (Includes sturdy carrying case.)

Woodsman's Pal Bush–Axe

A heavy duty tool, easily carried. Handy for a variety of jobs around camp, farm, orchard or traveling through back country. Has 9" chopping and cutting edge, brush-hooking sickle edge and trenching edge.

Specially processed high carbon manganese steel with black finish. Rust resistant. Hand fitting soft leather grip with metal thumb and hand guard. Metal sheath for safe carrying.
Overall length 16". Weight about 22 oz.
Price, $14.75 postpaid.

Outdoor Travel Camps

A privately organized professional leadership cooperative, *Outdoor Travel Camps, Inc.* sponsors meaningful vacation programs (both winter and summer) for secondary school students who are outdoor enthusiasts. The program below is one of their most popular.

New England Exploration

Twenty teenagers and four adult leaders explore about nine New England areas in 5-10 day blocks of time. The trips emanate from Trailside, a centrally located Green Mountain wildlife sanctuary of 200 acres. Activities and skills during the summer include camping, hiking, cooking, photography, wildlife observation, motorboating, exploring, cycling, square dancing, berry picking, rock climbing, cave research, guitar and banjo instruction, waterskiing, canoeing, swimming, folk music, nature lore and mountaineering.

Participants are involved in all aspects of trip planning and the small group affords the opportunity for active involvement in spontaneous activity.

Write for detailed information to:
Outdoor Travel Camps, Inc.
Killington, Vermont 05751

Leisure

Food for the Outdoorsman

Chuck Wagon Foods fulfills an ever-growing need — sustenance for camper and other outdoor enthusiasts. They supply meal packs for breakfast, lunch and supper, and emergency kits for woodsmen, which include band aids, waxed wood matches, plastic water bag, compass and other essential items to aid the lost, injured or isolated. A concentrated food kit weighing only 8 oz., provides the outdoorsman with a ready-to-eat instant meal. Each food item has been selected for compactness, flavor and high nutrition. Above all, Chuck Wagon meals taste good!

Chuck Wagon Foods
Micro Drive
Woburn, Massachusetts 01801

I went to the woods because I wished to live deliberately, to front only the essential facts of life, and see if I could not learn what it had to teach, and not, when I came to die, discover that I had not lived.

Henry David Thoreau

"The life of one camper — is beyond price"

GO PREPARED

8 Oz.
4¼" x 2⅜" x 1⅜"
650 Calories

$2.00 EACH before discount

The "POCKET SIZE" is completely dipped in wax so that it's waterproof and will actually float. It weighs only 8 ounces and fits any sports shirt pocket. And it's guaranteed for two years.

FAMILY CAMPERS • SPORTSMEN • MOUNTAIN CLIMBERS
HIKERS • SCOUTS • BOAT OWNERS • SUMMER CAMPS

CONTENTS

COMPRESSED CEREAL BAR	TOILET TISSUE
STARCH JELLY BAR	2 BAND AIDS
2 TROPICAL CHOC. BARS	3 FISH HOOKS
3 SALT PACKETS	15' LINE (12 lb. test)
SINGLE EDGE RAZOR BLADE	SHEET OF ALUM. FOIL
SURVIVAL INSTRUCTIONS	WAXED WOOD MATCHES

ALL U. S. GOVT. APPROVED FOODS

Instep Point Protectors
Rubber protectors for adjustable 4 point crampons.
EICP12 $.95

Crampon Case
A case with a metal plate for the crampon points to rest against and a canvas cover around everything, buckles shut. Measures about 14″ x 5″. Weighs 9 ounces.
S12G735 $5.00

Rubber Point Guards
These connected point guards for crampons are an easy way to carry your crampons in safety. The point guards come with 12 rubber sockets and can be cut for use with 10 point crampons. Weight about 6 ounces a pair.
Z01G731 $1.95

Neoprene-Nylon Crampon Bindings
Excellent two-piece crampon straps made of neoprene-coated nylon. Will not stretch. Comes in 36 and 44 in. lengths. ⅝ in. heel).
thick. Please order in sets of 4 (2 for each toe and 2 for each
Set of 4   Z01G720 $4.95
Custom crampon strap set.   CUSSTIX $5.95

Lightweight Camping and Mountaineering Equipment

Eastern Mountain Sports is proud of two facts: its quality camping equipment and its 176-page catalogue. First, of course, is what they have to sell and it's hard to conceive that anything could be lacking for the outdoor enthusiast. The catalogue alone is worth reading — the next best thing to being out on the range. In addition to a fine product display, many in full color, the contents include information on, for example, ski touring, trouble shooting your stove, general interest books, maps, USGS Quads, a technical climbing report, and do-it-yourself kits.

Mail Order:

Eastern Mountain Sports, Inc.
1041 Commonwealth Avenue
Boston, Massachusetts 02215

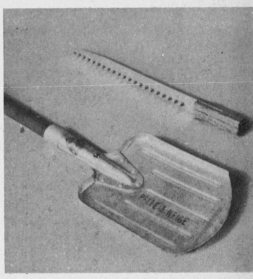

Snow Saw
Made from a high strength aluminum alloy. The blade (⅛″ by 1⅜″ by 15½″) has a tooth design developed especially for sawing hard frozen snow and ice. There are 21 teeth, each individually sharpened, and the end of the blade is tapered to a rounded point which will penetrate more easily on the forward stroke. The handle is hard mahogany and is permanently riveted to the blade. 20″ overall length. Weighs 6 oz.
SMSN21 $6.85

Collapsible Snow Shovel
A shovel with a removable 14″ ash handle and a slightly concave aluminum blade which measures 7½″ wide x 9½″ long. Blade can be used separately on the spike end of an ice axe.
1#   7 oz. $5.00

Doggie Pack
Let Fido carry his own food. 6 oz. blue waterproof nylon duck. Panniers are zippered. Leather reinforcement on the corners. Universal size.
GDP013 $20.00

Gloves

EMS Super Down Glove
Goose down filled. Outer shell is of supple deerskin. The palm, index finger and thumb are reinforced with additional layer of deerskin. Box finger construction. Lined with 2 oz. nylon taffeta. Fully baffled to prevent downshift. Knit cuff. Belt clip. Black. Pair of medium size weighs 10 oz. Sizes: XS, S, M, L, XL.
EMS1A1 $22.95

Get lost — Big Bella will lead you to safety

In Berlin, New Hampshire, when a person is reported lost in the woods, *Big Bella* is dispatched to perform her duty. Contrary to belief by many, *Big Bella* is not a bell but a fog horn type of unit which many years ago was used as a fire whistle. At the report of the lost person, the Berlin Department of Public Works springs to action, wheeling *Big Bella* into place near the last known location of the stray. Connecting her to the air compressor, while the search party is on foot, *Bella* blasts her strong horn at regular intervals into the wilderness. The wanderer, hearing her beckoning call, travels in the direction of the sound and happily into the arms of the search party.

Leisure

The Deacon Attends A Groundbreaking

Up here in the North Country we don't have too many social events so when one comes along we drop the hay making or the ditch digging or whatever, put on a clean shirt, and set sail for the merrymaking.

Such was the case recently when we hied ourselves up to Pinkham Notch (Porky Gulch) to take part in the groundbreaking ceremonies for the new Joe Dodge center of the Appalachian Mountain Club complex there. It was quite a shindig with an ex-governor of the state, officers past and present of the august A.M.C., old hutmen galore, friends and neighbors of Joe Dodge all rubbing elbows, and incidentally, bending a few.

I was asked to tell the group in three minutes who this Joe Dodge was. This proved to be an impossible task. It took four minutes. Of course, in the back woods a figure like Joe becomes a legend and many tales build up around him. Some are correct and others get stretched a bit in the telling. I tried to stick to the gospel as befits a deacon, but maybe we had just better say that the facts as presented border on the truth.

Joe started out being late for his first appointment. Planned as a Christmas present he arrived December 26th, 1898. He has never been late since, in fact he is usually ahead of time. He hiked the White Hills with his dad as a boy, and fell in love with them. Thus it was not strange, after a few years at sea and some schooling here and there, that he accepted the offer of the A.M.C. to become general manager at Porky Gulch. This proved a rather lonely post and so Joe, always a radio ham, got to thinking and asked another ham in the greater Boston area to contact one Teen Peterson living on the North Shore and ask her if she would marry him. The word came back, also by ham radio, that the answer was "Yes."

Life was simple and even more so after the children came along but Teen took it all in stride, as did the "Old Man." Anne and Brookie grew up to be stalwart citizens and skiers of repute. Meanwhile Joe continued to manage the ranch also acting as mayor, tax collector, town clerk, fence viewer, pound keeper, game warden, timber cruiser, and girl watcher, getting reelected to all jobs term after term.

He also filled numerous extracurricular posts such as chairman of the board of the Lakes of the Clouds Ferry Co., president of the White Mountain Jackass Corp. (Teen said she couldn't imagine a man better qualified on this one) and manager of the Porky Gulch Trading Co. which dealt in everything from Bear Skins to snowshoes. He also helped the ski teams at Dartmouth which earned him an honorary degree. He helped to organize the Mount Washington Observatory on the summit of the big hill and is still treasurer of that body. He's a good man with the weather and if you don't believe it just wait until you hear that he and Eight Ball Seller have gone fishing and see for yourself what kind of weather follows.

Then Joe came down out of the notch and into the sunshine. He became a hospital trustee, a vestryman at his church, a selectman of the town of Conway, and filled many other jobs too numerous to mention.

Well so much for history, a subject which always intrigued Joe by the way, and back to the ground breaking ceremonies. The committee had on hand five gold plated shovels, and so great were the number of friends and dignitaries that even so it took five shifts for everyone to get into the act. Then the shovels were auctioned off and brought $100 apiece. No better way can be found to show the esteem in which this mountain man is held by his friends.

And so today if you travel up thru Pinkham Notch you will note great activity at the site of the old trading post and a sign will tell you that here is being built a center to be known as — "The Joe Dodge Center — given by his friends and his wife Teen — Hut Manager 1927-1959."

H.H. (Bill) Whitney

P.S. If anyone reading these humble words would like to get into the act they can still do so by sending along a few bucks to the Appalachian Mountain Club, 5 Joy Street, Boston, Mass. 02108. Mark them for the Joe Dodge Center and mention this rag please.

Hosteling

In 1934, the first American Youth Hostel was established in Northfield, Massachusetts by Isabel and Monroe Smith. Today there are 31 hostels in the New England states (115 in the U.S.A.). Youth Hostels throughout the area open their doors — as they do world-wide — to those travellers seeking a place to lay their heads for a night or so. The only requirements are an AYH membership pass, sleeping bag, eating utensils and a wonderful sense of the open road. U.S. overnight fees range from $1.50 to $2.00 and in some ski hostels in season, $3.00. AYH members and pass holders may stay in any of the 4,300 hostels in 47 countries. The hostel, open to all regardless of race, religion, or economic circumstances, fosters the free exchange of experiences and ideas among people of many backgrounds. Its purpose is to help eliminate prejudices and to promote international understanding.

American Youth Hostels, Inc.
Greater Boston Council
251 Harvard Street
Brookline, Massachusetts 02146

Give Me The Hills

The author seems to have begun climbing and hauling herself up precipitous inclines about the time when most of us were casting cautious glances over the bars of our playpens. The most outstanding feature of this account of a woman's unfaltering desire to reach the topmost places of the world, is the joy and exhilaration she experiences while doing so. She emphasizes the fact that for sheer enjoyment one need not travel to the more renowned pinnacles of Europe or even our own Rocky Mountains. There are excellent "hills" right in New England which are quite as amusing (or abusing, depending on your point of view), especially if climbed during the winter.

One chapter entitled "The Four Thousand Footers in Winter," describes the ascents of seven peaks in New Hampshire. The cold, snow-filled winter months of this New England state are well-known, but Mrs. Underhill's accounts make one appreciate the intensity of these conditions.

Although not a "how-to" guide for budding mountaineers, the first-hand descriptions of the difficulties encountered will prove invaluable to the enthusiastic, but uninitiated.

Barrett S. Robbins-Pianka

Give Me The Hills
by Miriam Underhill
1971; 278 pp.
From: The Chatham Press, Inc.
        Riverside, Connecticut 06878
        $6.95

NATURAL HISTORY OF VERMONT

by ZADOCK THOMPSON

Natural History of Vermont

The charms of this book are many. Surely one of them lies in its quality of the unexpected. The author interpolates sprinklings of folklore among more objective observations (The fable of the fox and sour grapes, shows that the partiality of this animal for the fruit of the vine was understood in the days of Aesop.) Whenever required by personal knowledge, to contradict the insubstantiality of myth, he does that too. The relatively brief opening chapter, "Descriptive and Physical Geography of Vermont," predictably includes data on such phenomena as boundaries, mountains, lakes, streams, climate, and rainfall. The reader is less prepared for, but highly delighted with, wholly adventitious material on medicinal springs, sleighing, dark days, remarkable meteors and Indian Summer.

Fessenden Wilder

Natural History of Vermont
by Zadock Thompson
First Tuttle edition, 1972; 286 pp., paper
From: Charles E. Tuttle Company
        Rutland, Vermont 05701
        $3.50

Outdoor Fun

The first one published in a series of books aimed toward the young ecologist/naturalist, *Outdoor Fun* is a worthwhile learning tool.

Short, clearly illustrated articles tell about the salt marsh at work, succession of pond to forest and land erosion, to name a few.

MSH

Outdoor Fun
by Allan and Ellen Bonwill
30 pp., paper

From: Area Cooperative Educational Services
        Village Street
        North Haven, Connecticut 06473
        $1.00

A New England Simple — Uses of Powdered Starch

Powdered starch is an excellent silver polish; it also removes stains from wallpaper when nothing else will. If, when washing windows, a small lump of starch is added to the water, the dirt will be removed more easily.

Skinny-Dipping

CHARLES T. MORRISSEY

SKINNY-DIPPING has been a controversial issue in Vermont during the past two summers, and most likely it will continue to be a lively topic again this year.

Last summer a judge in Washington County sentenced a Warren man to 20 days in jail for skinny-dipping in the Mad River. The young man's father, an executive with *Life* Magazine in New York, expressed amazement in a telephone call to his son when he was told about this severe penalty. "Why didn't you try something simple," the father asked his son sarcastically, "like robbing a gas station?"

Everybody in Vermont seems to know what skinny-dipping means — swimming in the nude — and it's a rare Vermonter who hasn't experienced that thrill at one time or another. The 20-day sentence given the Warren dipper was ultimately dismissed when the state's attorney for Washington County, Kimberly Cheney, decided to drop the charges. A lot of Vermonters thought this was a wise move indeed, since the jails couldn't hold everybody who dipped occasionally in an isolated mountain stream or obscure swimming hole.

Responding to the public interest in the skinny-dipping issue, the state's attorney for Chittenden County, Patrick Leahy, offered these guidelines in a statement that received wide attention, including a story in *Time* Magazine:

1. In public areas (e.g. North Beach in Burlington) and semi-public areas: Nude bathing is not acceptable. In such instances, the officer receiving the complaint should order the person to dress. Failure to stay clothed should result in summons to Court.
2. On private land out of view of the public: The State has no legitimate interest and swimmers should be left alone.
3. In secluded areas sometimes publicly used (e.g. rivers, swimming holes, etc): If no member of the public present is offended, no disorderly conduct has taken place. If members of the public (e.g. families wishing to use the swimming area) complain, proceed as in No. 1 above.

But the part of Leahy's statement that received most attention was his explanation of how he derived these guidelines. "I ensconced myself at my family's summer farm near Montpelier during the Fourth of July weekend and researched the issue," he stated. "I began by reviewing the Norman Rockwell paintings, thoughtfully resurrected by the American Civil Liberties Union, showing such activities taking place allegedly in Vermont (along this line I was unable to either confirm or refute the persistent rumor that Vermont's number one politician, Calvin Coolidge, had also engaged in such activity within the borders of this State while subject to Vermont laws).

"I have also discussed — after grants of immunity — experiences of this nature enjoyed by some of Vermont's prosecutors, judges, law-enforcement officers and sailboat operators. After checking the Statute of Limitations, I have even reviewed past histories with some of my contemporaries during my teenage years in Montpelier. Also, each member of my office offered to investigate this matter in an undercover manner (so to speak).

"It appears that most Vermonters I've talked to have engaged in such scandalous activity at some time in their life (with the exception of a couple I didn't believe who claimed to have done so in May. Everyone knows the high probability of frostbite in May in Vermont)."

The pro dippers refer to Vermont's history to justify the innocence of nudity. They remind us that when two of Vermont's most heroic figures during the Revolutionary War, Ephraim Webster of Newbury and Richard Wallace of Thetford, swam across Lake Champlain from Fort Ticonderoga to Mount Independence in Orwell in the late fall of 1777, to deliver important dispatches without the British capturing them, they did so with their clothes bound behind their necks by cords across their foreheads. And by golly, they add, if the Vermont Bicentennial Commission re-enacts this feat in 1977, on its 200th anniversary, the swimmers should be skinny-dippers in order to be faithful to historical accuracy!

Critics of skinny-dipping who don't dismiss the whole business as dangerously immoral often complain that the practice is simply an inconvenience to others. Vermont residents, in letters to their local newspapers, have expressed dismay in recounting how they trudged through the woods to some favorite little oasis of beauty that they and only a few other people know about, and discovered the hide-away was "polluted" by someone swimming or basking in the nude.

Some dippers think their critics are simply "Peeping Toms" who "tut-tut" in disgust at nude swimming while riveting their eyes on it with complete fascination. Harpo Marx, of the famous Marx Brothers comedy team, has explained how a skinny-dipper can get rid of snoopers. In his memoir, entitled *Harpo Speaks,* Harpo recalls life on an island called Neshobe, in Lake Bomoseen, which Alexander Woollcott owned and used as a vacation retreat:

"Once I spotted a rowboat full of rubbernecks headed our way, towards the island. I stripped off all my clothes, smeared myself with mud, and went whooping and war-dancing down to the shore, making Gookies and brandishing a club. The tourists rowed away fast enough to have won the Poughkeepsie Regatta. That put an end to the snooping that season."

So far the debate about skinny-dipping has generally been good natured, and has produced some humorous stories. The late W. Arthur Simpson of Lyndonville was fond of telling about an attractive young lady in her middle 20's whose job required her to drive to farms along back-country dirt roads on hot and dusty summer days. On one particular "scorcher" in July she drove near an inviting pond in mid-afternoon, and decided to refresh herself with a quick dip into the cool waters. She piled all her clothes carefully on the bank and then waded in — and the sensation of the water enveloping her body was a complete delight. But then she heard a twig break in the underbrush along the bank, and she became very tense. Soon she heard more noises along the bank. "Who's there?" she called out nervously. A voice replied: "Henry." She couldn't tell by the timbre of the voice if Henry was a boy or a man. "How old are you, Henry?" she asked. Came back the answer: "I'm 85, dammit."

The debate about skinny-dipping can get emotional quite easily, more so when swimming in the nude and other aspects of nudity get all tangled up together. Although the issue may remain in the public eye, we hope *you* will avoid the public eye if you're a skinny-dipper. This would be one way to deflate the controversy. ∞

Reprinted by permission of the author and Vermont Life, Summer 1972 issue.

Standard Bear Paw—13 x 33

An old design which provides for excellent weight distribution, the Bear Paw is well suited for packing and hunting in the woods. The shoe is short and quite maneuverable but is not recommended for beginners.

Snowshoes

Vermont Tubbs, Inc.
18 Elm Street
Wallingford, Vermont 05773
$40.00

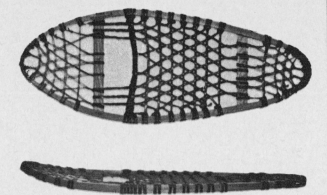

Snowmobiles – "Made in Pride Country"

According to Morton Melvin, president of *Memco*, the "Whip-It" is the only production model snowmobile manufactured in New England. Several models are offered with horsepower ratings from 32 to 40 — more than enough for normal needs. *Memco* is proud of its craftsmanship, pointing out that "Whip-It" is for those who enjoy quality snowmobiling in a safe, well-balanced machine.

Memco
Dryden, Maine 04225
Prices: $990.00 – $1200.00

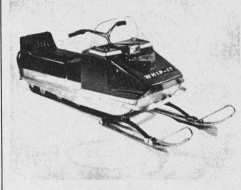

SNOWSHOES—

Snowshoes have been used in some form for 2500 years or more, their origin lost in antiquity. There is evidence of a primitive form being used in Asia and Northern Europe and Arctic regions. But only in North America has the snowshoe survived in time. The North American Indians through necessity developed this means of locomotion to such a degree that even today modern technology would be hard put to improve the design. The forest Indians found the short broad shoe best for woods and brush because of easier maneuverability and the plains Indians found the longer narrower shoe best for hunting and tracking the buffalo. Minor variations in these basic designs evolved through the years and this fine heritage of craftsmanship has left us many choices. So your choice of snowshoes will be a matter of personal preference.

SELECTING SNOWSHOES

In selecting the pair of snowshoes which is "right" for you, you should take into consideration several factors:

1. Terrain—flat, open, trails, brush
2. Snow conditions—light powder, deep, crusty
3. Usage—hunting, back packing, forestry, general recreation
4. Weight and height
5. Experience

Rawhide or Neoprene

Rawhide is still a favorite among sportsmen and recreational snowshoers. With the new finish that Tubbs has developed, the rawhide shoe is more abrasion resistant and consequently less prone to wear and sagging. The distinctive Tubbs overlay pattern on the toe and heel, give better all around purchase than the traditional fine weave style or the neoprene.

Neoprene is a synthetic material which represents the first material change in the manufacture of snowshoes in several hundred years. While not as aesthetically appealing as rawhide, neoprene resists snow build-up and consequently is comparatively lighter than rawhide under wet snow conditions. Neoprene is impervious to gasoline, oil, rodents and will generally give better wear. Professional woodsmen prefer the neoprene shoe because of its durability and low maintenance.

Leisure

Parachutes and Jump Suits

We hope you never have to use a Strong Enterprises product except by choice, but if parachute jumping is your thing, you probably already know about Strong. If you do not, you should.

Being an earthbound type with a reserve of courage I try never to put to the test, I was intrigued with the cost of parachutes. Of course, if a time comes when you need one, price is a somewhat secondary consideration, but you can buy a small reserve chute for as little as $63.90. "The Professional" is $667.90 and can go up to $685.90 if you want a harness container other than sage green. Personally I would stick to sage green to match my complexion if I ever jump.

But more than parachutes ... Strong has a tremendously wide line of accessories such as jump suits, gloves, instruments, and even decorations to pin on after you have returned to earth. If you served in World War II and envied the swaggering step of the paratroopers' boots, you can satisfy that envy with a pair of Strong Jump Boots for $31.95.

They have books and pictures on the subject, too.

RWW

Strong Enterprises, Inc.
542 E. Squantum St.
No. Quincy, Massachusetts 02171

THE 35' (T-10) MODIFIED
The largest of the surplus canopies, this parabolic shaped model is recommended for the heavier and/or older jumper and for all but the lightest students. Our tests show this canopy to descend significantly slower than either 28' or 32' "low porosity" models which are far more expensive. Your choice of steerable modification; our special Double L and TU alterations are suggested. Complete with risers, steering lines and knobs. Usually O.D. in color.
C-4 35" canopy, modified   Shipping weight 18 lbs $64.90

Camping Supplies

Just about everything for the camper at this equipment house run by members of the Gleason family.
162 page catalogue available.

Don Gleason's
Campers Supply, Inc.
Pearl Street
Northampton, Massachusetts 01060

JOHNNIE-SHOWER
Complete with shower bag, pulley and rope

$31.95
Ship. Wt. approx. 11 lbs.

JOHNNIE-HOUSE
Complete with grommeted polyethylene roof.

$23.95
Ship. Wt. approx. 10 lbs.

Here's the solution to the biggest problem of millions who love the outdoors . . . a portable private bathroom and shower that is clean, easy to set up, sturdy and inexpensive. Rustproof tubular aluminum framework fits together without tools. Center top-piece positions and locks framework for quick, rigid assembly. Wrap-around curtain is extra heavy-gauge polyethylene. Grommets in double-thick hem on all 4 edges attach to locking hooks in framework. Includes door-ties and sturdy ground stakes. (Toilet not included)

Cape Cod Compass

Each issue a collector's item.
MSH

Yankee, Inc.
Dublin, New Hampshire 03444
$1.50 yearly

Camper's Code of Conduct

Observe fire laws and use care with all fire. Park your vehicle off main roads; do not block side roads. Do not molest buildings, equipment, signs and gates. Be prepared to share your camping area with others. Leave your campsite clean. If there are no trash cans, carry your refuse out of the forest to an approved dump. Paper materials should be burned. Do not peel bark or disfigure live trees. Pets should be tied to stakes, not trees.

54   *ON AGAIN. OFF AGAIN*

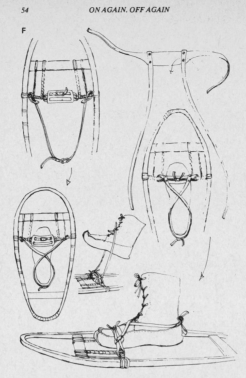

This simple *native Alaskan binding* looks difficult to manage but one soon gets the knack. *Suggested by Joe Delia*

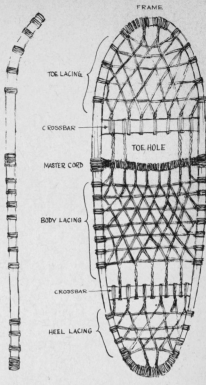

Green Mountain modified bearpaw, one of the most popular snowshoe models.

The Snowshoe Book

Anyone for snowshoeing? If so, the authors provide "a complete guide to how, why, when and where" to carry on this lost art. There was a time when snowshoes provided necessary transportation. Today it is pretty much of a hobby, in the same category as musket shooting. Snowshoeing is for those who want to enjoy the winter snows in peace and quiet.

Which snowshoes to buy? Which bindings work best? How about boots? What will it cost? Where do you go? What rations to take? How about emergencies?

These are only a few of the questions answered in this first comprehensive book on snowshoeing. Here too the reader will find chapters on the history of this age-old means of transportation, equipment and clothing, travel techniques, winter safety, races and games and much, much more.

Charles T. Letson

The Snowshoe Book
by William Osgood and Leslie Hurley
Drawings by Grace A. Brigham
1971; 127 pp., paper
From: The Stephen Greene Press
      Brattleboro, Vermont 05301
      $3.95

Did you know that a watch and a stick can be used as a compass?

An easy way to find direction is by means of a watch, stick and the sun. Hold the stick upright at the outer end of the hour hand. Turn the watch slowly until the stick shadow falls along the hour hand. South will lie halfway between the shadow and the 12 o'clock numeral. With this fixed, it will be easy to tell the other directions.

Adapted from The World Book Encyclopedia.
© 1972 Field Enterprises Educational Corporation.

Leisure

Car Magazines

Special-Interest Autos and *Hemmings Motor News* has everything for the car enthusiast. Classics, antiques, restorations, remodeling, performance specifications, how-to articles and hundreds of cars for sale pack the pages of these two magazines. Musts for buffs.

JCH

Hemmings Motor News
Bennington, Vermont 05201
Special-Interest Autos – bimonthly $6.00
Hemmings Motor News – monthly $3.50
Special combination rates available
Hemmings Motor News
Bennington, Vermont 05201

The Model A in all its glory

Antique & Classic Fords Bought and Sold
Page's Model A Garage
Haverhill, New Hampshire 03765

FRED PAGE reminisces occasionally about the first "A" he owned, a roadster, back in 1928, and many later ones including a couple he and his teenage boys fixed up in the '50's. Since then, Fred has owned literally hundreds of Model A's and other pre-World-War-II Fords.

Fixing up those cars with the boys was the start of a hobby that developed into an extensive sideline. Two years ago, after Fred retired from the American Express Company, where he was senior vice president and director, the Pages moved from New York's Greenwich Village to the Page family homestead in Haverhill, New Hampshire. Since then Fred has devoted himself fully to his hobby, which has grown to a full-time small business known as "Page's Model A Garage."

The Model A Garage is widely known among vintage Ford enthusiasts throughout the United States and Canada. The garage not only provides parts, information, repair and custom restoration services for Model A, B, and pre-War V-8 Fords but it also deals in remanufactured early Fords, some of which are perhaps better than when they were originally offered by authorized Ford dealers of the period. Owners of early Fords frequently come hundreds of miles for major service to their cars. The garage is able to supply and install such things as rebuilt engines, transmissions and rear ends for most thirty- to forty-year-old Fords. Except for the use of modern power tools and shop practices, time has been rolled back at the Model A Garage. The work in progress, the parts inventory, the parts books and reference manuals are all of another day.

Excerpted: Boston Sunday Globe
March 14, 1968

Museum of Transportation

The establishment of the *Museum of Transportation* was made possible through the generosity of the late Mrs. Larz Anderson of Brookline. Her will provided that the vast family collection of horse-drawn vehicles and antique motorcars be permanently displayed for the education and enjoyment of the public. The Museum is located in the Larz Anderson Coach House, built in 1885, and modeled after the famed Chaumont Castle in France.

From its beginning as a private collection, the Museum has grown to an active, involved institution. Its major focus is the examination of the social consequences of transportation technology; things that move man, change his life, give form to his cities, and allow him to expand the horizons of his existence.

Three periods of transportation history are presently covered in the collections: the era of the horse, the short but intriguing bicycle era, and the motorcar era. The Museum is involved in examining these eras because in them is found much relevance to the forms and patterns of life today.

Museum of Transportation
Larz Anderson Park
Brookline, Massachusetts 02146

Adults: $1.50   Children: $.75

Heritage Plantation of Sandwich

The inspiration for *Heritage Plantation* stems from the late Josiah K. Lilly's private collections. Covering seventy-six landscaped acres, there are ten exhibits, including the Round Barn (based on a similar structure built by the Shakers), the Military Museum, the Windmill, Flag collection, and exhibitions of early tools.

One of the high points of this delightful spot is the antique car exhibit, featuring thirty-five American autos, vintage 1899 to the mid-1930's. Here you'll find one of the great 1931 Duesenbergs, original price about $14,000. Also, Henry Ford's 1913 Model "T" touring car, or the beautiful 1930 "V16" Cadillac convertible that sold for $6,900.

Each car is restored to perfection, giving accent to the glory of the golden age of the automobile — an exciting story of American ingenuity.

Heritage Plantation
Sandwich, Massachusetts 02563
May 1 – October 15
Adults: $2.00   Children: $.75

Country Inns and Back Roads

This neat little book covers the inns and back roads of many parts of the U.S.A., but I couldn't resist reviewing the first ninety-four pages which discuss New England inns. (Confession: I couldn't resist the remaining 162 pages, either.)

One gets such an intimate feeling when reading about these delightful inns that whether or not you have any intention of visiting them is not important to the enjoyment of *Country Inns and Back Roads*. One of the important charms of country inns, as pointed out, is the opportunity to meet and talk to other guests in the convivial atmosphere of parlors and sitting rooms. Chandler Whipple's historic-fictional accounts of Lucian Willoughby, a Colonial innkeeper, reveal that problems facing 1972 innkeepers are miniscule compared with those of Willoughby and his wife two hundred years ago.

JCH

Country Inns and Back Roads
Editor: Norman T. Simpson
1972 Edition; 256 pp., paper
From: The Berkshire Traveller Press
        Stockbridge, Massachusetts 01262
        $3.50

Rod Ryder Engineering

Thatcher Kezer's grandson had difficulty riding his bicycle and at the same time carrying his fishing rod and reel. Neither the boy, bike nor rod were safe and secure. Grandpa changed all that. The result is Rod Ryder — a device which will keep the reel handle from engaging with the spokes of the bicycle wheel. The unit will accommodate seven different rod and reel construction designs.

Roy Ryder Engineering
241 Ferry Road
Salisbury, Massachusetts 01950
Rod Ryder – $7.95

Bicycling Tours

The following information provided by the Cape Cod Chamber of Commerce.

CAPE COD CANAL (Bicycling)

Service roads along the Cape Cod Canal provide a delightful area for bicycling enthusiasts and other recreational use, such as walking, jogging, etc. Also, to aid cyclists and pedestrians, the access roads are clearly marked.

Service Roads on *North Side* of Canal — Access Points
1. Scusset State Park
2. East side of Highway Bridge, Sagamore
3. Near Herring Brook Fishway, Bournedale
4. Northeast side of Bourne Bridge

Service Roads on *South Side* of Canal — Access Points
1. Sandwich, near the Boat Basin & U.S. Eng. Obs. Station
2. Pleasant St., Sagamore
3. Southeast side of Bourne Bridge

CAPE COD NATIONAL SEASHORE (Bicycling)

The Province Lands Bicycle Trail provides eight miles of paved bicycle trail through forests, ponds and bogs within the National Seashore.

Province Land Area Trails
1. Beech Forest Parking area to Bennett Pond
2. Bennett Pond Spur to Herring Cove Beach
3. Race Point Beach Spur to Beech Forest Parking area

Pilgrim Heights Area
1. High Head Road to Head of the Meadow Beach

The Eastham Bikeway Trail (Nauset area) provides two miles of paved trail, and the cyclist has a view of the "cedar banks", Nauset Marsh, old Nauset Coast Station, and other historical and natural history points of interest.

Nauset Area
1. Salt Pond Visitors Center to Coast Guard Beach

A New England Simple

Rust can be removed from iron or steel by rubbing vigorously with fine coal ash moistened with oil.

Bicycling Tour

Invitation to Adventure sponsors The Wandering Wheelmen, a bicycle touring group made up of 15 boys and two men who set out on two separate three-week trips during the summer. The trip originates at the *Invitation to Adventure* base camp in Ellsworth Falls, Maine. These trips are not designed to be an endurance test, but simply an opportunity to become better acquainted with your bicycle, your surroundings and yourself.

Their combination canoe/mountain climbing trips also offer a well-rounded, healthy outdoor experience for boys between the ages of ten and sixteen.

Write for more information.

Invitation to Adventure, Inc.
P.O. Box 296
Wilton, Connecticut 06897

Bikes

Bikes is the shortest title of the many new books about the popular sport of two-wheeling without a motor.

Its subtitle tells what you will find within its bright covers: "A How-to-do-it Guide to Selection, Care, Repair, Maintenance, Decoration, Safety and Fun on your Bicycle."

The author's clear drawings and interesting text make bicycles easy to understand and the open road seem so inviting.

Mary Goodrich

Bikes
by Stephen C. Henkel
1972; 96 pp.
From: The Chatham Press, Inc.
Riverside, Connecticut 06878
$4.95

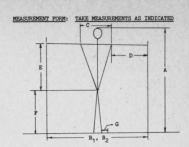

MEASUREMENT FORM: TAKE MEASUREMENTS AS INDICATED

A   HEIGHT:
B₁   ARM SPAN (TO OUTSIDE FOLDS OF WRISTS):
B₂   ARM SPAN (TO OUTSIDE OF KNUCKLES - FIST CLOSED):
C   SHOULDER WIDTH:
D   ARM LENGTH (FROM ARM PIT TO PALM JUST BEHIND KNUCKLES):
E   BACK LENGTH (FROM "LUMP" ON SPINE AT BASE OF NECK):
F   LEG LENGTH (NO SHOES, FEET TOGETHER, CROTCH TO FLOOR):
G   FOOT LENGTH (NO SHOES):
H   WEIGHT (IN LIGHT CLOTHING):
I   BODY TYPE:
     Average: similar weight distribution: hips-legs/arms-shoulders
     Type B: light hips-legs/ heavy shoulders-arms
     Type C: heavy hips-legs/ light arms-shoulders
J   NOTE ANY PARTICULAR BODY CHARACTERISTICS:

Custom-Made Bicycles: Why?

First, for maximum enjoyment, a bicycle must fit an individual as well as his clothes. No two persons have precisely the same length arms, legs, back, etc. Therefore, for a bicycle to fit properly, the dimensions of the various components will differ. The only way to get a bicycle with these "personalized" dimensions is to have it custom-made.

Second, the design of the bicycle frame; the choice of gears, brakes, tires and numerous other parts depends on what the bike will be used for — general riding, road racing, track racing or long distance touring. The better the equipment fills the need and usage, the chances are that bicycling will become a lifetime pursuit rather than a passing fad.

Many people have been turned off to the joys of the sport because of bicycle dealers who know nothing about the sport other than how to sell a bike. "Practice what you preach," I'm told. I ride as much as possible twelve months a year and know the problems a rider faces. Many of these problems can be avoided through meticulous selection and set-up of equipment.

Before building a bike, I prefer to get to know my customers. I want to know as much about them as possible — where they're going to ride, what are their physical capabilities. What I'm trying to find out is what is going to serve best the needs of the customers and give the greatest amount of satisfaction.

Components: I offer the best selection of European, Japanese and American parts available.

Measurements: Each bike is built with individual body measurements, weight and physical type in mind. (See the basic measurement form.) If a person has no experience in the sport, personal consultation is recommended.

Delivery Time: Primarily, it's a question of the work load. Delivery time varies from six weeks to six months. Quality will not be sacrificed. If a person has a special urgent need, I will try to arrange a production schedule to fit the need. But craftsmanship comes first.

Prices: Prices are subject to what is involved in terms of design, construction details and selection of components. The lowest price would be around $200 for a custom-design-built *Humberto* frame. The highest price would be just under $900 for an ultra-light, time trial bike built of space age materials. Typically, prices run between $450 and $650.

Humberto Pereira

Custom-Made Bicycles
Humberto Pereira
31 West Avenue
Essex, Connecticut 06426

Leisure

Mink Hills Post Office and General Store — Bygones Museum

Newmarket Road at Waterloo
Warner, New Hampshire 03278

The many items which have been gathered together to make up the general store museum and exhibits were not acquired in a fortnight or a year. They have been assembled over a period of many years during which time articles of yesteryear were secured by purchase or donation from attics, barns, second-hand and antique shops and as gifts from friends, interested firms and individuals. These items as they were acquired were laid aside waiting for the day when the self appointed storekeeper and postmaster would have the time, the place and sufficient "stock" to establish his own version of a general store of bygone days.

This country store is perhaps unique. It may not be an "original" country store, but it is a store museum and not a gift shop with a more or-less old fashioned "atmosphere". There is nothing for sale in the Bygones Museum.

Litter

I have, on many occasions, in this column written about the growing amount of trash to be found about the countryside. This is a problem that I feel should be brought to the attention of as many people as possible.

The trash I speak about — cans, bottles, discarded items of clothing, paper, etc., is not something left behind by hunters, fishermen or snowmobilers. This mountain of junk is being left behind by folks who picnic and camp throughout our beautiful White Mountains and other scenic spots in the North Country.

The past few summers have seen a large number of people coming to this area to camp out. The type of camper I mean does not go to a state, federal or private camp ground, but seeks out spots close to highways and waterways. This type of person, has no regard for the landowner, or the land itself. Trees are cut, fire places erected and when he leaves, the area looks like a small dump.

The following weekend he is back — or friends who have been told about the place arrive — and the campsite gets bigger and the amount of trash larger. On this goes throughout the summer so that by fall the spot has taken on the look of the local dump.

Some of these camping areas are on National Forest land but many are on private land. In some cases land owners have removed the trash at their own expense. Other people who have a feeling for the land cleaned up spots in many cases. Early this summer the 10th Special Forces, (Green Berets) spent a lot of time and manpower to clean up some of the worse spots.

It's not all the wayside campers either that are littering our countryside. There are many places where folks stop to eat a lunch and remains go into the woods when the picnic is over.

If you think I am playing this up, take a trip some weekend and get off the road a bit and you will see what I mean. You won't see this junk from the window of your car; you must walk a bit.

What is the answer to this question? Why do people abuse the great landscape they enjoy so much? Why won't folks carry out the empty cans and bottles after a few days of camping? With all the trash containers along our roadsides why must the remains of a picnic be thrown into the woods? I wish I knew the answers.

One answer, of course, is law enforcement. We have a good solid trash law in New Hampshire now, one that even provides that a judge could require the guilty persons to clean up the entire area. The

Exploring Connecticut

Whether tourist or history buff — this little book offers much.

MSH

Exploring Connecticut
by William J. Prendergast
1970; 54 pp., paper
From: The Pequot Press, Inc.
Chester, Connecticut 06412
$2.50

We Still Have Three Covered Bridges

Connecticut is one of 33 states that still have covered wooden bridges within its borders. We have three, including the one pictured above, which crosses the Housatonic River at West Cornwall. The others are Bull Bridge in Kent, and the Salmon River Bridge that spans the boundary line between the townships of East Hampton and Colchester.

For many years certain covered bridges in Connecticut were popularly supposed to be the rendezvous of "spooks." People coming upon them at night would be unmindful of the sign over the entrance "Walk Your Horses." They would hurry through at a brisk trot.

Hoboes found the covered bridges a haven, but after several had been burned because these uninvited guests wanted to warm themselves with little fires, a law banned these free hotel privileges.

A sad romantic story is still told about the old covered bridge which was formerly located in Ansonia. During the flood of 1852 a youth and maiden came upon the bridge to keep a midnight tryst. They lingered too long within its kindly shadows. The rushing water weakened the stanchions and the bridge was swept away with the lovers.

It has been many a year since the last covered bridge was built in the state. All the more reason why the three that remain ought to be cherished and preserved. What a pity, if in the name of progress they should be replaced with steel girders and concrete pillars.

---

law is good; next thing is to catch those who are doing the littering. This is not easy, believe me. In order to bring a person to court on these charges the law enforcement officer must see the act take place. This is not something that happens often. Pure rule of thumb will tell you that the litterers far outnumber the enforcement officers.

In the case of the off road campers, again the enforcement officer must see them leave the spot, for good, in order to make a case. When you talk with this type of people, they all assure you they plan to take everything with them when they leave. Of course they don't, and unless the man with the badge is hiding behind a tree when they pull out and break camp there is little he can do.

What is taking place is a move on the part of land owners to stop this type of camping. The U. S. Forest Service has, for example, put into effect a rule that does not allow roadside camping or camping beside any trail or stream, except in designated areas. This has become necessary due to the increasing use of the National Forest and the litter problem.

Private land owners who have seen their land abused have started to crack down. Several large land owners have passed the word to law enforcement groups they want no camping on their lands. In some cases they, the land owners, have regular patrols that are moving the campers out.

All this points to one thing — no regard for the other fellow's property. If those who come here from other places would follow the time honored rule — use the other fellow's land as you would your own — much of this problem would be solved. That rule has long been forgotten in recent years, however.

When I see signs of land abuse, pollution, and all else that troubles the country today, I think of the classic remark a good friend of mine made: "There is nothing wrong with the country today that less people wouldn't cure."

Paul Doherty

Reprinted with permission from the author and the Berlin Reporter, July 25, 1972.
Berlin, New Hampshire.

HABITAT

Habitat Index

A

Alcoholic Beverages 133, 134, 135, 137
Antiques 103
  bottles 101
  furniture 111
  ironware 113
  woodenware 130
Architecture 114, 115, 118, 124

B

Bags
  canvas 140, 145
The Berkshire Traveller Almanack 1973 121
Blacksmiths 114
Boats
  heating 102
  lighting 102
A Book of Cape Cod Houses 118
Brass
  lighting 102, 103, 104, 114
The Bug Book: Harmless Insect Controls 117
Buying Country Property 122

C

Candles 99, 135
Cape Ann: Cape America 119
Cheese 131, 132, 133, 135
Cider Press 136
Clocks 108, 109
  repair 111
Clothing
  canvas 140
  knitted 142
  leather 142, 145
  Shakers 144
  ski 141
Colonial Meeting-Houses of New Hampshire 118
Connecticut's Old Houses 124
Cookbooks
  breakfasts 133
  general 134
  herbs 132
  natural foods 134
  preserves 135
  Shakers 130
  special 132
  venison 138
Cooking
  fireplaces 105
  outdoor 100
  utensils 101
Copper
  lighting 99, 102
Country Stores in Early New England 139
Customs on the Table Top 134

D

*Doorways, Lanterns and Fences
  of Martha's Vineyard* 101

E

Early American Folk & Country Antiques 103
Early American Herb Recipes 132
Early American Homes for Today 118
Early American Ironware 113
Early American Wooden Ware 130
Early Houses of New England 114
*Easy Does It Furniture Restoration
  the Vermont Way* 110
Eat The Weeds 138

F

Fabrics 110, 140, 141, 142
Factory Store Guide To All New England 110
Farming
  supplies 136
Fireplaces 99
  building 105
  cooking 105
  equipment 100, 101, 102, 103
Flags 111, 116
Food 132
  apples 137
  candy 133
  cranberries 136
  farm produce 130
  ferns 136
  flour 137
  greens 136
  market 131
  natural 135, 138
  organic 133, 138
  preserves 132
  seafood 106
  smoked meat 134, 136, 139

Footwear
  leather 141, 142, 145
*The Forgotten Art of Building
  a Good Fireplace* 105
The Forgotten Art of Building a Stone Wall 121
Foundries 104
Fried Coffee and Jellied Bourbon 133
From Gunk to Glow 107
From The Galleys Of Nantucket 134
Furnishings 102, 109, 142
  kitchen 106, 109, 122, 129, 131
  repair 113
Furniture 106, 107, 108, 109, 110, 113, 123
  antiques 111
  leather 145
  plans 111, 112
  polish 109
  refinishing 107
  restoration 110
  Shakers 107, 144

G

Gardening
  insect control 117
Gardening for Health and Nutrition 138
Glass
  cutter 129
  jewelry 142
  lighting 100, 101
  stained 100

H

Hardware
  homes 101, 114, 122
Haymarket 131
Heating 99, 104, 106
  boats 102
Herbs
  cookbooks 132
Homes
  building 117, 118, 119
  hardware 101, 114, 122
  plans 119
  prefab 116, 117, 120
  restoration 117, 118
How to Build Your Home in the Woods 119
How to Mend China and Bric-A-Brac 113

I

Indian
  tobacco 140
Instruments
  precision 124
  sewage treatment 124

J

Jams, Jellies & Marmalades 135
Jewelry 108, 123, 141
  coin 140
  glass 142
Junkyard 107

L

Leather 106
  clothing 142, 145
  footwear 141, 142, 145
  furniture 145
Left-Handed Products 143
Lighting
  boats 102
  brass 102, 103, 104, 114
  copper 99, 102
  glass 100, 101
  pewter 101, 114
  restoration 110
  tin 99, 100, 101

M

Maple Syrup 133
Minerals
  slate 109
  soapstone 106
Museums
  Americana 128
  machines 128
  tools 128

N

The Natural Foods Cookbook 134
Needlecraft
  knitting 142
*The New England Meeting Houses
  of the Seventeenth Century* 115
The New England Village Scene – 1800 121

O

Old Vermont Houses 1763-1850 114
Optics 143

P

Pamper Your Possessions 102
Papers
  wall 110
Patterns
  stencilling 108
Pewter
  lighting 101, 114
Pharmaceuticals 141
A Pictorial History of the Shelburne Museum 128
Pill Crusher 143
The Pine Furniture of Early New England 111

Q

Quilt Making 112

R

Recipes
  applesauce 130
  apple wine 133
  cheese dish 134
  chokecherry jam 135
  drying apples 131
  maple treat 132
  preserving acorns 138
  punch 134
  rum drink 137
  salted mackerel 106
  sauerkraut 134
  venison mincemeat 138
Recollections of Old Stonington 113
Refinishing
  furniture 107
Restoration
  furniture 110
  homes 117, 118
  lighting 110

S

Sewage Treatment
  instruments 124
  system 125
Shaker Recipe Book 130
Shakers
  clothing 144
  cookbooks 130
  furniture 107, 144
Signs 120
Stores
  country 107, 131, 137, 139
  factory 110, 140, 141, 142
Stoves 104, 106
Supplies
  building 115, 120, 123
  drafting 106
  farming 136

T

Tin
  lighting 99, 100, 101
Tobacco
  Indian 140
Tools
  cutting 128, 129
  hand 125, 126, 127, 128
  museums 128
  power 124
  precision 127
The Transcendental Boiled Dinner 132

V

The Venison Book 138

W

Wall
  free-standing 127
  papers 110
  stencilling 110
Weaving
  rugs 107
Winemaking 133, 135

Y

Yankee Magazine 112
The Yankee Pioneers – A Saga of Courage 121
The Yankee Shun Pike 124

FirePot — A potbellied version of Ben Franklin's stove

Free standing ceramic *FirePots,* designed on a potter's wheel and fired in a kiln with rough, rich surface texture finished in earth tones, is their trademark. Hand wrought screens, andirons and flues are custom-made extras. Brochure available.

Strawberry Bank Craftsmen, Inc.
P. O. Box 475
Little Compton, Rhode Island 02837

O/A Dimensions:
24" diam. x 32" high

Opening:
17" high x 17" wide

Weight:
175 lbs. approx.
225 lbs. crated
$290* f.o.b. Little Compton

O/A Dimensions:
30" diam. x 34" high
(will go through 28" door)

Opening:
13" high x 19" wide

Weight:
250 lbs. approx.
400 lbs. crated
$395* f.o.b. Little Compton

GENERAL SPECIFICATIONS:

Material:
Silicon Carbide

Fuel:
Wood, Coal, Charcoal

Installation:
8" flue pipe for IGLOO &

TEPEE
10" flue pipe for BEACON tapering to 7" Roof Jack Assembly or existing flue

Colors:
Slate Grey
Woodland Brown
Smoke White

Candlemaking

Tour a candlemaking factory and watch experts dipping, molding, painting, decorating and wicking candles — using the same techniques colonials employed.

A New England Simple

If you wish to keep a candle burning all night — put powdered salt on the candle, until it reaches the black part of the wick. In this way a mild and steady light may be kept through the night, using just a small piece of candle.

Lanterns, Lamps and Sconces

Heritage Lanterns in Yarmouth, Maine, are still making handcrafted, solid copper reproductions of early American lighting fixtures.

We were especially attracted to a post-top lantern with an unusual middle section insert of amber seedy glass. It is called "Boston Post 42" and is still to be seen on the streets of Boston. As a tribute to the quality of our tastes [which we have great difficulty satisfying] it is their most expensive lantern @$238. But they have many, many more that range down to a low of $35.

Their catalogue is worth a review, as they have some designs we have not encountered elsewhere.

RWW

Heritage Lanterns
Sea Meadows Lane
Cousins Island
Yarmouth, Maine 04096

Essex Forge

The clock has stopped at *Essex Forge* where tin and wrought iron is lovingly shaped into decorative, functional pieces for the home. The resourcefulness of early New England craftsmen is no better displayed than in the products from this forge.

For candle $100.00
Electrified $120.00
Essex Forge
Dennison Road
Essex, Connecticut 06426

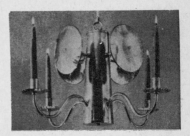

NO. 500. "THE NEW BEDFORD WHALER". Unique four arm chandelier with reflectors; original hung in master's cabin of an 18th century whaler. Center body was filled with sand to hold the lamp steady. Made for natural candles or wired for flame lamps with wax candle sleeves.

Finishes: All over bright tin, or black with bright tin reflectors

Dimensions: 14" h., 24" spread

Habitat

100

The Village Forge & Tin Shop

The tinsmith, once an important and busy tradesman, is today a rarity. These tinsmiths of Clinton are restoring an art which is part of the past — and doing it, with the skill of the 18th century craftsmen. The *Village Forge* offers a line of candle sconces reproduced in an authentic early 1800's manner. A handsome replica of a Nantucket Whaler lamp used in the galley of whaling ships is also one of their prized items. In addition to these and other pieces, the *Village Forge* makes a charcoal lighter which will get your outdoor grille glowing with no odor, taste or fuss in ten minutes or less. Also available is a grille holder for indoor fireplace cooking.

Village Forge & Tin Shop
Clinton, Connecticut 06413

Shipping charges extra

Lace Wall Sconce with Mirror Reflector 5" high $22.00

Charcoal Lighter, 12" high x 8" diameter — $3.75

Hooded Sconces, 12" x 4½" wide — $11.25 each, $22.00 pair

Nantucket Whaler Lamp, 14" wide x 13" high — $125.00

Functional Sculpture

Employing the "copper foil technique" first used by Louis Tiffany in the early 1900's, Richard MacDonald creates jewel-like sconces, candle-holders and lamps from stained glass sheets and chunks of hand-blown glass.

His future plans include one of a kind free standing sculptures, architectural walls and room dividers.

About the "copper foil technique", he writes: "Thin copper strips are wrapped around each piece of glass, then soldered into place. This allows for a wider range of forms, as it frees the glass from the cumbersome extruded lead cames used in two dimensional stained glass work."

Richard J. MacDonald
Wall Point, Lobster Cove
Boothbay Harbor, Maine 04538

Candleholder 7" high $40.00

Table Sconce 6½" high $40.00

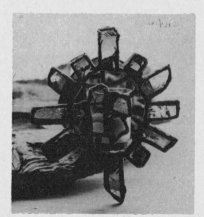

Star Wall Sconce with Mirror Reflector 7" high $26.00

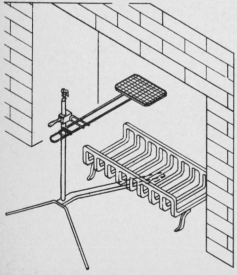

EZ Way Grille Holder, $14.95 each — $19.50 with grille

A New England Simple — To Remove Scorch Spots

To remove a scorch spot from linen, wet the spot and lay in the hot sun all day. Then wet again and repeat until spot disappears. A little chlorine water may be needed.

Habitat

Doorways, Lanterns and Fences of Martha's Vineyard

A charming photographic essay which might be of particular interest to anyone involved in building a colonial type home in which they wish to incorporate authentic detailing.

Gwen Orton-Jones

Doorways, Lanterns and Fences
of Martha's Vineyard
by Edith Blake
1969; 51 pp., 70 photographs
From: Vineyard Press
Vineyard Haven, Massachusetts 02568
$3.50 cloth; $1.95 paper

Lanterns

Down through the ages man has always been a complete fumbling fool in the dark, and therefore tried to overcome the situation as best he could with lamps. At first they were nothing more than saucers of animal or vegetable oil with a piece of rag for a wick. Later came candles and kerosenes.

In order to keep the lamps from being blown or splashed out, lanterns were used as containers. Some of these were hanging lanterns, and some were hand-held; some were heavy poop lanterns, and others were the kind that cows kicked over in barns.

Early lanterns had iron sides punched with holes. The holes let out the light and the iron sides kept out the wind. A similar iron-sided lantern had no holes, only a door by which the amount of light could be varied. This was called a "dark" lantern and proved an excellent tool for burglars wishing to sneak about undetected in the dark. After the use of glass became more prevalent, the bull's-eye lantern came into existence. This had a lens and cast a beam of light in the manner of flashlights.

Much later the calcium light or limelight was introduced. This was made by an oxygen-gas flame directed against a cylinder of quick-lime, heating the lime to a blazing brilliance. Hence the term "being in the limelight."

On Martha's Vineyard for many years there were no streetlights, and when they were installed it was only on the main streets of each town. Along the other streets, neighbors got together and contributed to the purchase of a lantern and then shared the tending of the lamp as well as its light.

When that wonder of wonders, the electric streetlight was erected, the lovely old lanterns were left to rot and some were reputed to have been dumped in Edgartown harbor. More times than not, some citizen on a clean-up binge would take them down and add them to the pile of growing junk in his barn.

In this age of the pseudo-antique many of these lanterns have been resurrected, electrified, and now serve as front door lights. Some of them still have the little crossbars with the buttons on the ends which held the lamplighter's ladder as he tended the lamp.

◆

Nothing astonishes men so much as common sense and plain dealing.

Ralph Waldo Emerson

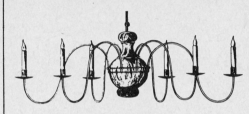
Wrought Iron and Tin

Doug Ryan: A man with strong opposition to progress and newfangled ways should have lived in another era. His work reflects the pride once taken in a man's labors — work done for the love of perfection.

He works in a carriage shed that he built himself, true to the style of the 19th century. It is a copy of the one now at Mystic Seaport. Constructed by using mortise, tenon joints and handmade "trunnels" instead of nails, 6 X 6 inch timbers, and ship lap joint siding, it will stand the test of time. When finished, he laid the bricks for the forge inside, where he makes early American iron and tin utensils and lighting fixtures. "Metal today," Ryan says, "is mostly stamped, rolled or molded with dies and presses because it is cheaper and quicker." He, however, uses no dies — all metal is hand hammered and fashioned. Doug Ryan works on special order only. He also does repairs on originals, the results of which are well worth the wait. Brochure available.

By appointment only.

Tinsmithing — one of New England's Oldest Trades

Using colonial tools and methods on pewter and tin, David Williams fashions lanterns, chandeliers, trays and other replicas of Early American tin work. Much of this is done from pictures of original colonial pieces. Some items are exact replicas, while others combine the detail of several.

"I make everything to order and sell direct to my customers only," he writes. "It takes anywhere from two to six weeks depending on my work load, the nature of the item requested (and sometimes on the humidity). Prices range from a minimum order of $10.00 to about $200.00, but I also produce giant chandeliers which can cost as much as $1500.00."

Once in a great while an exquisite example of Early American artistry comes to light.

This sconce is based on one shown in Wallace Nutting's collection; its simplicity is captivating.

#199 WALLACE NUTTING SCONCE

Candle $20.00
Electrified $28.00

Antique Bottles

Two New Hampshire couples with the ingenuity indigenous to this area have made a hobby into two profitable businesses. Guy and Betty Gosselin, and Janet and Lee Vincent are glass bottle enthusiasts whose growing collections were overrunning their homes. As a solution, several years ago, they founded *Antique Bottles* in Gorham.

Business was going well in the sale of their finds, but still . . . what to do with those broken pieces of bottles they found? You can't very well sell shards, even if they are old and rare, but you can, if you're clever, make them into electric lamps. The process took some time to perfect, but with the help of Guy Gosselin's glass smasher invention and contributions from other "diggers," production of the wooden framed glass inlaid lamps was under way.

Today, both businesses are successful, and the lamps are selling in *Antique Bottles*, as well as by special orders for individuals, motels, restaurants, etc. Write to them for prices.

The name Diogenes, incidentally, was selected for their bottle lamps in memory of the Greek Diogenes who went through life with a lighted lantern looking for an honest man. Good luck to Guy and Betty and Lee and Janet.

Claudia

Habitat

Plenty of Light — But No Genies, from Aladdin Lamps

The vagaries of electric service aside, no home or boat should be without the warmth and soft light of an oil-fired lamp. Aladdin provides lamps that convert from electricity to kerosene in seconds.

In New England these lamps, shades, parts and a line of portable boat heaters are available from:

RWW

Faire Harbour Boats
44 Captain Peirce Road
Scituate, Massachusetts 02066

23000

Height —	18-5/8''
Shade Ht. —	7¾''

Three Shades
C — Cabin Shade
D — Duck
W — White
Electric Converter Available

Mantle Lamp 23000 — $45.50 plus postage

W 6 — The Six-sided Light
$95.00

Deluxe
2300

Beautifully designed, solid brass or chrome finished bowls.

Choice of cranberry red, milk glass white or mint green glass shades, in attractive swirl design. Specify color

All other features are the same as Standard Lamp.

Height —	23¼''
Shpg. Wt. —	9 lbs.

Deluxe 2300 — $62.50 plus postage

TABLE LAMP
MODEL B-139M
Shade Standard
Height — 23''

Table Lamp B-139M — $29.75 plus postage

Colonial Hardware

Tucked away in towns and villages of New England are craftsmen of rare ability, proud of carrying on a skill long established, which might be lost lest persons like the Ridingers do not continue it. *S. Wilder & Co.,* founded in 1836, produces reproductions of colonial hardware — door knockers, sconces, and light fixtures — each tagged to indicate what it is and where it originated. All are solid copper or brass and have the mark of authenticity.

S. Wilder & Co., Inc.
400 Washington Street
Holliston, Massachusetts 01746

Pamper Your Possessions

This book is an authoritative, timesaving and lively guide to the care of your most treasured possessions. Step-by-step instructions are offered on the cleaning and preparation of most every valuable furnishing, implement, decoration or material to be found in an American home. What is the proper method of cleaning lace? Of cleaning crystal? Should you use wax on fine hardwood? What are the "enemies of silver?" How does excessive dryness — or wetness — affect objects in your home? These and hundreds of other questions regarding hard and soft woods, musical instruments, porcelain, lacquerware, marble, silk, linen, glass, gold, brass, silver, pewter, paper and leather, to name some of the subjects, are answered by the author.

From the Book Jacket

Pamper Your Possessions
by Veva Penick Wright
Illustrations by Grambs Miller
1972; 130 pp.
From: Barre Publishers
Barre, Massachusetts 01005
$6.95

A New England Simple — Smoky Lamps

Coal oil lamps that are subject to smoking may be improved by putting from two to three tablespoons of coarse salt into them. This will make the light brilliant and clear, keep the wick clean, and prevent smoking.

Fireplace Equipment

Do you get cold feet in bed in winter? There's a brass bed-warming pan for people like that at *Lemee's Fireplace Equipment.* There's also a lot of other "comfy" things for people decorating their homes with early American appurtenances. Catalog available.

Lemee's
Route 28
Bridgewater, Massachusetts 02324

Brass Bed Warming Pan	$19.95	No. BW-200
Wall Mirror	$ 7.95	No. 91
Eagle	$ 4.50	No. 90
Wood Box	$21.95	No. BB-100

No. BB-100 BRASS WOOD BOX Sturdily constructed in wood and covered on three sides and top with embossed solid brass. English courtyard scenes. 16" long, 10" deep, 11" high. Shipping wt. 12 lbs.

No. 90 EAGLE - Complete with screws for easy mounting. Finished in Gold or Satin Black. 19" long. Shipping wt. 2 lbs.

No. BW-200 BRASS BED WARMING PAN. – With wood handle. 36" long. 10-1/2" dia. Shipping wt. 5 lbs.

No. 91 – WALL MIRROR (Flying Eagle) - A classic in American design. Finished in Satin Black or Gold. Complete with mirror. 17-1/2" high, 13-1/2" wide. Shipping wt. 9 lbs.

Brass Lanterns

If you want a brass lantern — indoors or outdoors, wall, post, table or swag — try *The Brass Lantern*. They have assorted designs, all handmade with candle holder instead of electrified socket if you like. Satisfaction's guaranteed or your money's refunded upon return of the lantern. All handmade lanterns will be signed and dated inside by the craftsman to add to their heirloom quality. Your name as purchaser may be included too if you wish.

Fred Welsh

The Brass Lantern
353 Franklin Street
Duxbury, Massachusetts 02332

THE NIGHT WATCH

Indoor/outdoor wall, table, indoor swag, or post light. The combination of polished brass, antique rippled glass in amber or clear, and unusual square design, makes this lantern a charming addition to your home. This has been our first and most popular light because of its beauty, versatility and reasonable price.
8"Sq. X 15" High

THE BRASS LANTERN PRICE LIST

ITEM (Electrified)	POSTPAID
The Night Watch	
Wall Light	$27.00
Table or Post Light	$32.00
Swag (with 12' brass plated chain)	$37.00
The Night Watch II	
(Larger Post Light, 9" x 9" x 22")	$45.00
Nash's Lantern	$78.00
The Villager	$52.00
The Binnacle - - Post Light	$39.50
Also available as Wall Light or	
Table Light with legs	$39.50
The Riverboat	
Wall Light	$60.00
Post Light	$65.00
The Americana (12" x 12" x 28" high)	$95.00
The Americana II (14" x 14" x 36" high)	$130.00

All lanterns specified for outdoor use are weatherproof. Please specify if you wish a candle holder instead of electrified socket.

THE RIVERBOAT

Indoor or outdoor wall light. This distinctive lantern, although basically handcrafted of solid brass, has copper cross bars. It would serve well by the front door or as a decorative addition inside your home. Antique rippled glass in any color or frosted glass is recommended.
9"Sq. X 18" High

Early American Folk & Country Antiques

Mr. Raycraft states that his purpose in writing this book was to provide some insight into the field of collecting country and folk antiques as it exists today, including information useful for both neophyte and advanced collector. Being a searcher-after (should that be seeker-after?) myself, I found the book fairly interesting, but limited. The author's concern is mainly with 19th century furniture and artifacts. The former encompasses such essentials as dry sinks, benches, chests, chairs and tables, as well as such curios as pie-safes and salt licks. The latter category is broken up into four groupings: country kitchen antiques, early artificial lighting, country store antiques, and a "potpourri" — samplers, tin plaques of Lincoln, etc. Of these, the kitchen, store and lighting sections are the best, due mainly to the illustrations. Their subject material is varied, interesting and the group composition is well arranged for comparisons. The photography is excellent and the line drawings good. The actual text of the book as far as it goes is informative, and it doesn't pretend to be encyclopaedic, but the information could be better balanced — there is quite a description of dipping candles, but no description of how candles were made in candle molds!

Anne Ward

Early American Folk & Country Antiques
by Donald R. Raycraft
Sketches by Carol M. Raycraft
Photographs by Rick Imig & Jerry Hyman

1972; 148 pp.
From: Charles E. Tuttle Company
    Rutland, Vermont 05701
    $7.15

Men hang out their signs indicative of their respective trades: shoemakers hang out a gigantic shoe; jewelers, a monster watch; and the dentist hangs out a gold tooth; but up in the mountains of New Hampshire, God Almighty has hung out a sign to show that there He makes men.

Daniel Webster

Fireplace Screens

Using only the finest quality wire cloth, hand-clinched to a frame and painted with a semi-gloss black lacquer, *The John P. Smith Company* makes custom-built fireplace screens. These will be made to your dimensions *plus* one inch to each side and one inch on top to assure you of safe and proper coverage of the fireplace opening.

Prices vary according to the size ordered — send the proper dimensions and they'll quote a price for you.

The John P. Smith Co.
174 Cedar Street
Branford, Connecticut 06405

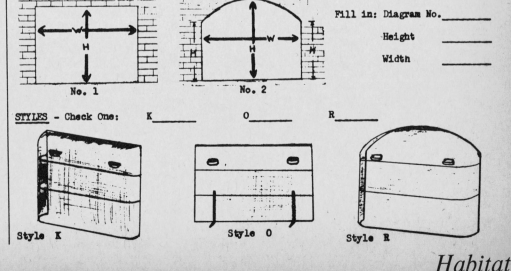

TO PLACE YOUR ORDER: Please recheck your dimensions according to appropriate diagram.

No. 1   No. 2

Fill in: Diagram No. _____
    Height _____
    Width _____

STYLES - Check One: K _____   O _____   R _____

Style K   Style O   Style R

Habitat

THE IDEAL BANQUET

A Plain Range, Easily Kept Clean

THIS NEW FAMILY RANGE
POSSESSES EVERY MODERN CONVENIENCE OF MERIT

GUARANTEED

Perfect in

Construction

and Operation

WE CAN FURNISH
Complete Gas Attachments for Baking, Broiling and Boiling; also Warming Ovens, Water Fronts of Iron or Brass, and Several Styles of Mantel Shelves

LARGE OVEN, REMOVABLE NICKEL RAILS, DIVIDED CENTERS
and Many Other New and Desirable Features of Merit. The Coal or Wood Grates may be drawn out through the front without disturbing the fire-box linings

PORTLAND STOVE FOUNDRY CO.
PORTLAND, MAINE

Portland Stove Foundry Co.

Come with us ... to a more pleasant day for a moment — just in your mind's eye. You're a child again and you've been out walking on one of those delightfully cold and still winter's nights. There's not a hint of a breeze and the stars seem so close you could almost reach up and touch them. The silence is so intense ... only marred by the happy crunch, crunch of the snow underfoot as you approach the kitchen window of your home.

You open the door and are greeted by a delicious warmth, not the sterile warmth of today's homes, a regal warmth with the burnt ochre smell of a real wood fire in the Franklin Stove.

The rest of the family is already gathered around the stove watching the kaleidoscope of infinite patterns traced by the friendly flame. They make room for you to warm yourself and you settle before the fire with happy thoughts of a warm drink and perhaps roasted chestnuts and some good talk before bedtime. All's right with the world.

Poor man indeed who can't summon up remembrance of such a memory. Too bad for today's generations that our preoccupation with chrome plate and plastic should deny them the pleasure of occasions like this.

The Franklin Stove has warmed the heart and hands of men great and small since this country was founded.

You can make this American tradition a part of your home. *The Portland Stove Foundry* has copied original patterns dating back to Revolutionary times in order to offer a complete line of authentic reproductions of the most famous and popular models.

Plain Box Stove $58.00
Ideal Banquet Stove
  Prices from $199.95 up to $549.00

Plain Box Stove

Early American Lighting Fixtures

Only the very best materials and craftsmanship are used in creating these authentic brass and copper reproductions of early American lighting fixtures.

A favorite is the Williamsburg Post Lantern, patterned after the giant street lanterns used in colonial days. Hand-turned or natural bark cedar posts are available at extra cost. Send for catalogue and price list.

Available at reasonable prices, they will add charm and distinction to any home.

R. Ingram Manufacturing Co.
Kelsey Hill Road
Deep River, Connecticut 06417
Post Lantern, Model No. 140 $68.00

Model No. 140 Post Lantern

Over-all height is 34" and lantern is 19" square. The post sleeve is 3½" in diameter. Large 12" frosted chimney will accommodate a 200 watt bulb. The lantern may be cleaned and serviced by the large door at side. Shipping weight 35 lbs.

Zack Gould — Itinerant Mason

Zack Gould "goes where the work is," building traditional fireplaces along the firebox and throat to smoke shelf design put down by Count Rumford (circa 1796). Zack writes:

"I'm more interested in doing good work than in monetary reward, so this gives me the freedom to 'barter' my fee. A pretty simplistic approach, I know, but then I live quite simply and have honestly met some nice people this way. I can pretty well sum up my feeling for this work with a quote by John Ruskin, found in the opening page of an old Audels Builders Guide.

" 'When we build, let us think that we build forever. Let it not be for present delight nor for present use alone. Let it be such work as our descendants will thank us for, and let us think, as we lay stone on stone, that a time is to come when those stones will be held sacred because our hands have touched them and that men will say, as they look upon the labor and wrought substance of them, See! This our father did for us'."

Suggested by Kathy Carrigan

Zack Gould
Sutton Island
Southwest Harbor, Maine 04679

The Forgotten Art of Building a Good Fireplace

The author feels that fireplaces built in modern times are not constructed as well as they were in the old days, when heating of the house and cooking of meals were dependent upon their efficiency. (There are surely many who will agree, as they struggle to get a fire going while smoke billows out into the room!)

Count Rumford, born a farmer's son in Massachusetts, was knighted by King George III of England because of his many contributions to society through his "scientific imagination and persistence." He was often compared to Benjamin Franklin. Count Rumford wrote the first book on fireplace design in 1795 and Mr. Orton feels his basic principles cannot be improved upon.

The book contains diagrams of fireplaces, showing front and side elevation, and giving plans and proper proportions for the construction of fireplaces and chimneys.

A.C. Ambrose

The Forgotten Art of Building a Good Fireplace
by Vrest Orton
1969; 60 pp. paper
From: Yankee, Inc.
Dublin, New Hampshire 03444
$2.50

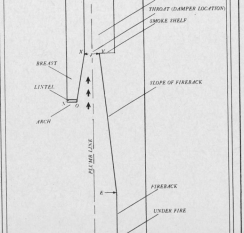

Fireplace Cooking

Since the start of summer backyard barbecue cooking, it was only a hop and skip to using indoor fireplaces during the winter months. It's often a necessary step, speeded up by electrical shortages and visits of tropical or snow storms.

What to do when your electric range won't function? That good old fireplace offers the handy, sensible, appropriate solution. Many of today's builders are putting fireplaces back into the kitchen, where they used to be in the days when fireplaces offered more than companionable warmth.

My fireplace cooking really began on the night of the great Atlantic Coast blackout. Prior to that, the four fireplaces in our 1740 Cape were used primarily for heat, the central heating not being up to the job.

It was dinner time and nothing worked. There were no lights, stove, plumbing or sink water. The refrigeration would only last just so long. Others along the coast were in the same boat. Some solved their dinner problems by streaming to restaurants that had their own generators. Others scurried around making peanut butter and jelly sandwiches by flashlight. Some mechanical types hooked up gas-powered lawn mowers to power generators temporarily.

At our house, we turned the emergency into a lark. All available candles were lit, the fireplace was stacked with quick-burning wood; the ornamental fireplace cookware was washed with water from our dug well. We poured a drink and waited for our first fireplace delicacies. Broiled chicken, cooked on a trivet over glowing coals; baked potatoes wrapped in foil under the ashes, and simmered green beans bubbling hot from the cauldron. We finished up with boiled coffee and satisfied smiles.

It was so much fun, we didn't wait for the next blackout but continued to use the fireplace, all the time broadening the range of fireplace cooking possibilities.

Pea soup, simmered four days over a slow-burning fire has a delectable smoky flavor; steak, charred over a wood fire surpasses any Tappan broiler. Waffles in an old waffle maker supply just the right touch for a Sunday night supper.

Friends who also like fireplace cooking make a hash that can't be beat and I already know that homefries done in a long-handle skillet make leftovers a treat. There are many ways to cook eggs, and most cuts of meat can be done in the fireplace. Vegetables are a little more difficult since most don't adapt to frying, but with a cauldron you can steam, simmer or boil.

For snacks, popcorn over hot coals has a marvelous smell, and encourages a camaraderie not likely to come from electrical contrivances.

There are all shapes and sizes of authentically reproduced fireplace cookware available today. A trivet, hanging pot and skillet will do for a start. Then, there's the reflector oven with its spit and drip spout. Friends cooked a Thanksgiving turkey in one of these. It took 22 hours, a mouth-watering aroma permeating the house, and was delicious.

My first attempt with a reflector oven was two ten-pound beef roasts, and even without the benefit of salt or pepper, they were simply mouthwatering. The meat cooked in just over three hours in front of a very fast burning fire, the spit being rotated periodically. The beef was served with 30 potatoes roasted in a bed of ashes, a salad, ale, apple pie, coffee and herb bread. Now, if I could just get my fireplace bake oven to work, I'd be all set for a new cooking adventure.

Sally G. Devaney

A New England Simple

Sometimes new kettles have an iron taste. To remove this, fill it with water and boil a handful of hay in it. This hay-water can also be used to sweeten wooden and tinware.

Habitat

Wood Products

Wood, Wood, Wood — tables, chopping blocks, toast tongs made from birdseye maple, butternut and walnut.

Adams also manufactures a group of engineering things — tripods, T-squares, straight edges and levelling rods, but only on a contract basis.

**J.K. Adams Company
Dorset, Vermont 05251**

4" x 3-1/2" x 3-1/4" $ 8.00

DESK CALENDAR

butternut
ICE CHESTS

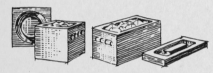

Cube. 4 tray capacity	$ 29.00
Cube. 10 tray capacity	$ 48.00
Longboy. 4 tray capacity	$ 32.00

Pine Furniture

A hand-rubbed finish, unique in these days of mass production, is offered by these makers of good New England pine furniture. Visit their workshop for substantial savings, or write telling them what you need and they'll quote a price.

**Colonial Vermont, Inc.
Shelburne, Vermont 05482**

Soapstone

Griddles, bootdriers, bun baskets, tables, carving stone and five varieties of stoves.

**Vermont Soapstone Co., Inc.
Perkinsville, Vermont 05151**
Stove $340.50 + shipping charge
Round Copper & Soapstone Griddle (12")
$18.85 + shipping charge

Soapstone is a granitelike rock (one formed under intense heat) which later was altered by hot, aqueous solutions containing silica and carbons. The result was a talc-carbonate rock, quite soft and greasy to the touch, and one which has several unusual and useful properties.

Soapstone and its close relative, talc, are found in a large area of Vermont ranging from Whitingham to Troy. Important quarries were being operated by 1842 at Grafton, Chester, Bridgewater, Plymouth, Bethel and Troy.

Commercial use of soapstone began here in about 1825 when water pipes, two and three feet long, were cut from three and four-inch blocks of soapstone and bored hollow. The finished pipe sold at the amazing figure of 6 cents per foot.

Because of the stone's great ability to absorb and retain heat, and its softness which allowed it to be worked easily, it was used as fireplace hearths and facing stone, as Franklin stove liners, for foot warmers, stoves, door sills and sinks.

While it is still in demand for its originally-discovered virtues, because of its astonishing heat-absorbing qualities the old stone may have an exciting future in space travel.

Courtesy of Vermont Life

BUTCHER BLOCKS

Great Butcher Block – without casters	$235.00
with casters	$250.00
Little Butcher block with knife	$ 12.50

end grain maple
CUTTING BLOCKS

8-3/4" x 7" x 2"	$ 8.50
same with magnet & knife	$ 9.75
10-1/2" x 8-3/4" x 2-1/4"	$ 11.00
same with magnet & knife	$ 13.00
12" x 10-1/2" x 2-1/2"	$ 15.00
same with magnet & knife	$ 17.50

◆

A New England Simple

Cockroach destroyer: A simple, harmless and most effectual remedy for driving away cockroaches is finely powdered borax. Sprinkle roaches' inhabit, and you will find that they will all leave. To be effective, continue its use for a few weeks, renewing every two days. It will not fail.

◆

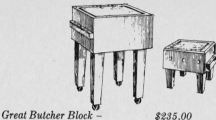

Dodges
Improved

Size: 16" x 21" x 29" High.
Weight: 225 lbs. Approx.

One of the favorite of the soapstone stoves. We still find many in use after a great number of years service.

Griddles

"A Stones Throw From the Best Pancakes". Our griddles are an old cooking item that have never been beaten. They make a light fluffy pancake of golden brown color. When the griddle is heated to the proper temperature (a drop of water dances when dropped on the surface) many pancakes may be cooked quickly. Never needs grease! Used correctly they give many years of superior service.

Steaks, hamburgs and omelettes may be cooked, also, resulting in a new, natural taste treat.

The griddle may be wiped clean with a damp cloth, or cleaned by rubbing with salt and a coarse cloth. If the color changes through cooking, it may be easily brought back to the original by a light sanding.

The more the griddle is used, the better it works!

Casco Bay Trading Post

So many good leather items that it's hard to list one — send for their catalog. The old-fashioned apple parer is one of the non-leather items which is particularly interesting.

**Casco Bay Trading Post
Freeport, Maine 04032**

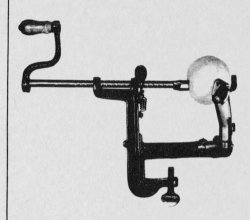

Apple Parer

Your mother used one — so did your grandmother. Here's a great rig to speed your "apple pie making," and besides, it's fun to use. In just five (5) seconds it will peel, core, and slice an apple to absolute perfection. So easy to work, even a child can use it.

Price: $5.95 plus 75c.

━━━━━━━━━━ ◆ ━━━━━━━━━━

**Embassy Seafoods, Inc.
P.O. Box 165
Gloucester, Massachusetts 01931**

Capturing the ocean-fresh taste of seafood is their business — and pleasure. Fish and lobster come from colorful Gloucester and the North Atlantic fishing boats which moor nearby. Embassy starts with just-caught delectable goodness.

Price list available

5 lb. pail Salted Mackerel $8.50 ppd.

Freshening salt mackerel: Salt Mackerel must always be freshened before cooking. Tastes differ in regard to the degrees of freshness required. From a few hours to twelve to forty-eight hours may be allowed, according to personal taste. The fish should be put in a large amount of fresh water, meat side down, and if convenient, raised a few inches from the bottom of the vessel, that the salt may drop away from the fish as fast as extracted. Change the water several times. For broiling or frying the fish should be freshened somewhat more than for boiling or baking with cream or cooking in any way with milk, as milk is very efficient in covering up the salty flavor.

Salt Mackerel Fried

Embassy Fillets, butter, tomato, lemon, flour.

Freshen the mackerel. Roll in flour and fry in hot butter. Garnish with quarters of fresh tomatoes and lemon. Serve with potatoes and desired vegetables and hot biscuits.

Salt Mackerel Baked

Embassy Fillets, small piece of butter, 1 pint milk or cream.

Freshen Fillets, then lay in a baking pan or earthen dish. Add the milk (or cream) and bake until milk is nearly gone, leaving simply a thin juice. Two minutes before serving, add the butter. This with the milk makes a thin sauce you pour over the fish when it is on the platter.

Habitat

Weston Village Store

Remember the doorbell on Grandma's front door — circa 1920? One quick twist of the shiny knob set up a jarring vibration that lasted an eternity — it seemed. It was guaranteed to bring the whole household to the door including the soundest sleeper. Robert Ballard, Prop. of the *Village Store*, will show you how it works as well as many of his other fascinating, timeless products.

Catalogue available.
Weston Village Store
Weston, Vermont 05161

Grandma did. Now some folks have fancy gadgets, but we prefer the pure and simple doorbell. No wires, no electricity, just a bell - - guaranteed to rouse you to your door for many melodious years.

$4.25

MOLD

Tin candle molds just like the ones our New England forefathers used to make.

two holder
$5.95

TANKARDS
to use and to collect

Armetale is a superior blend of 10 metals that looks exactly like pewter but which is extremely durable and light of weight. It is cast in sand, resulting in an aged and individual looking product. We find hot wine something special in these tankards. Holds about 8 ounces.

$7.95

GRANDMA SET

These kitchen utensils are here presented for your perusal. Grandma kept this perfectly sized knife and fork in close proximity at all times. We have a lot to learn from Grandma and we urge you to start with these. $4.95

mushroom candles

Unusual, perfectly formed candles. Many sizes and combinations available.

$1.75 ea.

Weston, Vermont 05161

Custom-Made Furniture

A piece of furniture designed especially for you? *P.H. Theopold* may be your man. He works only on order, but is willing to try anything if you're not in a hurry.

P. H. Theopold
RFD
Center Barnstead, New Hampshire 03225

From Gunk to Glow

One dollar doesn't go far today — but in this case, the value exceeds the price paid.

MSH

From Gunk to Glow
or
The Gentle Art of Refinishing Antiques
and Other Furniture
by George Grotz
1971; 64 pp.
From: The Pequot Press
    Chester, Connecticut 06412
    $1.00

LINSEED OIL, MY FOOT

FOR years now I have kept my big mouth shut while I listened to people talk about the glories of a boiled oil finish. But lately I find myself getting pretty cantankerous, and I'm going to tell you what I really think. I think that rubbing oil on a piece of furniture is the world's best way to make it look like something the cat dragged in on a dark, wet night.

In the first place, linseed oil darkens the wood. In the second place, it acts like a magnet to dust and grime, and each coat seals some more into the finish, dulling or concealing the grain. In the third place, hot plates — or even just heavy plates, if left long enough — will leave an impression in it. And in the fourth place, whiskey — which I keep in the house purely for testing purposes, of course — will dissolve it. (Wood alcohol will remove it almost as easily as it removes shellac — which is *supposed* to dissolve in alcohol.)

Just how this dirty idea of finishing furniture with linseed oil got started is hard to say. One source for much of its use is the famous Cornell Bulletin on "Refinishing Furniture." This otherwise excellent booklet sets forth the oil finish as something easy to do. And so it is. All you have to do is rub the oil into the wood about once a month for six months.

But most of its use, I think, goes back to a group of people who are trying to be their own ancestors. (Please don't hate me, Elmer, just think of me as ignorant.) Anyway, these people judge furniture purely by how old it looks. And getting it dirty with linseed oil unquestionably makes it look old.

But they can have it. I'll take shellac or varnish any day. For both are clear and hard. Both let you see right into the wood. Both set free the really thrilling beauty that God locked into the hearts of cherry and maple trees —the world's two most beautiful woods. Made in New England, of course!

Shaker Reproductions

This is a commission furniture shop, building to order for individual customers a variety of Shaker reproductions and other pieces in this style. Their catalogue describes a few of their products available. Pieces are finished with linseed oil and wax after the color has been sealed with a shellac or varnish wash. Shaker furniture, although outwardly simple, has a depth of sophistication which is captured by these craftsmen.

The North Family Joiners   RWW
Star Route 70, Box 73 A
Great Barrington, Massachusetts 01230

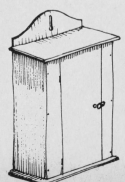

No. 3
The original of this cupboard came from the Sisters' Shop at Mt. Lebanon. It has a fine and light feeling, the effect of typical Shaker material economy. It measures 13½h x 11w x 5¼d. In pine; red, yellow, or brown.
$37.50

Junkyard

Normally, five acres of junk should repulse the conscientious citizen — a blight on the landscape. Not so with *one* junkyard. *United House Wrecking Company* is a delightful spot for the browser looking for anything from antiques to the kitchen sink.

United House Wrecking Company
328 Selleck Street
Stamford, Connecticut 06902

Handwoven Rugs

This talented craftswoman offers an interesting alternative to the wall to wall carpeting often found in today's homes.

With a lifetime of experience behind her, *Ina Uburtis* weaves 28" wide strips, any length, to your color specifications. A double threaded loom offers added durability to this fine product which is especially suitable to a colonial setting. If you like to see before you buy, order a sample wool rug which is perfectly suitable for a doormat. Sample wool rug — 28" wide x 16" long — $3.00. All prices are plus postage.

Ina Uburtis
179 Crescent Street
West Bridgewater, Massachusetts 02379

Wool	$3.00/running foot
Cotton Shag	$6.00/running foot
Wool Shag	$8.00/running foot

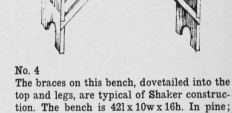

No. 4
The braces on this bench, dovetailed into the top and legs, are typical of Shaker construction. The bench is 42l x 10w x 16h. In pine; red, yellow, or brown. $30.00

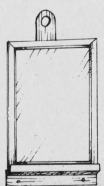

No. 2
The Shaker Millennial Laws stated: "A looking glass larger than this (12x18), ought never to be purchased by Believers." This reproduction glass is supported on a bracket designed to be hung from a peg. The top of the mirror is tied behind to the bracket by a thong which allows the hanging angle to be adjusted. Cherrywood, mahogany-colored finish. $40.00

Clock Parts and Whole Clocks

Mason & Sullivan do not manufacture but they do import a fascinating array of clock movements, clock parts, clock cases, and, indeed, whole ready-to-wind clocks with emphasis on Grandfather and Grandmother* clocks.

You can buy just the movement, or just the case, or just the face, or, even, just the brass numerals. They also have what they call "pampered lumber" and mouldings; so if you want to build a clock from tick to tock, or refurbish an old family heirloom, this seems to be the place to start.

*Either because of poor education or the recent rise of women's lib, this reviewer had never heard of a grand*mother* clock.

Complete catalogue is available.   RWW

Mason & Sullivan Co.
39 Blossom Ave.
Osterville, Massachusetts 02655
Postage additional

Stencilling

In colonial times, wallpaper was too costly for most homeowners and stencilling was used widely for decorative effects. Conventionalized motifs based on leaf and flower patterns were popular; borders accentuated windows, doorframes, ceilings and baseboards.

Anyone lucky enough to own an old house with original stencilled walls is fortunate indeed. For those not so lucky, but wishing to duplicate the stencilled walls of old, *Gloriana Goodenough* offers five stencil kits, each one copied from the wall of a different house, all patterns authentically accurate.

You provide the paint, brushes and stencil paper, and she provides the color-coded pattern and detailed instructions. Kits are reasonably priced at $1.25 each.

Gloriana Goodenough
Pomfret Center, Connecticut 06259

Unique Hand-crafted Tables and Jewelry

Jewelry from the seeds of Vermont trees — butternut, walnut and peachstones, sliced and polished, then mounted to make a unique item. Write for descriptive brochure.

Fairmont Woodcraft
C.A. Brown
Waterville, Vermont 05492

GRANDMOTHER CASE
75-in. high, 16-in. wide, 8¾-in. deep.

A nicely proportioned grandmother clock with clean lines and simplified construction. Uses fewer mouldings and turnings than most other cases and therefore is easier and cheaper to build.

Blueprint with specifications, full-size details, bill of materials and instructions for building case **No. M180** .... $ 1.00

Mouldings and turnings in Honduras mahogany, cherry or black walnut as follows:

	Mahogany	Cherry	Walnut
Moulding between feet and base (L on drawing)	$ 2.85	$ 3.15	$ 3.60
Moulding between base and waist (A on drawing)	5.40	5.95	6.90
Moulding under hood (B on drawing) ..	5.40	5.95	6.90
Crown moulding (DD on drawing)	4.00	4.40	5.30
1 finial for crown (C on drawing)	1.40	1.50	1.80
1 Hand-carved shell carving under hood (G on drawing)	2.50	2.60	2.70
Hardware kit consisting of 2 brass door pulls, 2 catches, 4 rubber-cushioned foot glides, and 4 hinges with satin brass finish, screws included	3.25	3.25	3.25
Complete set of M180 mouldings, turnings and hardware. Ship. wgt. 11 lbs.	**$24.80**	**$26.80**	**$30.45**
Mouldings and turnings listed above are the most difficult parts to make. The easier plain parts should be cut out of ¾" thick flat lumber. If not available locally, you may order this lumber from us. Every piece is top grade kiln-dried wood planed both sides. Ship. wgt. 46 lbs.	**$34.00**	**$37.40**	**$48.00**

A New England Simple — To Make Camphorated Ice

Take 1/2 lb. mutton tallow, cut it into small pieces, put into a saucepan and cover with boiling water. When fat has completely risen to the top — strain through a cheesecloth and while still warm, stir in a tsp. of essence of camphor, using 1 tsp. for every cupful of suet. Before it cools, pour into smaller receptacles and set in a cool place overnight.

If It Is Made of Wood We Have Probably Made It —

signs carved, bongo boards, coffee tables, potter's wheels, cupolas. My shop is in the factory where I used to work. I jokingly tell folks that I never got to sit in the office, so I bought it.

I do 'weekend logging' on my own woodland, and sometimes take small contracts for others cutting logs, rails and posts for fences, pulpwood and firewood, always following good forestry practice.

Last fall I made a hundred wooden doll carriages for the Vermont Wooden Toy Co. of Waitsfield, Vt. Acquisition of some wide pine planks prompted me to make some coffee tables. I thread the legs in and use little or no metal. I also make a cobbler's bench with dovetail joints in sides and drawers.

Most of my business is on a cash and carry basis. I sell a fireside bench or coffee table for $20.00. They average 4 feet long and about 16 inches wide. I can make many sizes, up to 2 feet wide and 5 feet long. Usually they are pine, but I will use butternut, maple, elm and birch on request. My milking stools are quite authentic and can be disassembled by screwing out the legs which are a wooden thread. I get $4.50 for these. A cobbler's bench sells readily at $40.00. My wife says I sell things too low priced and I guess she is right. I would have to make an extra charge of 15% for packaging a mail shipment. The 4 foot or over pieces have to go by truck as they are too large for parcel post.

I am 56 years old and the days are not long enough to do all the things I'd like to so I often get behind, but I keep my promises, though sometimes a little late.

Henry Chase

Henry Chase
1 Elm Street
Randolph, Vermont 05060

'TREEFORM' COFFEE TABLES

MAT: 2" Pine plank
FIN: Stain & Lacquer--lo-gloss.
SIZE: From 24" to 60"
Price: $10.00 per foot of length
Mailable.

Habitat

A Story About Slate

The story of Harpswell House slate began 300 million years ago. Finely divided particles of silt and clay were buried under tremendous pressures and temperatures during upheavals of the earth's surface, forming the compressed material we now call slate.

For centuries, slate has been quarried throughout the world with its first production in America taking place in 1734. Its unusual qualities of strength, resistance to the elements, fine texture and grain, and ease of fabrication have caused it to be acknowledged as one of the finest natural stones for architectural use.

Harpswell House, the first to adapt slate to the production of household and public area furnishings, has now originated the unique technique of combining slate and selected hardwoods and metals, using specially developed adhesives, in creating an appealing variety of distinctive gifts and accessories.

Harpswell House
Box 566
Brunswick, Maine 04011

WALL VASES

SIZE	APP. WT.	
2x2x9	1½ LB.	$10.00
3½x7x4½	2 LB.	12.00

Yankee Craft Products

Old Yankee Wood Tonic may sound like illegal "hootch," but those involved in the care and restoration of fine wood furniture and panelling know it as a top-drawer polish that makes wood "come alive."

Yankee Craft Products also manufactures a variety of carbon steel knives, from a 3" parer to a 10" butcher knife. Remember the two and three tine cooking forks that grandmother used? These are made of stainless steel with polished rosewood handles.

Old Yankee Wood Tonic – 8 oz. bottle $2.00

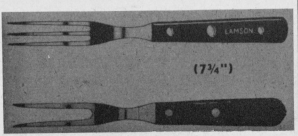

(7¾")

two for $3.25

ICE BUCKET

Ripple Slate and Teak
Plastic Liner
Fully Insulated
Felted Base
2½ Quart Capacity (2 plus trays)

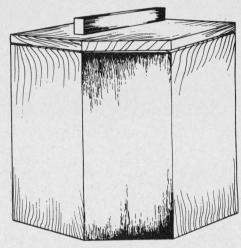

IB-3
Hexagonal - Alternate Ripple Slate and Teak - Teak Cover   8" hex. - 9" high
Approx. 5 lbs.   Retail $30.00

SALT AND PEPPER

SLATE AND ROSEWOOD

RO35
3½" High x 1¾" Square
Approximately ¾ lb.
Retail $15.00

YANKEE CRAFT PRODUCTS
30 WEST BRIDGE STREET
MANCHESTER, NEW HAMPSHIRE 03101

He Makes It — In Wood

"Every piece of wood is left as nature grew it. I try not to disturb the natural lines or any of the beautiful knots and grains that are in it," says Frank Henry. He will custom build anything, but tables, chairs, lamps and coat racks are sold ready-made at his shop.

Handcrafts by Henry
Route 7
Williamstown, Massachusetts 01267

Woodworking

For forty years, *George Jennings* designed and built pieces of furniture as a hobby, usually giving them away to friends and family. Now retired, he has selected 20 of his best loved items to sell by mail. Built only to order — using the wood and finish of your choice — every item is handcrafted. Send for illustrated brochure.

George Jennings
Heirloom House
Clinton, Connecticut 06413

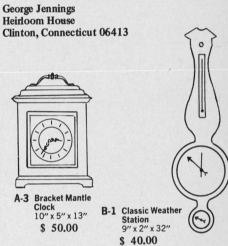

A-3 Bracket Mantle
Clock
10" x 5" x 13"
$ 50.00

B-1 Classic Weather
Station
9" x 2" x 32"
$ 40.00

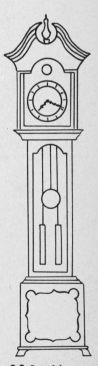

C-1 Majestic
Grandfather Clock
18" x 12" x 81"

$625.00

C-2 Graceful
Grandmother Clock
16" x 10" x 74"

$550.00

Habitat

WALLPAPERS
and
FABRICS
by
Old Stone Mill

Handprinted Wallpaper & Fabrics

The Old Stone Mill in Adams, Massachusetts, is where you want to go if you are looking for authentically reproduced Colonial-American wallpapers and fabrics.

They handprint their screen papers in a mill that is over 100 years old, and, delightfully, they welcome visitors during working hours. There is also a mill retail store that offers seconds and overstocked patterns. Might well be a bargain or two to be found here.

We would specially commend you to their booklet on their line of "Old Sturbridge Village Wallpapers and Fabrics."

You write to or go to [and a trip to Adams is great]

Old Stone Mill Corporation
Adams, Massachusetts 01220

SECTION I WHAT IS IT WORTH — AND IS IT WORTH REFINISHING?   11

SECTION II WOODS   12

SECTION III REPAIRS   14

SECTION IV PREPARING THE SURFACE FOR FINISHING   17

SECTION V STAINING   20

SECTION VI FINISHING   22

SECTION VII CARE OF FINISHED FURNITURE   29

SECTION VIII FRAMES   31

SECTION IX PIANO REFINISHING   33

SECTION X GILDING   35

Habitat

Fine Period Furniture — Designed, Reproduced, Restored

"Do as little as necessary to an antique and when in doubt 'don't'." Darn good advice from Harold D. Margolis — a man who knows what he is talking about.

Another bit of his philosophy concerns an original Chippendale chair.

"The owners wanted me to strip off the finish," he said, "but I wouldn't. After all, you don't refinish a Rembrandt painting if it's cracked."

Harold Margolis also makes fine reproductions to order. One of his finest works was a Duncan Phyfe dining table and 20 chairs for the Connecticut Governor's Mansion.

By appointment only.

The Nathan Margolis Shop, Inc.
30 High Street
Hartford, Connecticut 06103

Atlasta Farm Restorations

Restoring other people's precious antiques and lamps has become a full-time business for Mary-anne and Emile Smith.

Work on furniture ranges from complete restoration to French polishing. Lamp work is primarily wiring of old lamps for electricity, but done in such a way that oil and kerosene lamps can be easily returned to their original use.

Since the work is so highly individualized, it is difficult to give price information, but free estimates are gladly given.

Atlasta Farm Restorations
Codfish Hill Road
Bethel, Connecticut 06801

Easy Does It Furniture Restoration the Vermont Way

The clear step-by-step advice plus many how-to illustrations offered in this book made me take a long look at a favorite antique:

"Oh cracked paint, layer on layer
On my Windsor Chair, beware."

Mary Goodrich

Easy Does It Furniture Restoration
the Vermont Way
by William Farwell
1968; 40 pp., paper
From: Charles E. Tuttle Co., Inc.
Rutland, Vermont 05701
$2.00

FACTORY STORE GUIDE
To All New England

By A. Miser & A. Pennypincher

Factory Store Guide To All New England

If you want to do a little New England bargain hunting with savings of 30%, 40%, and even 50%, here is your guide.

Hats, shoes, clothing, lamps, clocks, and just about anything but sealing wax are all in one store or another scattered all over New England.

This is a book about factory stores, real factory stores, and not the shopping plaza discount type stores. This guide lists 150 locations, and the authors have visited each and every one; so have fun and save some money.

MSH

Factory Store Guide To All New England
by A. Miser and A. Pennypincher
1972; 150 pp., paper
From: The Pequot Press
Chester, Connecticut 06412
$2.95

Authentic Colonial Wall Stenciling

Through many years of study and practice in the art of stenciling, Mrs. John Syme has become somewhat of an expert, sought after by those who wish to duplicate authentically this old art in their homes.

Several years were spent studying with Esther Stevens Brazier, well-known among students of early American decoration as the pioneer of the return of this old craft. After Mrs. Brazier's death, her students formed the Historical Society of Early American Decoration, devoted to research of old patterns found on trays, chairs, stenciled walls, floors and all types of tinware.

Mrs. Syme will travel only within a twenty-five mile radius of her home. Please call or write ahead for appointment.

Suggested by Nancy Lyons

MRS. JOHN P. SYME
AUTHENTIC COLONIAL WALL STENCILLING

ESSEX, CONN. 06426

MEMBER HISTORICAL SOCIETY OF EARLY AMERICAN DECORATION

The Pine Furniture of Early New England

For the serious student of plain, early furniture, this book tells all. Excellent photographs of virtually every sort of chest, bench, table, desk, cupboard, mirror, weather vane and light, accompanied by descriptive text, give the reader a good knowledge of each. Fifty-five pages of clear drawings enable the amateur cabinet maker to copy most every piece.

Ellen Hill

The Pine Furniture of Early New England
by Russell Hawes Kettell
1949; 229 pp.

From Dover Publications, Inc.
180 Varick Street
New York, New York 10014
$10.00

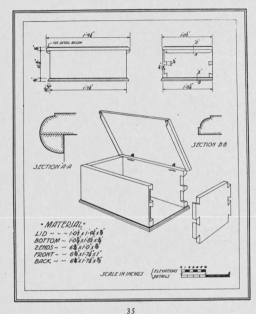

35
Desk Box [SEE PLATE 102]

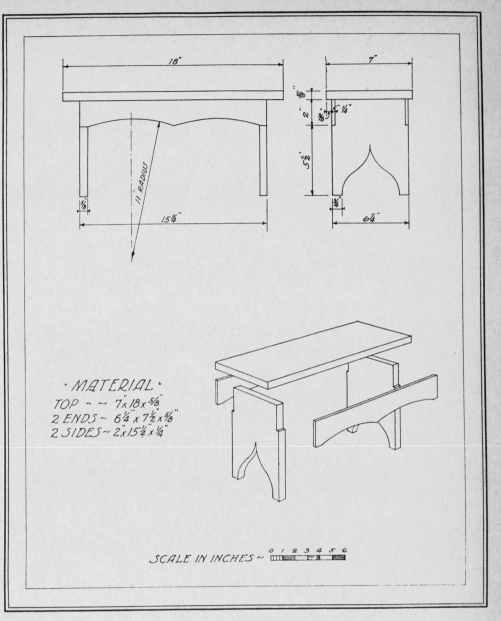

MATERIAL
TOP ~ ~ 7" x 18" x 5/8"
2 ENDS ~ 6¼" x 7½" x 5/8"
2 SIDES ~ 2" x 15¼" x ¼"

SCALE IN INCHES ~

17
Five-Board Footstool [SEE PLATE 53]

The Tick Tock Technician

I can't truthfully recommend taking your seven dollar, plastic encased alarm clock that you smashed off your bedside table one morning at 6:00 a.m. to Earl A. Nielson, the *Clock Mender* for "repair and restoration." When Mr. Nielson speaks of "repair and restoration" I don't think he's got this kind of job in mind. However, if you have any broken or generally run-down time-pieces around that you value and care for, the *Clock Mender* is waiting, with years of experience behind him.

Earl Nielson possesses a unique title — that of Certified Master Clockmaker. This was awarded to him by the American Watchmakers Institute after a three-part, five-month-long examination; part of which required "the repair of a deliberately damaged Westminster Chime clock, bringing its final accuracy within 15 seconds per day." In addition, Mr. Nielson is fully familiar with the inside workings of the most advanced clock movements. There is no standard price list, as each clock and its malady is considered individually. After repairs are made, your clock is kept in the shop for two more weeks to test steady going, as well as to "satisfy the implacable senses of touch, sight and hearing." If only your doctor was as thorough and thoughtful as the *Clock Mender* of Woodbury!

Claudia

The Clock Mender
Tick Tock Hill
Old Town Farm Road
Woodbury, Connecticut 06798

A New England Simple — To Remove Tar

Rub well with clean lard, then wash with soap and warm water.

The New England Flag

Historically, New Englanders were the first Americans to throw off forcefully the yoke of English dominance. This flag is based on one carried by the New England army during the Battle of Bunker Hill, June 17, 1775. The red cross signifies the Cross of St. George, the patron saint of England. The green pine tree represents our tall pine trees, and the six stars symbolize the New England galaxy.

May be ordered in a variety of sizes from:

Ebinger Brothers & Co.
Ipswich, Massachusetts 01938
Sizes: 12" x 18" Cotton — $1.25/ 2 for $2.00
16" x 24" Nylon — $3.50 each
3' x 5' Sewn Nylon — $15.00 each

Flags

American flags, state flags, or your own custom-made creation, for indoor or outdoor use are available from this firm. Send for their illustrated brochure.

The Flag Shop
85 Andover Street, Rt. 114
Danvers, Massachusetts 01923
Outdoor American Flag – Nylon 3' x 5' $16.20

CHOOSE THE PROPER FLAG SIZE

To determine the most effective size flag for a flagpole: the *length* of the flag should be approximately *equal* to one-fourth of the height of the pole above the ground: for example, the recommended size flag for a 40-foot flagpole is a 6 x 10-foot flag.

A New England Simple

To bleach white silks or flannel: Wash the articles clean, rinse in suds and smoke with brimstone while wet; the silk must be brushed or washed with a sponge; if rubbed it can never be pressed smoothly. Expose the goods to the air; the odor will soon evaporate.

Habitat

Yankee Magazine

What is *Yankee*? Some say it's nostalgia because it conjures up a longing for things, persons or situations that are not present. Others feel it is old fashioned — many of us fall for that. *Yankee* does create longings, it takes people out of themselves and sets their minds on things which don't have to be resolved, which aren't earth shattering.

On the other hand, *Yankee* is about today. "The Original Yankee Swoppers' Column," a major feature in each issue, is of today's world, involving today's people. There are houses for sale, places to visit, a guide for shoppers, recipes for the industrious, "Quips, Quotes and Queries," how-to articles, (see *Make Yourself a Pine Hutch!*) and answers from the "Oracle" to a variety of questions. Potpourri? Yes. And I suppose we could live without it — many do. But I think they're not as lucky as those who live with it.

Yankee softens the hard, raw edges of life today. Is there anyone around who can't use a little of that?

Yankee Magazine   JCH
Dublin, New Hampshire 03444
$4.00 yearly; 12 issues

REMEMBER THE GOOD OLD DAYS when a housewife didn't have to go to the market, because it came to her? There was the meat man, the fish peddler, the milk man and the ice man. Even the grocer came to the house, took the order and then delivered it. Items shown above were particular to this period and the various trades mentioned. The steelyard, foreground, was used to weigh items. Woven straw cuffs were worn by tradesmen to keep their sleeves out of whatever they were handling. Milk didn't come in bottles or cartons, but was poured into a pail such as that above, left out by the householder. Anyone wanting ice for their icebox would put a card in the window and, behold, the iceman cometh carrying a block of ice with a set of tongs. All items above are on display at the Watertown Historical Society Museum.

Reprinted with permission from the Town Times, July 27, 1972. Watertown, Connecticut.

Habitat

MAKE YOURSELF A PINE HUTCH!

With our men readers especially in mind this month, we are giving them the opportunity to do what Bud Dudley of Foxboro, Mass., has done — reproduce an early 18th-century pine hutch cupboard! The original stands in the dining room of the Old Stone House in Browington, Vt. — part of its collection of antiques and artifacts from Orleans County. (The Old Stone House is open to visitors for a nominal fee from May through October.) Now, without further ado, here are Bud Dudley's plans and list of materials

MATERIAL for the Pine Hutch:

1" (¾" finished) pine is used throughout.
Three 10" boards six feet long for back
One 10" board six feet long for shelf "A" and front of counter
Four 8" boards six feet long for sides
One 8" board twelve feet long for door and panels beside door
Three 8" boards ten feet long for top, bottom, shelves, and back of counter. There will be a five-foot piece left over for cleats under interior shelves and across front of counter to attach side panels, and back of door
One 8" board three feet long for front of hood and trim at top of hood

HARDWARE:

One pair 4" black "H" hinges
Forty-nine #9 1¼" flathead screws
Finish nails or reproductions of hand-made nails

Whittle out a turn knob and countersink for screw. Butt glue the boards for back, sides, counter, and door. Stain to suit your wife — the original is light. Two coats of linseed oil with a touch of stain on the interior surfaces gives a good finish.

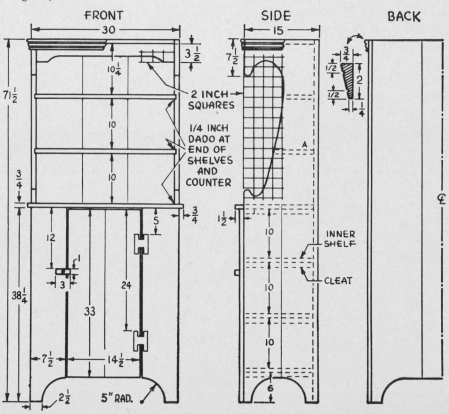

FRONT   SIDE   BACK

Reprinted with permission from the May 1972 issue of Yankee Magazine.

How To Mend China and Bric-A-Brac

This slim volume must surely be the most exhaustive study of a fascinating, not widely known, craft. In this day of plastic and paper, the services of a china mender are not needed nearly so often as they were years ago. Ironically, much of the work of the modern mender is to be found in museums, although the china mender can find ample clientele among the butterfingered of today.

The authors take pains to present the craft as a possible source of income for anyone reasonably adroit, and especially suitable for persons confined to wheelchairs. The final chapter, devoted to going into business, includes among other things, prudent advice about dealing with the china breaking public.

Be it the spout of a favorite teapot or a priceless antique, this book will tell you how to repair it.

Barrett Robbins-Pianka

How To Mend China and Bric-A-Brac
by Paul St.-Gaudens and Arthur R. Jackson
1953; 124 pp.

From: Charles T. Branford Company
28 Union Street
Newton Center, Massachusetts 02159
$2.95

Early American Ironware

Mr. Kauffman has spent a lifetime studying, teaching, fabricating and collecting early American metalware. This fine book is a culmination of his wealth of information. There are chapters devoted to blacksmiths, whitesmiths, farriers, edge toolmakers, cutters, locksmiths, gunsmiths, nailers, wheelwrights and tinsmiths, with over 200 photographs of examples of their work.

A whitesmith, incidentally, is described:

"Of all the trades combined with whitesmithing under one roof, blacksmithing was the most frequent and logical; for the work of the whitesmith was the filing, polishing, and assembling of objects made by the blacksmith. It appears that the blacksmith roughly formed such objects as irons, firetools, skimmers, rupture belts, etc. The finishing of these products required a more refined type of workmanship than is usually associated with blacksmithing, so they were passed on to the whitesmith."

CIE

Early American Ironware
by Henry J. Kauffman
1967; 166 pp.

From: Charles E. Tuttle Company
Rutland, Vermont 05701
$11.00

Plate 180. *Ironwork on the lid of a Conestoga wagon tool box, showing unusually fine craftsmanship in its symmetry and simplicity. (Courtesy of the Philadelphia Museum of Art)*

Recollections of Old Stonington

It is rather hard to believe that a book this small could be worth the price of $4.50, but it is an extremely limited edition and for those few who enjoy a lovely recollection of an old New England town, the price is secondary. Indeed, the exquisite drawings alone are worth $4.50.

When Anne Dodge writes, you *hear* the horses, *smell* the heat of a late summer day and return the neighborly wave from the porch partially hidden behind a maple.

And the author says, "All up and down the shady street was a froth of muslin skirts and a flutter of fans."

JPM

Recollections of Old Stonington
by Anne Atwood Dodge
Drawings by Richard D. Batchelder
1966; 48 pp.

From: The Pequot Press
Chester, Connecticut 06412
$4.50

The Hitchcock Chair Company

"L. Hitchcock — Hitchcocks-ville, Connecticut, Warranted." Lambert Hitchcock signed all chairs on the seat back. Legend has it the "warranted" meant the chair could survive a drop from the third floor of the factory where the chair was massproduced from about 1825.

Lambert Hitchcock's fortunes as a chairmaker rose and fell through the years. From a peak period of production in the 1820's to bankruptcy in 1829, and back to uncertain solvency during the next twenty years, Lambert's attention to the manufacturing of his famed stencilled chairs shared favor with his interest in politics and business ventures elsewhere. Eventually, the fortunes of the factory declined to a point where the operation was suspended in 1852. The rebirth of the Hitchcock chair is credited to John T. Kenney and a fishing trip he made late in the spring of 1946 on the Farmington River where he came upon the near-ruin of the old Hitchcock factory. Like all New Englanders, he had grown up with the "Hitchcock Chair" and had received one for a wedding present. Kenney became intrigued by the old factory and researched antique dealers in Hartford to learn that the original signed Hitchcock chairs were in constant demand — and no doubt, reproductions would command a ready market. Kenney took the plunge; the reborn Hitchcock Chair Company began operations on October 17, 1946.

A visit to Riverton (Hitchcocks-ville), Connecticut will be rewarding. It should include a tour of the factory and the Museum where 100 of the more than 300 home-furnishing pieces gathered by Mr. Kenney in his years of search for Hitchcock originals are located.

Hitchcock reproductions can be bought at the factory store in Riverton, and at select furniture shops throughout New England.

The Hitchcock Chair Company
Riverton, Connecticut 06065

A New England Simple

Cooking Utensils – Saucepans and other tin or granite dishes browned by use, may be cleaned by letting them remain half an hour in boiling soda water, then rubbing with a wire dish cloth or stiff brush.

Habitat

Old Vermont Houses 1763-1850

Vermont architecture – simple, strong, sometimes austere – like her people, her land. With marvelous photographs and text, Mr. Congdon points out the detailing – both interior and exterior – in houses from the earliest, 1763, to ones of the 19th century.

CIE

Old Vermont Houses 1763-1850
by Herbert Wheaton Congdon
1968; 192 pp., paper
From: Noone House
        Peterborough, New Hampshire 03458
        $3.95

Vermonters are not given to extravagance, . . . The men who built these houses and made these mantels and doorways really cared. Theirs was the spirit of true craftsmanship, not working with one eye on the clock, but, I am sure, with keen enjoyment as their mental vision took material form. Why, otherwise, "waste" hours of labor on the cornice and doorway of a remote hill-farm . . . , or elaborate the entrance to a seldom-used attic ballroom?

I stated in the beginning of this book that we have no great architecture, but I think Vermont has made a real contribution to the varied arts of home-building. Lacking breath-taking scenery or stupendous mountains, its little streams, green hills, simple homes and churches, are bound up with Vermont life in an endearing quality of friendliness.

The Time Betty Lamp

Jack Rogers, owner-designer of *The Colonial Brass Craftsmen, Inc.* delves into old books, journals and museums to come up with accurate reproductions of lamps used in colonial times.

The "Time Betty Lamp" was widely used in Holland at the time of the Pilgrims' departure to New England, so the design was not unknown to our early colonists, but only a small number of them were made. They are rarely found now, and are highly prized by collectors.

Jack Rogers has faithfully executed the "Time Betty Lamp" in pewter. Its most interesting feature is the glassfont which holds the oil and upon which Roman numerals marking the hours are embossed. The gradual lowering of the oil as it burned, marked the passing of time.

The Colonial Brass Craftsmen, Inc.
13 Summit Street
East Hampton, Connecticut 06424
Pewter Time Betty Lamp – $80.00 ppd.

Early Houses of New England

Contains some 50 sketches by the architect-author based on early American homes throughout New England. The sketches retain the original structure then go beyond to show how they could be built today with facilities for modern living. As an example, the author has at times added wings which were not generally a part of the original structure. In some instances, landscaping has been suggested, in keeping with the structure, as well as its natural setting.

Charles T. Letson

Early Houses of New England
by Norman Baker
1967; 144 pp.
From: Charles E. Tuttle Co., Inc.
        Rutland, Vermont 05701
        $7.50

Robert Bourdon – Blacksmith

Blacksmithing is one of the oldest crafts – requiring a natural ability, plus years of experience and practice. *Robert Bourdon* creates handmade functional items, skillfully forged in the old manner. Each piece is custom-made to order. Nothing is kept in stock. Few tools other than forge, anvil and hammer are used in his work, and all welding is done in the fire.

Early New Englanders practiced fire welding – but this tricky bit of the blacksmith's craft has nearly disappeared along with the "old time blacksmith."

"A blacksmith is expected to make or fix all kinds of things," Mr. Bourdon writes. "This winter I forged several ski sculptures for race trophies and individuals, repaired my neighbor's plow and 'ironed' his sugaring sled this spring. I made all kinds of hardware and lighting fixtures, forged a gun spring, made a tool for setting the sound post in a cello, fixed my neighbor's clarinet and I'm currently making a Chinese character in iron to decorate a fireplace in Arizona.

"Production is definitely limited to what one man can make with simple tools used with patience and skill in the old-fashioned way, so patience please, when ordering. Catalog $1.00."

Robert Bourdon
Greensboro, Vermont 05841
The Knocker Latch $45.00 plus $1.00 postage

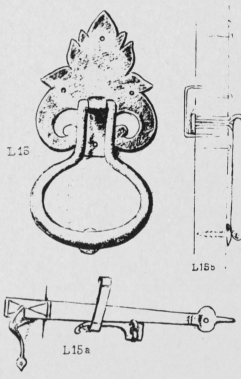

(L15) The Knocker latch is a clever and simple device of early origin and, as the name implies, is both a door knocker and a latch in one unit. The handle is used like any knocker but, by lifting and giving it a turn, the latch bar is released from its catch.

About eight inches by 4½" over-all. The escutcheon plate is from an early design.

Unless otherwise requested, the latch will be furnished with a single cam lift which operates by a turn in one direction only.

(L15a) Back latch showing bar and single cam lift. The bar is decorated with incised lines and beveled. About ten inches long. Furnished with a drive and clinch staple and braced catch.

(L15b) Cross section of a door and knocker latch, showing method of installation.

Habitat

The New England Meeting Houses of the Seventeenth Century

A scholarly work for the serious student of seventeenth century architecture, this book is well-illustrated, foot-noted, and contains a detailed chronological list of meeting houses.

Page 75 has line drawings of the longitudinal and cross sections of the original timbered roof of the Hingham, Massachusetts Meeting House II, built in 1681.

Jean Allen Skiff

The New England Meeting Houses
of the Seventeenth Century
by Marian Card Donnelly
1968; 165 pp.
From: Wesleyan University Press
Middletown, Connecticut 06457
$7.50

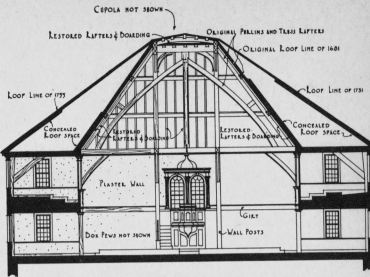

CROSS SECTION OF ORIGINAL TIMBERED ROOF

FIGURE 24. Hingham, Mass. Meeting House II. 1681. Cross section. Corse, "The Old Ship Meeting House," p. 25. *Courtesy* Old Time New England.

LONG SECTION OF ORIGINAL TIMBERED ROOF

FIGURE 23. Hingham, Mass. Meeting House II. 1681. Longitudinal section. Corse, "The Old Ship Meeting House," p. 24. *Courtesy* Old Time New England.

Weatherboard

"Our basic business is making kiln-dried Eastern white pine so that it looks like authentic barn board," so says *Vermont Weatherboard.* This fine company faithfully captures the true character and quality of old barn boards but without the dust, dirt, larvae, insects or even offensive odor. It's a distinctive siding and paneling — less expensive than hard-to-find old boards — for inside and out. Wrought head "old-fashioned" nails are also available. They lend antique charm to the paneling and have excellent holding power. An authentic appearing *Well House* may be bought at Weatherboard. If you don't have a well, use it as a decorative furnishing for your property.

Vermont Weatherboard, Inc.
Wolcott, Vermont 05680
Prices for New England:
$.44 — $.60 per board foot
Well House — Weatherboard Roof $88.00
            Shingled Roof $94.00
            FOB Wolcott, Vermont 05680

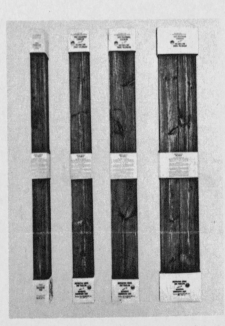

Homeowner's Convenience Packs

Homeowner's Convenience Packs come in four different units - separate widths 6", 8" & 10" (Packs A, B & C respectively) or Pack "D" containing 2 - 6", 4 - 8" & 2 -10" boards. The boards are 8' long, although each package does have at least one nested board. *Vermont* WEATHERBOARD is also sold in random width bundles.

Habitat

Yankee Barns

Barns have intrigued many of us for years. So keen is the desire in some to convert one into a comfortable home that their prize is dismantled piece by piece, each plank, beam and slat coded, then carted to another site. But the number of 18th century barns is limited. *Yankee Barn* may fill the gap with its designs which preserve the charm of the old barn yet acknowledge the life-style needs of the 20th century. The result is an aesthetically pleasing, practical home for full scale living upstairs, downstairs and outside. Three models are offered with a variety of optional component packages.

**Yankee Barn Homes
P.O. Box 1000
Boston, Massachusetts 02118**

Send $2.00 for complete information package.

Mark I – Partial specifications
Dimensions of basic house: 25'-4½" x 45'-4½"
Number of bedrooms: up to six
Square feet: 1,922
Cubic feet: 16,210
Approximate weight of
component package: 30 tons

The following Yankee Barn prices are for the basic house, exclusive of foundation and land costs.

Model	Component Package (F.O.B. factory)		Completed House (varies with location and options)		Average Total Cost of House Ready for Occupancy
Mark I	$15,400	+	$18,000 -$22,000	=	$35,400
Mark II	12,400	+	9,000 - 13,000	=	23,400
Mark III	7,795	+	8,000*- 10,000*	=	16,795*

*on concrete slab on grade

Optional component packages (F.O.B. factory)

Mark I	Living Room Ell	$3,775
Mark I	Shed Roof Foyer	975
Mark II	Anything Room	3,695
Mark III	Living or Bedroom Ell	3,180

Shipping Charges

Shipping charges vary from $1.25 to $2.85 per mile, depending on Model and options.

DRAWING
A-1-IV

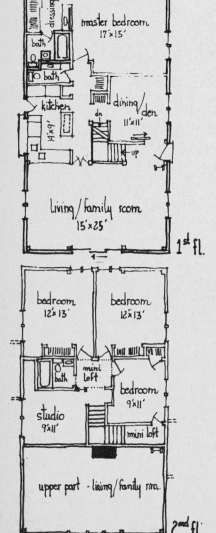

master bedroom 17'x15'
dressing
bath
bath
kitchen 14'x9'
dining/den 11'x11'
dn
up
living/family room 15'x25'

1st fl.

bedroom 12'x13'
bedroom 12'x13'
bath
mini loft
bedroom 9'x11'
studio 9'x11'
mini loft
upper part - living/family rm.

2nd fl.

***2nd fl. floorplan remains
the same in all models**

Habitat

Log Buildings

Northern's rustic log buildings are constructed of northern Maine timber which withstands arctic winters or blistering summers and temperates in between. These homes are erected easily on any type of foundation after the logs arrive at the building site pre-cut, marked and ready for easy assembly. A variety of models and floor plans are offered in basic and standard kits. The more expensive Standard Kit includes floor framing, subfloor, double roof, interior doors, interior partition stock and ceilings.

Northern Products, Inc.
Bomarc Road
Bangor, Maine 04401

The Northerner

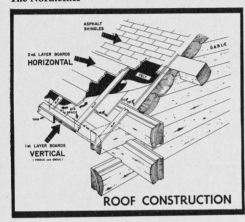

ROOF CONSTRUCTION

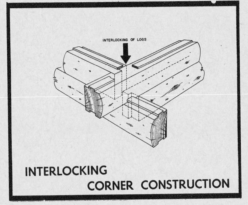

INTERLOCKING CORNER CONSTRUCTION

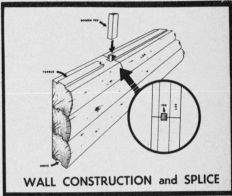

WALL CONSTRUCTION and SPLICE

MODEL	SIZE	STANDARD KIT	BASIC KIT
EASTLANDER	w/o Garage and Breezeway	$12,782	$9,060
OXFORD	Standard	12,022	8,527
GREENSBORO	Standard	10,575	7,270
SOMERSET	w/o Garage and Breezeway	9,770	7,065
CHADWICK	w/o Garage	9,677	6,747
LINCOLN	Standard	9,225	6,515
NORTHERNER	20 x 28	5,345	4,025
	24 x 32	7,115	5,135
	28 x 36	9,075	6,465
KENNEBEC	22 x 26	5,560	4,230
	24 x 28	6,475	4,915
	26 x 32	7,565	5,665
PENOBSCOT	24 x 30	7,885	5,985
	28 x 34	9,615	6,755
	28 x 38	10,367	7,647
TRAPPER	18 x 26	3,085	2,530
	22 x 30	4,105	3,335
	26 x 26	4,205	3,380
	26 x 30	4,915	3,945

Prices subject to change depending upon supplier and material costs.

The Bug Book: Harmless Insect Controls

Simple ways to control backyard pests without using toxic materials are the subject of this book; all the formulas and recipes for harmless home-made controls have been tested by the authors in their own gardens.

MSH

The Bug Book: Harmless Insect Controls
by John and Helen Philbrick
1963; 143 pp., paper
From: John and Helen Philbrick
P.O. Box 96
Wilkinsonville, Massachusetts 01590
$4.50

A New England Simple

Broken window glass can be removed by putting soft soap on the putty. In a few hours the putty will have softened and then can be removed with an ordinary knife.

◆

Anyone involved in building a home or clearing a site for one, should remember that trees produce oxygen, absorb carbon dioxide, cool the air, trap dust, reduce noise and stop erosion. To say nothing about beautifying our surroundings. So think twice before you cut down a tree and urge your builder to do the same.

◆

A New England Simple – Paint Removal

Try hot, undiluted vinegar to take paint off glass.

Northeastern Log Homes

A Northeastern solid log home may be just what you're looking for in authentic rustic charm. These homes are designed and manufactured from 6" x 8" eastern white pine logs, pre-cut and numbered to facilitate speedy construction. Pre-cut spruce timber trusses and roof purlin provide rustic cathedral ceilings with drop beam ceilings for bedroom and bath area. Northeastern also offers a complete custom design service. Scaled floor plans, drawings and price quotations are provided. Presently, fourteen different models are available in twelve floor plans. Prices of the homes range from about $7,500 to $16,000.

Northeastern Log Homes, Inc.
Kenduskeag, Maine 04450
Brochure of plans: $2.00

Restoration and Remodeling

Up Country Enterprise was started in October of 1968 by two people with a few hand tools and a love for the fine old house in which they lived. They began as a handyman business — washing windows, cutting grass, caring for pets, chopping down trees and driving people to the airport.

Through that diversified activity, they built up an inventory of trucks, snow plows, tractors, power tools, and other equipment to tackle almost any job. By 1970 they were painting houses and barns, installing bathrooms, remodeling kitchens and repairing sills.

During this time their eyes were focused on the restoration of fine old houses as a career. This goal they have now reached. They are delighted to work for a client who has an old house to remodel or restore. Increasingly, they are purchasing fine old New England houses in varying states of repair, restoring them to their early dignity and charm, then selling them to an interested buyer.

Up Country Enterprise is now a corporation, employing seven people full time and others part time. Its headquarters is still in the 18th century center chimney house in Peterborough. They are ready to do an exceptionally fine job in restoring or remodeling your home. It is interesting to note that its owners come to this business from an academic background, one as administrator and teacher of history, the other as teacher of English literature. One other unusual point about *Up Country Enterprise*: It is the only firm of building contractors in New England founded and run by two women!

Up Country Enterprise
Old Jaffrey Road
Peterborough, New Hampshire 03458

Habitat

Colonial Meeting-Houses of New Hampshire

An account of New Hampshire's meeting houses as compared with their contemporaries in New England. The photographs are the originals used when this book was first published in 1938 and are not as good as we might expect them to be today. An interesting book, nevertheless, though not as ambitious and complete a work as J. Frederick Kelly's two volume "Early Connecticut Meeting-Houses," Columbia University Press, 1948.

Gwen Orton-Jones

Colonial Meeting-Houses of New Hampshire
by Eva A. Speare
1955 Rev.; 237 pp.
From: Courier Printing Company, Inc.
Littleton, New Hampshire 03561
$6.00

On the Summit at Acworth

This front view of this masterpiece of colonial architecture possesses remarkable detail. Craftsmen carved the arches above the triple doors, and the frames of the Palladian windows. A scrutiny of its steeple on page one hundred thirty-six will excite admiration for the skilled artisans of a century ago.

Beneficent Congregational Meeting House

dedicated in 1810. This structure presents an unusual exterior for a New England church — a dome instead of a spire. The second house of the congregation "gathered" in 1743 during the "Great Awakening;" it was built under the leadership of its second minister, Rev. James Wilson, who came from Dublin in 1791 at the height of the classical revival in that city. In its early years it was known as "Paddy Wilson's Meeting House."

Habitat

HERBERT WHEATON CONGDON

EARLY AMERICAN HOMES FOR TODAY
A Treasury of Decorative Details and Restoration Procedures

CHARLES E. TUTTLE COMPANY
RUTLAND, VERMONT

Early American Homes for Today

The feeling of this book can be no better told than by Mr. Congdon himself.

"This book is intended to be a help to the do-it-yourself man who has had the good fortune to come into the possesssion of one of New England's old homes. It describes and illustrates a considerable variety of old-time designs of several periods, which might be used on its exterior or indoors. It should help the man who is 'handy with tools,' or any intelligent carpenter of the neighborhood, to make the most of a neglected but worthy old building. It could also be a safe guide in building a new house in the old style, which might be more vital than the usual undistinguished 'Colonial' too often seen in Suburbia. Materials may be bought at the local mill and mouldings altered in the home workshop.

"The most important preparation for such a project is to get the feeling of the best of the old work, to study the buildings themselves, if possible, as well as their details. As an aid to this, the illustrations in this book are not only general views of the whole but in many cases are accompanied by large-scale detail pictures. In addition, in the front of the book there is a list of all the illustrations which is arranged geographically — a suggestive guide to the back-road explorer. No photograph can take the place of a thoughtful perception of the real thing."

This is truly a worthwhile book, with a wonderful glossary.

CIE

Early American Homes for Today
by Herbert Wheaton Congdon
1963; 236 pp.
From: Charles E. Tuttle Company
Rutland, Vermont 05701
$14.25

A New England Simple for Milk Whitewash

Stir into a gallon of sweet milk enough unslaked lime in fine powder to make it thicker than cream. Add a teacup of turpentine, stir well, and put on at once with a paint brush. This sticks to smooth wood nearly the same as paint, and can be colored with earth paints almost any shade.

A Book of Cape Cod Houses

The pencil drawings of Cape Cod houses (more than forty of them) are so enchanting that one is drawn to this book over and over again for the sheer pleasure of looking at these familiar, appealing little houses that help make Cape Cod the picturesque peninsula everyone finds it to be. Half houses, three-quarter houses, whole houses, salt boxes, Greek Revival, Victorian and Gothic Revival — they are all here!

The text is informative and factual, telling how the styles of the houses of Cape Cod were developed to meet the needs and customs of the times. "An unusual treatment of the front stairs sometimes occurred in the full Cape. When the steep stairs from the front hall reached the chimney block, they stopped at a tiny landing, and one or two stairs were built at right angles on either side to lead to the attic chambers. These stairs were aptly called the 'Good Morning Stairs,' for when the occupants of the bedrooms arose each day they faced each other and could say 'Good Morning' before descending to the first floor."

There are also drawings of interiors, fireplaces, doorways and original floor plans of many of the houses. The reader will find this an exceptionally attractive book.

John D. Lyons

A Book of Cape Cod Houses
by Doris Doane, drawings by Howard L. Rich
1970; 91 pp.
From: The Chatham Press, Inc.
Riverside, Connecticut 06878
$7.95

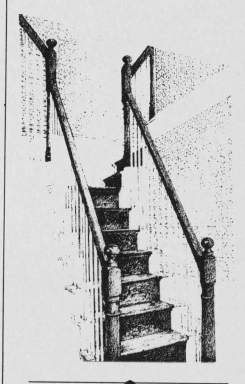

A New England Simple

Ivory handled knives which have darkened, may be cleaned by rubbing them with lemon dipped in salt, after which they should be washed in cold water.

The carpenter who builds a good house to defend us from wind and weather, is far more serviceable than the curious carver who employs his art to please his fancy.

From the Sloane-Stanley Museum
Kent, Connecticut

Yurt

Colonial Homes — Today

Old houses offer more than an investment to the purchaser. In addition to the fun of ownership and an historical feeling of continuity, they also enable the owners to be self-sufficient, especially in times of emergencies. With an old house in New England you're almost always guaranteed of having heat, light and water.

Old houses have fireplaces. Not only can you heat a room with a fireplace, but you can also cook in one.

They have dug wells in the backyards. All that you need is a bucket, a length of line and you have water.

Have you ever seen an old house without gas lanterns and candles placed strategically around? Often they're just for effect, but can be used to light your way when you need them.

The original owners of the lovely New England old homes knew how to take care of themselves. The houses that are left can show us the way.

Sally G. Devaney

Cape Ann: Cape America

An obvious love for his subject comes through in this well researched book on the history of Cape Ann. Museums, art galleries, gardens and old houses all are included.

There's a lyric description of "Beauport," now a museum, but formerly the home of Henry Davis Sleeper, one of this country's first interior decorators. There are thirty rooms, each one decorated in a different period, such as the Jacobean Room, the Paul Revere Room and the Franklin Game Room. These rooms were the inspiration for the American Wing at the Metropolitan Museum, as well as for the famous Winterthur Museum.

The garden of the Whipple House in Ipswich was designed by the man who supervised the Governor's Palace Garden at Williamsburg and it contains the chief flowers and herbs a Puritan mother needed. "Cleansing agents, dyes, insecticides, air purifiers and all her lotions and cosmetics came from her flower bed." The Whipple House is an elegant example of a seventeenth century wooden dwelling.

Jean Allen Skiff

Cape Ann: Cape America
by Herbert A. Kenny
Drawings by Tom O'Hara
1971; 294 pp.

From: J.B. Lippincott Co.
East Washington Square
Philadelphia, Pennsylvania 19105
$6.95

The Yurt — Sod-covered Roof and Walls of Pine

From far off ancient Mongolia comes the *Yurt*. There for thousands of years the prototype has withstood severe cold and violent winds of the unfriendly Steppes. As in years ago, today's *Yurt* shelters a family from the elements while offering an opportunity for living on a more personal, intimate relationship with the environment. The attempt in the design is to provide a dwelling that will not challenge nor dominate nor contend with nature. Instead, it seeks to be in harmony with it. The *Yurt* reduces skills needed in building to a minimum and still gives a beautiful, inexpensive, permanent shelter. One of the most significant qualities of the *Yurt* is the feeling of space it creates. Viewed from the outside it is unimposing. With its low profile, sod-covered roof and weathered pine, it blends easily into the natural landscape. The curved form gives as little resistance to the eye as to the wind, adding to the impression of its smallness. From the outside the possibility of standing erect within is questionable. Surprise. Upon entering one finds headroom throughout. The illusion is intended. The goal is to promote a feeling of being at home and in harmony with nature. All the structural elements described are functionally important and make the *Yurt* a stronger structure, less expensive and simpler to build. The esthetic qualities of the building are by-products of these elements.

The Yurt Construction Plan — $3.50
Wm. S. Coperthwaite
Bucks Harbor, Maine 04618

A New England Simple
Glazing for linen: To a pint of starch, add one teaspoon each of salt and finely scraped white soap.

How to Build Your Home in the Woods

With courage, spirit, and a little luck, along with a copy of Mr. Angier's comprehensive book, you can build your own home.

Nothing is left to chance in this bible for log cabin builders. Angier knows exactly what he is talking about — and what he talks about is every imaginable aspect of cabin raising.

Living as he does in a cabin in the Canadian Rockies, on the Peace River (over 100 miles from a railway and 3 miles from a neighbor), his credibility is staggering and is carried over to his discussion of the pursuit of happiness.

But first and foremost, it is a practical builders guide. Even if you've never so much as built a birdhouse, you can build a log cabin. You don't even need an axe!

Martin Robbins-Pianka

How to Build Your Home in the Woods
by Bradford Angier
Illustrated by Vena Angier
1952; 310 pp., paper
From: Hart Publishing Company, Inc.
719 Broadway
New York, New York 10003
$2.45

Use long laps
and spike stoutly

How logs are cut for splicing.

Shelter-Kit

Living in the lap of luxury in the wilderness? No. But living as one should with nature, not intruding upon the surrounding beauty. Architect designed — completely assembled by two persons — light weight and easy to carry to a remote site — low priced. These are some of the features of the Shelter-Kit Unit One camp designs. Unit One provides the outdoorsman with a weathertight habitable shell in a model which can be expanded from the basic design to a three-bedroom house. Complete instructions in detail, describe the step-by-step procedures to be followed when assembling the house. Shelter-Kit knows the importance of doing things "right." Instructions are sent a week or more in advance of Unit One's delivery. They recommend that these be studied before the work begins.

Shelter-Kit, Inc.
26 Franklin Street
Franklin, New Hampshire 03235
Basic One Unit $1,630.00

Elevations

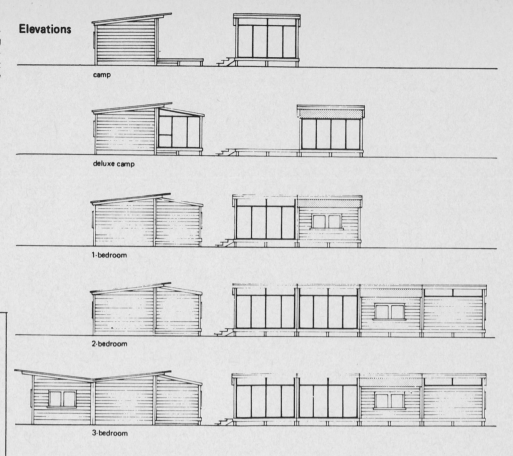

camp

deluxe camp

1-bedroom

2-bedroom

3-bedroom

Shelter-Kit Incorporated 26 Franklin Street Franklin New Hampshire 03235

Building Material of the Future

Urethane foam spray can be applied to most clean, dry surfaces without cutting or fitting. It becomes rigid, is an insulator and protects against rot or fungus. *Urethane* is used to shape small structures, even houses.

Urethane Applications Co.
Box 648
Waterville, Maine 04901
Each job separately priced.

MUSH . . . LITTLE URETHANE HOUSE!
(300 MILES OF WINTER)

Job:
    "House-on-Skis"

Builder:
    Urethane Applications
    Company
    Waterville, Maine

The "house-on-skis" is towed around the Maine countryside through rugged winter conditions—providing outdoor shelter for sportsmen. One inch of urethane foam insulation keeps the occupants comfortable.

This house-on skis is one of two which were towed behind snow-mobiles for 300 miles, from Ft. Kent to Oakland, Maine. Some 175 miles of the trek was through the Allagash wilderness, in -40° weather. Over snow and ice, uphill and downhill, through the woods and brush country—without mishap, except for one snowmobile breakdown which was repairable.

The ski-borne houses were built by Urethane Applications Company, Waterville, Maine, to prove the effectiveness of urethane foam insulation under adverse conditions. They were constructed of sheet metal with one-inch urethane foam insulation and mounted on ski runners. Isonate® CPR 385 rigid Urethane Foam, a PAPI -based urethane system supplied by the CPR Division of the Upjohn Company, 555 Alaska Avenue, Torrence, California, was specified for its low thermal conductivity. Each "house" included bunk beds for sleeping and a cooking kit. Gas lanterns kept inside temperatures comfortable—as warm as 80°.

Urethane foam proved such good insulation and so rugged that the ski-ing houses will soon be manufactured for sale. They can be built to just about any dimensions and will offer convenient comfort to wintertime outdoorsmen such as ice fishermen, skiers, snowmobile trippers, etc.

No. 344 — Size 4½ x 15 inches

No. 370 — Size 9 x 18 inches

You Name It They'll Nameplate It

Seton Name Plate Corporation makes more signs than a third base coach during a doubleheader, but they are basically a commercial outfit doing the bulk of their business via direct mail, and seem to be looking for orders of $25.00 or more at a clip.

If, however, you have suffered from those imperious notices that say, "Violators Will Be Prosecuted," or "Unauthorized Cars Will Be Towed Away," and would like to have one for yourself, Seton has them.

While I suppose it is against the law to put up signs on public streets, I am meanly bitten with an idea for two Seton signs. I would like to put them up near my house. One says "Parking Across Street" and then for across the street they have a nice red sign that says, "No Parking."

There's an extensive catalogue with every kind of nameplate and sign there is except a totem pole, and they might even make that on request.

RWW

Seton Name Plate Corporation
592 Boulevard
New Haven, Connecticut 06519

The Forgotten Art of Building a Stone Wall

Mr. Fields has written — with many walls of experience behind him — this grand little book on the practical ways of how to build a tailored stone wall without the use of mortar.

He includes a particularly good chapter on safety: precautions to take when splitting the stone, moving it to the site, and laying up the actual wall.

Curved walls, straight walls, walls with steps, some with stiles, retaining walls and garden walls. It all looks so easy!

CIE

The Forgotten Art of Building a Stone Wall
by Curtis P. Fields
1971; 61 pp., paper
From: Yankee, Inc.
 Dublin, New Hampshire 03444
 $2.50

Any one of these simple devices may help to save one's back while lifting numerous stones to the top of a wall.

The New England Village Scene — 1800

The farmers were the village.

MSH

The New England Village Scene — 1800
by Catherine Fennelly
1963; 16 pp., paper
From: Old Sturbridge Village
 Sturbridge, Massachusetts 01566
 $.50

. . . the economy of New England in 1800 was agricultural. More than ninety per cent of its people were primarily engaged in farming, and the backbone of the region was the inland rural village. The interior was still a countryside with the beauty left by God and the glacial ages — rushing streams and quiet ponds, mountain tops and hilly land and acres so filled with rock that to till them at all was a major triumph of man; while along the banks of the Connecticut, one of the main arteries of this region, lay some of the best farming land the new nation had yet acquired, rich and dark and fertile.

. . . The typical inland farmer owned only about a hundred acres of land, and of these he tilled but ten or so. The rest was pasture, mowing fields, wood lots, and waste or temporarily useless land. . . . The farmer's toil, like that of his whole household, was hard and unending. The round of clearing, plowing, planting, hoeing, and harvesting, the fences to be kept in repair, houses and barns to be mended, livestock to be tended, all took endless time and labor. In winter the farmer, often a craftsman as well, worked in his shop at making shingles or fashioning tables and chairs, turning bowls and dishes or making whatever he was particularly good at. His wife and daughters worked as hard in the house. They not only had the usual tasks of cooking, washing, and cleaning, but they made all the cloth used by the household, churned butter and pressed cheese for market, preserved food for winter with sugar, brine, and smoke, or by storing in the cool earth. The mere recital of the processes involved in making woolen and linen cloth is wearying.

The Yankee Pioneers — A Saga of Courage

"The greatest obstacles that faced the pioneers were neither the Indians nor the cold winters. They were the never ending forest and the absence of grass, which meant the absence of ox power. . . ."

"The early settlers had only the strength of their arms and backs between existence and extinction . . . They could not use animals because there was nothing in the woods for them to eat. Without their animals they could not bring their heavy tools such as grindstones and anvils, but only small tools such as axes and augers carried on their backs. . . ."

"The chief reason why the settlers chose the hills was that there were more beaver than people in the long-ago days, animals which had the inconsiderate habit of damming up brooks and rivers until the lowlands were an impenetrable marsh. The swarms of mosquitoes, gnats, blowflies and other insects that made life miserable for man and beast were not quite so thick on the hills as in the dank and swampy valleys choked with willows, alders and brush." These excerpts give only a glimpse of the many not-so-well-known hardships which our forebearers faced. It's a fascinating, sobering book which should awaken the reader today who is prone to complain about some of the shortcomings of modern living.

Louise Russell

The Yankee Pioneers — A Saga of Courage
By Samuel B. Pettengill
1972; 175 pp.
From: Charles E. Tuttle Company
 Rutland, Vermont 05701
 $5.50

The Berkshire Traveller Almanack 1973

Weather predictions play a minor role in this little journal — but if poems, epigrams and bits of wisdom appeal to you — keep the Almanack at your bedside.

Beautifully illustrated with old woodcuts and engravings, you'll be drawn to it again and again.

MSH

The Berkshire Traveller Almanack 1973
1972; 110 pp., paper
From: The Berkshire Traveller Press
 Stockbridge, Massachusetts 01262
 $1.95

The Berkshire Traveller
ALMANACK
1973
A Countryman's Ruminations

THE BERKSHIRE TRAVELLER PRESS
Stockbridge, Massachusetts 01262

Habitat

Buying Country Property

A very enlightening guide for anyone contemplating the purchase of country property — property anywhere for that matter. Such general considerations as knowing what you want, what you can afford, how to deal with real estate agents, and how to make the best mortgage deals should be valuable to all prospective buyers.

As for country acreage or a home in the country, the author offers specific advice on how to go about locating the property, how to judge it, how to improve it and pitfalls to avoid.

Charles T. Letson

Buying Country Property
by Herbert R. Moral
1972; 119 pp., paper

From: Garden Way Publishing Co.
    Charlotte, Vermont 05445
    $3.00

How to Judge The True Condition of a House

Your search for country property, of course, involves either the purchase of an existing house, with land, or a piece of land on which to build a house. This chapter concerns itself with the existing house. In evaluating such a house you are going to be subjected to perhaps the most difficult of all buying tasks.

The casualness with which most of us investigate houses we are considering buying is little short of amazing. What is the usual procedure? You take a look at the living room to ascertain the view, the number of windows, and the size. You cast an appraising eye at the fireplace: decide how you would like to have the room decorated, and that's that. You may be intrigued by the streamlined kitchen, and wonder how it would look with your own kitchen set. Someone reminded you that cross-ventilation is best for a bedroom, so, after you have counted the windows and figured whether the space was large enough for your bedroom furniture, you have checked that room off against your mental list. You take a hasty glance at the attic, look up at the rafters to make sure there are no leaks in the roof, and then make a quick trip to the cellar to poke at the furnace, if there is one.

That is the average house search.

There is no reason for such heedlessness. A little information and a few simple tests will give you a fair basis for judging, with some degree of reliability, any house you might consider buying. You won't become an expert appraiser of houses, but at least you will be able to recognize the most obvious defects, omissions and economies, as well as any downright fakes that may have been perpetrated. You will be able to satisfy yourself more assuredly as to whether the house is or isn't worth considering further.

Buying Country Property

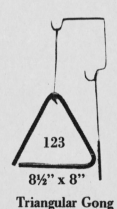

63 items to check in buying a house

1. Footing.	22. Jack rafter.	43. Rough sill.
2. Foundation wall.	23. Hip rafter.	44. Mantle.
3. Basement floor.	24. Purlin.	45. Ceiling joists.
4. Porch floor.	25. Chimney cap.	46. Studding.
5. Pilaster.	26. Chimney.	47. Floor joists.
6. Window sill.	27. Header.	48. Ribbon.
7. Key stone.	28. Bridging.	49. Gutter.
8. Transom.	29. Plate.	50. Handrail.
9. Column.	30. Corner post.	51. Balustrade.
10. Entablature.	31. Sheathing.	52. Newel.
11. Balustrade.	32. Building paper.	53. Leader head.
12. Cornice.	33. Siding.	54. Stair soffit.
13. Fan window.	34. Brick.	55. Wainscoting.
14. Valley.	35. Water table.	56. Base.
15. Dormer window.	36. Cleanout door.	57. Girder.
16. Flashing.	37. Subfloor.	58. Column cap.
17. Shingles.	38. Finish floor.	59. Basement column.
18. Roof sheathing.	39. Hearth.	60. Column base.
19. Ridge.	40. Stair landing.	61. Joist.
20. Common rafter.	41. Casement window.	62. Partition.
21. Collar beam.	42. Fire place.	63. Lath.

Heritage Metalcraft

In their "little foundry with a function," Wayne and Anita Holmquist turn out a line of decorative and functional gift items which are sold through their factory salesroom. Should you desire a trivet, buttermold, weathervane, sconce, or stringholder, Heritage is the place to visit. They also carry a line of reproduction firemarks. Illustrated price list available.

Heritage Metalcraft, Inc.
Route 202
South Windham, Maine 04082

Handcast Buttermolds $1.20 each

Flower B-26   Eagle B-27   Heart B-28

123

8½" x 8"
Triangular Gong
$6.50

Springs

Some springs spring and some springs sprung. There are extension types that resist pulling out and compression types that resist pushing in. Sort of reminds me of Dr. Doolittle's fey creation of the "Pushmepullyou," an animal with a head at both ends.

All that aside, *Hardware Products Company* has a simple and completely clear four-page catalogue that makes it easy to order the type, size, tension and/or elongation you want in a spring. They will be glad to send it to you on request. I stifled the urge to say they would spring for one.

Suggested by Stephen P. Baldwin   RWW

Hardware Products Company, Inc.
84 Fulton Street
Boston, Massachusetts 02113

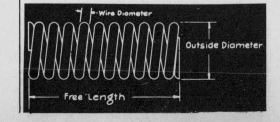

TREMONT NAIL COMPANY

THE NAIL MILL

The main mill building was constructed in 1848 and was named after the fulling mill (Parker Mills) whose foundation it now shares. Until the 1920's the main source of power was a centrifugal water wheel which powered the massive overhead shafting. The beams and trusses mostly wooden pegged are a study in strength and rigidity for which the ship-carpenters who designed and built them would have been justly proud today.

The bell in the cupola bears a date of 1851 and has called to work and to rest four generations of loyal workers. Since 1819, over a century-and-a-half, Tremont Nail Company has survived the tests of time. Loyalty, determination, fortitude and ingenuity have once again succeeded in preserving this early American industry. It is truly a living museum.

ELM STREET, WAREHAM, MASS. 02571
Just Off Cranberry Highway (Rt. No. 28)

ESTABLISHED 1819
Nail Makers for Over 150 Years

Tie Tac
for the Gents·

Nail Brooch
for the Ladies

Real nails from the World's oldest nail manufacturer. Add an antique gold finish, a finding, and you have a useful and unusual tie tac or brooch that are truly unique conversation pieces.

No. N-10 $1.98 ea. p.p.   Gift boxed

Overhead shafting, wooden pulleys and ancient lathes still serve faithfully in this early American machine shop.

Here our blacksmith does his welding, heat-treating and the making of machine parts.

Decorative Wrought Head Cut Nails

Fashioned after the hand forged nails of the late 1700's, these nails have the added feature of 70% more holding power than wire nails.

No. N-40 $1.00 lb.
Pkgd. 1 lb., 5 lb., and 25 lb. boxes
Available in 1½", 2", 2½" and 3"
Specify "Wrought Head" and Size

Nail Keg and Cushion

A stool, wastebasket or hamper, you name it. Can be painted, stained or left as is. The keg measures 11½" in diameter by 18" high. The keg alone is $4.95. The padded colonial print cushion is $2.00. Shipping weight is 9½ lbs. for the keg and 3 lbs. for the padded top.

Tremont Nail Company History

Nails in their crudest from date back to 3000 B.C. The Romans hand-forged them and they have been found in excavations and sunken ships from the period 500 A.D.

When our ancestors first stepped from the Mayflower onto that soil that was to become Plymouth County, they discovered a soil which was essentially sandy and difficult to cultivate. As they plowed for their first crops, they noticed that the earth yielded small deposits of crude iron ore mixed with the ooze of the swampy regions. From this ore and with crude smelters, they separated the metal from the ore and began the fashioning of nails and metal tools they had left behind them when they sailed into the unknown.

Cooking utensils; shipfitters hardware, nails and wagon treads grew from this ore dug in the swamps where the cranberries grow today. As the Massachusetts Bay Colony grew, the residents of Wareham were able to supply newcomers with nails for their homes. The industry had been born.

The original factory was established by Issac and Jared Pratt in 1819 on the site of an old cotton mill which had been shelled and burned by the British in the War of 1812. Known originally as Parker Mills Nail Company, it later became known as the Tremont Nail Company. The first cut nail machines appeared during the late 1700's and the first machine to cut and head a nail in one operation was invented by Ezekiel Reed of Bridgewater, Mass.

The present nail factory has about 60 nail machines and was completed in 1848. Among those who managed the business in the early days are men whose names are famous throughout New England: John Avery Parker, William Rodman, Charles W. Morgan, Bartlett Murdock, Benjamin Fearing, William Caswell, Horace Pratt Tobey and William A. Leonard.

For a century-and-a-half the company has achieved a reputation for skilled nail cutting that has made its product readily saleable throughout the markets of the world. Through all the changes and the hurried pace of modern industry the same product is still being produced for customers who prefer the superior holding power and durability of this time-tested nail.

Habitat

The Yankee Shun Pike

This newspaper of real estate and auction news may be your best bet for finding that "home away from home."

If collecting antiques is your bag — a variety of auctions, estate sales and shops are listed. Thrifty souls, who don't mind a bit of driving throughout Vermont and New Hampshire, might be well rewarded.

RWW

The Yankee Shun Pike
Miller Publishers, Inc.
Bellows Falls, Vermont 05101
$3.00 yearly; published monthly

Winches and Hoists

Nine different models in five series are offered by *Superwinch* — winches for snowmobiles, trucks, trailers, boats and one-man power loading for any trailered car. *Superwinch* says, ". . . they are dollar for dollar, the smallest, lightest, most versatile, most powerful 12 volt and 110 volt winches and hoists anywhere . . ."

Superwinch, Inc.
Pomfret, Connecticut 06258

Connecticut's Old Houses

This little book makes fascinating reading for those with a real interest in old houses. Why was the salt box a practical shape? How did houses really look in olden times? "Contrary to general belief, early houses were not painted white. The colors used were red, yellow and blue." Before 1700 few were painted at all — neither the outside nor the interior woodwork.

The author divides early Connecticut architecture into five periods from 1635 — 1830 and tells us how these house plans reflect the social and economic conditions of their times. There are descriptions of thirty-two houses now standing in chronological order of construction.

The book concludes with a chapter about churches and meeting houses, listing those in existence with architectural interest, and a final chapter on five Connecticut public buildings.

"Probably the very earliest chimneys were of logs laid crosswise, or of woven wattles, and plastered on the inside with clay. Such chimneys were obviously fire hazards and required periodic inspection: hence the office of 'chimney-viewer'."

Louise Russell

Connecticut's Old Houses
by J. Frederick Kelly, A.I.A.
1970; 73 pp., paper
From: The Pequot Press
         Chester, Connecticut 06412
         $2.50

The Foxboro Company

Foxboro produces instruments and systems to handle variables — industrial process and energy control variables. Among the many types are environmental variables for those encountered in water and fluids measurement control, waste disposal and treatment, desalination, incineration and other problems in our daily environment. More than sixty years of specialization in handling the control problems of industry is an assurance of competence of engineering and quality of product when you buy *Foxboro*.

The Foxboro Company
Foxboro, Massachusetts 02035

Pneumatic Consotrol Controller
130 Series Consotrol Indicating Controllers are pneumatic receiver-controllers operating on a 3-15 psi signal. Set point is manually set or pneumatically adjusted by a remote 3-15 psi signal. The controllers introduce many new concepts and design features including balanceless-bumpless transfer, full scale vertical indication, exceptional visibility of display, shelf-mounted versatility, and new packaging.

Panel Mounting Concept for Electronic Consotrol Instrumentation
Outstanding convenience is offered by shelf-mounted electronic Consotrol instrumentation packaging design featuring unit construction. Each instrument fits into its individual shelf position and slides easily in and out of the shelf for operating adjustments, without interfering with other instruments or interrupting control. The typical shelf shown contains (left to right) a controller, recorder, controller, auxiliary station, and controller.

Electronic Consotrol Controller
General purpose indicating control station providing proportional-plus-reset and proportional-plus-reset-plus-derivative control action. Input and output are standard 10-50 ma d-c signals. Transfer from automatic to manual and manual to automatic is completely balanceless and bumpless. Unique "T" switch performs both manual adjustment and transfer switching functions. Wholly solid-state and computer compatible.

Electronic Consotrol Recorder
Solid-state, panel-mounted instrument that receives standard 10-50 ma d-c inputs from remote measurement transmitters. Records one, two, or three variables on 4-inch roll or Scan-Fold strip chart. Easy loading, simple adjustment, long-term recording. Can be located up to several thousand feet from point of measurement. Designed for shelf mounting.

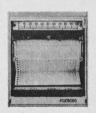

Tools
are extensions
of the human
hand —
They were the
first works of
Art.

From the Sloane-Stanley Museum
Kent, Connecticut

Hard-to-Find Tools

Their catalog of hard-to-find tools will delight all gadgeteers and people who like to work with their hands.

For the furniture fixer, there's a special plastic injector so glue can easily be squeezed into joints without taking the piece apart. A handy $5 torch lamp will remove paint without harming the wood.

Riffler files of unusual shape will appeal to sculptors, jewelers and handymen.

Their lightweight stainless steel garden tools will especially appeal to women gardeners. The steel parts are forged for utmost strength (not a mere stamping from sheet metal). These are available only from Brookstone.

Catalog $.50

The Brookstone Co.
Brookstone Building
Peterborough, New Hampshire 03458

Universal Hole Cutter	+ $1.40 handling
Upside Down Oiler	+ $1.15 handling
Slim Open-end Wrenches	+ $ .90 handling
Miniature Nutdrivers	+ $ .90 handling

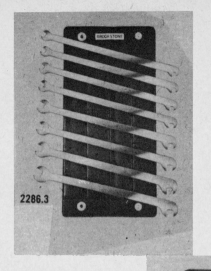

2286.3

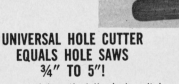

2316.8

AN OILER THAT PUMPS UPSIDE DOWN?

You bet—and it wasn't easy locating one, either. We have one now with TWO hydraulic pumps. It allows you to oil those hard-to-get-at places where you have to pump oil UP into the work area. The standard one-pump oiler just won't work on these jobs while ours will do the job in BOTH directions.

The quality is heavy duty. Deep-drawn aluminum body is a full 3/32" thick, practically unbreakable. Pumps are all brass and aluminum—built for a life-time of rugged use. Holds full half pint, enough for any job. 5" brass spout.

D-2481.0 Twin pump oiler **$5.25**

UNIVERSAL HOLE CUTTER EQUALS HOLE SAWS 3/4" TO 5"!

A most unusual invention! Here's how it is used:
1. Mark center of desired hole.
2. Drill at that point a hole to clear and insert Hole Cutter frame.
3. Drill a small starting hole anywhere on radius of desired hole.
4. Insert cutting blade and hook into cutter frame at corresponding slot. Hook other end into frame handle, adjusting handle and tension to suit.
5. Cut in either direction. Resulting disc comes out with frame (does not fall where not wanted).

Will cut holes for 1/2" to 4 1/2" pipe. Slots in frame are spaced to do this accurately.
Will cut practically any material.
Cuts arcs in tubing for branch connections.
Works as universal hacksaw, cutting in any direction, straight or curved. Blade is round, only 1/16" dia., has teeth all around. Ideal for cutting out odd, irregular shapes. Cuts steel, other metals and materials up to several inches thick (blade 8 1/4" long).
Cuts slots, rectangular holes, etc., freehand or using edge of material as guide.
Useable as a file.
Very nicely made. Rigid frame of 3/8" dia. steel, finely polished nickel plated. Nickel plated fittings. Comfortable hardwood handle, stained and varnished.
About 14 3/4" long, over all. 2 5/16" depth of cut. Comes with one blade.

D-2316.8 Universal hole cutter hacksaw . . . **$14.95**

NO SUBSTITUTES FOR MINIATURE NUT DRIVERS

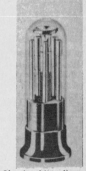

Without this handy socket wrench set, you just can't get at many of those tiny nuts buried so deep in instruments, clocks, models, controls, appliances, electronic devices.

Five tough steel socket wrenches, interchangeable in jeweler's chuck-type handle. Shanks 1/8" diam. Hex sizes 5/64", 3/32", 7/64", 1/8", 5/32" — fit thread sizes 00, 0, 1, 2. Deep counterbored to fit over studs.

Swivel-top handle, knurled for grip, about 3 3/4" long with wrench. Complete set in handy plastic stand with See-thru dust dome.

D-1071.0 Complete nut driver set **$4.95**

PURITROL
THE POLLUTION SOLUTION

Pollutrol

A clean answer to a dirty problem.

New Englanders take pride in workmanship and technological advances. *Pollutrol* subscribes to this. Their approach to sewage treatment is modern and advanced. What is it? The *Puritrol* sewage treatment manufactured by *Pollutrol* is a system of unique design whereby domestic waste is treated so the clear, odor free effluent may be safely discharged. *Puritrol* utilizes the extended aeration process of biological treatment while incorporating a patented batch principle.

Pollutrol Industries, Inc.
Box 3727
Portland, Maine 04104

Prices for *Puritrol Systems:* According to capacity in gallons per day from:
1,500 gals. – $4,300.00 to
25,000 gals. – $33,950.00
FOB, Gardiner, Maine 04345

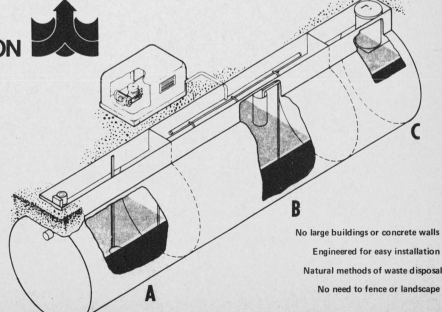

No large buildings or concrete walls

Engineered for easy installation

Natural methods of waste disposal

No need to fence or landscape

"Mister, if you can't shave with it, you can't carve with it"

That about sums up the honed edge of the thinking of the *Woodcraft Supply Corp.*, of Woburn, Massachusetts.

Their catalogue is 25¢, and has to be the best buy since Manhattan Island . . . 44 pages of fine tools, books, cutlery, workbenches, and other good things.

But let Rogers Welles of Woodcraft tell it in his own words:

Woodcraft was founded in 1928 by Mr. George S. Eaton who had for years been an industrial woodworking machinery salesman. As fate would have it, he started on his own, just as the machinery manufacturers began to produce small equipment suitable for the home craftsman; so, he dealt in both.

Eventually, however, it became increasingly difficult to obtain both the kind of and the quality of tools needed within the domestic market. Woodcraft, therefore, was forced to look elsewhere. High quality tools not otherwise available were located throughout Europe. Today, we have over 26 suppliers from five European countries — and the number is growing constantly.

Periodically, people frustrated with the difficulty of finding quality woodworking tools wrote in for tools — thus, the beginning of the mail order idea. Today, mail order constitutes the major part of our business.

It is the opinion of the writer and also of many customers that Woodcraft Supply has more types of quality tools under one roof than can be found anywhere in the world. However, our most invaluable *product* is free for the asking; the opinions, advice and accumulated experience of our *woodcrafters*. In conjunction with this experience, we carry a wide range of books for those who wish to *dig* the information out for themselves or who wish to pursue some subject in detail at their leisure.

Woodcraft Supply Corp.   RWW
313 Montvale Avenue
Woburn, Massachusetts 01801

SEWING AWL

No. 413

Ideal for sewing leather, canvas and similar materials. The awl carries a spool of thread on the handle Hollow handle holds extra curved needle and wrench. Directions furnished with each awl explaining how automatic lock stitch can be effected in repair work. Comes with one straight and one curved diamond pointed needles.

Mailing weight 1/2 pound. $2.50

TIMBER SCRIBER

No. 6930. Timber Scriber or "raise knife." Used to scribe the waterline of boats. Single blade. Closed 3½", open approx. 5 inches. Simulated stag handle. Mailing weight 1/4 pound. $5.15

CAULKING IRONS

#999 Straight blunt $2.60
#1000 Straight sharp   2.60
#1001 Bent sharp   3.00
#1001A Bent blunt   3.00
#1002 Single Crease   4.15

Mailing weight 2 lbs. ea.

#1001 #1001A #1002 #1000 #999

CHIP CARVING KNIVES

No. 600(6). Set of six knives as shown at the left . Length 5 to 6¼ inches. Mailing weight 1 pound. $8.70

Individual knives as shown at the left . Order by stock number as indicated. Mailing weight ¼ pound. $1.60

620   617½   619   624   623   622

CURVED RASP

No. 3556. "Curved Rasp. Technically a Staircase-Makers rasp, this tool is very handy, particularly for sculptors. Mailing weight ½ lb. $3.75

BEECH SPOKESHAVE

No. 2360. The old fashioned wooden spokeshave with Sheffield Steel Blade. Width of cutter 2". Mailing weight 1 lb. $6.75

DRAW KNIVES

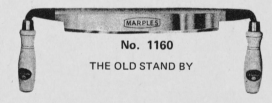

No. 1160

THE OLD STAND BY

No. 1160-10. 10" Draw knife. Mailing weight 2 lbs. $9.10

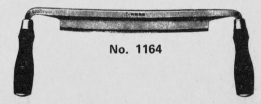

No. 1164

No. 1164. Draw Knife. Carpenters' American Pattern. Made of cast steel with black handles.

No. 1164-10 — 10" length of blade. Mailing weight 2 pounds. $8.40
No. 1164-12 — 12" length of blade. Mailing weight 2 pounds. $9.45

Habitat

"Polecats" and Ingenious Space Dividers

These "Polecats" are made of metal, and to describe them in words is like trying to describe a fish you caught while keeping your hands in your pocket. They are, basically, metal poles that go from floor to ceiling and are equipped with clamps to hold most anything at any height.

The Brewster Corporation (who make the "Pole-cat") also make "Sho Wall," free-standing partitions that divide space most imaginatively. They are burlap covered in a myriad of colors and are even supplied in chalkboard. Absolutely great for making two spaces out of one if you happen to have a couple of children who seem to be at each other's throat.

BURLAP

tacking • mounting
1st and 2nd surfaces

Specially refined fire retardant, 10 oz. prime fibre. Supports 20 lbs. per hanging point on picture hooks. Accepts: picture hooks, pins and tacks. COLORS: Sand, Gold, Moss, Tangerine.

Complete catalogue and price lists from:

The Brewster Corporation
Old Saybrook, Connecticut 06475

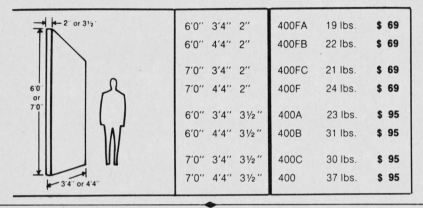

6'0"	3'4"	2"	400FA	19 lbs.	**$ 69**
6'0"	4'4"	2"	400FB	22 lbs.	**$ 69**
7'0"	3'4"	2"	400FC	21 lbs.	**$ 69**
7'0"	4'4"	2"	400F	24 lbs.	**$ 69**
6'0"	3'4"	3½"	400A	23 lbs.	**$ 95**
6'0"	4'4"	3½"	400B	31 lbs.	**$ 95**
7'0"	3'4"	3½"	400C	30 lbs.	**$ 95**
7'0"	4'4"	3½"	400	37 lbs.	**$ 95**

Brown & Sharpe

"Think Metric." At the 1972 International Machine Tool Show, the theme for hundreds of exhibits was centered on the metric system. *Brown & Sharpe,* one of the machine tool makers exhibiting, displayed a measuring device which converts the metric system into the present U.S. system. From its beginning in 1833, *Brown & Sharpe* has been a leader in precision metalworking. Now, as the U.S. gets ready for the day when it changes measuring standards, this New England manufacturer is completely ready for the conversion.

Joseph R. Brown, the founder, learned his trade from his father, David Brown, a master clock and watchmaker. In 1831, Joseph went into business for himself making lathes and small tools. On September 12, 1848, he made a momentous entry in his job book. "Lucian Sharpe came to work for me this day as an apprentice." Three years later, he became a partner and the company became "J.R. Brown & Sharpe."

Throughout their careers, both Mr. Brown and Mr. Sharpe were interested in the problem of setting up standards of measurement for the mechanical trades. The B&S wire gage system was eventually adopted as the American standard and is still in common use today.

Perhaps the outstanding standard-bearer of Mr. Brown's tradition for accuracy was Oscar J. Beale whose particular forte was the development of accurate measuring machinery that enabled B&S to manufacture gages with precision exceeding anything then available elsewhere in the world.

Over 14,000 products are manufactured by B&S. They are sold through local industrial distributors.

Brown & Sharpe Mfg. Co.
Precision Park
North Kingstown, Rhode Island 02852

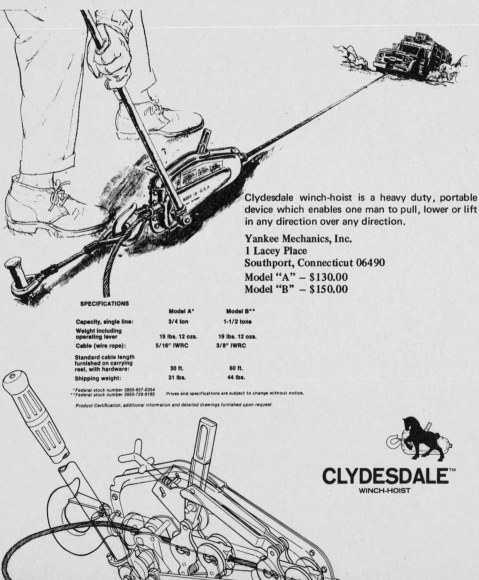

Clydesdale winch-hoist is a heavy duty, portable device which enables one man to pull, lower or lift in any direction over any direction.

Yankee Mechanics, Inc.
1 Lacey Place
Southport, Connecticut 06490
Model "A" — $130.00
Model "B" — $150.00

SPECIFICATIONS

	Model A*	Model B**
Capacity, single line:	3/4 ton	1-1/2 tons
Weight including operating lever	19 lbs. 12 ozs.	19 lbs. 12 ozs.
Cable (wire rope):	5/16" IWRC	3/8" IWRC
Standard cable length furnished on carrying reel, with hardware:	30 ft.	60 ft.
Shipping weight:	31 lbs.	44 lbs.

*Federal stock number 3950-857-0354
**Federal stock number 3950-729-6165   Prices and specifications are subject to change without notice.

Product Certification, additional information and detailed drawings furnished upon request.

CLYDESDALE™
WINCH-HOIST

A New England Simple – To Repel Mosquitoes
Kerosene applied to screens with a cloth or brush will keep away mosquitoes.

A New England Simple – To Drive Rats Away
Thoroughly besmear their door or passage into the room with coal tar, which will completely coat them from head to foot, and they will suddenly leave.

Habitat

The Sloane — Stanley Museum

Eric Sloane, Connecticut artist and writer, is also a collector of early American implements. He gave his collection to the State of Connecticut and it is displayed at the Sloane-Stanley Museum erected by The Stanley Works of New Britain. The Museum is on the site of the old Kent furnace where operations began in 1826. The furnace had produced high quality pig iron for nearly seventy years. Within sight of the distant hills and the Housatonic River, this scenic spot, which for many years was a town dump, is now made into an attractive park. The ruins of the old iron works add a note of interest for historians and antiquarians coming to see and learn more of New England's past. Inside the Museum, the tools, as arranged by Eric Sloane, present both an artistic and an educational display of early implements, many of them handmade. With the early settler's reverence for wood and his skill in designing ingenious tools, this collection tells a valuable story about our forefathers and the great American heritage of craftsmanship.

In the lobby of the Museum is a diorama of the Kent Iron Furnace as it appeared in the late nineteenth century. Also, books by Eric Sloane are on sale.

The Sloane — Stanley Museum
Kent, Connecticut 06757
Open: Memorial Day through October 31
Adults: $.50   Children: $.25

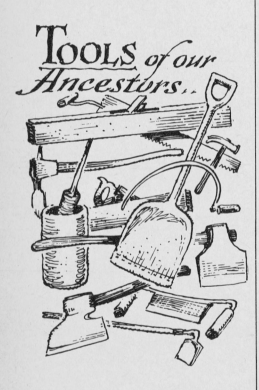

Cutting Tools

It may be a long time, it may be several lifetimes, in fact, before you ever experience the urge to have your knife blades reconditioned or replaced, or feel the necessity to purchase a wire rope cutter (available in three sizes), or know the need to possess a pair of wire nippers (available in two styles). On the other hand, *you* may be in chronic need of these services and items. If so, the *M.W. Robinson Co.* can supply all the reground knife blades, wire nippers and other cutting tools your heart desires.

Claudia

M.W. Robinson Co., Inc.
Laurel Brook Road
Rockfall, Connecticut 06481

The American Precision Museum

The *American Precision Museum* building, an exhibit in itself for its architectural grace and historic structure, houses an important collection of hand tools and machines, together with products illustrative of what the tools accomplish. The great drama of how tools and machines have been invented and applied in replacing manual labor, is the story of how tireless machines have relieved men from the drudgery of earlier days. It began with machines to apply the power of wind, water and steam in place of muscle. Good examples of these are the lathes and planing machines for wood and metal, sewing machines, riflemaking devices, typewriters.

The museum also collects drawings, photographs, correspondence, catalogs, periodicals, biographical materials and related data for its reference files. The largest present asset of this description is the 800-volume set of Patent Digests describing the scientific and technical inventions of American and important foreign patentees.

The building housing the museum was built in 1846, as an armory and machine shop. When built, it was the most modern armory in existence, with all new machinery to make army rifles having complete interchangeability. This system was a considerable advance in technology and is one on which we rely today for automobiles and countless other machines of our civilization.

The American Precision Museum
Windsor, Vermont 05089
Admission: $ .75

◆

CAREW

Cutting Nippers

D = MAXIMUM OPENING

DIMENSIONS IN INCHES

Model	A	B	C	D
8"	9-1/8"	2-7/16"	1-1/4"	5/16"
10"	11"	2-3/8"	1-5/16"	5/16"
12"	12-7/8"	2-11/16"	1-1/2"	5/16"
14"	14-15/16"	2-3/4"	1-9/16"	7/16"

The Stanley Works

The origin of the carpenter's plane goes back to the beginning of civilization. In its earliest form it was nothing more than a stone flattened at one end in much the same manner as our modern chisel. Pieces of this tool have been found dating back to 4000 B.C.

Stanley Works does not have its roots as deep as the dawn of civilization, nor does it claim to have invented the plane, but the company has had much to do with the refinement of this important tool. The "Bailey" plane is one of Stanley's most famous pieces of merchandise.

To Leonard Bailey, an employee of the *Stanley Tool Works,* goes the major credit for improving the carpenter plane to its present efficiency. It was in 1858 when the first patent was awarded Bailey. Today, his patents — and refinements by other Stanley engineers — have brought the plane to its present state of perfection. The story of the plane is only one part of the Stanley saga.

The company is famous for not only its quality line of hand tools, but its proficiency in manufacturing in such diverse fields as automatic door equipment, steel strappings, industrial hardware, hinges and cold rolled strip steel.

One of its latest expressions, designed to appeal to everyone, is the new Surform Sculpturing Kit. It contains a round file, flat file, pocket plane, coping saw, an outlined piece of wood and a 24-page instruction book.

Frederick T. Stanley and his brother William, founders of the company in 1843, were men of vision. They had their challenges and met them solidly by providing the tools and hardware to help build America. *The Stanley Works* today carries on this tradition in the same forthright manner.

The Stanley Works
New Britain, Connecticut 06050
Surform Sculpture Kit — about $13.00 at hardware stores and home center outlets.

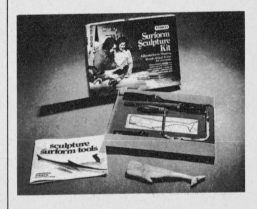

◆

A Pictorial History of the Shelburne Museum

This magnificent collection of colored as well as black and white illustrations depicts the grandeur and the homespun simplicity of Shelburne Museum in Shelburne, Vermont.

Compiled in celebration of its twenty-fifth anniversary, the book traces, in photograhic and editorial form, the museum from birth to its present day status, an outstanding coming together of Americana.

Sally G. Devaney

A Pictorial History of the Shelburne Museum
by Richard Lawrence Greene and Kenneth Edward Wheeling
1972; 127 pp., paper
From: Shelburne Museum
Shelburne, Vermont 05482
$5.00

Cutlery

Many of us haven't played mumble-peg or cleaned rabbits and squirrels or skinned coons, possums and skunks. Certainly, there is no one alive today who's heard the cry, "Up to Green River," but it all has to do with knives — Russell Harrington knives. The Harrington Cutlery Company was founded in 1818, the John Russell Cutlery Company was founded in 1834 in separate parts of Massachusetts — Southbridge and Greenfield. In 1932 they merged.

The story of these two companies is a saga with roots deep in the history and expansion of our country. While Harrington in Southbridge was winning favor with its forged steel razors, guns and jackknives (for cleaning rabbits, playing mumble-peg and many other things), 45 miles away to northwest as the crow flies the Russell Cutlery began operation. Its fame spread across the nation to the frontier and beyond on the merit of the Green River Blades it made. The Rocky Mountain men and free trappers used the name as a standard of excellence of things traded, from horse to trap. Anything done "Up to Green River" connoted quality. On the other hand, the cry of a trapper in a fight, "Give it to him, up to Green River!" meant something else again.

As the 20th oldest industry in Massachusetts in continuous service, the *Russell Harrington Cutlery Company* employs over 300 highly skilled people. It sells 1,000 types of cutlery to all countries where the dollar exchange is available. More than 4,000,000 knives are produced annually, using modern manufacturing methods and a quality control bred years ago in "Green River!"

Catalogue available.

Russell Harrington Cutlery, Inc.
Southbridge, Massachusetts 01550

The Fletcher-Terry Company

Individuals who work with a glass cutter take this handy tool for granted but try cutting glass without one! The glass cutter had an important impact upon the glass industry and it all started 102 years ago. Records show that the glass cutter — really, a small steel wheel — was the discovery, if not the invention, of Samuel G. Monce. The principal reason for the limited use of glass for practical purposes prior to the early 1860's was the difficulty of cutting it into desired shapes.

In 1868, a jeweler in Leverett, Massachusetts, named O. M. Pike successfully challenged the existing belief that only the diamond could cut glass evenly. He decided that a hardened steel rod with an angled tip would produce the desired result — a satisfactory cut — much more economically. After weeks of testings, Pike finally produced a rather clumsy glass cutting machine which he patented on December 29, 1868. Elated with his success, he began looking for a manufacturer.

How and why he chose the R. J. Ives Machine Shop in Bristol, Connecticut, is not known, but his decision gave Sam Monce, an employee of the shop, a chance for further experimentation in cutting glass. While working on the project, Sam discovered that a steel wheel would produce the same kind of scratch as the rod. He persisted with his idea and, when his efforts proved practical, Sam applied for a patent which was granted June 8, 1869. Named the Excelsior, and retailed from $1.50 to $2.50, it was widely used and so valued by glaziers that they called it the "Bristol Diamond." In 1870, Sam Monce went into business for himself.

From this beginning, members of Sam Monce's kin, the Fletchers and Terrys, expanded his small business through the years and for over a century have successfully carried on his manufacturing skill and ingenuity.

The Fletcher-Terry Company
Spring Lane
Farmington, Connecticut 06032

Fletcher-Terry's general purpose cutter (02–DC)
$.90

BASIC KNIVES .. AND THEIR USES

PARING KNIFE

Four styles of paring knives are most common... curved, spear, sharp, and clip point. Delicate pepper rings finely sliced or slivered olives or cherries, can be done with a curved or sharp point paring knife to dress up fancy salads. A cook's paring, or spear point knife, can be used to remove corn from the cob, break up heads of lettuce or cabbage, peel fruit or vegetables, cut beans, etc. The clip point is used for eyeing potatoes, seeding, peeling, and pitting.

UTILITY KNIFE

A sharp 6" utility knife is most efficient for slicing non-solid fruits and vegetables, such as tomatoes or squash. For acid fruits, a stainless steel blade is preferred. Useful for cutting large melon rings, cutting heads of lettuce into wedges, preparing cabbage for shredding, halving grapefruits and oranges, etc.

BONING KNIFE

Blades vary in length from 4" to 8". Many cooks simplify carving and get extra servings by boning out a roast when it is partially cooked. For boning roasts, whole hams, lamb legs, veal legs, and filleting fish, a narrow flexible blade is best. The wider stiff blade is used for cutting raw meat and many other trimming operations on less thick cuts of meat.

BUTCHER, CIMETER STEAK KNIFE, AND CLEAVER

For the odd jobs in the kitchen, the butcher and cimeter steak knives can be used for dicing salt pork, cubing cooled meats, cutting steaks or trimming raw meat. Many cooks substitute the favorite forged cook's knife for jobs normally done with these knives. The cleaver is used for opening lobsters, cutting poultry and joints.

FRENCH COOK'S KNIFE

Available in blade lengths from 8" to 14", this knife has more uses than any other one knife in the kitchen. The blade is wide at the handle and tapers to a point. Deep choil protects knuckles when dicing or mincing celery, onions, nut meats, parsley, peppers, etc. When properly used, the chef positions the point of the knife on the cutting board beyond the food to be diced or sliced and, without lifting the point, works the knife in a rocking motion to cut evenly and rapidly. Used for carving hot roasts also. The blade may be forged or not forged.

SLICERS AND CARVERS

The most important carving knife is the roast beef slicer, most often used to carve rounds, boneless roasts, boiled briskets, pot roasts, butt roasts, and standing rib roasts. The narrow cold meat slicer or ham slicer is used to slice ham or left-over cold roasts of all kinds. The wide, stiff blade does a better job on hot meats, whereas the narrow, more flexible blade cuts cold meat more efficiently. Although there are many patterns to select from, a slicer or carver should have adequate length to permit smooth slicing action.

Wilk says —

And then there is the old story of the Maine country store with about half of its shelves filled with boxes of salt of every type and size. The owner was showing a visitor through the store and took him to the ample attic which was floor to ceiling with more salt. The visitor was mightily impressed and said to the owner, "You must really sell an awful lot of salt."

"Nope," the owner replied, "I don't sell much salt at all, but that salesman from the salt company, boy, can *he sell salt!*"

Habitat

Early American Wooden Ware

The timber was cut by the time of the old moon in February, dried in the March winds, quarter sawed and fashioned mostly by hand, into the necessities of the early days.

With many photographs, the author gives a wonderful account of the origins, uses and manufacture of such things as splint goose baskets, burl bowls, cheese drainers, buckets, rolling pins, brooms and clothes pins. There is also a short chapter on the Powder Post Beetle — a must to know for anyone with wooden things!

CIE

Early American Wooden Ware
by Mary Earle Gould
1971; 243 pp.

From: Charles E. Tuttle Co., Inc.
Rutland, Vermont 05701
$9.35

Sieves were very important in long-ago days, as many things, such as sugar, salt, herbs, spices, soda and meals were ground, crushed and sifted before they could be used. Grandma in the kitchen and grandpa in the barn both had their sieves. Whether made of hair or of splint these sieves were works of art, and perhaps the finest examples of handwork found in any of the wooden ware.

The earliest type of sieve found in the old New England homes was made of hair — reds, browns, grays and blacks — taken from horses' manes and cows' tails. The hair was sorted and tied in bundles of several lengths, according to the size of the sieve to be made. The hoops were of ash or quartered oak, like those of the pantry boxes, made either in graded sets or in the regulation size of twelve inches. Each sieve had two hoops, one fitting into the other. The mat was woven, the edges sewed over and over with a coarse thread and clamped between the two hoops. Nails held it securely in the rims, so taut and even that after many years of use the mats are still firm.

In the Old Hadley Museum situated in Old Hadley, Massachusetts, there is a loom on which mats for sieves were woven. It stands about five feet high and is eighteen inches wide, and was operated from a high stool. With it are bundles of black hair in different lengths, a finished mat and a few hoops — silent memorials of labor performed many years ago.

This loom was originally owned by two sisters, Hattie and Sarah Marsh, who lived in the village of Old Hadley. They were the third generation to live in the house which had been built by their grandfather. Spinsters in the true sense of the word, they were very eccentric and remained indoors constantly, with the blinds drawn. A brother lived with them and attended to any contacts necessary with the outside world. The sisters made and sold sieves as a means of livelihood.

Fig. 1. Pig platter made from one piece of wood three feet long. A roasted pig was served head, feet and tail with an apple in its mouth.

Fig. 2. Remember when the bread was placed on a bread board and cut at the table? One says Bread, one says Spare Not. Still another says The Staff of Life. The small butter dish says Butter.

Fig. 3. A group of pantry mortars and pestles. The one at extreme right is lignum-vitae showing the heart and sap. The large central one is also of lignum-vitae, the heart wood. The one at the left is burl with an iron headed pestle.

Hickin's Mountain Mowings

Tucked back in the Dummerston hills, just far enough off the beaten path to give one the feel of the natural beauty of the Vermont countryside, is *Hickin's Mountain Mowings*.

Some Vermonters feel that Frank and Mary Hickin have one of the finest produce farms anywhere. The Brattleboro Reformer wrote in an article about them:

"Frank sells his produce with the enthusiasm of a proud father; as one acquaintance remarks, 'He is the only person I know who can work up a missionary zeal about a carrot'."

In an average season, they have more than 100 different kind of vegetables and fruits, including snowpeas, lemon cucumbers, 25 varieties of lettuce, raspberries, and tiny new potatoes the size of a marble. When not involved with harvesting, they make sugar in their own sugar house. From the stove in their farmhouse kitchen come such goodies as jams, jellies, pickles and their traditional maple fruit cake — rich, moist and flavored with pure maple syrup and wine. Brochure and price list available.

Hickin's Mountain Mowings
RFD 1
Brattleboro, Vermont 05301

Gift Box — 3 lb. wheel Vermont cheese, 1/2 pint pure Vermont Maple syrup, 1 lb. honey, 1 jar jam or jelly, 1 jar pickles, 1 lb. fruitcake, and extra space filled with apples. $13.50

Maple Fruit Cake — 2 lb. $5.50
Maple Butternut Fudge — 1/2 lb. $1.95

Maple Icicle Relish 9 oz. $.95
                          16 oz. $1.69

Shipping charge extra

◆

Shaker Recipe Book

Some very interesting facts about the Shakers are an added bonus to this wonderful little cookbook. All the recipes sound good, but the one for applesauce was particularly appealing.

MSH

Shaker Recipe Book
by Cynthia Rubin
1970; 32 pp., paper

From: Emporium Publications
Box 539
Newton, Massachusetts 02158
$1.00

Thanks to the fine canning process which the Shakers developed, their Shaker Applesauce was shipped by the gallons, sealed in Shaker pails and firkins, and sent far and wide to American markets.

The famous Shaker Applesauce was cooked in sweet cider, the proportion being something like 4 gallons boiled down to one, then slowly cooking the dried apples in this. The result was a rich and delicious applesauce.

SHAKER APPLESAUCE

2 pounds dried apples
1/3 gallon water
2/3 gallon cider, boiled down from 2 gallons fresh cider
1 pound sugar, if desired

Soak the apples overnight. In the morning add the cider to the apples. Cover and simmer for 4 hours. Add the sugar. Do not stir; let the apple slices remain whole.

Wooden Bowls

Bowls: large, small, round, oval — all beautifully turned from Vermont hardwoods and made to last a lifetime. Cutting boards, kegs, pails, children's toys and loads more wooden things are on sale. Catalog available.

The Weston Bowl Mill
Weston, Vermont 05161

We turn our round bowls mostly from the choicest of Vermont's hardwoods: maple and yellow, grey, and white birch. The wood is green—right from the stump—when it is brought to the lathe, and, once turned, the bowl air-dries for 6-8 weeks before it is ready for sanding and finishing.

Cat. No.	Size	Plain	Natural or Colonial	Shipping weight
*RB-6	6"	$1.70	$1.95	½ lb.
RB-9	9"	1.95	2.25	1 lb.
RB-11	11"	3.75	4.50	3 lbs.
RB-13	13"	6.75	7.75	4 lbs.
RB-15	15"	9.95	11.50	5 lbs.
RB-17	17"	14.95	16.95	10 lbs.

* Our enlarged, improved 5½" bowl.

Recommended: An unfinished* (plain) bowl—or set of bowls—hand-rubbed with mineral oil. This gives you a permanent, washable finish and base for your salad oils and allows the bowl to be used for chopping, as well. (We use mineral oil because it has no odor. Try it! your drugstore has the oil and it takes only a few minutes of elbow grease.)

*Warning: *An unfinished bowl subject to moisture without an oil finish is bound to crack.*

Suggested Sizes:

9" Bowl—King-sized individual salad, or salad for 2
11" Bowl—Salad for 2—4 servings
13" Bowl—Salad for 4—6 servings
15" Bowl—Salad for 6—8 servings
17" Bowl—For extra large families

The Plymouth Cheese Corp.

This firm, started by President Coolidge's father, is still in the family, and now being managed by the former President's son — John.

The Plymouth Cheese Corp.
Box 1
Plymouth, Vermont 05056

A true, old-fashioned
Granular Curd American Cheese,
carefully aged and naturally cured,
made by us in the real Vermont tradition.

2¾ lb. wheels of Plymouth Cheese
@ $5.50 per wheel, postpaid ($6.00 west of Mississippi River)
Please specify mild or medium sharp.
Also available in Sage, Pimiento or Caraway a $5.65 per wheel, postpaid ($6.15 west of Mississippi River)

Drying Apples

There were no short-cuts available to the early New Englander. They did things pretty much as their forefathers had done. Such as this method of drying apples:

Gather together the best apples; peel, core and quarter them. Plant four strong crotches in the ground, place poles horizontally on these and on them lay boards, close together. Thinly spread out the apples. Soon they will be covered with all the bees and wasps in the neighborhood, sucking the juice out. This actually accelerates the drying operation. At night cover them with blankets. If it might rain, gather them into baskets and bring into the house. Set them out the next day and repeat until they're perfectly dried. The amount of shrinkage will amaze you. (Today, the finicky person might cover the apples with a fine cheesecloth).

To use: Put a small handful in warm water overnight; next morning they are swelled to their former size. When cooked in pies or dumplings, it is difficult to tell that they're not fresh.

Haymarket

"A cuke is a cuke to a lady. They don't know whether they want a Sanford grape or an Olivia grape or an Amella grape or a Tokey grape or a seedless grape. See what I mean, so they don't know. A grape is a grape to them." The sights and sounds of Haymarket Square where the market men hawk their wares and discuss their lives have been captured by Wendy Snyder in a vivid and sensitive manner. Her camera does not have the dimension of smell, but it hardly needs it. Her perception for the lusty, hectic, confused yet efficient environment of pushcarts, produce vendors and meat men who operate from early dawn to dusk is dramatically caught in some 60 black and white photographs. Haymarket Square has its roots going back 300 years in the heart of Boston. This neat little book gives one the feeling that it is an important part of the New England heritage — and it is.

JCH

Haymarket
by Wendy Snyder
1970; 110 pp., paper
From: The MIT Press
      Cambridge, Massachusetts 02142
      $2.95

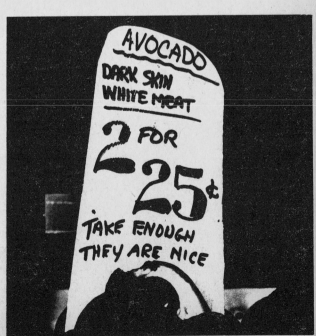

Jams and Jellies

The Jelly Mill, crafts, boutique, gourmet items, jams, jellies — 88 flavors!

All jams and jellies are pure fruit and sugar, no water added. Ninety-nine times out of one hundred they have the flavor you want.

A six-pack, 10 oz. assortment will be sent any-where.

Try their "wild" assortment of preserves: wild beach plum, grape, elderberry, blueberry, black-berry and strawberry.

Six-pack, 10 oz. $6.50 ppd. in N.E.
$6.95 ppd. elsewhere

A check must accompany order.

Natural Vermont Cheeses — not colored — not processed — not fussed with. Made of raw milk with all enzymes, vitamins and minerals retained.

Brochure available.

Green Mountain Jack Cheese (12" bar)
$2.45 + postage; $.80 East of Miss.; $1.05 West

Habitat

About Tomatoes

Tomatoes, untouched by frost, can be harvested green, wrapped individually in pieces of paper, and stored in a cool, dry, dark place. As needed, they may be sun-ripened on a window sill. When frost threatens, pull up the entire vine and harvest at your leisure. The juice of tomatoes whose plants have had their roots in close proximity to those of the stinging nettle will keep for several weeks without fermenting at ordinary refrigerator temperatures.

When tillage begins, other arts follow. The farmers therefore are the founders of human civilization.

Daniel Webster

Early American Herb Recipes

This is great reading for anyone interested in herbs and a lot of people are these days with the "back-to-nature" interest. A potpourri of practical and ludicrous herbal information, there are recipes for everything from perfume and soap to pastries, gravies and insecticides.

Herbal cosmetics are "in" things with today's teenagers and many of the recipes in this book will appeal to this group. Want to cure a red face? Spring water and oil of tartar or a pound of lime in two quarts of spring water are suggested for morning and night face washings. Ouch!

What about broom buds, pickled? Or a caraway cordial? A recipe from 1838 recommends rose water in macaroons. And a rose red conserve is said to be good for haemorrhages.

The book's contents are compiled from a collection of one hundred and twenty-eight old books and the more than five hundred recipes are reproduced exactly as they appeared in the original sources, complete with misspellings and quaint turns of phrases.

Although I don't recommend following many of the recipes, some would be fun to try and it's interesting reading. The illustrations add greatly to the book.

Sally G. Devaney

Early American Herb Recipes
by Alice Cooke Brown
1966; 152 pp.
From: Bonanza Books, Div. of Crown Publishers, Inc.
419 Park Avenue South
New York, New York 10016
$10.00

The Transcendental Boiled Dinner
JOHN J. PULLEN

The Transcendental Boiled Dinner

Delight? On the printed page? Yes, dear reader. This book by John J. Pullen of Maine, Pennsylvania and Connecticut is a combination of wit and practicality. The title pricks you with the possibility that you, too, may achieve perfection via (aluminum) pot.

The binding, typography, thick-cream pages, and jacket portraits of two Boilists, will all persuade you that this is a book to be enjoyed by the senses.

Read it — and find equal satisfaction for the mind. The beauty of Maine and the wise humor of New England are to be found here. Ponder the relative qualifications of Jonathan Edwards, Julia Child and Sophia Loren (!) in preparing this dinner. Next winter, when you would rather stay snowbound by the hearth, suit up, and answer the Call of the Meeting. You will be combatting the idea that "the New England Town Meeting is the epitome of participative democracy, when in reality it is only the normal domination of the interested over the apathetic that prevails everywhere else."

Mary Goodrich

The Transcendental Boiled Dinner
by John J. Pullen
1972; 92 pp.
From: J.B. Lippincott Co.
E. Washington Square
Philadelphia, Pennsylvania 19105
$3.95

A New England Simple — To Cure a Bronchial Cough

1 cup heavy pure honey, 3 T. vinegar, a pinch of ground alum. Take a tsp. as needed, keep throat covered.

Maple Treat

Mix 2 cups flour, 3/4 cups milk, 6 T. of shortening, 4 tsp. baking powder, and 3/4 tsp. salt. Roll out to a rectangle 3/4" thick. Place 2 cups sliced apples over this and spread with 1/4 cup sugar, cinnamon, nutmeg mixture. Roll as for jelly roll, slice in 1" thick slices and place in 2-3" deep, buttered pan. Pour 2 cups of warm maple syrup over all and bake at 375° for 35-40 minutes. Serve warm topped with whipped cream or ice cream.

Fried Coffee and Jellied Bourbon

Except for a very unusual Sunday or the hunt buffet in Williamsburg, breakfast in these United States is a dreary affair at best.

No longer, I am happy to report.

Willan C. Roux has put together a breakfast cookbook that not only covers all the standard fare really worth eating, but also some truly different breakfasts.

Except for deeply dedicated topers, I do not recommend Joe Palmer's jellied bourbon on page 36, but then again I have not tried it.

Above and beyond recipes, Will Roux has some sage advice on handling any women in your household and much solid information on what really goes into scrapple (and many other good breakfast staples).

Best of all, he sets down in good clear type the unbreakable rule that one makes an omelet only in an omelet pan and then eats it immediately. It is never to be warmed up, and, oh, how more pleasant would life be if the airlines did not pollute the skies with their vulcanized version of the omelet.

It is a good book to have. And, oh yes, excellent cartoons by Larry of the English magazine Punch.

RWW

Fried Coffee and Jellied Bourbon
by Willan C. Roux
Drawings by Larry
1967; 111 pp.
From: Barre Publishers
Barre, Massachusetts 01005
$4.95

Organic Foods

Erewhon supplies an impressive list of natural foods. Grains, cereals, stone ground flour, beans, seeds, granola, sea vegetables, pasta and unusual foods such as umeboshi — plums pickled in brine — are some of their specialties.

Erewhon
33 Farnsworth Street
Boston, Massachusetts 02210
12 – 1 lb. $6.60

Catherine's Chocolate Shop

A third generation of confectioners presiding over gleaming copper kettles perched on top of an old candymaker's stove brewing all manners of rich fillings with no preservatives added. Using recipes which date from the turn of the century — they hand dip chocolates at the rate of 1200 per hour.

Homemade caramel, nougat, pineapple, marzipan, cream and fondant fillings, as well as nuts, preserved ginger and glazed pineapple dipped in white, milk or bittersweet chocolate.

Brochure available.

Catherine's Chocolate Shop
Stockbridge Road
Great Barrington, Massachusetts 01230
Berkshire Assortment — hard and soft centers dipped in milk, white and bittersweet chocolate.
$2.25 lb.
Stem Cordial Cherries dipped in white, milk or bittersweet chocolate and individually wrapped.
$2.99 lb.
Rum Balls — covered with bittersweet chocolate.
$2.50 lb.
Old Fashioned Assortment — assorted fruits and creams dipped in bittersweet and milk chocolate.
$2.25 lb.

You May Safely Enclose Check or Money Order

PARCEL POST CHART

	Up to 150 miles	150-300 miles	300-1000 miles	West Coast & Florida
FIRST POUND TO ANY ONE ADDRESS	80¢	90¢	$1.00	$1.20
EACH ADDITIONAL POUND TO ANY ONE ADDRESS	20¢	20¢	20¢	20¢

Mailing Charges Include Postage, and Proper Packing. Include these Charges in your payments. Add 25¢ per package for Insulated Packing. Thank you.

A Loaf of Bread — — — and Thou

To fill in the missing words above write:

Winecraft
P.O. Box 94
Northboro, Massachusetts 01532

They have a catalogue of kits, and they tell us that if we have an empty gallon jug and fruit juice of our choice, they will supply everything else we may need.

And if you have wondered about the legalities of making your own wine, here is what they say in their catalogue:

Legal Requirements of winemaking

Write to the Assistant District Commissioner, Alcohol and Tobacco Tax Division of the Bureau of Internal Revenue nearest your home, for two copies of Form 1541. When you receive two copies of Form 1541 fill both out and return them. You will then receive one copy back carrying the Assistant Regional Commissioner's Stamp. There is no charge for this service. The form contains all pertinent regulations that you must observe.

Apple Wine

1 gallon of pasteurized apple cider or apple juice available in most grocery stores
1 Nutrient Tablet
1 Campden Tablet
1 Pectin Enzyme Tablet
1 Wine Yeast Tablet
1 lb. sugar (2 measuring cups)

If your juice was purchased in a one gallon glass jug, it can be used as your fermenting vessel. Otherwise obtain a one gallon glass jug, wash it thoroughly and rinse in very hot water. Pour about 1 quart of juice into a clean bottle, cap and save for future use. Next crush and dissolve the Nutrient, Campden and Pectin Enzyme tablets in a little warm water and add them to the remaining 3 quarts of juice. Add the sugar to the 3 quarts of juice in the gallon jug and shake gently until it is dissolved.

Rinse the air lock in moderately hot water and fit to the jug without water in the lock. Allow to stand overnight. Next add 1 whole uncrushed yeast tablet to the juice and re-fit the air lock. Shake the jug gently each day until fermentation starts (usually in 4 to 6 days). After the initial violent fermentation slows, fill the jug to the base of the neck with the juice previously set aside. Add water to the air lock and allow fermentation to proceed to completion. When there is no further sign of fermentation, siphon the wine into a clean glass jug, using care to be sure that no sediment is picked up from the bottom of the first jug. It is impossible to get all of the wine out of the first jug without picking up some sediment so do not try. Crush one Campden Tablet and dissolve it in a little warm water and add it to the jug. Fill the jug to the base of the neck with cool water that was previously boiled. Re-fit the air lock and let it stand until the wine clears and then bottle.

Cheese and Maple Syrup

Sell ten tons of cheese and 18,000 cans of maple syrup in one year? That's what they tell us at:

Dakin Farm
Ferrisburg, Vermont 05456
Dakin Sampler (1 qt. of maple syrup and 2 lb. block of sharp cheddar cheese) $10.00 ppd.

In early 19th century New England, the standard breakfast served in most farming families consisted of ham, beef, sausages, bread, butter, boiled potatoes, pies, coffee and cider. Of course, this was eaten about 5 a.m., and a good, hard morning's work put in before an equally filling, almost identical meal was served at noon. For supper, you might be served milk biscuits, short-cakes and pies, washed down with plenty of cider again.

From the Galleys of Nantucket

Lambs Wool, Beet Wine, and English Monkey, just a few of the interesting recipes offered in this cookbook. It would make a nice addition to a cook's bookshelf.

A note after a recipe for Castor Oil Cookies says, "two of these equal a dose of castor oil." As a child, this reviewer would have welcomed that method of getting her daily quota, instead of the "straight down-the-hatch" method commonly employed.

MSH

From the Galleys of Nantucket
by The Ladies Union Circle
1969; 251 pp., paper
From: The Ladies Union Circle
First Congregational Church
Nantucket, Massachusetts 02554
$4.50

Lambs Wool (In A Wassail Bowl) Traditionally Served on the 12th Night.

8 large baking apples	1 cup firmly packed
2 quarts apple cider	brown sugar
	2 T. mixed pickling spice

Wrap each apple in a double thickness of aluminum foil; place in a baking pan. Roast at 450 degrees until soft (about 1½ hours). Remove foil, put apples through a food mill or sieve.

Meanwhile, combine cider, sugar, and pickling spice in kettle. Stir over low heat until sugar dissolves. Bring to a boil. Lower heat and simmer for ½ hour, strain. Add hot cider mixture to the apple pulp. Serve hot in sturdy mugs. Makes 3½ quarts.

English Monkey

1 cup stale bread crumbs	1 cup milk
1 tablespoon butter	½ cup soft, mild
1 egg	cheese, cut in
½ teaspoon salt	pieces
Few grains of cayenne	

Soak bread crumbs 15 minutes in milk. Melt butter, add cheese, and when cheese has melted, add soaked crumbs, egg slightly beaten, and seasonings. Cook 3 minutes and pour over toasted crackers.

———◆———

LAWRENCE'S SMOKE HOUSE
RT. 30 NEWFANE, VT. 05345

Smoked Meats

For over twenty-two years, *Lawrence's Smoke House* has been turning out fine smoked meats. Their hams and bacon are hung for days in a smokehouse and have that natural old-fashioned flavor that only long, patient corn cob smoking can produce.

Lawrence's Smoke House
Route 30
Newfane, Vermont 05345

Sliced Bacon — 2 lbs. $3.95
Whole Ham — 10-11 lbs. $18.95
1/2 Ham — 6-7 lbs. $12.50

Customs on the Table Top

The story of the "table top" in the early days of the Republic reveals the New Englander in a little-known but unexpectedly friendly and human light. Most of us know about his native shrewdness, his inventiveness, his legendary conscience. Now we see him in the eighteenth and early nineteenth centuries as a good host, a hearty eater, and a prodigious drinker, at least until the temperance movement began. His were the pleasures of the table, extolled since the days of Solomon in spite of clerical warnings against their dangers; and, it might be added, many of the New England clergy were pretty good livers themselves. And the New England housewife "set out" a good table, proud of her cooking and its abundance and developing in connection with it a distinct social pattern of table setting, service, and eating habits.

. . . Today we can scarcely realize how important pewter was on the rural New England table — every poorest family boasted a piece or two. The thrifty housewife saved her white stoneware — today called "salt glaze" — or her plates and bowls of English delft or perhaps her few pieces of treasured Chinese porcelain, and displayed them in her parlor cupboard, using pewter on her daily table. There was scarcely an article not made in pewter, and in New England at least, there seems to have been a pewterer in practically every sizeable town. No matter where one lived pewter went by peddlar's cart to every village store and country crossroads.

No one worried about which fork to pick up first at table. There was only one fork, at the left of the plate, with tines turned down if the table setter was meticulous and somewhat old-fashioned, turned up if she was casual. On the right was the knife. A good trencherman picked up the knife and went to it. (How else would you have eaten those peas?) Its rounded, spatulate blade was designed for that purpose and the custom, like the knife, originated in England. ". . . the people, nearly all of them, eat with their knives, like the English, which are round at the point (the knives!) and they do not use their two-pronged forks," wrote Baron Louis de Closen in 1780. The dexterity with which one could scoop up the juice of a berry pie was simply amazing.

MSH

Customs on the Table Top
by Helen Sprackling
1958; 22 pp., paper
From: Old Sturbridge Village
Sturbridge, Massachusetts 01566
$.50

———◆———

Boil some apple skins in a little water, strain them and use the juice as thickening for jellies and preserves. A better pectin than any you could buy. Great for use in fruit pies, too.

New England's "emtins" is Pennsylvania's "sots"
Yeast Starter: 1 pound flour, ¼ pound brown sugar, salt, 2 gallons water. Boil for 1 hour and bottle when warm.

The Natural Foods Cookbook

A nutritionist's delight — no white flour, sugar, baking powder or soda. Honey is the chief sweetener and unhydrogenated oils have replaced the fats.

This cookbook offers you good cooking, good eating and good health.

MSH

The Natural Foods Cookbook
by Beatrice Trum Hunter
1972; 368 pp., paper
From: Garden Way Publishing Co.
Charlotte, Vermont 05445
$.95

Homemade Sauerkraut (in quart canning jars)

Remove outer leaves from firm, mature heads of cabbage. Wash and drain. Cut into quarters. Remove cores and shred. Allow 2 pounds of shredded cabbage for each quart canning jar. Sprinkle 4 tablespoons salt over each 2 pounds of cabbage. Mix thoroughly by hand. Pack mixture into jars. Press down firmly with wooden spoon or tamper. Brine will form over cabbage. Cover packed cabbage with pad of clean white cheesecloth. Fit two thin, flexible wooden strips crosswise into neck of each jar so that they press down on cabbage. Set jars in shallow pan or on folded newspaper, as brine may overflow during fermentation. Leave lids loose. After about 10 days, if jars have been kept a fairly constant temperature of 70° F., brine level will drop rather suddenly. This means that fermentation is about over. Remove cheesecloth and wooden strips. Fill jars to within 1 inch of top with 2½ per cent brine (1 ounce salt to 1 quart water). If kraut is to be used soon, simply close jars and keep cool. If kraut is to be kept longer than a few weeks, preserve in a boiling water bath. To do this, press cabbage down firmly with spoon to release gas bubbles. Fill jars with brine and cover but do not seal. Put in kettle with water to cover tops of jars. Bring to boil and continue boiling for 30 minutes. Seal and store.

When serving sauerkraut, flavor with one of the following: dill seeds, caraway seeds, celery seeds or ground juniper berries.

———◆———

That's The Spirit

Quite honestly, when I read through the tremendous list of alcoholic beverages that *Heublein* makes I was getting to the point where I had better not drive, but then, quite surprising to me, I found they also own Kentucky Fried Chicken, Colonel Sanders and all. This food notation brought me around.

Heublein, of course, launched the pre-mixed, bottled cocktail quite by accident in 1892. It seems the Governor's Foot Guard had ordered a gallon of martinis and a gallon of Manhattans for an outing. It rained that day and the following Saturday. An order to throw the stuff out found a helper nipping away at the jugs and reporting they tasted just fine. An idea was born.

But even as they will admit, some of their early efforts produced martinis that needed more than an olive to fix. Now, however, their pre-mixes are excellent, these are just a drop in the Heublein barrel. Their line goes from "Anisette" to "Zapple." Yes, "Zapple!" By the way, "Zapple" is listed as a new product immediately beneath something called "Waikiki Duck."

I did not investigate "Waikiki Duck" as that old headiness was beginning to return.

Heublein products, of course, are available in your local grog store, and in this part of the country, "Heublein" is pronounced "Hi-Bline."

RWW

Heublein, Inc.
Hartford, Connecticut 06101

Crowley Cheese

Lovers of cheese — and of Americana — will find the *Crowley Cheese* factory a delightful place to take the family. The best time is right before lunch for that's when the cheese-making process is at its most interesting stage. After more than 148 years in business, *Crowley Cheese* still prefers old fashioned methods, patient craftsmanship and a limited volume of a quality product that contains absolutely no additives, preservatives, flavor enhancers, artificial coloring, retardants or other questionable food improvements.

Crowley Cheese, Inc.
Healdville, Vermont 05147

CROWLEY CHEESE
HEALDVILLE, VERMONT 05147
ORDER FORM

QUANTITY		QUANTITY	
_____3 LB. CHEESES	☐ Mild	_____5 LB. CHEESES	☐ Mild
Area 1: $6.50 Area 3: $7.00	☐ Medium	Area 1: $9.00 Area 3: $9.50	☐ Medium
Area 2: $6.75 Area 4: $7.25	☐ Sharp	Area 2: $9.25 Area 4: $10.00	☐ Sharp
Postage Included (Check One)		Postage Included (Check One)	

SHIPPING AREAS

AREA 1: New England and N. Y.
AREA 2: Del.; Md.; N. Car.; N.J.; Ohio; Pa.; Va.; Wash. D.C.; W. Va.

AREA 3: Ala.; Ark.; Fla.; Ga.; Ill.; Ind.; Iowa; Ky.; Mich.; Minn.; Miss.; Mo.; S. Car.; Tenn.; Wis.
AREA 4: All other states and Canada.

Jams, Jellies and Marmalades

Great grandmother toiled for hours over a hot wood stove to keep her preserve shelves filled.

Beatrice Vaughan has simplified many of these old recipes so that they can be quickly prepared by today's housewives.

MSH

Jams, Jellies & Marmalades
by Beatrice Vaughan
1971; 32 pp., paper
From: The Stephen Greene Press
Brattleboro, Vermont 05301
$1.00

Old-Fashioned Chokecherry Jam

Remove stems from chokecherries and wash; drain. Combine 1 cup of water with every 4 cups of fruit. Place over low heat and simmer until fruit is tender, stirring occasionally. Rub through medium sieve. Measure and add equal amount of sugar. Place over moderate heat and stir until sugar melts. Bring to full rolling boil and cook until mixture sheets* from the spoon (220 degrees). Stir frequently. Seal in hot sterilized jars. 3 cups of pulp will make about 2 half-pints.

*To fall from the spoon in two distinct drops.

Aunt Mable Berry's Rose-Hip Jam

1 pound rose hips
1 cup water
sugar

Simmer rose hips and water until fruit is very tender. Rub through sieve and weigh the pulp. To each pound, add 1 pound of sugar. Return to heat and simmer until thick, stirring frequently. Seal in hot sterilized jars.

Rose hips should be gathered after the first frost of autumn. Be careful not to use those from bushes which have been sprayed with insecticides.

Egolites Candles

Not a product of urban, machine age mass production — *Egolites Candles* are made one at a time in a Vermont home workshop.

The wax is melted and poured each morning and wicks are treated and dried according to a 2000-year-old formula. In the afternoon, each candle is taken from its mold, and with patience and pride trimmed, wicked and glazed.

ERLEND JACOBSEN
R. R. 1
Plainfield, Vermont 05667
(802) 426-3565

Pillar Candles

Large	35 hrs.	$3.50
Medium	25 hrs.	2.50
Small	16 hrs.	1.50

One of the colonial housewife's many duties was that of making cheese. This was a long and demanding process that went on month after month. The endless pails of milk had to be turned into butter or cheese before they spoiled, so it was a never-ending job.

The Appleyard Corporation
MAPLE CORNER · CALAIS · VERMONT 05648

Pure Foods — No Additives

Located in a 100-year-old farmhouse, this corporation (six people) has developed a small, high quality line of foods. Pride is taken in the fact that no preservatives, additives, artificial sweeteners nor colors are used in any of the products, which include apple cider jelly, tomato conserve, cheeses and maple syrup.

Appalled at the ingredients and nutritional content of most cereals, they decided to make their own — using toasted rolled oats, monukka raisins, almonds, sunflower seeds, apricots, dried apples and whole powdered orange. All of the ingredients are natural, and the apples are dried on racks over wood stoves in their kitchen, just as they were a century ago.

Case of Cornucopia cereal (30 13-oz. bags) $22.50

Winemaking Supplies

Home winemaking is one of the fastest growing hobbies in America. Thousands are discovering that winemaking is simple and inexpensive, and not a form of alchemy which some seem to believe. Techniques used by the modern home winemaker allow him to predict how the wine will turn out, and to reproduce favorite recipes easily. These techniques eliminate spoilage, and prevent wine from becoming vinegary. The yeasty brew called "homemade wine" is a thing of the past. The wines you make can compare with the best available from the store.

It is legal to make wine at home. The head of a family can make up to 200 gallons per year. Before beginning, he should file Form 1541 with the nearest office of the Alcohol and Tax Division of the Internal Revenue Service. Form 1541 and the address of your local office can be obtained from the I.R.S., Washington, D.C. There is no cost.

Beer making at home is illegal!

Catalog and price list available.

BEGINNER'S WINEMAKING KIT: includes all ingredients you need to make eight gallons of good wine, except fruit and sugar. Bottles and kitchen utensils are all you need in the way of other equipment. Boxed for gift wrapping. Kit includes - step-by-step instructions, book, "First Steps in Winemaking," two fermentation locks, eight wine yeast tablets, nutrient tablets, campden tablets, citric acid, siphon hose, wine corks & labels. $5.95

Bacchanalia
273 Riverside Avenue
Westport, Connecticut 06880

Habitat

Haley's Grain Store — Old Hickory Smokehouse, Inc.

The Haleys seem to have both sides of Park Street pretty much to themselves. On one side is *Haley's Grain Store,* an old-fashioned farm and home store, carrying feed and accessories for all types of animals, from cows to goats, along with a complete selection of seeds, fertilizers, equipment and clothing for the farmer.

Across the street, the *Old Hickory Smokehouse* offers a line of gifts, a small restaurant, their own smoked hams and fresh killed turkeys, from Labor Day through September, for Thanksgiving and Christmas.

No mail order, but they are open from 9 to 5:30 every day. Sunday's they knock off at 3:00 p.m.

RWW

Haley's Grain Store, Inc.
Old Hickory Smokehouse, Inc.
Park Street, Route 20
Palmer, Massachusetts 01069

Ocean Spray Cranberries, Inc.

As our nation moved West — so did cranberries — the first commercially marketed ones being sent to Wisconsin, Oregon, Washington and Canada in 1830.

In the early 1900's, Marcus L. Urann, President of the United Cape Cod Cranberry Company, put cranberry sauce into cans. He perfected the recipe, stirred the first batch, sealed the containers, designed the labels, then went on the road to sell it.

Once strictly a seasonal thing, the cranberry has gone "year round." Grocers' shelves now offer a variety of cranberry products to be used in hundreds of ways.

Ocean Spray Cranberries, Inc.
Hanson, Massachusetts 02341

About Cranberries

Cranberries are truly native berries. Long before Columbus came to the new world, wild cranberries had an important place in everyday life. For instance, Indian squaws often used tangy cranberries to liven up their food. Food such as pemmican cakes made of dried deer meat and meal, and succotash made of corn, beans and fish.

The Pequod Indians on Cape Cod treated wounds from poisoned arrows with a cranberry dressing. Squaws made their rugs and blankets colorful with red cranberry juice.

When the Pilgrims came to America, they learned of this wild berry from the friendly Indians. The women brightened their clothing with the berry juice. When Mary Ring, a Pilgrim, died in "Plimouth" in 1633, her red petticoat was valued at 16 shillings — a small fortune in those days! Pilgrim women soon began to create their own ways to fix cranberries for the table. They made them into sauces, bubbling tarts and cranberry nogs.

Early American sailors found cranberries good for their health. The cranberries were stored in barrels of cold water and served regularly to crews at sea to provide Vitamin C and ward off the dreaded scurvy.

Cranberries were called "Sassamanesh" by the eastern Indians and "Atoqua" by the Algonquians in Wisconsin. In New Jersey, where cranberries were the symbol of peace, "Pakimintzen" meant cranberry eater. The word "cranberry" was not taken from any of the Indian names. It was a

W.S. Wells & Son

While a king might prefer caviar — any down-easter worth his salt will tell you that the very best caviar can't compare to a mess of dandelion greens cooked up with boiled potatoes and salt pork.

When those first tender shoots popped out of the earth on a fresh spring morning, my great-grandmother was out on the lawn, knife in hand, filling her basket. Backbreaking work it was — but a small price to pay for the health-giving, spring tonic benefits she believed they gave to her family.

Today, *Wells & Son* does all the work for you — including packing the greens in tins, so you can enjoy them year-round. In fact, to their knowledge, they are the only canners in the United States who process dandelion greens.

If the tender, unfurled shoots of the fiddlehead fern are more to your liking, they can those, too.

Vance Wells says, "I don't particularly like dandelion greens, but they're supposed to be good for the digestion, so I eat them once a week." Good enough reason for this reviewer at least to try them.

Suggested by Ruth Pullen   MSH

W.S. Wells & Son
174 High Street
Wilton, Maine 04294

contraction of crane berry, an early name given to the berries because their pale pink blossoms resembled the head of a crane. Cranes were often seen in the lowlands, enjoying the ripe berries.

Cultivation of cranberries began in Massachusetts nearly 200 years after the landing of the Pilgrims. By that time, popularity of the tangy wild berries was growing in this country. Moreover, England was happy to pay well for cranberries; a bottle of imported cranberries selling there for five shillings. The only way to meet the demand was through cultivation.

In 1816 Henry Hall of Dennis, Cape Cod, noticed that cranberries seemed to grow larger and juicier where sand from the dunes blew over the vines. Our cultivation methods today come from this simple observation made nearly 150 years ago!

Even though cranberry plantations are often called "bogs," the berries do not grow in water. They grow on swamp land near a water supply. This water supply provides frost protection and irrigation when they are necessary. To prepare a swamp for planting, trees and brush are cleared away. Narrow ditches are dug to drain off the water. Then peat soil, previously covered by the water, is leveled off. Over the peat soil goes a layer of sand, about three inches thick. Cuttings or branches from existing cranberry vines are planted deep enough so they take root in the peat soil beneath the sand. The cranberry vines, planted about six inches apart, gradually spread over the ground forming a thick green carpet. With care these vines produce berries indefinitely.

What kind of care? Weeding in the spring, pruning in the fall, fertilizing and resanding every three or four years. When frost threatens, the vines must be flooded for protection; in time of drouth, they must be irrigated. Birds are needed to control insects, bees to pollinate the blossoms. On the West Coast, sometimes a grower will use geese to help with the weeding.

It is about five years from the time a bog is planted until it yields its first full harvest. September, with its nip of fall which puts the brilliant red in the cranberry, is harvest time.

Apple Orchard

Harwood Hill Orchard grows apples (pick your own), pears and plums. Newly planted strawberries, raspberries and blueberries will be ready in 1973. Their wares may be ordered by mail, but most of the fruit is sold at their impressive 1793 pegged-beam barn. From September through March, a cider press operates producing the old-fashioned unpreserved type. Gift items, syrup, jams, jellies, cheese and home-made apple pies enrich the offerings of this Vermont farm.

Harwood Hill Orchard
Route 7
Bennington, Vermont 05201

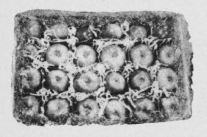

The Cracker Barrel

Dip candles — grind your own peanut butter — or sit on a cranberry box and munch on king-sized pickles at:

The Cracker Barrel
Route 132
Hyannis, Massachusetts 02601

Rum Fustian

A favorite drink in Puritan New England. Take a pint of beer, pint of sherry and a pint of gin, the yolks of a dozen eggs, sugar and a little nutmeg. Stir all together, then heat with a red-hot loggerhead (poker). Fustian means imitation, this drink supposedly being a good substitute for rum. There's a legend that this drink killed off a whole tribe of Indians who had incurred the Puritans' displeasure. It is said that they gave the Indians several barrels of rum fustian — it was easier than fighting them.

Johnnycake

The famous New England Johnnycake consisted simply of corn meal and milk, baked hard so that it might be carried as sustenance on long journeys. The actual name was "journey cake" and the hungry traveler usually dipped it into cider or any other beverage handy. This softened its crust and gave it a little flavor. Since that original recipe, there have been many variations.

Vrest Orton

A country store with genuine old-time flavor carrying everything from soup to nuts — and then some. Vrest Orton's catalogue is a pleasure to read and order from. It's filled with the countryman's sage product descriptions and recipes.

The Vermont Country Store
Weston, Vermont 05161

Vermont Country Store Wholegrains

BREAKFAST CEREALS

Below are 9 breakfast cereals of stoneground grains: directions for cooking appear on each bag. Like all wholegrains they should be kept in a cool place to remain fresh.

SAMP CEREAL: This delectable morning bracer is concocted of coarse cracked corn and wheat, and contains *all* the vitamins of both.

CRACKED WHEAT CEREAL: Composed of cracked wholegrain wheat, this cereal does not cook mushy but can be chewed.

CRUSHED WHEAT CEREAL: This wholegrain wheat cereal has been ground to meet a special need of folks who want a finer, softer breakfast cereal that cooks soft and creamy. It is also excellent for children.

WHOLE KERNELS OF WHEAT: The oldest breakfast food known to man is cooked *unground* whole kernels of wheat. Soak in water for 24 hours then cook in doubler-boiler with a dash of salt.

VT. LUMBERMAN'S MUSH: A medium ground soft and rich tasty cereal of corn, wheat, and oatmeal. Highly recommended by pediatricians for children and by gerontologists for elderly people. Good to fry also.

SCOTCH OATMEAL: That old-country breakfast porridge of wholegrains oats, with its rich nutty flavor, called *Scotch* or *Irish* Oatmeal.

WHITE OR YELLOW CORN GRITS: Natural, stoneground grits are NOT (I repeat NOT) the hominy grits you get in the south; hominy grits have the germ removed. Our *wholegrain* grits are coarse *cracked corn*, with *all* the rich vitamin-laden germ: nothing taken out. An excellent breakfast cereal or side dish. *White or Yellow; please indicate choice.*

CRACKED RYE CEREAL: Our nutritious hearty rye Breakfast Cereal is made of the coarsely cracked whole kernels of rye. Cook like oatmeal.

REAL WHOLEGRAIN OAT GROATS. The whole kernels of oats after the hull has been removed. Of all grains (except SOY) oats contain the highest percentage of protein, low in fat and calories, (each serving is 107 calories) for people who are worried about weight, cholesterol, and other hazards.

MEALS OR FLOURS

Below are our 9 different stoneground flours or meals for cooking everything from bread to cakes. For recipes for all our stoneground flours and meals see the book COOKING WITH WHOLE-GRAINS by Mrs. Vrest Orton on Page 66.

BREAD WHEATFLOUR. Sometimes called "Graham Flour" because years ago Dr. Graham advocated for good health, using stoneground wholegrains. Ours is the real germ-content *high protein* flour. The best dark bread and rolls can be made from this rich flour without using any white flour.

PASTRY WHEAT FLOUR is a wholegrain stoneground flour for making delicious pastries such as pie crust, tarts, cakes, cookies and other such delicacies. This flour contains less protein than bread flour and that's why some like it for pastries and the like.

YELLOW CORNMEAL: There are over 300 ways to use cornmeal. Our yellow cornmeal is rich and full-flavored and preferred by us folks up north.

WHITE CORNMEAL: The sweet fine *white* cornmeal is wonderful for southern dishes, and is preferred by folks south of the Mason-Dixon Line.

RYE FLOUR: Old-fashioned stoneground rye meal for bread and other uses.

OAT FLOUR: A ground oatmeal flour for use in making oatmeal bread, cookies, etc.

MUFFIN OR PANCAKE MEALS: By grinding together wholegrain corn, wheat and rye, this contains the good taste and the vitamins of America's three most nourishing grains! Easy to use for pancakes, muffins, rolls, etc.

BUCKWHEAT: Our 100% pure buckwheat flour (not a mixture) contains only buckwheat.

RICH HIGH PROTEIN SOY FLOUR. The richest vegetable source of vital protein, just a little added to other wholegrains gives you a zestful source of protein. Use one tablespoon of soy flour for each cupful of our other wholegrains.

Our Wholegrains are Refrigerated

We have our own stonemill and have gone to great expense to keep all our grains (both before and after grinding) in a temperature and humidity controlled refrigerated room. Our customers can be sure of getting fresh, safe flours and cereals, in our two stores and by mail.

That's why it's best to buy wholegrains from us.

"Your wholegrains are lovely, as you well know (I tried some for fun and am now clinging to them for survival, and proselytizing) and your coffee bean candy is far superior to other people's coffee bean candy." MRS. JAMES M. BEATTY, *Maryland.*

Habitat

Eat The Weeds

A guide to edible weeds of New England, stressing not only availability, but also the delicious and health giving qualities of uncultivated, naturally occurring grasses, fruits and vegetables. Three short introductory chapters deal with collection, preparation and use of weeds to enrich the soil, while the majority of the 223 pages are filled with tried and true recipes as unfamiliar as acorn bread and as universal as strawberry jam.

Lack of illustrations makes immediate identification of all but the most common weeds practically impossible for the amateur. Until you have become an authority, it is suggested that specimens be collected, preserved and presented to an expert (who might be your grandmother!) for identification.

An extensive bibliography provides more than adequate additional resources for the aspiring herbalist.

Barrett Robbins-Pianka

Eat The Weeds
by Ben Charles Harris
1972; 223 pp., paper
From: Barre Publishers
Barre, Massachusetts 01005
$3.95

Acorn Flour

Another and very different way of preserving acorns, practiced by the Wintoon Indians of western Tehama County, in California, was described to me by F.B. Washington, of Oakland. The acorns were buried in boggy places near cold springs, where they became swollen and softened and turned nearly black in color, but remained fresh for years. When needed, they were dug out and roasted, never dried or pounded for flour, the mush and bread being made of the dried acorns. White men, in plowing, have opened up caches of acorns that had lain in these cold, boggy places for fully 30 years, and found the acorns black, but still good.

When preserved dry in the usual way, the acorns are shucked as needed, and the dry meats, each splitting naturally in two parts, are pounded in stone mortars until reduced to a fine meal or flour. This at first is disagreeably bitter, but the bitter element is removed by leaching with warm water, which in seeping through acquires the color of coffee and the bitterness of quinine. The meal is then dried and stored to be used as required, for mush or bread.

Mush and bread made wholly of acorn flour are not pleasing to the taste, but leached acorn meal mixed with corn meal in the proportion of one part acorn to four parts corn makes excellent corn bread and pones, and mixed with white flour or whole-wheat flour in the same proportion makes palatable bread and muffins, adding to the cereal value the value of a fat nut product.

I have often eaten the pure acorn mush and bread as made by the Indians, but prefer the mixed product mentioned above. John Muir, during his arduous tramps in the mountains of California, often carried the hard, dry acorn bread of the Indians and deemed it the most compact and strength-giving food he had ever used.

Winter Storage of Vegetables

Some vegetables need to be frost-hardened before harvest and storage. Beets, carrots and turnips fit this category. After a few frosts, dig them for storage in a cold place, or mulch them and leave them right in the garden. Rutabagas, winter radishes, salsify, kohlrabi and horseradish fit this category, too.

EAT
THE
WEEDS

BEN CHARLES HARRIS

BARRE PUBLISHERS
BARRE, MASSACHUSETTS
1972

Organic Foods

Many people feel that organic foods, grown without added sugar, salt, preservatives or harmful chemicals, are the best you can eat. *Here and Now* offers such basics as: whole grains, beans, seeds, whole ground flour, rice products, honey and tea, as well as unusual things — dried bananas, sun-dried pineapple snacks and nori (a seaweed). Jeans, workshirts and vitamins are also offered. Brochure available.

Here and Now
P.O. Box 619
Stamford, Connecticut 06904

The Venison Book

If you expect more than dutiful cooperation from your wife in preparing your deer for the table, have her start this 77-page book on Page 41, Chapter V, entitled "Keep It Yourself."

The first four chapters, which are immensely valuable to the inexperienced deerslayer, and provide a darned good review for the Nimrod, deal with the humdrum details of where to shoot the beast, and the rather messy aftermath of field dressing and butchering. If the little lady reads this, she probably won't cook or eat it.

The more appetizing last three chapters deal with the preservation of the meat, including details of freezing, canning and smoking. A series of excellent and well-chosen recipes for preparing the feast in unusual ways and descriptions and recipes for some of the more esoteric dishes and desserts which can complement this proof of the hunter's prowess are included.

James Devaney

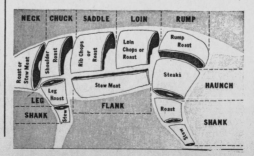

Gardening for Health and Nutrition

This concise how-to-do-it book gives simple instructions on making bio-dynamic compost, mulching, companion planting and poison-free bug controls.

Simple illustrations explain seasonal changes, planning a garden, soil bacteria and when to plant flowers and crops.

MSH

Gardening for Health and Nutrition
by John and Helen Philbrick
1971; 93 pp., paper
Published by Rudolf Steiner Publications
151 North Moison Road
Blauvelt, New York 10913
From: John and Helen Philbrick
P.O. Box 96
Wilkinsonville, Massachusetts 01590
$1.45

Window Gardening

Some indoor winter crops may be grown successfully in deep flats placed in sunny windows. Avoid high temperatures. These include parsley, chives, radishes, many herbs, possibly lettuce. Bean and bamboo sprouts may be produced in any warm room.

The Venison Book (How to Dress, Cut Up and Cook Your Deer)

by Audrey Alley Gorton
Illus. by George Daly
1957; 77 pp., paper
From: The Stephen Greene Press
Brattleboro, Vermont 05301
$1.95

Venison Mincemeat

This recipe was extracted with some difficulty from a Vermonter who hadn't reckoned to let it go out of the family. Some of her reluctance was based on the suspicion that the recipe might be used as evidence of possession of illegal deer! It makes enough mincemeat for about 15 pies. You might like to make a winter's supply and freeze it. The recipe can be halved or quartered very easily.

4 pounds venison (scraps are fine for this)
2 pounds beef suet
tart apples
3 pounds brown sugar
2 cups maple syrup (or dark molasses)
2 quarts cider
3 pounds currants
4 pounds seeded raisins
½ pound citron, cut fine
1 quart applejack (or brandy, wine, cider or grape juice)
1 tablespoon cinnamon
1 tablespoon ground clove
1 teaspoon allspice
1 teaspoon mace
1 teaspoon ground nutmeg
salt to taste

Cover the meat and suet with boiling water and cook until the meat is tender. Let it cool in the liquid. When it is cold and the fat has solidified, remove the meat and chop the cake fat (suet). Reboil the liquid until it is reduced to 1½ cups. Chop the venison and add to it twice as much apple, peeled, cored and chopped fine. Add the sugar and syrup or molasses, the dried fruits, the suet, the cider and the reduced liquid in which the meat was cooked. Boil slowly for 2 hours, stirring to prevent burning. Add the applejack or brandy and the spices. Mix thoroughly and store in crocks or jars.

It is by no means necessary to use exactly the ingredients given. You may want to add orange or lemon peel or chopped figs; or you may prefer a different proportion of spices. You may also use wine or sherry in place of the cider; or grape juice instead of the applejack or brandy.

Habitat

Country Stores In Early New England
Country Store — synonymous with New England.

MSH

Country Stores in Early New England
by Gerald Carson
1955; 16 pp., paper
From: Old Sturbridge Village
Sturbridge, Massachusetts 01566
$.50

As a social institution the country store influenced the standards and behavior of daily life as profoundly as our mass communications do today — radio, TV, magazines, newspapers, and national advertising. Viewed as a place of warmth and human contact the store was fully equal to all that can be said for the modern bus station, tavern, soda fountain, lodge or grange. Of all our senses, the sense of smell seems most closely connected with the remembrance of things past. Thus, the redolence of the old country store has taken a high place in family tradition and folklore. It was a powerful, complex, not unpleasant odor, varied according to the products of different time periods, such as the appearance after the Civil War of kerosene and the store coffee grinder. In the first quarter of the last century a man with a good nose might have distinguished molasses, fish, tea, the rolls of dress goods, a delicate tang of dried apples, medicinal herbs such as lobelia and tansy, a whiff of snuff, with a heavy stratum in the air, like a layer of smoke on a still day, of New England rum and the smell of horses.

Equally as celebrated as the smells were the store loungers, who made their own special contribution to the fragrance of the store, unregenerate and unwashed, exchanging "chaws" of tobacco or pulling on well-charred pipes with stubby stems. In pleasant weather they sunned, spat, and whittled out in front on a bench. Come October's bright blue weather, they moved inside. The regulars and the occasionals made a group ever shifting and reforming, sometimes boisterous and bawdy, getting off some guy or joke in a mood of high fantastical revelry, again earnest and disputatious. Here was the very seat of racial memory. Here the Oldest Inhabitant joined with the local Herodotus, perhaps it was the judge, to preserve orally the "remembrance of what men have done." They talked of forts and rendezvous in the Old French War, recalled the wonders of the Dark Day of 1780 — May 19th it was, on a Friday. There was the man who knew a man who knew General Washington, an oft-told tale. The young storekeeper entered the conversation long enough to say that he had seen Lafayette, held high on his grandsire's shoulders, while the old man's breast heaved with martial sentiment. The storeroom was an arena where conflicts and quarrels flared over town and school affairs, the church and its doctrine. A horse trade would do, or a disputed fence line. It was all a bit of theatre to relieve the tedium of isolated lives and a monotonous diet. And sometimes shy mountain women came to feast their eyes upon the marvels of the rural mart, pass a worn hand over some store pretty, and silently slip away, satisfied.

A New England Simple
To unite broken glass: Take a small quantity of isinglass and heat in spirits of wine until dissolved. This will mend broken glass so that the crack is nearly imperceptible.

A New England Simple
Pure white lead, or zinc white, ground in oil, and used very thick, is an excellent cement for mending broken crockery ware; it takes a very long time to harden. Put the mended article in some storeroom, and don't look at it for several weeks or even months. It will then be found so firmly united that if ever again broken, it will not part on the line of the former fracture.

Woodcut Showing the Places of Origin of Country Store Merchandise
From Emma Willard's Geography for Beginners, *Hartford, 1826*

Canvas Most Anything

From canvas ice bags to canvas hats, canvas tote bags, some jackets, and even a sweater (wool, not canvas). You can get them all from the *Port Canvas Company*. We infer from their letter that they will entertain making you any special canvas product with the possible exception of a Royal Top Gallant for your square-rigger.

From their growth in just four years, it appears they know canvas and how to make it into a good product.

Catalogues available. Add $1.00 shipping charge to your order.

RWW

Port Canvas Company
Dock Square
Kennebunkport, Maine 04046

Bea's Bonnet $ 7.00

Skate & Ski Boot Bag $12.00

——————————◆——————————

Homestead Wools

Fashion your new dress, suit, skirt or jumper from these fine Homestead fabrics in the season's newest, most popular colors, weaves and patterns. Prices for all wool, wool blends and synthetics are much less than retail store prices for the same quality. Samples on request. Mail orders filled. No requests accepted from outside the United States.

Homestead Woolen Mill Store
West Swanzey, New Hampshire 03469

Habitat

Artist's Portfolio $ 9.00
Brush Holder $ 7.00

Tennis Tote $14.00

KINNI-KINNICK

Kinni Kinnick — smoked by early Indians, settlers and frontiersmen.

Indians rarely smoked pure tobacco, but rather mixed it with the leaves of certain trees, shrubs, herbs and the bark of roots. There was a sense and logic in the way they used tobacco — not frequently — but at the right time or moment.

Kinni Kinnick is the Algonquin word for tobacco, meaning "what is mixed."

Order From:

American Indian Tobacco and Enterprises
Lamentation Mountain
U.S. Route 5
Meriden, Connecticut 06450

Eastern Woodland Indian Tobacco	½ lb.	$4.10
Ceremonial Indian Tobacco	½ lb.	$4.10
Pride of the Iroquois	¼ lb.	$2.10
Old Chippewa Straight	¼ lb.	$2.10
Kinni Kinnick (non tobacco blend)	¼ lb.	$2.10

Woolen and Yard Goods Mill Stores in Maine

The Cascade Woolen Mill Store in Oakland, Maine has pure, virgin wool fabrics with remnants, seconds and pound goods at savings. They fill mail orders and will send samples on request. Shop hours are 8:30 — 4:30 Monday through Saturday.

Then there is Cascade Fabrics in Ellsworth, Maine, with woolens as above, plus Hathaway yard goods at factory discount prices. This store is open 9:00 — 5:00 Monday through Saturday and 1:00 — 5:00 on Sunday. They seem to be a harder working bunch in Ellsworth than those mere six-day-a-week layabouts in Oakland.

RWW

AT
CASCADE WOOLEN MILL
OAKLAND, MAINE

CASCADE FABRICS
ELLSWORTH, MAINE

——————————◆——————————

Coin Jewelry

An old art has been revived by Henry Turek, Jr. His cut-out coin jewelry is handmade and handsome. He will design a wide variety of charms, pins, necklaces, earrings — pierced and regular, tie tacs and cufflinks from coins.

T-Coin
Box 53
East Hampton, Connecticut 06424

Indian Head (with rim):   Pin — $4.50
                               Earrings (pierced) — $12.00

Buffalo Face (without rim):   Charm — $4.00
                               Cufflinks — $10.00

Washington Eagle (with rim):   Necklace — $5.00
                               Tie Tac — $5.50

Ski Wear

Remember the heavy, sodden winter clothing you dragged around the ski slopes not so many years ago? They were enough to discourage even the most ardent skier. Times have changed and thanks in great part to *Profile*, the ski bunnies and bums and hundreds of thousands of other outdoorsmen now brave the trails, down-hills and ski lodge traffic in attractive, comfortable gear. According to *Profile*, being dressed correctly adds to the physical and psychological enjoyment of being active. A maker of outerwear in New England for over 100 years, the staff of this West Lebanon manufacturer has experienced first hand the truth in the tradition of the variable and rapidly changing weather in New England. The entire *Profile* line is tested under a variety of weather conditions and with its special all around *Omni Wear,* the garments provide protection from wind, cold and rain, yet they are flexible, lightweight, rugged and "breathe" to permit escaping moisture away from the body. A far cry from the days when we kept all that moisture on us.

Profile Sports Corporation
West Lebanon, New Hampshire 03784

Prices: Ski Parkas from $30.00-$70.00.

Available only at fine Ski Shops throughout New England.

The first left and right shoes in man's history were made by a New Haven, Connecticut tavern keeper, John Miles. For a long time people accustomed to sharp, pointed straight shoes laughed at his invention and called them "crooked shoes." It wasn't until after the Civil War that they were adopted for regular use.

Burgess Shoe Store

Bass — a well-known maker of good sturdy shoes — offers factory rejects at reasonable prices.

Brochure available from:

Burgess Shoe Store
Wilton, Maine 04294

G. H. BASS & CO. WOMEN'S
SIDE-LACED WEEJUN

If Perfect $20.00   **$12.**95

This popular Weejun is side laced and tasseled; your choice of either brown leather or scotch grain; supple leather uppers; double Neolite soles and heels. Sizes 5/10 (AAA); 4/10 (AA, A, B, C). Save $7.05.
E748 Brown
E745 Brown Pebble Grain

The Dorr Mill Store

The Dorr Woolen Company

The Dorr Woolen Company is perhaps the only textile mill in New England that can surprise the summer visitor, with green grass, attractive landscaping and a profusion of flowers surrounding it. This modern mill produces wool and wool-blend women's-wear fabrics in a wide variety of designs, colors and textures. Using the latest multi-color shuttleless looms, unusual and distinctive fabrics are made for the over-the-counter trade and the garment industry, including many of America's most famous makers and designers. Daily tours of the mill are a popular attraction for visitors to this summer vacation area.

The Dorr Mill Store. . .

is located across the road from the mill. This bright, attractive store carries the most extensive selection of wool and wool-blend fabrics (all made at the mill) in the eastern United States. These fabrics are dress, skirt, suit and coat weights. The store has a full notions and patterns section, and always displays an exciting assortment of remnants, seconds and pound goods. One department is devoted to hooking and braiding, featuring a full line of kits and supplies including 100% pure wool materials. Produced by the Dorr mill, these woolens are available in 60 shades (open stock) by the yard, and in over 200 shades made up into swatches — a service offered by no other mill in the country!

The Dorr Woolen Company
and Dorr Mill Store
Guild, New Hampshire 03754

Assortment of seconds/remnants $1.50 – $3.00 per yd.

Regular line of wool and wool blend fabrics $2.50 – $11.00 per yd.

Blankets and fringed "throws" $7.95 – $25.00

Hooking kits $4.95 up

A New England Simple

To clean kid gloves: Put on the gloves and wash them, as though you were washing your hands, in a basin of spirits of turpentine. The gloves should be hung in the air, or some warm place, to carry away the smell of turpentine.

Pharmaceuticals

Another enterprising Yankee has left his mark upon the New England scene. Parker J. Noyes, a Civil War veteran, came to Lancaster, New Hampshire and opened a drug store, and soon after began manufacturing drugs, powders, lotions and pills — selling them to physicians. One hundred and four years later, the *P. J. Noyes Co. Laboratories* still serve the medical profession. They manufacture 120 different products, mainly prescription items and an increasing amount of laboratory pellet foods for animals, as well as their own brand of aspirin and hand cream. A measure of the Noyes success is seen in the fact that the company has survived in the pharmaceutical field against the onslaught of the industry giants.

The P. J. Noyes Co.
Pharmaceuticals
Lancaster, New Hampshire 03584

The
P.J. Noyes Co.
PRICE LIST

PHARMACEUTICALS

*SERVING THE MEDICAL PROFESSION
FOR OVER 100 YEARS*

LANCASTER, NEW HAMPSHIRE
03584

Friar Tuck Sales

Primarily a wholesale distributor of costume jewelry, they also offer such varied items as smile stickers, coloring book assortments, children's activity boxes and New England scenes place mats. Unlike most wholesale businesses, you can order items separately. Of course, the larger the assortment, the less you pay — as individual pieces are priced higher. Those with the Yankee peddler instinct might be tempted to buy an assortment of earrings, pins or whatever strikes their fancy and resell them at considerable profit. Price lists available.

Friar Tuck Sales
19 Berkley Street
Quincy, Massachusetts 02169

Handmade Sterling Silver Rings
$3.50 each or three for $10.00

Habitat

Sandwich Glass Jewelry

It's interesting that the site of the original Sandwich Glass plant built in 1825 was selected not because of the sand (which was unsuitable for glass making), but because of the extensive woodlands that provided fuel for the furnaces, fired around the clock. Then, on the other hand, it may have been that Deming Jarves, the founder of the factory, wanted to work where he could take a few days off when he felt the urge to go fishing. Whatever the reason, out of such basic ingredients as lead, potash, manganese and sand, the beautiful, soft-shaded "Olde Sandwich" was blown, blown-molded and pressed.

At the time of peak production, the Boston and Sandwich Glass Company owned 28,000 acres of good timber that produced 20 cords to the acre. Unhappily, production ceased in 1888 because of a labor dispute and never again was Sandwich Glass produced. At the Museum in Sandwich there is a noteworthy collection of every pattern of glass made by the famous glassworks.

For those who want to own authentic Sandwich Glass at relatively inexpensive prices, *Sandwich Glass Jewelry* offers a fine selection of pieces made from dug up glass fragments which are processed and then mounted. What looks like a gem-like jewel, may well be a part of a Sandwich goblet, vase, oil lamp, perfume bottle or any one of the myriads of other Sandwich products.

Wee 3 Sandwich Glass Jewelry
Bourne, Massachusetts 02532

Tie Tacks
$2.00 to $5.00
(the $3, $4, and $5 are Collectors Gems)

$5.00

C18 Antique Pendant Necklace
20" chain
Have many rare "one of a kind"
fragments — $7.50 to $15.00
(reds, vasa murrhina, hobs, milk fiery,
opalescent, etc.)

Tie Clasp
$3.00 "Common Colors"
"Rarer Colors" up to $6.00

Handknits

Many years of knitting has led to a full-time business for Mrs. Persons. Brilliantly colored mittens are her specialty, though she will knit sweaters and afghans to order.

One of her most popular items is a pincushion kit, designed with the beginning knitter in mind. Allow up to 2 weeks for delivery.

Mrs. C. W. Persons
The Needle Shop
P.O. Box 49
Marshfield, Vermont 05658

Pincushion Kit $.75

Mittens — Your choice of color
Children's sizes $4.00 and $5.00
Adult sizes $6.00 and $7.00

WALTER DYER is LEATHER
244 Broad Street
Workshop Outlet
Lynn, Massachusetts 01901

MOD BOOT

This has become a classic and is worn by discriminating people all over the world. I am the biggest and best wholesaler (also retailer) in the world. The leather is Fould's Chrome Elk. It is very thick, long wearing and foot conforming. This will cling to your foot like a fat lady's girdle. You will love them. We repair the single sole and replace the double sole. Hand-stained for that rich look.

Men's No. 115   Price $20.95 ppd.
Sizes 6 to 13 Also ½ sizes
Widths A to EEE

No. 933 is a foot and a half across top, maybe two feet. At least 2 ft. deep 4 in. wide. If somebody wants a really big bag, roomy etc., this is it. If you dislike any bag, money back.
Price $60.95 ppd.

DAN COOPER
DESIGN CORPORATION

THE TEXTILE HOUSE — EFFINGHAM FALLS
CENTER OSSIPEE, NEW HAMPSHIRE — 03814

Textiles

Dan Cooper printed and woven fabrics have always been available through decorators. You can now order them by mail. Samples will be sent on request with no obligation only that you return them when through. Delivery is immediate except on special orders. Custom made curtains and bedspreads are available. Showroom is open Monday thru Friday, nine to five and Saturday from nine to four. No catalog.

Habitat

PIL-TAB PULVERIZER

EASY TO USE

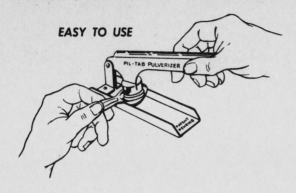

—DIRECTIONS—

With pill in the spoon hold spoon, as shown, in the notch in the side of the base. With the other hand, press the lever and crushing button down on the pill. If not sufficiently crushed, lift lever and tap the spoon to center the uncrushed particles, and press again.

After raising the lever, draw the edge of the spoon across under the bottom of the crushing button to scrape off all medication.

DO NOT CRUSH enteric coated pills made for delayed action.

Check the label, or, if in doubt, consult your druggist or doctor.

E. C. BULL & SON, Inc.
Hamden, Connecticut 06517

Hayfoot — Strawfoot

Finally! A company devoted entirely to the manufacture of left-handed products. Left-handedly, you can purchase playing cards, needlepoint instructions with sample piece, shears of all kinds, even a left-handed bread knife and a corkscrew. Also available is a selection of books written by and about left-handed people. Send for their brochure.

The Aristera Organization
Peter B. Nieman, President
9 Rice's Lane
Westport, Connecticut 06880

Postage and handling not included in price.

Pil-Tab Pulverizer is made of sturdy, anodized aluminum and stainless steel with "captive" spoon which cannot be mislaid. The return of only two from the 30,000 sold in the last few years is great testimony to its durability. "You just can't please everybody," Mr. Bull says.

E. C. Bull & Son
39 Wood Street
Hamden, Connecticut 06517

Pil-Tab Pulverizer — $3.50

A New England Simple

Bran water makes an excellent stiffening for dark materials.

PLAYING CARDS ▲

(2 Deck Set)

These cards have their identification "pips" on all four corners. Ordinary cards have these pips on just two corners. Now, leftys and rightys can always identify each card in their hand, no matter how they are held! The set contains one blue back and one red back deck of top quality plastic coated cards. This is one of our most popular products. Everybody loves them.

K 10 $3.00 per set

LEFTY NOTEBOOK ▲

Opens from left to right. No more need to get ridges from leaning on the spiral binding. 8½ x 11 ruled sheets with the holes punched on the left, so that the page will line up properly in a loose leaf 3 ring binder. Really customized for leftys.

B 10   2 for $1.18

Early AO spectacle shop . . . 1833

A-OK Since 1833

American Optical was founded in 1833 by William Beecher in Southbridge, Massachusetts, where its world headquarters and main plant complex are still located. Beecher was a jewelry craftsman who had an idea he could make silver spectacle frames better and sell them at a lower price than those available at that time, almost all of which were imported from Europe. The fledgling enterprise that Beecher started had its ups and downs for several years, but was greatly aided by the genius of a young man who became associated with the company in 1864, shortly after Beecher retired. This man, George Washington Wells, was to the optical industry what Henry Ford was to the automobile industry. Through Wells' inventive genius and ability to systematize production and reduce costs, the young company attained an outstanding position in its field. Eventually, Wells obtained a controlling interest in the firm and, for nine decades, the name of Wells was to be synonymous with American Optical as father, sons and grandsons guided AO's destinies until the company became publicly-owned in 1952.

AO's original product, spectacle frames, needed lenses. In the early years of its existence, AO imported lenses from Europe. However, when the Civil War curtailed this trade, AO began devising its own methods of lens manufacture.

As ophthalmic science advanced, simple lenses that merely magnified an object were gradually refined to provide built-in "corrections" for astigmatism and other visual deficiencies. The need to *protect*, as well as to correct, man's vision led to AO's entry into the safety field where its products now include hundreds of items designed to protect the individual from a multitude of industrial hazards. In 1935, AO purchased the Spencer Lens Company which was, at that time, the leading manufacturer of microscopes. That acquisition gave AO an important foothold in the area heavily dependent upon precision optics. It also enabled AO to expand into the educational field with audiovisual equipment. Subsequently, AO moved into the field of medical instrumentation. Today, many of these instruments are providing a means of visually determining conditions of the blood, heart and other organs of the body.

In addition to glasses — frames and lenses — AO's line includes such wide ranging protective products as clothing, accessories, respirators, hearing devices, headgear and eyewear.

American Optical Corporation
Southbridge, Massachusetts 01550

Orders and correspondence for safety products should be directed to established service centers. For New England:

American Optical Corporation
Putnam, Connecticut 06260

A New England Simple

Before putting away patent leather shoes that are not worn regularly, rub them with olive oil. This will preserve the leather.

The Shaker Cloak –
an American classic revived

From the last decades of the nineteenth century until the 1930's, the Shaker cloak was a highly-esteemed necessity of the well-dressed American woman. Mrs. Grover Cleveland ordered one from the New Lebanon, New York, Shakers for her husband's second inaugural. Through the 1920's the Shaker cloak was one of the most sought-after and prestigious articles of Shaker manufacture.

SHAKER WORKSHOPS has now revived the Shakers' classic cloak, taking infinite pains to assure that our version matches the original in every detail. Like the original, ours is cut from the finest 100% wool, and is available in three authentic colors: Deep Blue, Cranberry Red and Mink Brown. Like the original, ours has a cape collar, lined hood, pleated back and a 3-inch wide sash. And like the original, it is cut and sewn with faultless precision — a standard of workmanship rarely seen nowadays.

Our Shaker cloaks are made to order. Deliveries can usually be made within about four weeks. Please specify the length from the neck line to the floor. $125.00 postpaid.

Fabric samples can be supplied on request at 25¢.

Shaker Workshops
THE 1747 WRIGHT TAVERN
Two Lexington Road
Concord, Massachusetts 01742

"Form Follows Function"

Those words came from the Bauhaus School of Modern Architecture, but 150 years or so before that concept was put into words, it was part of the Shaker philosophy, and they translated it through their hands.

Now the exquisite-simplicity of their designs have been meticulously reproduced by the *Shaker Workshop,* and are available, reasonably priced, in kit form or ready made.

They have a catalogue which sells for $1.00, and is worth much more than that.

RWW

Shaker Workshops, Inc.
P.O. Box 710*
Concord, Massachusetts 01742
*Their going-to-see address is much more fitting:
The 1747 Wright Tavern
Two Lexington Road
Concord, Massachusetts 01742

SW4   ARM CHAIR

Many experts feel that this chair is a Shaker classic. It is sometimes referred to as an "elder's chair" because of its generous proportions and stately lines. Its dignified stature, however, perhaps belies its comfort which is truly remarkable, and suggests its suitability for nearly every room. Height of back 51½" Height of seat 18" Width 22" Depth 18"

Kit: $59.95 Weight 15 lbs. U.P.S. or Parcel Post

SW22   OVAL BOXES

These hand-made classics are considered by some to be the acme of Shaker design. Originals are sought at every auction as among the finest product the Shakers ever made in wood. The original tools made and used in a Shaker oval box factory were studied to re-establish and perfect the technique of making these rare items. These boxes make perfect gifts and can be used for storage in the kitchen, for sewing or decorative purposes, or as general household catch-alls. Stained with light or dark stain or unfinished. U.P.S. or Parcel Post

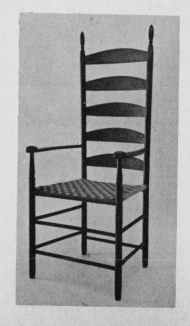

No.	Length	Width	Height	Price	Weight
1	6¼"	4¼"	2¼"	$12.00	1 lb.
2	8"	5-1/8"	2-7/8"	$14.00	1 lb.
3	9-1/8"	6¼"	3¾"	$16.00	2 lbs.
4	11½"	8¼"	4¾"	$18.00	3 lbs.
5	13¼"	9-3/8"	5¾"	$20.00	3 lbs.
Nested set of 5				$70.00	9 lbs.

Pooler's Moccasin Shop

The Poolers have been making leather things for four generations. Started in the 1890's as a repair shop, Pooler's now offers a wide variety of leather shoes, moccasins, custom-made clothing, belts and handbags. Their shoes and moccasins come in a wonderful selection of colors and sizes — and there is no extra charge for your shoes if your feet are different sizes! Send for their catalog.

Pooler's Moccasin Shop
Water Street
Skowhegan, Maine 04976

Heavy Supreme Krome Ring Boot

Men — sizes 7-12	$19.95
Young Men 4-6	$18.95
Ladies 4-9	$18.95
Misses & Boys 10-3	$17.95

Ladies & Misses Hand Laced Slipper Moccs —
No Sole $5.95

STYLE NO. 1204A
HEAVY SUPREME KROME RING BOOT

STYLE NO. 200A
LADIES & MISSES' HAND LACED SLIPPER MOCCS

NO
SOLE
with or without
BEADS & LACE

Boots and Sandals

With the help of an eighty-one year old bootmaker, *Super Sandal* of Bar Harbor, Maine, now offers handmade, fully lined, and made-to-measure boots and shoes. These are in addition to their regular line of unique sandals, moccasins, leather handbags, work aprons, belts, and wallets.

Prices are not the lowest but then they are not out of sight either. They have a modest catalogue with prices shown.

Super Sandal
9 Main Street
Bar Harbor, Maine 04609

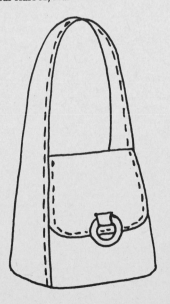

B) Shoulder bag with unique two piece construction - made of soft leather.
9" x 11" x 3½ - $30

Toni Totes of Vermont

These tote bags have "the fresh, clean look of Vermont!" They are good for carrying anything. Made of unlined canvas — navy, camel, toast and natural with contrasting trims — these totes come in many different styles and sizes. Especially nifty is the tote for toting tennis rackets — one or two of them at a time.

Toni Totes of Vermont, Inc.
Route 100
Londonderry, Vermont 05148

Hand Tote Tennis Bag
          15" x 3" x 12" $17.00

Wilk says —

New England feuds, while always less violent than the Hatfields and the McCoys along the Big Sandy River in Kentucky, are damn near as lethal if either party has a skin any thinner than an elderly rhinoceros. Once asked if he knew a rather prominent man in his home town, the Connecticut Yankee replied loud enough for all within earshot to hear, "Known him all my life. Haven't spoken to him in thirty-five years, 'cause he confuses intelligence and status with good sense, and he hasn't got any."

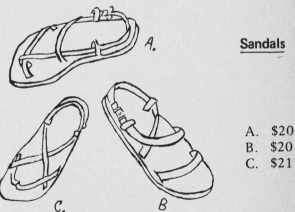

Sandals

A.	$20
B.	$20
C.	$21

To order sandals, send a drawing of feet on stiff cardboard. Drawings should be made following the outline of the foot with the pen perpendicular to the paper. Mark the space between the big & second toe. Also indicate end of little toe and the beginning & end of the arch.

Sandals are hand made with molded arch and adjustable straps. Please indicate choice of light or dark color. Sandals are available by mail from October 1 to May 15.

Morrow Leather Creations

Leather in several shades of brown, plus black, combined in such a way that each color is part of a shaded pattern, embellished with handcrafted silver, enameled, stained glass and sculptured metal belt buckles make *Morrow Leather Creations* belts more than just something to hold up a pair of pants.

Fifteen styles of sandals, leather furniture, garments and hats, along with handbags guaranteed for the life of the purchaser, are all part of designer/craftsman John Gaynor's extensive line.

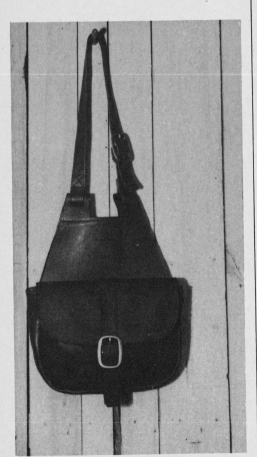

Morrow Leather Creations
Box 473
Avon, Connecticut 06001

Leather Handbag, Five Inside Pockets $28.00

Habitat

CRAFT

Craft Index

A
Adhesives 180
All Hands Aboard Scrimshawing 173
Antiques
 glass 169
Art Galleries 186
The Art of Bird Carving 158
The Art of Colonial America 167

B
Bags
 kits 151
 weaving 174
Baskets 154, 155
Batik
 artists 150, 170
 supplies 150
Birds
 etchings 185
 prints 177
 woodcarving 157, 158
A Book of Country Things 182
Brass
 furnishings 164
 rubbing 182

C
Candles 161
Clothing 148, 151
 weaving 153
Combmaker 159
Cooper 157
Copper
 weather vanes 166
Craft
 centers 148, 149, 167
 Indian 148
 organizations 149
 schools 149
 shops 148, 149, 153, 157, 160, 164, 171, 172
 supplies 150

D
Decoupage
 artists 184
 prints 183
 supplies 181
Drawing Aids 182

E
Early American Folk Pottery 168
Ecology
 recycling newspapers 176
Etchings
 birds 185

F
Fabrics
 dyeing 150
 weaving 153
The Folk Arts and Crafts of New England 167
Foundries 166
Furnishings 178, 180
 brass 164
 hand painted 186
 pewter 164
Furniture 161

G
Glass 172
 antiques 169
 blowing 169, 171
 fused 167, 170
 jewelry 160
 lighting 171
 stained 160, 167, 168, 169, 171
 stained, kits 169
 stained, supplies 168, 169
 works 171
*A Guide To Decoration
In The Early American Manner* 178

H
Hardware
 homes 161
Homes
 hardware 161

I
Indian
 craft 148
 museums 148
Ivory
 piano keys 173
 scrimshaw 173

J
Jewelry
 glass 160
 pottery 172
 silversmiths 164, 166
John Rogers — The People's Sculptor 177
The Jug and Related Stoneware of Bennington 171

L
Lead 168
Leather
 bags 148
Let's Have a Craft Show 149
Lighting 159
 glass 171
 lampshades 178

M
Mail Order Book Service 185
Majolica — Collect It For Fun and Profit 167
Maps
 prints 177
Museums
 art 186
 Indian 148
 maritime 156
 papers 180

N
Nantucket Lightship Baskets 155
Needlecraft
 kits 175
 patterns 174, 175
 rug braiding 174
 rug hooking 174
 schools 150
 shirret 175
 supplies 152, 154, 175
 yarns 152, 175
New England Glass & Glassmaking 172

P
Painting 186
 driftwood 185
 marine 184, 186
 reproductions 184
 supplies 179
 tole 164, 178
 tole, supplies 181
Papers
 cutting 184
 museums 180
 printing 179
 writing 176, 177, 178, 180, 181, 183, 184, 186
Patterns
 needlecraft 174, 175
 rug hooking 152, 174, 175
Pewter
 furnishings 164
Picture Frames 178
Pottery 160, 167, 168, 171, 172
 ceramics 167, 170
 ceramic tiles 167, 170
 equipment 165, 169, 170
 jewelry 172
 supplies 169, 170
Printing
 hand binding 181
 limited editions 176, 181
 linoleum block 181
 medieval illumination 179
 papers 179
 woodcuts 184
Prints
 birds 177
 charts 184
 decoupage 183
 maps 177
 mounted 177

Q
Quilt Making 151, 160

R
Rubber Stamp 182
Rubbing
 brass 182
 instructions 183
 kits 182, 183
 stone 182
 supplies 183
Rug Braiding 174
 equipment 174
 supplies 174
Rug Hooking 174
 equipment 152, 174
 instructions 152, 174
 kits 152, 174
 patterns 152, 174, 175
 supplies 174

S
A Sandwich Sampler 169
Schools
 craft 149
 needlecraft 150
Scrimshaw
 ivory 173
Scrimshaw and Scrimshanders 173
Sculpture 149, 161, 162, 167, 177
Shakers 159
Signs
 woodcarving 158
Silhouettes 184
Silver Design Competition 163
Silversmiths 162, 165
 guild 163, 165
 jewelry 164, 166
 supplies 162, 164
 tools 162, 163
Supplies
 batik 150
 craft 150
 decoupage 181
 needlecraft 152, 154, 175
 painting 179
 pottery 169, 170
 rubbing 183
 rug braiding 174
 rug hooking 174
 silversmiths 162, 164
 stained glass 168, 169
 tole painting 181

T
Tole Painting 164, 178
 supplies 181
Tools
 cutting 156
 hand 156
 precision 163
 silversmiths 162, 163
Toys
 kites 180
 stuffed 160
 wooden 160

W
Wall
 stencilling 164
Weather Vanes
 copper 166
Weaving 155
 bags 174
 chair seats 155
 clothing 153
 equipment 153, 154
 fabrics 153
 rugs 154
 spinning 151
 yarns 151, 152, 153, 154
Whales
 woodcarving 158
Winslow Homer 186
Winslow Homer at Prout's Neck 185
Woodcarving 157
 birds 157, 158
 letter openers 157
 pipes 158
 puzzles 157
 shipcarvers 156, 158
 signs 158
 whales 158

Indian Crafts

Mrs. Nowetah Timmerman of the Susquehanna-Cherokee Indian tribes began making beadwork when she was six. As time progressed she became more and more interested, not only in making Indian crafts, but also in preserving Indian artifacts and culture.

Now she owns the Indian Blanket Craft & Gift Shop, in which she carries her own handmade beaded jewelry, rugs, blankets, mats, leather garments, woven belts and many other items.

Nowetah also offers free educational programs for scouts, schools, churches and other groups. Call or write for appointment, or better yet, visit her shop.

Mrs. K. Nowetah Timmerman
1 Old Nod Road
Clinton, Connecticut 06413

Mid-Coast Arts & Crafts Center

The Mid-Coast Arts & Crafts Center was founded to promote and inspire arts and crafts in the mid-coastal area of Maine and to provide educational instruction and training, as well as to renew the older crafts that have slowly lost ground in today's world.

A permanent site has been developed at the Knox County Airport in Owl's Head. Items made by members of the center may be purchased at a privately operated sales facility located at the airport.

Mid-Coast Arts & Crafts Center
Box 213, Star Route 32
Owl's Head, Maine 04854

The Good Life

Muriel and Don Lawton are to be envied for they are among the decided minority who have turned wistful yearnings into enjoyable reality. Abandoning their busy professional life in Madison, Wisconsin, the *Lawtons* took the plunge in 1970 and opened an arts and crafts shop on Deer Isle, Maine.

What's most amazing about the shop is that all the merchandise is made by the couple themselves. Notable is their pottery output, but their paintings (in various mediums) are displayed as well. Not to mention handwoven towels and scarves, ashtrays fashioned from beer bottles, sandcast candles and a special specialty, "happies" — little handmade "vase people." They also display their creative wares at other stores and galleries around Maine.

Lest you've got your defenses up and are thinking the *Lawtons* have simply traded one hectic merry-go-round for another, here's a brief description of their life by Muriel. It should bring you a little nearer to your own Deer Isle. "Our winters are spent creating, designing and producing our ideas. Other seasons we are busy selling, meeting people and sharing the fruits of our large organic garden. We always have the time for relaxing, reading, long beach walks. We truly have a good life."

Claudia

The Lawtons
Reach Road, Box 120
Deer Isle, Maine 04627

Frog Hollow Craft Center

Lucky are those craft-minded people who live in the Middlebury, Vermont area. Not only does the *Frog Hollow Craft Center* offer working, selling and teaching opportunities for professional artists and craftsmen, it also offers a wide range of learning opportunities for residents of the area.

Three professional craftsmen have workshops and hold classes in the center. In addition, there is a group of associated artists and craftsmen who display and sell their work in the gallery located there. Any nonresident craftsman may display and sell items on approval of a jury of experts, and may apply to teach in the Craft Center when workshop space is available.

As a service to the Middlebury community, *Frog Hollow Craft Center* offers free craft courses to elementary school children in the area. These courses include weaving, macrame, batik, pottery, woodwork, carpentry, basket weaving and bookbinding.

Frog Hollow has a monthly newsletter describing current and prospective programs. Any individual or organization wishing to receive this letter should send their name to Rena Gearhart at the Center.

Suggested by Colonel William J. Slator
Editor, Addison County Independent

Frog Hollow Craft Center
Mill Street
Middlebury, Vermont 05753

Acadian Crafts

The Acadians came to the New World in the late 16th-and early 17th-centuries from the provinces of Brittany and Normandy. When they refused to swear allegiance to the crown of King George II, they were forced to leave Nova Scotia, and moved southward to the colonies. Many of them settled along the St. John River on the Canadian border. Descendants of these independent, hard working people, still living in the St. John Valley, banded together in early 1970 to form *Acadian Crafts Association, Inc.* — a co-op organized to market craft products as a supplement to their incomes. With the help of a board of directors, they decided to specialize in crocheted goods, and to limit their products to infants' and ladies' wear.

Acadian Crafts, along with their regular line of products, also produces custom-made items to your pattern or color requirements. Write for more information.

Acadian Crafts Association, Inc.
Box 246
Madawaska, Maine 04756

Arrand Art and Fine Crafts Studio

Designing and making leather handbags and soft toys keeps bread on the table, but Pamela and William Arrand would like to do more one-of-a-kind pieces, such as wall hangings, rugs, macrame, chess sets and furniture. If you have something special in mind — contact them. They'll be happy to quote you a price.

Arrand Arts and Fine Crafts
Schoolhouse
East Ryegate, Vermont 05042
Man's Shoulder Bag   13"x10"x4" $60.00
Colors: Tan, Cherry, Mahogany
Made of top-grain cowhide, with brass buckles

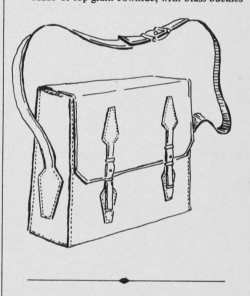

The Maine-Made Shop

Beatrice Bartol, owner of *The Maine-Made Shop,* sells products of Maine artists and craftsmen exclusively. She buys things outright — preferring not to work on the consignment basis that many craft shops adopt. She's proud of the craftsmen represented in her shop and has become a real "booster" of Maine crafts in general. She writes:

"You will find other New England states ahead of Maine in the production and marketing of crafts, but we've made tremendous progress in the last few years, and we're getting there."

The Maine-Made Shop
P. O. Box 144
Boothbay Harbor, Maine 04538

A Craft Center

The home of the village blacksmith — 1820 — has become a craft center. The Fayerweather House is a completely restored example of the typical middle-class villager's home a century and a half ago.

It now houses *The Fayerweather Craft Guild,* which conducts a year-round program of classes, workshops, lectures and demonstrations. It also sponsors a small shop where handcrafted items may be purchased.

The Fayerweather Craft Guild
Kingston, Rhode Island 02881

The Falmouth Craft Studio

There's always an interesting and colorful variety of crafts on display at the *Craft Studio.* Several years ago a group of professional craftsmen and eager amateurs of every age pooled their creative skills and founded this school. Some of the fine quality articles on sale are the pressed flower stationery, tissue paper collages, leaded glass and batiks. The *Craft Studio* welcomes professional craftsmen as well as amateurs and encourages more young people to become serious craftsmen. Several scholarships are awarded to deserving high school students each year.

The Falmouth Craft Studio
119 Palmer Avenue
Falmouth, Massachusetts 02540

The New Hampshire League of Arts and Crafts

A dedicated group of artisans whose aim is to encourage New Hampshire craftsmen to produce quality work, with a strong emphasis on design. Besides the eleven state-wide craft outlets created solely for the purpose of selling League members work, they sponsor many educational programs — with a particular emphasis on craft instruction for the elderly.

League of New Hampshire Arts and Crafts
Hanover, New Hampshire 03755

Gallery for Artists

Renaissance combines the excitement of contemporary art with the decor of the past. A converted ale warehouse is now a gallery for ceramics, macrame, weaving, silver and old prints. Visitors can enjoy a glass of sherry while listening to Renaissance or Baroque music.

A special feature is the craft work of Olaf Jensen, an ex-seaman from Norway. Mr. Jensen builds historic ship models with a careful eye to authentic detail.

Renaissance
207 Market Street
Portsmouth, New Hampshire 03801

Peter's Brook HANDCRAFTS

East Arlington, Vermont 05252

A Heart Warming Idea-At-Work in Vermont Sculptures on the Highway

Everyone who has yawned at the boredom and anonymity of our interstate highways should drop a note of appreciation to:

Vermont International Sculpture Symposium
University of Vermont
Burlington, Vermont 05401

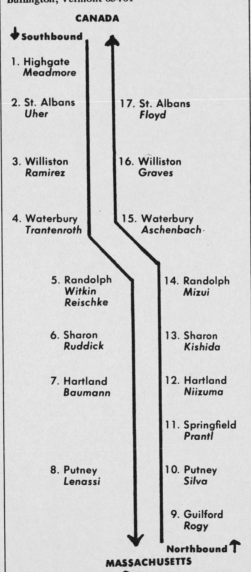

CANADA

↓ **Southbound**

1. Highgate
   Meadmore

2. St. Albans
   Uher

3. Williston
   Ramirez

4. Waterbury
   Trantenroth

5. Randolph
   Witkin
   Reischke

6. Sharon
   Ruddick

7. Hartland
   Baumann

8. Putney
   Lenassi

17. St. Albans
    Floyd

16. Williston
    Graves

15. Waterbury
    Aschenbach

14. Randolph
    Mizui

13. Sharon
    Kishida

12. Hartland
    Niizuma

11. Springfield
    Prantl

10. Putney
    Silva

9. Guilford
   Rogy

Northbound ↑

MASSACHUSETTS

Crafts are an important movement in New England today. The skills of our forefathers — craftsmen of rare quality — are being perpetuated by many people who are supporting themselves fully by their own artistry. In a holding action against the constant thrusts of our mechanized society, the cry of today's craftsmen is not to accept the mass-produced materials as the sole method of meeting man's needs. Hail to their effort.

Bennington Gallery

Situated in a lovely, tree-lined court, the *Bennington Gallery* offers original creative craftsmanship of the highest quality. As tempters — paintings, graphics, sculpture, free-blown glass, pottery and plants. Leaflet available.

The Bennington Gallery
125 North Street
Bennington, Vermont 05201

Summer School of Crafts

The purpose of *Haystack-Hinckley School* is to provide young people with well-equipped studios and freedom in an attempt to instill in the individual students the desire to create professional work in terms of quality and with regard to design and excellence of execution.

Summer sessions are held on the Hinckley School's campus in Maine. Classes in ceramics, foundry, fabric decoration, leather, glass blowing, weaving, graphics, jewelry and photography are taught by professional practicing craftsmen.

Haystack-Hinckley School of Crafts
Hinckley, Maine 04944
Write: Erling Heistad, Director
          7 Highland Avenue
          Lebanon, New Hampshire 03766

Let's Have a Craft Show

Let's Have a Craft Show is not only a frequent event around New England these days, it's also the title of a very practical publication of The Connecticut Guild of Craftsmen.

This organization numbers over four hundred members, and concerns itself with the interests of the producing craftsmen. One of its aims is to improve the quality of craft shows and to make them more profitable both for sponsors and participating craftsmen. Membership is open to anyone interested in New England crafts.

Those writing to the Guild for a free copy of *Let's Have a Craft Show* are encouraged, through an accompanying letter, to join the organization.

The editor of the brochure is Robert B. Norris, Executive Officer of the Connecticut Guild of Craftsmen. He starts with a warning to readers that "unfortunately, far too few groups realize that launching a craft show is much like walking a tight rope across Niagara Falls." He goes on to the selection of a date (at least six months from the first planning session), commissions, handling sales and all the other nitty-gritty items so essential to success.

Let's Have a Craft Show each month includes a newsletter, a list of members, a monthly calendar of craft events around the region and a host of other information valuable to those interested in handcrafts.

MSH

Let's Have a Craft Show
Edited by Robert B. Norris
Published by:
The Connecticut Guild of Craftsmen
P. O. Box 94
Storrs, Connecticut 06268
$5.75 yearly

Craft

150

Arts and Crafts Supplies

Copper enameling equipment, stained glass, jewelers supplies, clock movements, clay, paints, papers and much more available from:

Bergen Arts and Crafts
Box 381
Marblehead, Massachusetts 01945

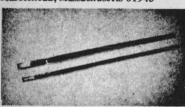

BRISTLE BRUSHES

For coating larger areas with wax

No. 9306-A .... large ..... $ .65
No. 9306-B .... small .... .50

BATIK FORMULA WAX

Specially formulated for use without the addition of paraffin.

No. 9302-A lb. ..... $ 1.50
No. 9302-B 10-lbs. 13.75

ALCOHOL LAMP

For keeping wax in liquid form.

No. 1652-JB

$2.00

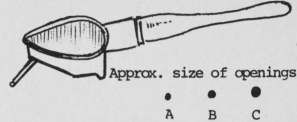

BATIK – TOOLS EQUIPMENT AND SUPPLIES

CHINESE BAMBOO BRUSHES

For free design work

No. 332-1 .... large .... $ .75
No. 332-2 .... small .... .60

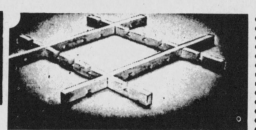

STRETCHER FRAME

Material is stretched over the frame for wax coating and for fine dye work. The wooden pieces of frame are 24" long and notched for adjusting.

No. 9308-AZ .... (4-pcs) $5.40

WAX PAPER   A re-usable

work surface for Batik. Sheets 18"x24".

No. 9309 .... Pkg. of 10 $1.65

Approx. size of openings

A   B   C

TJANTING NEEDLE

Traditional tool for applying wax on fine line work and for outlining areas. Melted wax is poured into Tjanting and wax flows through fine needle spout.

No. 9300-A ..... small $4.10
No. 9300-B ..... medium 4.10
No. 9300-C ..... large 4.10
No. 9300-AZ .. set of three 11.95

BOOKS ABOUT BATIK

No. BP-9325 Batik Handbook, by Craftools, Inc. Written especially to guide the beginner. Illustrated $1.25

No. BP-9307 The Hand Decoration of Fabrics, F. J. Kafka. Profusely illustrated step-by-step guide to all methods. 198 pp $5.50

BATIK KIT

Contains all supplies necessary to 'Batik' your material.

No. 9301-AZ $24.95

Arnold Print Works, Inc.

BLEACHERS · PRINTERS · DYERS · FINISHERS
ADAMS, MASS. 01220

Bleaching, Printing, Dying and Finishing

Do not write the *Arnold Print Works* to have your daughter's latest mini dyed shocking fuchsia. These people are a large commercial operation with some 650 employees who bleach, print, dye, finish, package, and store goods for draperies, slipcovers, shirtings, etc., for the largest and most prominent textile converting firms in the United States. They process tens of millions of yards of goods annually.

But it is rather nice to know that one of the original backbone industries of New England ... textiles ... has not completely moved away to the South.

They have a modest four-page pamphlet that tells their story.

Arnold Print Works, Inc.
Adams, Massachusetts 01220

Craft

GENTIAN MEADOWS SCHOOL

Gentian Meadows is a pleasant "one-room school" in a one hundred-year-old farmhouse in Bowdoinham, Maine.

The School teaches rug braiding, two methods for oriental-type rugs, crewel work and canvas embroidery, popularly called "needlepoint."

An open and informal schedule makes hours available either individually or in a class, at reasonable rates. Monday is reserved.

The School stocks materials and supplies.

Mrs. Verrill's successful and popular classes in adult education programs are well established.

For further information write, call or visit

GENTIAN MEADOWS SCHOOL
Needlework and Rug Making
Mrs. Thelma F. Verrill, *Director*
Richmond, Maine 04357

A New England Simple

Iron Rust can be removed from white fabrics by soaking them in sour milk.

Batik Artist

Stylized birds grace the batik wall hangings that *Nancy Hamilton* creates. Inquire about her natural fibre sculptures — woven, knotted and twisted — to be hung from a tree. The birds love them!

Nancy Hamilton
35 Creighton Street
Providence, Rhode Island 02904

Baby's Crib Quilt – Doll Quilts

Quilts are time-consuming to make, so this Maine housewife would not be able to fill large orders. But, if you want to give a new mother something very special, one of *Dawn Babbitt's* quilts is sure to be a treasured gift.

Dawn Babbitt
Douglas Hill, Maine 04023

Doll's Quilt – 36" square – $2.75 ppd.
(All cotton)

Baby's Crib Quilt – 47" x 34" – $8.00 ppd.
(Flannel pieces and cotton backing)

Maartje Knoppers – Spinner and Weaver

Maartje Knoppers moved to Maine about five years ago from Holland, where she had learned to spin and weave. Once here, she obtained her own Corriedale sheep, and now shears them, washes and dyes the wool, then weaves it.

She writes, "In this time of machine-made material and computers . . . a majority of people have forgotten the beauty and joy of creating with their hands. The art of doing for yourself has been forgotten, I hope to bring it back."

Maartje Knoppers
Mt. Auburn Avenue RR 3
Auburn, Maine 04210

Make Your Own Handbags

If you were asked to suggest a new use for upholstery webbing – what would you come up with?

The clever folks at *Barn Door Crafts* offer a delightful group of handbag kits, each one made of jute upholstery webbing. The lining material, a 10-inch zipper, needles, colorful embroidery yarn and complete instructions are also included.

Barn Door Crafts
Viets Road
Sandisfield, Massachusetts 02155

"ARROWHEAD" PATTERN
Kit No. 1004
$5.25 each

HOME Co-op

HOME stands for Homeworkers Organized for More Employment – a joint effort hardworking people are making to help themselves. Settled on the picturesque Maine coast, we have the beauty of woodlands and blueberry fields, lakes and hills – but few economic opportunities.

We're a determined people, eager to share our skills and learn new ones. We want to be productive in our own rural situation with its mixture of beauty and difficulty. Far from centers of commerce, we have to find a way to make talents and resources economically effective for ourselves and our families. These needs have brought HOME Co-op into being.

. . .On the backroads where the tarred highway ends, a senior citizen, not able to make ends meet with his social security check, holds up another red birdhouse to his admiring wife. Half a mile away, a family is gathered around the kitchen table, carefully cutting cotton pieces; the mother arranges them for a colorful hostess skirt. Across the bridge, a former shoeworker hums away as she stitches a leather vest on her thirty-three-year-old treadle. The ancient machine's sturdy construction handles suede easily. Birdhouses, skirts, and vests will meet at HOME's headquarters in Orland. . . .

HOME is concerned with people who have more than economic problems. Country areas lack the many assistance agencies that cities maintain. HOME sponsors projects in craft instruction and new developments in supplementary farming. It has programs in nutrition, remedial reading, basic literacy, and communication skills. Classes are a learning time, a laughing time and a get-together for folks gathered in from many miles.

HOME believes in people and their potential for independent, constructive living. It focuses on the rural families of middle Maine who continue, against many odds, a life style of simple realism, hard work and closeness to growing things.

We "Down East-ers" watch the change of sky and season, and our hands move as inspiration comes alive in wood and cloth. Our handiwork is one way of sharing Maine with you.

HOME Co-op
Box 408
Orland, Maine 04472

#203 Kimono Dress with Bib
Dolman sleeves - tie belt
black print skirt, red
and white apron $90

#205 Basic Black (or whatever)
black, red and navy - panel apron
and blet accessories $74

Craft

Specialty Wooden Products

High quality items to complement needlework. *Sudberry House* manufactures finely turned out Bermuda handle kits, footstools, luggage racks and serving trays.

Sudberry House
Wesley Avenue
Westbrook, Connecticut 06498

Queen Anne Footstool 9" x 11" x 7" high $24.00
Velcro Bermuda Bag 6" $10.95
Needlework Tray Table with Luggage Rack 16" x 24" $41.95 (other sizes available)

SUDBERRY HOUSE

NEEDLEWORK TRAY TABLE

Christopher Farm — Wool

Christopher Farm has over 400 sheep — primarily of the Montadale, Corriedale and Columbia breeds. These three breeds were developed especially for their wool.

The natural lustre of the wool is also imparted to the yarn. Dark fleeces are mixed with various proportions of white wool to achieve eight distinctive shades of browns and greys. The white wool alone yields the classic off-white color long associated with "Fisherman" sweaters.

Knitting yarns containing lanolin, primarily used in fisherman sweaters, are available in a wide range of colors, both two and three ply, for either indoor or outdoor sweaters. The "Icelandic type" of yarn is utilized for bulky knits and also by weavers who desire a marked change of texture in their weaving. The natural color rug yarns and warp yarns are extremely strong and popular among weavers.

Wool is sold directly from the farm via mail order throughout the country, and by a number of stores in the Northeast. Swatch card available — $.25.

Christopher Farm
R.F.D. #2
Richmond, Maine 04357

		4 oz. skein
Fisherman (2 and 3 ply)	per lb.	$6.00
Rug (4 ply)	per lb.	$4.36
Icelandic (4 ply)	per lb.	$6.00

For Rug Hookers Only

Over 700 patterns and a complete line of equipment in this illustrated catalog. A how-to manual as well, there are many interesting and unusual articles to aid the rug-hooker.

Joan Moshimer
Craftsman Studio
North Street
Kennebunkport, Maine 04046
Catalog $2.00.

A typical Maine coastal scene

#92 "THE LOBSTERMAN" 26" x 44" $5.95

A New England Simple

To make cold cream: 4 oz. of sweet almond oil and 2 oz. each of white wax, cocoa butter, rose water and lard. Cut the cocoa butter, lard and wax into small pieces and let them melt in a bowl placed in boiling water. Add the oil and rose water, blending and stirring occasionally until cold.

Onion Skin Dyeing (save the dry outer skins)

Onion skin dyeing is fun to do and the results are delightful. Can be used in pictorials, leaves, flowers, fruit, Orientals and geometrics. Keep a bag of these beautifully colored wools by your hooking frame, and you will use it constantly.

Gather together an assortment of colored flannels, new or used, in all sorts of odd sized pieces. The colors can be red, rose, orange, tan, green, blue, gray, lavender and some small checks and tweeds if you have them. Darker colors will result if you start with a lot of dark colored wools. Generally, for best results, use medium and light colored wools. Soak the wools for a few minutes in warm water, with a little Cushing's "Plurosol" or detergent in it, then arrange them in layers in a medium sized enamel pan, putting between each layer a handful of the onion skins and about one tablespoon of uniodized salt. Let these layers build up to within a few inches of the top of pan, then cover with boiling water. Let it all simmer for about 30 minutes, then rinse well and dry. The colors that emerge will be like no others you have ever seen — soft and subtly blended with a "golden glow" from the onion skins. The more onion skins you use, the more pronounced will be the "glow."

Wilk says —

Piney Allen's farm lies just a mile south of Greensboro, Vermont, and as the hardier northern Vermonters are wont to point out to a shivering visitor during one of their cooler July evenings, "Summer don't start til you pass Piney Allen's goin' south."

Craft

Waist Loom

A handcrafted waist loom — for the beginner or expert weaver.

$6.00 each

How to get started

Yarns

Contessa Yarns has been recommended by several craftsmen as a good supplier of yarns for the weaver. They offer a variety of quality yarns. Write for their brochure and samples.

Contessa Yarns
Lebanon, Connecticut 06249

Handweaving

The Ayottes create and produce an original line of apparel including wall hangings, coats, capes, dresses, skirts among many others. These enthusiastic Rhode Island School of Design graduates have combined their talents to produce beautiful, handwoven fabrics. For those who would like to do their own weaving, the Ayottes sell *Leclerc* looms. Robert Ayotte is convinced the only thing to wear out on these quality looms is the weaver.

Ayottes' Designery
Center Sandwich, New Hampshire 03227

1. Cut the Yarn

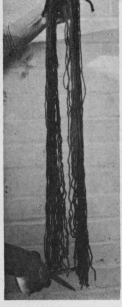

2. Thread the Heddle

3. Tie around the Dowel

ROBERT C. NELSON
69 Pleasant Street
Concord, Mass. 01742

Then, Lift the Heddle,

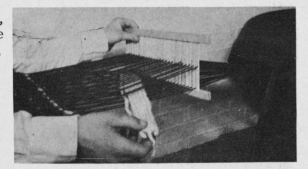

And Drop the Heddle.

You're Weaving!

Twenty-five-stick, rigid heddle.
Width of woven panel is up to 13".
Length is unlimited.
Wood shuttle, as long as the heddle for easy grasping in making a shot, and also for direct counting of the anticipated number of weft passes when winding a color on the shuttle.
One dowel included.
Waist string.
Instructions for stringing and straight weaving.

Baa, Baa Black Sheep

The Reimers family seem to have created "A Sound of Music" family operation in Hinesburg, Vermont, but their thing is weaving, not music.

There are seven Reimers and each has his own loom, but that is just the off end of their operation. They start with raising sheep, shear the wool, spin, and then weave. The one thing they do not do is dye the wool, preferring to work out their patterns in the natural wool colors. At the moment Peter Reimers is madly looking for a pure black Merino.

The looms they find or they build are much like the camel's nose in the arab's tent ... there are now looms in every room of their house and more on the way. They range from looms for beginners to looms for master weavers.

What started as a different family way of life has burgeoned into a business, albeit a modest one. The Reimers do have finished cloth for sale; write for patterns and prices:

Green Mountain Creative Crafts
Hinesburg, Vermont 05461

Craft

A Vanishing Art Still Thrives

The Taylor family, three generations of them, have been making ash baskets for years in Rindge, New Hampshire.

Basket-weaving was one of the first crafts practiced in New England by the earliest settlers. Originally, baskets were made of willow, birch or soft maple. Today's baskets are made of ash, a tough elastic hardwood ... the methods of manufacture are essentially the same as they were 300 years ago, with the exception of some power-driven tools.

The first step in basket-making is to cut thin, weavable strips of ash from the edges of selected planks. On this handmade rig, a motor provides power for the knife; but only the skilled hand and eye of an experienced craftsman can guide the draw blade to cut even, uniform strips, up to four feet long. These strips are used for the horizontal weaving of the basket.

Steam-treated blocks of ash are cut into sturdy "up-rights" on this slasher. A power-driven blade makes repeated cuts; the operator must judge just how the wood will split and control the thickness of each slashed-off strip. These "uprights" form the bottom and vertical side pieces of the various West Rindge Baskets.

Filling strips now are woven around the uprights, the ends carefully tucked in, until the correct height has been reached. Then, to finish each basket off, inner and outer hoops of oak are nailed on at the top. The hooper holds the basket tight against an anvil that forces the filler strips down and tightens the whole weave. Clinch nails driven around the perimeter hold it tight ... for years and years.

Forty-six separate hand-operations are needed to produce one covered basket. One of the most important of these is setting up the bottoms. Experienced weavers intertwine the uprights, and the finished bottoms are steamed. The projecting ends are then bent up to form the basket sides. Drying in wooden forms sets the wood permanently in the desired shape.

Each West Rindge Basket, before it leaves the Taylor's shop, is critically inspected for flaws in either materials or craftsmanship. Only perfectly sound baskets, ones that will serve at least two generations, are sold. You'll find that no two baskets are quite the same. There are minor variations in size, irregularities of the weave, slight checking or twisting of the wood ... these are the hallmarks of the individual touch that makes each hand crafted basket unique. If anything ever goes wrong with a West Rindge Basket — if a handle breaks or part of the bottom splits — even if it's years after you bought it, we'll fix it, free.

West Rindge Baskets, Inc.
Box 24
Rindge, New Hampshire 03461

◆

Craftivity

Weaving, rug yarns, rug canvas, hooks and needles are available from Reba Maisel at below wholesale prices. She offers a pleasing selection of colors, textures and weights. Enclose a self-addressed envelope in sending for samples.

Craftivity
P. O. Box 61
Wayland, Massachusetts 01778
Rug Wool $2.25/lb.
Weaving Yarns $1.75/lb.

Pepperidge Handspinners

This title bears reference to a vast assemblage of old and new looms, six or seven spinning wheels, collections of bits and pieces of antique spinning and weaving equipment, bags and baskets of raw fleece and multi-colored yarns reflecting nature's bounty of color. The yarn colors are drawn solely from weeds, barks, berries and an occasional bug!

WEST RINDGE BASKETS, INC.
Box 24 • RINDGE, NEW HAMPSHIRE 03461

LARGE WASTE
15 x 12½ x 12½
Weight 3 lbs.

SMALL WASTE
9 x 10 x 10
Weight 2 lbs.

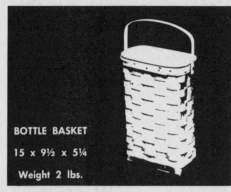

BOTTLE BASKET
15 x 9½ x 5¼
Weight 2 lbs.

SECRETARY LUNCH 9"
9 x 9½ x 5½
Weight 2 lbs.

LARGE WASTE	$5.00
SMALL WASTE	4.00
BOTTLE BASKET	6.00
SECRETARY LUNCH 9"	5.00
SECRETARY LUNCH 6"	4.50
MINI LUNCH (not shown) 4 x 8 x 5½	4.50

SECRETARY LUNCH 6"
6 x 9½ x 5½
Weight 2 lbs.

These brightly colored yarns, together with the natural wool, become scarves, sweaters, hats and wall hangings on old and new looms.

The products of loom and wheel have never been for sale, simply because the sole proprietor of the *Pepperidge Handspinners* — Warner Lord — works on a "when inspiration strikes and material is available, I'll get to work basis."

Warner Lord writes: "Service and information are two offerings that I do have. My main concern is spreading the word about handspinning and weaving in the colonial tradition. Instruction in hand-spinning and vegetable dyeing is available.

"The crafts of spinning and weaving offer the individual a chance to start from the raw material and, through the labor of his hands, produce a thing of beauty and utility. This satisfying accomplishment is within the reach of anyone with the proper equipment and the tricks of the trade."

Pepperidge Handspinners is in a position to supply the "tricks of the trade" and either supply or help you find the proper equipment. "This whole enterprise is a vast amount of fun and the more people I have contact with the 'funner' it gets!" says Mr. Lord.

Pepperidge Handspinners
503 Opening Hill Road
Madison, Connecticut 06443

Ellsbury Stevens, Handweaver

Fifty years' experience on the power looms of the American Woolen Company is the background Mr. Stevens brings to his weaving.

Both light and heavy weight woolen rugs are woven in two-color combinations — your choice.

Ellsbury Stevens
22 Elm Street
Newport, Maine 04953

Wool Rug	24" wide by 36" long	$ 8.00
	Up to 26" wide by 44-48" long	$10.50
	Postage and insurance extra.	

Chair Seat Weaving

"A chair is only as good as the seat that is in it."

Service is friendly and quick, advice freely given, and delivery almost immediate from the *H. H. Perkins Company*. Any materials needed for weaving chair seats can be found here — cane, rush, splint, wicker, and how-to instruction booklets, too.

The H. H. Perkins Company
10 South Bradley Road
Woodbridge, Connecticut 06525

AWLS

Used in clearing old holes — also used on last few steps of caning when holes become filled.
Tempered Steel Awl .... Priced each 35¢

SEAT WEAVING FOR PLEASURE AND PROFIT

Seat weaving is a fascinating and profitable craft offering opportunities for making home repairs as well as additional income. There are no particular skills or long periods of study required. Our instruction booklet offers detailed instructions and with our fifty years experience, we are in a position to help solve all of your problems.

As a sideline business, there are many potential customers right in your own neighborhood and once you have completed a few chairs you will find much additional business among your friends. Suggested prices for you to charge are as follows: (Including cost of material.)

CANE SEATS
Hand Cane
14¢ to 20¢ per hole
Counting holes around edge.

PRESSED CANE
Pressed Cane
55¢ front inch

Rush Genuine
95¢ to $1.00 front inch

Fibre Rush and Splint Weave
60¢ to 70¢ front inch

PORCH CHAIRS — Reeds or Fibre Splint
14" to 17" seats $7.00   Backs, Med. size $7.50
17" to 20" seats $8.00   Backs, Lge. size $8.50

ACCESSORIES
HARDWOOD PEGS
Hardwood pegs used in hand caning while work is in progress. May be used many times..............35¢ per doz.

NATURAL STRAND CANE
STRAND CANE — Is used in hand woven seats. The process consists of weaving strands thru holes in the seat frame to form the desired pattern.

All long select quality 14' to 18' lengths. Packed in bunches of about 1000 feet. Binding, enough for four chairs included free with each bunch. One bunch should seat from three to four chairs.

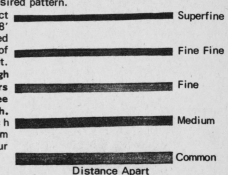

Superfine
Fine Fine
Fine
Medium
Common

Kind	Size of Hole	Distance Apart Center to Center	Bunch	½ Bunch
Superfine	3/16"	3/8"	$4.00	$2.15
Fine Fine	3/16"	1/2"	4.20	2.25
*Fine	3/16"	5/8"	4.35	2.40
*Medium	1/4"	3/4"	4.60	2.55
Common	5/16"	7/8"	4.80	2.65

Binder 500 feet to bunch $2.35 — Per strand 10¢

*Size most commonly used.
Postage on Cane — I lb. per bunch.

DISCOUNT ON CHAIR CANE
**5-1,000 ft. ASSORTED BUNCHES—LESS 10%
SPECIAL QUOTATIONS ON LARGER QUANTITIES.**

Size of cane determined by the diameter of the hole and space between center to center. See chart above, also page #1 instruction book. Cane is not sold less than ½ bunch lots.

Connie Coleman
Handweaver
Designer
51 Spring St.
Warwick, R.I.
02888

A New England Simple
Heat nails before using in plaster walls, and the plaster will not crack.

Nantucket Lightship Baskets

Nantucket mink, they call them. Young Island girls, off-Island girls — young and old — covet them. In fact, they're all the rage — they make friends quickly!

According to reports, the original baskets were made by the Indians from pliable willow twigs and native clay. The name "lightship baskets" originated from the floating lightships off Nantucket where the men aboard used much of their spare time in weaving these gems which became a necessary part of keeping house on early Nantucket Island. Many of their little charmers are in use today and are highly prized as collector's items.

In a new book, *Nantucket Lightship Baskets,* by Katherine and Edgar Seeler, published by The Deermouse Press in Nantucket ($9.95), are detailed instructions as to the method of construction of these baskets. Should an off-Islander have the gall to attempt to make one, they write, the perpetrator had best keep his product down cellar in a burlap bag, and not even mention the sacred name of Nantucket in connection with his work.

It's apparently allowable for an Islander to make Lightship Baskets. But only after certain well-defined conditions are met — he must serve the proper apprenticeship under an approved craftsman and he must have acquired the skill to proceed in exactly the same manner in which the originals were made in the mid-19th century. There are an elite few basketmakers now living on Nantucket

who have met these criteria. The prices of their work range from $25 for a small, simple open top basket to $500 for handbags with tops of ivory scrimshaw or other hand-carved ornamentation. Orders are not always filled immediately, so be prepared to wait. For many, the wait is worthwhile.

Files and Saws

The *file* is one of the oldest tools known to history. It is recorded that as early as the reign of King Saul (I Samuel XIII: 21), about the year 1090 B.C., "they had a file for the mattocks, and the coulters, and for the forks, and for the axes, and to sharpen the goads." The first files from which the modern tool has evolved may date back to prehistoric times. Primitive man shaped his stone hatchet by abrading it with a flat piece of granite or of some harder stone. *Saws* also date from the Neolithic Age. Archeological discoveries indicate that the principal was put to use closely following the origin of the axe and knife. The most primitive of these cutting tools appear to have been made from tapering flint or chips crudely sharpened to a thin edge.

Nicholson File Company has not been in business since prehistoric time, but long enough (1864) to be one of the oldest file manufacturers in the business, and to establish leadership in that field. They also make industrial hammers. Through solid Yankee tradition of pride in craftsmanship, Nicholson's fine products today are kept in the forefront of the industry by a pioneering spirit which promotes new designs for its tools and improved methods of operation.

Two informative books — "File Filosophy" and "Sawology," both brief accounts of the history, manufacture and uses of files and saws — are offered free by Nicholson.

Nicholson File Company
Providence, Rhode Island 02904

BALL SHAPE

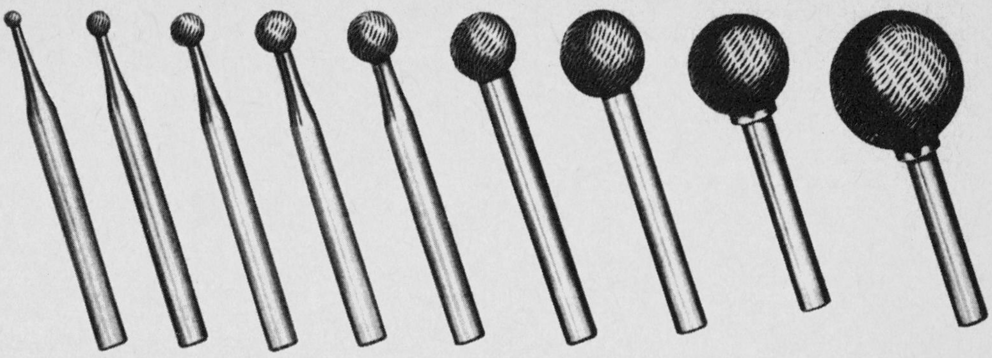

HAND CUT STYLE "C"

Number→	C1	C2	C3	C4	C5	C7	C9	C10	C14
Diameter Inches	1/8	3/16	1/4	5/16	3/8	1/2	5/8	3/4	1

BALL SHAPE	Diameter By Length	Coarse or Medium QUANTITY * A 1 to 11	Coarse or Medium QUANTITY * B 12 to 49	Coarse or Medium QUANTITY * C 50 to 149	Fine Cut QUANTITY * A 1 to 11	Fine Cut QUANTITY * B 12 to 49	Fine Cut QUANTITY * C 50 to 149
C1	1/8	2.18	2.03	1.86	2.62	2.43	2.25
C2	3/16	2.30	2.13	1.99	2.85	2.63	2.43
C3	1/4	2.35	2.18	2.01	2.89	2.67	2.48
C4	5/16	2.47	2.29	2.11	3.07	2.85	2.62
C5	3/8	2.74	2.55	2.35	3.38	3.14	2.89

	Diameter By Length	Coarse or Medium QUANTITY * A 1 to 11	Coarse or Medium QUANTITY * B 12 to 49	Coarse or Medium QUANTITY * C 50 to 149	Fine Cut QUANTITY * A 1 to 11	Fine Cut QUANTITY * B 12 to 49	Fine Cut QUANTITY * C 50 to 149
C7	1/2	3.29	3.06	2.83	3.99	3.68	3.41
C9	5/8	3.60	3.36	3.10	4.47	4.16	3.84
C10	3/4	4.20	3.90	3.60	5.37	4.98	4.60
C14	1	6.35	5.90	5.45	7.67	7.14	6.56

TREE SHAPE • RADIUS END

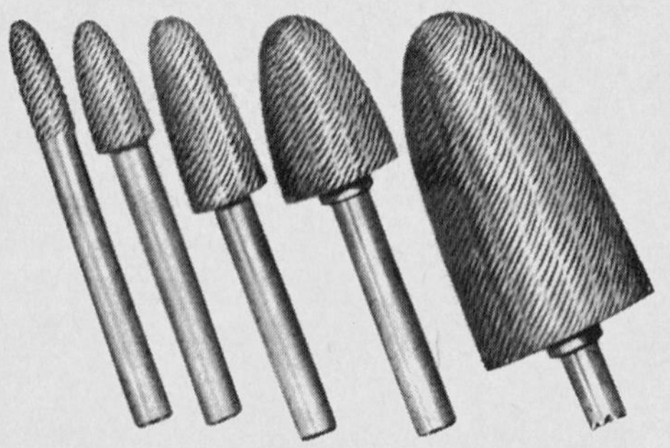

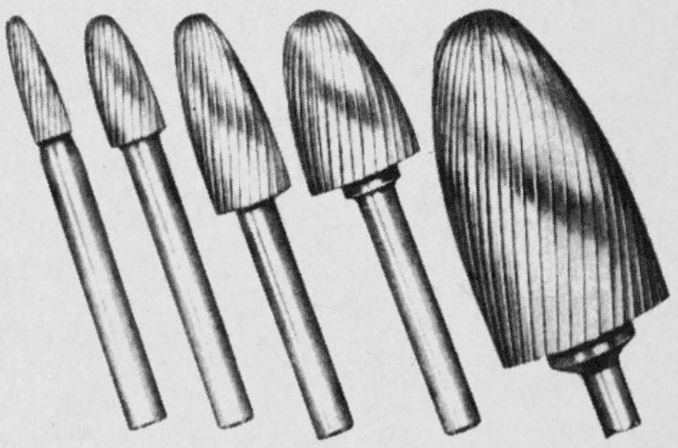

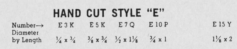

HAND CUT STYLE "E"

Number→	E3K	E5K	E7Q	E10P	E15Y
Diameter by Length	1/4 x 3/4	3/8 x 3/4	1/2 x 1 1/8	3/4 x 1	1 1/8 x 2

GROUND BUR STYLE "S"

Number→	S1F	S3K	S5K	S7Q	S10P	S15Y
Diameter by Length	1/8 x 7/16	1/4 x 3/4	3/8 x 3/4	1/2 x 1 1/8	3/4 x 1	1 1/8 x 2

TREE SHAPE RADIUS END							
E3K	1/4 x 3/4	2.74	2.55	2.35	3.38	3.14	2.89
E5K	3/8 x 3/4	3.07	2.85	2.62	3.69	3.43	3.16
E7Q	1/2 x 1 1/8	3.43	3.18	2.93	4.34	4.03	3.68
E10P	3/4 x 1	5.39	5.00	4.62	6.59	6.12	5.67
E15Y	1 1/8 x 2	11.89	11.05	10.17	14.61	13.58	12.54

TREE SHAPE RADIUS END							
S1F	1/8 x 7/16	2.63	2.44	2.24	3.23	3.02	2.80
S3K	1/4 x 3/4	3.02	2.80	2.58	3.60	3.36	3.10
S5K	3/8 x 3/4	4.12	3.82	3.54	4.92	4.58	4.22
S7Q	1/2 x 1 1/8	5.53	5.14	4.73	6.60	6.16	5.68
S10P	3/4 x 1	7.30	6.81	6.27	8.82	8.20	7.53
S15Y	1 1/8 x 2	15.71	14.57	13.46	18.84	17.50	16.20

Willard Shepard — Shipcarver

A life-long love of the sea coupled with a fascination for hand-carved objects and a strong desire to create with his hands have helped to make *Willard Shepard* one of the top woodcarvers in the country. He is resident shipcarver at the Seaport Marine Museum in Mystic, Connecticut, where, if you are so inclined, you may visit with him. He'll enjoy it and so will you.

The eagles are carved from white pine, finished with gold leaf.

Willard Shepard
Jordan Cove
Waterford, Connecticut 06385

Jenny Lind Figurehead — 32" long $220.00

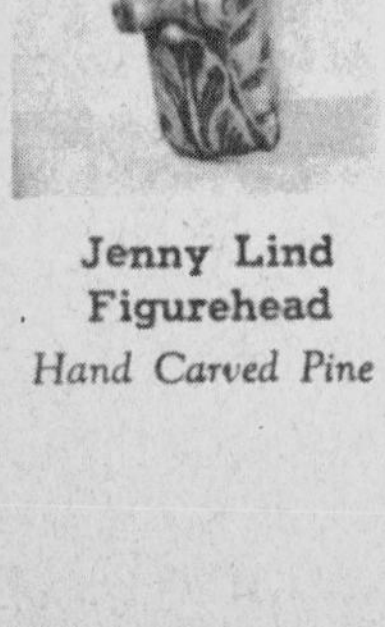

Jenny Lind
Figurehead
Hand Carved Pine

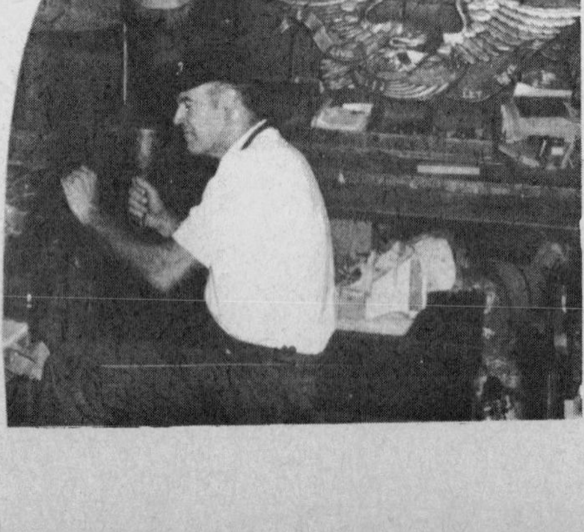

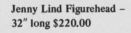

Salem Eagle — 28" long $66.00

Salem Eagle — *Hand Carved Pine*

Portsmouth Eagle — 28" long $47.00

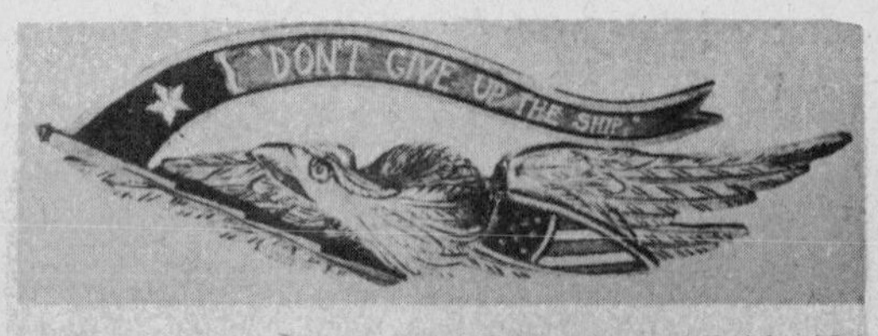

Portsmouth Eagle — *Hand Carved Pine*

An 85-year-old New Englander still doing his thing

Hugh Spencer, a well-known scientific photographer and recipient of many awards in that field, produces beautifully hand-carved letter openers in his spare time. Made of applewood, each has an exquisitely shaped animal balanced on one end. He started making them in 1914 and today, 58 years later, this well-made product of a New England craftsman is still in great demand. See or purchase them from:

Suggested by Gwen Orton-Jones

The Guilford Handcraft Shop
Guilford, Connecticut 06437

———————◆———————

If a man does not keep pace with his companions, perhaps it is because he hears a different drummer. Let him step to the music which he hears, however measured or far away.

Henry David Thoreau

———————◆———————

Puzzles in Wood

Polyhedral puzzles are handmade of the finest cabinet woods — cocobolo, paldao, rosewood, bubinga, teak, padouck and other kinds — with a natural finish. Each comes with an instruction sheet which includes, in addition to assembly directions, interesting observations and intriguing geometrical pastimes to be found in these beautiful many sided structures.

Stewart T. Coffin
Old Sudbury Road
Lincoln, Massachusetts 01773
Nova Puzzle. Symmetrical stellated polyhedron with 72 polished faces. $16.00
Jupiter. Super Spider-Slider Puzzle. Sixty individual pieces of wood. Symmetrical in design. $25.00

SIRIUS Puzzle. A new and improved variation of a classic design. Six identically shaped pieces, made up of three different woods, interlock to form a stellated rhombic dodecahedron. Two distinctly different symmetrical solutions are possible, in contrasting wood patterns. 3 inches. $10.00

SCORPIUS, The Spider-Slider Puzzle. Unique and original. Twenty-four individual pieces of wood, of four contrasting types, make up the six spider-shaped pieces of this diabolical design. SCORPIUS slides apart in four different directions, in a manner which is baffling, to say the least. Four possible symmetrical patterns provide added challenge. 3¾ inches. $12.00

The FOUR CORNERS Puzzle. An original design. Each of the six pieces is made up of three contrasting woods, selected for beautiful end grain effect. The four different woods which form the apexes of this tetrahedral solid come literally from the four corners of the world. The solution is simple and yet perplexing. Arranging the corner woods in different combinations of patterns results in four distinct symmetrical solutions. 3½ inches. $14.00

Country Cooper

If you want a handmade piggin or a keeler or perhaps a kannakin, the Country Cooper can reproduce one. "Each one a collector's item," says Warren Williams, and most customers agree they are. He takes pride in his craftsmanship with each item made with the care of Colonial days combined with modern knowledge and equipment.

What's a cooper you ask? According to the dictionary he's one who makes or repairs wooden kegs, casks or barrels. In the city that was pretty much the limit of his job. Supplying the barrels to carry the whiskey, rum, salt pork, fish and other commodities for Colonial shipping and commerce was more than a full-time job for the city cooper.

But the country cooper was a different breed, by necessity more versatile and practically indispensable to the farmer and homemaker. "Metal was so scarce and expensive," Williams explains, "that until after 1850 it was not commonly used for containers, except where exposed to cooking fires. So it was left to the local cooper to make the wooden buckets, pails, tubs, shovels, barrels and kegs for the farm. For the home," adds Williams, "he used his cooper's tools to make wooden bowls, dishes, spoons, scoops, piggins and kannikans."

For the uninitiated a kannikan was a handy storage container for sugar, lard, flour or cornmeal with a wide bottom and a narrow top. A piggin was a small wooden pail or tub with a staved handle. The most common of all the staved containers in the home, it came in many sizes to be used as a dipper, a salt box or a pail. The keeler was a shallow dish, much like a small tube with fingerhole handles, commonly used to cool milk and skim the cream. Excerpted by permission from Dec. 1971 issue of Contact. New England Electric, Westboro, Massachusetts 01581

W.W. Williams Industries
Falls Road
Royalston, Massachusetts 01368
May thru October 30
Closed Thursday-Friday
Winter months by appointment.

———————◆———————

Relief in Perspective

Is it a painting? Is it a woodcarving? Mr. Hatch says it is a bit of both. What Mr. Hatch creates are pictures carved in intricate relief and then painted. His most recent one is large (64"x23"), and depicts the harbor at Portland, Maine, from a delightful perspective. This painting/carving is priced at $625, but he does less expensive creations.

Kendall Hatch
Broad Cove Road
Cape Elizabeth, Maine 04107

Wooden Ware by Warren W. Williams

The Country Cooper

Sketch shows Cooper shaving bevel on staves

Gallo Birds in Ivoryton

Gallo Birds is a unique example of a Lesson in Patience. For over two years we struggled with our carving and painting finally to come up with what we think to be intricate and exacting miniatures of game birds. Each bird is carved of kiln dried pine and painstakingly painted in oils to the subtle and exacting tones of wild ducks and upland birds.

Our collection thus far includes ring-necked pheasant, quail, ruffed grouse, wood duck, woodcock, mallard, pintail, bluebill, redhead, black duck, green winged teal, Canada goose, bufflehead, golden eye and mourning dove.

Don and Mary Jane Gallo

Each bird sells for $21.50

Gallo Birds
Walnut Street
Ivoryton, Connecticut 06442

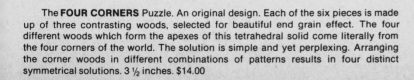

Craft

Andrew Marks — Pipemaker

Each one a masterpiece of design — not just a pipe — a piece of sculpture.

Using well-seasoned Grecian or Corsican root briar, *Andrew Marks* hand-carves these pipes. After the final form of the pipe is achieved through the use of files, the briar is hand sanded to a very soft finish and rubbed with oil, then left to darken naturally through the smoking and handling of its owner.

You may leave the design of your pipe entirely to Mr. Marks or he'll be happy to collaborate with you on a design of your own.

Each pipe is shipped in its own special carrying glove. Allow three weeks for delivery and one dollar for postage.

The Pipe Shop
Main Street
Middlebury, Vermont 05753

X $ 60.00

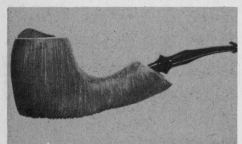

IV $250.00

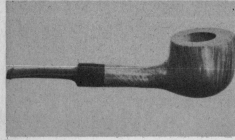

VII $ 35.00

Precision Carved Signs

These wood engravers specialize in precision carved signs. The customer may either provide the general idea or specific instruction for his sign. *Yankee Wood Engravers* turn out thoroughly done hand-crafted pieces.

Catalogue available.

Yankee Wood Engravers
Box 884
Amherst, New Hampshire 03031
$8.00

Craft

The Art of Bird Carving

A clear, concise and lavishly illustrated book on how to carve and paint all kinds of birds.

Mr. Gilley, self-employed for many years as a supplier of his own carved birds, has completed and shipped more than 6000 of them to all parts of the world. His enthusiasm for this art and his extensive knowledge, backed by years of experience, has led him to put forth his "tricks of the trade" in book form. Mr. Gilley explains how to make patterns for the various species of birds and gives complete and easy to understand instructions on how to proceed with a bird carving project from the selection of a subject to the finished product.

There are details concerning both hand and power tools — where to obtain them and how to use them safely and successfully. Also included are many fine drawings and illustrations to supply the proper information needed to carve and paint birds.

Bird carving is a rewarding and fascinating hobby. Its possibilities are as unlimited as the imagination of the carver. With the help of this book you should be able to produce exciting results and develop the basic skills which will enable you to continue to improve your work. Getting started, as with most accomplishments, seems to be the big hurdle. The experiences of Wendell Gilley will help build a desire to try your hand at carving.

This book provides a rare opportunity to enjoy some good reading by an established expert in the woodcarving field as well as a chance to learn from someone who is well schooled in the habits and beauty of birds.

MSH

The Art of Bird Carving
by Wendell Gilley
Publisher: Hillcrest Publications, Inc.
P.O. Box 242
Heber City, Utah 84032
Order From: Mr. Wendell Gilley
Southwest Harbor, Maine 04679
$9.00

A New England Simple

To clean oil-painted surfaces: Dip a piece of soft flannel into warm water, squeeze it until it feels dry. Apply it gently to some finely pulverized French chalk and rub the painted surface. The effect will be the removal of all dust, greasy matter and dirt. The surface is then washed with a clean sponge and clear water, and dried with a piece of wash-leather. This method does not injure the paint like soap, and produces a very good result.

Shipcarver

Clark Voorhees lives in a marvelous old barn that is also his shop. There he creates whales, ships' stern and transom decorations and other special order pieces, carved of wood, and painted in his own folk-art way.

Clark Voorhees
Weston, Vermont 05161

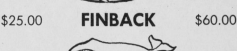

Wood Carvings

From picking up driftwood and observing shore-birds and other objects of the sea as a boy, Bob Clark developed his interest in bird carving. He began with miniature carvings and recently finished "Finger Bowl Ducks" measuring only 1½" in exquisite color and detail. Besides miniatures, he does carvings of whales, quarterboards, decoys and various sizes of song and shorebirds.

457 Boston Post Road
East Lyme, Connecticut 06333
Prices from $3.50

The Yankee Woodcarver

HAND CARVED BIRDS, WHALES, ETC.

First Combs Made in America

It all started in 1789 when sixteen-year-old Enoch Noyes of West Newbury, Massachusetts, boasted, "I'm the champion whittler of combs!" No one disputed him. For nineteen years, Enoch Noyes whittled combs in his cellar workshop and as soon as he had a batch ready, off he went to the surrounding farmhouses selling them — and sell them he did!

This could have been the whole story of Enoch Noyes and his whittling, until a knock on his door, and a man with a small bag of tools changed his future.

William Cleland, a Hessian and deserter from General Burgoyne's army, stood before Enoch and asked for employment. He had made combs in Germany. Enoch welcomed him at once, and when the stranger showed him the marvelous carving tools he carried with him, the whittler was elated. Up to then Enoch had used only a jackknife to whittle his combs of wood.

The demand for something better was there. Post-Revolutionary women yearned for combs made of natural shell, but transforming the carapace of the small turtles found in nearby ponds and brooks, with the limited tools available, was difficult. William Cleland with his equipment and expertise changed all that.

Enoch and his new partner discovered that cattle horns could be used to make combs. Children stopped at the open door of their shop and watched the combmakers as they softened the horn in a cauldron of hot oil. When ready, it was thrown on the floor, and to the accompanying squeals of delight from the boys and girls, the men stamped vigorously on the horn with their heavy boots. Next, they placed weighty stones on top of the horn until it cooled. The wrinkles left after this operation were removed by use of crude handmade tools called a "shave" and a "standing horse."

Cleland, with his knowledge of the proper finishing techniques, taught Enoch how to use his old-world tools. The quarnet was especially useful. It resembled a mason's trowel, but with teeth cut crosswise, about five teeth to an inch. Enoch was an apt pupil; in no time the combs were improved and found a ready market in a constantly enlarging group of appreciative customers.

From the combshop of Enoch Noyes there followed an incredible number of comb making enterprises. Horn combs that looked like amber or mother-of-pearl came on the market and much of the finishing work was now being done by women. The comb industry moved from its crude beginnings to more sophisticated production methods. It was found that steer horns were superior to cow horns because of their more ample size. In time, South American and South African horns were imported, these became preferred by combmakers.

In the latter part of the 18th century, Andrew Lord of Saybrook, Connecticut made the first ivory combs in America. By 1849, all ivory combs in the country were being made in the flourishing Connecticut towns of Meriden, Litchfield, Middletown and Mansfield. Later Leominster, Massachusetts became the greatest comb manufacturing center in the world.

And so it was that Enoch Noyes was the inspiration that fired ambition in others to carry on the comb business. His sons and grandsons and their sons continued the high standards Enoch set.

From the crude beginnings of whittled combs to the elegant, carved tortoise-shell high combs, worn by women of high fashion in later periods, was indeed a compelling accomplishment.

Margaret Kimball Herlihy

Geo-Tec Lamps

New England is not all "traditional" as you can see by these innovative lamps, created by *db Design*. Their Geo-Tec lamps are a combination of the ancient art of paper folding with 20th century plastic technology worked into bold, geometric designs. Write for their catalog which features such items as Ecology Lamps, with bases made from recycled soda and beer cans and topped by a glass globe.

db Design
Charlotte, Vermont 05445
Table Lamp with Acrylic Base $54.00

Heritage of the New England Shakers

The roots of Shakerism began in the Albany, New York area during the 18th century, but communities soon formed in New Hampshire, Maine, Connecticut and Massachusetts.

The organization of these communities is interesting in a modern context because living was communal. Although people were divided into "Families," the word itself had a very broad meaning. All were brothers and sisters in a consecrated communion of the spirit. This spiritual link related every Shaker to the founder, Mother Ann Lee, as well as to every other Shaker.

The original Elders were appointed by Mother Ann and, in the beginning, were responsible for setting up the Order of the Ministry, a self-perpetuating organ. Trustees, appointed by the Ministry and Elders, were named to handle business dealings with the "outside world." They were assisted by Deacons and Deaconesses who were responsible for the various trade shops. The Shakers never let religious zeal blind them to the fact that they must get along with other people around them — trade meant survival.

Divisions of the community into families had distinct advantages. Each family had its own store as a clearinghouse for incoming and outgoing articles, and a variety of agricultural work and craft industries led to great flexibility of production and labor, one person often having more than one occupation.

Once the organization of the Societies became established, various business endeavors were commenced with the "outside world." Fine craftsmanship, high quality and integrity led to success and an unsullied reputation. In 1790, the Shaker seed industry began; it lasted for well over a century. Broom corn was introduced and Shaker brooms became a well-known product. Raising livestock and sheep gave rise to the famous Shaker flannels and cloaks.

Many communities had their own specialities. Shirley and Harvard in Massachusetts, were leading producers of cider and applesauce. In 1874 Canterbury, New Hampshire produced between three and four thousand pounds of maple sugar. Sabbathday Lake, Maine was active in the lumber business and produced many wooden products, among them, the famous oval "finger" boxes. At the peak of this "fancy goods" production, Alfred, Maine offered the consumer some 21 different styles of boxes. Shaker herb shops provided New England druggists with a variety of herbs and fine medicinal products. They bottled muscadine wine, peach and rose water; their pickles, catsup, horseradish and dairy products were in demand throughout the country and Shaker stores in New Hampshire and Maine were well stocked with foodstuffs, homemade preserves and candies.

The Shakers' sole purpose in life was to establish God's Kingdom on earth. Their minds, hearts and hands were devoted to this ideal. Industry and efficiency were not confined to the workshop, but reached into the kitchens as well. Like their architecture and dress, Shaker cookery expressed simplicity and a high standard of perfection. The Shakers practiced organic gardening and served plain, wholesome meals. In the early days of the sects' development, meat was considered less beneficial than other types of foods, and pork was forbidden.

Technical problems challenged creativity. They were always looking for practical and more efficient timesaving devices and techniques. Furniture and architecture reflected this search. There were no moldings or ornaments to catch dust, and houses contained many built-in wall units and cupboards.

Shaker furniture was designed for utility; combination pieces were common. Benches enlarged to become tables; wood boxes doubled as towel racks. Inventive genius lent large wooden rollers to beds so they could be moved easily for cleaning. Ball-and-socket devices on the back legs of early sidechairs allowed a person to "tilt" in his chair after a good meal.

Today, only two Shaker communities exist: one at Canterbury, New Hampshire and another at Sabbathday Lake, Maine. The most important factor in the gradual extinction of the Shakers has been their belief in celibacy, one of the basic tenets of their religious convictions. During the Civil War, there were no formal orphanages and many orphans came to live in Shaker communities. Although these orphans could leave by choice at age sixteen, many remained. As the industrial age took hold and manufacturing led to the accumulation of material goods and jobs in the cities, many chose to depart. Converts became fewer and fewer in number.

Eventually, the original religious fervor was spent; revival and fanatical sermons became fewer and less meaningful. Older Shakers could no longer maintain religious enthusiasm; the younger ones were not interested.

Today, the few remaining Shakers live in peaceful serenity. During the summer, the Communities become museums, and guides lead tourists through the various rooms and houses. But Shakerism will survive the last remaining Shaker, and its story will long be told, for it has become part of the proud American tradition.

Cynthia Elyce Rubin

A Community of Craftsmen

A small group of craftsmen have banded together to create a nineteenth century community of craft shops in Charlestown, Rhode Island.

Headed by Ken Merrifield and Bob Bankel, they bought an abandoned farmhouse and its outbuildings in 1968. By fall of that year, they had turned the milkhouse into a colorful, gay nineties emporium, complete with poop-poop-de-doo music. The old cow barn became "The Palace Hotel Bazaar" with a fifteen foot stained glass window, a library, Victorian parlor and kitchen. After looking over the extensive collection of nineteenth century farm tools, clocks, cast-iron stoves, swords, canes and much more on display here, stop in at "The Crystal Cafe," possibly the only place in New England where a cup of coffee or lemonade sells for a nickel.

The "J. Halstead Brown & Co. Boutique" is decorated with old oak paneling and huge glass showcases rescued when buildings in a nearby town were being razed in a redevelopment project. Old Victorian lights, a tin ceiling and Dutch doors opening onto a formal garden complete the decor. Here Marion Muntimuri designs and makes clothes.

Upstairs is the Wood and Stained Glass Workshop where visitors can watch John Larner making wooden toys or creating jewel-like glass lamps and ornaments.

The Fantastic Umbrella Factory
Route 1
Charlestown, Rhode Island 02813

by John Larner: Natural Pine Hobby Horse
$4.95 ppd.

by Marion Muntimuri: Nickolas and Marion Dolls 15", washable $14.50 each ppd.

Stained Glass Cross 2-3/4" x 3-3/4" $5.50 ppd.
Colors: Ruby red, forest green, spring green, amber, sky blue, cobalt blue, clear.

Windswept Farm

Windswept Farm is nestled in an old New England farmyard surrounded by its original dry stone walls. Ann and Bruce Glen have converted the barn and other buildings into an original and happy shopping experience.

One barn is filled with antiques and local hand-crafted items. A Down-East Yankee country store will tickle your fancy with goodies and treats for adventurous souls.

New this year is a fabric mill outlet housed in another barn. Not only will one find just what one wants but will do so at fabulous savings, as the Glens buy directly from the manufacturer.

A third building houses all the pottery made by Bruce Glen (vases, lamps, pitchers, ash trays, candlesticks, and cooking casseroles), and displays work of other New England craftsmen. The pottery studio is adjacent to the barn.

As their hours are flexible, call before you visit the Farm.

Windswept Farm
Route 1
Charlestown, Rhode Island 02813

Candlesticks 6" to 8" high — $8.50 ppd.

The Great Noank Quilt Factory

Warm bed quilts were a must in Colonial homes, the early ones being made of plain colored linen. When a worn spot developed, it would be carefully patched with whatever material was handy. Over a period of time, the basic linen cover disappeared entirely beneath hundreds of bright patches. Thus, the American "crazy quilt" had its beginning.

At the *Great Noank Quilt Factory,* Sharon McKain makes quilts and teaches quilt making in the manner of our ancestors. Her innovative designs are worked into marvelous color combinations. Along with colorful bedcovers, she also makes quilted wall hangings, bags and back packs.

Beautiful to look at, Sharon's quilts are surely destined to become treasured heirlooms, to be handed down from generation to generation.

Suggested by James Scully

The Great Noank Quilt Factory
Sharon McKain
75 High Street
Noank, Connecticut 06340

Bags (all sizes)	$ 20.00 and up
Back Packs	$ 35.00

Baby Quilts	$ 30.00
Single	$150.00
Double	$180.00
King	$240.00

Candle Hurricane Lamp — $15.00 ppd.

Craft

OLD SALT

Wood & Wax Works Craftsmen's Showroom

Step into this shop and the aroma of scented hot wax, mingled with that of leather and wood welcomes you.

Yvette Saglio designs and handmakes all the candles sold here. Some are two feet in diameter, others just right for the dinner table — all have to meet her high standards of quality before being sold.

The focal point of the shop is Dean Saglio's natural slab hardwood tables. He seeks out unusual pieces of wood — sometimes diseased but magnificent trees — cuts them down, and mills them himself, while striving to preserve the natural beauty of the wood. Occasionally, this requires some intricate rigging and there's a degree of danger involved, since he uses chain saws with four and six foot blades.

Once cut, the wood is dried in a kiln on the premises. This drying process takes from two to three months before the piece is ready to be worked. The dried wood is sanded to a high polish and finished with oil. All wood is joined with dowels — screws or nails are never used. Though most of his work is traditional, Dean enjoys mixing the beauty of a natural slab of highly finished wood with materials such as plexiglass, chromed steel and wrought iron.

Tables are often made to the purchaser's specifications or needs. No two are ever alike. It is customary for a buyer to examine and choose from the raw dried wood selection kept on hand. It will take up to a month for a custom-made coffee table and three to six months for a dining table — though there are always a few in stock at the *Wood & Wax Works Craftsmen's Showroom*. Call before visiting.

Wood & Waxworks Craftsmen's Showroom
Off Route 138
Usquepaugh, Rhode Island 02892
Dining tables of native hardwood (maple, cherry apple, oak and walnut) range from $350.00 to $850.00.

Coffee tables and benches of the same woods range from $25.00 up to $250.00.

Nothing great was ever achieved without enthusiasm.

Ralph Waldo Emerson

Every Candle Handcrafted

If candles in the shape of things appeal to you, the *Innerlight Candle Company* is your spot.

While the lighthouse and the escargot rather please me, I have always had a strange feeling of apprehension in lighting a candle made to look like a person. I kept a Santa Claus candle for years as a child. Never would light it.

The lighthouse candle in any color is $2.00, the Snail $1.50, and the Old Man of the Sea $2.00, but they will send you descriptions and prices on their whole line . . . hundreds of different candles.

RWW

Innerlight Candle Co.
46 Freeman Street
York Beach, Maine 03910

A New England Simple — To Whiten Ivory

Boil alum in water, immerse your ivory and let it remain one hour. Rub the ivory with a clean cloth, wipe it with a wet linen rag, and lay in a moistened cloth to prevent it from drying too quickly, which causes it to crack.

Things

In 1968, we started making practical and impractical *things* in limited quantities to be sold at a profit (to make a modest living). These included articulated garden gloves, three handled wooden mugs, "sticky boards," and wooden toaster tongs. None of them was really profitable — so we developed a series of products based on the tail of a whale: book ends, door stops, door knockers and whatnots in cast iron or bronze. Should be profitable. Coming along presently are line drawing wire forms of birds, fish and animals (might make a product line).

Things we can and do make for other people include knots and splices for the Navy; machine assembly and package mechanical fasteners; trophies (wood plaques); commercial displays and signs (with a local artist); wood trailboards for nostalgic yachtsmen owning plastic boats; painted and mounted cast phenolic half-hull models of traditional vessels; rigging kits for small boats, and running rigging for new and old sailors.

Our manufacturing facility is almost an old-fashioned wedding. Something borrowed, something blue (bench tops), something old and nothing new (hate to buy new machinery).

Public and employee relations are enviable 'cause we fix things for people. Write me for prices of these *Things*.

E.B. Lawton, Proprietor

Things of Essex, Inc.
Essex, Connecticut 06426

Iron Whale's Tail Door Knocker
8″ high x 5″ wide $19.50
Wire Sculpture: The Bittern
16″ high $18.00 Limited Edition

About the New England Simples: These home remedies, most of unknown origin, may be of dubious effectiveness. They were used faithfully by housewives long before modern science surfeited us with "miracle" solutions to many of our problems. *Make your own judgment* as to whether or not the remedies are applicable today.

Craft

Everything for the Silversmith

If that guy you are married to (or going with) has not come through with a silver bracelet for the last 28 years, why wait for the clown to get the message. Make one for yourself.

The *C.W. Somers & Company* in Boston has absolutely everything you need from an alcohol lamp to yellow ochre. The complete catalogue (#D70) and price list are worth writing for if you have a serious interest in jewelry making and silversmithing.

C.W. Somers & Co.
387 Washington Street
Boston, Massachusetts 02108

Saw Frames	A $4.50
	B $5.75
Saw Blades	$.50 dozen
	$5.20 gross
Bench Pins	Fig. 12 $5.35
	Fig. 13 $ .60
Scribers	Fig. 14 $ .65
	Fig. 15 $1.75
	Fig. 16 $1.95

Filing Block with Clamp $1.25

Curtis LaFollette — Silversmith

The list of awards *Curtis LaFollette* has won for his silver is long. Now an Assistant Professor of Metalworking and Design at Rhode Island College, his work is limited to commission designs.

Hollowware and flatware executed in sterling silver are his specialties; he no longer accepts commissions for jewelry. Curtis writes:

"While it is impossible to state an upper price limit for work of this sort, I can say that the cost of a small vessel, a 4"x2" pitcher, for example, would be from $300 on up, depending on the design. A five-piece place setting of flatware would start at $185.

"The price of a design is submitted to my clients along with a sketch or sketches. There is a minimum waiting period of six months between acceptance of design and completion of the object."

Curtis LaFollette
136 Main Street
Hudson, Massachusetts 01749

Del Filardi — Sculptress In Metals

The wire and metal sculpture that this talented woman creates cannot be properly appreciated in a photograph. Her interpretations incorporate steel and brass, both new and salvaged "junk parts."

Miss Filardi has an extensive background in lapidary, jewelry and woodcarving and studied sculpture and welding techniques under John La Sala of Westport, Connecticut.

Her work may be seen by appointment at her studio and is on display continually at the Artists Guild & Gallery in Charlestown, Rhode Island.

Del Filardi
Greenwich, Connecticut 06830

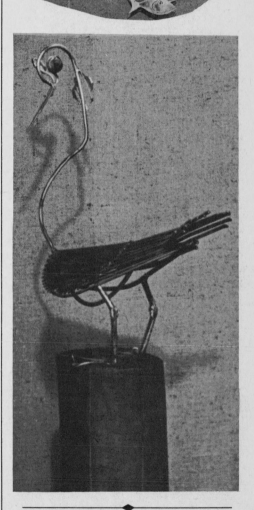

SAW FRAMES

A. 4" Deep
B. 6" Deep

Fig. 10

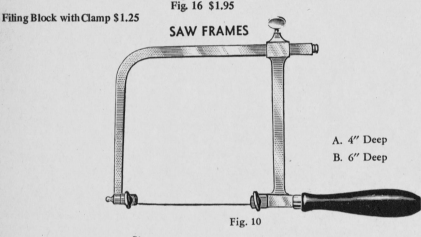

Sizes
4/0
3/0
2/0
0
1
1½
2
3
4
5

Fig. 11

SAW BLADES

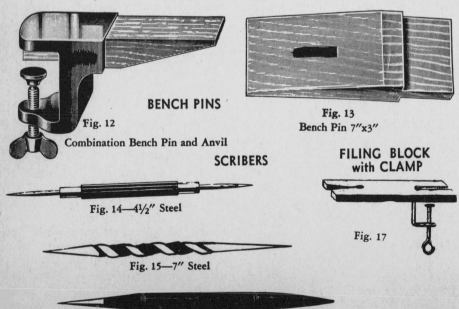

BENCH PINS

Fig. 12
Combination Bench Pin and Anvil

Fig. 13
Bench Pin 7"x3"

SCRIBERS

Fig. 14—4½" Steel

Fig. 15—7" Steel

Fig. 16
4½" Plastic with Steel Tip

FILING BLOCK with CLAMP

Fig. 17

Indian Devils

A clergyman in Massachusetts, more than a century ago, addressed a letter to the General Court on some subject of interest which was then under discussion. The clerk read the letter, in which there seemed to be this very remarkable sentence: "I address you not as magistrates, but as Indian devils. The clerk hesitated, and looked carefully, and said, "Yes, he addresses you as Indian devils." The wrath of the honorable body was aroused; they passed a vote of censure, and wrote to the reverend gentlemen for an explanation, from which it appeared that he did not address them as magistrates, but as individuals.

Starrett®

Precision Tools

Like many New England stories of small beginnings to world-wide recognition, L. S. Starrett Company grew from a single tool to a line of more than three thousand. Starrett's tools have to do with precision — instruments that can measure tolerances of ± .000001" for the decimal inch system and of ± .000027 mm for the metric system. As you might expect, fine craftsmanship is the hallmark of these toolmakers since its founder, Laroy S. Starrett, handcrafted his combination square in 1877.

Complete catalog with price supplement available.

The Starrett Book for Student Machinists
184 pp. $2.90
Training Aid Kit $1.25

The L. S. Starrett Company
Athol, Massachusetts 01331

Combination Squares With Square Head Only

4 to 24 Inch

No. 11H and No. 33H Series

With Reversible Lock Bolt,
Spirit Level (except 4 in.) and
Tempered Steel Machine Divided Blade

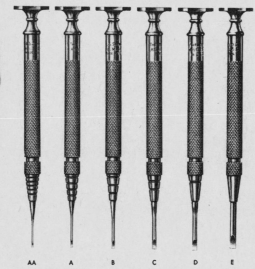

The Starrett No. 11H—12 inch Combination Square is illustrated below. This tool has a cast head and is available with wrinkled finish. Blade shown has No. 4R Graduation.

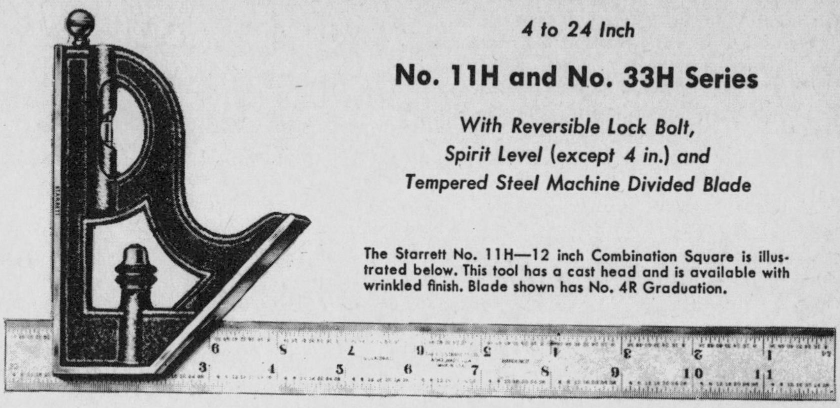

$12.95

Jewelers' Screw Drivers

No. 555 Series

Starrett No. 555 Jewelers' Screw Drivers are shown singly at right and above as a complete set in attractive red plastic case.

AA A B C D E

WATCH and clock makers, jewelers, opticians, toolmakers and others will find this set of screw drivers especially adapted for fine, delicate work. The bodies are made from steel tubing, knurled and nickel plated. The swivel knobs are concaved to fit the finger and hexagonal in shape to prevent rolling. The blades are of best quality steel, properly tempered. A slight turn of the knurled chucks securely locks the blade so that it will not turn or come out. The chucks are grooved to designate the size of the blades which vary in widths from .025 to .100 inch. Five grooves designate small size AA, four grooves size A, three grooves size B, two grooves size C, one groove size D and the largest size E is plain. Size F also available with blade for Phillips head screws. When not in use the blades can be reversed in the body for convenience in carrying the screw drivers in the pocket.

Available singly or in sets with or without attractive red plastic case.

SPECIFICATIONS

Catalog Number	Length	Diam. Body	Width Blade
No. 555AA	3¾"	¼"	.025"
No. 555A	3¾"	¼"	.040"
No. 555B	3¾"	¼"	.055"
No. 555C	3¾"	¼"	.070"
No. 555D	3¾"	¼"	.080"
No. 555E	3¾"	¼"	.100"
No. 555F, with #0 Phillips Blade	3¾"	¼"	

No. S555-6 Set of 6; AA, A, B, C, D, E, with or without Red Plastic Case

No. S555-7 Set of 7; AA, A B, C, D, E, F, with or without Red Plastic Case

Extra Blades, Any Size

SEE SEPARATE PRICE BOOK FOR PRICES

No. S555-6 Set Furnished Without Case Unless Otherwise Ordered
Individual Sizes Packed Six in a Box; Sets, One in a Box

555AA, A, B, C, D, E	SCREW DRIVER	260	1.60
	Extra Blades, any size	260	.40
555F	SCREW DRIVER With Phillips Blade	260	1.70
	Extra Blade	260	.50
S555-6	Set of 6, AA-E, Without Case	260	9.60
S555-6	Set of 6, AA-E, Complete in Case	260	10.30
S555-7	Set of 7, AA-F, Without Case	260	11.30
S555-7	Set of 7, AA-F, Complete in Case	260	12.00

Sterling Silver Design Competition

For 14 years, the Sterling Silver Design Competition, sponsored by the *Sterling Silversmiths Guild of America,* has encouraged the development of new design ideas. The translation of an idea into hard metal requires a high degree of craftsmanship which the Guild feels is more than adequately met in this competition.

A total of $1750 is awarded to five Guild Award winners and five Honorable Mention pieces. All entrants are reimbursed for the sterling weight of their entries. In addition, the metal working departments of design schools represented by the winning students each receive $1750.

Sterling Silversmiths Guild
1111 East Putnam Avenue
Riverside, Connecticut 06878

A 1972 Guild Award Winner
"Covered Bowl" by
Gretchen K. Williams of
Cleveland Institute of Art

Gold & Silver Wire

Suppliers of gold and silver wire and sheet stock to jewelry manufacturers, *Vennerbeck & Chase* have been in business since 1881. Their prices are wholesale only, but a jewelry craftsman may save some money if he wants to send a large enough order to take advantage of the discount.

Thistle

METAL SPINNING

NEW HAVEN VERMONT

05472

Brass Hurricane Lamp
4" diam. — 12½" total height
$15.75 per pair + postage

Compote Bowl, Brass
10" diam. x 5½" high
$12.25 + postage

Silver Rings

"Working at an old oak table in front of my kitchen wood stove, I fuse and twist silver wire into rings. Each one is different and some are set with brightly colored polished stones," writes Katherine Wills.

Plain rings are priced from $10.00 to $15.00, and rings with stones range from $15.00 to $30.00. Write her for more information.

Katherine Wills
Route 2
Freedom, Maine 04941

Unusual Handcrafts

A small shop carrying limited but unusual handcrafts of excellent quality. Owner is a craftsman jeweler specializing in silver, brass and gold.

Frances Holmes Boothby
Silver Workshop
Weston, Vermont 05161

Pewtersmiths

Hugh Bethell took to the hills of northwestern Connecticut from the caverns of New York City. several years ago. Those who appreciate handwrought materials turned out with exquisite care will be glad he did. (Bethell is.) Using the methods and tools handed down through generations of craftsmen, this pewterer engages the whole Bethell family. Bowls, pitchers and candlesticks are the main pieces produced in a variety of finishes from the highly polished silver-like sheen to his preference, the dull look, which is more commonly identified with pewter. Although as many as 10,000 hammer blows may go into every dish, Bethell works not in anger, but with painstaking patience and love. Much of the work is done on order using designs supplied by the customer. For those who do not have an inspiration, the Bethells will suggest one of their originals.

Hilcraft
Hickory Hill Road
Lakeside, Connecticut 06758

Prices vary according to the job ranging from $3.00 to $30.00.

Examples: Napkin Rings – $3.00
Plates 6" (rolled edge) – $5.00
Bowls 12" – $22.00 – $30.00
Ladles 4" x 13" – $12.00
Pitchers 9", 1¾ qts – $29.00

Reviving A Lost Art — Tole Painting

Ruth and George Wolf present furniture and accessories, beautifully decorated with "Tole Painting," using authentic designs of old.

This art originated in the Orient and was introduced to Western culture in the 1600's. After the rigors of settling in a new country abated, our torebearers began to enrich their surroundings with the artistic adornment which is our heritage today.

Ruth Wolf is also an authority on the early art of wall stenciling, and is often commissioned to stencil walls for people who wish to recreate this lost art in their homes. Brochure available.

Hayfields Studio, Inc.

DEERING, NEW HAMPSHIRE

Metal Spinning is the art by which a round-flat piece of metal is shaped over a form as it revolves on a lathe. This is done by means of a tool held under the arm of the operator. As the metal and form are turning, the tool is pressed against the metal thus causing it to take the shape of the form. The various shapes made depend upon the skill of the operator or spinner.

Mr. Edward Young, who is the owner and does the spinning, is the descendant of a long line of metal spinners. From all accounts handed down, his family was doing metal spinning when water was the means of getting power to turn the lathes. His background includes commercial work from aircraft, lighting fixtures and testing of new metals to the fine work in silver and gold. Because of his wanting to do creative work of his own, he started Thistle in an old barn in Vermont in 1954.

Here, at Thistle, we design all our own items and make our own forms as in the days when a craftsman had to know such things. Each piece is handcrafted and is given a satin finish after which it is lacquered to prevent tarnishing.

Craft

Silver

Sterling silver occupies the place of honor in American homes – and it wears its regal title well. For centuries the treasure of kings and emperors, it is today a beautiful necessity – the prized possession of those who seek excellence in everything they own. In America, the craft of the silversmith was one of the first to be established. Literally hundreds of silversmiths flourished in the Colonies, among them men of culture who frequently played leading roles in affairs of church and state. The beautifully simple pieces of silver which characterize this era have a truly wonderous grace of line and perfection of proportion. Because they were useful, not merely ornamental, their lean simplicity emphasized handsome form with little added decoration.

As the Colonies became wealthier, the desire for fine silver grew. It was during the stage of "Colonial life in the manner grand" (1750 – 1812) that the famous patriot, Paul Revere, together with his father and son, made their lovely pieces of silver tableware.

Today, we can still enjoy the unique beauty of these styles in the many Colonial-inspired designs and authentic reproductions which are available in sterling flatware and hollowware. And we can be justly proud of our heritage of silversmithing that began three centuries ago.

The sterling industry still depends to a great extent on the genius of the master craftsman. But since the days when silver was entirely wrought by hand, modern methods have greatly speeded up production. When old-time silversmiths made flatware, they hammered out their silver by hand. Today, a ribbon or sheet of sterling silver is fed into a grade roll where heavy steel rollers produce strips of exactly the right width, thickness and weight for each individual piece. Instead of shaping and ornamenting each piece by hand, the modern silversmith employs precision-made steel striking dies that eventually produce pieces of beautiful sterling flatware.

The visitor to a sterling silver factory today can see men performing tasks essentially the same as those which produced a work of art during the time of Cellini. As many as 60 hand operations may be employed in the crafting of a single piece, and the talents of artists, die-cutters, chasers and engravers may be needed before a piece of sterling reaches the final, glowing perfection which is demanded of it.

Excerpted from:

Sterling Silver . . .
Queen of the Table
Sterling Silversmiths Guild of America
1111 East Putnam Avenue
Riverside, Connecticut 06878

Many hand operations such as soldering, decorating and polishing go into the making of a piece of sterling holloware such as this bowl.

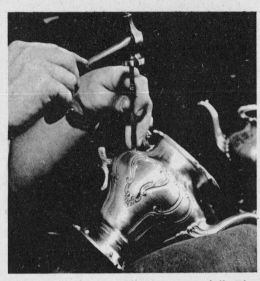

The art of chasing calls for great skill. The chaser must first transfer the design free-hand onto the holloware. The piece is then filled with molten pitch, and the chaser hammers the design into the surface with small tools.

Die-makers working in tool-steel with engraver's tools perfect by hand the details of the all-important dies. A master die-cutter usually spends three weeks perfecting a single die.

The modeller develops the designer's sketch as a third-dimensional form in wax. A mold is then made in silver, and the new design is studied in line, form, color and texture.

Wheels

A potter who not only teaches his craft, but also designed a wood-framed, stone-weighted kick wheel when he couldn't find a ready-manufactured one that satisfied him. Write for price information.

Wheels
Federal Station
P. O. Box 1077
Worcester, Massachusetts 01609

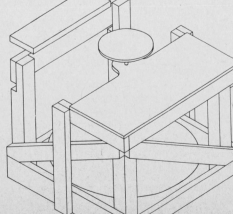

New England Silversmiths

There are six major old-time silversmiths in New England today – *Gorham, International, Lunt, Reed & Barton, Towle,* and *Wallace.* Each has at least two important things in common. They all manufacture fine silver and they share a birthright deep in New England history.

These silversmiths owe their beginnings to young, inventive craftsmen who, through curiosity and experimentation, brought to a burgeoning country a broad awareness of the beauty of silver.

Two hundred years ago William Moulton and his sons, predecessors of the Towles, were active silversmiths. Later, in the early 1800's, men like Robert Wallace and Deacon Hall, Jabez Gorham, Isaac Babbit and his artisan friends, Henry Reed and Charles Barton searched tirelessly to find better ways to produce high quality silver. Today, the same pride of workmanship which was their founders' hallmark, is carried on by these six great silversmiths.

The Gorham Co., Providence, Rhode Island
International Silver Co., Meriden, Connecticut
Lunt Silversmiths, Greenfield, Massachusetts
Reed & Barton, Taunton, Massachusetts
Towle Silversmiths, Newburyport, Massachusetts
Wallace Silversmiths, Wallingford, Connecticut

Perkins Silversmiths

This talented craftsman feels that craftsmanship and pride go hand in hand. Her jewelry has a light, airy quality, "Mainly," says Laura Perkins, "because it is designed by a woman for women."

The busy mother of two preschool boys, she not only finds the time to make a wide variety of bracelets, pins, pendants and earrings, but teaches her craft to others.

Perkins Silversmiths
Box 287
Nottingham, New Hampshire 03290
3" Sterling Silver Scroll Pendant with sterling chain
$12.00
2" Sterling Silver Scroll Pendant with sterling chain
$ 5.50

E. G. Washburne & Co.

Weather vanes of every imaginable kind have been intrinsic features of the New England scene for many generations. The subjects used for weathervanes represented a wide range of tastes, trends and trades.

Early New England craftsmen hammered them from sheet metal. Along with progress came the carved wooden mold, in which a piece of metal was molded into shape with a hammer.

By the 1800's, woodcarvers whittled full-bodied weather vanes, then took them to a foundry to be made into cast-iron molds from which a countless number of copper weather vanes could be hammered. But, the skilled craftsman's days were numbered — mass production by machine made him nearly obsolete.

Full-bodied weather vanes could not be adopted to the machine processes, so a few craftsmen survived to carry on their trade of hammering copper into cast-iron molds.

Continuing in the fine old tradition are the craftsmen of *E. G. Washburne & Co.*, established in 1853 — still hand hammering from original old molds, these celebrated copper weather vanes.

E. G. Washburne & Co.
85 Andover Street
Danvers, Massachusetts 01923

COW —SWELL-BODIED

Vane Complete	Figure Size
W40	28 inches long, 18 inches high

Antique Natural	$195.00
Gold Leafed	$260.00

The Mystic Foundry

This non-ferrous foundry was started in 1952 by Eliot Borges. Nonferrous means that they pour only brass, bronze, aluminum, zinc and lead. Being a sand foundry — for every casting produced — first a mold must be made of sand. After molten metal is poured into the mold, it is broken apart to claim the cast piece.

They specialize in repair work, using the piece of a broken or obsolete part as the pattern to cast a new usable piece. The foundry is a favorite of old car buffs. *Mystic Foundry* also designs and custom sculptures school and club emblems, memorial or historical plaques. By using drawings or photos they can put most any design into bas-relief in the metal of your choice.

Much of their work is custom-made and the prices are figured individually, but they do have a few standard items available which they make up on order.

The Mystic Foundry, Inc.
Broadway Extension
Mystic, Connecticut 06355

A New England Simple — To keep knives from rusting.

Scour them on a board, crosswise, with some dry brick, after having wiped them perfectly dry, and put them away without wiping off the brick dust.

Fused and Leaded Glass

Natalie Newhoff studied with well-known stained glass craftsmen and is well able to create the functional pieces often associated with glass artists. But a creative, artistic nature drove her to experiment — to go beyond the functional — and make lasting pieces of sculpture.

Mrs. Newhoff writes:

"This new form of glass fired into several layers has become a looser medium with the potential for more flexible design. It can also acquire a new degree of sparkle from the crackling which occurs after firing. Widely varied surface texture is possible, thick globs of glass can soften into each other and crushed sprinkled glass can give a uniform rounded or flowing texture. The clean chiseled painted blacks which have traditionally given stained glass much of its excitement are also possible to paint in fused glass, and fused glass sections can be combined with leaded areas. It is becoming one of the newest plastic media for today's color experiments. It promises grandeur and scope which paint on an opaque surface cannot hope to achieve, and delicate pleasure in smaller, intimate pieces.

"A two foot length of rich-toned antique stained glass viewed in the sunlight is an exciting experience. Handblown, antique stained glass streaked with filaments of tiny bubbles or sparkling from delicate, fine-line angles on the surface, thundering with powerful amethyst-purple tones, a blaze of cardinal red, or the silent majesty of deep blue lures the artist to use its power in stating his own message. An artist's most important message can come through fine glass. It is capable of being light, bright, delicate as well as very strong, simple, powerful and always provides an unmatched color quality because light is enclosed, contained within it."

Natalie Newhoff
Box 45
Brainard Road
Westbrook, Connecticut 06498

The Art of Colonial America

Examples of all kinds of early American art are included in this interesting and informative book. Not only are there many primitive paintings of rarely smiling ancestors and little girls in grown-up costumes, but also a good representation of engravings, buildings, silver, furniture, weather vanes and needlework. Americans indeed have a rich artistic heritage.

Sally G. Devaney

The Art of Colonial America
by Shirley Glubok
1970; 48 pp.
From: The Macmillan Company
866 Third Avenue
New York, New York 10022
$5.95

Majolica — Collect It For Fun And Profit

"Majolica, tin and lead glazed pottery, obtained its name from the fact that this distinctive type of pottery was made in Spain and shipped from the Balearic Islands, the largest of which was Majorica or Majolica."

Wildey Rickerson has put together a fine guide to collecting it. With honest, and sometimes humorous text, and clear photos, Mr. Rickerson has catalogued Majolica. Common, unique and hard-to-find pieces are discussed including designs such as shell and seaweed, begonia leaf, cauliflower, and corn. There are many good sketches of the identifying marks of Majolica. The rarer forms of pottery of this type — French Faience, Palissy and Whieldon — are included in a short discussion. I only wished the photos had been in color!

CIE

Majolica — Collect It For Fun and Profit
by Wildey C. Rickerson
1972; 70 pp., paper
From: The Pequot Press
Chester, Connecticut 06412
$3.50

Majolica

Collect it for fun and profit

Wildey C. Rickerson

Wesleyan Potters, Inc.

In 1948, a group of craftsmen founded Wesleyan Potters, Inc., a non-profit cooperative which promotes the learning and development of skill in crafts.

Classes are held year-round with lectures, exhibits, demonstrations, films and discussions scheduled as special events. Several times each year, visiting craftsmen conduct workshops and critiques. A marvelous craft sale is held each year around Christmas — ask to be put on their mailing list.

Visitors are welcome by appointment. Call Lucile Blanchard at the Center.

Wesleyan Potters, Inc.
350 South Main Street
Middletown, Connecticut 06457

A New England Simple — To cleanse the inside of jars.
Fill them with hot water, and stir in a spoon or more of pearlash; empty them in an hour and if not perfectly clean, fill again and let them stand a few hours.

Luta Studios

Versatile craftsmen create colorful figurines, chess-sets, birds, mirrors, casseroles, bird cages, hanging lamps and bells from clay.

Several artists working together, are particularly noted for their fine ceramic panels and friezes.

Hand-painted tiles may be ordered in any design — even to match a favorite wallpaper.

Prices range from $2.50 for individual 6" x 6" tiles, to $5.00 per square foot. Experienced Luta employees will lay the tile, if you wish.

Luta Studios
South Main Street
Deep River, Connecticut 06417

The Folk Arts and Crafts of New England

by Priscilla Sawyer Lord
and Daniel J. Foley

The Folk Arts and Crafts of New England

A panorama of the early settlers' lives is viewed through things they created for daily use. Well-illustrated, this volume offers a wealth of historic fact and folklore on the arts and crafts of early New England.

Unquestionably, an important addition to the bookshelf of every craftsman or collector of early Americana.

MSH

The Folk Arts and Crafts of New England
by Priscilla Sawyer Lord and Daniel J. Foley
1970; 282 pp.
From: Chilton Book Company
401 Walnut Street
Philadelphia, Pennsylvania 19106
$9.95

Decorative Ceramic Tiles

Richard Johnson specializes in custom designed ceramic tiles. Churches and organizations can submit sketches, snapshots or historical text to be made into single or multi-colored tiles. Great fund raising item. Minimum order is 200 tiles. Prices on request.

Richard Johnson
34 Coe Avenue
Portland, Connecticut 06480

Coran-Sholes Industries

c a m e (kām) n. A grooved lead bar used to secure the panes in stained glass windows. [Origin unknown]

Coran-Sholes Industries
509 East 2nd Street
South Boston, Massachusetts 02127

268 - 3780

CAME-LEADS

MOST POPULAR SIZES	Price Group	Approx. Wts.
1/16 x 3/16 FLAT U	1	4 oz.
3/32 x 3/16 ROUND H	1	5 oz.
3/16 x 5/16 ROUND H	3	11 oz.
3/16 x 1/2 FLAT H	3	18 oz.
3/16 x 3/8 FLAT H	3	15 oz.
1/4 x 1/4 ROUND H	3	13 oz.
1/4 x 5/32 ROUND H	2	12 oz.
1/4 x 1/8 FLAT U	1	9 oz.
1/4 x 3/16 FLAT U	2	11 oz.
3/16 x 3/16 FLAT H	2	9 oz.
1/4 x 3/8 FLAT H	3	13 oz.
9/32 x 5/32 FLAT U	2	7 oz.
11/16 x 3/16 FLAT H	3	24 oz.
3/8 x 3/16 ROUND H	3	12 oz.
90° ANGLE	1	22 oz.
120° ANGLE	1	13 oz.

CAMES ARE PACKED IN 25 lb., 50 lb., 75 lb. and 100 lb. WOOD BOXES. MINIMUM ORDER IS 25 lbs. ONLY ONE SHAPE CAN BE PACKED PER BOX.

THERE IS A $5.00 CHARGE ON ALL BOXES. THIS CHARGE IS REFUNDED IF BOX IS RETURNED IN A REUSABLE CONDITION. SOME CAMES MAY BE PACKED IN TWO 50 lb. BOXES RATHER THAN A SINGLE 100 lb. BOX, TO INSURE THAT THE LEAD WILL NOT BE CRUSHED.

ANY SHAPE CAN BE EXTRUDED. IN THE CASE OF A SPECIAL SHAPE FOR WHICH WE DO NOT ALREADY HAVE DIES THE MINIMUM QUANTITY IS 500 lbs. THERE IS NO CHARGE FOR THE EXTRUSION DIE.

PRICES ARE F.O.B. SOUTH BOSTON. IF YOU WISH, YOU CAN CALL AHEAD AND PICK UP YOUR ORDER AT THE PLANT. WE WILL SHIP ANYWHERE FREIGHT COLLECT.

LENGTH OF STRIP IS BETWEEN 66 AND 72 INCHES.

25# BOXES CAN BE SHIPPED VIA UNITED PARCEL SERVICE. THIS IS LESS EXPENSIVE IN SMALL QUANTITIES. PLEASE ADD $3.00 FOR SHIPMENT WITHIN NEW ENGLAND AND $5.00 OUTSIDE NEW ENGLAND.

50 AND 100 LB. BOXES MUST GO BY FREIGHT COMPANIES. FREIGHT CHARGES WILL BE COLLECT.

OUR 90° AND 120° ANGLE CAMES ARE ALLOYED TO BE STIFFER THAN PURE LEAD. THIS "TEMPERING" MAKES THE LEAD MORE RESISTANT TO SAGGING.

ASK FOR JOE SHOLES

ALL SHAPES CAN BE COMBINED FOR QUANTITY PRICING

PRICES ARE PER POUND. THEREFORE, SHAPE #1 IN A 50 POUND BOX, WOULD BE APPROX. 4 STRIPS FOR $.70

Price Group	25 lbs.	50 lbs.	100 lbs.	300 lbs.
1	1.00/lb	.70/lb	.65/lb	.60/lb
2	.85/lb	.55/lb	.50/lb	.45/lb
3	.75/lb	.48/lb	.43/lb	.38/lb

Sherrymike Pottery

Rich tones of brown, overcast with soft greens enrich the casseroles, bean pots, serving plates and other pottery creations of this talented Maine craftsman.

Sherrymike Pottery
Adele Nichols
19 Pleasant Street
Hallowell, Maine 04347

Two quart bean pot $20.00

Early American Folk Pottery

American folk potters were severely limited not only in time and materials but also by the demand for strict utility in their wares. They did, however, in spite of these limitations, create wares of great strength, integrity and beauty.

Harold Guilland has done a marvelous history of stoneware, tracing its manufacture throughout the southern states and New England. There are good, complete chapters on the potters, their designs, and the traditions of earthenware and stoneware. The photographs are wonderful, and many of the selected pieces are in themselves unusual for their unique design. A few excellent examples of stoneware and earthenware include a grave post, money bank, cheese strainer, and a Gemel bottle (two stoneware bottles fastened together like Siamese twins, used for storing oil and vinegar).

CIE

Early American Folk Pottery
by Harold F. Guilland
1971; 322 pp.

From: Chilton Book Company
401 Walnut Street
Philadelphia, Pennsylvania 19106
$12.50

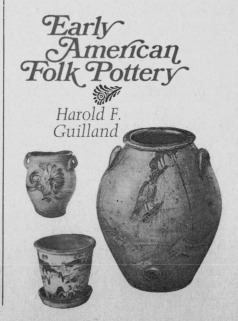

Early American Folk Pottery

Harold F. Guilland

Stained Glass

The Whittemore-Durgin catalog — pure entertainment, chock full of interesting things to buy. Obviously a business with a sense of humor.

Whittemore-Durgin Glass Co.
825 Market Street
Rockland, Massachusetts 02370

Catalog $.25

Basic Kit #10 — Contains complete instructions and pre-cut glass to make three ornaments, plus the necessary lead, liquid solder and hanging wire. You don't have to cut glass to make these ornaments — we've done it for you! You get plenty of additional material too — enough to cut at least a dozen more ornaments! You get 5 pounds of stained glass remnants, 18 feet of lead came, 3 big pattern sheets containing 26 patterns, and a special glass cutter for cutting stained glass. Our pamphlet "Getting Started in Stained Glass" which contains the complete, easy to follow basic steps is included in Basic Kit #10.

$11.95 postpaid

Peter Esak, Glassblower

Lampwork — A glassblowing technique done by rotating lengths of glass tubing over an open flame, then blowing into one end.

Employing a four burner, crossfire setup and various lengths and colors of lead crystal tubing, *Peter Esak* creates functional, decorative, one-of-a-kind pieces.

Before he set up the present studio in his home, he studied extensively with several professional glassblowers. His creations of wind chimes, bud vases, wine goblets, mobiles, fantasy animals and much more are fast becoming collectors' items.

Peter Esak
Bayview Avenue
Mystic, Connecticut 06335

4" high crystal bells, hurricane lanterns, bud vases, animals $3.00 ea.

#801 HORSESHOE NAILS - Recognizing that possibly some of our customers may not have access to a supply of farrier's material, or may not care to have dealings with persons engaged in horse type functions, we have made available our very own brand horseshoe nails, made to our own specifications. (A point at one end and a head at the other.) Every swift leaded glass person is well aware of the requirement for a nail which will hold glass in place (on the workboard) without chipping it, and be easily removable attractive, modest, and have just enough charisma to prevent the Cleaning Lady from throwing it out. Our #801 Horseshoe Nail meets every one of these requirements, and is recycleable to boot. (It can double as a cribbage peg, a hors d'oeuvre pick, or can be made into a finger ring for your high school sweetheart.)

12 for 30¢ postpaid.
100 for $2.00 postpaid.

$62.00

POTTER'S WHEEL HARDWARE KIT

A Sandwich Sampler

At first glance, this soft-cover book with its cross stitched cover looks like just an attractive introduction to the famous glass of that area. However, its innocent appearance is deceptive. There are nuggets of information throughout, and the line drawings on each page are well done and helpful to the collector. It covers a surprising range for its size and manages to be fun besides.

Alice Rosencrantz

A Sandwich Sampler
by Charles & Polly Gaupp
1970; 54 pp., paper
From: The House of the Clipper Ship Press
East Sandwich, Massachusetts 02537
$2.00

J is for Jewel Case

Now here is truly a great rarity. In fact, if you have one, you should have a special case for your jewel of a jewel case.

Wilk says —
New England most times gets short shrift from the larger states of our union as an insignificant gaggle of rather small states, but as a Vermonter once pointed out, "If you ironed Vermont out flat, it just might be a mite bigger than Texas."

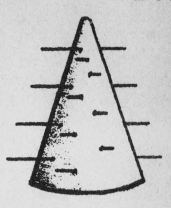

CERAMIC BEAD TREE
$ 4.95

Cole Ceramic Laboratories

As ceramic specialists, *Cole* will be glad to advise the potter in the selection of the finest quality kilns, potter's wheels, pug mills, clays, glazes and tools. If it's special equipment you need, they'll find it for you.

Informative literature available.

Cole Ceramic Laboratories
Gay Street
Sharon, Connecticut 06069

Developed for the rapidly growing ceramic bead business, the Bead Tree allows the artist to arrange properly the beads in the kiln without fear of their sticking to the shelves or each other. Bead Tree branches are made of high temperature Inconel for use up to cone 01. Each tree has a capacity of 40 to 50 beads, depending on size, and consists of a one-inch solid steel stress proof shaft, 32 inches long; an 11-3/8 inch cast aluminum wheelhead with ½ inch concentric circles scored into the accurately machined surface. Also included are two one-inch flangette sealed bearings with mounting flanges. Shaft and wheelhead are match threaded to assure a smooth, no wobble operation. A drawing of a suggested wood frame Potter's Wheel is included.

Scargo Potter's Wheel

Designed by a potter, this wheel is completely portable, weighing only 85 pounds. A boon to teachers and demonstrators, it fits easily into the back of a station wagon.

The designer, Mr. Harry Holl, writes us that it is particularly good for children who cannot control ordinary wheels.

The Scargo Potter's Wheel was chosen for exhibit and demonstration at the U.S. Trades Fair in Poland.

Scargo Stoneware Pottery
Box 304, Rt. 6A
Dennis, Massachusetts 02638

Scargo Potter's Wheel	$325.00
Two-Way Switch	$ 10.00
Casting Ring For Bats	$ 12.00
Crate	$ 10.00

Craft

Ceramics

This craftsman's favorite shapes come from nature, with insects, animals and plants inspiring many unusual designs. A versatile craftsman, *M.G. Martin* works in and teaches a variety of media, including ceramics, batik, tie-dye and papier-maché. Hand-painted and glazed ceramic tiles in original designs are also a specialty.

M.G. Martin
Upper Grassy Hill Road
Woodbury, Connecticut 06798

Black Ceramic Planters –
  11" high, $25.00
  16" high, $50.00
Ceramic Tiles – 4½" x 4½"
  $10.00 per sq. ft.

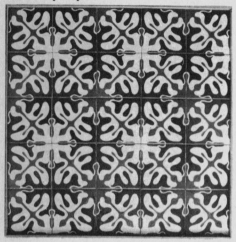

ANIMALS	Ea.
Birds (fanciful)	$3.00
Bluebird	4.50
Blue Jay	4.50
Cardinal	6.00
Chickadee	4.50
Red-winged black	4.50
Robin	5.00
Titmouse	4.00
Butterfly	3.00
Camel	10.00
Cats	4.00
Chicken (flossy)	7.50
Dachshunds (small)	4.00
Dolphins	3.00
Donkey	7.50
Dragonflies	1.50
Elephant	10.00
Fish	7.50
Fox	5.00
Frog (small)	4.00
Frog (large)	6.00
Giraffe	10.00
Grasshopper	5.00
Hedgehog	10.00
Hippopotamus	5.00
Kangaroo	15.00
Lion	6.00
Luna Moth	5.00
Mouse	3.00
Owl	5.00
Panda	5.00
Pelican	10.00
Penguin	5.00
Polar Bear	8.00
Rabbit	5.00
Sea horse	8.00
Snail	6.00
Squirrel	4.00
Tiger	12.00
Turtle	5.00
Unicorn	15.00
Whale	5.00
Zebra	10.00

Sheffield Pottery, Inc.

Located on top of their own source of clay — eleven acres with clay going down to a depth of **297 feet**— *Sheffield Pottery* sells a variety of clays, casting slips, glazes, kilns and potter's wheels.

For those not inclined to make their own, they market a good variety of pieces under the Sheffield Ware label.

There is no chemical coloring in Sheffield Ware, its natural rich charcoal browns and cinnamon tones come from the brown and white clay used. The top layer is cut away (sgraffito is the technical term) to reveal the under color of the pottery. When the outer layer of white is incised, the design shows through in brown. The white takes on a pearly gray cast from the brown. Each piece is then fired with a transparent glaze. Catalog available.

Sheffield Pottery, Inc.
Route 7
Sheffield, Massachusetts 02157

Fused Glass Pieces

Fusing glass is a relatively new ceramic technique. It started less than twenty years ago as an experiment in a Museum of Modern Art mosaics course. The teacher was Priscilla Porter. Miss Porter now shapes and bakes more than one hundred different varieties of transparent mosaics including everything from a simple little star for the Christmas tree to twelve-inch cake plates. Her glass menagerie ranges from a luna moth to elephants and giraffes. Not only are her pieces sold in the finest gift shops, but she also has had one-man shows and commissions from all over the country. The *Priscilla Manning Porter Studio* is now also working with sculptured forms and religious pieces. Tours of the studio with its six kilns, sheets of glass, busy artisans and bright jars of colored glass may be arranged on Thursdays by appointment. Brochure available.

Sally G. Devaney

Priscilla Manning Porter Studio
Plumb Hill Road
Washington, Connecticut 06793

2-quart casserole with cover.   It is suitable for baking and serving. $7.75.

  Bean pot with cover, approximately 2 quarts. Traditional style, two modified handles; for baking, or makes a very attractive cookie jar. $6.75

SO EASY TO FIRE

A favorite of thousands of hobbyists just beginning in ceramics, the A-66B will handle 14" plates easily. Its 14⅜" dia. x 13¼" deep dimensions may be extended in depth 6½" by the addition of the AA-6B extension collar. The A-66B features a 4-way switch for complete firing control, quality firebrick, full opening hinged lid, and heavy Kanthal elements. This kiln fires to 2300° either with or without the collar. The A-66B and AA-6B in Stainless; A-66 and AA-6 in Hammertone.

MODEL A-66B
Basic Kiln Price $109.50

Craft

The Pairpoint Glass Works

Except for the new *Pairpoint Glass Works* in Sagamore, the history of glassmaking in New England has come to a close. Pairpoint had its beginning in 1837 in Boston. It was then called the Mount Washington Glass Company and it prospered in the thriving and proud glassmaking industry during the mid-1800's. In 1880 the Mount Washington directors, having moved earlier to New Bedford, purchased, a small silver company. Its leading silver designer was Thomas J. Pairpoint. Appropriately, the new enterprise was named the Pairpoint Silver Company.

For the next seventy-five years a great variety of distinguished handmade crystalware emerged from the blowing room of the glassworks. Over the years, glass of every type and color was produced at the New Bedford works. Honors for the single best known product fell to the rare and beautiful Mount Washington rose paperweight.

When glassmaking operations ceased at the New Bedford works in 1957, Robert Bryden, its last manager, moved the operation to East Wareham. Operating a two-pot furnace, his firm produced a number of pattern-molded and other forms of Burmese ware. These pieces, despite their late date, are much sought after and highly prized by collectors.

Although the glassworks suspended business in 1958, Bryden continued the operations intermittently and in 1970 opened a newly built factory in Sagamore, where, once again, the *Pairpoint Glass Works* is in operation on a full-time basis. Catalogue available.

Pairpoint Glass Works
Sagamore, Massachusetts 02561
Colonial Style Candlesticks 9″ tall — $50.00 pair
Winged Chalice 11″ tall, without engraving
$75.00

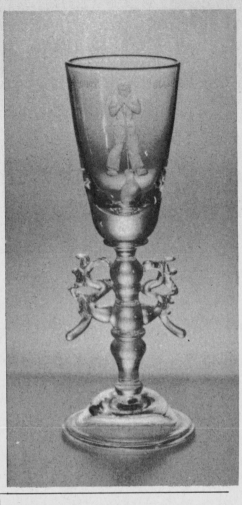

Pottery and Stained Glass

The Foster Studio offers a new line of traditional and modern leaded glass shades and also specializes in one of a kind lamps, windows and light sculptures for general sale and on commission. Christopher Foster approaches stained glass as an art. Each piece of glass is cut according to pattern, the edges are wrapped in copper tape, and fit together like pieces of a puzzle. They are then soldered in place. The lead lines are fine in the true Tiffany tradition.

On display in the showroom she shares with her husband, are Evelyn Foster's wheelthrown ovenware, pottery and sculpture. Evelyn offers classes in this field, as well as in drawing and painting.

Foster Studio
Route 82
Hadlyme, Connecticut 06439
Iris Lamp — 20″ Diameter, $550.00 ppd.

Kennebunk Railroad Station Craft Workshop

From Cambridge to Kennebunk came John and Carol Standish to become owners of a sadly deserted railroad station. They turned it into a charming home and craft workshop.

John's field is stained glass and Carol's is pottery. At first they sold only their own work, but soon realized that other craftsmen would be needed to help keep the shop going. Now they offer a wide selection of New Englander's crafts. Catalogue available.

The Kennebunk Railroad Station Craft Workshop
12 Depot Street
Kennebunk, Maine 04043

Gull — 7″ x 9″ in two shades of blue
    and white $12.00 ppd.

The Jug and Related Stoneware of Bennington

Cornelius Osgood, Professor of Anthropology at Yale University has produced a concise, detailed history of stoneware, beginning with the technicalities of its manufacture through the development of kilns throughout New England. Included is a fine history of the Norton family of Bennington and a glossary of ceramic terms.

This book is an outstanding guide to the identification of the shapes and marks of stoneware and related pottery.

CIE

The Jug and Related Stoneware of Bennington
by Cornelius Osgood
1971; 222 pp.

From: Charles E. Tuttle Co., Inc.
    Rutland, Vermont 05701
    $15.00

THE JUG and Related Stoneware of Bennington

by CORNELIUS OSGOOD

New England Glass & Glassmaking

This fine history of glassmaking in New England covers the range from our early history, when most was imported from England, to approximately 1952 when glassmaking in New England was no longer economically practical. Various plants were founded as early as 1639, but primarily for the making of window glass. By 1750 the industry was a thriving one, with Massachusetts and Connecticut leading in the number of producers.

With good photographs, line drawings where useful, and a comprehensive list of glass producers and their histories, this book is invaluable to the serious collector.

Alice Rosencrantz

New England Glass & Glassmaking
by Kenneth M. Wilson
1972; 401 pp.
From: Thomas Y. Crowell Company
201 Park Avenue South
New York, New York 10003
$15.00

Welcome Rood Studios

Betsy Zimmerman and her husband live and work in an old building which was once a tavern. Here Betsy has a studio and kiln and turns out some unusual pottery — each piece one-of-a-kind. Her shop also carries the work of neighboring craftsmen — macrame, wrought iron chandeliers, candles and rugs. It's worth a visit. Open Thursday through Sunday 1-5 p.m.

Welcome Rood Studios
S. Killingly Road
Foster, Rhode Island 02825

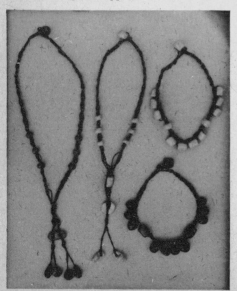

Mustache Cup $5.50 ppd.

Egyptian paste necklace: a combination of Egyptian paste beads and macrame in dark brown cord. There are three colors of beads to choose from: Yellow, royal blue and turquoise.

Choker $6.00 ppd.   Long Pendant $7.50 ppd.

Craft

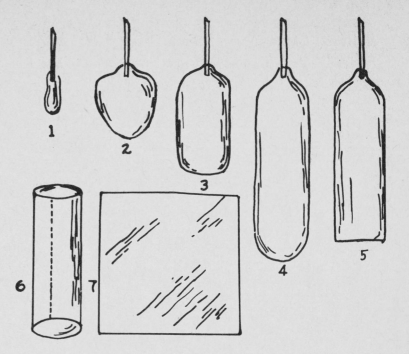

FIG. 41 Steps in the process of making window glass by the cylinder-glass method. A cylinder about five feet long and one foot in diameter was blown; then the end was cut off, the blowpipe was cracked off, and the cylinder was slit and opened out into a flat sheet. (*Photo by The Corning Museum of Glass, illustration copied from K. M. Wilson's drawing in* Glass in New England, *an Old Sturbridge Village booklet*)

Stone Soldier Pottery

Robert Burnell's pottery is hand decorated, and the glazes are applied by hand dipping and pouring. Through the use of a special technique — reduction firing — the fine variegated colors and mottled textures of his pieces are achieved.

Stone Soldier Pottery is sturdy and durable, contemporary and simple in design. It is made of the highest quality stoneware clays and is ovenproof.

Stone Soldier Pottery
Jacksonville, Vermont 05342

CANDLESTICK, Sm. — Green, brown, blue, white/blue and white/brown.

Small Candlesticks $2.50 pair

FLOOR PLANTER — Hand thrown and decorated. 10" to 12" high. Whites, browns, blues, and greens.

Floor Planter $20.00

CHOWDER BOWL
Wheel thrown, deep for chowders or stew. Holds a full meal.
White w/blue rim, white w/brown rim.

Chowder Bowls $5.00 each

A New England Simple

To whiten piano keys: Yellowed ivory keys may be made white again by washing them with a sponge wet with a solution of hyposulphate of soda, then exposing them to the sun. Repeat process until desired whiteness is attained.

All Hands Aboard Scrimshawing

A book with appeal for both the collector and the craftsman.

MSH

All Hands Aboard Scrimshawing
by Marius Barbeau
1966; 26 pp., paper

From: The Peabody Museum
East India Marine Hall
Salem, Massachusetts 01970
$1.25

The whaleman has left behind him one enduring monument . . . , the only important indigenous folk art, except that of the Indians — the art of scrimshaw. . . . Its practice was so widespread among the ships that it may be said to have been universal. In their spare time for a matter of seven or more decades, the better part of 20,000 whalemen, year in and year out, spent most of their leisure hours trying to fashion something beautiful. In their isolation they developed their designs along original lines, and the result was unique. . . .

The whaleman, in preparing the engraving, first used a coarse hand-made file to scrape off the ribs; then a finer file to work it down, while the bands of the ivory colors began to appear and disappear; then, sandpaper or a piece of sharkskin, ashes from the try work, also pumice. But the final polish was from the palm of the hand.

Now the sharp, pointed instrument — a sail needle in a bone handle; the Indian ink or the gunk and gurry worked into the striations, the final palming. There were also many tricks. Often the tooth was soaked in brine, to give the ivory an orange richness. And it was dipped in water for easier tooling. . . .

A hacksaw would be borrowed of the cooper, and a half a dozen men would stand around the work bench, giving advice while the tooth was sawed . . . The tools of scrimshaw were generally knife, files, and saw. Many ships had homemade turning lathes. Much fine turning was simulated with a file, and much of the pattern in scrimshaw that resembles scroll-sawing was also file work. Holes were drilled with gimlets made of nails. The countersinking for shell, silver, and mother-of-pearl inlay was scraped out with a knife, assisted maybe with a chisel. A grindstone at times proved useful in smoothing. Finishing was done with wood ashes, and polishing with the palm of the hand.

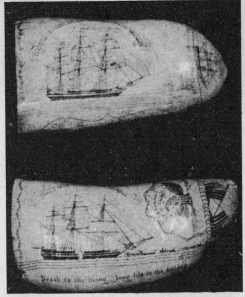

Etched sperm whale teeth.

Piano Keys

From an ivory comb, laboriously sawed out by hand, to a Steinway Grand is a long and seemingly illogical step.

But that giant step, although by no means taken in one fell swoop, was made over a period of years by Pratt, Read & Co., of Ivoryton (a village snuggled next to Essex, Connecticut). It all started in 1789, when the first ivory combs were hand-sawed by Andrew Lord, an Essex craftsman.

After making ivory combs and other ivory articles from elephant tusks brought over here from the jungles of Africa, the small Pratt, Read & Co. found a ready market for their ivory products in making piano keys, which were sold to piano manufacturers. For many years, more ivory was used for piano keys than for all other purposes combined. Genuine elephant ivory was said to have a "feel", a density, a permanence, a color and a suitability for piano keys never, up to some years ago, equalled in any other substance.

Pratt, Read & Co. has a business history which extends over a period of more than 172 years. It was only natural, perhaps, that during the middle of the nineteenth century, the company should have become a manufacturer of piano and organ actions, after having supplied the ivory veneers for keyboard instruments for so many years. An action is the intricate mechanism which transfers a blow on the piano key to the strings of the piano.

Today, Pratt, Read & Co. is the largest producer of piano and organ keys and actions in the entire United States, and supplies more than one-third of all keys and actions produced in the nation.

The headquarters of the company is a modern plant in (appropriately named) Ivoryton, there is another large plant in the South, as well as a woodworking plant, the Allen Rogers Corp., in Laconia, New Hampshire, and a hardware plant, Cornwall & Patterson in Bridgeport, Connecticut, both fully owned subsidiaries. The company has approximately 1,250 employees in its main and subsidiary plants.

The chances are, therefore, better than about one out of three that the next time you strike a chord on your piano or organ, its "inside workings" as well as its keyboard will have come from the hands of the skilled workers at Pratt, Read & Co.

Curtiss S. Johnson

Pratt, Read & Co.
Ivoryton, Connecticut 06442

Scrimshaw

Scrimshaw is one of the earliest folk crafts in the United States. It was developed aboard New England whaling ships by seamen during long monotonous days at sea. *Bernard Schneider* began doing scrimshaw as a hobby. His love of the sea and ships is expressed in the carving and engraving of whale's tooth ivory.

Scrimshaw
Cameos

Bernard Schneider
83 Foxcroft Road
West Hartford, Connecticut 06119

By appointment.

Scrimshaw and Scrimshanders

This handsome book has over 450 illustrations showing a range of work of incredible beauty. It not only pursues, in depth, the fine scrimshaw of the sailor, but other work equally impressive. The woven straw work, embroidery and the well-known Nantucket basket are all shown in detail.

The collection of scrimshaw is hard to believe, particularly in two examples of guillotines which are so intricate one wonders how men in their few hours of leisure could create such work. Their tools were handmade and limited in scope, yet the toys, with involved moving parts, religious tableaux of figures and decorations, all were created with care and great skill.

It's an impressive show, this book; a pleasure and an inspiration.

Alice Rosencrantz

Scrimshaw and Scrimshanders
Whales and Whalemen
by E. Norman Flayderman
1972; 291 pp.

From: N. Flayderman & Co., Inc.
New Milford, Connecticut 06776
$19.95

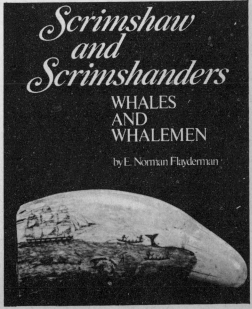

Craft

Rug Hooking

There are patterns for the young at heart, the Americana group, wall hangings, chair seats, Siamese cats, herbal runners and *Di Franza* kits for children and the beginner. "*Di Franza Designs* are significantly different from the usual patterns found for rug hooking. The purpose is to give this craft a new direction and offer those interested in a more contemporary approach something from which to choose. Creating fine designs is not the result of aimless doodling, but of keen observation and studied skill."

Di Franza Designs
118 Elm Street
North Reading, Massachusetts 01864
Prices vary from a small 14" x 14" "Sun" at $1.00 to a "Sunflower Kit" at $25.00
Catalogue available.

New England Motifs 40" x 58" $14.00

Alice in Wonderland 34" x 50" $12.00

Siamese Cat chair seat 14" circle $1.50

Hooked Rugs

Pearl McGown can be considered the originator of present day rug hooking. Her materials represent research started in 1931 to discover the designs and methods created by New England women in the 18th and 19th centuries. The techniques Mrs. McGown has taught go back to the days when housewives brought color and beauty into their homes by using woolen cloth which they dyed and cut into strips to "hook" rugs. These methods are taught today by her pupils. During the years, Mrs. McGown has trained thousands of teachers at her home, Rose Cottage, or through adult education courses, civic organizations and women's clubs. Now, there is a correspondence course for training teachers who cannot attend classes. Mrs. McGown has spread far and wide the interest and knowledge of rug hooking — truly a labor of love and an inspiration to all who have been reached. Rose Cottage was her shop until 1970. The house is a "ruggers" paradise with floors and walls covered with rugs and exhibits.

Ellen R. Hill

Books on Rug Hooking

The Dreams Beneath Design	$ 2.20
You Can Hook Rugs	$ 6.30
Color in Hooked Rugs	$ 6.80
The Lore and Lure of Hooked Rugs	$10.30
Persian Patterns	$ 3.70

Order From:

Pearl K. McGown, Inc.
Rose Cottage
135 Sterling Street
West Boylston, Massachusetts 01583

Pearl McGown designs and supplies — a selected list for beginners from an ardent "hooker" —

Letter Service — 10 issues	$ 3.00
Dye pamphlet	$ .75
So You Want to Hook — fundamentals of hooking	$ .75
Pick and Choose — catalog of rug patterns (97 illus.)	$ 2.20
Petites for Practice — catalog of small pieces (124 illus.)	$ 1.15
Hooked Rug Designs — catalog of rugs and small pieces (376 illus.)	$ 3.30
Rug Hooking frame	$14.00
Economy lap frame	$ 7.50
Hooks, hand forged	$ 1.10
Rug shears (8")	$ 5.25
Dorr's sample swatch card	$ 1.00
Dyed swatches	$ .85
Rug bindings	$.15 yard
Cutting Machine — send for catalogue	

Order From:

Lincoln House Fabrics
Sturbridge, Massachusetts 01566

SPECIALIZING IN
BRAIDING FOR YOU
FAST · BEAUTIFUL · EXCITING

Country Braid House
GEORGE AND MARION JURTA

CLARK ROAD
TILTON, N.H 03235

Rug Braiding Machine

A machine that braids rugs? Several years ago, Marion and George Jurta developed one. You can purchase their own braid by the yard, or they'll braid your materials for a fee. Better yet, rent their machine and do it yourself. If you really take to it, they build machines on special order.

Taaniko

This 300-year old method of non-loom weaving was developed by the Maori peoples of New Zealand. After spending a year in New Zealand, studying this age-old craft, *Joyce Smith* returned to the United States to practice and teach it. She writes:

"The technique is full of variations and possibilities, with a broad use of multiple colors and color changes. One can make wall hangings, window coverings, belts, purses and three-dimensional hangings."

The Taaniko shoulder purses sell for $35.00 and are available in any color combination.

Joyce Smith
15 Keene Street
Providence, Rhode Island 02904

Rugbraiding Supplies

This company's president created the first tools for faster and better braiding and has been adding to their line ever since. A complete catalog of rug making materials and equipment available.

Braid Aid
466 Washington Street
Pembroke, Massachusetts 02359
add $.05 postage

#12 Braidmaster Set of 3 $1.00

The first of the original tools developed by Braid-Aid Company to make reversible rug braiding possible. For those who prefer simplicity, this tool handles medium to coat weight fabric
Shipping weight............................. 2 oz.

Beginners — A word of advice!
1. Buy an instruction book and use it.
2. Use fabrics of uniform weight.
3. Make a small practice rug.
4. Notice that if you do not start correctly, you cannot finish correctly.
5. Pick out a pattern and follow it. You do not have to use identical colors.

The first YWCA dormitory in the country was opened in Hartford, Connecticut. It opened in 1872 at 58 Church Street with forty-five boarders.

Needle Arts

Exciting original designs for needlepoint, crewel and bargello.

For the truly creative designer the world is an exciting place, full of ideas. New ideas come from nature around us, the people we talk with and the books we read. Sometimes a flash of understanding will stimulate a wonderful new design idea. Fine design covers infinite moods and objectives. It may be bold, gentle, vibrant, subtle, pictorial, abstract, sentimental, youthful, mature, graceful, dramatic, etc. We will continue to develop designs representative of this wide range of opportunity. Our goal is constantly to be sensitive and perceptive to our environment so that our designs will always have a depth, quality and lasting beauty worthy of the beautiful and durable medium in which we work.

Needle Arts, Inc.
28 Washington St.
Camden, Maine 04843
Send $1.00 for catalog.

Craft

C. J. Bates & Son
Knitting Needles — Crochet Hooks
A New England Institution

How many remember bodkins, earspoon and toothpick combination, tiddlywinks and a nail file inserted into a bone needle? These were some of the first products to come from the C. J. Bates factory in 1873 — produced from odds and ends of scraps of ivory from nearby Deep River where ivory piano keys were made. Through the years this New England manufacturer has been in continuous operation and managed by the descendants of its founder, Carleton J. Bates.

Typical of the firm's forward look is an innovative sales approach to the display of knitting needles. Until 1946, needles were not displayed in any orderly fashion in stores. Most often they were kept in messed-up drawers with rubberbands binding pairs of needles. With the introduction by Bates of carded knitting needles, crochet hooks and accessories — where size, length and price are all clearly shown, eye appeal and "buy appeal" stirred interest and increased sales. Awareness of the importance of point-of-purchase displays has led Bates to win several national awards for packaging of their wares.

Today, in its modern plant in Chester, Connecticut, *C. J. Bates* makes only crochet hooks and knitting needles from steel, wood, aluminum and plastic. The knitting needles range in size from 5/64" to an inch in diameter. The products are distributed nationally under the trade name of *Susan Bates*.

C. J. Bates & Son, Inc.
Chester, Connecticut 06412

A New England Simple

To make transparent soap. Cut 6 lbs. of yellow soap into strips and put into a tin or copper kettle along with 1/2 gallon of alcohol. Cook over a slow fire until soap is dissolved, add 1 oz. of sassafras essence, stir until well mixed. Pour into pans 1½ inches deep and cut into bars when cold.

Patterns for Crewel, Hooking, Needlepoint and Embroidery

Heritage Hill supplies patterns, material, equipment and step-by-step instructions for needlepoint; embroidery, including crewel work; and hooking everything from brick covers to rugs. Along with the instructions are helpful hints for the novice as well as the expert. What materials to use, how to make a frame, and finishing your "work of art." In addition to the catalogue, single color sheets on various kits are also available such as "Your Favorite Birds in Needlepoint" and "Flower-of-the-Month Crewel Embroidery Kits."

Sally G. Devaney

Catalogue $1.00
Heritage Hill Patterns
Box 624
Westport, Connecticut 06880

Sunlit Yarns

Carol Bauer writes:

"Hand dyed in a backwoods Maine kitchen, each skein of wool has its own character, with varying shadings and hues — as if sunlight was playing over them. This is a yarn for the creative person, almost anything can be done with it. The color range is infinite; the weight is a heavy, one ply, sometimes handspun, in 4 oz. skeins selling for $2.00.

"I have designed and assembled kits for vests, smocks, sweaters and a baby bunting. I also have seasonal natural dyed roving (for spinning) and handspun yarn, which is considerably more delicate and costly.

"The wool is sold at craft shows and through the mail. If you would like samples, please let me know the colors and enclose what you can afford for handling."

Carol Gibson Bauer
Mt. Vernon, Maine 04352

Needlecraft Patterns

We wrote the Artisans Guild about their intriguing hot iron transfer stitchery patterns (average price $4.50) and a very nice Cynthia Tierney told us:

In answer to your questions, yes, your readers can buy directly from us. I am enclosing a copy of our $1.00 catalog which we are currently marketing. When the customer buys one of these catalogs, she receives a list of the stores in her area where she may buy these patterns direct. If there is no store in her area, she can buy through us.

The Artisans Guild
10 "B" Street
Burlington, Massachusetts 01803

Pattern No:	0708
Size:	20"x20"
Price:	$4.50

The perfect piece for you to combine techniques of quilting, applique and stitchery.

Shirret

Sew a needle — pull a thread — recycle old clothing, bedspreads, whatever else you have to create reversible rugs, chair pads, stair treads, table mats and many other useful objects.

Shirret (shur a): a new word added to the vocabulary of handcrafts, coined to describe an unusual combination of the needle arts of shirring and crocheting, it brings new dimension to these time-honored skills.

Created by *Louise McCrady* of West Hartford, Connecticut, this versatile craft is very satisfying, for work goes quickly and results appear almost immediately.

The Shirret needle has a long slender shaft which permits penetration of the fabric strips — a hook on one end is the correct size for making a crochet stitch of the carpet warp. Fold the strips of cloth accordion fashion and push the needle through until it is filled, then attach this section to the body of the work by making a double crochet stitch of carpet warp between the folds of the previous row.

The crochet stitches form a web of warp thread interlaced through the strips of fabric, giving the work great strength and durability. Because the warp stitches are hidden inside the shirred folds, each piece is completely reversible.

Basic Kit includes shirret needle, book of directions and patterns, illustrated, and carpet warp. Complete package — $8.00

Louise McCrady
30 Rockwell Place
West Hartford, Connecticut 06107

Printed Papers

Fanciful designs, whimsical people and fantasy flowers romp over the Christmas cards, ornaments and notepapers designed and made by two talented sisters — Diethild Beckman and Rotraut Postler. Please add $.25 for each item ordered.

Printed Papers
RFD 1
Newmarket, New Hampshire 03857

POSTCARDS pkg of 20/$1. (5½"×3½")

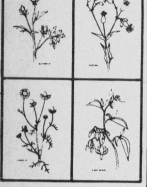

1. WAYSIDE BLOOMS
black on white

2. TWO FRIENDS
purple on white

NOTES with env. pkg of 12/$1.

6"×3½"
blue on white

3. PUPPETS ON PARADE

4. FRIENDSHIP QUILT GARLANDS
4½"×3⅜" – red on white

POSTCARD NOTES with env. pkg of 12/$1.50

black on moss green
9¼"×4"

5. MOON MUSHROOMS

black on bright green
8⅝"×4"

6. FAMILY REUNION

Craft

Recycled stationery *is made of 100 percent recycled paper. This one, by Editions Limited, is packaged in a cutting box as a continuous roll, and it is sealed shut with specially provided seals.*

Dear Friend,
[handwritten letter reproduction, signed ECOLOGUE]

The Bayberry Hill Press

Foster Johnson, after spending 40 years in the advertising business, now, for his own enjoyment and the pleasure of those who appreciate fine printing and binding, produces entire books himself. He sets the type by hand, prints the pages on a press once owned by famed American type designer, Fred Goudy, and finishes the production with a handsome binding. A perfectionist, Foster Johnson's limited editions (eight to twelve titles a year), are beautiful examples of book publishing at its finest. Each year for Christmas, he publishes children's books for ages 6 to 12. The stories are usually about animals and are available on a first come, first served basis at about $7.50 each.

The Bayberry Hill Press
Preston Avenue
Meriden, Connecticut 06450

There are three major elements in the product—the paper, the dispenser box and adhesive-backed labels. Pelkey said that all three are made from 100 per cent recycled paper.

"The only thing that isn't recycled paper," Pelkey said," is the metal cutting strip on the box, and I think that's recycled tin."

ECOLOGUE trademark is carried on the gummed label that is used to seal FOLDED NOTE

Rapping Paper

Editions Ltd.
P.O. Box 989
Pittsfield, Massachusetts 01201
$3.00 per box

Yankee Bundlar

Recycling newspapers is an important part of today's ecology scene. *The Yankee Bundlar* allows you to tie stacks of newspapers quickly. Place them on the specially designed rack, with a ball of twine concealed in a bottom compartment, pull up a length of twine, wrap around the stacked papers and tie two knots — that's all there is to it.

Another interesting feature; the twine is specially constructed for papers which can be recycled along with the newspapers.

Material Handling Systems, Inc.
67 Grassmere Avenue
West Hartford, Connecticut 06110
Yankee Bundlar –
  Black Finish $2.98 plus postage
  Brass Finish $3.98 plus postage

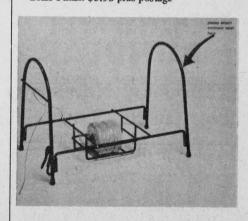

Grief can take care of itself, but to get the full value of a joy you must have somebody to divide it with.

Mark Twain

John Rogers — The People's Sculptor

The story of John Rogers' life and works gives the reader an intimate view of American cultural history. As a young man he worked at a number of enterprises — as a farmer, a mill worker, and a master mechanic. He had an inventive turn of mind and was always devising improvements and novel arrangements for his comfort. Did you think the water bed was a novelty of the late 1960's? For his bachelor apartment in Hannibal, Missouri, he writes his mother that he has built a "hydrostatic bed!"

"In the first place there is a water-tight tank the size of a bed. This is filled with about six inches of water. Then a water-tight cloth is spread over it loosely and fastened to the sides of the tank; on this a mattress is placed. You can't sink much because of the mattress and what can be a more perfect spring than water seeking its level. It will be so elastic as to fit every part of the body."

Always interested in drawing and working with clay, John Rogers finally got his family's support to go abroad after the panic of 1857 left him jobless. He studied art in Paris and Rome, but his independent spirit rejected formal teaching, and he developed his own style. He became the best known and most popular American sculptor ever, and his plaster statuettes of contemporary subjects, priced at about $14.00 each, found their way into almost every American parlor.

The second half of the book is a catalogue of his 208 known works with pictures of many of them and an appendix with information for collectors.

Ellen Hill

John Rogers — The People's Sculptor
by David H. Wallace
1967; 326 pp.
From: Wesleyan University Press
Middletown, Connecticut 06457
$20.00

110.

THE CHARITY PATIENT

Plaster, painted; height 22 inches
Signed JOHN ROGERS/NEW YORK
Patented December 4, 1866
Price: $15.00 (1866–76); $12.00 (1882);
$10.00 (1888–92); $8.00 (1895)
Collections: 1, 2, 3, 4, 5, 6, 9
Bronze master model: The New-York Historical Society, purchased in 1936 from Katherine R. Rogers

Small Printing Presses

Ninety years' experience in building and selling printing presses gives *The Kelsey Company* a right to say "ours is built to last." Type, ink, papers and other products enabling you to set up a complete printing business are also available. Send for catalog.

The Kelsey Press ranges in size from 3 x 5, $49.95 to 9 x 13, $305.95

The Kelsey Company
Meriden, Connecticut 06450

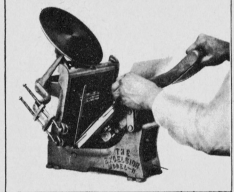

The Fascination of the Printing Press

EVER SINCE printing presses came into general use, men and women, rich and poor, famous and obscure, in all walks of life, have found pleasure in operating "private presses" a form of skilled and artistic creation as much as painting, etching, sculpture, drawing, or fine cabinet work. Some have it as a recreation, others adopt it as their life work. Gutenberg, Caxton, Walpole, Elbert Hubbard (of Roycroft fame), and more recently, Bruce Rogers and Douglas McMurtrie are distinguished examples.

Many people turn to printcraft for relaxation from the cares and fatigue of the office, factory, shop or studio. He who has not experienced the unforgettable moment of taking the first proof from a type form prepared by himself has so far missed one of those "thrills that come once in a lifetime."

The tremendously influential art of printing is open to everyone. Let it introduce you to a new way of enjoying your hours of relaxation, and incidentally, if you wish, a way which also has a cash reward.

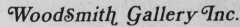

Woodsmith Gallery Inc.
Wardsboro, Vermont 05355

Product Of A Small Vermont workshop

Currier and Ives lithographs, rare antique map prints and reproductions of Audubon bird prints mounted on hand-carved 3/4" pine blocks and finished to a mellowed natural patina.

Full color reproductions (original lithographs ca. 1868) illustrate the changes of season on the American homestead. 9" x 12", hand-carved and antiqued, they evoke pleasant memories of the simple rustic life. One $5.95, two $9.95, three $13.95, complete set $17.95. Order #600 for full set. $1.00 postage and handling.

CURRIER & IVES FAMOUS FOUR SEASONS

Spring #601   *Summer #602*

Autumn #603   *Winter #604*

Jeanne Warner — Notepapers and Cards

Your boat, summer cottage, home, dog or whatever — sketched from your own photograph to make notepaper, Christmas cards or invitations. Don't forget to specify the inside greeting for cards.

Jeanne Warner
Fair Wind
Tenants Harbor, Maine 04860
First 100, envelopes included $35.00
Each additional 100 $10.00

A Guide to Decoration in The Early American Manner

Early settlers decorated their walls, floors, furniture, tinware and a variety of wooden objects with lovely handpainted designs, generally using a fruit or flower motif.

This book is a guide to help the reader master the different techniques which were employed, with much detail as to materials used.

Completely master the step-by-step approach used in this book and you'll be well on your way to being a fine tole painter.

MSH

A Guide to Decoration in the Early American Manner
by Nadine Cox Wilson
1968; 112 pp.
From: Charles E. Tuttle Company
   Rutland, Vermont 05701
   $4.50

Pilgrim Fathers

Within ten years after our Pilgrim Fathers first stepped upon the rock at Plymouth, they made an appropriation, out of their scanty funds, for the establishment of a college, "Christo et ecclesiae," (for Christ and the church.)

Elm Tree Studio

Elm Tree Studio offers an exclusive line of unique handmade gift items by two creative young people, John and Sally Dwyer. Especially exquisite are Sally's original pen and ink renderings, watercolored prints, handmade notepaper and Christmas cards. John's wood carvings, including candle holders, sconces, spoon racks and napkin holders have an antiqued quality and an authentic detail. Hand designed catalog is available.

Elm Tree Studio
Box 44
Prides Crossing, Massachusetts 01965

Handmade notepaper — Gift boxes from $3.75 — $5.95

Spoon rack with sconces and pegs, copper trim
   16" x 32" — $24.95

Elm Tree Studio

exclusive line of unique hand-made gift items
by
John T. Dwyer and Sally Parks Dwyer

Craft

APPLICATION OF THE STENCIL

PLATE 21. Stenciling. *a.* Units of composite stencil cut out of architect's linen. *b.* Applying cut-out units on tacky varnished surface with velvet square wrapped around forefinger. *c.* Close-up view of composite stencil and velvet-wrapped forefinger in process of applying bronze powders. *d.* Stenciling a one-piece unit. No shading can be left surrounding the units. Notice the open child's paint box which is lined with velour and used as a palette.

The Newtons

Dried grasses, leaves and flowers, laminated between sheets of fiberglass and plastic, are made into lovely place mats, lampshades and notecards by this clever Vermont woman.

Not to be outdone by his wife, Mr. Newton makes picture frames from rustic, weathered barn boards. These can be any size, are beveled and have a white liner along the inside edge.

Edythe and Granville Newton
Danville Township R.D. 64
Route 2
St. Johnsbury, Vermont 05819

Barn Board Picture Frames	$ .20 per inch
Nature Place Mats	$1.50 each
Note Cards	$ .35 each
Bridge-type Lampshade	$6.50
8" Lampshade	$4.00

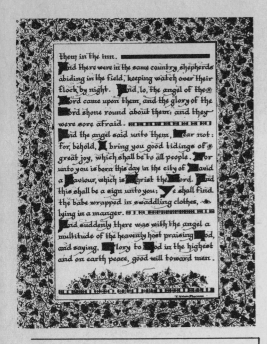

Medieval Illumination

Helene Sherman studied watercolor technique and calligraphy at the Vesper George School of Art in Boston. She started to copy the old manuscripts from book reproductions. Not satisfied with the results from copies, she later studied the originals at the Huntington Library in San Marino, California, and at the Morgan Library in New York City.

That first visit to the Huntington Library was a memorable one. Armed with a written introduction, she was allowed to examine the divine manuscripts — but only from afar, with hands behind her back and breathing subdued. (The gold is extremely perishable.) It was difficult for her not to touch and feel the ancient vellum. When asked what else she might like to see in the way of manuscripts, she answered that she would like to examine the Gutenburg Bible. No more temptation with the old manuscripts until she could have a closer look! But she vowed that on the next visit she would sketch in her notebook.

Over the years, Miss Sherman has illuminated numerous testimonials, bookmarks, Bibles, books for rare book collectors, and altar cards. Among her special commissions have been: the War Memorial for the Colonial Dames of New York, MIT and Fordham Universities' War Memorials, altar piece for St. Patrick's Cathedral, and altar cards, lettered in Latin, for the National Shrine of the Immaculate Conception in Washington, D.C. She takes great pride in having drawn the color citation that former President and Mrs. Case of Boston University took to Africa and presented to Dr. Albert Schweitzer for his 85th birthday in 1960.

Miss Sherman's works are executed on heavy sheepskin. "Mine never wrinkle as much as others," she says. The medium is mainly tempera and 23k gold, known as shell gold because originally the monks mixed it in mussel shells. Much of her work is characterized by a richness of complexity, performed with a jeweler's precision and outlined by a geometric frame dense with interlaced design and subtle movement. When asked how long it takes to complete a page, the reply was, "a long, long time. I don't advise anyone to study illumination who doesn't have a greater than normal degree of patience. The work itself is almost simple compared to the patience it demands."

With an inexhaustible vigor, Miss Sherman attends her beloved vocation, design. Greeting cards, miniature volumes, hooked rugs — all are planned with a deft hand and an intelligent, trained eye. Color, decoration and individual expression lend her works a unique and tasteful quality. Her religious writings embody an awesome feeling that can usually be found only in the holy books. Her own religious convictions are deep and intense.

Cynthia Elyce Rubin

Miss E. Helene Sherman
Sudbury, Massachusetts 01776

Tableau

The finest paper available for all types of artistic printing.

Block Printing Paper

Tableau block printing paper, among the finest for all types of artistic printing, is a domestic paper made from extremely long, imported vegetable fibers. The paper has been treated with a special wet strength treatment which bonds the fibers together without affecting the absorbency of the sheet. It can be purchased from most art dealers or directly from:

Technical Papers Corporation
729 Boylston Street
Boston, Massachusetts 02116
Sheet Sizes: 6¾"x8½" 9"x12" 18"x24"
20"x30" 24"x36"
Roll size 40" wide — 160 sq. yards to the roll

TABLEAU BLOCKPRINTING PAPER

PRICE LIST

Sheet Size	Minimum	Price
18" x 24"	100 Sheets	.15 per sheet
20" x 30"	100 Sheets	.18 per sheet
24" x 36"	100 Sheets	.24 per sheet
9" x 12"	500 Sheets	.04 per sheet
6¾" x 8½"	500 Sheets	.03 per sheet
Rolls		
40" x approx. 160 sq. yds. 1 Roll		60.00 per roll

Sheets 6-3/4" x 8-1/2" packed 500 sheets per package.
All other sizes packed 100 sheets per package, 500 sheets per bundle.
Rolls — 1 roll to the package.

All prices are F.O.B. Boston, Massachusetts

Artists Materials

Utrecht Linens is one of America's leading manufacturers and distributors of basic artists' materials of the highest grade — selling directly to schools and artists throughout the country.

Utrecht's direct distribution system results in remarkably low prices.

Utrecht Linens, Inc.
229 Newbury Street
Boston, Massachusetts 02116
Minimum orders of $20.00

UTRECHT Cotton Canvas Boards

Utrecht Linens cotton canvas boards meet the special demands of artists, students and schools. They are made from a fine quality canvas mounted over heavy weight, multi-ply board. The edges are turned over and trimmed. Our cotton canvas boards provide a fine surface to receive oil colors, which retain their brilliance without sinking in.

12" x 16"	$12.00 Per Four Dozen	$34.00 Per Gross
16" x 20"	$10.20 Per Two Dozen	$59.50 Per Gross
18" x 24"	$13.50 Per Two Dozen	$76.50 Per Gross

Superior Hand-Prepared Belgium Linen Canvas

Hand-Prepared · Finest Sizing & Priming Materials · Single Primed

Utrecht Canvas for oil painting is prepared of the finest 100% pure Belgian linen, of substantial weight, and tightly woven. Carefully and expertly done by able craftsmen, you are guaranteed the best single canvas that can be commercially made.

54" Wide $27.80 Per 6 Yard Roll	84" Wide $49.35 Per 6 Yard Roll
4 Six Yard 54" Rolls—$104.45	4 Six Yard 84" Rolls—$180.35

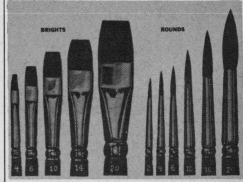

Rhenish Red Sable Oil Color Brushes are made with exacting craftsmanship, and of carefully selected 100% pure red sables. The pure red sable hairs are strong, extra-long and of great resiliency, which makes for durability and professional quality. The brights are used for broad and smooth brush work, and for blending colors. The rounds are excellent for outlining, painting details, and fluid brush work. Seamless nickel ferrules with long black polished handles.

	No. 2	No. 4	No. 6	No. 8	No. 10	No. 12	No. 14	No. 16	No. 20
PER BRUSH:	.62	.80	1.05	1.35	1.75	2.05	2.35	2.85	3.60
PER DOZEN:	7.13	9.20	12.07	15.52	20.12	23.57	27.02	32.77	41.40

	No. 2	No. 4	No. 6	No. 8	No. 10	No. 12	No. 14	No. 16	No. 20
PER BRUSH:	.49	.66	.80	.95	1.20	1.50	2.10	2.45	3.30
PER DOZEN:	5.63	7.59	9.20	10.92	13.80	17.25	24.15	28.17	37.95

1— 5 SETS: $7.65 Each
6—24 SETS: $7.60 Each

Utrecht's Complete Professional Oil Painting Set is designed to fulfill the needs of a basic course in oil painting.

CONTENTS: *UTRECHT PERMANENT ARTIST'S OIL COLORS* (Studio Size Tubes 37 cc) Yellow Ochre, Burnt Sienna, Burnt Umber, Ivory Black, Ultramarine Blue, Alizarin Crimson, Viridian, Cadmium Yellow Lt., Cadmium Red Lt., (in ½ lb. Size Tubes 1" x 6" 62 cc) Titanium White and Flex-Gel Oil Painting Medium. *BRUSHES:* Art Sch. Tested Bristle "Flat" #3 & #8; Highest Quality Pure Red Sable "Round" #4; One 9" x 12" *WOODEN PALETTE.*

The contents come in a heavy cardboard box with basic information for the beginning student.

Craft

CRANE & CO.
INCORPORATED
PAPER ══════ MAKERS
ESTABLISHED 1801

DALTON, MASS. 01226
U.S.A.

WHO EVER SAW A
WHALE FLY A KITE?

Kites and the Kiteman of Nantucket

If you are a kiteophile, Al Hartig is your man. Hartig's custom-made kites are not cheap. Prices range from $5.00 for an ACE up to $25.00 for the Maxim's soufflé of kites, THE NATIONAL EAGLE, with a wing span of five feet.

Many Hartig kites are patented, a development that surprised even him. He was interested in taking the kite route out and away from Manhattan Island and was merely making damn good kites. Suddenly he found that many of his innovations were novel enough for patents.

Hartig kites have such features as seamed pockets to hold the struts, rudders and keels for stabilizing, unusual bird shape kites that break through the normal 50 to 70 foot ceilings of such kites, and on and on and on.

Hartig's kite shop at "Derby Manor" is continually being assaulted by misguided, conglomerate type minds that want to see it expanded and enlarged. In the Spring 1972 issue of a magazine called "Best Western Ways" Al Hartig answered these warped minds with, "All you want to do is give me money; what else have you got to offer?"

There is a catalogue and kites are wonderful.

The Nantucket Kiteman
Box 1356
Nantucket, Massachusetts 02554

Crane & Co.

In 1801, Zenas Crane established the first paper mill in Massachusetts west of the Connecticut River in Dalton. Already an experienced paper-maker at the age of 24, he had chosen the site for its abundant, crystal-clear water supply and its accessibility to western markets. Six generations of the Crane family have guided the development of *Crane* from a hand-operated, one-vat mill to a modern papermaking complex.

Chances are you have had some *Crane* paper in your hands today — because *Crane* has been the principal supplier of crisp paper for currency to the U.S. Government since 1879. Each bill will be folded more than 4,000 times before it is taken out of circulation, therefore, strength and durability are primary requirements of the paper. If your folding money slips through your hands before you've had time to examine it, there are many other *Crane* fine papers which you can use at a more leisurely pace. Correspondence papers, wedding invitations, engraved stationery, tracing paper and synthetic fiber webs are some of their many other fine products.

Crane does not sell directly to the consumer. All their products may be purchased through appropriate stores — and banks — everywhere.

The Crane Museum housed in Crane's Old Stone Mill has exhibits tracing the history of American paper making from Revolutionary times. Open Monday through Friday, June — September. Free.

Ambroid Company, Inc.

Spruce gum held together the Indians' birch bark canoes. It did the job well, but there came a time, back in 1910, when the water-sensitive gum was not considered good enough for those involved in the manufacture of birch bark canoes and a substitute was sought. *Ambroid* created a waterproof glue that met specifications. Old Town Canoe Company and the Hudson Bay Company were their first customers. They still use *Ambroid* adhesives after 62 years — quite a testimonial! Birch bark canoes are no longer made by these companies, but *Ambroid* has branched out and now supplies adhesives for use with woods, leather, canvas, metal, most fabrics, glass and plastics. Available at fine hardware stores everywhere.

Ambroid Company, Inc.
612 Montello Street
Brockton, Massachusetts 02403

A True Cottage Industry

As we watch the conglomerates grow (and sometimes are awed by their bigness) there comes this whisper of a fresh business breeze from Maine. Nancy Lee Holland, Proprietor, tells us:

"We are a small, new business in Brunswick, Maine, mostly mail order, although we sell to some gift shops and book stores in Maine and Massachusetts. Our products are made individually in Maine homes, to our specifications and standards. There is a great need for work in the 'cottage industry' and we hope to continue to have our products made in this way."

Lee Crafts
P.O. Box 550
Brunswick, Maine 04011

The Lee Book Holder

Read and knit at the same time. The book holder becomes a third arm, allowing you to do two things simultaneously. Flexible brackets adjust to any thickness and the whole device folds flat for carrying.

$6.50 plus $.45 postage

The Lee Art Hanger

No more thumb tacks or tape — use this clever burlap hanger as a bulletin board, or to display posters and snapshots. Special hooks do not puncture walls or pictures so you may change things at whim.

19" x 25" $2.50 plus $.25 postage
Other sizes available, all in lovely colors.

Craft

Tole Painting and Decoupage Supplies

A complete line of supplies for the tole painter and decoupage artist available from:

Carson and Ellis
1153 Warwick Ave.
Warwick, Rhode Island 02888
East of Mississippi, send $1.25 postage, West $2.00

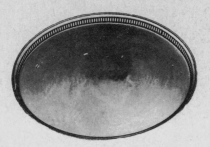

OVAL GALLERY TRAY

16 x 22 $6.50

An excellent reproduction of the early gallery trays. Fine for landscape or elaborate floral designs.

SC-9 4¾" wide and 14" high
Double candle holders on 2½" shelf with sunburst top. $4.30

SC-10 4¼" wide x 13" high
Has single candle holder on 2½" shelf. Sunburst top and bottom. $4.20

CUT CORNER TRAYS

8½ x 12 $4.00
12 x 16 $5.50

Made with heavy gauge bright tin with a flat rim and wire bound edges, soldered corners. A perfect reproduction.

The Chapeaux Box — A lovely little box, symmetrical and delightful to design for. Sponge painted backgrounds are easy on these straight sides.
L 5¾" x W 5¾" x D 4¼" 400017.........................$5.95

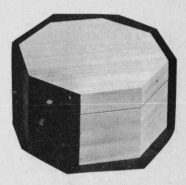

SC-6 10" high x 3" wide
Single cup set in crimped 3½" shelf. A simple effective sconce. $3.80

Italian Octagonal — As a vanity box this container would be adequate for jewelry or makeup accessories. The top can be used as a shadowbox for purse, or as shown for a truly roomy fashion accessory — soft maple.
L 7½" x W 7½" x D 3½" 400210.........................$8.75

Linoleum Block Designs

Distinctive, original linoleum block designs are this talented gal's specialty. Eight cards to a package, range in price from $1.50 to $2.50.

Anne De Maria
Russell Avenue
Rockport, Maine 04856

Harcourt Bindery

This is one of the oldest and possibly the only bindery left in New England doing handwork exclusively. The majority of work is done in imported leathers. Since the new owners, Sam and Emily Ellenport, took over the business, they have been encouraging restoration of old books and reproduction of period binding styles.

The bindery can do repairs, special one-of-a-kind jobs, and presentation copies as well as regular cloth work. No catalogue is available, but the owners will answer requests and send swatches if desired.

Harcourt Bindery
9 & 11 Harcourt Street
Boston, Massachusetts 02215

Prices range from cloth work, $8.00 to full leather work, $50.00.

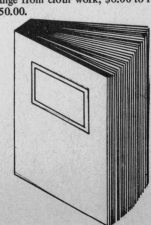

11111 11 22222 2
4 444 4 4 33 333 3
5 5555 5 66 666 6
8 8888 5 7 7777
9 9999 9 00000
00000 00 00 00
00000 0 000

Every Kind of Drawing Aid and Lettering

New Englanders have always been noted [and sometimes damned] for their precision,and a quick review of The C-Thru Ruler Company's catalogue can tell you why. Would you believe 71 different types of rulers alone. Then there are protractors, slide rules, french curves, lettering guides, graph charts, trimmers, T-squares, ship curves, and finally even dry transfer lettering sheets.

On the latter, they have three type faces available, among hundreds, that rather caught my fancy: "CONSORT BOLD," "DOM CASUAL," and "IN-SERAT GROTESQUE."

RWW

The C-Thru Ruler Company
6 Britton Drive
Bloomfield, Connecticut 06002

NANTUCKET

A Most Elegant Rubber Stamp

Rubber stamps can be rather dismal items, with use generally limited to the business world.

Two Nantucket Islanders found an old line drawing of a whaling ship executed many years ago by well-known Nantucket artist Rus Hillier. They had a rubber stamp created with the ship design carved into it. It wasn't long before this became a highly successful item in their shop. Its uses are many and varied, from creating your own bookplates to creating your own notepaper. Children buy them and stamp their arms with pseudo-tattoos.

These are available in two sizes, with or without the words "Nantucket" printed on them. If you prefer your own copy, write for an estimate.

The Havemeyer's
Mitchells Book Corner at The Chancellor
Nantucket, Massachusetts 02554

3" Rubber Stamp $6.70
4" Rubber Stamp $7.70

Oldstone Enterprises

Stone and brass rubbing is fun. An art that can be enjoyed by man, woman and child — no special skill is needed. To help you get a start, G. Walker Jacobs, well-known writer, lecturer and expert in the art of rubbing stone and brass, has created a kit, complete with informative guidebook and packaged in a convenient black leatherette carrying case.

Oldstone Enterprises
Box 462
15-17 Bassett Street
Marblehead, Massachusetts 01945

Kit plus 52-page guidebook: $7.50 ppd.

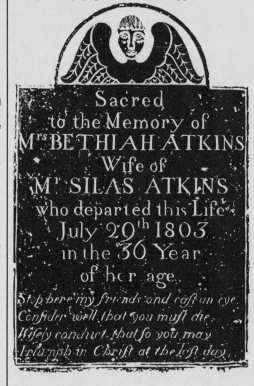

Sacred to the Memory of Mrs BETHIAH ATKINS Wife of Mr SILAS ATKINS who departed this Life July 29th 1803 in the 36 Year of her age. Stop here my friends and cast an eye Consider well that you must die Wisely conduct that so you may Triumph in Christ at the last day

One of the problems in the study of graveyard art is that it was not a conscious art form—the men who carved the stones did not keep records of them, nor did they keep sketch books of ideas for the designs. When their diaries mention carving a stone, it is usually only the name, date, and price of the stone that is recorded. While it is possible that some stonecarvers may have brought their designs with them from England, this is rather doubtful since there are no records of any practicing English carvers coming to this country. Most of our early stonecarvers were men whose sustaining occupations were ones such as woodcarving, masonry, leatherworking: they became stonecarvers only when the need arose. Perhaps, had New England stonecarvers thought more of themselves as true artists rather than as simple craftsmen, they would have left us a few more details concerning the origins and uses of their designs.

As one gains in experience, it is not difficult to identify the work of a given stonecarver throughout various graveyards. Nearly all New England stones were produced locally, and most stones have not been moved since the time of their original emplacement except within the confines of the graveyards.

The work of any one man is usually confined to one area, his home being in a town relatively near the geographical center of that area. For the most part, it is possible to assume that stones of similar or identical style were carved by one artist during his lifetime. Exceptions to this rule can be found however, as in cases where leftover precut stones were sold long after the death of the stonecarver. As the population of America grew, so did the need for skilled stonecarvers, so that by 1700 there were at least fifty stonecarvers in the Boston area alone. Some of these men, notably the Lamsons of Charlestown, became well known, and as their work was in great demand, they set up workshops and passed their craft on from father to son. The works of these talented men are still to be seen and admired in graveyards throughout the New England states.

1 2 3 4 5 6 7 8

A Book of Country Things

For those who have taken up the age-old, honorable profession of farming, this book is full of interesting and useful bits of information about the pioneer arts that were a way of life to Walter Needham's grandfather, over one hundred years ago. Sprinkled liberally with fine old yarns, real Yankee humor and many details of country life in the last century, the casual reader will enjoy it no less.

Homemade quill pens and ink, laying a slate roof, bullets from woodchuck pelts and much more is offered. The old ways may not be considered practical by today's standards, but they sure were more interesting!

MSH

A Book of Country Things
Told by Walter Needham; Recorded by Barrows Mussey
1965; 166 pp.

From: The Stephen Greene Press
Brattleboro, Vermont 05301
$4.50

Gramp made his own paint, and he made his own butternut dye, and he also made his own harness- or shoe-blacking, and his own ink. For harness-blacking, he saved up his saw filings, and dissolved them in vinegar. Leather dressing, for use instead of looks, was lampblack and tallow. Gramp always had lampblack in a little old can; he would take a fat pine knot, get it burning in the stove, and then hold it under a piece of metal to collect the smoke. Afterward he would scrape the lampblack off into the can.

As long as he lived he always made his own ink. The base was saw filings and vinegar, the same as for harness-blacking; then he would put in a little white maple bark to get tannic acid to make the ink more permanent. The vinegar ate up the saw filings, and made the color. That kind of ink turns light brown with age — iron rust is what it turns to; you've seen some of these old letters. Originally the ink was black.

He used steel pens in my time, but I've seen him make a quill pen, the same as he done when he was younger. It's quite a trick; it takes a very sharp knife and pretty good eyesight. Gramp cut the quill off at a slant, scraped out the pith, and then split it up the long side. If he didn't quite get it centered, he would have to work it down until the two points come even. It sounds simple enough, but it has to be well done in order to make a pen that will write much of any.

Pens was cut from goose quills, and Gramp generally had a few geese. I don't remember much about them except the old gander used to make my legs black and blue; he was always biting me and slapping me with his wings. They kept the geese for quills and feather beds and feather pillows and suchlike, but most stuffings was hen feathers. Everybody slept on cornhusk ticks with feather beds on top; I never see a mattress until I was quite a young man.

A New England Simple — Homemade Paste

A good homemade paste can be made by mixing 1/2 teaspoon each of starch, flour and moistening with a little boiling water. Then after allowing it to stand for a moment, add water, stir and cook the mixture til thick. To improve its lasting qualities, add 10 drops of oil of cloves to each half pint of paste.

The Art of Rubbing

Two Boston men have devoted much time to the development of techniques and equipment for making impressions of America's early gravestones.

Their kits, supplies and wall plaques reflect the well-being of a stone, a concern for accuracy in reproduction, ease and convenience in the techniques applied. They offer two booklets as well as a collection of decorative wall plaques carefully representing various regional style and carving found in the detail of gravestones from the New England area.

Reproducing

RELIEF SURFACES

A COMPLETE HANDBOOK OF RUBBING, DABBING, CASTING AND DAUBING
By
WILLIAM J. A. McGEER

$2.00

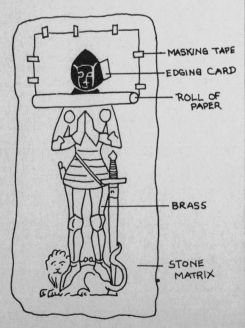

ENGLISH GOTHIC ART

BOX 873

WEST ACTON, MASSACHUSETTS 01720

Concord, Mass. 1799
A beautiful example of the primitive geometric carving style of rural New England.

Pewter or Brass, 15″ wingspread
$5.00 + $1.00 postage

THE EARLY AMERICAN
GRAVEſTONE
Aſ PRIMITIVE ART

FACES IN STONE

written
and illuſtrated by Richard Friſwell

$1.00

Handicapped Artists

"Your help will enable us to become dignified participants in the game of life — rather than mere spectators." This slogan of HAAI (founded in New England) is a modest statement by a group of courageous people with severe physical disabilities. However, their talent abounds and HAAI is anxious to discover the whereabouts of other handicapped artists to encourage them to join it. The cards for sale by the artists are painted well — not just for an incapacitated person, but for anyone with the full use of all his limbs! For information write:

Handicapped Artists of America, Inc.
8 Sandy Lane
Salisbury, Massachusetts 01950

Artprints Company

Colorful Gibson girls, antique maps, clipper ships, pirates, mushrooms and owls. A few of the many prints available for the decoupage artist — or just for framing.

Artprints Company
Box 26, Route 152
West Nottingham, New Hampshire 03291

| 1-152 | 8 x 16 | $2.00 |

| 9 x 11″ | 2641 | $1.00 |

| | OWL | |
| 2-104 | 11 x 14 | $1.50 |

Hand Printed Notepapers

Using live plants from her organic herb garden as models, *Adele Godchaux* makes intricate woodcuts which are then printed on Japanese rice paper to create lovely handmade notepaper. Descriptive price list available.

Adele Godchaux Studio
Upper Depot Road
Marshfield, Vermont 05658

All note papers — $1.50 per box of 8

Comfrey
Symphytum officinalis
var. caucasicum

Vignari Art Enterprises

The noted marine artist, John T. Vignari has put together an interesting catalog of fine art color reproduction prints which represent a span of over 300 years of marine art. Thomas Eakins' *Starting Out After Rail* is one of the fine examples. $6.00.
Add $1.00 for postage.

Vignari Art Enterprises, Inc.
2 Main Street — Box 335
Ogunquit, Maine 03907

STARTING OUT AFTER RAIL by Thomas Eakins (American 1844-1916) From the Museum of Fine Arts, Boston, Mass. He was one of the most important realist painters in America. Blue sky with land and boats on the horizon. Sea is brown and light blue, boat brown with white sail. Size 25 X 19. $6.00.

Hyssop
Hyssopus officinalis

Decoupage

Patience and meticulousness are two basic requirements for this delicate craft. *Hollis Schneider,* after years of using treasured old Victorian scrapbook motifs gleaned from New England attics, began drawing her own designs for decoupage. In the true tradition of the art, they are uncolored, leaving the artist the creative fun of choosing a palette and doing the actual coloring with oil-based pencils.

Hollis Schneider
83 Foxcroft Road
West Hartford, Connecticut 06119

By appointment.

Three sheets of assorted designs, mostly floral, available. $3.00 ppd.

Useful Materials from Old Charts

Chart Products printed on napkins, stationery, dinner mats, post cards and gift wrappings are made from century old copper engravings of sailing charts. This family business expresses the fine attention to detail typical of old-time New England craftsmen.

Descriptive catalogue available.

Sibley Industries
Ashby, Massachusetts 01431

A Family of Craftsmen

Handmade chests decorated with country paintings, decoupage, wall plaques and beautifully designed note paper — all produced by one family and sold through their own shop.

Partridge Workshop
Box 573
Boothbay Harbor, Maine 04538
Notepaper box of 10 $1.25

Silhouettes

An old-fashioned art practiced in modern-day New England. The name conjures up fantasies of dainty colonial ladies wrapped in silks and laces — sitting in their drawing rooms and painstakingly cutting likenesses of their children out of black paper; the tiny scissors employed just fitting over the tips of their fingers.

Natalie Garvin is one of a handful of people in New England who still practice the art of silhouettes. She began her professional career at Sturbridge Village where she "cut the likenesses of all who favored her with their custom." Having more work than she can comfortably handle, she is constantly looking for talent to train and follow in her footsteps. The requirements are an uncanny ability to make almost instant likenesses, good coordination of eyes and hands — plus unlimited patience.

For two copies of a silhouette mounted on a white, 5"x7" card, send a clear, side-view snapshot and $5.50 to:

Silhouette Studio
52 Woodhouse Avenue
Wallingford, Connecticut 06492

Your Own Stationery

Have a need for personalized memo pads or postcards? *Jacques Stationery* offers these, plus stationery and envelopes, custom printed in a good choice of type styles, paper textures and colors. Send for samples and quotes.

Jacques writes. "I might add that this is a hobby-business where profit is secondary to pleasing the folks with whom I deal and I have never once deviated from this policy."

Jacques Stationery
Wallingford, Vermont 05773

Wilde Birds

Sea-smoothed and sun-bleached wood can be found up and down the coast of Maine.

Incorporating beachcombing with painting, we collect such wood and then handpaint birds on separate pieces. Our most popular are sandpipers, sea gulls, the great blue heron, hawks, owls, blue jays, and cardinals.

Our particular favorites are shore birds, but any specific request can be fulfilled. Prices range from $7.50 on up, but you will find us most reasonable as we are not trying to make the Fortune 500 list of big companies. We love Maine, and in addition to teaching, we paint these birds. These two occupations are designed to satisfy a habit we have . . . we like to eat.

Sarah Wilde

Sarah & Bill Wilde
Box 98
West Boothbay Harbor, Maine 04575

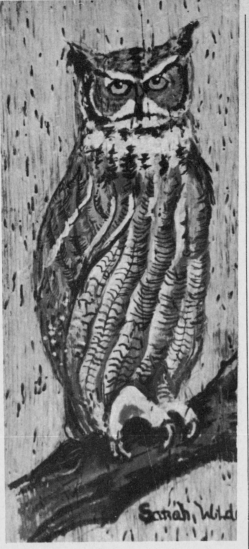

Scratchboard Etchings

Anatomically accurate birds hand etched on black scratchboard and mounted on wooden blocks or framed for hanging are offered by the Richard Edwards family.

Any common variety of bird will be made to order in any size, to satisfy the individual collector or someone seeking a special gift.

About scratchboard, Mr. Edwards writes:

"Scratchboard is a high-quality artist's board coated with a special clay. This coating is then covered with a thin layer of black India ink. The illustrations are done by scratching through the layer of black ink with sharp-pointed tools. This technique renders an illustration with a high fidelity of line and a completely different effect than is commonly seen in most etchings. Since the lines are actually cut through the ink layer into the underlying layer of white clay, the technique is actually an etching."

Richard's Corner
Box 364
Cheshire, Connecticut 06410
New England Winter Birds $4.00 each

Books for Craftsmen

Established in 1971 as a mail order book service, *Book Barn* specializes in books for craftsmen. Their catalog lists over 600 titles of craft and design books which have been reviewed and evaluated for the craftsmen's convenience. There is no shop, but anyone interested in what the Barn offers is invited to write or call for an appointment.

Book Barn also acts as a resource center for information.

Book Barn
P.O. Box 245
Storrs, Connecticut 06268
Catalog $.50

Winslow Homer at Prout's Neck

It is the author's intent that we become acquainted with Winslow Homer the man, as well as the artist. This is by no means an easy task. The aesthetic experience is by its very nature a profoundly individual one. Much of Beam's book is an apology, an attempt to refute those critics who have dubbed Homer a "naive naturalist" and an "illustrator of incidents." (Winslow must have been sensitive to these criticisms for when working from photographs it was his wish that all negatives be destroyed.) The text is illustrated with photographs of many of his paintings, some of which are compared to actual shots of the same scenes and accompanied by an analysis of the obvious differences between the two. This technique is used to convince the reader that Homer was not merely a copyist, but "an interpretive realist who imposed an abstract rhythm of his own creation upon everything he depicted."

All of the nearly one hundred illustrations in the book are black and white, therefore, one cannot really pass judgment on statements about Homer's superb use of color. It might have been better to have had only ten color plates.

That the author feels affection for Winslow Homer as a human being is obvious. Beam sees him as a rugged individualist and draws upon many local anecdotes in his writing.

The book succeeds in its attempt to stimulate an interest in Homer's works, and to make the artist a person with whom we can empathize.

B. Robbins-Pianka

Winslow Homer at Prout's Neck
by Philip C. Beam
1966; 282 pp., paper

From: Little, Brown & Company
       34 Beacon Street
       Boston, Massachusetts 02106
       $3.95

WINSLOW
HOMER
AT PROUT'S NECK

Philip C. Beam

The "Oliver Cromwell," the first American warship, was built in Essex, Connecticut in 1775. It had sixteen guns.

Craft

Stamford Harbor Light

The Artists Guild & Gallery

Perched on a hilltop, this gallery commands a panoramic view of Block Island Sound.

A marvelous collection of paintings and sculpture by contemporary and 19th century artists is on display. The enthusiastic owners of the gallery, which encompasses two charming buildings, take great pride in all the artists represented and the visitor is assured of a warm welcome.

Ten of Rhode Island artist Arthur Hayward's renderings of northeast coast lighthouses have been reproduced in postcard form, and are sold exclusively at the gallery.

Postcards — set of 10 — $1.25

The Artists Guild & Gallery

19th Century and Contemporary
Route 1, Charlestown, Rhode Island
(Mailing Address, Bradford, R I. 02808)

B. A. COOK
RUTH GULLIVER

Lyme Point Light

John D. Lutes — Marine Artist

John Lutes' paintings do not attempt to tell a story, but rather to interpret a mood. His favorite subjects are the working vessels from Rhode Island coastal villages — draggers, lobster boats and skiffs. All are perfectly beautiful and the attempt to create a mood is very successful.

Words do not adequately describe this talented man's work. It must be seen to be fully appreciated. Many of his paintings are on display at the Artists Guild & Gallery in Charlestown, Rhode Island.

John D. Lutes
Charlestown, Rhode Island 02813

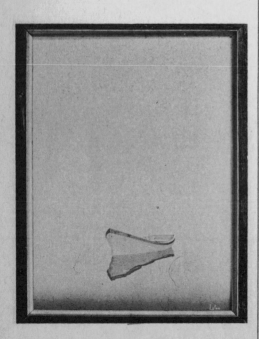

A New England Simple
Raw white potato is good to clean oil paintings.

Painting on Antiques

Ruth Bolster's interest jumped from painting, to buying and selling antiques, then back to painting again. Now she has combined both interests — she paints designs on the antiques — mirrors, chairs, tables, boxes, tin trays.

"I love the beach and am very concerned about oil pollution of our beautiful stretches of sand. I'm very aware of the importance of ecology and try to incorporate this feeling into my designs. I want people to see the beauty of nature's small things which are often overlooked and taken for granted."

Ruth Bolster
207 Main Street
Freeport, Maine 04032

Boston Museum of Fine Arts

The Boston Museum of Fine Arts houses man's visual world from remote antiquity to the present day. It ranks as the second most comprehensive museum in the Western hemisphere with collections which are often unsurpassed. Resources include a school, library, research laboratory and a varied educational program of lectures, films and musical performances.

Boston Museum of Fine Arts
The Fenway
Boston, Massachusetts 02115

Adults: $1.00 Free to members and children under sixteen.

Winslow Homer

Much has been published about one of America's favorite painters, but John Wilmerding's biography and selection of reproductions of Homer's works brings into sharp focus the artist's position in the ranks of great genre painters.

I'm not sure how one should look at this large, handsome volume, but one thing is certain: do not endeavor to absorb it in a quick, superficial manner. I was impelled to go first to the color plates and illustrations, then to the text. The way in which one approaches this book may be highly incidental, but there's a point to be made. Before reading the well-written biography, a visual impression of the works illuminates the text, thus leading to a better understanding of the man.

John Wilmerding's Homer is a masterful effort to present the whole man — "his life, the development of his style, and the meaning of his images." It is a fine publishing event, indulge yourself.

JCH

Winslow Homer
by John Wilmerding
50 color plates, 148 black/white illus.
1972; 224 pp.
From: Praeger Publishers
111 Fourth Avenue
New York, New York 10003
$30.00

Complete Subject Index   187

A

Adhesives 180
Alcoholic Beverages 133, 134, 135, 137
All Hands Aboard Scrimshawing 173
Amateur Sugar Maker 12
The American Boys Handy Book 63
The American Neptune 45
Animals 18, 25
  accessories 19, 20, 21
  bears 19
  birds 20
  cats 19, 20
  cows 18, 19
  deer 74
  dogs 19, 20, 21
  fowl 20
  frogs 19, 25
  goats 21
  horses 17, 18
  ointments 18
  repellents 24
  sheep 17, 18
  tonics 18
  wild 19, 23
  wildlife sanctuaries 29
  zoo 66
Animals Nobody Loves 19
Antiques 64, 70, 103
  automobiles 94
  bottles 101
  furniture 111
  glass 169
  ironware 113
  toys 63, 64, 65
  woodenware 130
Appalachian Mountain Club 86, 90
Archaeology in Vermont 39
Architecture 48, 62, 114, 115, 118, 124
The Art and Practice of Hawking 20
Art Galleries 186
The Art of Bird Carving 158
The Art of Colonial America 167
Audubon Societies
  Massachusetts 5, 15, 25, 29
  Rhode Island 25
Automobiles 94
  antiques 94
The Ayrshire Digest 19

B

Bags
  canvas 140, 145
  kits 151
  weaving 174
Baskets 154, 155
Batik
  artists 150, 170
  supplies 150
A Beachcomber's Botany 26
Bees 22
The Berkshire Traveller Almanack 1973 121
Bicycles 95
  custom-made 95
  equipment 95
  tours 95
Bikes 95
Bird Banding 23
Birds 21
  birdwatchers supplies 24
  etchings 185
  feeders 23, 24
  field guides 21, 24
  hawks 20
  houses 23
  prints 177
  taming 20, 23, 24
  woodcarving 157, 158
Blacksmiths 18, 114
Block Island Summer 31
Boats
  building 83
  canoes 84, 85, 86
  ferry 84
  footwear 76
  gear 76, 78, 80, 81, 82
  hardware 81
  heating 102
  kayaks 77, 84, 85, 86
  kits 77, 80
  lighting 102
  models 80, 81
  motor 78
  museums 83
  plans 79, 81
  racing shells 78
  reproductions 82
  row 77, 78, 79, 80, 82
  sail 77, 78, 79, 81
A Book of Cape Cod Houses 118
A Book of Country Things 182
A Book of New England Legends and Folklore 43
Boston Architecture 62
Boston Magazine 61
The Boston Marathon 61
Brass
  furnishings 164
  lighting 102, 103, 104, 114
  rubbing 182
The Bug Book: Harmless Insect Controls 117
The Building of a Wooden Ship 83
Buying Country Property 122

C

Camping 86, 87, 88, 90
  canoe trips 86
  equipment 87, 88, 89, 93
  food 88
Candles 99, 135, 161
Canoeing on the Connecticut River 86
Cape Ann: Cape America 119
The Cape Cod Compass 93
Cape Cod Journey 60
Cape Cod Pilot 28
Cheese 131, 132, 133, 135
Chemicals 42
Child Life In New England: 1790-1840 69
Cider Press 136
Clocks 74, 108, 109
  repair 111
  sundials 33
Clothing 148, 151
  canvas 140
  knitted 142
  leather 142, 145
  Shakers 144
  ski 141
  weaving 153
The Cod 75
Colonial Meeting-Houses of New Hampshire 118
Combmaker 159
The Community Press of New England 56
Companion Plants and How to Use Them 14
Conley's Gardening Handbook 6
Connecticut 47
The Connecticut Conservation Reporter 15
The Connecticut River 73
Connecticut's Old Houses 124
Connecticut Town Origins 44
Conservation Associations
  Chatham, Massachusetts 29
  Connecticut 25
Cookbooks 9
  breakfasts 133
  general 134
  herbs 132
  natural foods 134
  preserves 135
  Shakers 130
  special 132
  venison 138
Cooking
  fireplaces 105
  outdoor 100
  utensils 101
Cooper 157
Copper
  lighting 99, 102
  weather vanes 35, 166
Country Inns and Back Roads 94
Country Stores in Early New England 139
Craft
  centers 148, 149, 167
  Indian 148
  organizations 149
  schools 149
  shops 148, 149, 153, 157, 160, 164, 171, 172
  supplies 150
A Cruising Guide to the New England Coast 79
Cruising the Maine Coast 83
Customs on the Table Top 134

D

Decoupage
  artists 184
  prints 183
  supplies 181
Dolls and Miniatures 64
*Doorways, Lanterns and Fences
  of Martha's Vineyard* 101
Down East 13
Dowsing 30
Dowsing
  instructions 30
  kits 30
  society 30
  supplies 30
Drawing Aids 182
Drinking Water Filter 27
Duck Decoys 74
*Dynamics of Growth in New England's
  Economy, 1870-1964* 46

E

Early American Folk & Country Antiques 103
Early American Folk Pottery 168
Early American Herb Recipes 132
Early American Homes for Today 118
Early American Ironware 113
Early American Wooden Ware 130
Early Houses of New England 114
East of America 31
*Easy Does It Furniture Restoration
  the Vermont Way* 110
Eat The Weeds 138
Ecology 11, 14, 15, 25, 29, 90
  kits 54
  nature centers 6, 14, 15, 29
  recycling newspapers 176
  schools 52, 55
Enduring Friendships 81
Enjoying Maine Birds 21
Environ/Mental Essays on the Planet as a Home 14
Etchings
  birds 185
Exploring Cape Cod 60
Exploring Connecticut 96

F

Fabrics 110, 140, 141, 142
  dyeing 150
  weaving 153
Factory Store Guide To All New England 110
Farming 6
  haying equipment 11
  supplies 136
  tools 9
A Field Guide to the Birds 24
Fireplaces 99
  building 105
  cooking 105
  equipment 18, 35, 100, 101, 102, 103
Fish
  anglerfish 73
  cod 75
  exhibition 66
  lobsters 27
  whales 21
Fishing 73, 75
  eels 28
  gear 72, 88
  lobster traps 26
  regulations 75
  schools 52
Flags 111, 116
The Flora of New England 4
The Folk Arts and Crafts of New England 167
Food 132
  apples 137
  camping 88
  candy 133
  cranberries 136
  farm produce 130
  ferns 136
  flour 137
  greens 136
  hiking 88
  market 131
  natural 135, 138
  organic 133, 138
  preserves 132
  seafood 106
  smoked meat 134, 136, 139
Footwear
  boats 76
  canvas 76
  leather 141, 142, 145
*The Forgotten Art of Building
  a Good Fireplace* 105
The Forgotten Art of Building a Stone Wall 121
Foundries 104, 166
Fried Coffee and Jellied Bourbon 133
From Gunk to Glow 107
From The Galleys Of Nantucket 134

Furnishings 26, 102, 109, 142, 178, 180
  brass 164
  hand painted 186
  kitchen 106, 109, 122, 129, 131
  pewter 164
  repair 113
Furniture 106, 107, 108, 109, 110, 113, 123, 161
  antiques 111
  leather 145
  miniature 64, 65, 67
  plans 111, 112
  polish 109
  refinishing 107
  restoration 110
  Shakers 107, 144

G

Gardening 5, 6, 11, 14, 16
  blueberries 5
  bulb grower 10
  bulb planter 10
  bulbs 10
  center 6
  coldframes 10
  dwarf plants 11
  fertilizer 6
  flowers 4
  greenhouses 13
  herbs 8, 9, 12, 15
  indoor kits 12
  indoor plants 4, 7
  insect control 15, 117
  organic 15
  organic fertilizer 6
  plant food 5
  potting soil 4
  seeds 6
  soil conditioner 4, 5
  soil testing equipment 6
  strawberries 6
  tools 13
  wild flowers 8
Gardening for Health and Nutrition 138
Gardens
  botanical 8
  lighting 5
Give Me The Hills 90
Glass 172
  antiques 169
  blowing 35, 169, 171
  cutter 129
  fused 167, 170
  jewelry 142, 160
  lighting 100, 101, 171
  stained 100, 160, 167, 168, 169, 171
  stained, kits 169
  stained, supplies 168, 169
  works 171
Good Old Days 49
Growing Up In Old New England 64
A Guide To Decoration In
  The Early American Manner 178

H

Hands to Work and Hearts to God 57
Hand-Taming Wild Birds at the Feeder 23
Hardware
  boats 81
  homes 101, 114, 122, 161
Haunted New England 43
Haymarket 131
Heating 99, 104, 106
  boats 102
Heavy Equipment Repair 12
Hemmings Motor News 94
Herbs 8
  cookbooks 132
  gardening 8, 9, 12, 15
  insect repellent 15
  kits 9
  sprays 15
Hiking 86, 87, 88, 90
  equipment 87, 88, 89, 93
  food 88
Hill Country Harvest 11
Historic Mansions and Highways
  Around Boston 60
Home and Child Life in Colonial Days 63
Homes
  building 117, 118, 119
  hardware 101, 114, 122, 161
  plans 119
  prefab 116, 117, 120
  restoration 117, 118

The Horn Book Magazine 63
Horses 17, 18
  harnessmaker 19
  horseshoeing 18
  ointments 18
  riding equipment 19
Horticulture 5
The House on Nauset Marsh 26
How to Build Your Home in the Woods 119
How to Make Dolls' Houses 67
How to Mend China and Bric-A-Brac 113
Hunting
  decoys 74
  gear 88
  regulations 75

I

The Independent School Bulletin 44
Indian
  craft 148
  museums 50, 148
  tobacco 140
The Indian in Connecticut 45
Instruments
  music 63, 70, 71
  precision 124
  sewage treatment 124
  weather 32
Ivory
  piano keys 173
  scrimshaw 173

J

Jams, Jellies & Marmalades 135
Jewelry 108, 123, 141
  coin 140
  glass 142, 160
  minerals 48
  pottery 172
  silversmiths 164, 166
John Rogers — The People's Sculptor 177
The Jug and Related Stoneware of Bennington 171
The Junior Scientist Newsletter 42
Junkyard 107

K

Kalliroscope 42

L

Lead 168
Learning
  games 54, 68
  kits 54
  tools 53, 54, 61
Leather 106
  bags 148
  clothing 142, 145
  footwear 141, 142, 145
  furniture 145
  preservative 20
Left-Handed Products 143
Let's Go! Trips for Children in Connecticut
  and Rhode Island 66
Let's Have a Craft Show 149
Libraries 42
Life in an Old New England Country Village 47
Lighting 35, 159
  boats 102
  brass 102, 103, 104, 114
  copper 99, 102
  gardens 5
  glass 100, 101, 171
  lampshades 178
  pewter 101, 114
  portable 86
  restoration 110
  tin 99, 100, 101
The Lightning Book 36
Living the Good Life 15
Look What I Found! 23

M

Machinery Around Your Country Home 34
Mail Order Book Service 185
The Maine Catalog 51
Maine Fish and Game 74
Maine Mountain Guide 86
Maine's Treasure Chest — Gems and Minerals
  of Oxford County 39
Majolica — Collect It For Fun and Profit 167
Man and Nature 25
Maple Sugar 12
  equipment 11
The Maple Sugar Book 16
Maple Syrup 133
Maps 13, 16
  prints 177
Marblehead — The Spirit of '76 Lives Here 46
Massachusetts and Rhode Island Trail Guide 86
Mass. Soc. Prev. Cruelty to Animals 18

Medicine in New England 45
The Metaphorical Way of Learning & Knowing 53
Minerals 39
  granite 39
  guide 32
  jewelry 48
  slate 109
  soapstone 106
  stores 39
M.I.T. Technology Review 29
42 More Short Walks in Connecticut 87
Mountain Flowers of New England 86
Museums
  Americana 17, 47, 51, 57, 64, 94, 96, 128
  art 61, 186
  boats 83
  children's 61, 67
  Indian 50, 148
  machines 128
  maritime 26, 62, 156
  natural history 6
  papers 180
  railroads 60
  science 40
  tools 128
  toys 65
  transportation 94
  whaling 62, 85
Music
  books 71
  dictionary 71
  instruments 63, 70, 71
  records 71
My Own Cape Cod 27
Mysterious New England 43

N

Nantucket Lightship Baskets 155
The National Fisherman 75
The Natural Foods Cookbook 134
Natural History of Vermont 90
Needlecraft
  kits 175
  knitting 142
  patterns 174, 175
  rug braiding 174
  rug hooking 174
  schools 150
  shirret 175
  supplies 152, 154, 175
  yarns 152, 175
The New England Butt'ry Shelf Almanac 9
The New England Caller 70
New England Canoeing Guide 86
The New England Colonial Gardens 16
New England Glass & Glassmaking 172
The New England Guide 62
The New England Meeting Houses of the
  Seventeenth Century 115
New England Men of Letters 43
The New England Village Scene — 1800 121
New Hampshire Echoes 46
New Hampshire Folk Tales 49
Northwoods Tales and Unusual Recipes 87
The No-Work Garden Book 11

O

The Old Farmer's Almanac 32
Old Landmarks and Historic Personages
  of Boston 44
Old-Time New England 70
Old Vermont Houses 1763-1850 114
On The Sound 82
Optics 143
  microscopes 40, 41
  telescopes 41
Outdoor Fun 90
Overseas Travel Kit 61

P

Painting 186
  driftwood 185
  marine 184, 186
  reproductions 184
  supplies 179
  tole 164, 178
  tole, supplies 181
Pamper Your Possessions 102
Papers
  cutting 184
  museums 180
  printing 179
  wall 110
  writing 176, 177, 178, 180, 181, 183, 184, 186
Parachuting
  equipment 92

Patterns
  needlecraft 174, 175
  rug hooking 152, 174, 175
  stencilling 108
People From The Other World 43
Pewter
  furnishings 164
  lighting 101, 114
Pharmaceuticals 141
A Pictorial History of the Shelburne Museum 128
Picture Frames 178
Pill Crusher 143
The Pine Furniture of Early New England 111
Plantation in Yankeeland 46
Playground Equipment 66, 67
Pottery 53, 160, 167, 168, 171, 172
  ceramics 167, 170
  ceramic tiles 167, 170
  equipment 165, 169, 170
  jewelry 172
  supplies 169, 170
Printing
  Americana 51, 54, 64
  hand binding 181
  limited editions 44, 47, 176, 181
  linoleum block 181
  medieval illumination 179
  papers 179
  woodcuts 184
Prints 54
  birds 177
  charts 184
  decoupage 183
  maps 177
  mounted 177

Q

Quilt Making 112, 122, 151, 160

R

Railroad 60
  museums 60
Recipes
  applesauce 130
  apple wine 133
  cheese dish 134
  chokecherry jam 135
  drying apples 131
  frog's legs 19
  lobster stew 27
  maple treat 132
  preserving acorns 138
  punch 134
  rum drink 137
  salted mackerel 106
  sauerkraut 134
  venison mincemeat 138
Recollections of Old Stonington 113
Records
  music 71
  Yankee humor 31
Refinishing
  furniture 107
Restoration
  furniture 110
  homes 117, 118
  lighting 110
Rhode Island Yearbook 49
Rock Hound's Guide to Connecticut 32
The Rocky Shore 26
Rubber Stamp 182
Rubbing
  brass 182
  instructions 183
  kits 182, 183
  stone 182
  supplies 183
Rug Braiding 174
  equipment 174
  supplies 174
Rug Hooking 174
  equipment 152, 174
  instructions 152, 174
  kits 152, 174
  patterns 152, 174, 175
  supplies 174

S

Sail 79
The Salt Water Sportsman 73
A Sandwich Sampler 169
The Sandy Shore 26
Schools
  alternative 53
  bartending 52
  craft 149

  ecology 52, 55
  film 54
  fishing 52
  maritime 52
  needlecraft 150
  private 44, 55
  travel 52
Scrimshaw
  ivory 173
Scrimshaw and Scrimshanders 173
Sculpture 149, 161, 162, 167, 177
Sea Born Island 30
Sea Fever — The Making of a Sailor 27
Seaweeds of the Connecticut Shore 14
Sewage Treatment
  instruments 124
  system 125
Shaker Recipe Book 130
Shakers 57, 159
  clothing 144
  cookbooks 130
  furniture 107, 144
The Shepherd 18
Short Walks in Connecticut 87
Signs 120
  woodcarving 158
Silhouettes 184
Silver Design Competition 163
Silversmiths 162, 165
  guild 163, 165
  jewelry 164, 166
  supplies 162, 164
  tools 162, 163
Skinny-Dipping 91
Sky & Telescope Magazine 42
Snowmobiles 92
The Snowshoe Book 93
Snowshoes 92

Soundings 77
Square Dancing 70
Starting Right With Bees 22
Starting Right With Milk Goats 21
Starting Right With Poultry 20
Stores
  country 107, 131, 137, 139
  factory 110, 140, 141, 142
  minerals 39
The Story of Dorset 47
Stoves 104, 106
Striped Bass & Other Cape Cod Fish 75
Successful Ocean Game Fishing 75
Summer Island: Penobscot Country 31
Sundials
  clocks 33
Supplies
  batik 150
  building 115, 120, 123
  craft 150
  decoupage 181
  dowsing 30
  drafting 106
  farming 136
  needlecraft 152, 154, 175
  painting 179
  pottery 169, 170
  rubbing 183
  rug braiding 174
  rug hooking 174
  silversmiths 162, 164
  stained glass 168, 169
  tole painting 181

T

Tales of Old Wallingford 48
Teachers Services 61
That Quail, Robert 24
Tin
  lighting 99, 100, 101
Tobacco
  Indian 140
Tole Painting 164, 178
  supplies 181
Tools
  cutting 128, 129, 156
  farming 9
  gardening 13
  hand 125, 126, 127, 128, 156
  learning 53, 54, 61
  museums 128
  power 124
  precision 127, 163
  silversmiths 162, 163
Toy Review 68

Toys
  antiques 63, 64, 65
  doll houses 66, 67
  dolls 63, 65, 66, 68
  games 66, 68
  kites 63, 180
  stuffed 67, 69, 160
  wooden 66, 68, 69, 160
Toys and Banks 64
The Transcendental Boiled Dinner 132
Trees 6, 7, 8
  dogwood 6
  rare 6
  seeds 12

U

Understanding Boat Design 81
Using Wayside Plants 13

V

The Venison Book 138
Vermont Afternoons with Robert Frost 49
Vermont General Fish and Game Laws and Regulations 75
Vermont Life 49

W

Wall
  free-standing 127
  papers 110
  stencilling 110, 164
Weather
  forecasting 32
  instruments 32
  lightning 36
  snow removal 34
Weather Vanes 18
  copper 35, 166
Weaving 155
  bags 174
  chair seats 155
  clothing 153
  equipment 153, 154
  fabrics 153
  rugs 107, 154
  spinning 151
  yarns 151, 152, 153, 154
Weekly Market Bulletin 6
Whales 21
  woodcarving 158
Whaling Wives of Martha's Vineyard 76
What Is It? . . . at the Beach 27
The White-Flower-Farm Garden Book 5
White Mountain Guide 86
White Water Handbook for Canoe and Kayak 86
Wild Flowers of Martha's Vineyard 13
The Wild River Wilderness 50
Windmills 16
Window of Vermont 45
Winemaking 133, 135
Winslow Homer 186
Winslow Homer at Prout's Neck 185
Witch Hazel 7
Woodcarving 157
  birds 157, 158
  decoys 74
  letter openers 157
  pipes 158
  puzzles 157
  shipcarvers 84, 156, 158
  signs 158
  whales 158

Y

The Yachtsman's Guide to Dining Out in Maine 79
The Yankee Guide to the New England Countryside 61
Yankee Magazine 112
The Yankee Pioneers — A Saga of Courage 121
The Yankee Shun Pike 124
The Year of the Whale 21
Your Happy Valley Guide 86

Z

Zeb, A Celebrated Schooner Life 83

Geographic Index

CONNECTICUT

Avon
Morrow Leather Creations 145

Bantam
Sam Richards Trader 4, 86

Bethel
Atlasta Farm Restorations 110

Bloomfield
The C-Thru Ruler Company 182

Branford
The John P. Smith Co. 103

Bridgeport
The Guitar Shop 63

Bridgewater
The Connecticut Conservation Association 25

Cheshire
Richard's Corner 185

Chester
C.J. Bates & Son, Inc. 175
Norman A. Ross 81

Clinton
Indian Blanket Craft & Gift Shop 148
George Jennings 109
R.D. Symonds 19
Village Forge & Tin Shop 100

Deep River
R. Ingram Manufacturing Co. 104
Luta Studios 167

East Hampton
The Colonial Brass Craftsmen, Inc. 114
T-Coin 140

East Lyme
The Yankee Woodcarver 158

Essex
Custom-Made Bicycles 95
E.E. Dickinson Company 7
Essex Forge 99
Mrs. John P. Syme 110
Things of Essex, Inc. 161
Valley Railroad Company 60

Fabyan
Grandmother's Soft Toy Shop 67

Farmington
The Fletcher-Terry Company 129

Greenwich
Del Filardi 162

Guilford
The Guilford Handcraft Shop 157

Hadlyme
Foster Studio 171

Hamden
E.C. Bull & Son 143

Hartford
Bartending School of Mixology, Inc. 52
Colt Industries 48
Criterion Manufacturing Company 41
Heublein, Inc. 134
The Nathan Margolis Shop, Inc. 110
Mark Twain Memorial 25

Higganum
Scovil Hoe Co. 9

Ivoryton
Gallo Birds 157
Pratt, Read & Co. 173

Kent
The Sloane-Stanley Museum 128

Lakeside
Hilcraft 164

Lebanon
Contessa Yarns 153

Litchfield
White Flower Farm 4

Madison
Pepperidge Handspinners 154

Meriden
American Indian Tobacco and Enterprises 140
The Bayberry Hill Press 176
International Silver Co. 165
Kelsey Company 177

Middle Haddam
C. Sherman Johnson Co., Inc. 81

Middletown
Elizabeth Andrews Fisher 63
Wesleyan Potters, Inc. 167

Milford
The Ames Laboratories, Inc. 42
Christopher's Travel Discoveries 61

Mystic
Peter Esak 169
The Mystic Foundry, Inc. 166
Mystic Seaport 62

Naugatuck
Sperry Top-Sider 76

New Britain
The Stanley Works 128

New Haven
Alan-Whitney Co., Inc. 63
Seton Name Plate Corporation 120
Wff 'N Proof 54

New London
The Connecticut Arboretum 14

Noank
The Great Noank Quilt Factory 160

Noroton Heights
P.B. Enterprises 27

North Coventry
Caprilands Herb Farm 12

North Grosvenordale
Toncoss Miniatures 67

Norwalk
Browser's 5

Norwichtown
The Bean Hill Whittler 84

Old Lyme
Mile Creek Boat Shop 78
Edith Twining 112

Old Saybrook
The Brewster Corporation 127
Douglas C. Ryan 101

Orange
Midas Coin Auction Shop 64

Pomfret
Superwinch, Inc. 124

Pomfret Center
Gloriana Goodenough 108

Portland
Richard Johnson 167

Riverside
Sterling Silversmiths Guild 163
Sterling Silversmiths Guild of America 165

Riverton
The Hitchcock Chair Company 113

Rockfall
M.W. Robinson Co., Inc. 128

Sharon
Cole Ceramic Laboratories 169

Southport
Off The Beaten Path 9
Yankee Mechanics, Inc. 127

South Woodstock
Woodstock Pottery 53

Stamford
Here and Now 138
United House Wrecking Co. 107

Stonington
Old Stonington Foundry 67

Storrs
Book Barn 185

Uncasville
Tantaquidgeon Indian Museum 50

Wallingford
Silhouette Studio 184
Wallace Silversmiths 165

Washington
Priscilla Manning Porter Studio 170

Warrenville
Mrs. Blake Prescott 64

Waterford
Willard Shepard 156

Westbrook
Custom Miniature Reproductions 65
Natalie Newhoff 167
Sudberry House 152

West Hartford
Material Handling Systems, Inc. 176
Louise McCrady 175
Bernard Schneider 173
Hollis Schneider 184

Westport
The Aristera Organization 143
Bacchanalia 135
Heritage Hill Patterns 175

Wethersfield
Brimfield Gardens Nursery 6

Wilton
Invitation to Adventure, Inc. 95
The Saddler 19

Woodbridge
The H.H. Perkins Company 155

Woodbury
The Clock Mender 111
M.G. Martin 170

MAINE

Auburn
Maartje Knoppers 151

Bangor
Northern Products, Inc. 117
Prentiss & Carlisle Co., Inc. 13

Bar Harbor
College of the Atlantic 52
Super Sandal 145

Belgrade
The St. Croix Voyageurs 86

Boothbay
Boothbay Railway Museum 60

Boothbay Harbor
Conley's Garden Center 6
Richard J. MacDonald 100
The Maine-Made Shop 148
Partridge Workshop 184
The Schooner Museum 83

Brunswick
Harpswell House 109
Lee Crafts 180

Bucks Harbor
Wm. S. Coperthwaite 119

Camden
Needle Arts, Inc. 174

Cape Elizabeth
Atlantic Sails 78
Kendall Hatch 157

Deer Isle
The Lawtons 148

Douglas Hill
Dawn Babbitt 151

Dryden
Memco 92

Ellsworth
Cascade Fabrics 140
Ellsworth's Doll Museum 65

Freedom
Katherine Wills 164

Freeport
L.L. Bean, Inc. 88
Ruth Bolster 186
Casco Bay Trading Post 106

Fryeburg
Western Maine Forest Nursery Co. 7

Gorham
The Gorham Flag Center 116

Hallowell
Sherrymike Pottery 168

Hinckley
Haystack-Hinckley School of Crafts 149

Hurricane Island
Outward Bound School 52

Kenduskeag
Northeastern Log Homes, Inc. 117

Kennebunk
The Kennebunk Railroad Station
Craft Workshop 171

Kennebunkport
Joan Moshimer 152
Port Canvas Company 140

Kittery Point
Alden Ocean Shell 78

Limerick
David Court 18

Lincolnville
Charlotte Hatch 68

Litchfield
The Rock Garden 11

Madawaska
Acadian Crafts Association, Inc. 148

Mt. Vernon
Carol Gibson Bauer 175

Newport
Ellsbury Stevens 154

Oakland
Cascade Woolen Mill 140

Ogunquit
Vignari Art Enterprises, Inc. 184

Old Town
Old Town Canoe Company 85

Orland
HOME Co-op 151

Orrington
Baldwin Boat Company 84

Owl's Head
Mid-Coast Arts & Crafts Center 148

Oxford
Pinewood Products 26

Portland
Pollutrol Industries, Inc. 125
Portland Stove Foundry Co. 104

Richmond
Christopher Farm 152
Gentian Meadows School 150

Rockport
Anne De Maria 181
Searsport
The Penobscot Marine Museum 26
Skowhegan
Pooler's Moccasin Shop 145
South Thomaston
Harold H. Payson 79
Southwest Harbor
Zack Gould 105
South Windham
Heritage Metalcraft, Inc. 122
Tenants Harbor
Jeanne Warner 177
Waterville
Urethane Applications, Inc. 120
West Boothbay Harbor
Sarah & Bill Wilde 185
West Paris
Perham's Maine Mineral Store 39
Wilton
Burgess Shoe Store 141
W.S. Wells & Son 136
Yarmouth
Heritage Lanterns 99
York Beach
Innerlight Candle Co. 161

MASSACHUSETTS
Adams
Arnold Print Works, Inc. 150
Old Stone Mill Corporation 110
Amherst
Teacher Drop Out Center 53
Arlington
Multi-Mer Science 5
Ashby
Sibley Industries 184
Athol
The L.S. Starrett Company 163
Barre
Imprint Society 44
Belchertown
Wheeler Saw Co. 13
Belmont
Habitat 55
Boston
American Science and Engineering Co. 61
Appalachian Mountain Club 86
Boston Museum of Fine Arts 186
The Children's Museum 67
Children's Zoo 66
The Francis A. Countway Library
of Medicine 42
Downeaster Mfg. Co. 32
Eastern Mountain Sports, Inc. 89
Erewhon 133
Isabella Stewart Gardner Museum 61
Harcourt Bindery 181
Hardware Products Company, Inc. 122
Museum of Science 40
New England Aquarium 66
William Post Ross 70
Society for the Preservation
of New England Antiquities 70
C.W. Somers & Co. 162
Technical Papers Corporation 179
Utrecht Linens, Inc. 179
Bourne
Wee 3 Sandwich Glass Jewelry 142
Brewster
The Cape Cod Museum of Natural History 6
Bridgewater
Lemee's 102
Brockton
Ambroid Company, Inc. 180
Brookline
American Youth Hostels, Inc. 90
Museum of Transportation 94
Burlington
The Artisans Guild 175
Cambridge
The Film School 54
Kalliroscope Corp. 42
John D. Lyon, Inc. 6
Synectics Education Systems 53
Urban Systems Products, Inc. 54
Chatham
Chatham Conservation Foundation, Inc. 29
Chelmsford
A.S. Margulies Co. 10

Concord
Moor & Mountain 87
Robert C. Nelson 153
Shaker Workshops, Inc. 144
Dalton
Crane & Co. 180
Danvers
The Flag Shop 111
Turen, Inc. 20
E.G. Washburne & Co. 166
Dedham
James Bliss & Co., Inc. 80
Dennis
Scargo Stoneware Pottery 169
Dunstable
Edward A. Larter, Jr. 16
Duxbury
The Brass Lantern 103
East Falmouth
Ashumet Holly Reservation 5
The Salt Water Tackle Box 72
Easthampton
Arcadia Nature Center
and Wildlife Sanctuary 14
Connecticut River Watershed Council 15
Falmouth
The Falmouth Craft Studio 149
Foxboro
The Foxboro Company 124
Gloucester
Embassy Seafoods, Inc. 106
Granville
The Herb Farm 8
Noble & Cooley Company 71
Great Barrington
Catherine's Chocolate Shop 133
The North Family Joiners 107
Greenfield
Lunt Silversmiths 165
Hampden
Laughing Brook Nature Center 29
Hanson
Ocean Spray Cranberries, Inc. 136
Holliston
Child Life Play Specialties, Inc. 66
S. Wilder & Co., Inc. 102
Hudson
Curtis La Follette 162
Hyannis
The Cracker Barrel 137
Hyannis Port
Old Harbor Candle Co. 99
Ipswich
Common Fields Nursery 5
Ebinger Brothers & Co. 111
Jamaica Plain
Arnold Arboretum 8
Lexington
Information Resources 54
Lincoln
Stewart T. Coffin 157
The Massachusetts Audubon Society 25
Lynn
Walter Dyer 142
Marblehead
Bergen Arts and Crafts 150
Fore 'N Aft 19, 76
Oldstone Enterprises 182
Nantucket
The Havemeyer's 182
The Nantucket Kiteman 180
New Bedford
Cape Cod Cupola Co., Inc. 35
Whaling Museum 85
Newbury
Palumbo 35
Parker River Marine, Inc. 76, 82
Newburyport
Towle Silversmiths 165
Newton
Education Development Center, Inc. 54
Selective Educational Equipment, Inc. 41
Newton Highlands
ARP Instruments, Inc. 71
Unitron Instrument Company 40
North Dartmouth
Gull of Bristol, Inc. 78
Northboro
Winecraft 133
Northampton
Don Gleason's 93

North Marshfield
Village Lantern 101
North Quincy
Strong Enterprises, Inc. 92
North Reading
Di Franza Designs 174
North Wilmington
Arthur Eames Allgrove 12
Orleans
The Herbary and Potpourri Shop 15
Osterville
Mason & Sullivan Co. 108
Palmer
Haley's Grain Store, Inc. 136
Pembroke
Braid Aid 174
Pittsfield
Editions Ltd. 176
Prides Crossing
Elm Tree Studio 178
Quincy
Friar Tuck Sales 141
Rockland
Whittemore-Durgin Glass Co. 169
Rowley
The Jewel Mill 48
Royalston
W.W. Williams Industries 157
Sagamore
Pairpoint Glass Works 171
Salisbury
Handicapped Artists of America, Inc. 183
Rod Ryder Engineering 95
Sandisfield
Barn Door Crafts 151
Sandwich
Heritage Plantation 94
F.M. Schumacher Co. 12
Scituate
Faire Harbour Boats 102
Sheffield
Sheffield Pottery, Inc. 170
South Boston
Coran-Sholes Industries 168
Southbridge
American Optical Corporation 143
Russell Harrington Cutlery, Inc. 129
South Carver
Edaville Railroad 60
South Dartmouth
Manchester Yacht Sails, Inc. 82
South Deerfield
Lewis Farms, Inc. 6
South Hamilton
P. DeJager & Sons, Inc. 10
South Wellfleet
Wellfleet Wildlife Sanctuary 15
Springfield
Milton Bradley Company 68
Stockbridge
The Little Doll House 65
Sturbridge
Lincoln House Fabrics 174
Old Sturbridge Village 57
Sudbury
E. Helene Sherman 179
Sudbury Laboratory, Inc. 6, 24
Taunton
Reed & Barton 165
Waltham
Frank Hubbard 71
Ward Hill
The Railroad Enthusiasts, Inc. 60
Wareham
Cape Cod Shipbuilding Company 77
Tremont Nail Company 123
Watertown
Workshop for Learning Things, Inc. 53
Wayland
Craftivity 154
West Acton
English Gothic Art 183
West Bridgewater
Cape Dory Company, Inc. 77
Ina Uburtis 107
Westfield
Kamper Kraft 74
West Lynn
Dedham Kayaks 77

Williamstown
  Handcrafts by Henry 109
Woburn
  Chuck Wagon Foods 88
  Woodcraft Supply Corp. 126
Woods Hole
  The New Alchemy Institute East 29
Worcester
  Verandel Company 13
  Wheels 165

RHODE ISLAND
Charlestown
  The Artists Guild & Gallery 186
  The Fantastic Umbrella Factory 160
  John D. Lutes 186
  Windswept Farm 160
 Foster
  Welcome Rood Studios 172
Greene
  Greene Herb Gardens 9
Kingston
  The Fayerweather Craft Guild 149
Little Compton
  Strawberry Bank Craftsmen, Inc. 99
Newport
  H.M.S. Frigate Rose 82
North Kingstown
  Brown & Sharpe Mfg. Co. 127
Peace Dale
  Narragansett Pier Railroad 60
Providence
  The Audubon Society of Rhode Island 25
  Beneficent Congregational Meeting House 118
  Cosmo Glassworks 35
  The Gorham Co. 165
  Nancy Hamilton 150
  Nicholson File Company 156
  Joyce Smith 174
  Vennerbeck & Chase Co. 164
Usquepaugh
  Wood & Waxworks Craftsmen's Showroom 161
Warren
  Blount Marine Corporation 84
Warwick
  Carson and Ellis 181
  Connie Coleman 155

NEW HAMPSHIRE
Amherst
  Yankee Wood Engravers 158
Center Barnstead
  P.H. Theopold 107
Center Harbor
  Norvik Kennels 21
Center Ossipee
  Dan Cooper Design Corporation 142
Center Sandwich
  Ayottes' Designery 153
Deering
  Hayfields Studio, Inc. 164
East Kingston
  Dowsing Supply Company of America 30
Franklin
  Shelter-Kit, Inc. 120
Gorham
  Antique Bottles 101
Greenville
  Henri Vaillancourt 86
Guild
  The Dorr Woolen Company
    and Dorr Mill Store 141
Hanover
  League of New Hampshire Arts and Crafts 149
Haverhill
  Koch Recorders 70
  Page's Model A Garage 94
Lancaster
  The P.J. Noyes Co. 141
Manchester
  Yankee Craft Products 109
Marlow
  Sand Pond Publishers 64
Marshfield
  Mt. Washington Cog Railroad 60
New Ipswich
  Sundials 33
Newmarket
  Printed Papers 176
North Stratford
  Bambé 4

North Woodstock
  The White Mountain Central Railroad 60
Nottingham
  Perkins Silversmiths 166
Penacook
  Duncraft 24
Peterborough
  The Brookstone Co. 125
  Up Country Enterprise 117
Portsmouth
  Renaissance 149
Rindge
  West Rindge Baskets, Inc. 154
Tilton
  Country Braid House 174
Warner
  Mink Hills Post Office and General Store
    Bygones Museum 96
Wentworth
  Bernier Studio 168
West Lebanon
  Profile Sports Corporation 141
West Nottingham
  Artprints Company 183
West Swanzey
  Homestead Woolen Mill Store 140
Winchester
  Jeremiah J. Thibault 23
Wolfeboro
  The Wolfeboro Railroad Company 60

VERMONT
Barre
  The Barre Granite Association 39
  The Foto Shop 30
Bellows Falls
  Steamtown, U.S.A. 60
Bennington
  The Bennington Gallery 149
  Harwood Hill Orchard 137
Brattleboro
  Hickin's Mountain Mowings 130
Burlington
  Vermont International
    Sculpture Symposium 149
Calais
  The Appleyard Corporation 135
Charlotte
  db Design 159
Chelsea
  H.N. Sanborn & Son 19
Chester
  The National Survey 16
Craftsbury
  Stephen Parker 18
Danville
  The American Society of Dowsers, Inc. 30
Dorset
  J.K. Adams Company 106
East Arlington
  Peter's Brook 149
East Ryegate
  Arrand Arts and Fine Crafts 148
Ferrisburg
  Dakin Farm 133
Greensboro
  Robert Bourdon 114
Healdville
  Crowley Cheese, Inc. 135
Hinesburg
  Green Mountain Creative Crafts 153
  Vermont Ware 13
Jacksonville
  Stone Soldier Pottery 172
Jeffersonville
  Uni-Bass 71
Killington
  Outdoor Travel Camps, Inc., 52, 88
  Trailside Country School 52
Londonderry
  Toni Totes of Vermont, Inc. 145
Lunenburg
  The Stinehour Press 47
Lyndonville
  Dairy Association Co., Inc. 18
  Green Mountain Horse Products 20
Manchester
  The Jelly Mill 132
  The Orvis Company, Inc. 72
  Orvis Vermont Fly Fishing School 52
Manchester Center
  The Enchanted Doll House 66

Marshfield
  Adele Godchaux Studio 184
  The Needle Shop 142
Middlebury
  Cornwall Crafts 66
  Frog Hollow Craft Center 148
  The Pipe Shop 158
Newfane
  Lawrence's Smoke House 134
New Haven
  Thistle Metal Spinning 164
Perkinsville
  Vermont Soapstone Co., Inc. 106
Plainfield
  Erlend Jacobsen 135
Plymouth
  The Plymouth Cheese Corp. 131
Putney
  Natural Organic Farmers' Association 15
  Putney Nursery, Inc. 8
Randolph
  Henry Chase 108
Richmond
  Harrington's 139
Rochester
  Student Hosteling Program
    of New England, Inc. 87
Rutland
  G.H. Grimm Company 11
Shelburne
  Colonial Vermont, Inc. 106
  The Shelburne Museum 51
St. Johnsbury
  Edythe and Granville Newton 178
Townshend
  Mary Meyer Mfg. Co., Inc. 69
Waitsfield
  Vermont Wooden Toy Company 69
Wallingford
  Jacques Stationery 184
  Vermont Tubbs, Inc. 92
Wardsboro
  WoodSmith Gallery, Inc. 177
Waterville
  Fairmont Woodcraft 108
Weston
  Frances Holmes Boothby 164
  The Gallery Shop 71
  Vermont Country Store 137
  Clark Voorhees 158
  The Weston Bowl Mill 131
  Weston Village Store 107
Windsor
  The American Precision Museum 128
Wolcott
  Lowther Press 136
  Vermont Weatherboard, Inc. 115
Woodstock
  Sugarbush Farm 132